PROMISES AND CONTRACT LAW

Promises and Contract Law is the first modern work to explore the significance of promise to contract law from a comparative legal perspective. Part 1 explores the component elements of promise, its role in Greek thought and Roman law, the importance of the moral duty to keep promises and the development of promissory ideas in medieval legal scholarship. Part 2 considers the modern contract law of a number of legal systems from a promissory perspective. The focus is on the law of England, Germany and three mixed legal systems (Scotland, South Africa and Louisiana), though other legal systems are also mentioned. Major topics subjected to a promissory analysis include formation of contract, third party rights, contractual remedies and the renunciation of contractual rights. Part 3 analyses the future role which promise might play in contract law, especially within a harmonised European contract law.

MARTIN HOGG is a Senior Lecturer at the School of Law, University of Edinburgh. He has researched and published extensively in the field of obligations law, in both a national and comparative context.

D1388693

PROMISES AND CONTRACT LAW

Comparative Perspectives

MARTIN HOGG

CAMBRIDGE
UNIVERSITY PRESS

CAMBRIDGE
UNIVERSITY PRESS

University Printing House, Cambridge CB2 8BS, United Kingdom

Published in the United States of America by Cambridge University Press, New York

Cambridge University Press is part of the University of Cambridge.

It furthers the University's mission by disseminating knowledge in the pursuit of education, learning and research at the highest international levels of excellence.

www.cambridge.org
Information on this title: www.cambridge.org/9781107416970

© Martin Hogg 2011

First published 2011
First paperback edition 2014

A catalogue record for this publication is available from the British Library

Library of Congress Cataloguing in Publication data
Hogg, Martin.
Promises and contract law : comparative perspectives / Martin Hogg.
p. cm.
Includes bibliographical references and index.
ISBN 978-0-521-19338-2 (hardback)
1. Promise (Law) 2. Contracts. I. Title.
K845.P76.H64 2011
346.02–dc22
2011013371

ISBN 978-0-521-19338-2 Hardback
ISBN 978-1-107-41697-0 Paperback

For Alexa

CONTENTS

vii

PREFACE

It is the thesis of this work that promise has played an important role in the contract law not only of those jurisdictions whose legal culture derives directly and unashamedly from Roman law and the medieval *ius commune* but also in those systems forming part of the Common law world, systems which are somewhat more reticent in acknowledging a debt to Roman or medieval European legal influences. The importance of promise in contract law derives from a mixture of sources: from the natural law tradition of Aristotle, Aquinas, and the late scholastics; from Roman law itself; from the canon law; and from the emphasis placed in later centuries upon the will, of which the promise is one specific manifestation. It is argued that, while promise was the paradigm voluntary obligation in medieval and early modern law, its primacy was largely supplanted by a model of agreement with the contract as its concrete expression, one in which promise was relegated largely to a description of the nature of agreement (as an exchange of promises) and of some unusual transactions which could not easily be accommodated within an agreement model, such as the promise of reward. Promise survived, however, as a discrete obligation in one European system, that of Scotland, and the functions which it is capable of performing in that system offer some inspiration for a possible rediscovery of the value of promise in other systems. Many transactions analysed in this work are only with difficulty fitted into a contractual model, whereas, it will be argued, it would be more honest to recognise that the unreciprocated or unilateral promise provides a neater and more apposite explanation for the basis of liability. It will also be suggested that the promise in the wider sense of a contractual promise is a concept which still illuminates much of the substantive content of contract law, despite attacks which have been made against promise by the reliance theory of obligational liability and other non-promissory theories.

It is not the intention of this work to suggest that *all* of contract law can be explained by the idea of promise. Indeed, it will be admitted that many controls upon parties' promises are imposed externally, without

xiii

reference to the will or promise of the parties, in order to enforce societal norms embodying values, such as objective good faith. Nonetheless, the case will be put that the promise, especially the unilateral promise, might usefully be given a greater role in contract law than it currently plays in most legal systems, and that it is heartening that just such a view appears to have been taken by the drafters of model legal projects such as the Principles of European Contract Law (PECL) and the Draft Common Frame of Reference (DCFR). At the present time, the probable future of promise in European legal systems, and conceivably further afield in the US and South Africa, is a bright one.

This work contains, particularly in Part 1, a discussion of the various legal theories which have over the centuries been suggested as explanations for the normative force of contract law. It must be stressed, however, that the search for an 'ideal' theory of contract law is not the objective of this work, as it is for many works on contract theory. Too much contract theory gives the appearance of being based upon an ideal of what the law should be, rather than what it actually is, and of thus being disconnected from the law with which the courts are concerned. Projects for the construction of utopian contract law and theory are all very well, but the approach adopted in this work is largely one of attempting to discover what role promise has played, and still plays, in the law of concrete legal systems. Nonetheless, some suggestions are offered as to how will theory, in a reinvigorated form, might continue to offer an overarching explanation for the normative force of promises and contracts, given that there is a perceived crisis in the minds of some about how to justify the enforcement of voluntary obligations. In offering ideas concerning such a reinvigorated will theory, it will be suggested that promissory theory cannot realistically hope to explain all of contact law, as it once tried to, but that this incompleteness need not be seen as a weakness.

The present study is, as the title indicates, a comparative one. Promise as a field of study comes alive in a comparative context, in both a legal jurisdictional as well as disciplinary sense. In terms of legal systems, the primary focus is on one system from each of the three great western legal families: England (representing the Common law), Germany (representing the civilian family) and Scotland (for the mixed legal systems). Given the comparatively small size of Scotland as a jurisdiction, the mixed legal systems of South Africa and Louisiana are also considered in Parts 2 and 3 of the work. There is in addition some reference to Common law cases from the USA, Canada and Australia. In respect of non-legal disciplines, observations on the idea of promise are offered from the field of philosophy (especially linguistic philosophy), theology and anthropology.

I am indebted to a number of people and organisations for assistance rendered with the research which I undertook for this book. I am grateful to my two research assistants, Gemma Grant and Michael Johnston, for work which they did for me over two successive summers. The Edinburgh Law School allowed me a period of sabbatical leave in which to conduct my research and to prepare the manuscript of this work, and I extend my thanks both to the Head of School, Professor Douglas Brodie, for supporting my application for leave and to colleagues who covered my teaching and other duties during my absence. I was a guest at Tulane University in New Orleans, and at Stellenbosch University in South Africa, during that sabbatical leave, and I am grateful to the Dean and Faculties of both institutions for a desk and library access. I am especially grateful to Professor Vernon Palmer at Tulane for his support, which was an invaluable contribution to my successful time in New Orleans. That visit to New Orleans was funded by an award from the Carnegie Trust for the Universities of Scotland, for whom sincere appreciation for their generous assistance is gratefully extended. I was also the happy recipient of a Max Planck Society Scholarship which enabled me to visit the Max Planck Institute for Comparative and International Private Law in Hamburg to conduct research on German law, and I owe a great debt of thanks to Professor Reinhard Zimmermann for supporting me in my scholarship application to the Society and in arranging accommodation for me at the Institute. Lastly, I should not omit to thank Laurence Marsh for his eagle-eyed copy-editing and all of the staff in the Law division of Cambridge University Press who assisted with the production of this book, especially Finola O'Sullivan and Richard Woodham.

ABBREVIATIONS OF COURT NAMES

(given in brackets after case citations in the table of cases)

A	Appellate Division of the Supreme Court of South Africa
BCCA	British Columbia Court of Appeal
C	Cape of Good Hope Provincial Division of the Supreme Court of South Africa
CAS	Court of Appeal of Singapore
CC	Constitutional Court of South Africa
CExC	Court of Exchequer Chamber of England and Wales
Ch	Chancery Division of the High Court of England and Wales
CP	Court of Common Pleas of England and Wales
CPD	Common Pleas Division of the High Court of England and Wales
CSC	Cape Colony Supreme Court
CSIH	Court of Session (Scotland), Inner House
CSOH	Court of Session (Scotland), Outer House
D	Durban and Coast Local Division of the High Court of South Africa
E	Eastern Cape Local Division of the Supreme Court of South Africa
EWCA	Court of Appeal of England and Wales (incl. cases heard prior to 1875 by the Court of Appeal in Chancery)
FCA	Federal Court of Australia
HCA	High Court of Australia
HL	Appellate Committee of the House of Lords
KB	King's Bench Division of the High Court of England and Wales
KZNHC	KwaZulu-Natal High Court
LAC	Labour Appeal Court of South Africa

NC	Northern Cape Provincial Division of the Supreme Court of South Africa
NSCA	Nova Scotia Court of Appeal
NZCA	New Zealand Court of Appeal
NZSA	Supreme Court of New Zealand
OCA	Ontario Court of Appeal
PC	Privy Council
QB	Queen's Bench Division of the High Court of England and Wales
SCA	Supreme Court of Appeal of South Africa
SCC	Supreme Court of Canada
SCNSW	Supreme Court of New South Wales
SCQ	Supreme Court of Queensland
SCWA	Supreme Court of Western Australia
T	Transvaal Provincial Division of the Supreme Court of South Africa
UKSC	United Kingdom Supreme Court
W	Witwatersrand Local Division of the Supreme Court of South Africa

TABLE OF CASES

ARRANGED BY JURISDICTION

Australia

Canada

England and Wales (and Channel Islands)

Germany

Reichsgericht

Bundesgericht

Other courts

New Zealand

Scotland

South Africa

United States – Common law cases

United States – Louisiana law cases

Other jurisdictions

Netherlands

Belize

France

Singapore

TABLE OF LEGISLATION

ARRANGED BY JURISDICTION

Australia (Commonwealth and State / Territory Acts)

Austria

England, Wales and Scotland

(a) Statutes:

Subordinate legislation:

France

Germany

Civil Code (BGB):

Commercial Code (HGB):

Code of Civil Procedure (ZPO):

Italy

Netherlands

New Zealand

Quebec

South Africa

Switzerland

United States – Common Law jurisdictions (and Federal Acts)

United States – Louisiana

Civil Code (1870 version, now repealed) Articles:

Civil Code (current version) Articles:

Individual Laws:

Model Law

Draft Common Frame of Reference ('DCFR') Articles:

PART 1

Theoretical and historical introduction

1

The concept of promise

There are a number of principal arguments advanced in this work, among them that promise has played a central role in obligations theory and practice (in part, though not merely, because it has been used to describe the nature of contract),[1] that the idea of promise as a manifestation of human will and commitment is central to an understanding of contract, that this idea explains much of the body of contractual rules and doctrines applied by the courts, and that promise narrowly defined (as a unilateral promise) is a better explanation for a number of circumstances in which voluntary obligations are intended than is the bilateral obligation of contract. However, none of these arguments can sensibly be advanced without first settling the fundamental definition of the idea of a promise and the characteristics of the practice or institution of promising. For that reason, this chapter will address some very basic matters, including: the constituent elements of a promise; how promises are formed; what the party making a promise (the promisor) must intend before a promise can exist; whether the beneficiary of a promise (the promisee) must also intend anything before the promise can be constituted; whether promises must be accepted before they bind the promisor; and whether promises may be made subject to conditions.

These questions will not be posed simply with legal understandings of promise in mind, but also with regard to other disciplines, including linguistics and morality. Such an inter-disciplinary approach recognises that promise, and the institution of promising, is not the preserve of lawyers alone, but is a feature of human society the effects of which cannot be neatly contained within the boundaries of a single academic field. There will, however, be some specifically legal discussion later in the

---

[1] The description of a contract in the US Restatement (Second) of Contracts is typical of such a usage of the promissory idea: contract is 'a promise … for the breach of which the law gives a remedy, or the performance of which the law in some way recognizes as a duty' (§1).

3

chapter, when the focus will be on three aspects of promise which are crucial for the law's conception of promise, these being whether a promise is by nature gratuitous, conditional and unilateral. Lack of precision about what these three concepts mean has been productive of much confusion in the debate as to the nature of promise and as to whether contract can be said to be about promising. It is hoped that clarity as to the meaning of these terms will enable such confusion to be resolved.

1. What is a promise?

(a) A definition of promise

To begin with, an attempt will be made to provide a definition of a promise; without such a definition, it must inevitably be unclear which types of transaction or behaviour can constitute promises and which cannot.[2] In seeking to construct such a definition, an attempt will be made not only to be as inclusive as possible, but also as jurisdictionally and disciplinary neutral as possible. In attempting this definitional task, a number of suggestions about the nature of promises will simply be stated, without (to begin with) any attempt to explore whether they are valid, so that a possible basis can be laid out for exploring the whole of the potential field of enquiry. The suggestions to be made are empirically based, deriving from observations of commonly conceived features of promise. Though this methodology may seem somewhat arbitrary, it is justified on the basis that, because promising is an institution constructed by human societies, it is therefore legitimate to examine how such societies conceive of the institution. Some might dispute the assertion of promise as a human institution, but challenges to such a view will require to wait until later in the chapter. It is hoped that the end result of this process will be a definition of promise which accurately describes the institution of promising

---

[2] It is surprising that in some of the leading modern works on promise this task of defining promise is not attempted. Thus, in Atiyah's *Promises, Morals and Law*, no clear definition of a promise is offered at any single point in the text, it merely being noted (p. 8) that the discussion will include both morally binding and non-binding promises. As a result, one is never clear exactly what Atiyah means by his reference to a promise at any stage of his argument. His treatment of vows (p. 54) is also undertaken without the provision of a definition. Consequently, he seems to conceive that a vow can lack a party to whom the vow is addressed, which is a quite different understanding of a vow to that taken in this work. Fried similarly fails to provide a comprehensive definition of a promise, saying simply that 'when I promise I commit myself to *act*, later' (Fried, *Contract as Promise*, p. 9), which expresses only some of the necessary elements of a promise. More recently, Kimel, in *From Promise to Contract*, also fails to offer a definition of promise.

and the promises to which it gives rise (the problem of different linguistic constructions with a similarity to the promise, as well as different cultural understandings of the phenomenon of promising, are also considered later in the chapter). The elements of the suggested definition produced by this process will then be tested for accuracy.

A good place to begin in creating a definition of promise is to ask who is conceived of as being able to make promises. Societies generally seem to wish to include human beings (both adults and children), as well as legally recognised entities such as companies, partnerships, governments, clubs and societies.[3] There is also a general wish to include supernatural beings, such as God, as promise makers, even if some may doubt the existence of God, for it is incontrovertible that religions have historically conceived, and do still conceive, of divine promises, and that such conceptions have been influential in the development of understandings of promise (as the discussion in later chapters will indicate). Given this range of persons who make promises, it can also be observed that, from whichever category of human, juristic, or supernatural they come, persons from one category are generally conceived of as being able to make promises to any of the other two categories of person (so a human being may make a promise to a company, two partnerships may exchange promises, God may make promises to human beings, and so forth). Second, it seems that promises are commonly conceived of as being more than merely internal thought promises. A promisor must do something other than mentally intending something: he must demonstrate his intention in some objectively observable fashion. Third, many promises seem to be made without any expectation on the part of the promisor that he will get any benefit from making the promise: they are what may be called gratuitous. So, for instance, a person may promise to mend another's garden fence for nothing. On the other hand, some promises seem to be given in the hope, or even with the legal entitlement, of some reciprocal benefit being received by the promisor. Thus, a company may promise to allot shares to an individual in exchange for money. Fourth, some promises are made without any condition attached, so that there is no uncertainty surrounding the fact that the promisor will be obliged to undertake the promised act. On the other hand, some promises are made with conditions attached. Thus, one person may promise another a lift in his car if the latter is unable to buy a ticket for a particular train. In such a case,

---

[3] Though these last two are not always conceived of as having personality in some legal systems, and thus not being able to make promises in their own name.

the promisor is only obliged to fulfil the promise if the condition is met. Fifth, a promise is understood to entail the idea that the promisor is placing himself under some obligation, an enforceable duty or commitment to the promisee, whether of a moral or legal nature (a subject discussed more fully in Chapter 2). Last, it seems that it is generally conceived that the nature of the duty which the promisor is undertaking is the performance of some future act (which may include *not* doing something) which will be of benefit to the promisee.

These commonly held features of a promise allow a definition for a promise to be proposed. Such a definition is one which, it is suggested, is capable of satisfying the understanding of a promise held by different human disciplines, including those of sociology, psychology, theology and the law. Drawing on what has been said above, therefore, the following definition of a promise may be proposed:

> A promise is a statement by which one person commits to some future beneficial performance, or the beneficial withholding of a performance, in favour of another person.

Some examples of statements which might constitute promises have already been suggested above. Given the proposed definition, a few more statements which would seem to qualify as promises may be suggested:

> 'I promise to pay you what I owe you next week.'
> 'I promise to marry you when I get a job.'
> 'I promise to pay my taxes promptly in future.'
> 'I promise to give you a lift to the shops in my car on Saturday.'
> 'I promise to stand as guarantor for my son's debt.'
> 'I promise not to trespass on your land again.'
> 'I promise that I will visit you in hospital tomorrow.'

In fact, given what was suggested earlier, that a promise must objectively demonstrate an intention to accept an obligation,[4] there would in addition seem to be no objection to a promise being constituted by a simple affirmative response to an enquiry as to whether a stated commitment was being undertaken. Thus, the question 'Do you undertake to ensure that I will receive the package tomorrow?' met with the reply 'Yes' would seem to give rise to a promise on the part of the person giving the positive

---

[4] See, for a recent exposition of the idea that the essence of contract lies in the acceptance of, or assumption of, an obligation, Coote, *Contract as Assumption*. Coote summarises his view (p. 42) thus: 'In essence, a contract is a promise or undertaking in respect of which legal contractual obligation has been assumed by means which the law recognises as effective for that purpose.'

response.[5] Additionally, there is no reason why the idea of a promissory 'statement' might not be interpreted sufficiently widely to allow inclusion of non-verbal conduct manifesting promissory intent. So, a handshake, or the handing over of a key to a safe in which were contained funds sufficient to satisfy a debt, might equally be considered a 'statement' indicative of promissory intent.

In all of the above examples, the use of the phrase 'I promise that …' would reasonably be interpreted by the hearer as an indication of an intention on the speaker's part to be bound by the commitment described in the statement. In other words, what the speaker would be doing in each of the above examples by uttering the phrase 'I promise that…' could, in the alternative, have been done by uttering the more expansive phrase 'I am hereby promising that …'. So, to utter the phrase 'I promise that …' is, in this first sense of the phrase, to intend to undertake a promise in the act of the utterance. It must, however, be appreciated that there is a second sense which may be intended by use of the phrase 'I promise that …', a sense which operates merely as a description of the act of promising, rather than as a phrase constitutive of a promise itself. In this second sense, a narrative rather than an active form, the phrase could be used by someone seeking to describe an act of promising and who was asking another to consider what the import of such a promise might be. So, 'I promise that …' could be intended to mean 'Imagine that I were to promise that …'.[6] Alternatively, also in this second sense of the phrase, it might be intended to describe a frequent habit of the promisor in making promises, as in 'On a regular basis, I promise that I will help my friends'. In this second sense therefore, the speaker is not making a promise, but merely describing the act of promising. What sense is meant by a speaker should be evident from the surrounding circumstances in which the phrase is uttered.[7]

It is important at this early stage of the analysis of promises to note that it is generally considered that it is not necessary to employ the verb 'promise' in order to make a promise, even though it is that verb which in

---

[5] As the discussion in Chapter 3 will indicate, such an answer and question format was the method by which the form of contract called *stipulatio* was undertaken in Roman law: see p. 111.

[6] For instance, as in this phrase, which might be used by a legal tutor to pose a question to a class: 'I promise that I will marry someone: what consequences would follow from such a promise?'.

[7] Similar observations might be made of other words indicating commitment, e.g. 'I pledge that …' or 'I swear that …'.

English is most commonly used.[8] Any other verb which unequivocally indicates, from the context of its usage, an intention to commit to a future performance in favour of another will suffice. Thus, in English, alternative words or phrases such as 'accept', 'assure', 'dedicate', 'undertake', 'guarantee', 'give you my word that …', 'commit', and 'pledge' will each suffice, in an appropriate context,[9] to indicate an intention to enter into a promise.[10] The words 'vow' and 'swear' may perform a similar function, though, as is discussed further below, vows and oaths have been the subject of somewhat distinct treatments by different societies and cultures and therefore require separate consideration. Some forms of words cause problems, however. The use of the form 'I will do x' is one such difficult case, as the intention communicated by the phrase 'I will' is ambiguous. Thus, if rather than stating 'I promise to pay you what I owe you next week', the speaker instead says 'I will pay you what I owe you next week', does such a statement indicate commitment of a promissory type or is it a mere prediction as to a future event or a statement of future intent? The phraseology when considered alone fails to convey a clear meaning, and any proper determination of the presence or absence of the commitment of the speaker to be bound to an obligation in such a case will inevitably require to have regard either to the circumstances in which the statement was made or conceivably to an operative presumption against or in favour of interpreting ambiguous words in a promissory way.

(b)   Promise: objectively existing phenomenon or human construction?

The discussion thus far has assumed that promising is a legal institution (in the sense of a legal structure governing a specific type of human

---

[8]   The English verb (as with similar verbs in other languages with classical origins) derives from the Latin verb *promittere*.

[9]   The context, however, is everything. Use of none of the words listed, not even promise, is conclusive in every case that a promise will be intended or constituted by the speaker's words, a point which has been made by many linguists, psychologists and jurists, in their respective writings. For instance, as Searle has commented on the phrases 'I promise' and 'I hereby promise', 'we often use these expressions in the performance of speech acts which are not strictly speaking promises, but in which we wish to emphasize the degree of our commitment' (Searle, *Speech Acts*, p. 58).

[10]   A useful promissory analysis of many of these phrases, from a linguistic perspective, is found in Hickey, 'A Promise is a Promise'. Hickey does not mention 'commit' in his list of promissory synonyms, because commitment is the concept he uses to define the foundational meaning and content of a promise. He defines commitment as 'binding oneself to a certain course of action' (p. 70), such binding usually being of a moral, but also possibly legal, nature.

interaction) of human origins, the nature and boundaries of which are therefore determinable by human societies.[11] An alternative view would be that promising should properly be seen as having an externally determined and constant nature (much like gravity), which it is the task of human beings to discover rather than determine for themselves as a matter of social agreement. A similar debate might be had in respect of other institutions with similarities to promise, such as the vow or the oath which are considered later in this chapter. Whichever view of the nature of the institution of promising were adopted, one would expect its existence to be recognised in a foundational legal rule or norm, that norm being something like 'If A makes a promise in favour of B in the correct form, then that promise must be kept'.

If promising is a given objective reality, rather than a human social construct, describing the nature of promising would be an enquiry focused on discovering its objective nature, rather than an exercise of constructing a definition that seemed to match the human institution of promise. Can a belief in promising as an objective reality be maintained? Theologians might argue that God makes promises and, as human beings, formed in the divine image, we derive our capacity and disposition for promising from God, and that therefore the very concept of the promise has boundaries which are defined by reference to divine acts of promising. Natural lawyers might argue that promising is a fundamental, innate aspect of the human condition, an aspect of the way the world is and thus not something simply created by man through particular instances of social interaction. Linguistic philosophers might argue that even though the promise is a type of human 'speech act', it is one which is employed to describe specific instances of the species of promise, a species which has an existence quite apart from any specific instance of it or of the parties to a particular promise.[12] It is not the intention of this work to explore in depth the complexity of such arguments, but they will be touched on so far as they throw light on the law's conception of promises and the functions the promise plays in contract law. In particular, Chapter 2 (which explores the nature of promise as a moral and legal obligation) will consider the sources of the obligatory nature of promises, and will thus necessarily consider contrary

---

[11] There is an extensive body of literature on the subject of legal institutions. See for instance MacCormick, *Institutions of Law*; Del Mar and Bankowski, *Law as Institutional Normative Order*; Ruiter, 'A Basic Classification of Legal Institutions' and 'Structuring Legal Institutions'.

[12] Not all linguistic philosophers would agree with such an argument, but it is advanced in the writings of Adolf Reinach (see, principally 'Die apriorischen Grundlagen', trans. by Crosby as 'The Apriori Foundations of the Civil Law').

arguments to the position that promising is a human institution the content of which is determinable by those to whom it applies.

For the moment, however, it will continue to be asserted, without providing a detailed justification for such assertion, that the concept of promising may be determined, as with other human social institutions, by human beings themselves, though it is not denied either that human beings may be predisposed (perhaps genetically, perhaps by virtue of our nature as divinely created beings) to promising, or that the boundaries they give to the institution of promising may not be affected by a theistic belief in an objective and supernatural nature to promising, issues considered further in the next chapter.

The nature of promise will now be explored further by reference to component elements of the working definition suggested above. In this examination, it will become evident that the promissory analysis of non-legal disciplines can often be of assistance to juridical understandings of promise.

(c)   Testing component elements of the definition of promise

(i)   A promise is more than merely an internal mental process: promises as speech acts demonstrating commitment

It was observed when suggesting a definition of a promise that mere internalised mental processes or unarticulated statements – the 'promise' made only in the mind of the promisor of the type 'I shall see to it that my daughter is financially supported while at University' – should not count as promises properly so called. It is generally accepted across disciplines having an interest in the idea of a promise that some manifested commitment of the person undertaking a promise – whether that commitment be expressed by way of spoken words, writing, or behaviour (for instance, a nod of the head in response to a question asking whether a promise is intended[13]) – to another is required before there may be a promise. So the speaker, uttering the promissory words, must know and intend that in so doing he is undertaking a commitment, that commitment being

---

[13] Atiyah suggests that, where it is conduct, such as a nod of a head, which is held to demonstrate the promissory intent, what is happening is that a promise is being implied from the conduct (see *Promises, Morals and Law*, pp. 173–4). But why must an implication be made? Where conduct unequivocally indicates assent to an obligation, no implication need be made any more than where words indicate assent: each is simply a mode of communicating assent to the obligation.

to assume an obligation (a binding duty) towards another. Why is the necessity for such a commitment maintained?

Different ways of justifying the necessity of such a requirement are emphasised by different disciplines. The lawyer may emphasise the onerous nature of what is being undertaken when promising (especially if the promise is to be a gratuitous one), and may therefore stress the need for certainty before the speaker be held to have assumed such an onerous obligation. The psychologist may emphasise the different stages in the process of deliberating upon, and then committing to, a decision, noting that it is only when human beings manifest some behaviour external to their thought processes that they may be taken to commit irrevocably to a decision which has been the subject of mental deliberation, and that, before this stage is reached, human beings generally feel that they are operating within a private, personal realm, and thus are free to change their minds. The sociologist might emphasise the importance to the functioning of human society of certain types of publicly declared and manifested conduct, and highlight the ceremonial attendant upon, for instance, making vows or oaths, the notarisation of legal documents, or simply the form and context within which words must be placed before public recognition is given to certain types of acts. The linguist may explain how certain words have developed a usage which best allows the speaker to manifest commitment to the undertaking of duties in favour of others. Taken together, these disciplinary observations doubtless explain that a number of factors have led to the universally accepted requirement that promissory intent be more than mere internal mental commitment to a course of action. In fact, the various disciplinary observations have not been confined to their respective spheres; those, for instance, writing on the law appear at various times to have drawn upon the analysis of other disciplines when justifying and explaining the rule that undertaking a valid promise at law requires the promisor to demonstrate some objective consent to the obligation.[14]

---

[14] For instance, the theologian Thomas Aquinas noted the mental processes preliminary to making a binding vow as (i) deliberation, (ii) a purpose of the will, and (iii) a promise. Similarly, in the seventeenth century, the Scottish jurist James Dalrymple (Lord Stair) seems to have drawn upon the behavioural observation that human beings typically demonstrate three stages of the will when deciding whether or not to commit to an obligation, namely (i) desire, (ii) resolution, and (iii) engagement. The third of these stages is crucial for the law: without some act of engagement to what is desired and has been resolved, no obligation can arise (see Stair, *Institutions*, I.x.2). The similarity of the analysis of Stair to Aquinas's is marked, though there is no indication that Stair had this passage of Aquinas

That there be some external conduct manifested by a speaker before he can be held to have undertaken a promise suggests that the crucial perspective for judging a promise is an objective one. This is not to say that the subjective intention of the speaker to promise is unimportant, merely that, in practical terms, such internal, subjective intention can only ever be judged and assessed through externally manifested, and objectively judged, conduct.[15] A baldly stated preference for an objective approach, however, skates over the complexity of how one judges and interprets the intention of a speaker from his external conduct. People often use words ambiguously. How should such ambiguous words be interpreted? And what of the speaker who uses a word incorrectly, thinking that its meaning is x, when in fact it is commonly understood to mean y in the context in question? Such questions are very challenging for the courts, touching both upon the fundamental question of whether a promise should be taken to have been intended at all, or, if it should, what promissory content was intended by the promisor in using the words in question. In this work, these questions will primarily be considered in the context of specific topics considered in the later chapters (formation, error, and so forth). They are also, however, quite properly questions which shape and influence the discipline of the construction or interpretation of promises and contracts, a field in which there has been much uncertainty of late in (to choose but two systems) English and Scots law. Such uncertainty has resulted largely from an ongoing philosophical and linguistic debate between judges and academics about whether words have any objective meaning beyond that which contracting parties may choose to give them in a particular context, and whether, if they do, courts should begin the

---

in mind when framing his own observation. One may also note Grotius's three 'modes of speech' (*De iure belli ac pacis*, II.xi.2–4).

[15] There are numerous judicial statements to this effect in relation to voluntarily assumed obligations. For instance, see the following comment of Lord Clarke, delivering the unanimous judgment of the UK Supreme Court in *RTS Flexible Systems Ltd* v. *Molkerei Alois Müller GmbH & Co. KG (UK Production)* [2010] UKSC 14: 'Whether there is a binding contract between the parties and, if so, upon what terms depends upon what they have agreed. It depends not upon their subjective state of mind, but upon a consideration of what was communicated between them by words or conduct, and whether that leads objectively to a conclusion that they intended to create legal relations ...'. To similar effect, see Lord Steyn in *Deutsche Genossenschaftsbank* v. *Burnhope* [1995] 4 All ER 717, 724e: 'the court must not try to divine the purpose of the contract by speculating about the real intention of the parties. It may only be inferred from the language used by the parties, judged against the objective contextual background.' The same objective approach is taken in the Draft Common Frame of Reference (DCFR): see Art. II.-4:302.

task of construing a contract from the standpoint of such objective meaning unless a clearly absurd result is reached.[16] The debate is also affected by the unresolved question of whether contract should be seen primarily as a private concern of the contracting parties (a view which tends towards a preference for the parties' subjective understanding of the words they use), or whether contract should be recognised as inevitably having a public aspect, given that contracts may affect third party interests or require to be acted upon by third parties (a view which tends towards a preference for the objective meaning of words).[17] The complexity of such debates is, however, beyond the scope of the present enquiry, the focus of which is on the distinction between internal mental processes and external behaviour.

Returning to that focus, given that objectively manifested and interpreted behaviour demonstrating a commitment to act (in other words, to be bound to an obligation to do something), rather than mere internal thought processes, is suggested as the crucial means for determining whether a promise has been formed, what role then does intention have

---

[16] The nature of the debate may be appreciated by contrasting the ground-breaking approach to interpretation of Lord Hoffmann in judgments such as *Investors Compensation Scheme Ltd* v. *West Bromwich Building Society* [1998] 1 WLR 896 and *Chartbrook Ltd* v. *Persimmon Homes Ltd* [2009] UKHL 38, an approach which emphasises the subjective understanding attributed by parties to words and the wide context against which such subjective understanding may be judged, with that displayed recently by the Scottish courts, who have expressed a preference for a narrow interpretative context and for beginning with the 'natural meaning' of words. Thus, for instance, paraphrasing Lord Mustill's words in *Charter Reinsurance Co.* v. *Fagan* [1997] AC 313, Sir David Edward QC stated in his judgment in *Multi Link Leisure Developments Ltd* v. *North Lanarkshire Council* [2009] CSIH 96 (affd., on other reasoning, [2010] UKSC 47) that the court's enquiry 'should start (and will finish) by asking what is the ordinary meaning of the words used' (para. 25). A preference for an objective meaning to words is entrenched in some civil codes: in the Louisiana Civil Code, for instance, Art. 2047 (Meaning of words) provides that '[t]he words of a contract must be given their generally prevailing meaning'. Even the further provision of Art. 2048 that '[w]ords susceptible of different meanings must be interpreted as having the meaning that best conforms to the object of the contract', makes sense only on the presumption that the different possible meanings referred to are objectively determinable.

[17] For instance, a third party may rely on, or be required to enforce, contractual provisions: thus a third party seeking to enforce a benefit in its favour, an insurer or bank with an interest in the contract, or a party such as the keeper of a public register in which the contract has been lodged. A particularly troubling case is that of collective workplace agreements between employers and trade unions: such agreements may be relied upon by many employees, who will naturally give to the words in the agreement their ordinary meaning, and may be wholly unaware of absurd or unusual subjective meanings attached by the contracting parties to the language they have used.

in defining the concept of a promise? Most disciplines would agree that, in theory at least, a speaker must manifest a commitment to the performance of a future act in favour of another (and not just an intention to so commit himself or an intention to act), albeit that that commitment is to be judged objectively.[18] So statements whose language merely expresses a hope, intention, or prediction of doing something are excluded as promises: for instance, 'I hope to pay you the money next week', 'I intend to send you a cheque in the post tomorrow', 'I expect to be able to leave you my house in my will', or 'I will have dinner with you this evening'. But must the speaker (the promisor) also manifest other types of intention? And is any intention on the part of the hearer of the speaker's words required before a promise may be constituted? Some promissory writers have suggested that some such further indications of intention are required.

To explore these questions further, it is useful to refer to the arguments of some of those writing in the field of linguistic philosophy. This is a specialised field, and not all of its complexities can be considered here. However, the crucial contribution of linguistic philosophers of relevance for present purposes is their categorisation of promises as a form of 'speech act'. The concept of a speech act may be exemplified by one of its most famous instances in literature:

> And God said, Let there be light: and there was light.[19]

A speech act, like this one from the book of Genesis, denotes an utterance which does not describe a state of affairs (for instance 'the cat sat on the mat'), but, in the act of its utterance, *does* something. Consider for instance the words 'Stand up!', a phrase which functions as an instruction, so that the speaker, in speaking, does the act of issuing a command. The example quoted from Genesis is a particularly direct speech act: the speech act is a command which, by its very utterance, is immediately given effect to in physical reality by divine power. Not all speech acts are so immediately effective in relation to the act in question, a promise being one such less immediately effective speech act, given that it requires a future performance to bring the promised reality into being.

Promises are categorised by linguistic philosophers as a type of speech act. It is said that a promise, when uttered, does something, because it

---

[18] So that an insincerely meant promise which had the appearance of one genuinely meant by the promisor would count as a valid promise, a view supported by Atiyah, who frequently refers to insincere promises as valid promises, and also Robbins, *Promising, Intending and Moral Authority*, pp. 145–6.

[19] Gen. 1:3.

binds the promisor to a future performance. In the modern era, it was the linguistic philosopher J. L. Austin who most clearly developed the idea of speech acts for an English-speaking readership, though he was not the first to point out that words can function as acts.[20] Austin conceived of speech acts as either illocutions or perlocutions, illocutions being acts that we perform by uttering the words alone, whereas perlocutions are acts requiring some particular effect to be produced in order for the act to be successful, in other words they must persuade or convince the hearer.[21] Later linguistic philosophers proposed further, more detailed classifications of speech acts. For instance, Searle proposed a classification of speech acts which divides them into assertives (which assert the truth of what is said), directives (such as requests and commands), commissives (which commit a speaker to some future action, such as, crucially for the present discussion, promises and oaths), expressives (communicating some emotion or point of view of the speaker), or declarations (which have the effect of producing an alteration in the state of affairs, for instance court judgments).[22]

Austin classified promises as illocutions, as have some other linguistic philosophers who followed him (including Searle),[23] but this classification has not been followed by all. By contrast, Hickey characterises promises as perlocutionary, arguing they are only effective if the hearer is convinced of the commitment of the speaker of the words.[24] Hickey makes a specific claim which is of direct relevance to the question being presently considered of the mental processes and intentions underlying promises: he asserts that, if the hearer to whom a speech act of commitment is made does not accept it, the commitment is taken to be invalid: '[i]n other words, one needs the hearer's consent.'[25] This suggests an understanding of promise in which the promisee must not only hear but assent to the promise, and thus a view which requires a specific intention on the part of the promisee to be present also. Hickey's justification for this position is that:

> When looking at acts of commitment one sees that the consent of the hearer, which is an integral part of them, is important so that the speaker

[20] The Spanish scholastic Leonardus Lessius, for instance, had stated that a promise effects what the promissory words signify: *De iustitia et iure*, 2.18.5.

[21] Austin, *How to Do Things with Words*, especially Lectures IX and X.

[22] Searle, 'A Taxonomy of Illocutionary Acts'.

[23] Robbins also sees promises as illocutionary: see *Promising, Intending and Moral Authority*, pp. 143–4.

[24] Hickey, 'A Promise is a Promise', p. 69.   [25] *Ibid.*, p. 70.

> may achieve his purpose … The reason why can be seen in the motivation
> for performing a speech act of commitment. One can ascertain that such
> speech acts have a perlocutionary effect on the hearer and reflexively the
> recognition of success for the speaker on perceiving this effect.

Hickey's view is that promises are designed to persuade or convince the hearer, and so, unless such persuasion is secured, and the hearer 'consents' to what is promised, there is no promise in place. Persuasion of the hearer is an integral part of the promissory act for Hickey.

What are we to make of this argument? From a legal point of view (as the discussion in Chapter 3 will indicate), divergent positions are taken in different jurisdictions. Although most jurisdictions require a promise to be accepted before it binds the promisor, this is not universally the case, and suggestions by jurists, such as the natural lawyer Grotius, that promises had to be accepted before they were binding were not universally adopted. The present day law of Scotland, for instance, does not require an acceptance, or the demonstration of any 'persuasion' on the part of the promisee, before a promise can bind in law (although an outright rejection negates any promissory effect); some civilian jurisdictions require some promises to be made before a notary to be binding, without requiring any consent of the promisee; whereas Common law jurisdictions generally require promises to be accepted before they bind (though promises made by way of deed or under seal do not). Moving beyond the confines of the law, it seems a somewhat narrow conception of a promise to suggest that it should be a requirement that the promisor persuade the hearer of the commitment being made, so that the hearer 'accepts' the promise. Doubtless promisors will *hope* that the promisee will be convinced of the sincerity and commitment of the promise, but why should this be a prerequisite of a promise? Were such a restriction to prevail, we could not concede that a promise could ever be made in favour of an unconscious person, an absent person, or a person as yet unborn, at least not until any such person possessed the capacity or knowledge to be persuaded of the promise, yet there is clearly a desire (of many, at least) that the institution of promise be able to accommodate such examples as promises. And what of the hearer who may doubt the speaker's sincerity of commitment, but nonetheless keeps an open mind as to the possibility that the speaker may be sincere? While it has been suggested that the requirement that a promisee accept a promise demonstrates its voluntary nature by excluding 'forced promises',[26] such a requirement is unnecessary: so long as

---

[26] See Fried, *Contract as Promise*, p. 43.

a promisee is able to reject a promised benefit, non-compulsion can be assured.[27]

Hickey's argument that the hearer must assent to the promise naturally follows from his categorisation of promises as perlocutionary rather than illocutionary speech acts. As noted earlier, other linguistic philosophers do not share his view, and do not require persuasion of the hearer before a promise can be considered to be formed. This does not mean, however, that they necessarily consider that the only type of intention relevant to promises is (as was suggested earlier) the simple intention of the speaker to undertake a commitment by uttering the words in question. Searle, for instance, suggests the following necessary conditions for the making of a promise.[28] Some of these conditions (numbers (3) and (5) – (9)) relate to specific intentions or states of mind that the speaker (S) or hearer (H) must possess when S makes the relevant utterance (t) in the presence of H:

(1) S expresses the proposition p (the promise) in the utterance of t – by which Searle means that there must be present an utterance which can be isolated from the rest of the speech act, and analysed by reference to the following conditions;

(2) in expressing p, S predicates a future act (a) of S;

(3) H would prefer S's doing a to not doing a, and S believes that H would prefer this;

(4) it is not obvious to both S and that S will do a in the normal course of events;

(5) S intends to do a;

(6) S intends that t will place him under an obligation to do a;

(7) S intends to produce in H the knowledge that t will place S under the obligation to do a;

(8) S intends to produce such knowledge by means of the recognition of his intention; and

---

[27] Fried concedes as much – 'there must at least be the option to refuse or reject not just the benefit, but the promise of the benefit' (*ibid.*, p. 43) – while remaining unwilling formally to abandon his view that acceptance of a promise is essential, even if he admits that a tacit acceptance will suffice.

[28] One of Searle's conditions (which he numbers (1)) has been omitted from this list, as not being relevant to the present discussion, that condition being that 'normal input and output conditions obtain': Searle is referring to a collection of basic conditions without which meaningful communication cannot take place, for instance that the speaker and hearer each speak the same language, are conscious of what they are doing, are not deaf, and so forth.

(9) S intends to make his intention recognised by means of the hearer's knowledge of the meaning of *t*.

Atiyah has attacked this approach to defining promises on the basis that Searle 'makes no empirical inquiries of any kind at all as to how people in fact use the concept of promising'.[29] As will be seen below, there is force in this criticism, given that some of the conditions Searle lists do not seem to match with statements commonly taken to be promises.

Some of Searle's list of conditions were not mentioned in the definition of a promise proposed earlier because they were taken for granted,[30] while others match up with elements of that working definition, though not in precisely the same terms in which Searle puts them.[31] What, more particularly, of Searle's conditions which relate to intentions or states of mind of the speaker or hearer?

First there is condition (3), that H would prefer S's doing *a* to not doing *a*, and that S believes that H would prefer this. This correlates in part to the definition suggested earlier, which required that a promisor must commit to some performance 'in favour of' the promisee. This suggests that the promise must be of benefit to the promisor, rather than being detrimental. Searle also accepts this, as he notes that a commitment to do something disadvantageous to another should be classified as a threat and not a promise.[32] However, this does not explain why Searle couches this condition in terms of H's 'preference' and S's knowledge of this preference. This puts the matter in a subjective fashion, whereas it has been suggested earlier that intent ought to be judged objectively. The same objective approach, it is suggested, out to apply to the assessment of the nature of the beneficial act to be performed: such assessment should be an objective exercise, not one dependent upon

[29] Atiyah, *Promises, Morals and Law*, p. 108.
[30] For instance, condition (1), that there must be some words capable of being isolated as a promise, was assumed for present purposes, though fleshed out to some extent in the earlier discussion of words which can be used to demonstrate promissory intent.
[31] Thus, condition (2) agrees with the suggestion in the definition of a promise offered earlier that a future act of the promisor must be intended as the subject of the promise, and condition (6) corresponds to the suggestion in the definition that a promise must be a commitment of a promisor to some future performance, though it has been suggested that it is the objective assessment of S's intention which is crucial, rather than actual subjective intention (for that reason, Atiyah's objection to an intention to be bound providing the obligatory force of the promise – that this would release the false promisor from being bound – is not a valid one: the false promisor is bound because the objective interpretation of his state of mind is that intent was present).
[32] Searle, *Speech Acts*, p. 58.

the subjective opinion of the promisee. The promisor is in no position conclusively to know the subjective state of mind of the promisee: he can only guess at it, if he chooses to. Moreover, such guesswork will be problematic if the promisee's state of mind is such that he unreasonably considers an objective benefit not to be of benefit to him. Consider the following examples: S's commitment to H to demolish H's illegally built house might express an act which H would rather not wish to be done (because H does not want to see his house demolished), but nonetheless it could properly be seen as conferring the objective benefit of putting H into a position of complying with the relevant planning laws and thus arguably ought to be considered a benefit in favour of H. Or, to take another example, S's statement committing himself to extracting the rotten tooth of H, a child, might be a commitment to undertake an act which H would not wish done (because H is afraid of dental treatment), but nonetheless, as the act can be seen as objectively conferring a benefit on H, it ought surely to qualify as a promise. So, it is suggested that an objective assessment of whether the act in question is 'in favour of' another ought to be taken, rather than Searle's subjective approach, otherwise undertakings such as the two examples suggested here will not qualify as promises.

Condition (4) also seems suspect. Why cannot things which might very well happen in the normal course of things be the subject of a promise? It may be that the promisor wishes to put the matter beyond doubt or publicly to acknowledge an existing duty, or it may be that he wishes to comply with a third party requirement that a promise be made in respect of the act (the requirement for instance might be a legislative one, such as a rule of tax law stating that, if one wishes a transaction to fall within a certain tax regime, it must be supported by a promise).[33] It is unsurprising that things which are likely to happen anyway are not usually made the subject of promises, but it seems unduly restrictive to write this in as a requirement of a promise.

---

[33] For instance, a charitable individual might be intending to give a certain sum of money to a charity every year for the next few years. The charity might very well know that this is going to happen, because the individual has made such donations every year for a number of years, and has furthermore expressed his wish to continue doing so. Nonetheless, the individual concerned might now decide to make the giving which he was in any event planning to undertake the subject of a legally binding Deed of Covenant, because to do so confers certain tax advantages on him. The point is that sometimes things which we expect to happen in any event can nonetheless be made the subject of binding undertakings, and this may occur for reasons other than the relationship between the promisor and promisee.

Condition (6) addresses an issue – the source of the obligation which the promisor will come under – which was not the subject of treatment in the working definition, on the basis that different types of promise might find their source in different places.[34] Searle suggests that the promisor needs to intend that his statement will bind him. That agrees with the law's analysis (which requires an intention to be bound),[35] and it seems a valid requirement so long as it is recognised that such an intention may be tacitly present simply by virtue of the fact that the promisor *knows* that uttering the words will place him under an obligation because that is what the law (or the moral system) provides. So an intention might be either an intention that the promisor, in speaking, is binding himself, or an intention that in speaking he will be bound by virtue of externally applicable moral or legal norms.

Condition (7) raises the question of whether it makes sense to talk of intending to produce knowledge in someone else's mind, given that the production of such knowledge is something beyond the control of S. Surely all S can do is utter the words, and *hope* that H comes into the knowledge that S intends a promise.[36]

Condition (8) is also suspect – why must S intend this? Surely H's knowledge that S has come under an obligation by uttering *t* might not derive from H's recognising S's intention that that be so, but rather, for instance, from H's knowledge that the legal system will impose the requisite obligation upon S. This condition seems too restrictive.

Condition (9) – that S must intend to make his intention recognised by means of the hearer's knowledge of the meaning of *t* – suggests that the promisor must intend to bind himself by virtue of the promisee's hearing and understanding his promise. This too seems somewhat restrictive. It certainly seems correct to suggest that the promisor must intend that some other person must hear and understand the nature of the commitment (so a promise uttered in English to a group of persons who spoke and understood only Swahili would not seem to count as an utterance

---

[34] These issues are explored more fully in the next two chapters.
[35] See for instance the late Spanish scholastic, Lessius, who required that there be an 'intention of obligating oneself absolutely', and identified this intention as source of the obligatory power of a promise (*De iustitia et iure*, 2.18.1); also Rawls, who says 'promising is an act done with the public intention of deliberately incurring an obligation' (*A Theory of Justice*, p. 52).
[36] A similar point is made by Smith in *John Searle*, p. 66. Rawls suggests that it is S's *wanting* the requisite knowledge to exist in the mind of H which is important, rather than an intention by S that that be so: 'we want others to know that we recognize this tie [i.e. the promise] and intend to abide by it' (*Theory of Justice*, p. 52).

intended to be a promise), but it is not clear why it must be the promisee who hears and understands the promise. This would prevent promises being made to absent promisees, or to promisees not yet in existence. So all that seems necessary is that the promisor and some other person, even just a third party, hear and comprehend the nature of the promissory utterance,[37] though as a matter of practicalities the promisee will need eventually to learn of the promise, and understand its nature as a promise, if it is to be enforced.

This somewhat involved analysis of Searle's conditions for promising has been undertaken to demonstrate that focusing upon the subjective intention of promisor or promisee when defining the conditions for a promise leads to difficulty. While it seems correct that a promisor must intend to undertake performance of a future act in favour of the promisee when he utters the promissory words, an attempt has been made here to indicate how assessing such an intention must be an objective exercise, and how making reference to any further intentions of the parties both excludes undertakings that ought properly to be considered promises as well as insists upon knowledge by one party of the subjective state of mind of another party which is not practicable.

(ii) A promise is a commitment to a performance of the promisor

So the statement 'I promise that the sun will come up tomorrow' does not relate to any promised conduct of the speaker and so is not a promise. Similarly, a statement by Michael that 'I promise that Mary will pay you tomorrow' cannot be a promise of Michael's unless Michael has the ability to compel Mary's performance, in which case Mary would be acting on Michael's behalf and the statement could properly be construed as a promise by Michael. A promisor can of course promise that he will use his best endeavours to ensure that a third party does something, but such a promise creates no duty on the part of the third party.

A promise to tell the truth is more problematic. It might be said that truth-telling is of itself a beneficial act, something of value to the hearer, so that to promise to tell the truth is to commit oneself to perform a beneficial service to another. However, that might be to stretch the idea of performance too far. It may be more accurate to classify a so-called

---

[37] Melden, 'On Promising', takes a similar view to Searle and suggests that both promisor and promisee must be moral agents who hear and comprehend the nature of what is promised as a promissory utterance.

'promise' to tell the truth as a declaration made in solemn form, or an oath (if put in oath form, as in 'I swear to tell the truth'). If that is so, then it serves as an important reminder that the mere use of the word promise does not necessarily make something a promise, at least not in the sense suggested earlier.

(iii)   A promise must manifest more than an illusory commitment or one which the promisor is patently unable to fulfil

The context in which a statement is made may suggest that, despite the promissory language used, no promise is intended, because either (i) the context suggests that there is no serious commitment to performance,[38] as for instance in the case of a boastful or rash promise made in the heat of the moment, a joking promise, a promise of affection ('I shall love you forever'), or a political promise ('I promise that this government's first priority will be education reform'),[39] (ii) a promissory intent is present, but the circumstances suggest there is little chance of the commitment being fulfilled, or at least that there is a strong possibility that the commitment may not be fulfilled, for instance the commitment by the alcoholic, given for the twentieth time, that he will give up drinking alcohol for good,[40] or (iii) it is clear that the performance promised is one which the promisor has no control over ('I promise not to bore you during my lecture'[41] – clearly the promisor making such a statement has no power over whether or not his listeners will be bored by what he says, as being bored is an entirely subjective reaction of the listener).

In any of these three types of case, despite the use of promissory language, the statement made ought not to be considered a promise.

(iv)   A promise must relate to the future

So, for instance, a statement cannot be a promise if it merely confirms a past action or state of affairs ('I promise that it was not I who broke your

---

[38] For discussion of the idea that promissory language may, in a particular culture or society, not generally be considered to give rise to promissory obligations, see the discussion below at pp. 52–6 of the use of promissory language in Tongan and Iranian society.

[39] Note in this respect §118 of the German Civil Code (BGB): 'A declaration of intent not seriously intended which is made in the expectation that its lack of serious intention will not be misunderstood is void.'

[40] Such commitments by alcoholics to loved ones have been explained from a psychiatric viewpoint as not genuinely promissory but as 'acts of propitiation' and 'an invocation of pity and forgiveness that make use of the syntactic form of the promise, but lack the intention or ability to follow through' (Schlesinger, *Promises, Oaths and Vows*, pp. 9, 13).

[41] An example given by Hickey, 'A Promise is a Promise', p. 72.

vase' or 'I accept responsibility for the accident') or confirms a present action or state of affairs ('I hereby give you my car' or 'I promise that I am not having an extra-marital affair'). As such statements do not relate to the future they are not promises, though they may be something else, for instance a conveyance of property which effectually transfers real rights in goods, or a warranty of a present state of affairs. Of course, as argued earlier, the mere presence of a future prediction (as in 'I will ...' or 'I intend') is insufficient to denote promissory intent, so that the element of future performance is a necessary though not sufficient condition for promising.

This requirement of a future action clearly has implications for contractual theory. It might, for instance, be argued that a contractual theory built solely upon the idea of promise would be unable to explain contracts based upon an exchange of goods, money or services, for immediate payment, for instance the immediate purchase of, and payment for, a newspaper, given that, as such transactions indicate the consent of the parties to an immediate exchange, they may appear not to contain any promises as to future conduct. This question is explored in more detail in Chapter 4, where it is suggested that promissory theory can deal with such immediate exchanges. Another possible conclusion, however, would be that promise is merely one means to demonstrate an intention to be bound to an obligation, another means being just the sort of conduct which is demonstrated in transactions where contract formation occurs contemporaneously with performance.

(v)   A promise must state a commitment in favour of another party

So, a statement by the speaker to do something to benefit himself ('I promise to give up smoking for the good of my health') is not a promise, even if seriously intended.[42] Such statements may however amount to vows, such as a vow of chastity or poverty.[43]

It is an interesting question whether a promise in favour of another must be made directly to that other (as is held to be the case with an offer of a contract), or whether A might utter in the presence of B a promise to

---

[42] Some accounts of promising nonetheless suggest that a promise does not necessitate a promisee: see for instance Downie, 'Three Accounts of Promising'.

[43] On the assumption that a divine promisee does not count as a regular promisee, being unable to compel performance of the vow (at least in the present world). See further on vows below, at pp. 39–41.

benefit C and thereby bind himself to the stated promise. One ought to be more specific in relation to the latter case, and distinguish two cases:

(1) a case where A says to B 'I promise to you that I shall give C £100';
(2) a case where A says to B 'I promise to give C £100'.

In the second of these two cases, A is in essence using B as a witness to his promise to the absent C. Is this a validly constituted promise? There seems to be no overriding objection to this being a promise: A has certainly objectively demonstrated a commitment to be bound to C, even though C may not be immediately aware of this commitment, being absent. C's presence does not seem to be required in order to make the promise valid. This view is consistent with the approach taken in a number of jurisdictions that it is possible to make a promise in favour of a party which has not yet come into existence (clearly such a party cannot be present). Given that neither is C's presence required for the promise to be constituted, nor his acceptance necessary, there remains the question of whether notification of the promise to an absent promisee is required before the promise can come in to existence. Since the suggested essence of a promise lies in a unilateral voluntary act of the promisor, this again seems unnecessary,[44] though as a practical point the promisee would evidently require to learn of the existence of the promise in order for enforcement of the promise to occur.

In the former of the two cases, the promise appears to have been made by A to B and not to C. Does this mean that C cannot compel performance of the promise, given that it appears not to be the promisee? If it cannot, can B compel such performance, given that B may well have no interest in the performance of the promise (though this will depend on the facts, and there will be cases where B does have such an interest)? These questions are quite complex, and fall within the area of law commonly referred to as third party rights or *stipulationes alteri* which are the subject of detailed discussion in Chapter 5. Suffice it to say at this point, that in this type of case it may be possible to argue that where A makes a promise to B to do something for C he may also be taken to have made a promise to C to undertake the performance. This promise may be express if A's statement to B is of the form 'I promise to you that I hereby undertake to pay C £100', the words 'I hereby undertake to C' in effect amounting to a promise within a promise, but, even if there is no express promise to C contained

---

[44] This is the position adopted in Scots law: see *The Laws of Scotland*, vol. xv, para. 618.

within B's promise, it may be possible to infer from B's promise that he is also making a promise in C's favour.

(vi)   Things which are not components of the definition

It should be noted that the definition offered makes no reference to certain matters; some of these have been noted above, especially in the section examining the idea of promises as speech acts. For instance, it is not suggested that a promisee has to accept a promise before it can exist (though it has been suggested that a promisee has the power to reject the promised performance). It is further asserted, as a general point, that the effect produced by a promise in the promisee's mind and in any actions of the promisee are not relevant to the definition of a promise. The focus is properly on the promisor, as it is his intention and actions which may constitute the normative act of promising and may give rise to a binding obligation. Thus, although a promise may, and often does, produce reliance, or trust, or some other effect in the promisee, these are mere secondary results and not of the essence of the promise itself.[45] This assertion clearly puts the position adopted here at odds with certain theories of promise, such as reliance theory, discussion of which will follow in the next chapter.

2.   Three crucial qualities of relevance to promises: gratuitousness, conditionality, unilaterality

In addition to the qualities of a promise listed above, fundamental to any general, but especially to any legal, debate about the nature of promise is the question of whether a promise must possess one or more of three important qualities which may pertain to obligations: gratuitousness, conditionality and unilaterality. These terms have not usually been defined with care in debates about promise, and this lack of clear definition has been productive of much confused and unnecessary arguments about promises and about whether contract concerns promise. It will be essential then to define these terms clearly here, and to keep the definitions in mind in the succeeding discussion. It should be noted that the three qualities discussed below are applicable across the field of obligations,[46]

---

[45] A similar view is taken by Kimel, *From Promise to Contract*, pp. 14–32, who, in criticising Fried's views, argues that, though trust usually follows on from the making of a promise, it is not a necessary condition for promising.

[46] In Ch. 1 of my book *Obligations*, I endeavoured to test the qualities of gratuitousness and unilaterality in relation to the various obligations recognised by the law.

not just within promise or contract, so that a proper understanding of the concepts aids comprehension of obligations as a class, and not just promises.[47]

(a)   Gratuitousness

Obligations may be gratuitous or non-gratuitous (otherwise 'onerous'), the two being opposites. What does an obligation's being gratuitous mean?

Sloppiness of thought has crept in through discussions about the nature of obligations proceeding simply on the basis that gratuitous means 'done for nothing'. That is indeed the general idea underlying the concept of gratuitousness, but one needs to explore more precisely what the concept of 'done for nothing' means. On close inspection, it might signify one of at least three different situations: (i) something done without the legal right to compel any counter-performance; (ii) something done without the hope or expectation of a counter-performance; or (iii) something done which in fact is not met with any reciprocal counter-performance, whatever the hope of, or legal entitlement to, counter-performance might be.

To explain the difference between these three meanings, consider the following examples:

> (1) I promise to give a friend £500 as a birthday present. I neither hope for, nor am I legally entitled to, nor do I receive, anything in return.
> (2) I promise to give a friend a gift for his new home, in the hope that he will invite me to the party to celebrate his moving in, but without any entitlement to compel him to invite me.
> (3) I promise to pay an electrical store for a new laptop computer in return for its promise to supply the computer.
> (4) I promise to pay for a friend's rail ticket, without hoping for anything in return or being entitled to require any such reciprocal benefit. My friend decides nonetheless to thank me by giving me a bottle of wine.

In the first example, the promisor neither hopes for anything to accrue to him as a result of his promise, nor can he compel any such thing, nor in fact does he receive anything in return for it. On any understanding of the concept of gratuitousness, we would say that the promise is gratuitous. All that the promisor might conceivably get by way of his promise is pleasure in making the promise and at seeing the reaction of the promisee

---

[47] They are, in other words, qualities which relate to the 'general part' of the law of obligations as it was labelled by Smith in 'The Limits of Contract', pp. 1–24.

when the gift is given, but such a benefit is too ephemeral for it to count as a benefit in a legally relevant sense.[48]

In the second example, the promisor makes the promise hoping, or perhaps even expecting, that he will receive the benefit of an invitation to the promisee's party, but he cannot compel an invitation to the party. Some might say that the presence of this expectation or hope means that the promise is not gratuitous. On such an understanding of gratuitousness, it is the subjective intention to act out of liberality or generosity which is important; a subjective hope of receiving something in return for undertaking an obligation is sufficient to mean that it is not gratuitous, rather it is onerous. The difficulty with this view, however, is that it requires us to classify an obligation based upon a subjective intention of a party. While such a subjective intention may be determinable in many cases, or we may suspect such intention to be present, in some cases it may be impossible to form such a determination or suspicion. This would result in its not being possible to say whether or not the obligation was gratuitous, an undesirable result. A subjective approach also raises the difficulty of what happens where the motives for undertaking an obligation are mixed, partly gratuitous, and partly not. An answer to that problem may be that, so long as the predominant motive is gratuitous, a transaction will count as gratuitous, but an assessment of predominance of motive must be equally (if not more) difficult to undertake.

In the third example, the promise described is essentially what is classified in some jurisdictions as a 'contractual promise'. Here the party undertaking the commitment is able legally to compel a counter-performance from the other party in exchange for his performance. One could describe

---

[48] The first example describes the concept of gratuitousness in the law of Louisiana, as, under the Louisiana Civil Code, a gratuitous contract is one entered into for reasons of liberality (its cause, or motivation) and which results in obligations only on the contracting party pledging a performance (its effect): 'A contract is gratuitous when one party obligates himself to another for the benefit of the latter, without receiving anything in return' (CC Art. 1910). The words 'for the benefit of' refer to the motivation, or cause, of the undertaking. The Code goes on to provide a definition of a unilateral contract: a contract is 'unilateral when the party who accepts the obligation of the other does not assume a reciprocal obligation' (CC Art. 1907), a definition which focuses entirely on effect, without reference to motivation. Some scholars argue that the result is that in Louisiana Law a gratuitous contract and a unilateral contract are one and the same thing, the difference being that the focus in the idea of a gratuitous contract is the motivation for the undertaking, whereas the focus in the idea of a unilateral contract is the effect produced. A different view is that, while all gratuitous contracts are unilateral, not all unilateral contracts are gratuitous, in other words that gratuitous contracts are merely a subset of unilateral ones.

such a legal entitlement as the crucial issue for determining whether or not an obligation is gratuitous or not. The benefit of such a definition of gratuitousness is that it is judged by reference to an objective criterion, not by reference to subjective mental intent. There ought thus, on such an approach, to be little if any difficulty in determining whether an obligation such as a promise is gratuitous or not.

In the final example, though the promisor neither hopes for, nor is entitled to, anything from making his promise, the promisee just happens to give him a reciprocal benefit. If a definition of gratuitous is based upon whether as a matter of fact a promisor has received something in return, then this promise is not gratuitous, but onerous.

On any of the three definitions of gratuitous, example (1) is gratuitous. The other examples describe circumstances which may or may not be gratuitous depending on which definition of gratuitous is chosen. It has been suggested that an objective determination is preferable, which rules out using the second possible definition of gratuitous (the definition focusing on the hope or expectation of the promisor). That leaves the possibility of basing the definition either on the legal ability to compel a counter-performance, or on the question of whether, as a matter of fact, a counter-performance is received, either of which is an objective question. While it is a matter for specific legal jurisdictions to choose which definition they prefer, it is suggested that the preferable definition should be the promisor's ability to compel a counter-performance. If, instead, the focus is on the factual question of whether a benefit has been received, this would mean that a contracting party who had made a promise to perform, but who was met with a breach of the other party's duty to counter-perform, and did not therefore as a matter of fact receive the expected counter-performance, would be held to have made a gratuitous contractual promise. That would seem rather an odd conclusion. For that reason, it is suggested that gratuitousness is best judged by whether or not the party undertaking the obligation can or cannot compel a counter-performance at the time he undertakes the obligation. It is therefore that understanding of the idea of gratuitous which shall be used in this work.

Having settled on an understanding of gratuitousness, one then has to ask: must promises be gratuitous? This is clearly crucial, as if a promise *must* be gratuitous, then the common model of a contract, where A is described as offering something to B in exchange for B offering something to A, could not be characterised as an exchange of promises. For Common lawyers, used to describing a contract as an exchange of promises, the decision is therefore clear: promises need not be gratuitous (according to the definition suggested here), rather they may either be gratuitous or onerous (and in contracts of exchange, they must be onerous).[49] On the other hand, in a jurisdiction which was not used to describing contracts as an exchange of promise, there would seem to be less of a need to include onerous undertakings of a future performance as promises. Such jurisdictions might decide, for whatever reason, to take a more restrictive view of promise, and say that it was only the gratuitous commitment to a future performance which can count as a promise. Such an attitude would necessitate defining contract in some other way (for instance, as an agreement, rather than in promissory terms). We shall return to this question later when looking at the relevance of promises to contractual theory in more detail.

Outside legal debate, however, ordinary speech seems to encompass both gratuitous and onerous promises within the concept of a promise (and so would accord with the understanding of the Common law), though it is difficult to suggest whether or not occurrences of one type are more prevalent than the other, and if so which.[50] In the conception of non-legal disciplines, promises may certainly be exchanged, and thus given in the hope of or with the ability to compel something in return for the giving of a promise. For present purposes then, it seems sensible to allow a definition of a promise to be wide enough to encompass both gratuitous and non-gratuitous (onerous) promises. However, such a concession is made on the basis of the meaning ascribed to the concept of gratuitous here, namely an obligation undertaken without the ability to compel any counter-performance in favour of the party undertaking the obligation.

A final definitional point worth noting is that where non-gratuitous (onerous) promises are exchanged in a contract, the contract is sometimes said to be mutual. It is certainly possible to say that an onerous contract, one in which both parties are bound to certain performances, can in the

---

[49] The Common law tradition follows in the footsteps of the late scholastics, who held that promises might be either gratuitous or onerous. Thus, Lessius states: 'the word promise is general and can be extended to all contracts. I can promise a thing subject to the other party taking on some burden, for example, to give a price or some other thing, or I can do so gratis' (*De iustitia et jure*, 2.18.1; cf. his earlier statement, at 2.17.1, that both donations and promise are 'not properly speaking contracts since if they produce an obligation it is only in one party', a statement which it seems must be interpreted as referring to unilateral promise, given his assertion that the word promise can be extended to contracts).

[50] Atiyah states that it is 'highly probable' that the non-gratuitous promise is the more common type of promise, though he gives no evidence for this assertion: *Promises, Morals and Law*, p. 143.

alternative be called a mutual contract, onerous and mutual thus being held to be synonymous. However, some jurisdictions choose to distinguish onerous contracts from mutual contracts, on the basis that a mutual contract, while certainly onerous, must have the additional feature that at least some of the duties of each party under the contract are reciprocal, or synallagmatic. This distinction is made because it is conceivable that a contract might be onerous, imposing duties on both parties, but the duties of each may not find a counterpart in the duties of the other. An example of an onerous but non-mutual contract is mandate, where the duty of the mandatory to concern himself with the task allotted to him is not the synallagma of the mandant's duty to pay any expenses of the mandatory, each duty being independent of the other. By contrast, a mutual contract is one where there are at least *some* reciprocal undertakings, even if others are independent. In jurisdictions with a doctrine of mutual consideration, all contracts[51] should in theory be seen as being mutual to at least some extent, as the consideration paid by each party is viewed as having been given in exchange for the other's undertaking.

The distinction between mutual and onerous contracts is recognised in South African[52] and Louisiana[53] law, and in theory in Scots law too, though it is hard to find any theoretical discussion of the distinction in the latter. This distinction between onerous/non-gratuitous contracts and mutual/reciprocal contracts is a useful one, the latter being a subset of the former.

(b)   Conditionality[54]

Obligations like promise may be conditional or unconditional (otherwise 'absolute'), the two being opposites.[55] This is a crucial flexibility of

---

[51] Save those undertaken by way of deed or under seal.
[52] See Van der Merwe *et al.*, *Contract*, p. 10, who state that in South African law the mutual or synallagmatic contract is a 'particular type of multilateral contract. It differs from other multilateral contracts in that – according to the intention of the parties – the one party is bound to perform in exchange for performance by the other party.'
[53] The Louisiana Civil Code defines synallagmatic contracts at Art. 1908, and onerous contracts at Art. 1909.
[54] The discussion here seeks to be as inter-jurisdictional as possible. To that end, jurisdiction specific meanings of the term 'condition' or ideas of conditionality are avoided. Thus, there is no discussion of certain peculiarly Common law meanings of the word condition, such as a contract term in general, or a contract term performance of which goes to the root of the contract and which therefore gives a right to terminate the contract if the term is not fulfilled.
[55] See DCFR, Art. III.-1:106.

promise, as it enables the idea of promise to be employed to describe the nature of contract as an accepted conditional promise (or an exchange of promises, if mutual consideration is held to be a requirement for a contract). But what does conditionality mean? It is important to distinguish a number of meanings.

In a promissory setting, the idea of conditionality can be used to denote whether or not a binding obligation has been assumed by the speaker of the potentially promissory words. With that possible meaning in mind, the following four types of statement can be tested for their conditionality:

(1) Type 1 examples:
'I promise to pay you £100 next Monday.'
'I promise to marry you.'

(2) Type 2 examples:
'I promise to pay you £100 if you pass your driving test.'
'I promise to employ you if your current employer dismisses you.'
'I promise to buy you dinner if my football team wins its game today.'
'I promise to pay to have you flown home for medical treatment if you contract malaria.'

(3) Type 3 examples:
'I promise to buy the painting if my wife likes it.'
'I promise to pay you £100 if you give me your clock.'
'I promise to go to the cinema with you tonight if you pay for the tickets.'

(4) Type 4 example:
'I promise to pay you £100 every Sunday unless and until you cease going to Church.'

Note, that in each of these types of case, the condition must not be certain to happen, or else the promisor will be bound to fulfil the promise on the occurrence of the certain event, and the promise cannot be said to be conditional.[56] For instance, if the promise is 'I promise to pay you £100 the next time it rains', although the time for performance of the promise is as yet uncertain, we know that it is going to rain (precipitation being a universally recurring phenomenon), and thus the performance of the promisor is not conditional even if the time for performance remains uncertain until it rains. By contrast, a promise to buy an umbrella on condition that it rain tomorrow is a valid conditional promise, as whether it will rain tomorrow is an uncertain future event.

---

[56] As the first sentence of Art. 1767 of the Louisiana Civil Code states: 'A conditional obligation is one dependent upon an uncertain event.' The same requirement of uncertainty is stated in respect of conditional obligations in the DCFR, Art. III.-1:106.

In the first type of case, there is nothing in what is said to suggest that the promisor is not immediately bound by an obligation (whether it be of a moral or legal kind), so the promise is unconditional.

In the second type of case, however, the promise is, in some sense, conditional, but in what sense? Here, it could be argued, the person making the statement intends to be bound to the promise immediately it is uttered, but that performance is not intended unless and until the stipulated event (for instance, the promisee's passing his driving test) occurs. This is, of course, a matter of interpretation, and it might be argued that a different state of affairs was intended by the promisor (namely, that no binding obligation was intended until the contingency was met), but it is certainly one reasonable interpretation of the examples given under type 2 that the statements give rise to an immediately binding obligation, albeit one where performance is contingent upon the occurrence of the stipulated future event. The importance of that analysis would be that, once the statement had been made, the speaker would not be free to withdraw from the obligation. However, in those examples of this type where the contingency relates to some stipulated conduct of the hearer, the hearer is under no obligation to perform the conduct indicated (for instance to pass his driving test), though he is at liberty to attempt so to perform; if he does so perform, then he has fulfilled the condition of the promise and may seek the promised benefit from the promisor. Thus, with this sense of conditionality, the promise is conditional because, though immediately binding on the promisor once uttered, its performance is contingent on the occurrence of an uncertain future event. So, the idea of conditionality can relate to the performance of the promise, without there being any doubt that there is an immediately binding obligation.

In the third type of case, one interpretation of what is objectively intended by the promisor is that the nature of the statement as a binding obligation is itself conditional, the condition being that the person to whom the statement is made is himself willing to undertake an obligation of the type indicated (for instance, the obligation to transfer ownership in some goods). Here, therefore, the conditionality relates primarily to the nature of the statement as an obligation. It is not intended to be treated as an immediately binding obligation, but is, *pro tem*, merely a proposed obligation, and is to retain such nature until the condition is fulfilled. This type of conditionality, where the condition denotes that the obligation is not binding unless and until a future contingent event occurs, is in many jurisdictions styled a condition 'suspensive' of the obligation.[57] In this third type of case, the statement is also conditional in the sense applicable in the second type of case, namely that there is uncertain conduct of the other party upon which performance rests, but the primary sense of conditionality is as to the nature of the statement as an obligation at all. Neither offer nor acceptance has obligational force unless it is met with a reciprocal conditional commitment from the other party. It is the sense applicable to this type of case which allows contractual offers and acceptances to be characterised as conditional promises, and thus for the contract as a whole to be characterised in a promissory fashion.

In the fourth type of case, the type of conditionality concerned is likely (as with the third example) to be objectively interpreted as relating to the nature of the statement as an obligation. In this case, however, the promise gives rise immediately to a binding obligation, but such obligation may cease to be binding if and when a contingent future event occurs (in the example given, that the promisee ceases to go to Church). In many jurisdictions, this sort of conditional obligation is referred to as 'resolutive' (or 'resolutory').[58]

Are any types of condition impermissible? Some conditions may stipulate unlawful or immoral conduct, and so for those reasons may invalidate a promise. In addition, however, a condition which undermines the very idea that a binding commitment was being undertaken in the first place would seem to be impermissible in the sense that it would prevent fulfilment of the requirement that a speaker must commit to a future act. Thus, if the condition stipulated related to whether or not the person making the commitment still wished to perform the commitment at a future date, this would bring in to question whether any commitment was seriously being undertaken to begin with. So, for instance, the statement 'I promise to pay you £100 next Monday, if I have not changed my mind by

---

[57] The situation is in fact even more complex than suggested. In some jurisdictions, a so-called suspensive condition may *either* prevent an obligation from coming into being until the condition is fulfilled, *or* there may be an obligation in force immediately, from which neither party is permitted to withdraw, but the parties rights and duties under the obligation will not be enforceable unless and until the suspensive condition is purified. Which type of effect is intended by the relevant party or parties is a matter for the court to interpret. See, for instance, for Scots Law, the discussion at McBryde, *Contract*, paras. 5–35 to 5–40. In the DCFR, a suspensive obligation is one which, until fulfilment of the condition, does not have obligatory effect: see Art. III.-1:106(2).

[58] As the third sentence of Art. 1767 of the Louisiana Civil Code states: 'If the obligation may be immediately enforced but will come to an end when the uncertain event occurs, the condition is resolutory.' The DCFR also makes provision for resolutive conditions: see Art. III.-1:106(1),(3).

then' would not seem capable of being considered a promise because the condition attached undermines the very notion that any definite commitment has been undertaken to begin with.[59] On the other hand, a condition which permits the promisor to revoke the promise at some future point, but is not so sweeping as to be suggestive of a lack of an original intention to be bound at all, might be argued to be a permissible condition. Thus, a promise of the type 'I promise to pay you £1,000 on 1st January, but I retain the power to revoke this promise should I deem the changed nature of our relationship so to warrant' might fall within the category of valid promises, albeit that a fairly wide power of revocation is retained by the promisor.[60]

Are any other senses of conditionality relevant to the debate about the nature of promises? What of the argument referred to earlier of some linguistic philosophers that it is essential to the idea of a promise that the words spoken produce in the hearer an understanding of the binding nature of what is being said: without such a 'condition' being fulfilled, there can be no promise. That might seem to give rise to a further sense of conditionality, one which holds that *all* promises are conditional because they depend upon a subjective understanding in the hearer being attained before the statement can be considered a promise. However, as the argument that the words spoken by a promisor require to induce such an understanding on the hearer's part before a statement can count as a promise has been argued earlier to be controversial and probably misguided, it is proposed to discount this meaning of conditionality.

A further possible sense of conditionality has been said to lie in the fact that all promises are conditional because they relate to future acts, and all future acts are inherently uncertain because we cannot know whether circumstances prevailing in the future will permit performance of the

---

[59] Such reasoning would appear to underlie the first sentence of Art. 1770 of the Louisiana Civil Code: 'A suspensive condition that depends solely on the whim of the obligor makes the obligation null.' This point has long been acknowledged by jurists. For instance, Pufendorf states in his *Elementorum* that '[i]t must be observed, furthermore, that promises are unavailing and null, when the condition under which the promise is made has been put under my own pleasure, for example ... "You will have ten pieces of gold from me, when it pleases me"' (I.xii.11).

[60] Atiyah suggests that a promise of future performance is by nature irrevocable (*Promises, Morals and Law*, pp. 178–9) unless the promise is made for no consideration or is not relied upon (p. 181). This suggestion is made in the context of an argument that a promise is a type of consent to an obligation, and while present consents can normally be later withdrawn, a promisor is committing himself to a future performance which usually indicates that his consent will not be revocable.

intended act.[61] This sense of conditionality is based upon the rarely held belief that no obligations requiring a future performance can meaningfully be entered into. It is a position which therefore denies the obligatory force of most contracts. As a highly sceptical position, the sense of conditionality to which it gives rise is discounted here.

Given the various meanings of conditionality outlined above which *are* accepted, do any of these describe circumstances which would render a statement not to be a promise under the definition suggested earlier? That definition suggested that a promise is a statement by which a speaker places himself under a *commitment* as to a future act. Commitment denotes a present obligation (whether of a moral or legal nature). Given this definition, conditionality of the type mentioned in example three – the condition suspensive of the existence of an obligation – would prevent a statement from being a promise. If the nature of the statement as a binding obligation is postponed until some future contingent event, then unless and until such a contingency creates an obligatory effect, there can be no promise as there is no commitment. On the other hand, a condition which relates only to the performance of a firm commitment (example 2), or which is a resolutive condition (and thus relates to the possible future termination of an existing firm commitment), are types of condition which do not prevent a statement from being a promise.

It seems therefore that promises may be unconditional, or may be conditional in any sense other than suspensive of the obligation undertaken by the promisor. A speaker who is not yet bound to any commitment, and who may therefore withdraw from making any commitment until a stated event occurs, has not made a promise.

(c) Unilaterality

Most people's paradigm image of the promise is probably a unilateral act (though as will become clear in later chapters of this work, there is also a long tradition of conceiving of bilateral contract as an exchange of promises). It is useful then to begin by examining those promises which are unilateral. To do so, one must ask: what is meant by a promise being unilateral?

---

[61] A concern which is said to explain the absence of the phenomenon of promising from Tongan society, where the future is considered uncertain: see further discussion of this below, at p. 53.

As with gratuitousness and conditionality, the concept of unilaterality is one which can be utilised to analyse the whole spectrum of obligations, not simply the promise. To begin with, just as with the other two features we have been discussing, unilaterality has its opposite: bilaterality (or multilterality, in multi-party obligations). However, as with gratuitousness, there are conceivably a number of possible meanings of unilateral, which is where confusion may creep in. First, a unilateral obligation might mean one which is constituted by one party only, in other words, where it requires the actions or behaviour of only one party to give rise to the obligation. Alternatively, a unilateral obligation might be one where only one party assumes any duties or commitments under the obligation. In that sense, unilateral would be meant in a way synonymous to one of the meanings of gratuitous outlined earlier, that is an obligation undertaken without any ability to compel a counter-performance. These two distinct senses of the concept of unilaterality may be demonstrated by reference to the following examples:

I promise to pay £100 to my brother.
I promise to draft a will for my client for no consideration. My client accepts my promise.

In the first example, if we assume for the moment that a promise needs no acceptance on the part of the promisee before it can bind (an assumption which would not, in legal terms, hold good in every jurisdiction), then this promise might be unilateral either in the first sense outlined (because the promise may be constituted by the undertaking of the promisor alone, whether orally or in writing) or in the second sense (in that no duty or commitment is assumed by the promisee). On the other hand, in the second example, which essentially describes a contract lacking mutual consideration (again, this is not possible in all jurisdictions), the promise of the lawyer to draft a will for his client would be unilateral in the second sense (in that it imposes a duty on only one party, the lawyer) but not in the first: as a contract, it would require at least an indication of assent to the contract by the promisee, typically in the form of an acceptance, before the obligation could be constituted.[62]

In any legal system which requires mutual consideration before voluntary obligations may be constituted, the idea of a unilateral obligation

---

[62] In the Louisiana Civil Code, a further possible sense of unilateral is stipulated, that being non-mutual: '[a] contract is unilateral when the party who accepts the obligation of the other does not assume a reciprocal obligation' (CC Art. 1907). A synallagmatic, or mutual, contract arises 'when the parties obligate themselves reciprocally, so that the obligation of each party is correlative to the obligation of the other' (CC Art. 1908).

in either of the two senses of the term discussed above would be anathema: there could be no voluntary obligations constituted by only one party or which impose duties on only one party. However, even the Common law, with its doctrine of mutual consideration, allows unilateral voluntary obligations to be undertaken by deed.[63] In jurisdictions where obligations may be constituted by the actions of one party alone, or where there is no requirement of mutual consideration, obligations might be unilateral in either sense. Which sense of the word a jurisdiction chooses to use is, of course, entirely a matter for it, though if the second sense of the term unilateral were to be chosen (the sense of an obligation which imposes a duty on only one of the parties) there would then be a somewhat unnecessary and perhaps confusing overlap with the meaning of gratuitous defined as an obligation in which one party cannot compel a counter-performance. There might therefore be thought to be good sense in choosing the first definition of unilateral rather than the second, as for instance the drafters of the Draft Common Frame of Reference (DCFR) have done,[64] though such a course has not invariably been adopted by national jurisdictions.

The complications with understanding the idea of unilaterality do not end there. Some jurisdictions use the term unilateral both to refer to obligations constituted by only one party as well as to refer to obligations where only one party comes under any duties. The first usage describes what is called the nature of the juridical act, which is to be distinguished from the second sense, which describes the number of parties having duties under such an act. In such systems, while contract is always defined as a bilateral juridical act, two parties being required to constitute a contract, if mutual consideration is not a requirement of the law then contracts can be described (in the second sense of the term) as unilateral or bilateral, depending on whether one or two parties come under contractual duties. This can result in the confusing situation where a contract can be described as both bilateral and unilateral at the same time: bilateral because it is a bilateral juridical act, but unilateral in that it imposes duties on only one party. Such an analysis is, for instance, adopted in South African law.[65] The same position prevails

---

[63] See later discussion of contracts in deed form at p. 166. The separate and unusual phenomenon of English Law's 'unilateral contract' is ignored for the moment (for discussion, see Ch. 4, at p. 220).

[64] See DCFR Art. II.-1:101, II.-1:103. The DCFR restricts use of the term unilateral to undertakings (including promise) which are constituted by one party alone; there can therefore be no such thing as a unilateral contract in DCFR terms.

[65] See Van der Merwe et al., Contract, p. 9; see also p. 32, where it is explained that multilateral juristic acts are those 'in which at least two persons must participate, in contrast with

in Louisiana.[66] Because of the confusion which such usage can create, it is suggested that the terms unilateral/bilateral should be restricted to describing the number of parties constituting the obligation (the juridical act sense), and the terms gratuitous/onerous to describe the number of parties having duties under the obligation (as suggested earlier).

Jurisdictional policy reasons aside, there is no theoretical reason why promises may not be unilateral in any of the three senses mentioned above. Going further, ought unilaterality (in either sense) to be a requirement of a statement being a promise? Going against such a suggestion, it is certainly true that, in ordinary speech, one hears people talking about an exchange of promises, or mutual promises, particularly in Common law jurisdictions (which commonly still conceive of the law of contract in this way). Naturally, if a promissory view of contract were ever to be abandoned, there would be less need for the law to continue to conceive of promise in a way which encompassed bilateral as well as unilateral promises. One might then maintain a 'purer' doctrine of promise which excluded from the definition anything other than unilateral promises; mutual contracts would require description by reference to some concept other than an exchange of promises. There is no indication that such a development is imminent, however, and therefore in this work the concept of a promise will be drawn widely enough to continue to allow both unilateral as well as bilateral (or multilateral) commitments within the definition of that term. What sense of the word is meant at any particular point of the discussion should be evident from the context.

3.   Acts having some similarity to, but which are distinct from, promises

It was noted earlier that there are a number of English words which commonly act as synonyms for promising and which, in appropriate circumstances, may be taken to signify the act of promising when used by a speaker. There are in addition, however, some terms denoting concepts similar to, but not identical to, the promise, concepts from which promises need to be distinguished. As will be seen, one is in fact a special type of promise, and some of the others also involve acts of commitment.

---

unilateral juristic acts ... such as the making of a will or dereliction of ownership, which can be performed by one person'.

[66] On the distinction between unilateral and bilateral juridical acts, see Levasseur, *Louisiana Law of Obligations*, §1.1.2.

Six such concepts sharing similarities with promise are discussed: vows, oaths, threats, gifts, warranties and agreement.

(a) Vows

Vows and oaths are often treated as if they were interchangeable concepts, largely it seems because some references in classical texts as well as biblical sources have been variously translated either as vows or as oaths. Such conflation is unnecessary, however, because whatever translation of the original source language is adopted, it is possible to draw a conceptual distinction between the vow and the oath: a vow is a promise made to God (or one or more deities in a pantheon),[67] whereas an oath is a statement of personal commitment, often made in the presence of others, where God is called as a witness to the sincerity of the statement but where there is not necessarily an identified party intended to benefit from the commitment. As will be seen from the following discussion, vows are generally regarded as laudable acts and, given their nature as promises made to God, commitments requiring strict fulfilment; oaths, by contrast, do not receive such universal approval, especially when made rashly; however, if made, the calling of God as witness also creates strong expectations (if not a strict requirement) that the commitment should be fulfilled, such that, at least in the historical literature, divine punishment was to be expected for breach of the oath (or indeed, in some cases, for having made it at all).

The Old Testament contains five examples of vows (the Hebrew verb is *nadar*) in which the full nature of the vow is set out within a narrative context.[68] These examples also demonstrate a further feature of the Old Testament vow, not one which seems to be conceived as a generally necessary part of a vow: it is expressed in the conditional form, that is, in the form 'If God will do *x*, then I/we will do *y*.' The conditional nature of each of these Biblical vows may be demonstrated by the first of them (in chronological terms), that of Jacob: Jacob vows that, if God will look after him and provide for him, then he will be faithful to God and set up

---

[67] Atiyah, *Promises, Morals and Law*, provides no definition for a vow but conceives of the concept of a vow so broadly that he can speak of a 'vow to oneself' (p. 54), which contradicts the definition of a vow provided here. Atiyah's musings leave the reader unclear as to what he conceives of as the essence of a vow.

[68] These being Jacob's vow of fidelity to God (Gen. 28:20–22), the vow of the people of Israel to attack certain Canaanite cities (Num. 21:12), Jephthah's vow before his victorious battle (Judges 11:30–31), Hannah's vow to give her son to God's service (1 Sam. 1:11), and Absalom's vow to worship God (2 Sam. 15:8).

a temple to him at Bethel. The condition attached to this vow, as with the other biblical examples, being a counter-performance of God, the vow seems to take on almost the appearance of a contractual offer, though that is perhaps to attempt to analyse the matter too legalistically given the non-legal nature of the texts. In fact, the later Thomistic characterisation of vows suggests, as will be seen below, that they are to be seen as promises (of a religious nature) rather than as contractual offers. The narrative working out of these five biblical vows (they are each fulfilled, in response to God's positive response to the vow) clearly indicates a biblical approval of vows as commendable sacred acts.[69]

Aquinas considered vows in the *Summa Theologica*, defining a vow as 'a promise made to God',[70] the promisor being the human party and the promisee God. In Aquinas's view, a vow is by nature a virtuous act.[71] Unlike the narrative accounts of biblical vows discussed earlier, much of Aquinas's treatment of vows relates to unconditional vows, such as the vows taken upon reception of holy orders or by those accepting the religious rule of monastic life, though his analysis is also broad enough to include the conditional vow. As with the understanding explained earlier that a promise requires more than a mere internal act of the will, Aquinas rejects the idea that mere deliberation or intention is sufficient for a vow: a concluded manifestation of the will, sufficient to demonstrate a promise, must be present before a vow is constituted.[72]

Aquinas posits, as part of the case why vows cannot be dispensed with, that he who makes a vow 'makes a law for himself, as it were',[73] and thus that vows cannot be broken any more than the law may be. However, in favouring the view that vows may be dispensed with, and that this is not contrary to their origins in 'natural law and Divine precept',[74] Aquinas argues that such dispensation is consonant with natural law precisely because vows are self-made and may therefore have been undertaken without the maker being able 'to consider every circumstance'. Here again the natural law is seen to be sufficiently flexible to take account of changed circumstances and not the rigid creation it is characterised to be by utilitarians. Aquinas contrasts the enforceability of vows with the status in

---

[69] Indeed, Aquinas explains Jephthah's vow (see Judges 11) as an example of a good act even though it had an evil consequence (the death of his daughter): *Summa Theologica*, II-II, Q. 88, Art. 2.

[70] *Summa Theologica*, II-II, Q. 88, Art 1.

[71] *Ibid*, Art. 2. This conception of the vow emphasises its distinction from a threat (the latter is discussed further below, at p. 45).

[72] *Ibid.*, Art. 1.   [73] *Ibid*, Art. 10.   [74] *Ibid.*, Art. 10.

Roman law of the ordinary promises made between men: whereas the latter may require the fulfilment of certain conditions before they were binding, the former are binding unconditionally upon men and must therefore always be honoured.[75]

While it is important to have an appreciation of the specialised nature of vows in order to distinguish them from the general idea of promises, given this specialised nature it seems that the influence of biblical and medieval rules concerning vows can only have been of very restricted influence so far as the overall impact of promissory ideas on contract law was concerned. As Chapter 2 will indicate, it was late scholastic thinking about the moral importance of promises in a secular context which was to have the far greater effect upon contractual thinking.

(b) Oaths

Oath swearing is commonly conceived of, both by writers of the Christian and pre-Christian periods, as a statement by a speaker either of commitment to some future action (for instance, 'I swear that I shall hunt down my father's murderer'), or of the truth of a statement presently made or about to be made ('I swear that I shall tell the truth when giving this evidence'), by which the speaker invokes God (or a god) as a witness to the commitment to act or to the truth of what is said (by adding '... so help me God', or '... as God is my witness', for instance). Aquinas styled these two types promissory oaths (oaths committing to future action) and declaratory oaths (testifying to the truth of a statement).[76] In addition, the swearer of the oath may call down some punishment upon himself in the event that he breaks the oath, an addition to the form of the oath especially prevalent in the classical and pre-classical period.[77]

While the person swearing an oath may commit to the performance of some conduct in favour of another person, this is not a necessary component of all oaths. For that reason, many oaths do not conform to the definition of a promise suggested earlier, in that they lack a commitment to

---

[75] *Ibid.*, Art. 3.   [76] *Ibid.*, Q. 89, Art. 1.

[77] The addition of a conditional self-curse to an oath was also a feature of early medieval oaths: see Ibbetson, *Historical Introduction*, pp. 4–5. See further on classical oaths, Sommerstein and Fletcher, *The Oath in Greek Society*; Sommerstein *et al.*, *The Oath in Archaic and Classical Greece*. The idea of vengeance as an element in oaths continued into some early modern literature: thus in Hobbes's *Leviathan*, the author states that the swearer of an oath binds himself so that, if he is to break the oath, 'he renounceth the mercy of his God, or calleth to him for vengeance on himself' (1,14,31).

do something for another. Often, they are simply commitments to future conduct by the speaker declared before the world in general[78] or to a group of people, perhaps members of a local community, by which the speaker wishes to demonstrate the seriousness of his intent through the invocation of a divine witness. The conceptual overlap between promises and some oaths, however, has meant that oaths have often been compared to and analysed alongside promises.

References to oaths abound in classical literature, in both dramatic as well as historical and philosophical texts. In the dramatic context, it has been observed[79] that in classical Greek drama the form of the oath (as well as the vow) was often used as a dramatic tool in the recitation of the story of a tragic hero, the oath swearing being conceived of as a foolish act designed to usurp the divinely pre-destined fate of man. Outside the use of oaths as an element in Greek drama, however, classical references to oath swearing are often positive in nature. It is clear from the Greek writers that oaths were often made on solemn occasions, such as the making of treaties, alliances, and contracts, in which context the making of oaths was approved of.[80] Indeed, the literature suggests a certain pride taken by the Greeks in their making and honouring of oaths, a practice by which they saw themselves as being distinguished from the barbarian peoples, who frequently equivocated.[81] Plato mentions oaths favourably in his *Republic*, conceiving of oath-keeping as a virtuous act. The significance of this for Plato was that the highest aim of moral conduct and thought was human well-being (eudaimonia), and the achievement of such well-being was arrived at through leading a life of excellence (aretē), otherwise called 'virtue'.[82] Oath-keeping, being a virtuous character trait, contributed in Plato's view to the well-being of the oath keeper.[83]

---

[78] For example, as with the oath of Oedipus that the killer of Laius is not living in his house (Sophocles, *Oedipus Tyrannus*, 249–51) or the oath of the chorus in *Electra* that those who do not pay their dues will not go long without suffering (Sophocles, *Electra*, 1063–65).

[79] See Schlesinger, *Promises, Oaths and Vows*, especially Ch. 9 ('Promising as an element of form and content in Greek drama').

[80] See, for instance, the presence of oaths to confirm the decision of the Greeks and Trojans to determine their dispute by single combat (Homer, *Iliad*, 3.276) and the alliance between Croesus and the Lacedaemonians (Herodotus, *Histories*, 1.69).

[81] See for instance the comments on such an attitude recited in Aelian, *Historical Miscellany*, xiv.2 (Of *Agesilaus*, and the *Barbarians* breaking their Oaths).

[82] This 'virtuous' approach to human life and conduct was developed by Aristotle: see further discussion in Ch. 2, pp. 69–72.

[83] Plato also mentions the judicial use of oaths by various Greek states in his *Laws*, for instance the practice of *exomosia*, an oath by a witness that he does not believe a statement put to him to be true (*Laws*, 936e – 937a) as well as the imagined oath in the ideal

The view of swearing oaths which may be gleaned from classical Greek writers is thus mixed: dramatists used the device of the oath in tales of tragic heroes to suggest that the feature of oath taking which was a prediction about the future of the swearer, in opposition to his fate, was a usurpation of the divine prerogative to determine the future, whereas references to oath swearing in religious or solemn ceremonies, or as simple commitments to tell the truth, rather than as attempts to avoid one's fate, clearly put oaths in a more positive light. It seems then that for the Greek writers, one needs to distinguish the context of the making of an oath in order to judge whether it is to be seen as a laudable act or not.

In Roman society, oath taking was generally conceived of as a positive act, reflective of fidelity,[84] hence Cicero's remark that the 'foundation of justice, moreover, is good faith – that is, truth and fidelity to promises and agreements'.[85] Oaths were to be 'sacredly kept'.[86] On the other hand, the more mixed attitude to oath swearing seen in Greek society is also visible in the Bible, a source of evident significance and influence in later Christian attitudes to the permissibility and desirability of oaths, as seen from Aquinas's discussion of biblical texts in his analysis of oaths.[87] The overall impression given by passages from the Old Testament of oath swearing is that righteous oaths, though not lightly to be entered into, are not strictly forbidden, and, if made, must be honoured, but that the rash oath, which will often be made for a dishonourable purpose, is a reprobate act and will have undesirable consequences.[88] This attitude is consistent with the pattern seen in the classical Greek tests, a similarity which has been argued to indicate a cross-fertilisation of ideology between ancient Greek societies and Hebrew culture.[89] There are fewer instances of oath swearing in the New Testament,[90] though a difficult passage (in the

---

state of Magnesia of a *dikastes* that he will judge a matter fairly (*Laws*, 948e). There was a similar practice of *exomosia* in the actual courts of Athens: see the example related in Aeschines, *Speeches*, 'Against Timarchus', 67–9.

[84] The Roman concept of good faith has been intimately linked to the cult of the goddess *Fides*: see Nifong, 'Promises Past'.

[85] '*Fundamentum autem est iustitiae fides, id est dictorum conventorumque constantia et veritas*' (Cicero, *De Officiis*, 3.7.23).

[86] '*est enim ius iurandum affirmatio religiosa; quod autem affirmate quasi deo teste promsieris, id tenendum est*' (Cicero, *De Officiis*, 3.29.104).

[87] *Summa Theologica*, II-II, Q. 89.

[88] Lev. 5:4–5, 6:3,19:12; 1 Kings 2:23–24 (alternatively 3 Kings 2:23–24 in the Vulgate).

[89] See Schlesinger, *Promises, Oaths and Vows*, pp. 180–1. Schlesinger cites in support of this view the argument advanced by Albright, *From Stone Age to Christianity*.

[90] But see Rom. 1:9; 2 Cor. 1:23; Heb. 6:16.

Gospel of Matthew) stands out which, if taken literally, seems to prohibit any act of swearing.[91] The text was, however, subject to later interpretation which resulted in a received view (though not without dissent)[92] that oath-making was not strictly prohibited.

This mixed biblical attitude towards oaths is reflected in Aquinas's view that, while 'an oath is in itself lawful and commendable'[93] it 'becomes a source of evil to him that makes evil use of it, that is who employs it without necessity and due caution.'[94] While oaths and vows are, as previously indicated, sometimes conflated, Aquinas distinguishes the two clearly in the definitions (cited earlier) which he gives to each and also in terms of their theological significance: a vow, being directed towards God, is an act of religion; an oath, by which God's name is called in confirmation of something, is not such an act of religion. The distinction is an Aristotelian teleological one, made by reference to the respective end of each act.[95] While there is thus a Thomist distinction between oaths and promises, a promise might be backed up by an oath. This is an important point, for, where this occurred, medieval canon law gave the ecclesiastical courts jurisdiction for the breach of the promise, as such a breach would also constitute breach of the oath, which was seen as a breach of faith (*fidei laesio*) and thus a religious matter.[96] Significantly in Aquinas's treatment of promissory oaths, the promissory nature of such oaths mandates that they be kept, for the same reason that, in the Thomist view, promises in general must be kept: the requirement of the virtue of honesty.[97] This virtue of honesty, as it is emphasised by both Aristotle and Aquinas, is discussed further in Chapter 2.

Oath swearing was still in Aquinas's day a common feature of community life, which explains why a comprehensive study on promises must include some discussion of oaths. In the present age, the making of oaths is largely confined to judicial procedures where a confirmation of the truthfulness of evidence to be presented is sought, and to the admittance to office of public officials, officers of important private societies,

---

[91] Matt. 5:33–37.

[92] Various strands of Protestantism have doubted the acceptability of swearing oaths. For instance, the Puritans refused to take certain types of oath, a stance which put them in direct conflict with the Anglican ecclesiastical and juridical authorities of their day. For an historical summary of the competing ideologies underlying this conflict, see Greaves, *Society and Religion in Elizabethan England*, pp. 680–92.

[93] *Summa Theologica*, II-II, Q. 89, Art. 2.   [94] *Ibid.*   [95] *Ibid.*

[96] See further discussion of this point in Chs. 2 and 3.

[97] *Summa Theologica*, II-II, Q. 89, Art. 7.

or certain professionals (physicians being the most significant example). Breach of such oaths is normally conceived of as being governed by public law procedures, or disciplinary proceedings by the relevant society or professional body, rather than through a civil law action for breach of promise, the requisite conditions for which would often not be met in the circumstances of breach of the oath. Though such examples of modern oath-making therefore describe a much reduced field in which the oath is used, the matters in which the swearing of oaths continues to be used all have legal significance. Lawyers cannot thus ignore the function and consequences of the oath, albeit the private law consequences of a breach of oath tend to be less significant than the public law ones.

(c) Threats

Threats, if seriously made rather than as boastful attempts to coerce others, share the similarity with promises that they both declare a commitment by the speaker to perform some future act which will affect the hearer of the statement. The distinction lies in the fact that the promisor commits to a future beneficial act in favour of the party to whom the promise is addressed, while the maker of a threat commits himself to some act harmful to the party to whom the threat is directed.[98] As the late scholastic Lessius put it in his definition of a promise, a promise 'concerns something that is good'.[99]

This distinction is an important one: as threats, unlike promises, do not disclose virtuous intent, they are not looked upon favourably by the law. On the contrary, they may give rise to negative consequences for the maker of the threat, who may, by making the threat, have committed a criminal act, or, in a contractual setting, may be deemed to have committed an anticipatory breach of contract if, for instance, the threat is not to perform a contractual obligation when it falls due. Threats are, from a legal perspective, not susceptible to actions of enforcement by the party to whom they are addressed should the maker of the threat not perform the

[98] Páll Árdal provides a different definition of a threat, as a commitment to act which is unwelcome to the hearer: see Árdal, 'And That's a Promise', 231. Thus, on Árdal's view, a threat may be constituted by something unwelcome to the hearer even though the promised act is objectively of benefit to him, such as a threat issued to a child to correct its bad behaviour. This alternative definition provides an uncertain distinction between promises and threats, as the distinction can only be determined once the subjective attitude of the hearer of the statement is discovered. For that reason, the objective definition of a threat given in this text is suggested as preferable.

[99] Lessius, De iustitia et jure, 2.18.1.

threatened act: a court will not compel a harmful act by a private person. However threats are treated, they are not to be considered promises under the definition proposed earlier.

Promise thus shares with contract the feature that there must exist, at the time the obligation is constituted, an intention on the part of the debtor to protect or improve the other party's interests (even if that is not the effect which they in fact produce),[100] and thus to undertake something which is of benefit to that other party. This distinguishes voluntary obligations from involuntary or imposed obligations: in tort/delict, unjustified enrichment and *negotiorum gestio*, the party upon whom the duty is imposed is required to remedy a worsening of the other's position.

(d) Donation (gift)

A further act which can be distinguished from a promise is that of donation/gift (the two terms are synonymous).[101] Promise and donation are sometimes equated on the basis that the intention of the party undertaking each act is that another is benefited by the act, and also that a promise may be, and a donation is, made on account of the liberality of the party undertaking the act, that is out of a motive of generosity.[102] However, donation and promise may be distinguished in that:

(1) a promise may or may not be gratuitous; donation, *per contra*, is by nature a gratuitous act,[103] and

---

[100] Promises or contracts may unintentionally worsen the other party's position, if changing circumstances have rendered the originally intended benefit harmful to the other party's interests, but this does not prevent the promise or contract from having being validly constituted.

[101] This topic is discussed further in Hogg, 'Promise: The Neglected Obligation', and at greater length in Hogg, 'Promise and Donation in Louisiana and Comparative Law'.

[102] D. 39.5.1: 'A person makes a donation ... for no other reason than to display his liberality and munificence.'

[103] Though in some systems, a transaction may be partly donative, and partly remunerative, and still count as donative; see also the DCFR, Art. IV.H-1:202. Non-gratuitous receipts of benefits are likely to give rise to a legal inference that the transferor should receive something for the transfer, whether by virtue of the obligation of contract, unjustified enrichment, or *negotiorum gestio*. Such an inference can be countered by demonstrating that the transfer was made for reason of liberality on the part of the transferor. Even where the transfer is made out of liberality, and thus a donation, it is sometimes maintained that the transferee owes at least a counter-duty of gratitude, and that if this is not forthcoming the donation may be revoked. This was a rule of Roman law, and was adopted in some civilian and mixed systems, such as Scotland (see Stair I.8.2) and Louisiana (where ingratitude is given a very restricted meaning: CC Art. 1557).

(2) a promise is a commitment to confer a benefit in the future; donation, *per contra*, is an act which presently confers a benefit upon the donee rather than commits to a future beneficial act.

One may of course promise (or contract) to make a donation, by promising (or contracting) to confer a gratuitous benefit upon another at some point in the future. Different legal systems stipulate different requirements for such a promise, such requirements often varying according to whether the promise is to make a donation during the lifetime of the promisor (an *inter vivos* donation) or upon the death of the promisor (a *mortis causa* donation). But the fact that one may promise to make a donation in the future merely serves to highlight that promise and donation are two separate juristic acts.

The idea of donation as defined above restricts the concept to the gratuitous act of transference of the asset in question. Some systems, however, extend the concept of donation not just to the act of transfer but also to any preceding undertaking by which a party binds itself to effect a donation. Where such a view is taken, then it is consistent to talk of a 'contract of donation' or even a 'promise of donation', in the sense of a binding voluntary obligation to effect a donation. In South African Law, for instance, donation has been described as a contract, under which 'both parties must agree to effect delivery',[104] albeit, because only one of the parties is required to perform, it is a 'unilateral contract'.[105] In German law also, the idea of donation extends not only to the gratuitous disposition of an asset but also to any preceding contract of donation.[106] Where the concept of donation is taken to mean not just the act of transfer but any preceding undertaking to effect such transfer, then of course the idea of a promise to donate makes perfect sense, though the preceding promise and the subsequent act of donation are not one and the same thing.

The concept of donation is usually restricted, in a legal context, to transfers of property rights, rather than contractual rights of a transferor (when assignment would be the appropriate term for the transfer) or services. Thus one may talk properly of donating a car, or a house, or intellectual property, but not of donating a right to receive money or one's employment for a period of time. Admittedly, however, in a non-legal context, one does encounter references to donations of contractual rights or services. For instance, one may hear the statement that 'A has donated his

---

[104] Van der Merwe *et al.*, *Contract*, p. 6.
[105] *Ibid.*, p. 9. [106] BGB §§516–34.

(future) services to B'. For present legal purposes, however, references to donation will be restricted to a transfer of property rights. On that basis, a so-called donation of future services by A to B should in fact be described as a promise by A to B of future services and not as a donation.[107]

(e)   Warranties (guarantees)

It is important to recognise that the word warranty may be used in a number of different senses. In English law, for instance, the word has been used to refer variously to a term of a contract, as opposed to a mere representation; to a term not going to the root of a contract, as opposed to one that does (a condition), so that its breach only gives rise to a right to damages but not to terminate the contract; or to a statement of fact held out ('guaranteed') as true (sometimes annexed to or contained within a contract, sometimes issued separately to a contract, as in a so-called 'collateral warranty').[108] It is in this last sense that the term is meant here, a sense in which the term 'guarantee' is often used synonymously.

Some commentators have characterised promise sufficiently widely to include a warranty as a type of promise,[109] but much depends on the definition adopted for both a promise and a warranty. A definition of a promise was offered earlier, and a warranty has just been defined as a statement by which a party holds out that something is the case, that is, that a state of facts exists at the time of the making of the statement (or existed at a previously stated time). Examples might include statements such as 'I warrant that the pollution which affected this land has been cleaned up' or 'I warrant that these goods have been owned since manufacture by one party alone'. The distinction with a promise, as defined earlier, will be obvious: a warranty thus defined would not appear, on the face of it, to commit the maker of the statement to any future action. However, that is not the end of the matter, as a breach of the warranty, in the sense that the statement is found not to have been true when made, would normally be expected to give rise to remedies on the part of the person to whom the warranty was made, remedies which would oblige the party in breach to do something (for instance, pay damages). Such remedies might be seen as arising by operation of law, and thus not to be characterised as promissory, or they

---

[107] A useful comparison of donation and promise, from the perspective of various European legal systems, may be found in Schmidt-Kessel, *Principles of European Law: Donation*.

[108] In *Finnegan* v. *Allen* [1943] 1 KB 425, 430, the term warranty was said to be 'one of the most ill-used expressions in the legal dictionary'.

[109] See Atiyah, *Promises, Morals and Law*, p. 161.

might be seen as arising voluntarily, as an implied consequence of the warranty itself, and thus properly characterised as a conditional promise implicit in the statement of warranty itself. The 'voluntary but implicit' characterisation seems, however, a somewhat strained one, and the analysis underlying it would seem to suggest that all contractual remedies imposed by courts should be classified as voluntary and promissory in nature, which is not commonly held to be the case.

Where the maker of a warranty expressly binds himself to a future conditional act if the warranty is untrue, and thus the warranty is conceived of more extensively, then the totality of the statement is more easily classifiable as a promise, or at least as containing a promise. Consider, for instance, the statement

> 'I warrant that this land is clean of all pollution; if it is not, then I undertake to effect such cleaning or to pay damages.'

If one were to call the whole of this statement the warranty, then the warranty so defined would incorporate both a statement of fact as well as a promise; on the other hand, if the statement were to be conceived of as breaking down into a warranty (the statement of fact) followed by a promise (conditional on the warranty being untrue), then the warranty and the promise would be distinguishable, though a promise would certainly be present.

What the above discussion shows is that whether one should classify a warranty as a promise or as something else depends first on whether warranties are defined narrowly or broadly. The narrowly defined warranty – the mere statement of fact – is, on one view, not a promise, as it contains no undertaking to do anything. On another view, however, even such a simple statement of fact ought to be seen as containing an implicit duty to do something, such as pay damages, if the statement is found to be untrue, in which case the question is how one defines such an implicit undertaking: is it an implied promise, or is it merely a remedy imposed by law? With more widely conceived warranties (those including an express undertaking to do something if the statement of fact is found to be untrue), it is easier to characterise the warranty as including a promise, though the question remains of whether the promise should be distinguished from the warranty, or whether they are an indissoluble unit.

There seems no obvious objectively correct answer to these definitional questions, and different jurisdictions might conceivably have a narrower or a wider definition of a warranty. Given, however, that it seems theoretically possible with a warranty (especially those containing express undertakings on the part of the maker of the warranty) to separate out a statement of fact from any conditional undertaking (whether of a promissory nature or not) applicable should the statement be untrue, it may be safest to conclude that, while warranties can be viewed as containing a promise, they amount in total to more than simply such a promise.

(f)   Agreement

The concept of an agreement has been defined in varying ways, not all of which are relevant to the present discussion. Nearly all definitions would suppose a number of persons (at least two) to be involved in an act of agreement, though one occasionally encounters descriptions of a single person 'agreeing' in a unilateral act to do something. Ignoring that unusual and arguably misguided sense, an agreement is usually said to denote a 'meeting of the minds', in the sense that the parties concerned each express a concurrence in a posited state of affairs or course of action. Thus, the idea that two persons 'agree' that the weather is bad today would suggest that they concur as to that proposition (though not being omniscient beings, we can never be wholly sure what each subjectively understands by the idea of the weather's being 'bad', the very problem which often produces alleged subjective disagreement despite apparent concurrence). A concurrence suggests an externally demonstrated declaration of such concurrence, so that the mere fact that two individuals might both separately think that the weather is bad does not mean that they agree that it is: they must declare their adherence to the proposition in question before an agreement can be said to exist. Such an objective concurrence of parties is often arrived at through consecutive individual declarations, in which case use of the term agreement can denote the declaration of one of the parties to a previously stated proposition by the other: thus, the expression 'he expressed his agreement' often, in a contractual context, indicates an acceptance by one party of a prior contractual proposal made by the other.

The agreements with which the law is concerned do not however relate to statements of fact,[110] such as the nature of the weather, but rather to duties which the parties are (or at least one of whom is) to perform. The concurrence of wills which is of the essence of contract can (though need not) be described in promissory terms, an approach which was the tradition

---

[110] Save where such statements take the form of a warranty, and are thus guaranteed as true by one of the parties: see the discussion in the previous section of the main text.

of the medieval jurists and the late scholastics, and has been maintained clearly in the contract language of Common law jurisdictions, but also in other systems too.[111] Parties agree to be bound contractually either (in the case of a gratuitous contract) by the promise of one party being accepted by a simple 'yes' of the other, or (in the case of a mutual contract) through an exchange of conditional promises (the performance of the one being the condition imposed by the other for its performance). Agreement is thus the end result produced by a promissory mechanism which demonstrates concurrence of the parties' wills in the substance of what has been promised.

One can of course, as some theorists do, reject a promissory view of contract, and argue that contract is based on a non-promissory understanding of agreement or on some other basis altogether. On a non-promissory view of agreement, it might for instance be argued that the essence of agreement lies in a consent mutually to be bound at law. On such a view, when A contracts to sell his house to B for an agreed price, the parties are consenting to be bound to the obligations they have proposed (and, additionally, to any obligations imposed on them by the common law or legislation). The attraction to some of such an approach is that it is said to assist in explaining the binding force of some contracts which it is alleged do not embody any promises (because no *future* performance is pledged by either party). However, if the problem allegedly posed by such contracts for a promissory view of contract can be dealt with (and it will be argued later that such alleged problematic examples of contract can adequately be analysed in promissory terms),[112] then the need to eschew promissory language when describing agreement flies off. Though agreement is the end result, promise is the mechanism by which it is reached, and there is no reason why a promissory conception of such an exchange needs to be eschewed in favour of the language of a 'consent to be bound'.[113]

Agreement then, though different from promise, can be argued to be achieved in a contractual context by the means of promise. Crucially,

---

[111] It can be found in civilian conceptions of agreement too, as, for instance, in §861 of the Austrian Civil Code (AGBG), concerning the conclusion of contracts, which speaks of the making and acceptance of a promise (*ein Versprechen*) as the method by which the mutual consent or agreement (*der übereinstimmende Wille*) of the parties is achieved.

[112] See discussion in Ch. 4, at pp. 215–17.

[113] In any event, as will be evident from the definition offered earlier of a promise, a promise is an expression of a consent to be bound, so the language of 'consent to be bound' (or 'assumption of duty') can in any event be said to apply to the idea of promise.

however, whilst promising is a means to reach agreement, one can agree without promising, and thus agree without yet being bound to the agreement. This is so because there can be consensus between parties to the effect that, *if* they decide to bind themselves contractually, certain agreed terms will govern their relationship, without the intention to be bound yet having been manifested. This shows the importance, when determining whether a contract exists, of looking beyond mere agreement, to verifying whether the consent to be bound demonstrated by the making of a promise is present. Agreement does not equate to promise because one can reach a consensus that *x* will be so without yet binding oneself to undertake *x*. Agreement therefore, of itself, is not enough to create a contract: a concurrence of the wills of the parties is required, such concurrence being demonstrated by the mechanism of promise.

4.   Promise as a culturally universal and significant idea

The discussion of promise thus far as a human institution has doubtless given the impression, from the broad historical perspective taken, that promising has been a universal feature of all human societies since the earliest times. Indeed, over the centuries a number of legal philosophers have confidently asserted that promising is just such a universal institution.[114] Is such an assertion correct, however, or can one identify any cultures, whether current or historic, which lack a concept of promise? Theoretically, one might suggest that any culture which had no concept of the future, or of the predictability of future events, or of the reasonableness of relying upon human commitments to future acts, might lack a concept of the promise.

The sociologists Fred and Shulamit Korn have attacked the assertion that promising is a necessary aspect of all human societies, arguing that it is not based upon empirical anthropological study but rather 'assumptions about the nature of society and what is necessary for it to flourish'.[115] In support of their argument, they claim to have identified one such society where there is no concept of promising: Tonga. While they admit that Tongan society has a concept of oaths (for instance, as used in courts of law) as well as pledges (such as a pledge of allegiance), neither of these acts embodies a commitment of future action, which is of course an essential

---

[114] See, for instance, Hart, *The Concept of Law*, pp. 189–95; Hume, 'Of the Original Contract', pp. 160–1.
[115] Korn and Korn, 'Where People Don't Promise', p. 446.

component of the definition of promise given earlier. Moreover, they assert that this absence of promising from Tongan society is not a linguistic matter:

> it is not just that the Tongan language has no word equivalent to the English word 'promise' … Rather what is important is that in Tonga there is no performative equivalent to our speech act of promising whereby the speaker undertakes an obligation to perform some future act.[116]

They add, however, that while Tongans do make utterances couched in language which others might interpret as promissory, those making them do not perceive these utterances as giving rise to any obligation: there is no promissory intent present. Rather, such words are uttered because they are 'an expression of solidarity and concern' for the hearer's position.[117] One might imagine that such repeated false utterances would lead others to doubt the sincerity of the speaker, and indeed Korn and Korn concede that experience shows that, of themselves, such false utterances cannot sustain significant relationships: practical assistance and aid to the other must be forthcoming.[118]

The argument presented by Korn and Korn is, in essence, that the cultural norm in Tonga is simply entirely different to that elsewhere, and that a Tongan can, in consequence, say with impunity that he will do something yet not do it. Why is this so? Precisely, suggest Korn and Korn, for one of the theoretical reasons suggested above as likely to prevail in a society which lacked a concept of promising:

> To Tongans, the future is indefinite and uncertain. Plans for the future are not regarded as fixed, for there is no telling how things will work out.[119]

One might imagine that such an attitude would make any law of contract meaningless, and indeed in formal legal terms that would appear to be the position presented by Korn and Korn. Many Tongans, however, clearly do have confidence that others will do what they have said they will do, but the reason for this, it is said, is that

> confidence depends not on what is said but on a judgment about the other person's commitment to the relationship.[120]

Korn and Korn assert that those Tongans seeking to evade expected performance for short term gain find that others will be reluctant to form

---

[116] *Ibid.*, p. 447.   [117] *Ibid.*, p. 448.   [118] *Ibid.*, pp. 448–9.
[120] *Ibid.*   [119] *Ibid.*, p. 449.

a relationship with them,[121] though this seems to be an assertion based on game theory principle rather than upon any empirical evidence.[122]

What is to be made of the argument of Korn and Korn? If they are right that Tongans do not conceive that it is possible to undertake binding obligations relating to the future, and that any language they use suggesting otherwise is merely illusory, then it would seem to follow that the necessary requirement for a valid promise of an intention to be bound to a future act cannot be present when Tongans appear to be promising. On the other hand, one wonders whether, assuming such is indeed the Tongan attitude, it can be preserved in the long term, given Tongan interaction with outside cultures. It would be surprising if at least some Tongans had not adopted a non-Tongan view of the binding nature of promises. Furthermore, given that Tongans at least give the impression of undertaking promises, in that they use language which is couched in promissory terms, one might argue that, on an objective assessment of their intentions, they should in fact be taken to undertake promises, whatever their subjective understanding might be, especially in their interactions with non-Tongans, or else how could the Tongan Government, for instance, be expected to honour promises made to other national governments or foreign corporations. A society which at least has words which function in a promissory way clearly has some concept of promissory ideas even if, as Korn and Korn argue, the members of that society do not subjectively mean what they say when using that promissory language. Finally, the assertion by Korn and Korn that what matters is not words used but the 'commitment' of another to a relationship, seems to be a recognition that a commitment in some form to the future of a relationship is important in Tonga; that idea is hard to reconcile with the assertion that Tongans have no concept of the future or of committing to it. These points cast some doubt on the view that Tongans neither have a concept of promise nor undertake promises, and suggest that, even if any such position does prevail, it is unlikely to persist in the long term if Tongans wish to interact with the outside world.

In actuality, Tongan society may be more like Iranian society. Iranians appear to view promises in a different way to Western cultures, not because, as Korn and Korn argue in respect of Tonga, there is no concept

---

[121] *Ibid.*

[122] Game theorists recognise likelihood of performance as one of the variables to be inputted when analysing contractual negotiations: see, for instance, Katz, 'The Strategic Structure of Offer and Acceptance'.

of promising, but rather because the art of deception, being insincere in what one says, is, it is said, an established feature of Iranian society. This at least is the view of one Western observer of Middle Eastern society, Michael Slackman.[123] Slackman refers to a concept in Iranian society called *taarof*,

> a concept that describes the practice of insincerity – of inviting people to dinner when you don't really want their company, for example. Iranians understand such practices as manners and are not offended by them.

The practice of *taarof* beyond the field of social engagements has, Slackman argues, far-reaching consequences for international political relations. The same might be said for its consequences for contract and interpersonal promises too: insincere promising would seem to render contracting an unreliable and unpredictable field. There are further similar features of Iranian society, such as *taqiyya* (religiously sanctioned deception or dissimulation to conceal one's true intentions and beliefs), *kitman* (deception) and *khod'eh* (trickery or claiming one's true position by half-truths rather than outright lies or deception),[124] which evidently colour Iranian perceptions of the nature of what is being undertaken when promissory language is used.[125]

Such concepts suggest not that Iranians have no concept of promising, but rather a cultural norm where it is expected that promises which have been made may be insincere and unreliable. The language used by apparent promisors should not be taken to mean what it purports to. It seems then that apparent promissory language is not expected to be considered formative of promises, given a lack of subjective intent to promise.

Seana Shiffrin has expressed doubts about the alleged conclusive anti-promissory evidence of Tongan and Iranian society:

> Some reports about Tongan and Iranian culture may complicate claims about the universality of promising, but it is difficult to determine exactly what they show … Some of this evidence could be interpreted to show that in some cultures, it is hard to tell when sincere commitments are expressed, but not that promises as such have little or no significance. Further, the purported departures from the culture of promising take place in contexts of hierarchical, unequal structures; thus, they may not

---

[123] See Slackman, 'The Fine Art of Hiding What You Mean to Say'.
[124] See further on these, Campbell, 'Iran and Deception Modalities'.
[125] Slackman, 'The Fine Art of Hiding What You Mean to Say', quotes Iranian social psychologist Muhammad Sonati as saying 'In Iran … [y]ou promise things, and you don't mean it. People who live here understand that.'

serve as counterevidence of the importance of promising in maintaining social relations of equality amid local conditions of vulnerability. Tongan society is so pervasively hierarchical that much of its social interaction and dialogue is colored by status differences.[126]

Whether or not Korn and Korn or Slackman are correct in the conclusions they draw about an absence of promise or about the insincerity of promise in the societies they observe, it does seem correct that an assumption about the universality of promise usually goes hand in hand with a natural law stance about the fundamental nature of promise in human society. Such a belief in the natural law basis of promises raises questions as to the source of the moral force of promises, an issue which is addressed in Chapter 2.

5.   Preliminary conclusions

What may be concluded about promises from the discussion thus far, a discussion which has been largely definitional in nature? A definition of a promise has been suggested, namely that a promise is

> a statement by which one person commits to some future beneficial performance (or the beneficial withholding of a performance) in favour of another person.

This definition, which proved sufficiently robust to withstand a number of suggested criticisms of it, will be maintained for the purposes of the analysis to be undertaken in the remainder of this work, though it must be borne in mind that individual legal systems may (as will be seen) have somewhat differing conceptions of a promise.

It has been argued that promising is a human social institution whose nature is therefore determined by human beings. It has further been argued that, while the theory of promise rests upon the presence of a subjective intention by the promisor to be bound by the commitment, such an intention not only requires to be externally and objectively manifested by some words or conduct before it is held to give rise to a promise, but the existence and extent of such intention can only realistically be assessed from just such an objective perspective.

It has been noted that the definition proposed is sufficiently broad to encompass both conditional and unconditional promises, gratuitous and non-gratuitous promises, and unilateral and bilateral promises. The

---

[126] Shiffrin, 'The Divergence of Contract and Promise', p. 714, n. 8.

definition is thus capable of describing the undertakings of offeror and acceptor in a contractual relationship. As will be argued later in this work, promise so defined may also be susceptible of describing other features of contract law, such as the nature of some remedies, third party rights and renunciations of contractual rights.

The definition offered enables a promise to be distinguished from the more specialised idea of a vow (a promise made to God), an oath (a commitment where God is called as a witness), a threat (a commitment to harm the hearer of the statement), and a donation (the present act of a donor, rather than a future commitment to act).

Thus far, no possible source of the moral or legal normative force of a promise has been suggested. That question is the subject matter of the following chapter.

2

Promises as obligations: morality and law

1. Introduction: promise as a type of obligation

A promise is considered as a type of obligation, both in morality and law, but what does it mean to call promise an obligation? Having explored that question at the beginning of this chapter, the source of the obligatory nature of promise will be considered. The focus of the study of that second question will, in this chapter, be on promise within morally obligatory systems; the question of the binding force of an obligation in legal systems is largely considered in the next chapter. However, the question of the moral and legal force of an obligation such as promise cannot be wholly separated, as many theories of law and morality see the two systems as inextricably linked. Thus, a dominant theory of law posits that the force of contract derives from the fact that a contract is a promise, and that contracts should therefore be kept because promises should be kept. Such a theory evidently necessitates that one asks why promises ought to be kept. That fundamental, and essentially moral, question requires an exploration of the various theories concerning why promises ought to be kept, an exploration of which comprises the bulk of the discussion in this chapter.

To begin with, however, a description must be given of the meaning of an obligation. Such a description in fact properly locates the seminal nature of an obligation in the law, and not morality. This is not because there is no sense of being held or bound to a promise beyond the legal conception of a binding duty, but because, semantically, the historic origins of the term 'obligation' in fact lie in the law, and in Roman law to be more precise. The development in Roman law of the concept of an obligation out of an early power over the body of a wrongdoer has been chronicled.[1] This physical bond over wrongdoers explains the etymology of the word obligation: the Latin verb *ligare* means to bind, and an

---

[1] Zimmermann, *The Law of Obligations*, pp. 1–3.

obligation (*obligatio*) was literally a physical bond in the early days of Roman law. By the classical period of Roman law, the concept of an obligation had developed beyond a literal power to bind a wrongdoer and had come to incorporate the class of interpersonal legal relationships – bonds or ties only in the figurative sense – deriving both from harmful conduct (said to arise *ex delicto*) as well as those arising voluntarily (*ex contractu*). At least by classical times, this idea of a figurative obligation encompassed the whole of the relationship binding the relevant parties, and thus both the duty imposed on the one and the corresponding right given to the other.[2] In Western legal systems which derive from Roman law, an obligation thus entails a corresponding right and duty deriving from a legal bond or tie between the obliged (debtor) and the obligee (creditor). Such a bond naturally implies a power in the obligee to compel the obliged to perform the relevant duty. Bearing in mind the element of performance of a duty, it will be obvious why promise falls within the class of obligations. The power given to promisees at law to enforce performance are considered at various later points in this work.

2.   Taxonomies of obligations in morality and law

Recognising that promise is a type of obligation leads to the question of where promise fits in taxonomically with other obligations recognised by moral and legal systems. The law and morality tend to give somewhat different answers to that question, even though each sees the place of promise within its own system as determined by the nature of the binding force it ascribes to promise. In morality, there are a number of possible classifications of interpersonal duties.[3] For instance, one basis of a classification would be to use the class of person to whom the moral duty is undertaken: to God (as with those promises which are constituted as vows),

---

[2] While commonly, in modern layman's usage, the term obligation denotes only the duty side of such a bond, in this work the classical sense will be maintained unless the context indicates otherwise.

[3] What is offered in the main text is not a comprehensive analysis of moral systems or a comprehensive classification of the moral rules or principles operating in such a system, about which much has been written (see, for instance, Sheng, 'On the Nature of Moral Principles'), but rather a discussion of some possible moral classifications of obligations, a much more narrowly focused question. Promise as a type of obligation can, of course, be said to derive from a moral principle (whether it be a broad moral principle such as virtue or utility, or a more focused principle such as that one should keep one's word), but the source of the obligatory force of a promise as perhaps lying in such a moral principle is the subject of later discussion in this chapter.

family, friends, community, strangers, or even perhaps to self (though the concept of a duty, including a promise, owed to oneself is not one which fits with the definition of a promise suggested in Chapter 1). The rationale behind such a classification would be to stress varying degrees of importance to be attached to the nature of the obligation, with promises made to God or family being considered stronger bonds than those made to strangers. Such an approach is quite different to that taken by the law, which sees all properly constituted obligations as having the same legal force.[4] An alternative way of classifying moral obligations would be by reference to the nature of the duty undertaken: thus a promise made by A to B to go on holiday might be seen as less morally binding than one made by A to a dying B to provide for B's child. Again, because all legally recognised duties have a unitary obligatory effect, none being more or less of a powerful bond at law than others, the law would not recognise that sort of division either. The point about morality's distinction between duties owed to one type of person and another, or between those concerning one type of conduct and another, is that such classifications can be thought useful to human beings in helping them to decide how to prioritise undertakings, and thus to rank them in case of conflict, so that, for instance, a duty to one's spouse would, in case of conflict, trump that of one owed to a stranger. Moral rankings of duties also act as badges of the varying degrees of importance attached by people to certain relationships and to certain types of conduct, and thus operate socially as signs of the social hierarchy and of the hierarchy of types of laudable conduct. How are such moral classifications arrived at? That is a complex sociological question, but it seems to depend in large part upon how promises are seen to derive their moral force. This is a far from uncontroversial question, and much of the substance of this chapter will be taken up with considering it.

Given the traditional linkage of morality and law by human societies, an inevitably related question to the moral classification of promises is how the class of obligations is arranged by the law, that discipline from which the term obligation sprang. Because much of the detail of this question is discussed in Chapter 3, only a summary is offered at this point. Obligations as a legal taxonomic category describe the class of private law duties arising between persons. As interpersonal duties they give rise to so-called rights *in personam*. Such are to be distinguished from property law duties, which arise in relation to things and not persons,

---

[4] Human law is, of course, not concerned with promises made to God, the law being concerned with relationships between human beings.

and so give rise to so-called rights *in rem*. Within the class of obligations, further subdivisions are possible. The classical Roman division was a two-fold one between those obligations arising by wrongdoing (*ex delicto*) and those arising by agreement (*ex contractu*), a division later expanded to a fourfold one of (1) those arising by wrongdoing, (2) those arising *as if* by wrongdoing (*quasi ex delicto*), (3) those arising by agreement, and (4) those arising *as if* by agreement (*quasi ex contractu*).[5] The Roman classification is no longer adhered to by modern legal systems, which typically prefer to conceive of obligations as arising either voluntarily or involuntarily (though this distinction has some connection with the Roman categories of *ex contractu* and *ex delicto*), that is to say by virtue of a voluntary acceptance of the duty or without reference to such voluntary acceptance. Thereafter voluntary and involuntary types can be further subdivided. Within the voluntary class there is, of course, primarily contract. Many systems would not go further than recognising this single member of that class. However, if unilateral promises are given effect by a legal system, then it is possible (though not necessary) to conceive of such unilateral promises as a separate category of obligation within the class of voluntary obligations.[6] Within the involuntary class are placed delict/tort, unjustified enrichment and (where recognised in a legal system) *negotiorum gestio*.

Thus, just as moral classifications of obligations can be said to depend upon the alleged source of the moral nature of the duty (an issue explored later in this chapter), so too the typical modern legal classification of obligations hinges crucially upon the alleged source of the obligation's force, whether as arising voluntarily or involuntarily, that is whether deriving from the free acceptance of the obliged to be bound to the duty or without reference to such free acceptance but rather by force of law. It was fashionable in the 1970s and 1980s to attack such a division,[7] but such attacks have ultimately proved unconvincing, having failed both to take account of the importance attached by the law to personal freedom as well as to propose a better working classification for the law.[8]

[5] See further discussion in Ch. 3.
[6] There is also the question of where to place third party rights arising under contract, either as part of contract, or as a sui generis species of voluntarily assumed obligation. This question is discussed in Ch. 5 of this work.
[7] See, for instance, Atiyah, *Essays on Contract*, and Gilmore, *The Death of Contract*.
[8] Apart from the standard modern classification of obligations into voluntary and involuntary species, there are other criteria which can be used to describe obligations. Some of these were discussed in Ch. 1. Hence, obligations may be described as unilateral or bilateral (or multilateral), gratuitous or onerous, and as revocable or irrevocable.

Apart from the force of promises in morality or in law, can promises be considered obligatory in some other sense? Such a question might seem nonsensical: surely an obligation is either enforceable at law, or not; and, if not, only morality can suggest a duty of performance, albeit not a duty which can be used to compel anyone legally. This is essentially the case, though there is the problem of how to classify so-called 'natural obligations' (*obligationes naturales*), these being obligations which, though strictly not legal obligations (in that they lack the quality of enforceability), are considered more than merely morally binding obligations. An example of a natural obligation is a debt which has been extinguished through the passage of time. Such a debt can no longer be enforced at law, though the party who owed the debt may be said still to have a moral duty to repay that which he borrowed. Such a natural obligation is more than just a moral duty, however, because it has some secondary, indirect effects, recognised at law, albeit that it cannot be directly enforced. Thus, if the party who was formerly the legal debtor before the debt was extinguished nonetheless pays the debt, thinking it due, he cannot claim the money back under unjustified enrichment, as he would be able to do had there never been debt at all. Natural obligations therefore give rise to a type of limited legal relationship and effect between the parties, albeit not one which is recognised as a fully valid legal obligation. Such a natural obligation has therefore been said in modern South African law to give rise to 'a legal (and not a mere moral) relationship' revealing 'some of the characteristics of civil obligations', a description which seems apt to describe such obligations in general.[9] It seems therefore that we must recognise that some promises are neither fully legally enforceable, nor merely moral, but have an awkward interstitial status affording some legal protection against claims without giving rise to any right of action in law.

3.   Promises as moral obligations: the practice of promising

For a promise to be constituted as an obligation, the actions of the promisor must conform to the practice of promising, a practice whose requirements were explored in Chapter 1 by reference to the constituent elements of a promise. This practice of promising, it was suggested, is a universal (or near universal) feature of human societies, the boundaries of which

---

[9] Van der Merwe *et al.*, *Contract*, p. 4.

have been fixed by such societies. Whether these boundaries are properly to be seen as fixed by reference to natural law, by the exigencies of human existence and intercourse, or with some other consideration in mind, is explored by reference to the various theories of the moral force of promising considered below.

The exploration of morality and promises to be undertaken puts the focus squarely on the practice or institution of promising, rather than on individual promises.[10] A promise will have or will lack moral force depending on whether the constituent requirements for making promises in general have been complied with. Individual promises which conform to the practice will have prima facie normative force as moral obligations, though there may be specific reasons why a promise lacks moral authority in the circumstances of the case, as the discussion will show.

While the nature of the practice of promising is often a dual one, in that many morally binding promises will also be legally binding, it is evident that each source, morality and the law, can be distinguished. Some promises considered morally binding are not enforced by the law. Such might include promises made in a social context, those reflecting duties of a family or religious nature, or those intended to have legal force but affected by some invalidating factor or want of proper form. More controversially, it might be argued that some legally enforceable promises are immoral, either because the nature of that which has been promised is exploitative of the promisor, for instance one who borrowed money at a high rate of interest, or because that which has been promised is to do something immoral albeit legal, such as the supply of weapons to a dubious though not proscribed government. The counter-argument might be put that, given that the law takes account of moral concerns through a policy that promises *contra bonos mores* are not enforceable, any promises which are enforceable must therefore be moral, but such an argument depends upon publicly accepted moral norms being objectively moral, a position which some would dispute.

If then, moral and legal norms can be distinguished, even if they often coincide, it is necessary to explore whether, and why, it is that the practice of promising is considered a moral act.

---

[10] The proper focus of the enquiry suggested here agrees with the view of MacCormick, 'Voluntary Obligations and Normative Powers I', p. 61.

(a)   Promising as moral, immoral, or amoral?

It may be useful to recall the suggested definition of a promise given in
Chapter 1:

> a statement by which one person commits to some future beneficial per-
> formance (or the beneficial withholding of a performance) in favour of
> another person.

In that a promise, under this definition, is intended to secure a beneficial performance for someone by giving that person a right to compel the
pledged performance, it is often simply assumed, without considering the
matter too closely, that promising must by its nature be a moral act. Such
an assumption rests upon the view that the improvement of another's position is a morally good act, either because, in the case of a unilateral promise, it is a liberal, benevolent action, or because, in the case of the making
of a reciprocal promise, it is a mutually beneficial exercise. In either case,
the improvement of the human condition is often assumed to be a morally
good thing.

   Such an assumption takes no account of the nature of the individual
circumstances under which specific promises are made or are to be performed, including any possible change in such circumstances from those
envisaged at the time the promise is made, such as whether performance
of the promise might, inadvertently, make matters worse. It also takes no
account of the actual motivation for which the promise was made, whether
such was selfish, charitable, or liberal. The failure to consider such matters
has been argued by some to be a weakness in the assertion that the making of promises must be an inherently moral act. A promise made from
selfish motives might be argued to be immoral, if assessing the morality
of an act is taken to include not just its external characteristics but also the
subjective intent for which it was undertaken. A promise which, though
beneficial when made, is, due to changing circumstances, harmful to the
promisee or no longer desired by him, could likewise be argued to have
become an immoral undertaking.

   Concerns such as these have been thought by some to lead to the conclusion that the general practice of promising must necessarily be amoral,
albeit that specific promises might be moral or immoral according to
their circumstances.[11] That conclusion reflects a situationist ethics view of

---

[11] For a view that promising is amoral, see Smith, 'A Paradox of Promising'. Pratt, 'Promises,
     Contracts and Voluntary Obligations', also appears to take an amoral view of promising,

human behaviour, and one that is therefore subject to the usual criticisms of situation ethics, principally that such an ethical view, in denying universally objective qualities of certain types of acts and in attacking the idea of fundamental qualities to types of human behaviour beyond individual actions, fails to take account of the reality that human practices, customs, and institutions (such as promising), are employed by societies precisely to permit people to engage in types of behaviour which are considered moral. It is, after all, *types* of act which are encouraged or forbidden by legislative authorities, rather than individual acts of particular human beings, demonstrating that it is such types of act or practices which are seen by those operating within moral systems as facilitating or hindering a moral life. Promising is one such practice, and its permissibility and encouragement in all human societies is properly seen as a sign that it is considered by such societies to be a moral practice or institution. It would seem then that the view that promising is amoral is flawed, in that it fails to consider the institution of promising as it exists and operates, focusing instead on specific acts of promise which are only possible because they are manifestations of the general practice of promising.

Though there is some body of opinion asserting that the practice of promising is amoral, it is rarer to find the view advanced that promising is by nature an immoral act. Though such a position is rare, it has its proponents. Fox and Demarco, for instance, have argued that promising is necessarily an immoral act, because to bind oneself to a certain future conduct without knowing what competing moral obligations might subsequently mitigate against performance of the pledged conduct is an abnegation of the responsibility we have to make moral choices according to the circumstances prevailing at the time when we are to act. They ask:

> Can people justifiably obligate themselves, in advance, to keeping their promises, in the face of other possible moral obligations? We argue that they cannot. Promising is, as a rule, immoral: it is either an advance declaration of the intention to do the immoral under knowable or

arguing that the rule that we should adhere to promises is in fact 'derivative', 'does no real moral work', and therefore that it provides no assistance in answering the question of whether or not a promisor should adhere to a specific promise in the circumstances (p. 571). In trying to resolve that dilemma, argues Pratt, the promisor does not appeal to rules, because his case is 'not one that has been decided before' (p. 573), a classic situation ethics argument. See also McNeilly, 'Promises De-Moralized', who argues that for a practice of promising to exist it is not necessary to have the assent of most, or even any, members of society to the moral principle of promising. His argument is, however, largely detached from the actual world, and proceeds from discussion of an imaginary world and persons in it.

unknowable contingencies, or else it is a deceptive, and thereby immoral, offer of assurance.[12]

The principal concern of Fox and Demarco thus seems to be that it is immoral to bind oneself to do something in the future when doing that something may in the circumstances then prevailing infringe moral norms. Such a reckless commitment, as embodied in a promise, must therefore necessarily be an immoral act.

This concern is, in fact, not a new one. Many philosophers and jurists who have considered the nature of promising have raised the spectre of the promised act which may be harmful when the time for performance occurs. Plato considered the question in his *Republic* by reference to the example of a promise made to return weapons lent by an owner who had since become mad and might conceivably harm himself if he regained possession of them.[13] Aristotle recognised that the dilemma necessarily led to the conclusion that not all promises should be honoured, if to adhere to a promise would lead to an unjust or unvirtuous result. In Aristotle's view, human actions are directed towards the ultimate end of man, an end achievable through a virtuous life and virtuous practices. Promises are a means to that end, but, if keeping a promise no longer helps to achieve that end, because of changed circumstances, then keeping the promise would no longer be a virtuous thing to do. This does not mean that Aristotle can be described as a situation ethicist, for he was not; but it does indicate that a natural law approach to promising (of which, more later), under which it is deemed possible and desirable to make normative statements about types of human behaviour like promising, is not so rigid an approach as to require that adherence to every instance of a promise will be good. Promising can be seen as a morally good thing, but there may be other competing moral norms which can trump adherence to a promise in specific circumstances. An appreciation that this is so contradicts the view of Fox and Demarco that promising must be bad because one promises in the dark, so to speak, without knowing whether what one has promised may turn out to be undesirable and hence immoral in the circumstances.

In addition to the Fox and Demarco objection, others have objected to the idea that promising is moral on the ground that individual human

---

[12] Fox and Demarco, 'The Immorality of Promising' (1993), 81. Their theory was later expounded at greater length in Fox and Demarco, *The Immorality of Promising* (2001), and the passage quoted above is also found in that work at p. 69. For a response, see Mills, 'The Morality of Promising Made in Good Faith'.

[13] *Republic*, 331c.

beings ought not to be permitted to create obligations, whether moral or legal, simply through a declaration that they pledge to do something. From a moral point of view, the objection is that such a power both deprives the community of the right to decide those duties which ought or ought not to be undertaken, and is thus a usurpation of the function of the proper law-making organs, as well as being open to abuse by those who wish to distort just allocations of resources through selfish acts. In short, the tolerance of individual determination of resources which promising allows is deemed immoral. Can the morality of promising be defended against such a criticism? It is true that the institution of promise-making has been described as allowing people to, as it were, make laws for themselves,[14] and so to bind themselves where they were not bound before. Such a power is, however, subject to control by moral and legal systems, so that unlawful promises or those *contra bonos mores* are not recognised as validly made, this illustrating that ultimately the promisor is bound because it is the moral or legal system that determines that he is so bound, not because he is himself a being capable of determining moral norms. So, it is the moral being's operating within the system which binds the promisor, not the promisor himself, this negating the argument that promising usurps rightful normative authority. It remains true, however, that the law does indeed permit individuals to trigger, through promising, the binding effect of a moral norm, and thereby to allocate resources as they see fit. Such a liberty can surely, however, only be subject to a blanket objection from a position which utterly negates the worth of individual autonomy and the respect due to it. Anyone with a concern for personal autonomy and the individual's right to dispose of his property and services will find nothing in principle objectionable about the ability to promise and thereby bind oneself to an allocation of such property and services, even if some regulation of this power may be deemed desirable.

If the views that promising is necessarily immoral or amoral both seem flawed, that still leaves competing theories as to why promising is a moral practice. These competing theories require examination.

(b) Source of the morality of the practice of promising

A multitude of theories concerning the moral force of promising have been advanced from the classical period down to the present day. Such

---

[14] See Aquinas, *Summa Theologica*, II-II, Q. 88, Art. 10.

theories can be categorised along various lines, and it would be impossible to do full justice to the myriad types of theory here, so only the major types of theory will be analysed.[15] In any event, as noted earlier, this work is not one primarily of abstract legal theory, but seeks to consider legal theory to the extent that it assists an understanding of the role of promise within contract law in an historical context.

The theories considered below do not always provide a justification or explanation for specific rules governing promises or contracts (for instance, as to when damages will be available for breach of a promise, or when performance by a promisor may justifiably be withheld), such rules often being the result of more practical considerations, but they do purport to provide a reason why promising is considered a moral practice and one capable of creating obligations.[16]

(i)   Promising as a virtuous act; the natural law tradition

The first of the varieties of theory which hold that the act of promising is moral is embodied in the Aristotelian-Thomist tradition. This tradition has a long pedigree, which, following a considerable period during which it appeared to have been defeated by rationalism and utilitarianism, has undergone something of a renaissance in the past few decades.[17] The tradition sees the utterance of a promise as a virtuous act, for in undertaking to benefit another at some future point we have engaged either in an act of liberality towards that other (if the promise is gratuitous) or in an act of commutative justice (if the promise is given in exchange for some

---

[15] Even then, some will quibble with the definitions and descriptions of the different types of theory described. This, however, seems inevitable in a field in which so many nuanced and overlapping theories have been offered.

[16] For this reason, the main thrust of Craswell's argument, in 'Contract Law, Default Rules and the Philosophy of Promising', that too much time is devoted to trying to answer the philosophical question of why promises should be kept given that the various theories do not explain the choice of the specific rules of contract, seems unjustified. Theories seeking to explain why people are bound to perform certain duties cannot necessarily hope to provide definitive reasons why a particular position is adopted in relation to the consequences of breach of contract, damages, specific performance, error, and so forth. The detail of such rules will seldom be able to be deduced directly and unequivocally from the fundamental justifications offered by theories of morality for doing or not doing acts, but that does not detract from the value of such theories.

[17] There are a number of current proponents of various varieties of virtue ethics: see, for instance, Oakley, 'Varieties of Virtue Ethics'. For a summary of some of the current debate in the field, see Hacker-Wright, 'Virtue Ethics without Right Action'. For an exposition of modern contract law through the lens of virtue see, for instance, Cimino, 'Virtue and Contract Law'; for the wider use of the concept of virtue in modern law in general, see Farrelly and Solum, *Virtue Jurisprudence*.

counter-pledge of the promisee). In either case, through promising we have also manifested the virtues of truthfulness and fidelity to the promisee, having declared as a matter of truth that we consider ourselves bound to that person and as a matter of faithfulness that we are committed to benefiting him. The objective truth of these statements about the nature or promising is held in the Aristotelian-Thomist tradition to be evident from the nature of the world around us, in particular from our human nature and the natural relations between human beings, as well, in theistic strands of the tradition, as being revealed in religious texts and through divine-human relations. This summary of the nature of the Aristotelian-Thomist tradition's view of the morality of promising contains a number of important concepts and ideas which require some explanation.

The explanation requires us to begin by considering the writings of the Greek philosopher and ethicist Aristotle,[18] who, strange though it may seem given the following consideration of his views, did not discuss promise as such. However, he had much to say about truth, virtue, and justice, the relevance of each of which to promising will become apparent. A great deal has been written by others on Aristotle's views on these subjects, and so only a summary of his philosophy is necessary here.

Aristotle conceived of the highest end of man as *eudaimonia*, a Greek word which has been variously translated in to English as 'happiness', 'flourishing', or 'well-being', each of which translations attempts to convey Aristotle's idea of a life lived in favour with the gods. To this highest end of man are subordinated all other human goals, whether of wealth, health, or pleasure, each of which is to be sought only in so far as it promotes the end of well-being. To enable people to live in such a way as to achieve this highest end, they may employ and develop certain innate character traits or virtues (*aretē*, literally 'excellence'), these virtues being achieved through moral training.[19] Included among such virtues are justice, liberality and truthfulness, each of which requires some elucidation.

In Aristotle's writing, justice (*dikaiosunē*) is distinguished in to two types, distributive and commutative justice.[20] There is a tendency today to

---

[18] Aristotle lived *c*. 428–348 BC Though space does not permit a fuller treatment, mention ought also to be made of Aristotle's precursor, Plato, who also held to a philosophy of virtue. While, however, Aristotle examined commercial transactions for their conformity with justice, Plato was roundly dismissive of them (see for instance his view that commercial contracts ought to be unenforceable: *Republic*, 556a–b). Virtue and money-making are largely inconsistent in the Platonic conception, a view which marginalised Plato's thought on contractual matters in the emerging mercantile Europe of the medieval period.

[19] *Nicomachean Ethics*, 1098a; 1106a.   [20] *Ibid.*, 1130b–1138b.

think of distributive justice as meaning an absolutely equal distribution of wealth or resources among members of society, a division perhaps to be overseen and achieved by the state. That was not the Aristotelian conception of distributive justice, however. On the contrary, Aristotle's view of the world was a hierarchical one, in which merit (*axia*) was possessed in different measure by human beings. Some people demonstrate greater merit through demonstrating certain qualities (hard work, natural ability, courage, fortitude, and so forth), and so are more worthy than others. Such meritorious individuals are conceived of by Aristotle as more deserving of a greater share of wealth and resources, and so it is in keeping with the dictates of distributive justice that they should receive such greater share. Distributive justice is thus distribution *proportionate to human merit*. Human transactions which help to achieve such a distribution may be said to accord with the ends of distributive justice, such transactions including voluntary contracts[21] and other exchanges, as well as benevolent and gratuitous transactions in favour of meritorious persons, including those founded upon promises, all of such transactions according with the end of distributive justice in so far as they assist the endowment of the meritorious with an appropriate share of wealth and resources.

Commutative justice (or, as it is alternatively translated, 'corrective justice'[22]) is more evidently of relevance to voluntary transactions, of which Aristotle mentions a number of types, though it is also said to apply to involuntary transactions. Aristotle lists a number of contracts to which commutative justice clearly applies: sale, loan (with or without interest), pledge, deposit and hire.[23] Commutative or corrective justice does not relate to the qualities, or merit, of the parties in a specific relationship,[24] but rather relates to their interdependence (*synallagma*). In particular, it requires an equality in the relationship of the parties. It is in keeping with this form of justice that those who give something under an exchange should receive an equal value back for such giving. Similarly, in involuntary transactions, a party who loses out ought to be compensated for this or to receive back what he lost.

The above descriptions of the nature of both distributive and commutative justice indicate how, in Aristotelian thinking, both of these varieties

---

[21] On contracts and distributive justice, see Kronman, 'Contract Law and Distributive Justice'; Lucy, 'Contract as a Mechanism of Distributive Justice'.

[22] It is corrective justice in that it 'supplies a corrective principle in private transactions' *Nicomachean Ethics*, 1131a.

[23] *Ibid.*   [24] *Ibid.*, 1132a.

of justice ought to inform the undertaking of promises and contracts, commutative justice especially so.

Another virtue of relevance to promise is that of liberality (*eleutheriotēs*),[25] by which Aristotle meant the observance of a mean in relation to wealth, neither giving away too little, nor too much:

> Acts of virtue are noble, and are performed for the sake of their nobility; the liberal man therefore will give for the nobility of giving. And he will give rightly, for he will give to the right people, and the right amount, and at the right time, and fulfil all the other conditions of right giving.[26]

The relevance of liberality to promising is evident, for someone might promise, out of the virtue of liberality, to give of his wealth to others by promising to donate a portion of his wealth to them.

Lastly there is the virtue of truth (*aletheia*). In the following passage from his *Nicomachean Ethics*, Aristotle suggests that, in those actions where human beings have nothing to gain for themselves, if they are truthful 'in word', they behave in a praiseworthy fashion, and are therefore more likely to be trusted in those matters in which they do have an interest:

> Let us discuss ... first of all the truthful man. We are not speaking of the man who keeps faith in his agreements, i.e., in the things that pertain to justice or injustice (for this would belong to another excellence), but the man who in the matters in which nothing of this sort is at stake is true both in word and in life because his character is such. But such a man would seem to be as a matter of fact equitable. For the man who loves truth, and is truthful where nothing is at stake, will still more be truthful where something is at stake; he will avoid falsehood as something base, seeing that he avoided it even for its own sake; and such a man is worthy of praise. He inclines rather to understate the truth; for this seems in better taste because exaggerations are wearisome.[27]

The reference here to truth-telling is usually understood to include the truth which is inherent in making gratuitous promises (and indeed 'truth-telling' is sometimes translated in this text as 'promising'), those who truthfully pledge their wealth through making such promises doing so in a matter in which they have no interest themselves and therefore also demonstrating their trustworthiness in transactions in which they do have an interest.

For Aristotle then, the virtues of justice, liberality and truth-telling might all be made manifest in making promises to others. Promise-making

---

[25] *Ibid.*, 1119b.   [26] *Ibid.*, 1120a.   [27] *Ibid.*,1127a–b.

might thus be one of the vehicles to achieving that virtuous life which is the highest end of man. The long-term significance of this Aristotelian-virtue approach to promising lay in the influence it was to play in medieval philosophical thought, especially in the uses to which it was put by the most important medieval philosopher, the Dominican friar St Thomas Aquinas. This influence has been well documented, especially in a legal context by James Gordley. Gordley has examined in detail how Thomas, and after him the Spanish scholastics, used the Aristotelian idea of the 'end' of man, and the virtues which assist in the achievement of that end, and applied them to specific human transactions and institutions, identifying an end which they served and the virtues which they manifested (for instance, liberality, commutative justice, and so forth).[28] In so doing, Aquinas and those following him ensured that Aristotelian conceptions of virtue and the good life would be of continued relevance to contract law.

Aquinas's development of virtue ethics in relation to promise and contract merits some examination. In matters of contract, Aquinas's interest, as a theologian, largely related to the contract of marriage, though application of the Aristotelian approach to other contracts was made by later writers, as is explained in Chapter 3 of this work. Aquinas accepted the Aristotelian division of justice into commutative and distributive forms, defining the former as relating to 'the mutual dealings between two persons' and the latter as 'the order of that which belongs to the community in relation to each single person'.[29] Like Aristotle, Aquinas saw distributive justice as relating to proportional distribution, and not signifying an absolute equality between all persons in society, whereas commutative justice concerned ensuring equality between specific persons.[30] Aquinas divided commutative acts into those which are either voluntary or involuntary. Voluntary commutations might be for no value, such as a donation, in which case the virtue of liberality explained the transfer; or they might be undertaken because of indebtedness to another, in which case the virtue of justice would explain the reason for the transfer. Aquinas lists a number of the recognised Roman contracts to exemplify such justice-based transfers: sale and purchase, usufruct, loan, hire, deposit, pledge and security.[31] Though Aquinas cites no Roman law source when giving this list, it seems clear that he must have had the Roman law in

---

[28] Gordley, *Philosophical Origins* (esp. Ch. 2) and 'Enforcing Promises'. The views of the Spanish Scholastics are discussed further in Ch. 3, at pp. 118 – 19.
[29] *Summa Theologica*, II-II, Q. 61, Art. 1.   [30] *Ibid.*, Art. 2.   [31] *Ibid.*, Art. 3.

mind. In Aristotelian fashion, Aquinas provided a definition of each of these transactions according to the purpose, or end, which they serve.

A potential difficulty with Aquinas's definition of commutative justice is that, as with Aristotle's own somewhat imprecise conception, it is never clear exactly how one is to calculate in specific instances whether someone has gained too much by a transaction, and in so doing offended against commutative justice. Aquinas's explanation is that

> it is necessary to equalise thing with thing, so that the one person should pay back to the other just so much as he has become richer out of that which belonged to the other. The result of this will be equality according to the 'arithmetical mean' which is gauged according to equal excess in quantity.[32]

This presupposes that it will always be clear how one values the two sides of a transaction, but in practice that cannot always be so. In a case of an overpayment, for instance, it will be easy to conclude that the payee has received too much and to determine by how much. But how is the performance of a service to be valued? And how much, for instance, is part, defective performance of a contract worth? The Aristotelian concept of value seems to presuppose that there is an objective value which is an intrinsic quality of a service or an object, whereas neoclassical economics understands value as being subjective[33] and as fluctuating according to the estimation made by human beings of something's worth in a particular transaction (its so-called marginal utility[34]). The problem with the nice Aristotelian idea of an 'arithmetical mean' in calculating the justice of a transaction is that it gives the impression of a simple mathematic computation, which, given the subjective nature of value, will hardly ever, if at all, be the case. The point is a not unimportant one, for, if the concept of commutative justice is to be used to attack extortionate bargains for instance, then one needs to know at which point a bargain ceases to become simply a good one and becomes unjustly unbalanced in one party's favour. The answer for Thomists lay in the conception of the 'just price', discussed by

---

[32] *Ibid.*, Art. 2.

[33] Though some economists in various centuries have continued to promote objective theories of value. One such theory is the labour theory of value of objects, which argues that the value of an object is relative to the labour put into producing it: see the writings of Adam Smith, David Ricardo, and Karl Marx, among others; for a standard modern treatment of the theory, see Meek, *Studies in the Labour Theory of Value*.

[34] A concept advocated by the Austrian Economic School from the late nineteenth century onwards. The marginal utility of a good or service is that of the last unit purchased, measured by the price paid by the consumer.

Aquinas,[35] a concept developed by the late scholastics (as will be seen in Chapter 3) to mean a market price. Clearly a market-based approach to assessing commutative justice is less likely to be one which interferes in parties' contractual arrangements, in that it recognises fluctuating values, though even then it does not eradicate all difficulties in assessing transactions according to the criterion of commutative justice.[36]

If the market-price approach to assessing equality of exchange for the purposes of commutative justice helps to allay some fears about undue interference in contract, no such easy solution appears to apply when one has to judge human behaviour by reference to distributive justice. As Aquinas himself admits, the relevant 'proportion' for determining this will differ depending upon whether the government of a society is aristocratic, oligarchic, democratic, or one of the other various forms of government regulated according to 'various forms of community'.[37] The difficulties for using the concept of distributive justice in any way likely to produce self-evidently correct answers in contractual disputes must be obvious, and should be a warning against attempting to use this form of justice as a basis for regulating specific contracts. Indeed, as Fried once remarked,

> liberal political theory (and practice) accept distributive justice as a goal of collective action, but one to be pursued by the collectivity as a whole, funded by the general contribution of all citizens.[38]

Fried, in consequence, took the view that individual contracts should *not* be subject to redistributive action on the basis that they were unconscionable, because 'it is unfair (and in the end unrepresentative) to force particular persons, who are making their private arrangements against the background of conditions they did not create, to bear the burden of remedying these conditions'.[39]

Aquinas discusses promises principally in the context of vows,[40] and of marriage (including betrothal) in particular.[41] As discussed in Chapter 1, a vow is a special type of promise, a 'promise made to God' as Aquinas succinctly puts it.[42] A promise is a voluntary act[43] by which one undertakes

---

[35] *Summa Theologica*, II-II, Q. 77, Art. 1.

[36] For instance, what of the seller who has good reason for selling below the market price, as a favour to the buyer or because he requires to sell his stock quickly? Is such a contract not in conformity with commutative justice because of the lower-than-market price?

[37] *Summa Theologica*, II-II, Q. 61, Art. 2.   [38] Fried, *Contract as Promise*, p. 106.

[39] *Ibid.*   [40] *Summa Theologica*, II-II, Q. 88.

[41] *Ibid.*, Supplement, Q. 43 (betrothal), Q. 46 (promise of marriage).

[42] *Ibid.*, II-II, Q. 88, Art. 2.

[43] 'Something that one does voluntarily for another' (*ibid.*, II-II, Q. 88, Art. 2).

to benefit another,[44] 'since it would not be a promise but a threat to say that one would do something against someone'.[45] Aristotle had located promising within the virtues of liberality or justice, depending on the reason for their being made, but Thomas adds that the virtues of honesty[46] and fidelity require the fulfilment of promises, as does the natural law.[47] This fusing of Aristotelian teleology and the concept of the virtues with a Thomistic theory of natural law was part of the genius of Aquinas's use of the Greek philosopher's ideas.

Though the kernel of the idea of natural law can be located in an Aristotelian discussion of natural justice in Book V of the *Nicomachean Ethics*, it was Aquinas who developed this into a fully worked out theory which taught that certain immutable laws are inherent in the (divinely ordered) natural world, and that these laws may be discovered through man's divinely given reason.[48] The significance of this for present purposes is that the duty to adhere to promises made and contracts entered into (as well as to vows) is conceived of in the Thomist worldview as one of the duties deriving from the natural law, though Aquinas recognises that, while the natural law might enjoin adherence to all promises, it was entirely proper that the civil law might require certain formalities of promising before a promise could be held to give rise to legal rights.[49]

The natural law/virtue conception of promise does not necessarily exalt the moral requirement to keep a promise above all other natural laws, such that no circumstances could ever permit the breach of a promise once made (a telling point against those like Fox and Demarco who argue that promising must be immoral given its non-receptivity to other moral norms)[50]. While, in general, says Aquinas, a failure to adhere to a promise shows a lack of fidelity to the promisee, there may be a reason excusing such a failure.[51] First, where a promise is made to do something unlawful,

---

[44] 'We promise something to a man for his own profit' (*ibid.*, II-II, Q. 88, Art. 4). By contrast, continues Aquinas, a vow is a promise made to God *for our profit*, not for God's profit, which poses some difficulties for the definition of a promise adopted in this work, namely a commitment made to benefit another.

[45] *Ibid.*, II-II, Q. 88, Art. 2.

[46] For Aquinas, it is a lie if one does not do what one has promised: '*mendacium est, si quis non impleat, quod promisit*' (*ibid.*, II-II, Q. 110, Arts. 3, 5).

[47] *Ibid.*, II-II, Q. 88, Art. 3.

[48] Aquinas discusses the nature of law, including natural law (*ibid.*, II-I, QQ. 90–7). For a treatment of the history of natural law theory see McCoubrey, *The Development of Naturalist Legal Theory*.

[49] 'But for a man to be under a civil obligation through a promise he has made, other conditions are requisite' (*Summa Theologica*, II-II, Q. 88, Art. 3).

[50] See the earlier discussion of Fox and Demarco, at p. 66.

[51] *Summa Theologica*, II-II, Q. 110, Art. 3.

the promisor is excused, it being better that the unlawful act is not committed. Second, if the circumstances have changed, such that performance of the promise cannot be achieved, this may also act as an excuse.[52] Admittedly, this second excuse seems somewhat wide in its potential ambit, especially as expressed in the words of Aquinas ('if circumstances have changed with regard to persons and the business in hand'), but we may reasonably assume that Aquinas did not have in mind every conceivable change which might occur since the making of the promise, but rather more restricted types of change (such as what might in the modern law be called frustrating circumstances beyond the control of the parties).

The natural law conception of fundamental moral duties, such as that created by a promise, is not unique to Thomistic writing, or even to the wider Christian tradition, for one can conceive of there being a natural law without belief in a Christian deity, or even in any deity at all, but rather because of a belief that nature and human beings just happen to be the way they are, and that part of such human nature is that we are predisposed to make and to adhere to promises. The attraction of the natural law approach, especially when posited on a theistic basis, is in providing an objective foundation for the moral force of promises, one which, because of human nature, is permanent, non-fluctuating, and not therefore subject to human whim or alteration. In the Western legal tradition, however, the close association of natural law theory and Christian theology subjected such theory to increasing criticism in a post-Enlightenment, sceptical, increasingly humanist society. However, by this stage, as will be seen in the following chapter, natural law ideas had become welded to the concept of the force of promise as lying in the human will, a concept which was entirely in keeping with the approach of Enlightenment philosophy and thus able to be utilised as a continuing basis for respecting promises even as the popularity of natural law ideas waned.

Thus far, the discussion has shown how the Aristotelian/Thomist tradition explained promising to be moral because it was a vehicle giving effect to those virtues which contributed to the ultimate end of man. In addition, the tradition held the view that the moral nature of promises

---

[52] Aquinas cites here in support a passage from the writing of Seneca (*De Beneficiis* IV) as well as the changed circumstances related in 2 Cor. 1 which prevented the Apostle Paul from honouring a promise to go to Corinth. Similarly, someone may be released from a vow or an oath if the circumstances have changed: *Summa Theologica*, II-II, Q. 88, Art. 10; II-II, Q. 89, Art. 9.

was made manifest by the unchanging laws of nature, which predisposed man to make promises. These views, originally pagan in nature, became fused with Christian theology in a way which provided a further justification for the morality of promising. Two important theological sources furnished the required material for such a process: Scripture and the canon law.

Scripture   There is a large repository of promissory textual material in the Bible, and both theological and legal discussion of biblical promissory ideas has not been insignificant.

Quite apart from an approach that promises derive their moral force from being virtuous acts mandated by the natural law (which, in the Christian tradition, is ultimately an expression of the divine law), another strand in the theological understanding of the moral value of promises considers promises as human reflections of divine acts of promising. This approach posits that, in so far as human promising borrows its nature and form from divine promising, it also takes its moral force from the divine source of promising. Clearly, whether or not one adheres to this view is dependent in large part upon a personal belief in the divine, but regardless of such personal belief or lack of it, it is undeniable that biblical conceptions of promise and of the importance of adherence to promises have been influential in the development of Western promissory philosophy. The writings of Aquinas, Scotus, the Spanish scholastics, and the Northern natural law school on the subject of promises are littered with biblical references. In Scotland for instance, Stair, when discussing whether natural law mandated the keeping of promises or gratuitous contracts, rejected the view of Connanus that it did not; in asserting the contrary, Stair stated that 'especially this is confirmed by the law of God', which he illustrated by citing from both Old and New Testaments.[53]

There are in both Old and New Testaments references to promise in relation to promises made by God, those made by human beings, and also frequent references to the 'Covenant' between God and his people, a covenant which can be described in promissory terms.[54] References to divine promises abound in both Old and New Testaments. In the Old

---

[53] He cites Prov. 6:1, Neh. 9:8, and Heb. 10:23.

[54] There has been much debate among scholars as to whether biblical covenant references are best seen as referring to unilateral promises made by God, or to bilateral contracts entered into between God and his people (contractual promises), though the detail of such debate cannot be considered here.

Testament, divine promises are made both to the community[55] as well as
to individuals,[56] a pattern repeated in the New Testament. Divine promises are seen as everlasting and unshakeable, an important template for
the theory of the sanctity and irrevocability of promises in the human
sphere.[57] On the other hand, the references to promises made by humans
in the Bible are less felicitous[58] as well as less numerous; more often
humans are seen making vows or oaths, rather than ordinary promises
to their fellow men. There is a difficult passage from the Letter of James,
which has on occasion been argued as forbidding human beings from
making promises at all: James appears to say that human plans about the
future are arrogant because 'you know not what shall be on the morrow'.[59]
However, the view of later scholars, including Aquinas,[60] was to the effect
that the passage did not forbid promising outright, so long as those making them appreciated that all human plans are subject to God's will.

Promising is a central feature of the biblical narrative, and indeed in the
later reformed theological tradition it has been argued by some to be the
central theme of the Bible.[61] The biblical references to promise provided a
fertile source of promissory material for the development of promissory
and contractual doctrine in Western legal systems. That source material
stressed the divine importance accorded to adhering to promises, as well
as their inherently moral nature (given that God is portrayed as making
promises), and thus proved useful for developing a theory of voluntary
obligations which required adherence to that which was promised. Biblical
sources were not relied upon as the sole justification for the moral force
of promises, but, as in the writings of Aquinas, as one aspect of the argument deployed in defending particular views. The Reformation increased
the direct usage of biblical source material in support of legal arguments,
for, while in the pre-Reformation period, it was the canon law which was
the paramount source in the development of the enforceability of promises, in Protestant countries at least the reference to canonical materials
fell away after the onset of the Reformation, when the canon law came to

[55] Ex. 12:25, 19:8; Deut. 27:3; Josh. 23:5; Neh. 9:15, 9:23; Acts 7:5, 7:17.
[56] 1 Kings 5:12, 8:20, 9:5; 2 Chr. 1:9.   [57] See, for instance, 1 John 2:25.
[58] Mark 14:11; Luke 22:6; Acts 23:31.   [59] James 4:13–17, 14.
[60] Aquinas explains why these verses from James should not be seen as prohibiting a
promise of a future marriage: *Summa Theologica*, Supplement, Q. 43.
[61] The reformed strand of theology dubbed 'epangelicalism' (from the Greek root, *epengel-*,
meaning promise) characterises the fundamental theme of *all* Christian history as being
the fulfilment of the divine promises made to man: see Kaiser, 'The Old Promise and the
New Covenant'.

be viewed with suspicion given its papal source. A good example of this change is seen in the writing of Grotius, who in his chapter on promises in *De jure belli ac pacis* includes a number of references to Scripture, but none to canon law.[62]

The canon law The contribution of the canon law (by which is meant primarily the canon law of the Western, Roman Church) to the development of the idea of the inherently moral nature of promises, and in the importance of enforcing such promises, began to diminish with the Protestant Reformation of the late fifteenth and sixteenth centuries and was certainly over by the end of the eighteenth century. By then, however, that important contribution had transformed the idea of promise from a purely moral one to one which had become embedded, to varying degrees, in the private law of the various European legal systems, as will be seen from later discussion. The influence of the canon law on private law was more or less direct, and more or less profound, in different jurisdictions for various historical reasons which are referred to below.

The depositories of the canon law are numerous, the two most important from the medieval period being:

(1) the *Decretum*, a series of extracts from Scripture, the Church Fathers, and the various Councils of the Church. The *Decretum* was compiled between around 1130 and 1140 by Gratian, a canon lawyer and professor at the University of Bologna. Added to the margins of the *Decretum* is a gloss written by Johannes Teutonicus (who died in 1252), a Master General of the Dominican Order, supplemented by Bartholomew of Brescia (who died in 1258). The *Decretum* falls into three parts: the *Ministeria*, being general norms of canon law together with a tract on ecclesiastical persons and their functions; the *Negotia*, taking the form of questions and answers relating to administrative matters and the law of marriage; and lastly, *De Consecratione*, comprising maxims and canons on sacramental matters; and

(2) the Decretals, a collection of papal laws, compiled at the request of Pope Gregory IX by St Raymond of Penafort between 1230 and 1234.

---

[62] Grotius cites various scriptural passages referring to God's promises, stating that 'God Himself, who cannot be bound by any established law, would act contrary to His nature if he did not make good His promises' (II.xi.4,1). Another example of the new Protestant attitude is found in the Scottish jurist Sir John Skene, who chose to annotate his 1609 reprint of *Regiam Majestatem* with a concordance including not canon law sources but biblical texts: see Cairns, '*Ius Civile* in Scotland', 169.

Again the margin of the text as we have it today was supplemented by a gloss written by the canonist Bernard of Parma (who died around 1263), which incorporates references to, among other sources, the subsequent Code of Pope Boniface VIII commonly called the *Liber Sextus.*

These two collections, together with a number of other works, are collectively referred to as the *Corpus Iuris Canonici.*[63]

The *Decretum* and Decretals contain a number of texts relating to promise which were influential in the development of promissory ideas in private law. Thus, from the *Decretum,* the following texts among others exerted an influence on jurists of the time and later periods:

(1) D. 23 c. 6: The maxim that '[t]he breaking of promises is more to be feared than the breaking of general vows';[64]

(2) C. 22 q. 2 c.14: A passage in which St Augustine,[65] following Cicero,[66] says that one need not keep a promise to return a sword to a person who has become insane (as mentioned earlier, Plato had used a similar example). A gloss to this passage explained that 'this condition is always understood: if matters remain in the same state'.[67] The Italian jurist Baldus de Ubaldis read this condition concerning promises into the civil law, holding that all promises were subject to it. The rule thus established is still known in the civil law as that of *clausula rebus sic habentibus,* or, as Common lawyers will more readily recognise it, as the doctrine of frustration or failure of basis. The rule is clearly an inroad in to the sanctity of promises, and so requires some justification, whether that of the civilian justification of an implied condition (justified therefore by reference to the tacit agreement of the parties) or that of equity (as in the Common law).

(3) C. 22. q. 5 c. 12: The maxim that '[t]here ought to be no falsehood in our words',[68] a maxim supported by the text from St Matthew's Gospel 'let your speech be yea, yea: no, no: and that which is over and above these, is of evil'.[69] The maxim bears a striking resemblance

---

[63] A reprinted edition of the Latin text of the *Corpus Iuris Canonici* was published in two volumes in 2000.

[64] *Solet enim plus timeri quod singulariter pollicetur quam quodgenerali sponsione concluditur.*

[65] *Enarrationes in Psalmos,* 5.7.   [66] *De officiis,* 3.25.95.

[67] The gloss is that of Johannes Teutonicus, *gl. Furens, ad.* C. 22 q. 2, c. 14.

[68] *ita quoque in verbis nostris nullum debet esse mendacium.* The maxim is included with a reference to Wis. 1:11 and Prov. 14:5.

[69] Matt. 5:37: *sit autem sermo vester est est non non quod autem his abundantius est a malo est.*

to a passage of Aquinas quoted earlier,[70] as well as demonstrating a continuity with the classical Greek thinking noted earlier concerning the importance of truth-telling. Helmholz has said of the significance of this passage for the development of the law that '[t]his ethical principle ... furnished the first principle upon which the canon law of contracts was constructed. The hands of the canonists fashioned it into an instrument capable of enforcing promises of virtually unlimited character'.[71] The maxim was a central plank in juristic development of the doctrine of promissory liability.

From the Decretals, further significant texts are worthy of note:

(1) A number of texts deal with the jurisdiction of the ecclesiastical courts in respect of promises, some founding, others excluding, such jurisdiction. Thus we have both a gloss on Sext 2.2.3 noting that ordinary contracts between laymen for commercial purposes do not fall within ecclesiastical jurisdiction,[72] as well as Sext 2.11.2 stating that only promises conjoined with an oath give jurisdiction to the ecclesiastical courts. This jurisdiction over promises backed by oath was to be profoundly influential in developing the role of promise in European legal systems. Oral promises could, with the simple addition of an oath when made, easily be litigated before church courts, an evident advantage over the secular law position in most jurisdictions, where formalities were required to validate promises. This fact explains the rise in promissory cases before the ecclesiastical courts during the medieval period,[73] though this eventually led to conflicts with secular courts which in England, for instance, prompted a dramatic curtailment of ecclesiastical jurisdiction in promissory cases.[74] By this point, however, the ecclesiastical jurisprudence had in any event begun to result in a greater willingness to enforce promises in the secular courts (a development discussed further in Chapter 3).

(2) Specific texts justified the universal enforcement of contracts, embedding the principle of *pacta sunt servanda* in canon law, and eventually,

---

[70] See p. 75.   [71] Helmholz, 'Contracts and the Canon Law', p. 50.

[72] Glos. ord. on Sext 2.2.3: *Ex tribus tenebatur: ex iure communi, ex pacto, et vinculo iuramenti; ex ultimo coram ecclesia convenitur.*

[73] An interesting study of English and Spanish ecclesiastical causes concerning promises is Helmholz, 'Contracts and the Canon Law'.

[74] At the end of the fifteenth century, the penalties provided for under the English statute of *Praemunire* (originally enacted to regulate appeals to Rome) were utilised to curtail commercial claims before the English ecclesiastical courts.

through such texts, in the civil law.[75] The principle was only formulated in the precise words of the maxim by Pufendorf, but there is no doubt that the principle could itself already be identified in canonical texts, not just from the *Corpus iuris canonici*, but also, for instance, in the writing of Hostiensis, Cardinal-bishop of Ostia in the thirteenth century, who in his published works made an important contribution to the idea of universal contractual enforcement. [76]

Further canonical texts relevant to promise and contract which were to have an influence on secular law included texts relating to, amongst other matters, the just price (*pretium iustum*) of a contract, error (enunciated in a canonical setting largely in relation to marriage), specific performance, and rescission of contract for breach.[77]

As noted earlier, the pattern of influence of the canon law on the civil law differed according to jurisdiction. In England, the influence was felt largely in remedies which came to be granted in equity in the Courts of Chancery. This itself was a feature of the fact that most Chancellors who held office before St Thomas More were churchmen, and many equity drafters also had experience as ecclesiastical lawyers or were at least familiar with ecclesiastical forms of action. Many of the maxims which found their way into equity show a marked resemblance to those of the *Liber Sextus*. The totality of this effect might be described as an 'indirect reception' of canon law into the equitable jurisdiction of England.[78] By contrast, the influence of the canon law's position relating to promises in Scotland has been described as 'positive and direct',[79] a conservative approach to legal change resulting in the pre-Reformation ecclesiastical jurisdiction over promises (which, as in England, had been extensive, but had also, unlike in England, suffered no pre-Reformation restriction),[80]

---

[75] Gregor. IX, Lib. 1 Tit. XXXV *De Pactis* cap. 1 (*Pacta quantumcunque nuda servanda sunt*): '*Dixerunt universi: Pax servetur, pacta custodiantur*' ('all said: peace should be preserved, pacts respected'); and cap. 3 (*Iudex debet studiose agere, ut promissa adimpleantur*): '*Studiose agendum est, ut ea, quae promittuntur, opere compleantur*' ('one ought to conduct oneself with care, so that, that which is promised will be achieved').

[76] See Hostiensis, *Summa aurea* and *Lectura*. A very thorough analysis of the meaning, origins, and influence of the maxim is provided in Hyland, '*Pacta Sunt Servanda*: A Meditation'.

[77] For the influence of the canon law on some such areas in the Common law, see Martinez-Torron, *Anglo-American Law and Canon Law*, pp. 136–42.

[78] See Martínez-Torrón, *ibid.*; Vinogradoff, 'Reason and Conscience', p. 198.

[79] Sellar, 'Promise', p. 266.

[80] The legal historian Gordon Donaldson, having examined the records of the Court of the Official Principal of St Andrews (an ecclesiastical court) from the sixteenth century, has

simply being taken over by the civil courts at the Reformation. By contrast with England, the Scottish experience resulted in a 'very significant fusion of canon law and Scots common law'.[81] This may still be seen today in the continued existence of a discrete obligation of promise in Scots law.

These differing jurisdictional experiences of the canon law's relationship with secular law and courts make it difficult to state a concise view on the overall effect of canonical principles, rules, and maxims relating to promise (and to contract in general) on the civil law of Europe as a whole. Helmholz has expressed the view that the canonical interest in promises was somewhat restrictive for developing contract law, given the form of promises as unilateral acts in contrast to the bilateral nature of contract.[82] This though states too narrow a conclusion for the present field of study, given that promise has been defined widely in the introductory chapter so as to include contractual as well as unilateral promises. Quite apart from this definitional point, however, it is virtually certain, as will be seen in the next chapter, that the canonical enforcement of promises was largely responsible for the rise of assumpsit in English law, a promissory action which was to provide one of the principal strands of modern English contract law. In addition, the canonical enforcement of unilateral promises was unequivocally incorporated into Scots law, albeit with an added requirement of form that had not been present in the canon law. The canonical position on certain remedies as well as on error was also certainly to influence secular contract law, as again will be seen in the next chapter. Helmholz's conservative view seems to underestimate the influence of the canon law on the development of the secular law of contract.

Objections to the morality of promising as having a natural law/virtue basis   Thus far, the case for recognising the morality of promises based upon the idea of their contribution to the virtuous life, upon natural law, and upon scripture and canon law, has been put largely without any criticism of these various foundations. There are, unsurprisingly, a number of objections to this view; some of these will be developed in the recitation of alternative theories concerning promise later in the chapter, given that such later theories were often reactions against the earlier natural

---

expressed the view that, excluding appeals, 24 to 27 per cent of judgments concerned 'the rendering of money or goods by one party to another for the fulfilment of contracts' (Donaldson, 'The Church Courts', p. 366).

[81] *Ibid.*, p. 266. See also Cairns, '*Ius Civile* in Scotland'.

[82] Helmholz, *Contracts and Canon Law*, p. 52.

law tradition. Such objections will not, however, be considered in detail, as the purpose of this work is not primarily to promote a specific view of the foundation of promise, but rather to explain its historic role in the development of contract law. Such an historic role can be explained without necessarily expressing a view in favour or against the beliefs which supported it. Some brief consideration of the principal objections to the virtue/natural law theory of the morality of promises described above will, however, now be undertaken.

The first common line of attack focuses on the characteristically Aristotelian component of the tradition: the virtues, and the alleged 'ultimate end' of man. It might be argued that Aristotle's identification of man's ultimate end, and of the means to achieve that end (the virtues), is entirely arbitrary; other societies, at other times, might conceive of a different 'ultimate end' for humanity, and might thus identify quite different virtues appropriate to that end. One response to such an argument is to accept its truth, whilst not agreeing with its conclusion that virtue ethics is worthless. One could agree that virtue ethics must inevitably develop out of particular societies with particular values, and that the virtues identified in Aristotle's Greece may not necessarily be those of the twenty-first century Western world. Such an agreement would mean only an admission that virtue ethics is societally contextual, a quality which might be thought to be a positive one in its ability to make such ethics adaptable to the needs of the modern world.[83] Other defenders of virtue ethics may baulk at such a concession, however, concerned that it contains within it the danger of subjectivism and relativism. They might rather point out that the virtues identified by Aristotle – such as truth-telling, and justice – are timeless and valid everywhere: it is inconceivable that a virtuous life would not be one lived in accordance with such timeless virtuous practices.

A related objection to the virtue strand of the tradition is the argument that the Aristotelian-Thomist view of the nature of man and the universe, including the theory of the ultimate end of man and the virtues attendant upon a good life, has been decisively falsified by subsequent scientific and philosophical developments. It is certainly true that modern science disputes the theory adopted by Aristotle and Aquinas about the nature of being, including, for instance, the view that one can distinguish the fundamental essence of a thing (its substance) from its external features (its accidents). That theory of substance and accidents supported various

---

[83] See further, on the changing nature of virtues, MacIntyre, *After Virtue*.

contractual principles, including a distinction between types of contract terms (those being the essential, natural and accidental). Rationalists are sceptical about the idea that certain types of contract can have specific ends, from which one may deduce the appropriate *causae* or reasons for which such contracts are properly undertaken. The scepticism of rationalist science and philosophy was largely accepted by subsequent thinkers,[84] an acceptance which Gordley has argued has robbed modern contract theory of an underlying philosophy sufficient to explain its principles and rules.[85]

There are certainly few in the present age who would subscribe to an Aristotelian-Thomist view of the physical world. However, not only has virtue ethics undergone a revival which is not dependent upon an acceptance of the Aristotelian view of the nature of matter and the physical world, but, by its own standards of scientific proof, the rationalist, scientific theory of human nature has not been able to demonstrate the falsity of the concept of virtue or of a virtuous life, such ideas lying beyond the field of scientific proof. Moreover, even if one does not accept the ideas espoused by new virtue ethicists, concepts such as liberality and commutative justice and the attribution of specific ends to types of contract have to some extent found new form and substance in currently popular ideas such as good faith. That concept has come to supplement and regulate the idea of the autonomy of the will in a not wholly dissimilar way to that in which the Aristotelian virtues once did. Whether, however, the idea of free will tempered by good faith can be considered a coherent basis upon which to build a modern contract philosophy is explored later.

The second line of attack on the virtue/natural law theory of the moral force of promises focuses on the natural law element of the tradition. The criticism, simply put, is that the assertion that there is a natural law is false. Such criticism holds that there are no moral laws evident from the nature of the world around us, and that it is therefore not self-evidently the case that promising is morally virtuous. This was the position adopted by the positivists who flourished in the period from the Enlightenment onwards. Their contrary views are discussed below, so it suffices to say at this point that these alternative theories rest largely upon the view that there is no moral quality to actions (including promising) apart from the

---

[84] Though, for instance, much theology continues to be based upon Aristotelian ideas, such as the distinction drawn between substance and accidents which is used to explain the Eucharistic doctrine of transubstantiation.

[85] See Gordley, *Philosophical Origins*, pp. 230–1.

effect they have upon surrounding society, particularly, for instance, in the happiness they produce, or in the utility that they offer to the functioning of that society or of more specific interests such as commerce. For positivists, the moral quality to behaviour is thus relative. A frequent criticism of such positivists is that, bearing in mind that all theories of law have to accept the reality that not all promises are held to be binding, natural law's explanation for not upholding all promises – based upon the idea of implied conditions deemed to affect promises – is unconvincing.[86] This, however, is not a wholly accurate criticism, as the natural law tradition does not rely solely upon the idea of implied conditions to explain invalid promises: in addition, natural lawyers have used the concept of the just or appropriate *causa* required to support promises and contracts, they have considered whether consent has truly been given in specific circumstances, and have had regard as well to external considerations of justice (for instance in relation to the just price of a contract).

A third line of attack on the virtue/natural law foundations of the morality of promising focuses on theistic conceptions of natural law: it is thus an attack on the religious basis of the moral worth of promises. The criticism is that canonical and scriptural texts cannot prove the inherent morality of promising, given that they presuppose but cannot demonstrate a specific theistic belief, a belief which is rejected as unjustifiable.[87] There is little that can be said of this criticism, save that one either accepts its sceptical, humanist premise, or rejects it and, in so rejecting it, affirms the value and place of the insights about human nature and the moral quality of human actions such as promising which is provided by canonical and scriptural sources. Admittedly, however, even those who do accept these insights are often slow at advocating them in an avowedly secular age.

(ii) Promising as an act of the will: respect for personal autonomy

One of the great themes of obligations theory in the western legal tradition, both from a moral and legal standpoint, has been the view that promises (and thus the contracts formed by an exchange of promises) are acts of the human will.[88] Such a conception opens up a second approach

---

[86] This attack is advanced by Atiyah in *Promises, Morals and Law*, pp. 22–4.

[87] An interesting recent philosophical study of whether it is justifiable to commit oneself 'by faith' to a religious claim when its truth appears to lack adequate evidentiary support is Bishop, *Believing by Faith*.

[88] On the will in the law, see Pound, 'The Role of the Will in Law'.

to viewing the act of promising as moral, by positing that, as a function of the human will, promising is moral because it is the free choice of an autonomous moral being, worthy of respect as such, to create or subject himself to an obligation.[89] A promise can thus be said to embody a moral principle forged by such a moral being about what it is right to do. As Raz put it:

> What one ought to do depends in part on oneself, and this is not just because the behaviour, needs, tastes, and desires of the agent count just as much as those of any other person, but because the agent has the power intentionally to shape the form of his moral world, to obligate himself to follow certain goals, or to create bonds and alliances with certain people and not others.[90]

The rise to prominence of the will theory as a means of explaining the force of promises, and hence of contract, is often ascribed to nineteenth-century legal and moral thought.[91] This development, it is said, took the idea of the will, which had already been a feature of contract law prior to this point, and gave to it the pre-eminent position in the philosophical and moral explanation of the force of promises and contracts.[92] As will be seen when considering the other theories of promise discussed later in this chapter, the counter-attacks on the idea of the will as the explanatory moral force behind promise and contract has left the theory somewhat battered but not, it will be suggested, dethroned from its position as the standard modern explanation for the moral and legal force of promises.

It should be noted that there are different strands of will theory. One view posits the will itself as the source of the obligation created, whether it be of promise or of some other type, and so conceives of the moral agent as endued with normative power. By that agent's willing to make a promise, the agent thereby wills a moral obligation in to being. On such a view, the promissory obligation is seen as having both its source and force (moral

---

[89] 'According to the classical view, the law of contract gives expression to and protects the will of the parties, for the will is something inherently worthy of respect' (Cohen, 'The Basis of Contract', 575).

[90] Raz, 'Promises and Obligations', p. 228.   [91] See Gordley, *Philosophical Origins*, Ch. 9.

[92] 'Logically central to Will Theory was the idea that contractual liability depended on the voluntary, intentional, act of the parties. There was nothing new in this; it was an idea that had been familiar to Common lawyers for at least half a millennium. What was new was the greater depth given to the idea, and the greater weight placed on it' (Ibbetson, *Historical Introduction*, p. 232). The nineteenth-century timescale suggested is doubtless true of the Common law, though arguably the will had already played a more prominent position in the legal theory of some non-Common law systems before this point, a matter explored in more detail in the next chapter.

as well as legal) in the act of the human will. A slightly different strain of will theory sees the promisor as merely, in making the promise, expressing a consent to be bound in law to an obligation, the difference being that, while on this view the consent of the promisor remains an act of the will, the source and the force of the promissory duty is found not in that act of will but in the law's imposition of the duty in response to the freely given consent of the promisor.[93] On this view, the promisor wills undertaking a legal obligation, but the obligation has its source in the normative power of the legal system. This may seem a neat distinction, depending on the moot point of whether it is better to see the law as allowing individuals to create obligations by their actions or whether the law permits them voluntarily to submit themselves to externally imposed obligations, but it is a distinction which often makes a difference to the question of whether or not objections to will theory strike home (as the discussion of Hume's views below will indicate). Both of these strands of will theory suggest that the act of promising is moral, though in the case of the latter strand the moral nature of the promise need not simply rest on the idea that it is the free choice of a moral being, but can further be said to lie in the fact that, as the law will only ever impose moral and not immoral duties upon a promisor, any promise which has legal effect through such imposition must necessarily be a moral one.[94]

The will theory of the moral force of promises is the foundation of a number of more specialised theories of contract law. Theories of contract based upon the idea of an agreement[95] or the idea of a bargain[96] are both

---

[93] Coote's theory of contract as assumption might be classified in these terms. He sees contract as stemming from an expression of the parties' will, made manifest in their promises, to submit to the imposition of contractual duties upon them (an assumption of contractual duty). His theory thus contains elements of promise, will and intention to contract, but it ultimately rests upon the basis that the law permits voluntary assumption of duty in some cases: see further Coote, *Contract as Assumption*, Ch. 2.

[94] This, of course, presupposes a belief in the view that obligations imposed by a sovereign normative power upon a promisor will necessarily be moral, a view which would not be universally accepted given that sovereign normative powers appear not to be universally morally good.

[95] Thus Peel, *Treitel on Contract*, has contract as 'an agreement giving rise to obligations which are enforceable or recognised by law' (para. 1–001), this definition being almost verbatim the definition adopted in early editions of *Chitty* (the newest editions of *Chitty* discuss definitions both in terms of promise and agreement, without definitively settling for either).

[96] The bargain theory has, as an essential component, not just the idea of the will but of exchange, and is thus a theory peculiarly designed to explain the Common law idea of *quid pro quo* or consideration, as it later became. Furmston, *Cheshire, Fifoot and*

dependent upon will theory, given that the will, as the faculty of human decision-making, is self-evidently the seat of the ability of human beings to agree or to bargain with others. If the concept of the will is attacked as unable to explain why promises are enforced, then logically agreement or bargain theories of contract must necessarily fall with it.

There are a number of common criticisms of the will theory of the moral force of promises. First, given that human beings can choose freely to do that which is immoral, a promise might conceivably be used as a vehicle for implementing just such an immoral choice. Such a promise would seem logically to be as immoral as the choice prompting it. This problem can be argued, however, to relate only to specific promises, and not promising as an institution. Despite individual bad choices and thus bad promises, promising as an institution remains moral because, taken as a whole, the practice of promising is supportive of the autonomy of moral beings capable of undertaking moral choices. Even were this defence not to be accepted, then it might yet be conceded that at least those individual promises reflecting good choices must be recognised as moral

More fundamentally, one might choose to challenge the idea that there is such a thing as free will, and thus the idea that promise is based upon an exercise of such free will. Scientific views about the nature of causality since the Enlightenment have led some to adopt a sceptical view of free will for the reason that, it is said, science has shown the universe to be essentially deterministic.[97] What appears to be a freely made choice, whether it be a promise or some other human act, is in reality determined by the factors preceding it and not the human will. On such a view, a promise is neither moral nor immoral, for human beings are no longer seen as moral agents capable of making moral decisions. However, adherence to such a view depends crucially on a belief in an entirely deterministic universe, a controversial belief within the scientific community.

A slightly less sceptical view of free will, though one which nonetheless rejects any relationship between the will and promising, is represented in David Hume's view that the human will can only have a causal effect

Furmston, refers (p. 37) to 'the idea of bargain, fundamental to the English conception of contract', noting that, because this idea is absent in obligations undertaken by way of deed, such obligations should not properly be considered as contract. Such a view seems entirely logical if the essence of contract is located in bargain or agreement: the contract by way of deed is essentially a unilateral promise (much like the Scots unilateral promise), put into a required form, rather than such a bargain or agreement.

[97] Views differ on this point, however. The apparent unpredictability of the decay of uranium-238 atoms, for instance, would appear to indicate that at least some things are not determinable (at least from a human perspective).

on present actions. A promise, by contrast, relates to the future, and any binding effect said presently to be produced by a promise can thus only result from human convention and not from an act of the will.[98] Morality, including the morality of adhering to promises, is, on this view, mere sentiment, the idea of promise-keeping being said to be virtuous resulting merely from the fact that honouring promises creates pleasing results. Hume asserts that anyone unacquainted with society's conventions would not even grasp the idea of a promise; on the contrary, it would be unintelligible to him.[99]

Hume's points require to be broken down. Firstly, one must consider his objection that the will alone cannot give rise to binding obligations. This is essentially an objection to the idea of the will as a normative power. This criticism only raises any serious problems for that strand of will theory which posits that obligations arise directly from the will of the parties, but, as noted above, that is but one strand of will theory. The alternative is to say that what a promisor is doing is simply consenting to the law's imposition of a duty upon him. On that view, the will merely triggers the assumption of a binding duty which finds its force and origin in the law and not the human will itself. If that view is taken, then Hume's objection to seeing the human will as the source of an obligation is irrelevant. The human will has apparent normative capacity only because it is exercising a discretionary power to bind itself delegated to it by the sovereign normative power. On such a view, Hume's objection that the will can only have a causal effect on present actions is also irrelevant, as a consent to be bound at law can be said to be just such a present action of the will, the duty being imposed by the law as soon as the consent to it is given. At least one strand of will theory can thus offer a powerful riposte to Hume's insistence that the use of free will to explain promises necessarily involves seeing the force of promise as deriving from the human will.[100]

---

[98] '... promises are human inventions, founded on the necessities and interest of society' (Hume, *A Treatise of Human Nature*, III.ii.5).

[99] *Ibid.*

[100] A different response to Hume's concern would be to take the idea of an intention to act, formed by the human will, and add to it some other element, such further element being the source of the obligatory force of the promise rather than the act of will alone. The philosopher Michael Robins, for instance, has suggested that pure will or intention alone does not furnish a moral content to promises, but requires the additional element of 'commitment', a 'relation that binds together the very concept of intention with that of volition' and is 'irreducibly normative' (Robbins, *Promising, Intending and Moral Authority*, p. 12). The moral imperative here derives from the moral agent's committing himself to an intended course of conduct in favour of another, a commitment which Robbins believes is by its nature normative.

A second comment on Hume's position is that, in order to reject the view that promising is an essential feature of human nature, he somewhat unsettlingly rejects the social nature of human beings, portraying them as essentially isolated and self-concerned beings (humans are 'naturally selfish' in Hume's conception)[101] rather than as naturally cooperative creatures. Yet it is this latter conception of the human species which many would say represents a more accurate anthropological critique of human nature. And, if we are indeed cooperative and not isolated by nature, it is not hard to see a promise-making disposition as an inherent part of that cooperative nature: as Hume's contemporary Lord Kames put it when considering promises, '[a]s man is framed for society, mutual trust and confidence, without which there can be no useful society, enter into the character of the human species'.[102]

Thirdly, a substantial concern for Hume is that the theory that the human will can give rise to binding obligations would seem, Hume asserts, to allow people to turn that which is immoral (or indeed amoral) into a moral action simply by promising to do the act, which forces Hume to question whether morality can really be so subjective as to allow this.[103] Such a concern can be refuted through rejecting Hume's premise: promissory theorists do not assert, as Hume suggests, that promising can turn what was an immoral into a moral act. All that the promising does is to turn an act which was not the object of a moral duty into such an object, thereby creating a moral imperative or duty where there was none before. So Hume's objection is based on a false premise; promises do not undermine the objective moral or immoral nature of acts. A cruel father who neglects the care of his child by binding himself to give all his money away to a stranger would still be acting immorally in spite of his promise, and the fact that he has bound himself to give his wealth to another merely creates a duty to that party without affecting the nature of his conduct towards his child.

As a final comment on Hume's position, from a legal realist perspective Hume's view that human beings cannot bind themselves to an obligation by an act of the will suffers from comparison with the reality of what actually occurs in moral and legal systems, which *do* conceive of the human will as exercising normative power (whether primary or devolved) and

---

[101] Hume, *Treatise of Human Nature*, III.ii.5.   [102] Kames, *Essays on Morality*, II.vi.
[103] Hume asserts that we cannot 'by a single act of our will, that is, by a promise, render any action agreeable or disagreeable, moral or immoral; which, without that act, wou'd have produc'd contrary impressions, or have been endow'd with different qualities' (*Treatise of Human Nature*, III.ii.5).

do assert that obligations may be constituted simply by a voluntary act of such will.[104] That being the reality, it seems somewhat futile to argue that this is inconsistent with legal philosophy.

A further and significant attack on the moral nature of promises as acts of the human will has been said to lie in the fact that it is not, in fact, the actual, subjective intentions of promisors which are usually (if ever) given effect to, but rather the objectively manifested indication of such intentions, the words or behaviour of the promisor as manifested to the reasonable promisee or to the reasonable third party observer.[105] If there-fore, it is said, it is not the actual will of the promisor which creates a promise, then such act of will cannot be the source of the moral (or indeed legal) authority of the promise. Such 'objectivist' objections have been raised both in the Common law[106] as well as civilian jurisprudence.[107] The subjective/objective debate is one of the hardest fought in the law but, at least in the field of promise and contract, middle ground is possible. Such middle ground may be found in a number of ways. First, as discussed in Chapter 1, if one accepts the practical reality that internal thought proc-esses, such as acts of the will, can only ever (short of the invention of mind reading technology) be judged objectively,[108] then it seems reasonable to assert that, in general, the human will is best defined and characterised in its objective, external form. Second, however, one can concede, as some will theorists have done (and as seems reasonable), that while a subjective intention to make a promise at all should be considered necessary (even if, in the absence of an error-based challenge, such intention is usually

---

[104] As Cohen put it, on the question of taking account of the moral realities of the world around us: 'If, then, we find ourselves in a state of society in which men are, as a matter of fact, repelled by the breaking of promises and feel that such practice should be discour-aged or minimized, that is a primary fact which the law must not ignore' (Cohen, 'The Basis of Contract', 572; *Law and Social Order*, p. 90).

[105] There has been a lively debate in many legal systems as to whether taking an objective perspective of a party's conduct means the perspective of an entirely detached, disinter-ested, third party observer (what can figuratively be called 'fly-on-the-wall objectivity') or whether it means the perspective of a reasonable party in the shoes of the other party to the transaction (what can be called 'objective subjectivity', given that it is an attempt to bring a reasonable perspective to the other subject of the contract): for some interest-ing discussion in the Common law tradition, see Howarth, 'Objectivity in Contract'; Vorster, 'A Comment on the Meaning of Objectivity in Contract'. The DCFR takes the 'objective subjective' approach that it is how words or conduct were 'reasonably under-stood by the person to whom [they are] addressed' which counts: see Art. II.-4:302.

[106] In the USA, in the writings of Holmes and Williston, for instance.

[107] In Germany, in the writings of Schlossmann and Kohler, for instance.

[108] A practical approach which essentially constitutes the view of Pollock.

presumed from objective appearance), the entire content of a promise so intended need not necessarily be seen as deriving from subjective intention. On the contrary, some of the content of contracts may quite properly be externally and objectively imposed on contracting parties, on the basis of 'good faith', 'trustworthiness', or for some other compelling reason.[109] This distinction between the existence of and the content of a contract can be used to provide a narrower field which will theory has to defend. Such a possible reformed will theory is discussed at the end of Chapter 3.

(iii)   The 'contract theory' of promising

With the advent of an increasingly sceptical and rational age, it became popular to dismiss the idea of objective morality, derived from the natural law or a divine creator, as superstitious and unscientific. Attempts were made to justify the morality of promises by reference to matters external to the act of promising itself. One such approach was to justify the morality of promising by reference to its congruity with the rules adopted by surrounding society, specifically by reference to the 'social contract' alleged to exist between the members of that society. This 'social contract' was said to be constituted by that tacit consent which all were deemed to give to modes of acceptable behaviour and conduct which would govern society and human actions. Those acts deemed under the social contract to be acceptable could be described as morally good, and those unacceptable to be morally reprehensible. It was society whose practices and whose members' agreement were to determine the moral quality of actions. As promising had been agreed by societies everywhere to be an acceptable and desirable form of human conduct, the practice of promising thus constituted a moral one.[110]

While the contract theory of promises has had a number of variations to it, two main sub-types of the theory have attracted the names contractarianism and contractualism. The central thesis of contractarianism was espoused by Hobbes in *Leviathan*.[111] Contractarians, like all social contract theorists, see the duty to adhere to promises as rooted in the social contract. Additionally, they place great stress in the view that it is rational to adhere to promises, and that it is this rationality which leads individuals to realise that it is right to adhere to specific promises made by them.

---

[109] See, for the advocacy of such an idea in German law, Bechmann, *Der Kauf nach gemeinem Recht*, ii, §120.

[110] See further Darwall, *Contractarianism/Contractualism*.

[111] See Hobbes, *Leviathan*, xiii–xv.

Reason leads people to understand that adherence to promises facilitates trust between members of society, which in turn leads to human endeavour being realised through commerce and other human interaction. While Hobbes describes adherence to covenants as a 'law of nature', such natural law is not of the type espoused by Aristotle and Aquinas, but rather signifies the 'dictates of reason'.[112] However, because man's reason is often overtaken by his passion, something more is needed to give promises force, and that is the fear of punishment by the sovereign power if promises are not adhered to. This fear is a rational fear, says Hobbes: it cannot be rational to break a promise, given that the sovereign will punish such breaches.[113] This seems a somewhat naive view, however, if one considers that in some cases the punishment for breach may be less than the gain to be made by breach, if breach allows a pledged performance to be used more efficiently and profitably elsewhere. In such cases, reason might be thought to argue in favour of breach, despite Hobbes's assertion that that can never be so. Moreover, there are cases where a party may, for reasons of principle, break a promise knowing that punishment will be meted out. The decision to break a promise in such a case would seem to have nothing to do with reason, but rather with an emotive attachment to a principle. Despite such difficulties, contractarianism continues to attract modern advocates.[114]

As for the other major strand of the social contract approach to the morality of promises, contractualism, a notable modern advocate has been John Rawls. Rawls sees the duty to adhere to promises as a matter of justice, the various principles of justice having been determined by the agreement of the members of society. Promise is a type of what is styled 'institutional obligation', as it is an obligation governed by certain rules which determine the nature of the institution. In particular, the institution of promise is founded upon a constitutive rule that promises must be kept. This constitutive rule derives from the general moral principle of fairness, a principle agreed upon by members of society which holds that we are not entitled to gain from others without doing our fair share in return.[115] Thus, someone who accepts the benefits of a promise must in turn do his fair share by keeping his promises. In addition to the principle of fairness, a derivative of this principle, the principle of fidelity, further mandates adherence to promises.[116] What this theory states is thus

---

[112]   *Ibid.*, xv.   [113]   *Ibid.*

[114]   See Gauthier, *Morals by Agreement*; Narveson, *The Libertarian Idea*.

[115]   Rawls, *A Theory of Justice*, p. 112.

[116]   The principle of fidelity states that bona fide promises are to be kept: *ibid.*, p. 347.

that the duty to adhere to promises is not itself a fundamental moral principle: rather it is a duty founded upon a convention, the convention deriving from a fundamental moral principle (fairness, and its derivative fidelity).[117]

A notable criticism of contractualism as an explanation for the moral force of promises has been that the original principles of justice referred to by Rawls can themselves be described as coming into force only as the result of members of society promising to uphold them. But if that is so, then the institution of promising only has moral force because of promises that that should be so: but in what do these founding promises find their moral force? There seems to be a circularity here, as Robbins has pointed out.[118] Another objection is that it would be very difficult, if not impossible, in a modern world where societies are becoming increasingly pluralistic, to identify any fundamental principles of justice upon which we would all agree, or which none of us would reasonably reject,[119] although it has been suggested that one such is the 'rescue principle' (which states that, if a slight or moderate sacrifice would prevent serious harm to another, we should make such a sacrifice).[120] It does not, however, seem to be self-evidently the case that such a principle is more likely to find universal acceptance than the principle that 'promises should be honoured'; after all, all legal systems enforce promises to some extent, whereas not all impose a duty to go to the aid of those in danger.

(iv)   Consequentialism (utilitarianism)

A further theory of the source of the morality of promising is that of consequentialism, or utilitarianism as it is also known. On this view, promising is a moral practice because it generates trust, reliance, confidence, happiness, economic security, or other good consequences. It is therefore useful to society's functioning and the well-being of its members, as Hume argued when he observed that promises are 'artificial contrivances for the convenience and advantage of society'.[121] While the natural law and will approaches to promising also recognise such beneficial effects of promising, the consequentialist argues that it is *only* by

---

[117] A variation of contemporary contractualism is also espoused in Scanlon, *What We Owe to Each Other*.

[118] Robbins, *Promising, Intending, and Moral Autonomy*, p. 128.

[119] See Nagel, *Equality and Partiality*. The difference between seeking principles which either we could all agree on, or else which none of us would reasonably reject, is a distinction between Rawls's and Scanlon's versions of contractualism.

[120] Scanlon, *What We Owe to Each Other*, p. 224.

[121] Hume, *Treatise of Human Nature*, III.ii.5.

virtue of these effects that one may define promising as morally good. Utilitarian accounts of the morality of promising can overlap to some extent with the contract theory of promising just discussed, as part of the explanation provided by both of these types of theory relates to the effect that promising has in supporting the trust which is a foundation of the social contract.[122]

As with the contract theory of promising, consequentialist theorists fall in to two principal classes: rule utilitarians and act utilitarians. Rule utilitarians assess the utility of specified rules or practices, for instance the rule that promises should be honoured, while act utilitarians seek to evaluate the utility of specific human acts, the focus of the enquiry thus resting upon the effect produced by a specific act (such as a promise), whether that be a net good or bad effect. A rule utilitarian therefore, having concluded that promises should be kept as this maximises societal well-being in general, would argue for a rule that all promises should be kept; an act utilitarian would permit individual promises to be kept or broken depending on the likely outcome on well-being in the particular case. So, if a promisor were reasonably to conclude that breaking a specific promise would now be productive of more happiness (or greater economic benefit, or whatever other good effect is argued to be the desired outcome) than honouring it, he would be morally released from any duty to perform the promise.

Whether a real division between act and rule utilitarianism really exists has been doubted by some, who argue that rule utilitarians are compelled to accept the need for sub-rules, and then sub-sub-rules, leading in the end to such highly particularised rules that one arrives at the position of act utilitarians.[123] Whether or not this criticism is valid, the utilitarian approach in general is open to a number of criticisms.

First, utilitarianism struggles to explain why a promise is said to be binding (a commonly adopted view) even if it would, all things considered, be better to break the promise. This is a criticism which really only bites against rule utilitarians, as the act utilitarian's answer is simply that such a promise is not binding. This response, however, triggers the further more generalised criticism of utilitarianism, that it leads to unpredictable and uncertain results, for promisors and promisees will never know which promises are binding unless and until a weighing up of the effect of

---

[122] Narveson, for instance, advances an argument about promising which is both utilitarian and contractarian in nature (see Narveson, 'Promising, Expecting, and Utility').

[123] See Lyons, *Forms and Limits of Utilitarianism*.

the promise (to be carried out by whom, it might be asked) is undertaken. Such uncertainty is not conducive to the efficient working of society, or to the predictability for individuals of their own affairs.

Second, utilitarianism's definition of that which is good as that which maximises human happiness (or well-being, or whatever other good outcome by which the utilitarian chooses to judge morality) seems essentially arbitrary and subjective. One might plausibly choose some other equally reasonable criterion as the qualifier of a 'good' action. It is far from clear that 'happiness' or 'well-being' would be agreed upon by everyone as the relevant criterion upon which to build a definition of morality, given that such ideas are essentially subjective perceptions.

Third, utilitarianism presupposes that people act in the interests of the general well-being. In fact, it can just as plausibly be argued that people act in the interests of a more restricted group, whether it be their circle of family and friends, or their town, or institutions to which they belong. Thus, where promises are kept, it is just as consistent to say that the promisor sees an advantage to a specific class or group in so doing, rather than a benefit to society as a whole; and, where promises are broken, it is just as consistent to say that it is because the promisor perceives an advantage to a member of the specific class in so doing, not an advantage to the common good.

Fourth, utilitarianism opens up the danger of people being held to statements which they never intended to be binding on them. If A says something, and B acts upon it thinking that it will produce a beneficial result for him, then such a circumstance can be argued to give rise to promissory liability on A's part, *whether or not the statement was intended as a promise*, simply on the basis that it might maximise B's happiness or well-being. If such an outcome were to prevail, then freedom *not* to promise or to contract would be seriously undermined.

Fifth, by favouring the maximisation of happiness or well-being over the certainty of the promisee's entitlement, in whatever circumstances, utilitarianism favours a mere subjective arithmetic calculation of happiness over the interests of justice, trustworthiness, and certainty. Such an approach falls into the trap of assuming that it is better for A to judge what is best for B's happiness than it is for B (who has decided that his happiness is best served by the promise in his favour). In so doing, it diminishes the worth of others' decisions and patronises them. It, moreover, assumes that relative values can be given to 'amounts' of well-being and happiness, which hardly seems to be the case, unless perhaps one is dealing with economic well-being to which a specific monetary value can be given.

Sixth, utilitarianism seems to be at odds with certain fundamental values of society and legal systems. Most evidently, it is at odds with trust, and therefore with good faith in human relationships. The utilitarian lack of concern for keeping one's word as a matter of normative principle must inevitably erode trust and fundamentally undermine the good faith which is said increasingly to be an inherent part of promises and contracts.

Some criticisms of utilitarianism seem, however, less robust. For instance, Atiyah's point that, if a promisee knows a promisor is a utilitarian, the promisee will not rely on the promise because he will realise that the promisor may not keep it, and, by extension, if everyone were then utilitarian there would be no promises because no one would rely on them, seems an argument constructed upon a fanciful world in which everyone has adopted a utilitarian worldview.[124] This sort of legal theoretical argument divorced from the real world does not address the institution of promising at it operates in reality. In practice, most people place a high value on a promise, and will continue to do so. Atiyah's concern is a phantom one.

The utilitarian view of the moral worth of promising seems subjective, arbitrary and antagonistic to core values of human societies, quite apart from not reflecting the attitude of many promisors and promisees to the value of the promissory act. It will not do as an explanation of promising.

(v)   Reliance theory

Reliance theory, popularised largely in the twentieth century,[125] and advocated in different forms by Atiyah and MacCormick, among others, is based on the view that promising is moral because a promise generates reliance in others, in particular reliance which would be productive of detrimental results for the party acting in reliance if the promise were not upheld. Promises are only morally (and indeed legally) worthy of

---

[124] See Atiyah, *Promises, Morals and Law*, pp. 49–50.

[125] There are however earlier manifestations of a reliance approach to promises, often focusing on the idea of the expectations (a form of reliance) engendered by the giving of a promise. Adam Smith, for instance, stated that a 'promise is a declaration of your desire that the person for whom you promise should depend on you for the performance of it', such dependence evidently being reliance by another name (Smith, *Lectures on Jurisprudence*, 'Of Contract', p. 472). In his *Lectures*, Smith mentions the reasonable expectations engendered by contract at various points, as for instance when he comments of contract that '[t]he origin of this right is the expectation raisen in him to whom the promise was made that the promiser will perform what he has undertaken. Thus if one promises to give an other five pounds, this naturally creates an expectation that he will receive five pounds from him at the time promised' (p. 12); see further references by Smith to the expectations engendered by promises in his *Lectures*, pp. 87, 89, 400.

being kept on a reliance approach when such reliance is generated; where it is not, it would not be immoral for the promisor to fail to adhere to the promise. Some theorists locate the source of the obligation squarely in the presence of such reliance, while others locate it in an intention of the promisor that reliance be generated (and therefore do not insist that actual reliance be present).[126] It might seem that adoption of the latter view is in reality a modified kind of will theory, given that what is crucial is an act of will of the promisor that reliance be generated; as, however, what the promisor must will is not the obligation itself, but merely the reliance of the promisee, such an approach is not really a variant of will theory.

The reliance theory, conceiving of reliance as the central explanatory force of the value of promises, goes much further than the natural law or will theories of promise. Though such theories accord a role to the idea of reliance in explaining certain types of outcome (such as remedies in cases of induced errors), reliance is in such theories merely an extraordinary, additional consideration which can affect the finding of liability in certain circumstances, but it does not explain the worth of promises in general. Genuine reliance theorists hold that it is the very presence of the reliance which generates the moral obligation: a promisor is responsible for doing what he said he would *because* he has created a dependency by the promisee on his actions, such dependency being a source of moral duty (much as other types of dependency, such as that of a child upon a parent, can create moral duties).

Reliance theorists have laid claim to the central importance of reliance to contractual liability. Thus Atiyah has very grandiosely claimed that

> [f]ew would today deny that, in a broad and general sort of way, the fact that promises tend to be relied upon, that they positively invite reliance, is one of the chief grounds for the rule that promises should be kept, and that contracts should be legally enforced.[127]

Many would in fact deny any such thing, though they might concede that reliance is important in explaining the outcome in certain types of case. Reliance theorists like Atiyah have a tendency to repeat such broad, generalised statements about reliance theory, but such statements crucially do not reflect the law as it exists and is applied by the courts, certainly

---

[126] MacCormick argues that it is the intention of the promisor to generate such reliance which is the source of the obligation: see 'Voluntary Obligations and Normative Powers I', p. 66.

[127] Atiyah, *Promises, Morals and Law*, p. 36.

when one considers systems other than Common law ones, but even when just considering the Common law position.

As the principal proponent of modern reliance theory, Atiyah's views merit further consideration. In fact, Atiyah does not just propose his theory as an explanation for contractual liability, he suggests that liability in the whole of the law of obligations can be explained by a grand, unifying principle that wherever a benefit has been conferred upon another or detrimental reliance exists on that other's part, liability will be found. Whence does this principle arise? It arises, says Atiyah, from the agreement by a social group whose judgment determines the initial question of entitlement that it should be so.[128] Such a view leaves little room for individual choice about whether or not to subject oneself to obligations, as Atiyah explains:

> We thus find a decline in the belief that the individual has the right to determine what obligations he is going to assume, and an increased strength in the belief that the social group has the right to impose its own solution on its members, dissent as they may … it is the social group which makes the decisions and creates the obligations or entitlements.

This strikes a twenty-first century reader as an incredibly centralised, authoritarian view of the law of obligations. While it may well have been reflective of the decade in which Atiyah was writing, it strikes a very discordant note to modern ears. Perhaps it is unfortunate that Atiyah's great work on promises and morality was published on the cusp of an era in which personal autonomy and responsibility were to become reinvigorated (both in the minds of politicians and judges); had Atiyah taken a longer term perspective, this might have prevented the exposition of a view which now looks very much a fossilised product of its time. Such a longer term view would have led to the appreciation that, as Fried once remarked, 'the principle of fidelity to one's word is an ancient one' and that the 'validity of a moral, like that of a mathematical truth, does not depend on fashion or favor.'[129]

It would, however, be unfair to dismiss Atiyah's views too completely without giving more notice of the principal and serious criticisms of reliance theory. Amongst many possible criticisms, it is suggested that five in particular stand out as worthy of highlighting:

(1) Reliance theory is based upon a flawed historical description of the importance of the idea of the promise to contractual liability.

---

[128] *Ibid.*, p. 129.   [129] Fried, *Contract as Promise*, p. 2.

(2) Reliance theory does not describe accurately the state of the law as it exists, and is unable to provide a comprehensive explanation of contractual liability.

(3) Reliance theory represents a fundamental attack on personal freedom, and seeks to turn contractual liability into a sort of quasi-delictual liability.

(4) Reliance theory undervalues truthfulness and trust.

(5) Reliance theory would create uncertainty and confusion if adopted by the courts.

Each criticism merits elaboration.

There is firstly the criticism that reliance theory is based upon a flawed historical description of the importance of the idea of the promise to contractual liability. As the discussion in the next chapter will show, promise held a central role in obligations theory from the classical period until the beginning of the eighteenth century, and the idea of universal contractual enforcement was prominent in the canon law and subsequently in the civil law from the medieval period onwards. Yet this history is overlooked or distorted by Atiyah, who largely ignores the importance of unilateral promise and who maintains that the enforcement of bare mutual promises was a late development, only reaching its apogee in the nineteenth century. The confusion seems to arise because of the prominence of will theory in the Common law in that century, a theory which (as discussed earlier) stressed the enforcement of mutually agreed contractual arrangements. But the *pacta sunt servanda* principle had come to prominence well before the nineteenth century. Atiyah, ignoring this history, engages instead in ahistorical and unnecessary speculation: executory contracts, he muses, 'may have been thought a sufficient benefit to justify a promisor as bound by his own promise ... Perhaps it came to be felt that mere receipt of the counter-promise was enough.'[130] Such speculation allows him to downplay the importance of the executory contract, yet his narration is at complete odds with the recorded history of the *pacta sunt servanda* principle. Even Atiyah's description of the typical executory contract as it developed historically is distorted. Giving the example of a sale of a cow, he argues that a promissory explanation of contract cannot explain why, if someone has agreed to buy a cow, he is also obliged to accept it when it is delivered: the promisor, says Atiyah, only promised to pay for the cow, not to accept it.[131] This is an absurd distortion of the

---

[130] Atiyah, *Promises, Morals and Law*, p. 203. [131] *Ibid.*, pp. 205–6.

nature of the promise made by the buyer, and does not reflect the way in which such executory contracts are conceived of. Sale of goods contracts are typically held to give rise to duties of contemporaneous performance, so that the buyer's promise will be 'I promise to pay £100 for your cow upon my taking delivery of it'. Such a promise, which expressly stipulates the acceptance of delivery, would necessarily imply a duty to accept the very delivery which is requested. Were that not the case, not only would the seller be unable to earn the contract price (given that delivery is stated as the condition triggering the duty to pay), but it would be impossible for a seller which had contracted out of a desire to divest itself of an item which it could no longer maintain (such as a good requiring expensive repairs, or an asset the possession of which was attracting a tax liability which the seller could no longer afford) to achieve its purpose in undertaking the contract.

Secondly, reliance theory does not describe accurately the state of the law as it exists, and is unable to provide a comprehensive explanation of contractual liability. Reliance theory attempts to squeeze every example of an enforceable contract into a model of benefit conferral or of the protection of detrimental reliance. Yet courts in all jurisdictions enforce executory contracts, where no such benefit/detriment is present. Unilateral promises are enforced, whether generally (as in Scotland) or exceptionally (as in Germany and England, for instance). Reliance theorists attempt to find imaginary reliance to explain such promises, but such reliance is simply lacking in many cases. Reliance theory looks more like a vision of what the law might be like, rather than what it actually is.

Thirdly, reliance theory represents a fundamental attack on personal freedom, which seeks to turn contractual liability into a sort of quasi-delictual liability. This will be easily appreciated when it is remembered that many reliance theorists want to use reliance to explain the whole of the law of obligations, not just contract. On such a view, what matters is the prevention of harm. If the prevention of harm (or the possibility of compensating for harm caused) is not present, then there is no reason for the law to provide a remedy, and in consequence there is said to be no entitlement for persons to provide for liability. Yet surely the question of why a person should be able to create an obligation just by saying that he has[132] finds an adequate answer in the response that the law should allow an individual to do so because of respect for individual autonomy and trust.[133] Only such an attitude ensures that people are viewed as

---

[132] *Ibid*., p. 208.   [133] Fried, *Contract as Promise*, p. 16.

individuals, whose decisions are worthy of respect, not just as cogs in the macro-economic machine, only significant if in receipt of a benefit or the victim of a harm.

Fourthly, reliance theory undervalues truthfulness, honesty and trust. Why is this so? Reliance theory focuses on the result produced by promising. It says that the morality of promising arises from certain effects (the conferral of a benefit, or detrimental reliance) which may result from a promise. If, however, such effects do not result, the promisor is excused from liability and can renege on his promise; though the promisor said he was binding himself to do something, it turns out he was not. The ability to renege on a promise without any adverse consequences would have the potential for undermining truthfulness, honesty and trustworthiness generally in society. Perversely, by reliance theory's focus on detriment in individual cases, a wider detrimental effect would be produced through the failure to enforce promises in which reliance was absent.

Lastly, there is the concern that reliance theory would create uncertainty and confusion if adopted by the courts. The problem is that, under reliance theory, a promisor will not know whether he is bound to an obligation until such moment, if it occurs at all, that the promisee receives a benefit under the promise or relies upon it to his detriment. Any such moment of detrimental reliance may well be unknown to, or unknowable by, the promisor; even if it is, it may be challenged by a promisor who wishes to escape from the promise on the ground that no actual detriment has been suffered. Moreover, even assuming one knows that reliance has taken place, the idea of reliance does not assist in determining the nature of the right conferred. Thus, for instance, the mere fact of reliance cannot tell you whether a third party has a right which is that of an assignee or that of a third party under a *stipulatio alteri*: only the intention of the original contracting parties allows that determination to be made.

Disputes caused by debates about reliance would create unnecessary litigation and be difficult for courts to adjudicate. The danger of uncertainty which reliance theory creates is well illustrated in this comment of the reliance theorist Páll Árdal:

> The promiser in many cases ceases to have any obligation when he comes to *know* that the promisee could not care less whether the promise is kept or not ... Similarly our obligation tends to be stronger the more important the content of the promise is to the promisee.[134]

---

[134] Árdal, 'And That's a Promise', p. 234.

Such an approach provides a wholly unhelpful theory of when a statement does or does not have obligatory effect, given the stated contingency of knowledge by the promisor of the promisee's view of it, and the promisee's attitude to the content of the promise. Such a hugely subjective, reliance-based approach, would create vast uncertainty in any legal or moral system.

These criticisms of reliance theory are significant. Taken together they suggest that reliance theory is unhistorical, distorts existing legal practice, undermines personal autonomy and responsibility, and would create legal uncertainty if used as the basis for determining the existence of promises.

A more limited role for reliance   If it is clear that reliance theory cannot explain the whole of contract law, then it may yet have a more limited role in explaining liability in certain types of exceptional case. For instance, it is clear that in many jurisdictions wasted expenditure undertaken in preparation for performing a concluded contract (and therefore undertaken in reliance on the validity of such a contract) is claimable in some circumstances.[135] Reliance may also be one element in the availability of remedies designed to compensate for wasted expenditure incurred in the legitimate expectation of concluding a valid contract,[136] as well (in jurisdictions with a doctrine of mutual consideration) for founding liability in promissory estoppel.[137]

The role given to reliance should, however, be kept within tightly controlled boundaries. The enthusiasm for reliance-based liability, if allowed too free a rein, has the potential to distort established features of contract law. One good example of such a potentially distorting effect may be seen in Louisiana, where the ill-conceived general introduction of reliance-based liability to mirror the Common law's promissory estoppel has been both conceptually problematic as well arguably as unnecessary. Louisiana has no doctrine of mutual consideration, so gratuitous contracts are perfectly valid. The absence of the need for mutual consideration evidently excludes many cases that would have to be resolved in the Common law using promissory estoppel. Quite apart from this, the position of reliance-based liability within the text of the Civil Code is puzzling. It forms part of Article 1967, which follows on directly from Article 1966's stipulation

---

[135] See discussion in Ch. 6.   [136] See discussion in Ch. 4.   [137] See discussion in Ch. 4.

that every obligation requires a lawful cause. Article 1967 is in the following terms:

> *Cause is the reason why a party obligates himself.*
>
> A party may be obligated by a promise when he knew or should have known that the promise would induce the other party to rely on it to his detriment and the other party was reasonable in so relying. Recovery may be limited to the expenses incurred or the damages suffered as a result of the promisee's reliance on the promise. Reliance on a gratuitous promise made without required formalities is not reasonable.

Conceiving of reliance-based liability in this way is profoundly problematic. It suggests that reliance is a type of cause, that is, a 'reason why' a party contracts. But people do not enter contracts *in order* to create reliance in others; on the contrary, where reliance arises, it is as a *result* of a valid contract. The context of this reliance-based liability thus muddles up the reasons for making contracts with the results contracts produce. The purpose of such liability is also unclear. It looks like a version of promissory estoppel, but if it is, then it has been introduced without much thought as to the existing codal provisions, especially the legality of gratuitous contracts. As Gordley has commented, it is 'not wise ... to take a remedy for a disease you do not have'.[138] Gratuitous loans, loans for consumption, deposit and irrevocable offers, are all valid under other provisions of the Louisiana Code, and thus not in need of reliance-based liability or promissory estoppel to explain them. Article 1967 thus seems to ignore existing flexible civilian solutions to problems, and has introduced largely unnecessary reliance-based liability into the law. If Louisiana law lacks a solution in one area, it is perhaps to the problem of wasted expenditure undertaken in the legitimate expectation of a contract being concluded. The provision of a solution to that problem, however, does not need the very broad-based liability provided by Article 1967.[139] Despite these criticisms, it has been remarked that '[i]t can no longer be denied that reliance has conquered a place for itself in the Louisiana jurisprudence.'[140]

What may be concluded about the proper role for reliance in contractual liability? Principally two things: that the need for general reliance-based liability is absent in systems without the problems caused by the doctrine of consideration or overly strict formality requirements; and

---

[138] Gordley, 'Louisiana and the Common Law', p. 199.
[139] Pre-contractual liability is discussed further in Ch. 4.
[140] Litvinoff and Scalise, *The Law of Obligations in the Louisiana Jurisprudence*, p. 173.

that, where reliance liability has a residual, secondary role to play, strict control has to be kept over the limits of such liability, or else it has the potential to undermine the primacy given to declarations of parties' wills.

(vi)   Conclusion on the competing theories of the moral value of promises

The above discussion of different theories of the source of the morally obligatory force of promises discloses a preference for theories which emphasise the inherent, objective morality of the act of promising, over those which concentrate merely on the subjective effects of promising in specific circumstances. The latter have been characterised as productive of uncertain effects and as failing sufficiently to emphasise personal autonomy and responsibility. Though natural law theories have been largely supplanted by will theories, it would be possible to provide a justification for the moral value of promises which combined both approaches. One might, in natural law fashion, recognise human beings as predisposed by nature to promise, but also say, in will theorist fashion, that we only respect human beings as free, autonomous individuals if we respect the promises they choose to make.

Such theoretical preferences are, however, of secondary importance to an historical narrative of the rise of promissory ideas in the law. Therefore, in the next chapter the history of promising as a legal institution will be traced, in order to explain which theories of the value of promise influenced the development of the law. As will be seen, moral theories of the binding nature of promises were to have a profound impact upon the legal force of the promise in the Western legal tradition.

4.   Powers and sanctions relevant to breach of morally binding promises

Where promises have legal force, then of course legal remedies exist to enforce such promises and legal sanctions apply to the breaking of such promises. But what of breach of promises which are not recognised as having legal effect: how are such purely moral promises regulated?

Evidently such regulation has to be by non-legal means. That would seem to suggest that, for instance, compulsion by the promisee of the promised performance cannot be procured, as non-legal compulsion would lack a lawful basis. Some might argue that, in any event, it is always immoral to compel a promisor to do something, though such an approach would suggest that legal remedies such as specific performance must be immoral, a view evidently not shared by the law.[141]

A number of non-legal, regulatory methods might conceivably be employed in cases of breach of promise. The promise breaker might, for instance, suffer social exclusion, that is to say he might be shunned by associates and friends for his faithlessness, or might suffer social pressure to make reparation for the breach of promise. A party who, for instance, breaks off a promise to marry, though he can no longer be subject to a civil legal claim for breach of contract as was once the case, is still likely to suffer social stigma unless the breach of promise occurs for very good reason, and he might be expected by his peer group to repair any harm he has done through his breach of promise. Alternatively, a promise breaker might suffer adverse economic consequences. For instance, a commercial party which has strung another along into thinking that a contract was on the verge of being concluded, only to pull out without stating any good reason, might find that, even if it is not able to be sued at law, its reputation is badly damaged, with a consequent drop-off in business. Such possible social or economic effects of breach of morally binding promises are, however, somewhat hard to assess, and tend to be anecdotal. Additionally, an individual promise breaker might conceivably be a member of a group which enforces adherence to moral obligations through its own structures, such as a religious group or other unincorporated association. In such cases, breach of a morally binding promise might render the promisor liable to sanctions under the rules of the group concerned. Such cases are of interest in that they lie at the interface between law and morality, given that, though the group concerned may be entitled under its own rules to enforce penalties against the promisor in default, its decision might be justiciable before a civil court if its own procedures are not properly followed or if application of those procedures is held to amount to a breach of natural justice or some constitutionally guaranteed right.

At the divide between morality and law, sometimes a promise which appears at first examination to be binding only morally, as for instance one made within a religious context, may in fact be deemed by the courts also to have civil legal effect. A good example of such a promise is seen in the facts of the Canadian Supreme Court case *Bruker* v. *Marcovitz*.[142]

---

[141] See on this question Gilbert, 'Scanlon on Promissory Obligation'. Hart's view was that coercive force in implementation of moral rights is not improper, and may be justified: see Hart, 'Are There Any Natural Rights?'.

[142] [2007] 3 SCR 607.

The case concerned a promise made by a Jewish man to his wife to facilitate a *get* (a divorce under Jewish law) as soon as their civil divorce had
been obtained. Despite the promise, and following the civil divorce, the
man consistently refused to agree to the *get* for fifteen years. The woman
eventually sued in the civil courts of Quebec for breach of contract. The
man denied that his undertaking was intended to have civil legal effect.
The wife won at first instance, but on appeal the court held that, because
'the substance of the … obligation [was] religious in nature', the obligation was a moral one and thus unenforceable by the courts.[143] On further appeal to the Supreme Court the decision of the appeal court was
overturned, it being held that an agreement between spouses to take
the necessary steps to permit each other to remarry in accordance with
their own religion constituted a valid and binding contractual obligation
under Quebec law.[144] Abella J, for the majority, noted that whilst Quebec
law distinguishes between moral and civil obligations, and that it 'is true
that a party cannot be compelled to execute a moral duty … there is nothing in the *Civil Code* preventing someone from transforming his or her
moral obligations into legally valid and binding ones'.[145] The decision
is a valuable reminder not only that many civil legal obligations have a
moral basis, but also that such moral character is no bar to a promise also
having legal effect. The question of whether a morally binding promise
is also intended to be clothed with legal effect is a matter of the context
of the promise and thus ultimately of the intention of the party or parties
concerned.

[143] Abella J, para. 36 (quoting from the Appeal Court judgment of Hilton JA, para. 76).
[144] Abella J, para. 16.   [145] Abella J, para. 51.

3

The historical development of promissory ideas in the law

Having considered in the last chapter the idea of a promise as an obligation, as well as competing theories for the moral force of promissory obligations, in this chapter an historical analysis will be offered of the role which promise has played in the legal enforcement of voluntary obligations. As this analysis will disclose, after showing early signs of performing a likely major role in obligational theory and practice, promise dwindled in importance from the seventeenth century. Such a development might have surprised earlier generations of jurists: promissory actions played a central role in both Roman law (in the *stipulatio*) and the Common law (in the action of assumpsit), and promise was a core idea in the scheme of voluntary obligations of the scholastics, late scholastics, and canonists. Rather, however, than continuing to occupy this central role, promise pollinated contract, enriching it with the idea of the universal enforceability of contracts (expressed in the maxim *pacta sunt servanda*), and provided an analytical tool for explaining the nature of contract formation as an exchange of conditional promises. Having performed these roles, promise was eclipsed by the flowering of the very obligation of contract which it had enriched. What was left of promise at the end of this process was a continued independent existence in only one major Western legal system,[1] and an explanatory[2] and supplementary[3] function in the others. It will be suggested in this chapter that the eclipsing of promise was a great loss to Western legal systems: many transactions are best analysed in promissory terms, contract providing a second best and not wholly apt analysis.

---

[1] That being Scots Law.
[2] Explanatory in that it came to be used as one explanation for the nature of contract (as an exchange of conditional promises).
[3] Supplementary in the sense that the idea of promise was used in exceptional cases to explain circumstances which orthodox contract law found hard to explain, such as the offer of reward, the rights of a third party under contract, or the contract under seal (essentially a contract in promissory form).

The historical sweep of the present chapter is necessarily broad, given the antiquity of the influence of promissory ideas in the law. In consequence, much of the analysis is necessarily condensed in nature. There is, however, merit in such a broad historical view, given that prior analysis of the history of promise has tended to appear only as a small element in larger treatments of private law in general or of the law of obligations as a whole, while the present treatment seeks to take promissory developments as the sole focus of analysis. With this point in mind, it is to Roman law that attention must first be turned when explaining the role of promise in the contract law of the *ius commune*.

1.   Roman law

(a)   *Formal contracts: the* stipulatio

Classical Roman law was a law of actions and related rules rather than one of concepts or principles of general application. It had no general law of contract, and precious little contract theory.[4] It did, however, as a result of the classificatory work of the jurist Gaius and later development, conceive of a central division in the law of obligations between those actions arising *ex contractu* (from a contract), *ex delicto* (from a delict), *quasi ex contractu* (as if from a contract), or *quasi ex delicto* (as if from a delict). It has been conjectured that Gaius may have developed this divisional scheme from his understanding of Aristotle, but that cannot be proved.[5] In any event, the scheme itself, while one which allowed the pursuit of certain analytical goals by scholars, was not of much practical significance. What mattered in practice were the specific types of Roman contract, and the rules governing their use. It is within these specific contracts that the original influence of promise in Roman law may be seen.

The contracts recognised in Roman law were both formal and informal. Though the latter came to have the greatest significance for later contract theory, it is within the former that the promise took root. Formal contracts were those which were required to be made according to a specified formality in order to be valid. The formalities were simple and clear, and allowed for certainty in the undertaking of basic transactions. Formal contracts were either verbal (*verbis*) or written (*litteris*). An example of the latter was the *insinuatio*, a written contract, registered before a court,

---

[4] Gordley, *Philosophical Origins*, p. 30; Watson, *The Law of the Ancient Romans*, p. 58.
[5] See Gordley, *Philosophical Origins*, p. 31, citing German sources for this view.

by which a gift was effected. An example of the former was the *stipulatio*, a contract by which one party promised something to another. As both *insinuatio* and *stipulatio* demonstrate, in Roman law one must avoid the misconception that the essence of contract was in every case mutual performance: this was not necessarily the case, for both *insinuatio* and *stipulatio* were gratuitous in nature, one party alone undertaking a duty in favour of another.

The focus of the present analysis of Roman contract lies in the *stipulatio*, for it is in this action that one finds the enforcement of a promise. The promise itself might be of any nature whatsoever, a flexibility of content which made the *stipulatio* incredibly useful to parties. Any duty might be made enforceable in a *stipulatio*, so long as the promise was made in the correct form. This potential universality of content gave the *stipulatio* a flexibility comparable to modern contract law. Though a *stipulatio* required a valid supporting *causa* or purpose, such *causa* need not be mentioned in the verbal promise, so the promise might be framed either causally or abstractly.[6] The undertaking of a *stipulatio* was achieved through a simple verbal exchange. The promisee (creditor) asked the promisor (debtor) whether he undertook the promise in question. Thus, for instance, he might ask 'do you promise to pay a hundred [denarii]?' (*spondesne centum dare?*), the promisor answering 'I promise' (*spondeo*). With the giving of the response, a *stipulatio* was immediately created, and no witnesses or recording of the act were required. The immediacy and simplicity of the binding effect of the undertaking was one of the benefits of the *stipulatio*.

It is striking that it is the promisee who frames the content of the promise to which the promisor is to give his simple, unqualified assent. This is quite different to modern promising, where it is the promisor who asserts what he is willing to promise with (in some systems) a simple acceptance required by the promisee. The result of the Roman process is, of course, that the obligation created by the *stipulatio* is a gratuitous one, the promisee coming under no mutual obligation. If a mutual arrangement were desired, then a *stipulatio* would have to be made by each of the two parties. This would open up the danger that the second intended promisor might not make his promise following the making of the first. That, however, could be accommodated, in later law, by both stipulators

---

[6] See Zimmermann, *Law of Obligations*, pp. 91, 550. A *stipulatio* was however required to have a *causa*, even if unexpressed. If the *stipulatio* was framed abstractly (without any specification of the underlying *causa*) then the failure of the underlying cause could be raised by the promisee by way of an *exceptio doli*: D. 44.4.2.3.

making conditional promises. Take, for instance, the example of a sale of specified property at a price of one hundred sestertii. To enable this mutual arrangement to be achieved, two conditional *stipulatones* might be framed thus:

FIRST STIPULATIO: 'do you promise to give me one hundred, if I give you Pamphilus?' 'I promise.'

SECOND STIPULATIO: do you promise to give me Pamphilus, if I give you one hundred?' 'I promise.'[7]

Such an exchange is somewhat redolent of a modern contractual offer and acceptance, though in the case of the *stipulationes* each conditional promissory question requires its own unqualified assent rather than the giving of a mutual counter-promise.

Although the *stipulatio* created a gratuitous obligation, binding only the promisor to do something, the fact that a question posed by the intended promisee as well as the consent of the promisor through his utterance of the promissory words were both required indicates that a stipulation required the agreement of both parties to the pledged undertaking. Consequently, if there was a fundamental disagreement between the parties, there could be no valid stipulation: 'a *stipulatio* is complete only if both parties agree'.[8] Evidently the idea of disagreement affecting a stipulation relates to underlying, latent disagreement, not evident from the parties' exchange; agreement was always patently, hence formally, present by virtue of the stipulator's '*spondeo*' in response to the questioner's '*spondesne?*'. If a different verb to that used by the questioner were used in reply to the question, no valid stipulation was undertaken. Originally, the only valid verb form which could be used was that of *spondere*;[9] later however, other verbs were permitted, such as *dare, promittere* and, for securities, *fideipromittere* and *fideiubere*.

By the classical period, the practice had developed of embodying the terms of the stipulation in writing for evidentiary purposes.[10] Thereafter, the fate of the *stipulatio* is a matter of academic dispute. On one view, by the Justinianic period the use of writing as evidence of a *stipulatio* had evolved further, so that a stipulation might be undertaken entirely

---

[7] First *stipulatio: Centum mihi dare spondes, si Pamphilum tibi dederim? Spondeo*; second *stipulatio: Pamphilum mihi dare spondes, si centum tibi dederim? Spondeo.*

[8] D. 45.1.137.1.

[9] *Spondere* had, for Romans, sacred connotations, as the word was associated with the making of oaths: Zimmermann, *Law of Obligations*, p. 71.

[10] Zimmermann, *ibid.*, pp. 80–2.

by way of written transaction, there being no formal oral requirements.[11] However, an alternative view has been advanced that writing was never more than evidentiary, and that the essence of the *stipulatio* remained an oral undertaking, a position which finds support from some later Roman texts.[12]

By the Justinianic period, some discrepancies between question and answer were tolerated: for instance, a request for 100 sestertii, met with a promise to pay 500, would be interpreted as a promise good for the lesser amount, it being included within the greater amount; likewise if A promised the property Pamphilus, and B the properties Pamphilus and Stichus, there would be a good agreement for Pamphilus alone.[13] This is not quite the modern law of offer and acceptance, where an offer met with a qualified acceptance can still be the basis of a contract by treating the qualified acceptance as a counter-offer; rather, on the Roman conception, the valid lesser undertaking was severable from the invalid greater.

By 469, the development of the *stipulatio* in its final form was complete, that year seeing the promulgation of a law of the Emperor Leo that

> All stipulations, even if they are not expressed in formal or direct words, but in any words whatsoever, with the consent of the contracting parties, and they are in conformity with the laws, shall be valid.[14]

With such a development, Roman law dispensed with the need for the use of specific formal words for the creation of a *stipulatio*: any question and answer form might now be used as the basis of a valid stipulation.[15] Though the parties still both had to be present at the time the stipulation was made, there was a presumption that they were present if that were represented to be the case, rebuttable only if it could be shown that the parties were not present in the same town on the day in question.[16]

---

[11] Zimmermann (*ibid.*, p. 85) describes this change as having occurred under the influence of Hellenistic practice and tradition, citing Kaser, *Das römische Privatrecht*, pp. 76f, 376ff on this point.

[12] The debate is discussed by MacCormack, 'The Oral and Written Stipulation in the Institutes', who advances the alternative view. See also Nicholas, 'The Form of the Stipulation in Roman Law', who likewise maintains that in Justinian's time writing remained merely 'juridically evidentiary'. Meyer, *Legitimacy and Law in the Roman World*, argues (p. 264) that at the end of the fifth century AD there was evidence to suggest that the formal and ceremonial aspects of *stipulatio* were still being adhered to.

[13] D. 45.1.1.5. See Johnston, *Roman Law in Context*, p. 77.   [14] C. 8.37.10.

[15] See Nicholas, 'The Form of the Stipulation in Roman Law', p. 77.

[16] See the Law of Justinian of 531 to that effect, recited at C.8.37.14.

One of the major uses to which the *stipulatio* was put in Roman law was in providing for a penalty payable if a party did not perform an obligation to which it was bound, a use encouraged by Justinian.[17] Such a function of the *stipulatio* was especially useful given that specific performance of a contract could not be compelled; instead, the *stipulatio* was used as a means to encourage performance, including performance to a third party (again, especially useful given the absence of a general doctrine of third party rights in contract) and adherence to an arbitrator's decision (against which no appeal lay).[18]

It has been said of the *stipulatio* that 'its usefulness and flexibility made it the cornerstone of the Roman contractual system'.[19] The prominence of this promissory action assured it a continuing role in later European legal thinking through the reception of Roman law into the later European *ius commune*.[20] However, despite relaxation of its attendant formalities, it did not develop into the general contractual action of the later law; for that, recourse was had to Roman law's consensual contracts. One further thing which the *stipulatio* did was to endow, in due course, the general law of contracts with the notion of *causa* which had been employed in relation to the *stipulatio*: in the medieval law, as is discussed later, the idea of *causa* was used to clothe bare pacts and thus render them enforceable in a way that had not been so in Roman law, given the rule *ex nudo pacto non oritor actio*.

(b)   Informal contracts

Informal contracts in Roman law were of two types: those binding upon consent (the 'consensual contracts' which were to provide the theoretical basis for the modern law of contract), namely sale (*emptio venditio*), lease/hire (*locatio conductio*), partnership (*societas*), and mandate (*mandatum*); and those binding only on delivery of a thing (the 'real contracts', or contracts *re*), namely the loan for consumption of money or another commodity (*mutuum*), the loan for use (*commodatum*), pledge (*pignus*), and deposit (*depositum*).[21] There was some interaction between the formal and informal contracts, because, for instance, if parties wished to add to the default duties of the parties under one of

---

[17] Inst. 3.15.7.   [18] C. 2.55.1.   [19] Zimmermann, *Law of Obligations*, p. 89.

[20] On which process, see generally Cairns and du Plessis, *The Creation of the Ius Commune.*

[21] Barter was originally unenforceable, but was given legal recognition towards the end of the classical period.

the informal contracts they might do so by embodying further duties in a *stipulatio*.[22] Moreover, sometimes the potential of the informal and formal contracts taken together offered a number of possible means for effecting a certain type of transaction: thus, a gift might be effected by way of a *stipulatio donationis* or simply by delivery of the subject of the gift.[23]

Taking together the scope of both the informal contracts and the formal contracts considered in the previous section, a number of arrangements still remained unenforceable, these being the bare contract and bare unilateral promise ('bare' in the sense of not being clothed in any particular form). The bare contract, or *nudum pactum*, was to remain unenforceable until the medieval period, when the attitude expressed by the maxim *ex nudo pacto non oritor actio* gave way to that of *pacta sunt servanda*. Though the bare unilateral promise (*promissio*) was unenforceable, an exception was made in respect of a promise made to a municipality to support public works or in gratitude for some honour received (the *pollicitatio*).[24]

(c)   Conclusion on Roman law

The above analysis of the role of promise in Roman law discloses that the idea of promise featured in two main ways:

(1)   It formed the basis of the most important formal contract, the *stipulatio*, a formal promise to another person of variable content, this contract undergoing some substantial development over the period of Roman law's history. Such development allowed it to be used as a means of embodying any contractual undertaking, albeit eventually in the somewhat restricted form of a written undertaking. It could, for instance, be used to effect the gratuitous transaction of donation. As the *stipulatio* both embodied a gratuitous undertaking by one party to another, but also took the form of question and answer demonstrating the agreement of the parties, the *stipulatio* was at one and the same time gratuitous and consensual in nature. The permissibility of making conditional stipulations allowed the *stipulatio* to effect mutual undertakings.

---

[22]   Johnston, *Roman Law in Context*, p. 78.

[23]   And, indeed, by the Justinianic period, a mere contract of donation (*pactum donationis*) gave rise to a personal action: Inst. 2.7.2.

[24]   D. 50.12.

(2) Informally, it was the basis of the *pollicitatio*, a unilateral promise in favour of a municipality. This was a somewhat restricted role
for the informal promise, such a promise being otherwise generally
unenforceable.

Promise thus had an established role in Roman contract law. It was not
the only idea animating the law, but it was a powerful one, albeit one
which came to have a somewhat restricted practical importance given
the later development of the *stipulatio* as a purely written arrangement.

The *stipulatio* was the locus for an idea that was to be influential in later
European contract law: *causa*. The notion of *causa*, taken from Roman
law and mixed with Aristotelian ideas, became a generalised contractual
requirement in the medieval period through the developmental scholarship of the glossators.[25] The fact also that, while the *stipulatio* was a contract, it was based on an essentially unilateral act, a promise, set a pattern
for analysing contract as an exchange of promises which proved to be an
enduring analysis. It persists not only in descriptions of the basis of liability in contract in promissory terms, but also in the way in which offer and
acceptance are traditionally conceived.[26]

The Roman *stipulatio* was also one of the sources used by the canonists to develop the canonical action for the enforcement of bare promises, a development discussed below. This borrowing by the canonists
further ensured that promissory ideas continued to be influential in
later contract law.

2.   Medieval contract law

(a)   Continental legal thought

Following the collapse of the Roman Empire in the West, the study of
Roman law was largely abandoned for 600 years or so, before being redis-
covered and taught again in the Continental universities. The greatest of
the teachers of Roman law in this period of its rediscovery added their
own opinions on the classical texts in the form of glosses, hence the name
given to them of glossators. The founder of the glossators' school is generally considered to be Irnerius, who taught Roman law at Bologna and
died some time after 1125. The school effectively ended with the last, and

---

[25] See discussion below at pp. 116–17.
[26] This latter point is discussed further in Ch. 4, at pp. 212–13.

greatest, of its members, Azo, and his pupil Accursius (who wrote in the early thirteenth century).

It is important to note that none of the glossators seems to have been familiar with the ethical writings of Aristotle, which had also been lost in the West and were not to be generally available again until their translation in to Latin in the mid-thirteenth century. This means that, while the glossators developed the doctrine of *causa*, teaching that the absence of *causa* did not simply give rise to a defence (the *exceptio doli*) as in classical Roman law, but meant that the contract was seen as invalid *ex nunc*,[27] they did not put *causa* to the same Aristotelian uses as later scholars were to. Nonetheless, what the glossators *did* teach tended to the exclusion of undertakings given without any underlying *causa* or reason for the transaction.

The glossators' great achievement was in discovering and enunciating general principles in the Digest, which, as was discussed earlier, was not one of the great strengths of the classical Roman law. Accursius, for instance, noted the passage at D. 2.14.1.3, stating that all contracts require consent, an observation which was clearly of use in developing the law's later stress upon the idea of consent and agreement in contract. The glossators' interest in general principles bore fruit in a tendency to coin general maxims or brocards expressing legal rules, though it was not until the sixteenth century that the most important maxim, *pacta sunt servanda*, was to be coined by the canonist Hostiensis.[28]

The glossators were followed by the so-called 'post-glossators', or 'commentators', writing from the mid-thirteenth century onwards, of whom the two greatest were Bartolus de Saxoferrato (who died in 1357) and his pupil Baldus de Ubaldis (who died in 1400). These scholars had the benefit both of the Roman texts, as well as the ethical writings of Aristotle. Bartolus, for instance, knew that, under the Roman law, a *stipulatio* might be binding even if made gratuitously, but also that it required a *causa*. Bartolus therefore, applying an Aristotelian approach to the idea of *causa*, explained that *causa* must mean either the receipt of something in return for what was promised or the undertaking of the promise out of liberality.[29] In similar Aristotelian vein, Baldus discussed when a contract might be presumed to have been made foolishly rather than out of liberality.[30] He also used

---

[27] See further Zimmermann, *Law of Obligations*, p. 551.
[28] See earlier discussion in Ch. 2, at p. 82.
[29] Bartolus, *Commentaria* to D.44.4.2.3.
[30] Baldus, *Commentaria* to C. 4.30.13, no. 14.

his understanding of *causa* to explain the canonist rule that an informal
executory agreement was binding. This was so, as long as the agreement
had a *causa* (in the sense described by Baldus).[31] This approach of the
post-glossators was clearly in keeping with the view of Thomas Aquinas
expressed in the previous century, but the significance for legal development lay in the fact that the post-glossators were first and foremost legal
scholars rather than theologians with an interest in law.

The apogee of medieval legal scholarship is found, however, neither
in the scholastic writings of the glossators nor of the post-glossators, but
in that of the late scholastics, or Spanish natural law school. It was this
school which combined most fully Roman law with Aristotelian ideas to
produce a systematic theory of law, and one in which promise found a
prominent place. The Spanish scholastics were heavily influenced by the
Aristotelian-Thomist stress upon the virtues of promise-keeping, commutative justice and liberality,[32] and used the concept of the promise to
explain both the unilateral promise as well as the pact or agreement, the
latter being a promise accepted by another and made either for reasons
of commutative justice or liberality.[33] They debated questions such as
whether it was unjust to break a promise made for reasons of liberality if
the promisee would merely be disappointed but not worse off as a result
of the breach, Connanus (a French contemporary of the Spanish schoolmen) and Cajetan holding it was not, Lessius and Molina disagreeing.[34]
Lessius was concerned that Cajetan's view would lead to the conclusion
that merely executory contracts were not binding. The view of Molina,
that the intention to undertake a gratuitous promise was sufficient to create a valid and binding obligation was to become especially influential
in the enforcement in Scots law of unilateral gratuitous promises.[35] Such
debates were to continue in to the twentieth century, where, as discussed
in the last chapter, reliance theorists would argue for a position similar to
that advocated by Connanus and Cajetan.

Those scholastics who held that all promises were binding, regardless
of the effect upon the promisee, had to answer the question of whether
a promise had to be communicated and whether it had to be accepted
before it was binding. Soto and Molina were of the view that, while the

---

[31]   Baldus *Commentaria* to C. 3.36.15, no. 3.
[32]   Gordley, 'Philosophical Origins', p. 71.
[33]   See for instance Lessius, *De iustitia et jure*, 2.17.1; Molina, *De iustitia et jure*, disp. 252.
[34]   See Cajetan, *Commentaria* to *Summa Theologica*, II-II, Q. 88, Art.1; Q. 113, Art. 1;
       Connanus, *Commentariorum*, 1.6.1; Lessius, *De iustitia et iure*, 2.18.2; Molina, *De iustitia
       et iure*, disp. 262.
[35]   See later discussion of the views of Stair, at pp. 134ff.

positive law might require an outward declaration of a promise, under the natural law and as a matter of principle even a silent promise could bind the promisor. It was not this impractical view that won out, but rather the contrary view of Lessius that an outward declaration of the promisor's will was required,[36] a view supported in the fundamental requirements for a promise suggested in Chapter 1. There was an equally lively debate as to the question of whether an acceptance of a promise was necessary: Covarruvias, Soto, and Molina said that, as all promises were binding, an acceptance of a promise was not required in principle; Lessius disagreed, holding that an acceptance was necessary because it was the promisor's condition for being bound, an argument which clearly conceived of the nature of an offer as a conditional promise. This debate is noteworthy in being conducted in promissory terms; had the focus of contract been rather on agreement, no debate could have been seriously entertained as to whether an acceptance (or some other sign of agreement) was needed. The shift to thinking of contract primarily in agreement terms had not yet come.

The Spanish scholastics represented the penultimate flowering of the ancient natural law tradition, its final proponents being the Northern natural law school discussed below, whose members stood on the cusp between late medieval and early modern legal thought.

(b)   English law

Though it is a standard observation to contrast the Common law with the Romano-civilian heritage of Continental Europe, one remarkable shared feature of both English law and Roman law is the extent to which legal development in each came about as a result of changes in forms of pleading rather than as a result of legal theory. While their content might be different, English law and Roman law were both essentially legal systems based upon actions. As will thus be seen, the eventual rise of will theory in the Common law should not really be seen as the triumph of any overarching theoretical or moral perspective, but rather the result of gradual development in legal and commercial practice.

The history of the development of English law narrated below will highlight the importance of promise to contractual thought in England.[37]

---

[36] Lessius, *De iustitia et iure*, 2,18,5.

[37] A short, though now somewhat dated, summary of the place of promise in the law, largely from a Common law perspective, is found in Farnsworth, 'The Past of Promise: An Historical Introduction to Contract'.

This is clearly observable in the rise of the promissory action of assumpsit, which was to became one of the cornerstones of the unified law of contract of the nineteenth century. To that observation must, however, be added the crucial further remark that the promissory nature of assumpsit was to become, in time, a reciprocal rather than a unilateral promissory one, given the development of the doctrine of consideration. English contractual development, like that of the Continent, was to be one of a shift from promise to mutual agreement.

A noteworthy feature of English law between Glanvill in the late twelfth century and Blackstone in the mid-eighteenth century is the dearth of theoretical treatments of contract law. Such an absence means that the focus of the discussion below will be on court practice and decision in relation to the three medieval actions of debt, covenant and assumpsit, out of which modern English contract law largely grew. There is also some discussion of the form of contracts and the doctrine of consideration.

(i)   Debt

The early form of the English writ of debt[38] is narrated in Ranulf de Glanvill's late twelfth century Treatise on the Laws and Customs of England.[39] The writ could be raised for a debt deriving from any cause, which need not be narrated in the writ itself. The form of the writ asked the court to order the debtor to pay a specified sum of money (or to hand over specific goods due) to the creditor. Though the debt might conceivably derive from an underlying agreement, it could be due as a result of some other cause. Glanvill lists two forms of proof of debt, witness or sealed charter.[40] Thus, an underlying verbal agreement which gave rise to a debt might be proved by the bringing of witnesses; otherwise, a sealed instrument embodying the debtor's obligation might be produced. Agreements unsupported by anything except the allegation that the other party had pledged the faith of the agreement (that is, given his word to perform) did not fall within the jurisdiction of the King's court, such mere breaches of the faith of the parties falling instead within the jurisdiction of the ecclesiastical courts.[41] The connotations of the writ

---

[38] See further Simpson, *A History of the Common Law of Contract*, pp. 53–135.

[39] Glanvill, *Tractatus de legibus et consuetudinibus regni Angliae*.

[40] Glanvill, x,12.

[41] Glanvill, x,12: 'When the debtor appears in court on the appointed day, if the creditor has neither gage [a pledge] nor sureties nor any other proof except a mere pledge of faith, this is not sufficient proof in the court of the lord king. Of course, any breach of faith may be sued upon in an ecclesiastical court.'

with shame and dishonour have been remarked upon, this being a point of contact between the action of debt and the early idea of an obligation in Roman law.[42]

Glanvill was familiar with Roman law, so it is not surprising that at least four of the five *causae* which he lists as supporting the writ of debt are highly reminiscent of Roman actions: consumption, sale, loan for use and lease, as well as 'any other just cause of indebtedness'.[43] The influence of Roman law, at least in terminology if not in substance,[44] was evidently too great to be extinguished by its study being banned by King Stephen around 1150.[45]

The action of debt was evidently useful as a means of enforcing an underlying agreement if a claim for a specific sum could be proved before the court; it was not available where such a specific sum could not be stated, for instance because the parties had left the price of an agreement to be fixed at a later date. Another difficulty with using the writ of debt was that the debtor might repel the action by swearing that the debt was not due and by producing eleven 'oath helpers' who would testify to the same effect.[46]

(ii)   Covenant

The second action out of which the modern law of contract grew was that of covenant.[47] Like debt, the form of the writ simply narrated that the party bringing the writ was entitled to some performance and begged the court to order the other party to perform it or to pay damages (as assessed by a jury). The action developed in the course of the thirteenth century out of the action of trespass: again, like the Roman concept of an *obligatio*, it thus grew out of the redress due for wrongful behaviour. The idea of covenant meant no more than agreement, such agreement being narrated in the writ, but the origins of covenant in trespass gave the writ

---

[42] Ibbetson, *An Historical Introduction*, p.19.   [43] Glanvill, x,3.

[44] Unlike the Roman law, Glanvill's discussion of the various types of consensual contract which he lists places great stress upon pledges of performance, such as delivery in a contract of sale. Scrutton, *The Influence of the Roman Law*, argues that the Continental influence on English law was mainly terminological (see p. 74f). A similar point in relation to the Roman legal influence on the action of debt is made by Ibbetson, *An historical Introduction*, p. 19.

[45] Hall, in the introduction to his translation of Glanvill (p. xviii), surmised that Roman law continued to exert some influence on England because it had proved indispensable to the canon lawyers.

[46] Ibbetson, *An Historical Introduction*, p. 32.

[47] See further, Simpson, *A History of the Common Law of Contract*, pp. 9–52.

a certain ambiguous nature, part contractual, part tortious, which was to prove enduring.

Given that the idea of covenant was explicitly agreement based, one might have expected it to develop in time into a general contractual action. That it did not seems to be due to two procedural developments. First, in the late thirteenth and early fourteenth century the rule developed that an action of covenant could only be brought if the covenant was embodied in a sealed document.[48] Thus covenant, unlike debt, suffered the same restriction upon its development as had the *stipulatio* in later Roman law. Had this development not occurred, English law might have developed a general idea of contract much earlier than it did. Second, lawyers began to embody many agreements in the form of a conditional bond.[49] A bond to pay a sum of money would be written out, and endorsed with the condition that it would not have to be paid if the debtor had performed a certain duty by a specified day; non-performance would thus give rise to the action of debt. The attractiveness of an action for debt was that it was for a clear sum, rather than for an uncertain amount of damages, and that it could be brought for any deviation from the clear terms of the condition attached to the bond. The conditional bond was used to encourage performance of an underlying agreement in a similar way to the *stipulatio poenae* in Roman law. These two developments are prime examples of how wider, theoretical development of English law was constrained by practice and pleading.

In addition, another limiting aspect of covenant was that, because the form of the action of covenant was geared towards performance or damages, it was not ideal as a means of complaining about defective performance. As time passed, pressure was exerted by litigants to allow pleas of defective performance to be remedied, but where this occurred it was under the guise of the writ of trespass, alleging 'disturbance of the king's peace' by the defective performance, a not theoretically convincing, though increasingly successful, plea.[50] The difficulty of pleading defective contractual performance in covenant (contract), and the increasing hiving off of defective performance claims (including breach of warranty claims) into trespass (tort), drove a wedge between two common types of claim which were only reunited much later in the history of English contract law. Such developments inevitably hampered the conceptualisation of contract as a single obligation.

---

[48] Ibbetson, *An Historical Introduction*, pp. 26–7.
[49] *Ibid.*, pp. 28ff.   [50] *Ibid.*, p. 44.

(iii)   Unilaterality and bilaterality in early
English contract law

As the above discussion of debt and covenant disclose, the underlying contractual agreements in early English law which, prior to the rise of assumpsit, might trigger these two actions could be either formal or informal. If formal, the contractual agreement essentially took effect unilaterally: a debtor committed his pledged performance to writing, sealed the document, and delivered it to the creditor. If informal, the contract took effect bilaterally: consent to the agreement was exchanged by the parties, often accompanied by acts expressing agreement such as a handshake, the sharing of a drink, or the exchange of tokens (such as a coin) as a symbol of agreement.[51] A formal contract, a sealed document pledging the performance of the one party, thus had very much the characteristic of a unilateral promise, whereas the informal contract had more of the bilateral nature which one associates with what today would be called a genuine contractual agreement. Even today in English law, the successor to the sealed document, the document declared to be a deed, remains a valid, if exceptional, way of effecting a contractual undertaking by way of unilateral act.

There was no doctrine of consideration in English contract law before the mid-sixteenth century. Rather, there was an understanding that informal contracts (though not formal ones) must demonstrate reciprocity, a requirement which became settled during the fourteenth and fifteenth centuries.[52] Thus, neither an agreement to pay damages, nor to pay for past services, would be enforced.[53] In support of this position, reference might even occasionally be made by the courts to the Roman law maxim *ex nudo pacto non oritor actio*.[54] This development was, in time, to assist the law in developing from Glanvill's list of recognised informal contracts, with their reciprocal causes, towards a generalised understanding of contract as a reciprocal relationship.

(iv)   Assumpsit

Promise provides an appropriate characterisation not only for contracts under seal, but also for the action of assumpsit which had, by 1600, largely

---

[51] On such symbols of agreement, see Ibbetson, *ibid.*, pp. 73–4.

[52] See Simpson, *A History of the Common Law of Contract*, pp. 148–60; Ibbetson, *An Historical Introduction*, p. 81.

[53] Ibbetson, *ibid.*, pp. 81–2.

[54] YB M.9 Hen V f.14 pl.23; YB P.11 Hen VI f.35 pl.30 at f.38; YB T.17 Edw IV f.4 pl.4; *Luyt* v. *Boteler* (C1/60/142); *Grene* v. *Capell* (C1/94/22) (all cit. by Ibbetson, *ibid.*, p. 82).

taken over the field previously occupied by the action of debt.[55] Assumpsit, in form an action for breach of promise, grew out of the older action of trespass on the case. Though trespass on the case was originally used in a contractual context to deal with cases of misperformance, by the end of the fifteenth century it was beginning to be recognised as applicable to cases of non-performance also.[56] In such cases, the plaintiff would allege that the defendant had 'assumed and faithfully promised' (*assumpsit et fideliter promisit*) to do something for the plaintiff, but had failed so to do. This wrongful behaviour was what constituted the trespass on the case, though it is clear that courts were willing to see the substantial contractual nature of the claim which lay below the trespassory form of the action. This is evident from the granting of damages for non-performance in the performance measure,[57] as well as by decisions such as *Fyneux* v. *Clyfford* from 1518, in which the substance of the claim was non-performance under a sale of land constituted by mutual promises.[58] By 1530 the action was also being used for non-payment of monetary debts, where it was called *indebitatus assumpsit*.

The language of the claim of assumpsit – that the defendant had 'assumed and faithfully promised' something – was evidently promissory. It was also clearly unilateral, there being no requirement to mention any agreement by the plaintiff or other action on his part which might be necessary to perfect such promise. To begin with, this formal language also mirrored the substance of the action. However, as the seventeenth century wore on, assumpsit was transformed into a bilateral, contractual claim. This transformation may be seen in judicial statements such as this from *Hurford* v. *Pile* in 1618:

> A person who promises cannot countermand and recall his own promise, because every assumpsit is made by the mutual agreement of both parties and on reciprocal consideration, and through this creates a contract ... and because of this the person who assumes cannot make a countermand, for a bargain is a bargain and a contract is a contract.[59]

Indeed, from the middle of the sixteenth century, the nature of assumpsit had become fairly clearly established as contractual in substance and merely promissory in form. The judges had begun to doubt whether the

---

[55] See Simpson, *A History of the Common Law of Contract*, Part II (pp. 199–620).
[56] Ibbetson, *An Historical Introduction*, pp.139–40.
[57] See Baker, *Oxford History of the Laws of England*, vol. vi, ch. 49, esp. pp. 848–51, 860.
[58] (1518) KB 27/1026.
[59] Ibbetson, *An Historical Introduction*, p. 140, citing HLS MS 105f f.291.

presence of a promise actually made any difference to the nature of the transaction, and began to assert that what mattered was the underlying agreement of the parties.[60] Though the promissory language remained, it did not denote a unilateral promise but merely a promise in the broader sense of a contractual undertaking.[61]

It has been argued by a number of legal historians that the promissory language which found its way in to the action of assumpsit was borrowed from the canon law, in particular the canonical action of *fidei laesio*.[62] The *fidei laesio* had proven to be a popular action before the ecclesiastical courts for the reason noted earlier: those courts were willing to grant a remedy based purely on the violation of the faith of a contractual undertaking backed by an oath.[63] The popularity of this action was decreasing precisely at the time that assumpsit was becoming more popular, which has given rise to the conjecture that pleaders in assumpsit cases were borrowing the language and ideas popular in the ecclesiastical courts. The wording of claims in assumpsit and *fidei laesio* is virtually identical,[64] and though this does not conclusively prove a borrowing by the former from the latter, this is hardly surprising: if pleaders were borrowing from the canon law, such a borrowing would most likely have been an unacknowledged process.

The apparent borrowing from the canon law was important not simply in linguistic terms, but also because the canonical insistence that promises have a valid *causa* to support them was, it seems, influential in the common law's development of the doctrine of contractual consideration.

(v)   The doctrine of consideration

A great deal has been written about the origins of the doctrine of consideration in the common law of contract,[65] though this has produced

---

[60] *Ibid.*, pp. 137–8.

[61] Ibbetson remarks that, after *Slade's Case* in 1602, 'if the action of assumpsit was an action based on promise, it was a promise only in the weakest sense of the word, denoting nothing more than a voluntary undertaking' (*ibid.*, p. 138).

[62] See Martínez-Torrón, *Anglo-American Law and Canon Law*, and Ibbetson, *ibid.* Helmholz has argued that there is a possible correlation between the decline of *fidei laesio* and the rise of assumpsit, but that no definitive case can be made out: see Helmholz, 'Assumpsit and Fidei Laesio'; 'Contracts and the Canon Law', 62.

[63] See Jones, 'The Two Laws in England: The Later Middle Ages', 125; Ibbetson, *ibid.*, p. 136.

[64] Helmholz, 'Contracts and the Canon Law', p. 62.

[65] See, for instance, Simpson, *A History of the Common Law of Contract*, Part 2, chs. 4–7; Ibbetson, *An Historical Introduction*, pp. 141–5, and 'Consideration and the Theory of Contract'; Baker, 'Origins of the "Doctrine" of Consideration'.

no universal agreement on the precise nature of those origins. Simpson, for instance, has argued that the origins of the doctrine lie in the equitable doctrine of consideration which applied in the law of uses, itself developed from the common law of real property, and has accordingly argued that the influence of the canon law was much less than have other writers.[66] However, even Simpson has recognised the likely influence of Christopher St Germain's work *Doctor and Student*,[67] an imagined discourse between a Doctor of Divinity and a student of the common law. The work contains a lengthy discourse on the nature of promise, including a passage where the Doctor equates the canonical notion of *causa* with the idea of consideration,[68] though, as Simpson notes, much of this passage is concerned with whether promises bind *in conscience* rather than at law. The appearance of this work at the very moment to which the origin of the doctrine of consideration is commonly attributed strongly suggests that the central idea of the doctrine of consideration was at least popularised by the work, if not the details of the doctrine as it came to be applied in the common law.[69] Ibbetson has presented a case for a clearer connection of linguistic and ideological borrowing, though again not necessarily of substantive content, while Martínez-Torrón believes that '[w]hether the action of *assumpsit* and the doctrine of consideration were the result of canon law influence, or rather emerged from within the common law, will likely remain one more of those secrets which are jealously guarded by history'.[70] If there was any equation at this stage between the civilian and canonical notion of *causa* and consideration, it was gradually lost sight of, and not confidently reasserted again until the English translation of Pothier's *Treatise on Obligations* began to circulate freely in England in the early nineteenth century.[71]

Whatever borrowing by the common law from canon law that there may have been, this produced different long-term effects for the common law than those produced by the assumption of canonical jurisdiction by the civil courts in Scotland. Whereas the common law chose to interpret the canonical idea that *causa* clothed a bare promise and gave it enforceability as excluding unreciprocated promises, the Scottish courts took the exact opposite view and interpreted the notion of *causa* in a wider sense

---

[66] Simpson, *ibid.*, pp. 327–74.
[67] Published in Latin (the first English edition appearing in 1528).
[68] *Doctor and Student*, ch. 23.
[69] Simpson, *A History of the Common Law of Contract*, p. 396.
[70] Martínez-Torrón, *Anglo-American Law and Canon Law*, p. 135.
[71] See further below on this, at p. 154.

than that determined by the idea of consideration, thus permitting the enforcement of unilateral promises.

The doctrine of consideration was subtly different to the older common law idea of *quid pro quo*. Consideration was conceived of as the thing which motivated the giving of a promise,[72] whereas such motivational criterion was not present in the idea of *quid pro quo*. Consideration, moreover, might be constituted not merely by a benefit to the other party, but could include a benefit conferred upon a third party, or the incurrence by the other party of a detriment.[73] An undertaking to marry was good consideration, having formerly been, only by the turning of a conceptual blind eye, an act of reciprocity.

3.   The Northern natural law school

By contrast with English law, the contract law of Continental Europe and Scotland of the early modern period was the subject of a number of important theoretical treatments. The principal writers of the law in this period belong to what has been styled the Northern natural law school. It is their works which form the vast majority of the following discussion of this period, with an occasional reference to decisions of the courts.

The Northern natural law school were the last group of jurists to espouse unashamedly the natural law tradition of Aristotle and Aquinas, though as Reformed, early Enlightenment scholars, they did so from a Protestant perspective, and placed a greater emphasis upon reason than those natural lawyers who had gone before them. The greatest members of this school were the Dutchman Hugo de Groot (Grotius), the German Baron Samuel von Pufendorf, and the Scottish judge James Dalrymple, Viscount Stair.[74] The writing of each of these men was characterised by a blend of natural law thinking and an early modern view of the importance of man as a rational being. The natural law and reason were seen as going hand in hand, the latter informing the former. Each of the three gave a prominent place to promise in his writings, though with Pufendorf we see the abandonment of promise as the central concept of the law of

---

[72] Ibbetson, *An Historical Introduction*, p. 144; Simpson, *A History of the Common Law of Contract*, p. 424.

[73] Ibbetson, *ibid.*, p. 142.

[74] Other members of the School included: Petrus Gudelinus (1550–1619) of Leuven University; the French Huguenot translator of Grotius, Jean Barbeyrac (1674–1744); and the Scottish judge, Henry Home (Lord Kames, 1696–1782), Kames being one the last writers to merit the description of a natural lawyer in the ancient tradition.

obligations and its replacement with that of agreement. The writings of the Northern natural lawyers were to be influential in the development not only of modern civilian systems but also of the modern law of the mixed legal systems of Scotland and South Africa.

(a)   Hugo Grotius[75]

Hugo Grotius devotes a chapter of Book II of his work *De jure belli ac pacis* to promises.[76] This title follows an opening chapter on the causes of war (identified as self defence and property) and a succession of chapters on matters concerning rights relating to property and persons.

It is notable that Grotius deals separately with promises,[77] moving on to contracts,[78] then oaths,[79] before looking at all three as they relate to sovereign powers[80] and treaties.[81] Why does Grotius treat promises separately, and why does he place his treatment of promises before that of contract? He gives us little idea of the reasons for this in the chapter on promises itself, as he opens his chapter on promises by saying simply that the 'order of our work has brought us to the obligation which arises from promises'.[82] However, promise's appearance before contract, and the fact that (unlike Pufendorf) he gives it a separate treatment, does give the impression of its holding a primacy in Grotius's scheme of obligations. This may well be because Grotius saw himself as a scholar within the scholastic tradition, with all that that meant for the traditional scholastic emphasis of promises and vows.[83]

Grotius was not however a slave to scholastic opinion.[84] He begins his discussion with a strong refutation of Connanus's views that only reciprocated promises should be enforced and that it is not unjust not to fulfil a promise but only dishonest. Grotius cites in support of the contrary view, that promises ought to be honoured even when unreciprocated or not yet performed, the opinion of Hebrew jurists, passages of Paul from

---

[75] 1583–1645.

[76] The citations of the English translation of *De jure belli ac pacis* used are from the 1925 translation by Kelsey of the 1646 edition.

[77] *Ibid.*, II.xi.   [78] *Ibid.*, II.xii.   [79] *Ibid.*, II.xiii.

[80] *Ibid.*, II.xiv.   [81] *Ibid.*, II.xv.   [82] *Ibid.*, II.xi.1.1.

[83] See Zimmermann, *Law of Obligations*, pp. 567–8.

[84] He remarks of the scholastics that, because they lived in an age deprived of knowledge of the liberal arts, 'it is less to be wondered at if among many things worthy of praise there are also some things which we should receive with indulgence' (*De jure belli ac pacis*, Prologue, 52).

the Digest, the natural law, good faith, and 'the nature of immutable justice'.[85]

He says that those promises which are binding in law are those where an intention to promise is 'manifested by an outward sign of the intent to confer the due right on the other party.'[86] He compares the effect of such a promise to an 'alienation of ownership' because in making the promise we are intending either to alienate a thing or some portion of our freedom of action. Notably, he requires an acceptance before a promise can bind, though he admits that '[t]his effect does not follow from the law of nature but merely from the civil law'.[87]

Grotius admitted that promises might be made the subject of 'burdensome conditions', stating that this was so obvious from 'natural equity' that 'it does not need many proofs' (he does not offer any).[88] Grotius might have used this idea of the conditional promise as a means of connecting promise with contract by describing contract as founded upon conditional promises, but he does not do so. On the contrary, the language of promising is almost entirely absent from Grotius's treatment of contract in his succeeding chapter, which distinguishes him clearly from Pufendorf, as we shall see.

In fact, the definition of contract offered by Grotius, that it encompasses 'all acts of benefit to others, except mere acts of kindness',[89] is hardly a serviceable definition of the obligation, as clearly not all acts beneficial to others are in fact contracts. Contracts are described as 'reciprocal acts', of either beneficence or exchange (his own conceptualisation of the Aristotelian ideas of liberality and commutative justice), and being either such as 'separate the parties' (in that each party undertakes it to further his own interests) or such as 'produce a community of interests' (contracts for a common purpose).[90] The latter distinction seems a somewhat minor one to posit as of primary importance in understanding the field of contract, though, given that the latter class is held to include associations for the purposes of war, the reader is perhaps expected to grasp a certain relevance in this classification to a work on war and peace. Regardless of any such relevance, it hardly provides the most useful primary taxonomy for contracts in general. Grotius then spends some time discussing what it means to say that the law of nature enjoins that contracts are characterised by equality,[91] though, like Stair after him, Grotius is willing to leave it to the parties themselves to estimate what seems fair to them

---

[85] *Ibid.*, II.xi.1; II.xi.4.   [86] *Ibid.*, II.xi.4.1.   [87] *Ibid.*, II.xi.14.
[88] *Ibid.*, II.xi.19.   [89] *Ibid.*, II.xii.7.   [90] *Ibid.*, II.xii.3.   [91] *Ibid.*, II.xii.8–13.

by way of exchange,[92] an approach which does no more than pay lip service to Aristotle's idea of commutative justice. Grotius is, however, well acquainted with Aristotle: he characterises human acts as either 'kind' or 'reciprocal', citing Aristotle, and the first chapter of his first book contains a lengthy discussion of Aristotelian classifications of justice and law.[93] It is also more than abundantly clear that his text shows a clear support for natural law philosophy, though like Stair natural law and reason are inherently linked in Grotius's view.[94]

The remainder of Grotius's discussion of contract seems somewhat jumbled and disjointed, for he deals, in no apparent order, with a number of seemingly unrelated issues, such as the estimation of the price in a sale, monopolies contrary to nature, money as the medium of exchange, interest, partnership, joint undertakings for maritime operations, and a number of other topics. The result, for those looking for a logical treatment of the field, is unsatisfactory, far less elegant and structured than that of his treatment of promise, and certainly less satisfactory than the structured treatment offered by his near contemporaries Stair and Pufendorf.

A comparison of Grotius's treatment of promise and contract is instructive. He stands as perhaps the last writer in the natural law tradition who gave promise a central role in obligations theory. With his passing, contract and mutuality were to replace promise and unilaterality as the central themes in the first treatments of obligations which ushered in the modern era of obligations theory. However, as will be seen, though mutuality was to become the dominant model, the idea of promise had become so entrenched that the conceptualisation of mutual agreement was still discussed in promissory terms.

(b) Samuel von Pufendorf

At the cusp of this era of modernity stands another member of the Northern natural law school, Samuel von Pufendorf.[95] Although he treats of promise in his writings, he gives it much less emphasis than did Grotius

---

[92] *Ibid.*, II.xii.11.1: 'Whatever, in fact, the parties promise or give, they should be believed to promise or give as on an equality with the thing which is to be received, and due by reason of that equality.'

[93] *Ibid.*, II.xii.2.

[94] 'The law of nature is a dictate of right reason ... an act, according as it is or is not in conformity with rational nature, has in it a quality of moral baseness or moral necessity; and that, in consequence, such an act is either forbidden or enjoined by the author of nature, God' (I.i.10.1).

[95] 1632–1694.

or other natural lawyers before him. For Pufendorf, promise is a way of analysing contract, but it is contract which takes on the dominant role in obligations. Pufendorf's views on promise and contract are set out in his works *Elementorum jurisprudentiae universalis* (The Elements of Universal Jurisprudence) and in his most famous work, *De iure naturae et gentium* (The Laws of Nature and Nations).

In the *Elementorum*, he begins his treatment of obligations by laying out some conceptual ground. Obligations may be classified according to various criteria, including whether they are congenital or adventitious, equal or unequal, and mutual or non-mutual.[96] Congenital obligations derive from our human nature, and include the duties we owe to God and each other under the natural law; adventitious obligations are those which do not follow from our birth, but either we assume voluntarily or are imposed upon us by law. Unequal obligations are due from inferior beings to their superiors, whether to God or some superior human power; equal obligations, as the name suggests, exist between those of the same state in life. Most relevant for the present discussion is the division between mutual and non-mutual obligations.[97] A mutual obligation is one to which 'another obligation corresponds',[98] a concept of mutuality still employed by the modern law; by contrast, a non-mutual obligation is one to which no other obligation corresponds (Pufendorf gives the example of the duty of obedience owed by men to God, which has no corresponding duty on God's part).[99] In Pufendorf's view, no such non-mutual obligations exist between men under the natural law, because it is 'repugnant to the natural equality of men among one another for one to be bound to another in such a way that the latter is in his turn bound to the former in no way at all'.[100] This statement appears to suggest that it would be impossible for someone to undertake a gratuitous obligation in favour of another. That would fail to appreciate, however, that Pufendorf, like other natural lawyers before him, saw the recipient of a gratuitous promise as under a reciprocal natural obligation of gratitude, even if such an obligation of gratitude could not be legally enforced. Seen this way, gratuitous obligations have a place in Pufendorf's thinking,[101] the making of such a promise entailing that 'we must now follow the directions of our promise'.[102]

Pufendorf's general discussion of obligation is littered with promissory language. For instance, he illustrates a further obligational

---

[96] *Elementorum*, I.xii.1–5.
[97] The idea of mutuality was discussed in Ch. 1, at pp. 29–30.
[98] *Elementorum*, I.xii.6.   [99] *Ibid.*, I.xii.5.   [100] *Ibid.*, I.xii.5.
[101] *Ibid.*, I.xii.7.   [102] *De iure naturae*, III.v.7.

classification – that between perfect and imperfect obligations – with examples of promises of both type. A perfect obligation is one which creates a legal entitlement to enforce the obligation; an imperfect obligation does not. Like Grotius before him, Pufendorf insists upon an acceptance on the part of a promisee before a promise may become perfect and thereby bind the promisor.[103] This seemingly minor point is in fact of great significance. Because promises must be accepted, and because contracts evidently involve acceptance of the terms offered, contract can be characterised by Pufendorf as an accepted promise. Pufendorf's train of thought in this respect may be seen from the following progression in the text of the *Elementorum*: first he stipulates the need for promises to be accepted,[104] next discussing that promises may be conditional or unconditional,[105] before finally characterising a contract as constituted by conditional promises.[106] It is significant that an author who (as will be seen below) saw contract as the central obligation, nonetheless continued the existing tradition of analysing contract in promissory terms. Such a carrying over of promissory language into the analysis of contract by Pufendorf and others laid the foundations for a modern analysis of offer and acceptance which can still be classed in promissory terms and as having unilateral characteristics.[107]

Though in his *Elementorum* Pufendorf discusses promises before contract, when the chapter on Obligations is considered as a whole (and indeed when his later work is considered) it will be seen that he devotes far greater time to contract than to promise, and gives contract a much more extensive place in the scheme of obligations than did Grotius. Furthermore, having (as has been noted) characterised the duties of parties under a contract as conditional 'promises',[108] he mixes this conceptualisation with the language of mutuality.[109] A contract is a 'perfectly mutual obligation' arising from 'the agreement of two or more persons ... in such wise that on both sides there is an obligation of the same kind regarding one another mutually'.[110] This is a strikingly modern agreement-based conception of contract. The concept of mutuality he has expounded enables him to

---

[103] *Elementorum*, I.xii.10.   [104] *Ibid.*, I.xii.10.   [105] *Ibid.*, I.xii.11.

[106] *Ibid.*, I.xii.12.   [107] See the discussion in Ch. 4, at pp. 210–13.

[108] See for instance the discussion in the *Elementorum* at I.xii.12 of what good faith requires in the performance of each party's obligations.

[109] For that reason, Ibbetson's view that '[f]or Pufendorf, contractual obligation derived from the duty to keep one's promise' (*An Historical Introduction*, p. 218) perhaps somewhat overstates the significance of promise in Pufendorf's conceptualisation of contract.

[110] *Elementorum*, I.xii.12.

explain why it is that the good faith engendered by such reciprocity means that a contracting party who has not received performance is no longer bound to perform on his side (an entitlement still operative in the modern law under the name of 'retention' or 'justified withholding of performance'), and also why a breach of one of the various promises made by a contracting party enables the whole contract to be dissolved[111] (a concept also maintained today in somewhat modified form in the concept of fundamental or material breach).

Even though Pufendorf does not state that he is specifically turning his attention to contract until much later in his chapter,[112] a significant number of his illustrations in his general treatment of obligations are in fact contractual ones, as will be seen from his treatment of error, extortion, obligations undertaken with enemies, the right of others to bind persons, illegality, formalities, pledge and suretyship. The overall impression conveyed by such attention to contract in the *Elementorum* is that Pufendorf saw contract as the primary vehicle by which voluntary obligations might be assumed; by contrast, the genuinely unilateral promise is given little specific treatment.

The primacy given to contract in Pufendorf's approach to obligations is continued in his later, great work, *De iure naturae et gentium*. In the general chapter on obligations in this work,[113] the place of contract as the principal obligation comes out even more clearly than in the *Elementorum*. Pufendorf begins his analysis of obligations with the idea of the agreement: agreements, he tells us, are necessary to human societies.[114] He continues by explaining in the next section of the chapter (for which, building on canonical ideas, he coins the maxim *'pacta sunt servanda'*) how it is a 'sacred precept of natural law' that everyone must keep his word, that is to say, carry out his promises and agreements.[115] In this paragraph, Pufendorf recaps the development visible in the preceding centuries from enforcement only of contracts in specific form, through canonical enforcement of bare contracts and promises backed by oath, to a rule of general civil enforcement of what is promised or contracted.

There is also in Pufendorf's later work a refutation of the position of Connanus, Pufendorf citing Cicero at length (as well as others, including Grotius, whose similar refutation of Connanus was mentioned earlier) to demonstrate why Connanus's view would negate gratuitous promises and thereby 'destroy all kindness and liberality'.[116] Pufendorf also devotes

---

[111] *Ibid.*, I.xii.12.   [112] *Ibid.*, beginning at I.xii.51.   [113]   *De iure naturae*, III.iv.
[114] *Ibid.*, III.iv.1.   [115] *Ibid.*, III.iv.2.   [116] *Ibid.*, III.v.9.

a separate chapter to the different types of conditions affecting promises and contracts,[117] concluding with an explanation of what differentiates a conditional promise and a pact. He explains that where a condition attached to a promise is 'arbitrary' (that is, relates to a matter which the promisee has the discretion to perform or not), the promisor has no interest to sue if the condition is not fulfilled; whereas, with a pact, if someone undertakes to perform something on the condition that the other party does something, if that other fails to do what he has performed, the first party is entitled to sue for performance (as well as entitled to withhold his own performance).[118] The treatment of such issues relating to conditionality in a single chapter serves to remind us that Pufendorf continued to see contractual obligations as types of promise, even as he was expounding a theory of contract as characterised by mutuality and agreement.

In Pufendorf's writings we can identify the beginnings of the transition from promise to contract as the central idea of European obligations theory, even if, crucially, the language of promise is still employed by Pufendorf to describe the nature of contractual undertakings. While his stress on agreement and mutuality was to become the central concept of contract law, promissory ideas were to remain a feature of the law by virtue of the characterisation of the contract formation process in terms of the conditional promises embodied in offer and acceptance.[119]

(c)　James Dalrymple (Viscount Stair)[120]

The defining treatment of the law of contract and promise in Scots law is that of James Dalrymple, later Viscount Stair, in his work *The Institutions of the Law of Scotland*.[121] Whilst Scotland might be thought geographically remote from traditional centres of legal learning, Stair (like many Scots jurists among his contemporaries and of later generations), had both visited the Continent and studied civilian writers.

The medieval canonical view that unilateral promises were to be enforced was hugely influential in Scotland, in a way that was not the case elsewhere in Europe. The result of the fusion of ecclesiastical and civil jurisdictions in Scotland produced a taxonomy of obligations which recognised both contract and promise as separate obligations. The link

---

[117]　*Ibid.*, III.viii.
[118]　*Ibid.*, III.vii.8. The observations about contractual mutuality were, as noted earlier, also made in Pufendorf's earlier work.
[119]　See discussion in Ch. 4, p. 210.　　　[120]　1619–1695.
[121]　The first edition was published in 1681, with a second following in 1693.

between the two lay in the fact that an offer could be described as a type of promise, albeit one made conditional upon acceptance. In the case of such an offer, no obligation would be assumed by the promisor until the acceptance was forthcoming, whereas a 'pure' promise was intended by the promisor to be binding immediately. Neither type of promise required mutual consideration (indeed such consideration was evidently irrelevant in the case of pure promise). Given the uniqueness in contemporary Western legal systems of this characterisation of promise as an obligation distinct from contract, a somewhat more detailed analysis is merited of Stair's treatment of promise than has been given to the other writers mentioned thus far.

By Stair's time, and in fact since at least the middle of the century before,[122] the *nudum pactum* was enforced in Scots law, the principle of *pacta sunt servanda* having won out in Scotland. Whereas Connanus had disagreed, holding that gratuitous obligations did not even give rise to moral obligations, Stair rejected this view,[123] and further asserted that, even if a promise is not enforceable as lacking a necessary formality, it still obliges the 'conscience and honesty of the promisor'.[124] As the rule of Scots law is proclaimed by Stair to be that, subject to any particular formalities applying in certain cases, all that is required to contract is the consent of the parties – 'every paction produceth action'[125] – a study of the differences between the Roman classes of contract was rejected by him,[126] even though Stair immediately proceeds to divide his study of particular contracts in Scots law according to the Roman categories of loan, mandate, custody, sale, and lease and hire.[127] While the Roman categories are preserved, they are each conceived of as having the unifying theoretical base of an agreement between the parties, a conception largely absent from Roman law.[128] The formalism which characterised the *stipulatio* was to have no place in Scots law.

---

[122] Bare promises had been enforced at least since the decision in *Drummond* v. *Bisset* (1551) Mor. 12381.

[123] *Institutions*, I.x.10. All further references to Stair's writings below are to this work.

[124] The reference to honesty makes one think of the Aristotelian conception of promising as truth-telling.

[125] I.x.10.   [126] *Ibid.*

[127] Respectively, titles xii, xiii, xiv, xv and xvi of Book I.

[128] Though not all of the categories Stair discusses were always conceived of in terms of mutual contracts by Scots Law. The history of lease, for instance, discloses first a conception of lease as a bilateral contract, then a unilateral grant, before finally reverting to a bilateral contract once more: see Hogg, 'Leases: Four Historical Portraits', pp. 380–1.

What of the Roman *pollicitatio*? It seems implausible that Stair conceived of the Roman *pollicitatio* as having any place in Scots law: there is a single mention in the *Institutions* to 'pollicitation', where it appears in the phrase 'promise, pollicitation or offer, paction and contract'.[129] There has been a great deal of ultimately inconclusive debate amongst academics as to what Stair meant by a pollicitation,[130] though there is nothing to suggest that he meant it in the Roman sense of an enforceable unilateral promise in favour of a municipality. It is more likely that he was using the term as either a synonym for a unilateral promise in general, or for an offer. The question is not helped by the fact that in the first edition of the *Institutions* the phrase reads '… pollicitation, or offer, …', but the comma is not present in the second edition. As Sellar has commented, we shall probably never know what sense Stair intended, though this is not problematic: as the word is never used by him again, it can be safely ignored.

Stair can say that 'pactions, contracts, covenants, and agreements, are synonymous terms'.[131] As no mutual cause or consideration was required for a valid contract, gratuitous contracts were perfectly valid,[132] though requiring the assent of both parties. Further than this, however, Stair definitively upheld the obligatory nature of a seriously intended unilateral promise, which he described as that 'which is simple and pure, and hath not implied as a condition, the acceptance of another'.[133] The contrary view of his fellow Northern natural lawyer, Grotius, is specifically rejected. The reason for Scots law adhering to the enforcement of the unilateral promise is stated to be that 'the canon law having taken off the exception of the civil law, *de nudo pacto*'.[134] There is no citation of canonical sources here, but Stair may perhaps have been confident that his readers would have been so familiar with this aspect of canon law that no such citation was necessary, though some indication of how the cross-over from canon to civil law had occurred would have been helpful. Nor is there citation of Spanish scholastic sources in support of Stair's view, though, as noted earlier, Covarruvias, Soto and Molina all held to the view that, as all promises were binding, an acceptance of a promise was not required in principle (though a contrary Scholastic view was held by Lessius).

As noted earlier, Molina had justified the exception that a promise to contract (in other words, an offer) had to be accepted as a rule peculiar

---

[129] I.x.3.
[130] Smith, 'Jus Quaesitum Tertio', 15; Ashton Cross, 'Bare Promise in Scots Law'; Rodger, 'Molina, Stair and the *Ius Quaesitum Tertio*'; MacCormack, 'A Note on Stair's Use of the Term *Pollicitatio*'.
[131] I.x.10.   [132] I.x.12.   [133] I.x.4.   [134] I.x.4.

to onerous contracts: because onerous contracts created mutual obligations, they required mutual assent and thus had to be accepted. Stair also describes an offer as a conditional promise (a 'promise ... pendent upon acceptation'), to the same effect that it does not bind until acceptance. Thus, in a similar vein to Molina, Stair reasons that 'an offer accepted is a contract, because it is the deed of the two, the offerer and accepter'.[135] The early adoption of the civilian offer and acceptance analysis, in contrast with the Common Law's late borrowing of this approach from Pothier, is noteworthy.

Evidently, in Stair's scheme, which classifies both an offer and a unilateral promise as species of promise, it becomes crucial to identify which was intended by a promisor. While this may be a difficult task in some cases, especially given that a unilateral promise may be subject to a condition, the distinction is crucial for the obligatory effect. Stair makes this plain by distinguishing the types of condition which can be attached to a promise: there are those conditions which are, 'as in mutual contracts' (in other words, as contained in an offer), suspensive of the obligatory force of the promise, but there are other conditions which do not prevent a promise from being immediately obligatory, albeit that the obligation cannot be enforced against the promisor until the condition is performed by the promisee.[136] The distinction in effect between these types of condition Stair sees as exemplifying a division between those obligations which he calls μονοπλευρος ('monopleuros': one party, or unilateral) and those which are δευπλευρος ('deupleiros': two party, or bilateral).[137] There is further discussion of the difficulties faced by courts of distinguishing offers and conditional promises in the modern law later in this work.[138]

While we have seen that Stair rejected the natural lawyers Connanus and Grotius in certain matters, he follows them in others. For instance,

---

[135] I.x.4.   [136] I.x.5.

[137] While it had been suggested that the terms may have been invented by Stair himself (see Mersinis, 'Stair, *Institutions*, 1.10.5: A Linguistic Note'), this view overlooked the fact that the terms were also used roughly contemporaneously by Pufendorf in his *De jure naturae*, III.v.1: 'adventitious obligations arise from an act, either μονοπλευρος or δευπλευρος, of which the former is a gratuitous promise, the latter a pact.' More recent scholarship suggests that both Stair and Pufendorf may have taken the terms directly from the source where they seem first to have been used, that being Arnold Vinnius's Commentary on Justinian's *Institutes*, published in Amsterdam in 1658 (the relevant passage is his Commentary on Inst. III.xiv, then numbered III.xiii). While Stair may subsequently have become familiar with Pufendorf's writings, the relevant chronology suggests that Stair found his direct inspiration for adoption of the terms in Vinnius: see further Richter, 'Did Stair know Pufendorf?'.

[138] See discussion in Ch. 4, pp. 213–14.

the view of Lessius, Grotius and Pufendorf is adopted (though without citation of them) in relation to the outward expression of consent necessary before a promise can bind; the silent, inward promise is not (contrary to Soto and Molina) effective. While, says Stair, conventional obligations (like contract and promise) arise from 'our will and consent',[139] outward expression of that will or consent is required in order to indicate that the party binding himself has moved beyond the first two 'acts in the will', namely 'desire' and 'resolution', to the third and crucial act, that of 'engagement'.[140] A resolution, being merely a purpose to do that which is desired, can be altered without any fault on the part of the resolver (unless, says Stair, we declare the resolution in order to assure others, when its alteration might import 'levity and inconstancy, and sometimes deceit and unfaithfulness'[141] when presumably some remedy might arise, though Stair does not indicate which).

Stair's affirmation of the obligatory nature of the unilateral promise also permitted his description of the enforceable right in favour of a third party, styled a *jus quaesitum tertio*, as a species of promise,[142] though as this subject is treated at length in Chapter 5, nothing more will be said of that case here.

What of Stair's general contractual philosophy? He stands at the cusp of the change between the natural law tradition and later rationalist conceptions of law, demonstrating an artful blend of the established tradition with the emerging preference for rationality. Whilst the natural law tradition is marked in Stair, and he demonstrates a thorough knowledge of the Northern as well as Spanish natural law schools, distinctively Aristotelian-Thomist ideas become subjugated in Stair to other considerations. Thus, while one finds in Stair's writing a blend of natural law, reason, Scripture and Aristotelian virtues, the last of these is very muted: essentially the autonomy of parties and the will triumphs over ideas of commutative justice (such as the just price) and liberality.[143] Reason is cleverly used to bolster the idea that nothing is more in conformity with the natural tendency to adhere to the faith of promises.

Stair makes an express reference to the Aristotelian typology of commutative and distributive justice,[144] though this is not explicitly drawn

---

[139] I.x.2.   [140] I.x.2.   [141] I.x.2.   [142] I.x.5.

[143] Reid has posited the plausible argument that the positive role accorded by Aristotle to virtue was supplanted in the mind of Protestant jurists such as Stair by 'a deep sense of the depravity of human nature' ('Thomas Aquinas and Viscount Stair', p. 201).

[144] I.i.2. Stair comments of distributive justice that it is 'now almost wholly devolved upon public authority'.

upon by him in his analysis of contract law.[145] Likewise, though liberality is mentioned,[146] it does not appear in his treatment of promises, which is a noteworthy absence: had Stair wished to underpin his exegesis of obligations with Aristotelian virtues, his discussion of gratuitous promise would have been an obvious place for such virtues to be mentioned. Instead, in rejecting Connanus's position that gratuitous promises do not give rise to any moral obligation to perform, as lacking an onerous mutual cause, Stair cites the canon law, trust between men, natural equity, divine law and commercial considerations, but not the virtue of liberality.[147] In what little Stair says of donations, there is also barely a reference to liberality.[148] As for the just price, though he mentions the concept of enorm lesion (based upon the Roman *laesio enormis*), its ambit is restricted to transactions undertaken by minors.[149] For contracts in general, Stair ultimately rejects any estimation of the value of the exchange than that of the parties themselves. Though he says that it is 'the property of permutative contracts [that is, mutual contracts of exchange], that the purpose of the contractors is to keep an equality in the worth and value of the things', he notes that Scots law has rejected the Roman rule,[150] approved of by Grotius, that sales of land at less than half their just value are invalid. There follows a thoroughly modern discussion of how value in exchanges is to be estimated, demonstrating Stair's appreciation of the subjectivity of value, with citation of the *Codex* and Seneca in support of his view. Stair ultimately concludes that 'the equality required in these contracts [of exchange], cannot be in any other rate than the parties agree on'.[151] The departure from Aristotelian ideas of commutative justice and the fair price is striking: in effect, though Stair pays lip service to the idea of an

---

[145] Reid has commented on Stair's use of Aristotle that 'there are slim pickings in the search for explicit borrowings from either Aristotle or Aquinas for the Aristotelian character of Stair's work lies in its underlying method, argument and conceptual framework' ('Thomas Aquinas and Viscount Stair', p. 197).

[146] I.viii.2.   [147] I.x.10.

[148] He refers to it by name (at I.vii.2) in relation to the gratitude due by a donee, rather than in relation to the liberality of the donor. Stair says that such gratitude is not due by a donee in cases of necessity (see D. 5.3.25.11). He also discusses (at I.iii.5) natural obligations of 'beneficence', noting that these cannot be enforced at law, as well as the 'inward obligations' of 'affection, love, kindness, &c'. The status of these virtues as moral but not legal obligations is telling in an author writing at the boundary of the natural law and enlightenment eras.

[149] I.vi.44; II.xii.31.   [150] *Codex*, 4.44.2.

[151] I.x.14, though he notes the exception made for penalty and irritancy clauses, which are properly regulated at law, as well as in the case of contracts obtained through 'fraud or guile', where the obligation of delinquence (i.e. delict) provides a remedy.

equality of price, by allowing such a price to be measured according to the free choice of the parties, he substantively rejects the external regulation of bargains that was inherent in the Aristotelian-Thomist approach.

Though the values of liberality and commutative justice are sub-dued in Stair, with the will of the parties ultimately triumphing, there remains in Stair something which is uncommon in the modern law but was common in the Thomist tradition, and that is frequent reference to the 'cause' of obligations. However, these references are included to emphasise that obligations may be validly undertaken for any cause, whether onerous or gratuitous, those two terms supplanting the lan-guage of commutation and liberality. The admission that *any* cause may support an obligation, and the primacy given by Stair to enforcing the faith which had been pledged by a promisor,[152] represents a diminished role for *causa*. No longer must one look, as in Roman law, for a *causa* in order to clothe the bare pact with legality. Despite this abandonment by Stair of the earlier significance of *causa*, his treatment of the Roman categories of contract indicates that the underlying purpose which a transaction was designed to achieve might still be of some taxonomic and pedagogic assistance.

One field in which it might be argued that the Aristotelian tradition influenced Stair is that of error. As explained in the last chapter, the concept of man's end, the *summum bonum*, was central to Aristotelian philosophy. This idea was developed by Aquinas and later the Spanish scholastics to enumerate specific ends for particular transactions. One could not achieve the end desired in undertaking a transaction if one were mistaken as to the 'substance' of what was being undertaken, substance having a specific Aristotelian meaning distinguishing it from the exter-nal 'accidents' of a transaction. This Aristotelian interpretation on the substance of a transaction was able to be superimposed by the glossators and late scholastics on to a fragment of Ulpian in the Digest[153] stating that, in contracts of sale, an error as to the substance (*error in substantia*) of the subject being transacted precluded consent. Stair would have been well aware of this understanding of the Roman text, given his familiarity with scholastic writings, but to what extent did it influence him? When he comes to consider error, he states that a deed entered into between parties is to be taken as valid unless there is error 'in the substantials of the deed, and then there is no true consent, and the deed is null'.[154] Later, Stair states

---

[152] '[T]here is nothing more natural, than to stand to the faith of our pactions' (I.x.1).
[153] D. 18.1.9 (Stair cites this text at I.x.13).   [154] I.ix.9.

more generally, without specific reference to deeds, that '[t]hose who err in the substantials of what is done, contract not'.[155] Stair's conclusion is that, unless the error is substantial, its being the cause of a transaction will not invalidate consent.[156] The language of error in the substantials to describe relevant error is not conclusive of an Aristotelian approach, however, as the language is already found in the Roman texts, and it is a matter of debate whether the Roman authors had the Aristotelian sense in mind when using the term.[157] However, Stair also uses the standard scholastic example of marriage to draw out his point about error in the substantials: he contrasts the example of a marriage undertaken to the wrong party, which he classifies as just such an error in the substantials, with a marriage to a woman undertaken in the mistaken belief that she is a virgin, or rich, or well-natured, each of which errors would go not to the substance of the transaction but rather to the accidents (though Stair does not use the latter Aristotelian term). This distinction between types of error affecting a marriage had been discussed by Aquinas, as well as by the Spanish scholastics, who showed a typically canon law interest in errors *in persona*. This might suggest a scholastic approach by Stair to the question, though the contrary view has been argued.[158]

Though Stair does not very often cite directly from the canon law, and does not do so in relation to the obligatory force of promises, from the discussion above it will be evident that the authority of the canon law towards promises was decisive for Stair.[159] The canon law was not of course leading Stair to argue for a new position, given that he was describing an already established Scottish common law jurisprudence of his day, but his view certainly solidified the position given the authority which his *Institutions* came to have. Why the canon law position had come to be adopted by Scots common law has been explained in Chapter 2: essentially it prevailed through a fusion of the ecclesiastical and common law jurisdictions in Scotland. More often in Stair, however, there is direct reference to primary scriptural sources, indicating that Stair was not content

---

[155] I.x.13.   [156] I.ix.9.

[157] It is arguable that Ulpian had in mind Greek philosophical concepts in his discussion given that, in D. 18.1.9.2, when he cites the example of vinegar sold as wine, he refers to the ουσια (ousia), the being or essence, of an object, a Greek philosophical notion found in both Platonic and Aristotelian works: see further Schermaier, *Materia*, pp. 131–62.

[158] See Macleod, 'Before Bell: The Roots of Error in the Scots Law of Contract'.

[159] He says of the canon law generally that 'even where the Pope's authority is rejected, yet consideration must be had to those laws … as containing many equitable and profitable laws, which because of their weighty matter, and their being once received, may more fitly be retained than rejected' (I.i.14).

to adopt a more humanist version of natural law, such as is found in some treatises of continental natural lawyers, but was keen to stress the inherent link between reason, natural law, and the Christian (particularly the Protestant) faith. In support of the common law's upholding of naked pactions and promises, for instance, Stair specifically cites a passage from the Book of Proverbs enjoining the listener to adhere to the 'words of thy mouth',[160] as well as a verse in Hebrews stating that 'he is faithful that promised',[161] the reference being to the faithfulness of divine promises. It is significant that this reference to divine fidelity to promises is used to underpin Stair's approbation of the legal force of human promises. This is consistent with Stair's overarching view, expressed earlier in the same title on conventional obligations, that it is God who obliges us to the performance of voluntary obligations.[162] For Stair, the pattern of human fidelity to pledged performances is found in the fidelity of God to what He has promised.

Stair's magisterial treatment of voluntary obligations gave Scots law a distinctive approach to promise that was to endure, as discussion of the modern law in Part 2 of this work will indicate.

4.   Eighteenth and nineteenth centuries

(a)   English law

There are some pre-eighteenth century indications in English law of a general concept of contract. For instance, in a case from 1550, *Reniger* v. *Fogossa*,[163] it was remarked that an

> agreement concerning personal things is a mutual assent of the parties, and ought to be executed with a recompence, or else ought to be so certain and sufficient, as to give an action or other remedy for recompence: and if it is not so, then it shall not be called an agreement, but rather a nude communication without effect.

This is a late usage of the term 'recompence', which together with *causa* and consideration are three terms commonly encountered until consideration alone came to dominate from around 1560 onwards. This definition of a contractual agreement, including the requirement for mutual

---

[160] Prov. 6:1.   [161] Heb. 10:23.

[162] '[God] hath given that liberty in our power, that we may give it up to others, or restrain and engage it, whereby God obliges us to performance by mediation of our own will' (I.x.1).

[163] 1 Plowd. 1, 75 Eng. Rep. 1 (KB 1550).

performance, is remarkable given the date of its pronouncement: it was not generally until the end of the eighteenth century that contract as a distinct concept was generally conceived of separately from the various actions recognised at law, the approach of Blackstone being a good example of such later understanding.[164] Prior to this point, contractual material in the few legal treatises available was scattered between treatment of the various actions, nominate contracts, and torts.[165] In the early to mid-eighteenth century, there is very little of what might be called contractual theory, though occasional, somewhat unsatisfactory examples crop up.[166] Where, for instance, in Gilbert's unpublished 'Treatise on Contract', theoretical matters such as seriousness of intent to contract were raised, the discussion was cut short by a simple reference to consideration as demonstrating such intent without any exploration of whether other ways might conceivably demonstrate such intention.[167] Similarly, Blackstone defined consideration as the 'reason which moves the party contracting to enter into the contract' but qualified this by referring without demurring to the civilian view that it must be 'something mutual, reciprocal – something given in exchange' without explaining why unreciprocated reasons for contracting cannot count.[168] Such unsatisfactory references to consideration demonstrate the problem which the doctrine was to pose for the emerging will theory of contract, discussed in Chapter 2 and further below: if the will was paramount, why was it necessary in addition to demonstrate the presence of consideration, or an undertaking under seal, before a contract or a unilateral promise would be enforced?

This difficulty was perceived by the courts, and some judges attempted to restrict the ambit of consideration as a result.[169] Chief among those who attempted to do so was Lord Mansfield, who famously suggested in *Pillans* v. *van Mierop*,[170] a case concerning consideration in relation to a

---

[164] Blackstone defined contract as 'an agreement upon sufficient consideration to do or not to do a particular thing' (*Commentaries*, ii.442).

[165] Ibbetson, *An Historical Introduction*, p. 215.

[166] An example is Henry Ballow's *Treatise on Equity* (1737), which contains some brief statements on contract plundered from Pufendorf, overlaid with the Common law requirement of consideration.

[167] The relevant passages from Gilbert's 'Treatise on Contract' (BL MS Harg 265, ff 39–40, 43) are discussed by Ibbetson, *An Historical Introduction*, p. 237, and Swain, 'The Classical Model of Contract', 517.

[168] Blackstone, *Commentaries*, ii.443–4.

[169] See further generally on the development of the doctrine of consideration during this period, Swain, 'The Changing Nature of the Doctrine of Consideration'.

[170] (1765) 3 Burr 1663. Lord Mansfield remarked that 'I take it, that the ancient notion about the want of consideration was for the sake of evidence only: for when it is reduced into

bill of exchange, that the requirement for consideration should not apply in mercantile contracts. This general rebellion against consideration was disapproved of by the House of Lords in its later judgment in *Rann* v. *Hughes*,[171] though the precise result in *Pillans*, excusing the need for consideration in cases of bills of exchange, was upheld as a matter of mercantile practice. Other situations which caused difficulty for the restrictive requirement of consideration, such as charitable promises and family arrangements, were able to be dealt with under the law of trust.[172] Such solutions were not, however, as simple and as elegant as would have been a development allowing the general enforcement of a unilateral promise (including one in favour of a third party) or a gratuitous contract so long as it was seriously intended to have legal effect.

It is in the late eighteenth century that one begins to see common law writers and judges using the idea of agreement as the basis upon which to build a general notion of contract as an obligation out of the existing law of assumpsit, covenant and other actions possessing elements of agreement.[173] Not that such definitions did not exist before, because, as is evident from the quotation from *Reniger* v. *Fogossa* above, they did, but these were isolated attempts which did not catch on. This transition to seeing contract as having a conceptual basis and force in the agreement of the parties, albeit augmented by the necessary additional requirement of consideration and occasionally writing, was solidified by the appearance of, and frequent reference to, Pothier's *Treatise*, with its clear treatment of contract as a will-based obligation defined by reference to the agreement of the parties. The principles of the French law of obligations, as expounded by Pothier, provided the basis of developing the law of England in a number of fields. They provided, for instance, a basis for the emerging analysis of the contract formation procedure

---

writing, as in covenants, specialities, bonds etc there was no objection to the want of consideration. And the Statute of Frauds proceeded upon the same principle.'

[171] (1778) 4 Bro PC 27, 7 TR 350n. Lord Skynner, taking a natural law approach, did remark however that 'It is undoubtedly true that every man is by the law of nature bound to fulfil his engagements.'

[172] In relation to family arrangements settled by way of trust, the natural love and affection of family members was considered adequate consideration to support the trust. The need for such consideration in trusts was dropped at the beginning of the nineteenth century. See further on these points, Ibbetson, *An Historical Introduction*, pp. 206–8.

[173] Gordley, *Philosophical Origins*, p. 136. Nineteenth-century treatise writers who defined contract in agreement terms included: Comyn, *Law of Contracts and Promises*; Colebrooke, *Treatise on Obligations and Contracts*; Chitty, *Treatise on the Law of Contracts*; Addison, *Treatise on the Law of Contracts*; Leake, *Elements of the Law of Contracts*; and Pollock, *Principles of Contract at Law and in Equity*.

in offer and acceptance terms.[174] Pothier's views on the entitlement of the victim of a breach of contract to damages in the performance measure also influenced the decision in the seminal English damages case *Hadley* v. *Baxendale*.[175] The judgment of Alderson B in that case demonstrates some marked similarities to the views of Pothier as adopted in the Louisiana Civil Code of 1825:[176] the influence of Pothier stretched not just across the English Channel but the Atlantic also.

The increasing focus in English law on the will of the parties, manifested in their agreement to contract, has been characterised as an external imposition, rather than an internal development,[177] though it could surely be rejoindered that the movement away from the action of debt, with its emphasis upon the factual question of whether a debt existed, to the action of assumpsit, with its emphasis upon whether a party had willed, under a promise, to contract with another, had already represented an earlier, if rather more muted, emphasis upon the will.

Where did this leave the promise as a way of describing contract? While the idea of agreement was now in vogue, this did not obliterate promissory descriptions of contract. Sometimes agreement and promise were used as interchangeable descriptions. Thus, in Addison's *Treatise on Contracts*, a contract is described as a either a promise or an agreement, though the promissory description presupposes consideration being given for the promise and thus excludes gratuitous promises.[178] Moreover, in general the individual undertakings of contractual parties were still referred to as promises, albeit promises which had to be exchanged before there was a contract.

The growing emphasis upon agreement meant that, in conceptual terms, genuinely unilateral undertakings were inevitably further squeezed out from the category of valid transactions. On the other hand, some relief for bilateral though gratuitous transactions was provided through judgments in which the courts managed to concoct consideration to suit the needs of particular cases or in which further exceptions to the rule were created. It was settled, for instance, that the courts would not question the adequacy of consideration, for, as Pollock put it, whatever 'a man chooses to bargain for must be conclusively taken to be of some value to him'.[179]

---

[174] See discussion of Pothier's writings below, at pp. 152–7.
[175] (1854) 9 Exch 341.   [176] Ibbetson, *An Historical Introduction*, pp. 229–32.
[177] Ibbetson argues that the will theory 'was imposed on the Common Law from the outside rather than generated from within' (*ibid.*, p. 221).
[178] Addison, *Treatise on Contracts*, II.i.
[179] Pollock, *Principles of Contract* (9th edn, 1921), p. 186.

This clearly prevented the development of any line of cases which would have prevented contracts being challenged as extortionate bargains, and gave the common law a character which was far removed from Aquinas's insistence upon the just price and commutative justice.

The rise of agreement, with its focus on the will of the parties, as the basis and source of contract had a number of other effects. It posed more urgently a theoretical problem for the privity rule: if parties wanted to confer an enforceable right upon a third party, why should not such a right be recognised? Despite there being no good answer to this question, the privity rule was maintained, being reaffirmed in 1861 in *Tweddle* v. *Atkinson*.[180] The notion of agreement posed a similar question to promises made under seal: if agreement were so essential, how was it that simply by using the form of a seal the need for such acceptance could be dispensed with? Again, this question was never satisfactorily answered. Will theory also produced a tendency to dress some things up as implied agreements of the parties, which ought more honestly to have been described simply as legal rules. Thus, rather than take the approach of the civil law and state that there is a rule that destruction of the subjects of a contract subsequent to formation of contract terminates the contract, courts chose to talk in terms of an implied condition of the contract that the subjects continue in existence.[181] This sort of reasoning takes the idea of the will to extremes, and did much to discredit in the eyes of some the theory of contract as resting upon the human will. A further effect of the rise of will theory was that it provided the basis, when borrowed by Pollock from the German jurist Savigny,[182] of the idea of the intention to create legal relations, allowing English law to explain why certain transactions, such as family arrangements, did not have effect as contracts.

The ideas of agreement and will do not provide an obvious solution to the perennially difficult question of contractual error, and in the eighteenth and early nineteenth centuries, though common law and equitable courts granted relief in cases of mistake, they did so without providing any clear conceptual basis for so doing.[183] Nor, until 1860, does one find

---

[180] (1861) 1 B&S 393, 121 Eng. Rep. 762.
[181] See Blackburn J, in *Taylor* v. *Caldwell* (1863) 3 B & S 826.
[182] Ibbetson, *An Historical Introduction*, p. 233.
[183] Equity provided relief in two main types of case. There was, first, a general Chancery jurisdiction to rectify documents which did not properly reflect the underlying agreement of the parties; second, in cases of unilateral error, if there was evidence of dubious practices taking advantage of such an error, relief would be afforded. See further Ibbetson, *ibid.*, pp. 210–11, and Gordley, *Philosophical Origins*, pp. 140–6.

any treatise writer attempting a systematic examination of the conceptual nature of error.[184] When such academic analysis was forthcoming, it was in the civilian terms of 'essential' or 'substantial' error, with appropriate citation of civilian authority. Pollock took a different line, preferring the approach of Savigny that mistake mattered when there was a failure of the will of the party to match its apparent declaration (an error in transaction) but not if there was a simple error in motive.[185]

What is interesting from a comparative perspective is how many of the eighteenth- and nineteenth-century common law developments had clearly been waiting for a solid doctrinal basis to allow them to happen. If one compares continental systems, or Scots law, it is noticeable how such developments were present in earlier centuries precisely because of the existence of such general contractual doctrine and an earlier focus on the idea of agreement and the *pacta sunt servanda* rule.

(b)   Scots law

Following Stair's approach to contract and promise, at first natural law thinking continued. Andrew MacDowall (Lord Bankton), produced a similar work to Stair's own, his *Institutes of the Laws of Scotland* (the first volume being published in 1751). Like Stair, Bankton stressed the nature of man as a rational being, and saw law as embodying that which was 'just, right and good'.[186] Where the law did not command or forbid man, the 'freedom of man's will'[187] was paramount. Like Stair, Bankton extensively discussed the law of nature.[188] He also recognised the Aristotelian division between commutative and distributive justice,[189] equating commutative justice with the law of contract: '[c]ommutative justice is that which is incident to contract and mutual intercourse of negotiations among man'.[190] While he seems to suggest that an equality in contractual

---

[184] See Macpherson's work on Anglo-Indian Contract Law, *Outlines of the Law of Contracts as Administered in the Courts of British India*. See also Leake, *Elements of Contracts*.

[185] Pollock, *Principles*, Ch. 8 (mistake) (Pollock refers to Savigny's 'masterly essay' on error). This essentially Germanic view of error is gaining in favour in a number of legal systems in the early twenty-first century.

[186] *Institutes*. I.i.1 (all further references to Bankton's writings are to the *Institutes*).

[187] I.i.1.

[188] I.i.18–28. Like Stair, he sees nature and reason as intimately entwined: 'This original [i.e. natural] law is frequently termed the law or dictate of reason, because by the use of reason, duly improv'd, the laws of nature may be discovered.' (I.i.24)

[189] I.i.7. Bankton gives no specific citation of the Aristotelian source of this classification.

[190] I.i.8.

performance must be observed,[191] elsewhere he specifically rejects the idea that a failure to observe the precepts of this species of justice gives rise to any actionable claim at law, thus elevating the human will over external criteria for judging contractual justice.[192] Like Stair, Bankton asserts that conventional obligations derive 'from the will of the parties'[193] and that contract is based upon agreement.[194]

The similarity of Bankton's own thought with Stair marked a pattern of acceptance of Stair's ideas and legal structure which was to be continued by later writers. Bankton's one distinctive feature is perhaps that he follows each of the subject headings in his work with a discussion of the English law on the matter. Thus, on the taxonomy of obligations, he states that obligations in England 'may be divided into such as arise from contract, or quasi contract; or from a delinquency and crime, or a quasi delinquency, as they are termed in the civil law'.[195] This in fact seems rather generous to contemporary English understanding of the law. Bankton appears to have been projecting on to the then English law a civilian structure which he thought might usefully explain it, rather than a structure which English lawyers would themselves have generally recognised the law as possessing. It is only to the judgments of Lord Mansfield, appointed as a judge in 1756, some five years after Bankton's first volume appeared,[196]

---

[191] Bankton states that commutative justice means that 'an equality must be observed in our contracts, and we must perform the terms of our contracts … without distinction' (I.i.10).

[192] I.iv.12.   [193] I.xi.

[194] I.xi.1. Bankton states rather oddly that contract is the agreement of 'one or more persons', in contrast to the usual understanding, following Stair, that contractual agreement requires the consent of two or more persons to be bound at law. One must conclude that Bankton had in mind to include gratuitous contracts, where only one party comes under any onerous duty, but the reference to the agreement of a sole party expresses that idea rather clumsily, as even in gratuitous contracts the recipient of the benefit must at the very least accept the offer in his favour and hence agree to what is offered.

[195] I.iv.19.

[196] The seed planted by Lord Mansfield did not always find receptive soil. On the one hand, in the third edition of Chitty's Practical Treatise on the Law of Contracts (1841), it was still being asserted that 'English lawyers generally use the word obligation, in reference to … only a particular species of Contracts, that is, Bonds' (p. 1). By contrast, one may note Colebrooke's Treatise (1818), which contains a detailed discussion of obligations, and their various characteristics, with citation of the Digest, Pothier and Erskine; Leake's Elements of the Law of Contracts (1867), containing an introduction setting contract within the wider obligational framework; and, Anson's Principles of the English Law of Contract (1879), which includes discussion (pp. 6–8) of the 'various modes' by which obligations originate, including from agreement, delict, quasi-contract and breach of contract.

that one can really date the origins of a genuine understanding of a 'law of obligations' in the Common law.

Bankton's rough contemporary, Henry Home (Lord Kames), was the last major Scots jurist who merits the title of a natural lawyer. Kames was particularly interested in refuting the view of his fellow Scot David Hume that justice was an entirely human creation and that there was no such thing as the natural law. In Kames's *Essays on the Principles of Morality and Natural Religion*, first published in 1751 (the same year as Bankton's first volume), he considered, before rejecting, Hume's view, advanced in his *Treatise of Human Nature*,[197] that '[t]he sense of justice and injustice is not deriv'd from nature, but arises artificially, tho' necessarily from education, and human conventions'.[198] Kames asserted a similar defence of the natural intuition of man (his 'moral sense or conscience') in relation to right and wrong in his later *Principles of Equity*.[199] Kames grounded both contract and promise in the natural law, saying they had 'a solid foundation in human nature'.[200] He refuted Hume's view that promises have neither moral value nor are intelligible to human beings without having been established by human convention. On the contrary, says Kames, promises and contracts are based upon human nature: 'mutual trust and confidence, without which there can be no useful society, enter into the character of the human species'.[201] Thus, even though a promise made to someone might not be enforceable by anyone after that person's death, the promisor would suffer 'reproach and blame' if he neglected to do that which he had promised.[202] Flatly contradicting Hume's view, Kames asserts:

> The performance of a deliberate promise has, in all ages, been considered as a duty. We have that sense of a promise, as what we are strictly bound to perform; and the natural stings which attend other crimes, namely remorse, and a sense of merited punishment.[203]

Having grounded promise in human nature, and explained the consequences of breach of promise, he adds an interesting remark on the source of a promise's obligational force:

---

[197] First published in 1739.   [198] Hume, *Treatise*, 3.2.1.17.
[199] *Principles of Equity*, pp. 1–5. See also, for instance, pp. 8–9: 'That there is in mankind a common sense of what is right and wrong, and an uniformity of opinion, is a matter of fact, of which the only infallible proof is observation and experience.'
[200] *Essays on the Principles of Morality and Natural Religion*, p. 113.
[201] *Ibid.*, p. 114.   [202] *Principles of Equity*, p. 16.
[203] *Essays on the Principles of Morality*, p. 116.

> Were there by nature no trust nor reliance upon promises, breach of promise would be a matter of indifferency. Therefore the essence of a promise consists in keeping faith. The reliance upon us, produced by our own act, constitutes the obligation. We feel ourselves bound to perform: we consider it as our duty.[204]

This view bears a degree of similarity to the position advanced by modern day reliance theorists, as well as to the views of contemporary utilitarians.[205] Although Kames has been defending natural law theory, he does not here ground the obligational force of promise (or contract) in the duty of obedience we owe to God, and hence derivatively to others, as Stair would have it, but rather in the effect a promise has upon the party to whom it is made. This is a somewhat weaker argument for the force of promises, as it would seem to exclude from the category of valid promises those which have not yet been relied upon because, for instance, the promisee has yet to hear of it or, even having heard of it, has yet to take any course of action which might cause him detriment were the promise to be avoided.

Kames's defence of promises and contracts as binding, primarily because they are expressions of fidelity which give rise to reliance, is, within the Scottish tradition, an unusual justification of voluntary obligations. It is not advanced by any other prominent Scottish jurist, save by the twentieth-century legal theorist MacCormick, who argues that intention to create reliance, or knowledge of likely reliance, grounds promises.[206] To do justice to Kames's position, however, it should be noticed that his reliance justification is but one of a number of reasons he advances for the force of promises.

The other notable Scots jurists of the late eighteenth and nineteenth century added little by way of contract theory. John Erskine, in his *Institute of the Law of Scotland* published in 1773, had almost nothing on the theory of contract,[207] and George Bell made equally scant mention of contract theory in his *Commentaries*.[208] Indeed, by the end of the

---

[204] *Ibid.*, p. 117.

[205] See, for instance, the utilitarian justification of promises advanced by the contemporary English philosopher Paley, *Principles of Moral and Political Philosophy*, p. 106.

[206] MacCormick, *Legal Right and Social Democracy*, Ch. 10, especially pp. 202–3.

[207] His view that '[c]onsensual contracts are those, which, by Roman Law, might be perfected by consent alone, without the intervention either of things or of writing' both fails to express the proper breadth of contract in Scots law as well as to mention the non-enforceability in Roman law of the very bare pact (*nudum pactum*) which he cites.

[208] He simply follows Stair and Bankton in noting that contract is an act of the human will and has its obligatory force for that reason: *Commentaries*, iii.1.

eighteenth century, when the age of Enlightenment ideas were giving way to the Age of Commerce, Scots contractual theory seems to have gone into abeyance. It appears that Stair's view was so soundly entrenched and universally accepted that no need was perceived for continued theoretical debate. While Stair's natural law views were no longer required, their paring off from the basis he posited for contract and promise, as lying in the voluntary undertaking of liability, proved perfectly suited for the needs of commercial practice. Where courts felt the need to pronounce on matters of contract theory, they asserted just such a will-based approach, though one which emphasised, for commercial reasons, the need for objective interpretation of the will. Thus, it could be confidently asserted by the great, late Victorian judge, Lord Dunedin, that 'commercial contracts cannot be arranged by what people think in their inmost minds. Commercial contracts are made according to what people say.'[209]

(c) Civilian systems

(i) German law

Discussion in Chapter 2 disclosed how, in the canon law, the *pacta sunt servanda* principle of general contractual enforcement came to replace the restrictive Roman rule of *ex nudo pacto non oritor actio*. It seems that the maxim *pacta sunt servanda* was coined in those precise terms by Pufendorf, building perhaps on the work of Matthew Wesenbeck, a Dutchman who taught at Jena and Wittenberg in Germany and who disseminated the canonical idea to civil lawyers. A similar approach was adopted by the French jurist Charles Dumoulin, who also taught for some time in Germany. The teaching of this canonist rule combined with mercantile law and natural law principles, resulting in a general acceptance of the *pacta sunt servanda* rule in Germany by the end of the eighteenth century.[210] While such an approach was stated frequently to have been in accordance with existing Germanic customary laws, the evidence for this is scant.[211]

By the nineteenth century, German jurists had ceased to utilise the concept of *causa* when describing the fundamental nature of contract, the question of whether parties had seriously intended to contract being now considered matters of procedure and evidence.[212] Jurists were now describing contract instead as a declaration of will of the parties to the

---

[209] *Muirhead & Turnbull v. Dickson* (1905) 7 F 686, 694.
[210] Zimmermann, *Law of Obligations*, pp. 539–40.
[211] *Ibid.*, p. 541.   [212] *Ibid.*, pp. 541–2.

contract, and as a type of juristic act. Though some juristic acts were unilateral (such as a testamentary provision), contract was bilateral, requiring the presence and concurrence of the will of both parties to constitute the act.[213] Such a will-based approach, criticised by some jurists,[214] gave little room to the unilateral promise, save for exceptional occurrences such as the promise of reward. German law might have gone in another direction, however. The editor responsible for the codification of contract law in the German Code, Franz Philipp von Kübel, initially developed a radical model, quite at odds with the then existing law and the Pandectist approach, providing that the promise to render a performance to another would not necessarily require an acceptance on the part of the party to whom performance was to be rendered.[215] This radical approach was justified by von Kübel on the basis of modern German legal development, the needs of commercial communication and legal life,[216] as well as the free will of the promisor. As to free will, von Kübel argued that, if the promisor wished to exercise his will by binding himself, he should not require to justify such an exercise of the will by the need to have the concurrence of a second will.[217] Von Kübel's model was the subject of much discussion at the meeting of the First Commission of the drafters of the BGB, but did not receive support. Following the discussion, von Kübel decided to withdraw his general proposal on promises, to concentrate instead on the application of the promissory principle to certain specific cases. The specific uses for the promises which were agreed at the Second Commission (such as promises of a reward) are discussed in later chapters of this work. Notably, one important case that von Kübel saw as an example of a unilateral promise – a right given under a contract to a third party – was not so classified in the final text. Von Kübel's defeat was to set modern German law's face largely against the idea of the binding unilateral promise.

(ii)   Robert Pothier

Pothier[218] stands as a figure of towering influence on European legal thought, both because of the direct and immense influence which his views had on the content of the French Civil Code (and through it, the

---

[213] Savigny, *System des heutigen Römischen Rechts*, iii, §104, pp. 5–7; Puchta, *Pandekten*, §§49–54; Windscheid, *Lehrbuch*, i, §69.

[214] One critic of German will theory was Jhering, who argued that will theory ignored the underlying purposes for which contracts were entered into: Jhering, *Zweck im Recht*.

[215] See on this history, Zimmermann, 'Vertrag und Versprechen'.

[216] Von Kübel, 'Das einseitige Versprechen', pp. 1171 f.   [217] *Ibid.*, p. 1176.

[218] 1699–1772.

Louisiana Civil Code), but also because of the remarkable influence he had in England. For that reason, his views deserve a prolonged analysis, despite the fact that French law is only slightly mentioned elsewhere in this work. His standing in the Common law is demonstrated by the remark of Best J in *Cox* v. *Troy*, that 'the authority of Pothier ... is as high as can be had, next to the decision of a Court of Justice in this country'.[219]

Pothier's views are set out in his *Traité des obligations*, published in 1761. Pothier posits the necessity of all obligations having a 'cause from which the obligation proceeds',[220] a position which continues to be maintained down to the present time in French law.[221] Pothier first treats of contract, defining it as a 'kind of agreement',[222] as such requiring the assent of two or more persons. An agreement is also characterised as something 'by which two parties reciprocally promise and engage, or one of them singly, promises and engages to the other to give some particular thing, or to do or abstain from doing some particular act'.[223] The description of an agreement by reference to the concept of promise is noteworthy: as in Pufendorf, though we have moved to agreement as the central idea, the promissory language remains. It is also noteworthy that Pothier's description allows for gratuitous as well as onerous contracts. Only promises which disclose an 'intention of engaging and binding ourselves' count as promises capable of constituting a contract. With this definition of contract, Pothier distinguishes the 'pollicitation', which he defines as a 'promise not yet accepted by the person to whom it is made'.[224] It is evident from Pothier's definition that his notion of pollicitation is capable of encompassing not only a contractual offer but also the traditionally conceived unilateral promise. Pothier states that under natural law pollicitations are not obligatory (a view not shared by all natural lawyers), but he recognises that under Roman law the *pollicitatio* properly so called (that is, the promise in favour of a municipality) was enforced, but he adds that that is clearly not the case in contemporary

---

[219] Best J in *Cox* v. *Troy* (1822) 5 B & Ald 474, 480. Swain has recently cautioned, however, that the 'role played by Pothier, whilst significant in helping to shape contract doctrine in a period of flux, should not be overstated' ('The Classical Model of Contract', p. 529).

[220] Vol. 1, §1. The first translation in England, undertaken by William Evans, was published by J. Butterworth in 1806, though an earlier translation by F.-X. Martin had been published in 1802 by Martin & Ogden, Newbern, North Carolina, and it was this edition which influenced US Common law usage of Pothier's ideas. The English quoted in the main text is from the 1806 Evans translation of vol. 1, unless otherwise noted.

[221] See Art. 1108, *Code civil*.   [222] Pothier, *Treatise*, §3.   [223] §3.

[224] §4. This definition bears interesting comparison with the apparent conception of Stair of a pollicitation as a contractual offer (see earlier discussion at p. 136).

French law. Citing Grotius, he affirms the need for an acceptance before a promise creates any obligation.

Pothier continues[225] with a discussion of the difference between essential, natural and accidental contract terms, though there is no discussion of the Aristotelian underpinning of this distinction. What Pothier states of these types of term gives a very non-Aristotelian flavour to the concepts of substance and accident: substantial elements of a contract are those 'without which such contract cannot subsist';[226] natural elements are those which, although not being of the essence, 'form a part of it, though not expressly mentioned',[227] and can therefore be implied into it; accidental elements being part of a contract only by virtue of a special agreement of the parties. So, price is essential to a sale, and gratuitousness to a contract of mandate; warranties are implied in to sale; and the time allowed for performance in a contract is an accidental matter. This treatment is far removed from the philosophical and ontological debates of Aristotle and Aquinas on the nature of things.

Pothier rejects out of hand the old Roman contractual scheme of named and unnamed contracts, and contracts *bonae fidei* and *stricti juris*; instead, he posits a division between synallagmatic (or bilateral) and unilateral contracts, which he defines as a distinction between those where both parties bind or engage themselves to each other, and those where only one so binds or engages himself to the other.[228] Further classification is possible, and Pothier suggests additional divisions such as that between consensual and real contracts (that is, between those formed by simple consent and those requiring delivery of a thing),[229] and (as Grotius did) that between contracts of beneficence and those of interest to both sides.[230]

Following some discussion of defects of consent, including error and extortion, Pothier comes to a section of his treatise that was to prove very influential in English law. In the original French, it is entitled '*Du défaut de cause dans le Contrat*', that is, 'Of want of cause in Contract'.[231] This clearly identified the subject matter as that of cause, as it is understood in the civilian tradition. Yet, in the text of the 1806 translation, the leading English edition of Pothier's work of the time, the heading is rendered 'Of the want of a good consideration'. In translation the doctrine of cause is thus equated with the Common law concept of consideration. The translation of Pothier's statement that '*Toute engagement doit avoir une cause honnête*' thus becomes '[e]very contract ought to have a just cause (or

---

[225] §5 f.   [226] §5.   [227] §7.   [228] §9.   [229] §10.   [230] §12.   [231] §42.

consideration)', making the suggested equation very clear. It is hardly surprising that, presented with this equation, contemporary Common lawyers were quick to suggest that the English rules on consideration could be fitted into a logical scheme of contract, such as Pothier offered, and that in the enterprise of constructing such a logical scheme Pothier was cited in support, both in later English treatises and judgments. In the leading 1802 translation of Pothier published in the United States, the transformation of cause to consideration is even greater, in that the word cause does not even appear in the translation at all, but merely the term consideration. In the American edition, Pothier's opening statement on cause simply becomes '[e]very engagement ought to have a lawful consideration'. Though the transformation of cause to consideration is thus more complete in the American translation, the equation of cause with consideration in the later English edition was sufficiently clear. The great influence which Pothier's translated text had upon the development of English law in the nineteenth century was discussed earlier in this chapter.[232]

Pothier continues with an explanation of the rule against the *stipulatio alteri*, that is the rule against an enforceable promise made in the interests of a third party, a rule of Roman law which Pothier explains as applicable in the modern French law also.[233] Pothier explains the basis of the rule as being that someone who stipulates for performance in favour of a third party has himself no pecuniary interest in seeing the duty performed. This would mean that the party under the duty of performance could breach it with impunity, something which Pothier says could not be 'more repugnant' to the nature of a civil (as opposed to a natural) obligation. This explanation of course ignores the possibility of seeing the third party as itself entitled to seek performance, but Pothier clearly does not conceive of a possible third party right in those terms. Had such a conception been raised in Pothier's understanding of the relationship of the parties, then the objection he posited to obligations in favour of third parties might have been refuted.

Despite the rule against third party rights in contract, Pothier lists a number of common situations where it is not seen as applicable, among them: cases where the third party is in fact a principal to the agreement, the apparent stipulator having been merely an agent for the third party;[234] cases where a contracting party promises to engage a third party

---

[232] See earlier discussion at pp. 144–5.   [233] Pothier, *Treatise*, §54.
[234] §55. He discusses agency more fully at §§74 ff.

and vouch for his work;[235] cases where a contracting party merely des-
ignates a third party agent to whom the price is to be paid;[236] cases of
stipulations in favour of heirs (because 'they are as it were the continuation of ourselves');[237] and stipulations in favour of successors in title to
property.[238] Importantly, Pothier also recognises as exceptions to the rule
against *stipulationes alteri* cases where, unless performance to a third
party occurs, payment of a sum of money is to be made to the stipulator,
and cases where the stipulator transfers some money to the other party
on condition that a performance in favour of the third party is to occur.[239]
In both of these cases of conditional performance, the stipulator has a
pecuniary interest in the performance of the condition, and so the performance in favour of the third party may indirectly be enforced through
enforcement by the stipulator of the condition. These last two types of
case are important, for they in fact encompass many of the traditionally
conceived cases of third party rights, such as the life insurance contract
where a stipulator makes payments to an insurance company on condition of payment to a named third party after his death. Pothier concludes
his discussion of exceptions to the rule with the rules on agency (contracts 'through the ministry of another').[240] The totality of the exceptions
mentioned by Pothier constitutes a large inroad into the rule against the
stipulatio alteri, and demonstrates the extent to which continental jurists
of the time were seeking to avoid its application without yet dispensing
with the principle and conceding direct enforcement by the third party, as
happened in contemporary Scots law.

In his *Treatise*, Pothier offers a clarity of thought and expression, and
a highly organised scheme for the classification of obligations, which was
to prove immensely popular with contemporary and later lawyers. His
treatment of obligations was far removed from the involved discussion of
the minutiae of the law which had so characterised the treatments of the
schoolmen and which had come to be so despised by the rationalists of
the eighteenth century. By contrast, Pothier offered a rational, systematised and modern view of the law of obligations which appealed to those
seeking to make sense of the law. Though rejecting liability for unilateral
promises in favour of mutual undertakings, Pothier continued to employ
promissory language to describe such undertakings.

Pothier's approach not only provided the model for both the French and
Louisiana Civil Codes, but set the tone for later, nineteenth-century French
jurists. These jurists took a similar line to Pothier in holding that contract

---

[235] §§56, 58.   [236] §57.   [237] §61.   [238] §67.   [239] §§70,71.   [240] §§74 ff.

was formed by the will of the parties to undertake an obligation,[241] and described the process of formation in offer and acceptance terms.[242] There was some development of doctrine: Jean Demolombe, for instance, suggested that an offer should be deemed to be irrevocable even if the offeror did not expressly promise this, since a promise to this effect should be implied in to the offer; such an implied promise was itself an offer which the offeree should be deemed to accept as soon as he learnt of it.[243] A similar solution was advocated in German law by Ferdinand Regelsberger,[244] the approach being eventually adopted, in modified form, in the provisions of the BGB.[245] It is a solution which bears some similarities to the description used in the Common law (and discussed in Chapter 4) in the more restrictive circumstances of breach of pre-contractual tendering conditions.

5.   Contract theory and practice in the twentieth century

In German law, the adoption of the BGB in 1900 solidified an approach to contract (*Vertrag*) as clearly based upon the will of the parties, as expressed in their respective declarations of intent (*Willserklärungen*), and resting upon agreement. Contract is the general method prescribed under the BGB by which an obligation may be created by 'legal transaction' (*Rechtsgeschäft*), as opposed to by operation of law.[246]

German lawyers see the legal transaction constituted by a contractual relationship as comprising two 'declarations of intention' or 'declarations of will'. These declarations of intent are comprised in an offer and acceptance, though that basic statement is not iterated in the text of the BGB itself. In the *Motive* (the published deliberations of the First Commission on the BGB) the theory underlying the notion of a legal transaction was expressed in strong and explicit will terms thus: 'A legal transaction is a private declaration of intention aiming at a legal consequence which the law sanctions because it is intended.'[247]

---

[241] See, for instance, Duranton, *Cours de droit*, x, §§51–2; Demante and Colmet de Santerre, *Cours analytique*, v, §§2, p. 2 *bis*, 3; Demolombe, *Cours de Code Napoléon*, xxiv, §12; Laurent, *Principes de droit*, xv, §§ 424–7; Larombière, *Theorie et pratique des obligations*, i, § 41.

[242] Aubry and Rau, *Cours de droit*, iv. §343; Demolombe, *Cours de Code Napoléon*, xxiv, §45.

[243] Demolombe, *Cours de Code Napoléon*, xxiv, §66.

[244] Regelsberger, *Die Vorverhandlungen*, §13.   [245] §145 BGB.   [246] §311(1) BGB.

[247] *Motive*, vol. 1, p. 126 (contained in Mugdan, *Die gesammten Materialien zum Bürgerlichen Gesetzbuch*).

Such language and conceptualisation clearly discloses the prime importance given to the concept of the will in modern German contract law. This concept finds a ready expression in the large freedom of will which was originally given to contracting parties under the BGB (though subject to the duty of good faith). There is no requirement of a just price; there is no doctrine of *laesio enormis*;[248] and the parties can generally contract out of the default BGB rules. As with other legal systems, however, this freedom is increasingly being constrained as a result of the interest of EU legislators in consumer protection and in a growing human rights jurisprudence. Markesinis has opined that the time may have come 'when one should treat these developments as prompted by a socio-economic environment which is different from that which gave rise to the classical law of contract'.[249] In addition to such socio-economic factors, one might add a prevailing political culture with an emphasis on state regulation which has held sway over the European political landscape since the latter half of the last century.

A further remark of Markesinis is worth highlighting (though it is made without any citation of sources), that in German law the obligation of contract

> arises out of the promise of the parties (with its almost religious connotations in the Middle Ages) and not, as in the common law, from the notion of a bargain or (in later times) the idea of detrimental reliance.[250]

Given that the role of unilateral promise suggested by von Kübel was distinctly scaled down in the final text of the BGB, these remarks must be interpreted either as relating to the distant origins of German contractual doctrine or else, if intended as a description of the current law, as referring to conditional promissory conceptions of offer and acceptance, rather than to unilateral promise. Even so, the comparison made between German and English law fails to capture the historic role of promise in English law, even if that role was not as directly influenced by the canon law as was the case in Germany.

In German law, contracts are interpreted objectively. Declarations of will forming a contract are, by virtue of the doctrine of the 'objective horizon' of the recipient of the declaration (*Empfängerhorizont*), interpreted in a way that a reasonable addressee of the declaration would understand it. An exception is where both parties share a common misconception

---

[248] Which was rejected by the drafters of the BGB: see *Motive*, vol. 1, p. 321.
[249] Markesinis *et al.*, *The German Law of Contract*, pp. 47–8.
[250] *Ibid.*, p. 55.

about the meaning of the contract, when the shared mistaken understanding of the contract prevails over the objective meaning.[251] The wisdom of such an approach was questioned in Chapter 1 of this work, especially given that contracts often have effects on third parties, it having been suggested earlier that it is preferable to judge language objectively in order to avoid giving effect to absurd common mistakes. Apart from this case of common misconception, subjective intentions only become relevant in German law if one of the parties raises an objection which triggers the rules on mistake.[252]

The unilateral, unaccepted promise (*Versprechen*) has no place of general application in the BGB. As the late Karl Larenz put matters, the 'delivered unilateral promise is not enough ... to found a legal obligation; to this must be added the acceptance on the part of the promisee'.[253] Very exceptionally, however, a unilateral promise is given legal effect to in the BGB, in which event a single declaration of will suffices for the creation of a legal transaction. One such exceptional case is the public promise of a reward (*Auslobung*), discussed in some detail in the next chapter. Another example is found in the title on bearer bonds.[254] The issue of a bearer bond is described as having 'promised payment' to the bearer, and the article states that the holder of the bond may demand such performance. This exceptional provision deals with a duty which appears from the text to have been intended as an instance of a genuine unilateral promise, though the section simply states that the bearer may demand performance without stating what the nature of his entitlement is. This interpretation is borne out by the fact that this provision in the BGB was the third of the specific proposals of von Kübel (the other two being promises of reward and third party rights) concerning unilateral promise which he wished to see in the Code. In this specific instance, he had received German jurisprudence since the mid-nineteenth century on his side, the view being taken in such jurisprudence that through the issuing of the bond the promisor was making a binding promise to pay.[255] However, Zimmermann has commented that 'in this case, the law did not decide the dogmatic issue',[256] so that prevailing doctrine today, despite the original intention that this provision be seen as an instance of unilateral promise, treats the bearer bond as a contractual matter (albeit than no acceptance is required under the contract). The reasons for this current interpretation have been explained

---

[251] RGZ 99, 147.   [252] See later discussion in Ch. 4.

[253] Larenz, *Lehrbuch des Schuldrechts*, i.14.   [254] Title 24 (§§793–808) BGB.

[255] See Zimmermann, 'Vertrag und Versprechen', p. 475.   [256] *Ibid.*

as being a desire to minimise exceptions from the ordinary contractual principle set out in §311, and a concern that viewing bearer bonds as a type of promissory liability would create a danger of forcing an unwanted benefit upon a party.[257] It has, however, been doubted whether this prevailing contractual construction of bearer bonds remains appropriate in the present age.[258] Care must be taken with the BGB, as sometimes the language of promise is used when it is contractual liability, rather than unilateral promissory liability, which is meant.[259]

In the mixed legal systems, agreement had, by the twentieth century, come to dominate explanations of the basis of contractual liability, to the near exclusion of other bases; promissory language was largely reserved for describing unilateral promises. In Scotland, the modern era has seen continual judicial recognition of contract as founded upon the agreement of parties on all the essentials required at law. Agreement is concluded when the parties reach (as Stair, quoting from the Digest, put it) *consensus in idem*.[260] There are numerous judicial statements to this effect: in *Walker* v. *Alexander Hall & Co.*,[261] Lord Blackburn observed that the crucial feature of the case before him was that 'there was no *consensus in idem* between the parties'; in *Elcap* v. *Milne's Executor*,[262] Lord Penrose remarked that the 'pursuers' averments are not apt to support contract. There is no reference to consensus'; and in *Avintair* v. *Ryder Airline Services*, the Inner

---

[257] See Kleinschmidt, *Der Verzicht im Schuldrecht*, p. 70. As to the concern that a promisor might be able to force an unwanted benefit upon a promisee, a contrary view could be put that, by the very nature of the fact that no duties can be imposed upon the recipient of a unilateral promise (who is indeed entitled to reject a promise in his favour), the alleged danger of the unwanted but enforced promise is not a genuine legal concern; cf., however, for an iteration of the concern, Carter, 'On Promising the Unwanted', and Kimel, *From Promise to Contract*, pp. 24–5. The concern appears to have prompted the drafters of the DCFR specifically to provide that a right or benefit conferred by a unilateral juridical act may be rejected by the beneficiary: Art. II.-4:303.

[258] Koller, 'Wertpapierrecht', p. 1438.

[259] See for instance §641(2) BGB, which addresses the remuneration due to a contractor for a work whose production 'the customer has promised to a third party' (*der Besteller einem Dritten versprochen hat*). Though this does not make clear the nature of the 'promise' to the third party, it seems that what is meant is a contractual obligation to the third party on the part of the customer, so that 'promised' here must be taken to mean 'contractually obliged'. See also similar contractual uses of the word promise in §§611 and 316 BGB.

[260] See, for instance, references to consensus in the following: *Seed Shipping Co* v. *Kelvin Shipping Co* (1924) 19 Ll L Rep 170; *Pickard* v. *Ritchie* 1986 SLT 466; *Beta Computers (Europe) Ltd* v. *Adobe Systems (Europe) Ltd* 1996 SLT 604; *Percy* v. *Board of National Mission of the Church of Scotland* [2005] UKHL 73, 2006 SC (HL) 1 ('contract is an agreement'); *Advice Centre for Mortgages Ltd* v. *McNicoll* 2006 SLT 591.

[261] (1919) 1 Ll L Rep 661.   [262] 1999 SLT 58.

House remarked that there was 'no doubt that parties must achieve *consensus in idem* upon all the essential matters before there can be said to be a contract between them'.[263] The agreement of the parties must, however, be accompanied by a clear intention to be bound; without such intention, mere agreement is insufficient for a binding contract.[264]

The unilateral promise has continued as a separate obligation in Scotland, though under-utilised and seldom litigated on, and (from 1995) subject to a revised requirement of form which stipulates the need for a unilateral and gratuitous promise to be in subscribed writing unless undertaken in the course of business.[265] The neglect of this obligation, even in the one jurisdiction which has explicitly recognised it as a separate species of obligation, is marked. This is regrettable, as there are a number of transactions for which the gratuitous and unilateral promise is the most natural obligation, in the sense that it most accurately describes the nature of the relationship between the parties. Such transactions include offers of reward, IOUs, negotiable instruments, duties undertaken at the contract negotiation stage, third party rights, and options.[266] Some of these transactions are discussed in later chapters of this work, where the utility of a promissory analysis is explored.

I have previously suggested that, given the current state of Scots law, defence of the will approach to contract liability is easier in Scotland than in the Common law.[267] This is so for a number of reasons. First, because descriptions of contract liability in Scotland are typically agreement and not promissory based, this means that the oft levied charge that it is inappropriate to use the idea of promise to explain contract (because promise is a unilateral act whereas contract is bilateral) is evidently irrelevant. Scots law does indeed confine the language of promise to unilateral acts. This is so even in the one case where promissory language is used in a contractual context, namely to describe the nature of a third party right in contract, because (as the discussion in Chapter 5 will show) both of the contracting parties can be conceived of as making separate unilateral promises to the third party. In any event, the charge itself is somewhat suspect, given that it was suggested in Chapter 1 that the idea of promise is quite able to accommodate mutual, conditional undertakings.

---

[263] *Avintair Ltd v Ryder Airline Services Ltd* 1994 SC 270, 273.

[264] *W. S. Karoulias, S. A. v. The Drambuie Liqueur Company Ltd* [2005] CSOH 112, 2005 SLT 813; *Aisling Developments Ltd v. Persimmon Homes Ltd* [2008] CSOH 140.

[265] Requirements of Writing (Scotland) Act 1995, s. 1.

[266] See further Hogg, *Obligations*, Ch. 2, and 'Promise: The Neglected Obligation'.

[267] See Hogg, 'Perspectives on Contract Theory'.

Second, as the history of contractual theory narrated above has shown, the origin of will theory in Scots law can be traced to Stair's idea of law as the dictate of reason, and contract as an expression of the rational will, and not to much later nineteenth-century, mercantile free trade ideas, even if such ideas reinforced Stair's approach. Given this history, attacks on will theory which argue that such free trade ideology is outdated as a basis for explaining the underlying force of contracts have much less force. Third, as the discussion of remedies in later chapters will demonstrate, will theory is more easily supported in Scots law because of the importance placed upon performance remedies. As a result, modern Scots contract law can withstand the criticism that contracts are really only about making reparation for breach, as reliance theorists like Atiyah have argued.[268] Last, Scots law's lack of a doctrine of mutual consideration means it is immune from any arguments that consideration undermines a will-based approach because the law is actually about putting things in the correct form rather than enforcing the will of the parties. In a system with no mutual consideration requirement, the emphasis can be argued much more naturally to lie in enforcement of the will of the parties.

This last Scottish aid to defending will theory (the absence of a doctrine of consideration) is also shared by Louisiana and South Africa. Though no separate obligation of promise exists in each of those two systems, by the twentieth century each had clearly accommodated gratuitous contracts, any requirement of consideration having been rejected, with each supplementing the general approach by giving a limited role to promissory estoppel.[269] It is not uncommon to see in older South African cases descriptions of contract in promissory terms. Thus, in *Rood* v. *Wallach* the essential elements of contract were described as

> the promise to do or forbear some act made by one and accepted by the other party and the intention that the legal relations of the parties shall be governed by the promise in matters to which it relates, or, as is sometimes put, there must be consent and an intention to create legal relations.[270]

In more recent times, however, the preference has been for describing the essential element of contract as *consensus ad idem*.[271] Roman-Dutch

---

[268] Atiyah, *Essays on Contract*, Ch. 2.

[269] In South Africa, what have been referred to in this work as gratuitous contracts are usually referred to as unilateral contracts.

[270] 1904 TS 187, 219, per Mason J.

[271] See, for instance, *Bloom* v. *The American Swiss Watch Co.* 1915 AD 100, 105; *Saambou-Nasionale Bouvereniging* v. *Friedman* 1979 (3) SA 978 (A), 993.

law, the precursor of modern South African law, had in addition required *iusta causa* for a valid contract. In the late nineteenth and early twentieth century, de Villiers CJ tried to equate *iusta causa* with the common law doctrine of consideration, but this approach was eventually conclusively rejected in *Conradie* v. *Rossouw*,[272] in which the Appellate Division conclusively held that consideration was not part of the law of South Africa. This left the idea of *iusta causa* in a somewhat uncertain state,[273] though as recently as 1979 *iusta causa* was still being said judicially to be a component aspect of contracts.[274] Hutchison has expressed the ardent hope that 'when it next has an opportunity to pronounce on the matter, the Appellate Division will unequivocally declare that the *iusta causa* requirement, having served its historically important purpose, has now become redundant'.[275] In South African law both options and offers of reward are analysed as contracts; binding offers are unenforceable, showing up a weakness in the non-recognition of unilateral promises.

An important element in the development of contract law in South Africa since 1994 has been the influence of the values and rights established in the new Constitution. The Constitutional Court has had occasion to remark that

> the approach of the Constitutional Court is that contractual obligations are enforceable unless they are contrary to public policy, which is to be discerned from the values embodied in the Constitution and in particular the Bill of Rights. Where the enforcement of a contractual provision would be unreasonable and unfair in the light of those fundamental values it will be contrary to public policy to enforce the contract or the contractual term in question.[276]

Importantly, however, freedom of contract has itself been described by the Constitutional Court as supporting constitutional values:

> public policy, as informed by the Constitution, requires in general that parties should comply with contractual obligations that have been freely and voluntarily undertaken. This consideration is expressed in the maxim *pacta sunt servanda*, which, as the Supreme Court of Appeal has repeatedly noted, gives effect to the central constitutional values of freedom and dignity. Self-autonomy or the ability to regulate one's own affairs, even to one's own detriment, is the very essence of freedom and a vital part of

---

[272] 1919 AD 279.   [273] See Hutchison, 'Contract Formation', p. 170.

[274] See the comments of Jansen JA in *Saambou-Nasionale Bouvereniging* v. *Friedman* 1979 (3) SA 978, 990–92 (A).

[275] Hutchison, 'Contract Formation', p. 173.

[276] Wallis AJ in *Den Braven SA (Pty) Ltd* v. *Pillay & Anor* 2008 (6) SA 229, para. 32.

dignity. The extent to which the contract was freely and voluntarily concluded is clearly a vital factor as it will determine the weight that should be afforded to the values of freedom and dignity.[277]

This view was referred to approvingly in *Den Braven* v. *Pillay*, where Willis AJ added:

> suggesting that contractual autonomy is not in appropriate circumstances reflective of freedom and gives effect to the central constitutional values of freedom and dignity ... is contrary to the views of both the Constitutional Court and the Supreme Court of Appeal.[278]

All of this means that where restraints operate upon freedom of contract in South African law, they tend to do so by way of flexible public policy considerations underpinned by constitutional values, rather than by hard and fast legislative restrictions as in the UK.

In Louisiana, there is a clear codal statement that contract derives from the will of the parties, Article 1757 of the Civil Code stating that obligations 'arise from contracts and other declarations of the will'. This leaves no room for doubt that the contract theory of Louisiana is will based, in the sense that contracts are created *through* the operation of free will; any academic arguments to the contrary would be in contradiction to this clear statement of the Civil Code. Of course, the fact that this statement has been legislatively made also makes it clear that, while contracts are to be seen as arising through acts of the will, their obligatory force derives ultimately *from* the normative power of the state, channelled through the discretionary exercise of the will of contracting parties. Will theory in Louisiana thus has that form discussed in the last chapter which was characterised as seeing the will as exercising a devolved rather than an independent normative power.[279] In addition, as discussed earlier, there is in Article 1967 of the Code a limited reliance-based type of liability, criticised earlier for its equation of reliance with lawful cause.[280]

In the Common law world, the twentieth century was marked by a number of developments in contract theory. The reliance theory, discussed in Chapter 2, came to prominence, with some arguing that the convergence of contract and tort under a general reliance basis essentially marked the end of contract.[281] This prediction proved to be premature, as

---

[277] Ncobo J in *Barkhuizen* v. *Napier* 2007 (5) SA 323 (CC), para. 57.
[278] *Den Braven SA (Pty) Ltd* v. *Pillay & Anor* 2008 (6) SA 229, para. 33.
[279] See the discussion in Ch. 2, at p. 88.
[280] See the discussion in Ch. 2, at p. 105.
[281] Gilmore, *The Death of Contract*.

reliance as a general explanation for contract fell from favour from the 1980s onwards. Will theory in fact underwent something of a resurgence, though there was no attempt to explain the whole content of contracts or every contractual rule by virtue of the actual or presumed will of the parties. On the contrary, increased state regulation of the content of contracts emphasised that much of the content of contracts or rules affecting the rights and remedies of the parties necessitated the acceptance that, while the will might still explain the existence of a contract in the first place, it could not explain the whole of the contractual relationship.

Inroads continued to be made into the doctrine of consideration, both in England and elsewhere in the Common law world. In the US, there was a movement to hold offerors to promises to keep offers open. In the Uniform Commercial Code, for instance, it was provided that an offer by a merchant to buy or sell goods in a signed record that stated it would be held open was irrevocable for the stated time, or for a reasonable time if none was stated.[282] Some state laws went further. Thus, in New York State, the General Law of Obligations provided that, except for the commercial cases dealt with under the UCC, a signed offer pledging the offeror to keep the offer open for a fixed time was irrevocable during the stated time, or for a reasonable time if none was stated.[283] This rule is significant as being generally applicable, rather than confined to commercial offers, and puts the law of New York on the same footing as, for instance, German and Scots law. US state legislation also made promises to pay a debt, to modify an obligation and to pay for past favours enforceable.[284] In England, Denning J boldly tried to develop the law by holding in *Central London Property Trust Ltd* v. *High Trees*[285] that, following a gratuitous agreement to vary the terms of a contract, it would be inequitable to hold the parties to the original contract terms. Denning J's judgment, giving effect to the promises of the parties, was founded on the intention of the parties, not any detrimental effect which might be caused by not enforcing those promises. While such an approach might have led to the overturning of the consideration rule and to the general enforcement of gratuitous promises, later judgments restrictively explained the decision as an example of promissory estoppel and not direct enforcement of the promise itself. In a further development, in *Williams* v. *Roffey*[286] it was controversially held that a promise to pay for services already contracted for was supported by the consideration that a commercial advantage was

---

[282] UCC §2–205.   [283] New York State General Obligations Law, §5–1109.
[284] See Fried, *Contract as Promise*, p. 28.   [285] [1947] KB 130.   [286] [1991] QB 1.

obtained (that advantage being the certainty that the other party would now be able to perform). In 1989, contracts under seal were abolished and replaced with a much watered down procedure for declaring a document a deed, thus making the undertaking of a unilateral and gratuitous promise much easier in English law.[287] There was greater regulation of the substantive fairness of contracts, through the development at common law of economic duress and undue influence,[288] and under statute through the Unfair Contract Terms Act 1977 and later regulations.[289] The device of unilateral contract was used to deal with some perceived problems of pre-contractual fairness,[290] and there were signs of the courts becoming more receptive to the idea of good faith playing a role in contract law.

Many of these specific developments in English law are considered in later chapters of the work. In total, they represent a greater willingness of the Common law both to enforce bare promises but also to regulate the content and effect of such promises. Ultimately, however, the continued unwillingness of the Common law to recognise and enforce unilateral promises as such, but rather to treat them as imagined bilateral contracts, distorts the nature of many transactions having a genuinely unilateral nature, as will be argued later in this work.

6.   A revitalised will theory

It has been remarked at a number of points that the primary intention of this work is not to champion any particular theory of contract law, but rather to attempt to explain the role that promise has played, continues to play, and might play again, in the law. However, in the final section of this chapter, an attempt will be made to see whether a modern, revitalised will theory can continue to provide an overarching structure for the force of voluntary obligations. The reason for attempting such an exercise can be simply put. Will theory remains the dominant explanation for the force of contracts in western legal systems. Indeed, as has been seen, it is entrenched in some civil codes. However, that dominant theory has been attacked by a number of prominent contract scholars over the past century or so. If such attacks were to be accepted as valid, then this would be a

---

[287] Law of Property (Miscellaneous Provisions) Act 1989, s. 1(2).
[288] See, on undue influence, *National Westminster Bank* v. *Morgan* [1985] AC 686, *Barclays Bank* v. *O'Brien* [1994] 1 AC 180, *CIBC Mortgages* v. *Pitt* [1994] 1 AC 200.
[289] Unfair Terms in Consumer Contracts Regulations 1994, subsequently 1999.
[290] See further discussion of this in the next chapter.

matter of profound disquiet: any system of law which purported to enforce contracts on the basis of a theory of their normative force which could not be justified would be discredited. Moreover, if such attacks were accepted as having substance, then the suggestions to be made in later chapters of this book that promise ought to play a greater role in modern contract law than is currently the case in many jurisdictions would be liable to be undermined: if the will, of which promising is one manifestation, were no longer to be seen as a valid source of obligations, then any argument promoting a greater role for promise would seem to be fatally flawed. In order then to provide a theoretical defence for the later argument in this work for a greater role for promise, it seems prudent to undertake some consideration of the theoretical question of whether a continued defence of the dominant will theory is possible.

Whilst some have argued that the twentieth-century developments represent an attack on the continued sustainability of will theory,[291] not only does this view fail to take proper account of the distinction which should be made between the very existence of contracts on the one hand, and their content on the other (the latter, but not the former, certainly being less easily explicable by reference to the will of the parties), but no alternative theory has yet been advanced which more successfully explains the moral and legal force of contracts and promises in the modern age.

It is obviously absurd to ignore definitive statements by legal systems as to the basis of their contract law. Louisiana and Germany, for instance, both clearly posit the exercise of the human will as the means by which contracts are formed. Contract theory should not take place in a vacuum, but must reflect the law as it is, and to ignore such statements as to the force of contracts would be foolish in the extreme. Even where the will theory has no codal basis (as in Scotland and England), it remains the dominant theory for explaining contract law. The reliance-based attacks of the 1970s and 1980s proved ephemeral distractions which withered along with the collectivist, centralist political ideologies which were their political counterparts. That will theory still dominates is to be applauded because, whether or not historically it owed its popularity to political liberalism,[292] it can properly be seen as a juristic manifestation of respect for personal autonomy and responsibility, and, as such, a safeguard against the intrusive and overweening power of the state.

---

[291] Ibbetson, *An Historical Introduction*, p. 261.
[292] Gordley devotes an entire chapter (Ch. 8) of *Philosophical Origins* to arguing that it does not.

The will theory which can be confidently advocated in the present age is, however, inevitably a modified version from that which has been asserted at various points in the past. For one, a realistic will theory must view the will not as an independent source of obligations, but, as it is already conceived of in some systems, as a faculty through which parties are permitted to assume obligations which ultimately derive their binding force from the sovereign power of the state. This, in fact, is not a new idea: the natural lawyers of the past, including the late natural lawyers of the Northern school, saw human beings as free to undertake obligations in so far as God had left them so free. The will, as manifested in promises and agreements, was clearly seen as the means by which obligations might be assumed, but their force was derived from God (or, as less theistic proponents of modern law might prefer, from a temporal sovereign lawgiver). Modern will theory, if it is to continue to be a useful explanation of the source of obligations, must again recognise the derivative normative power of the will, rather than seek to locate in the will some wholly independent normative power. In such a scheme the will is merely one element of a larger set of conditions which in total explain promissory and contractual liability: the will is the faculty (or means) by which parties are permitted to assume voluntary obligations, and promising is a manifestation of such will.

Second, a revitalised will theory will have to be one that is slimmed down from the more expansive versions popular in past centuries. It should not seek to explain *all* of the content of contract law, as in former days, but merely the act of concluding a contract, as well as the content of the contract in so far as agreed by the parties and in so far as not objectionable under statutory or other legal policy. It should not seek to explain, for instance, the rules relating to illegal contracts, or to frustration, or to other external controls. Such controls, whether operating via legislation or common law policy, evidently operate to modify or strike down agreed content, or to impose further content. Though it is true that such interference is a restraint on the pure will of the parties, so what? That does not negate any respect for free choice, it merely limits such choice within socially acceptable boundaries, as ideas of liberality and commutative justice once did. The question, however, is whether the various common law and statutory restrictions on the will can be grouped together in any coherent way which would help to complete an overall general theory of contract which was based upon the will as the means by which contractual obligations are assumed.

What then would a revitalised will theory amount to? Doubtless there might be a number of ways in which such a theory might be defined, but one attempt is as follows. A new will theory would posit that a contract is formed through an expression of the human will (the promise)[293] by which the contracting parties demonstrate their willingness to be bound in law and thus to assume obligations. Such a contract would be seen as being concluded either through an exchange of promises (in cases of mutual contract) or through the acceptance by one party of another's promise (in a gratuitous contract). The obligations assumed by the parties through such a promissory manifestation of the will would be such as they expressly determine for themselves, as well as those which were imposed upon them by the law through legal rules (otherwise styled 'implied terms'). Both express and imposed contractual content would apply within the context of an overarching relationship characterised in terms of equity, fairness and good faith.

Such a definition of a revitalised will theory could be argued to offer a viable new general theory of contract. In the paradigm prevailing under such a new theory, the pure exercise of the will could, if that were desired, be restrained in ways analogous to those which applied by virtue of the older, Aristotelian constraints of liberality and commutative justice. That might be achieved by virtue of the fact that the law would be able to:

(1) take account of the concern about illiberal and unconsidered giving by imposing stricter requirements of form for transactions undertaken out of liberality or (to classify such transactions in slightly different terms) which were gratuitous ones; and

(2) regulate the justice of exchanges in ways which, to some extent, gave effect to the concerns which underlay the old value of commutative justice ('equality of exchange'), doing so through the application of ideas of equity, fairness, and above all the doctrine of good faith.[294]

On such an approach, the reason underlying a transaction would still be of relevance, even if the former doctrine of *causa* had largely disappeared. It

---

[293] Though it was suggested earlier that all contracts can be characterised in promissory terms, the alternative possible view was mooted that some contracts might be said to demonstrate a present consent to bound to an obligation in law even in the absence of a promise. On such an alternative view, the promise is merely one type of manifestation of the human will demonstrating contractual intent, other conduct being equally capable of so doing. Such an alternative theory is clearly also will-based, and so is suited to the revitalised will theory suggested in the main text. See, as an example of a non-promissory but will-based view of contract, Pratt, 'Contract: Not Promise'.

[294] Gordley does not discuss the concept of good faith in *Philosophical Origins*, though that work was published in 1991, before the modern resurgence of the idea of good faith had begun to occur.

would not have to be the case that the law would consider that 'the choices people make are the best or only guide to their welfare', as has been suggested to be the necessary position of will theorists,[295] because under a revitalised will theory promises could be constrained if their fulfilment conflicted with societal values and protective policies, such constraint applying both through requirements of form and via the moderating effect of the value of good faith.

As to concern (1), that relating to the question of liberality and illiberality, the law clearly has regard in the present age both to liberal intentions, through permitting transactions motivated by generosity to be given effect, but also to the concern about the potential for unconsidered liberality, by often imposing more onerous formal requirements in respect of gratuitous transactions. The willingness of the modern law to recognise that someone may wish to confer a benefit unilaterally and gratuitously, and to give legal effect to such an act of the will (at least in *some* transactions in all systems), embodies a recognition that people may quite properly wish to confer things on others out of generosity. Giving effect to such transactions may not be quite the same as an explicit acceptance of the Thomist understanding of liberality, but giving effect to an intention to confer a benefit gratuitously on another, while usually requiring a special form for it to ensure that such giving has been properly considered, surely comes at least close to recognising such a liberal motivation. This is particularly true of a system like Scotland, which has a separate obligation of unilateral promise: what clearer evidence could there be of the legal value placed upon the generous, unreciprocated promise?[296] It is also clear, however, that the revitalised will theory, which best explains why the law respects and gives legal effect to the desire to enter such transactions, is thought able to coexist with legal constraints that propose stricter requirements for achieving such effect, albeit that it will be argued in the final section of Chapter 4 that caution should be demonstrated in stipulating unduly burdensome constraints on such gratuitous

---

[295] Gordley, *Philosophical Origins*, p. 235.

[296] It would, however, be stretching the argument beyond reasonable bounds to argue that Scots law, with its separate obligations of unilateral promise and contract, chose to entrench the values of liberality and commutative justice structurally and taxonomically, by recognising an obligation which embodies each value. This argument would be unsound for a number of reasons: (i) there is no evidence that this was the chosen rationale for the creation of two separate obligations, (ii) given that Scots law allows gratuitous contracts, contract can equally be the medium for an arrangement embodying liberality, and (iii) unilateral promises are often given in a business context, where liberality is thus not the reason for the promissory undertaking.

undertakings: a preference ought to be shown for party autonomy over paternalism, the parties themselves often being the best judges of when gratuitous acts of the will should be enforced.

As to concern (2), the regulation of the justice of exchanges, while it is true that the rationale underlying the restraints that are imposed externally on the free will of parties to an onerous contract appear muddled, it is suggested that a coherent rationale can be offered. The mechanisms presently operating to enforce justice in exchanges seem to be a mixture of ideas of general equity, fairness, reasonableness and, above all, good faith. These values, especially good faith, embodied both in statutory regimes[297] as well as the common law, might be said to contain, as one major strand within them, the idea of commutative justice. If that is so, then the recent re-emergence of the importance of good faith in European legal philosophy might be seen as a re-emergence of the idea of commutative justice under another name. Good faith could be seen as a secularised, commercialised and non-philosophical yearning for good behaviour and decency, a value capable of application without a necessary reference to the morality of virtue and Christian theology in explaining why people should behave fairly and non-exploitatively towards others.

Whilst a recognition of the validity of type (1) and (2) restraints on free will, taken together with the modified will theory argued for above, may not amount to as grand and organised a general theory of contract law as existed in the days of the natural law schoolmen, it nonetheless presents a workable framework to explain what lawyers observe legislators and courts doing when they enforce some promises but not others. Though many would argue that the revitalised doctrine of good faith is vague and unhelpful, that is surely no more so than with the ideas of liberality and commutative or distributive justice; if it interferes in contractual freedom, then again this is no more so than would be the case by reference to commutative and distributive justice. Any concepts of general application which restrain contractual freedom are necessarily going to be somewhat imprecise and sweeping, whether they stem from philosophical or religious understandings, or from a more humanist and mercantile concern for fairness. So although, without a shared philosophy, it may be true that 'discovering general principles or doctrines that can explain the rules of positive law or the results that most people regard as fair'[298] will be harder,

---

[297] Consider, for instance, the law of marine salvage, which provides a regime for recovery by the salvor which displaces any promise which the owner may have made *in extremis*.

[298] Gordley, *Philosophical Origins*, pp. 230–1.

given that we live in a modern world where we no longer share common assumptions about the nature of humanity or its purpose, it can be argued that it is still possible to explain how courts continue to insist on caution in the exercise of liberality through formal means, and to regulate equality in exchange by reference to the concept of good faith. The language may have changed, and there may not be as solid and complete a general theory of contract law as prevailed until the eighteenth century, but the view suggested here still represents more by way of a theory of contract than had Roman law or the Common law before the nineteenth century. It is suggested therefore that we need not abandon the idea of seeking to set out some general contractual theory as it is currently articulated and applied by modern courts.

Utilising a revitalised will theory, it would not be necessary to resuscitate the idea of cause, any more than it would to continue to use that of consideration. Cause has withered away in most jurisdictions, and, even where it continues formally to be insisted upon, as is the case in France,[299] Louisiana,[300] and perhaps South Africa,[301] such formal insistence adds nothing of use to contractual analysis or enforcement. Indeed, in systems which continue to insist upon cause, the courts often ignore the actual intention of the parties and treat the cause as something else in order to allow the transaction to be validated.[302] There is no longer any clear universal understanding of what cause means, unless it is the very general idea of the reason or motive for entering into a contract. If it does mean no more than the reason or motive for contracting, then it seems an irrelevancy: it is self-evident that any parties who in fact contract must have had a reason for so contracting, as human beings possessing ordinary contractual capacity and intelligence do not act randomly and without motive when entering contracts. If there is a need to exclude some causes from giving rise to valid contracts – for instance, the contract entered into as a result of unlawful extortion – then specific legal rules (such as a rule that extortion invalidates contracts) can do the job of cause in a much better and targeted way. If there is a perceived need that parties should

---

[299] *Code civil*, Arts. 1131–33.   [300] CC Art. 1966.

[301] In 1979, it was suggested that *iusta causa* was still a component aspect of contracts (see Jansen JA in *Saambou-Nasionale Bouvereniging v. Friedman* 1979 (3) SA 978, 990–2 (A)), but there has been no judicial pronouncement on the matter from the higher courts since that date.

[302] This is particularly seen in the case of donation, where some national courts are unwilling to see some types of transaction fall for failure to comply with the restrictive form required of donations.

demonstrate seriousness of intent to contract, again a simple rule stating that that be required, and that such can be demonstrated by any relevant means, will do the job. If there is a perceived need to subject some promises to greater formality, then this can be done by reference to the objective nature of the transaction, rather than the motives for it. Such an objective approach works perfectly well in some systems in the case of donation. True, the reason why such strict requirements were first thought necessary was because of the nature of the cause – they arose from benevolence, rather than exchange – but recognising why such benevolent transactions might require cautionary measures designed to protect one of the parties need not involve a full-blown doctrine of cause.

The suggested general modern theory of contractual liability can still be said to rest upon respect for the will, as manifested in objectively interpreted promises made in favour of others. Such respect for promises has been a universal feature of human society, despite occasional and rather trifling examples said to demonstrate the contrary. One might explain such respect as part of natural law if one wished (and, indeed, if one is seeking a moral basis of promises, rather than just a legal one, such a natural law basis may well be thought necessary[303]), though a non-natural law view, resting upon general observations of human behaviour and societies, is also tenable. It is simply and actually the case that societies believe that promises should be upheld, for a variety of reasons, and therefore provide that this is so in their law. It helps if one believes that promising is a virtuous act, or that one is bound to keep promises because one has agreed expressly or tacitly to be bound by the rules of society, but lawyers do not need to share such beliefs to understand contract law. As for the restraints placed upon free promising, one can explain these as based largely upon formal requirements regulating gratuitous unilateral undertakings, and upon ideas of equity and good faith regulating equality in exchange.

Searching, however, for a single and universally correct theory of contract, one that will hold good at all times and in all places, seems a flawed exercise. It is an attempt to search for a Platonic form of 'contract' which simply does not exist. Contract is a tool for regulating human social interaction, and its nature is always changing, just as societies change. The

---

[303] The revitalised will theory suggested is certainly adequate to explain the legal force given to promises, but those seeking a moral basis for promises may quite reasonably search for something more than the normative power delegated to private persons by a legal sovereign, or else the moral worth of promises will rest upon a mere subjective and changeable basis, rather than one that is objective and unchanging.

best that lawyers can seek to do is observe why, in particular societies, legislatures and courts say they are enforcing contracts, how they determine the content of them, and then accurately describe what they have observed. If that means articulating a different theory of contract for, say, Soviet Russia, where one might argue there was no real private law of contracts but rather a state distribution of assets, from that prevailing in, say, sixteenth-century Spain or present day England, then so be it. Accepting that there is no universal general theory of contract which explains the law of contract in all societies is not to admit defeat, it is simply to realise that human societies are free to determine the basis of legal liability as they see fit.

PART 2

The modern law

4

Formation of contract

In this chapter, various circumstances surrounding the formation of contract will be considered from a promissory viewpoint.

Traditionally, the Common law and mixed legal systems have been against the idea that any liability of a promissory type might exist between negotiating parties before formation of contract, though that has not precluded duties arising between the parties based upon tort. By contrast, as will be seen, German law has a developed notion of *culpa in contrahendo*, a type of liability which appears to lie in the interstice between contract and tort. Increasingly however, even the Common law is recognising that some situations (such as breach of conditions of tender) merit liability, and promise can provide a rationale for such liability. The making of a so-called 'firm offer' is another circumstance where some systems consider that duties ought to arise, though this view is not shared by English law or South African law; in those systems where liability does arise, promise can again be used to explain the origin of the duties. Promises of reward and options are also considered: again, where these are legally enforced, promise provides an attractive solution to explain their basis in law. Letters of intent and the question of error in the formation of contract are trickier: the simple idea of promise does not provide an obvious solution to the problems that each raises, and some consideration is given as to how best therefore to characterise the results in cases raising those issues. The doctrine of consideration evidently plays a major role in the practical resolution of some of these debates, and a review of whether that doctrine ought to be maintained is undertaken later in the chapter. Lastly, as requirements of form or notarisation restrict promissory potential in some areas, some attention will be given to whether these restrictions ought to be maintained.

By way of some further preliminary remarks, it will be useful to restate briefly some of the classificatory terms and ideas set out in Chapter 1, as the solutions to some of the scenarios that follow entail an understanding of these terms:

(1) *The distinction between juridical acts and obligations*: a juridical act is a legally effective transaction which may be constituted by the actions of only one party (a unilateral juridical act) or more than one party (a bilateral or multilateral juridical act, depending on the number of parties); an obligation is merely one such type of juridical act, some obligations being unilateral juridical acts (unilateral promise and, in some jurisdictions, so-called 'unilateral contracts') and some being multilateral juridical acts (contract, delict, unjustified enrichment, and *negotiorum gestio*). Even where an obligation has been constituted by a bilateral juridical act (contract being one example), it may be affected by a subsequent unilateral juridical act, such as termination for breach.

(2) *The distinction between gratuitous and onerous obligations*: a gratuitous obligation is one in which only one party comes under any duties, an onerous obligation one where both (or all) parties do. In some jurisdictions, a gratuitous obligation is called a 'unilateral' obligation, but this causes confusion with the use of the term unilateral in relation to juridical acts, so such use has been avoided in this text. In jurisdictions where the doctrine of consideration applies, all contracts are onerous;[1] where the doctrine does not apply, a contract may either be gratuitous or onerous. Promise (in its narrow sense of a unilateral promise) is always gratuitous, as a promisor can never compel the performance of any counter-obligation by the promisee: if the promisor can do so, then there is an exchange of conditional promises constituting a contract.

(3) *The distinction between mutual (or synallagmatic) and onerous obligations*: mutual obligations are those where a duty or duties on one side of the relationship are offered in exchange for one or more on the other side. As such, mutual obligations are but one class of onerous obligation: an obligation may be onerous, in that both parties may come under a duty or duties, but the duties of each may not be reciprocal to any duties on the part of the other.

Having provided this brief restatement of some important fundamental terminology, the discussion now proceeds by way of consideration

---

[1] Save those undertaken, exceptionally, in deed form or under seal.

of a number of issues around the formation of contract which might conceivably have promissory characterisations.

1. Wasted pre-contractual expenditure following termination of contract negotiations

One of the most lively areas of debate surrounding formation of contract at the present time concerns whether a party negotiating a contract ought ever to incur liability for the negotiating expenses of the other party if negotiations for a contract are broken off. Such cases of failed contract can often result in the substantial costs of the negotiation process falling on one of the parties, particularly in cases where the negotiations are protracted or where one party has repeatedly requested the other to produce detailed information related to the intended contract. Where the money expended by one negotiating party has conferred some objective benefit on the other, then unjustified enrichment may provide a remedy; where this is not so however, and the expenditure is thus genuinely 'wasted', recovery is more problematic.

A strict dualist (or 'light switch')[2] view of the contract formation process would assert that there are but two states: the negotiation state, where no voluntary duties can arise between the parties, and the contract state, only achieved when the parties' wills have concurred in the formation of a contract, when duties will be assumed by each to the other (which duties rarely include any duties to pay for the other's negotiating or preliminary costs). There being, on this view, no intermediate state, no liability can arise for wasted pre-contractual expenditure (unless it be as a result of some tortious act, such as misrepresentation): any party undertaking such expenditure is held to do so at its own risk.

An alternative and emerging view is that there are (or ought to be) some circumstances where, if no contract is concluded, one of the contracting parties should be held to have undertaken liability for the other's wasted pre-contractual expenditure. Such circumstances must necessarily be limited, or else the allocation of risk between the parties will be fundamentally skewed against one of the parties and freedom *not* to contract will be threatened. Whether such liability should exist, if so how it should be delineated, and how conceptually it should be seen as arising, are questions with which all systems have to struggle. As the discussion which

---

[2] A characterisation given by the 'relational contract' theorist Ian Macneil, as recounted in Macaulay, 'Relational Contracts Floating on a Sea of Custom?', p. 778.

follows indicates, in Common law, civilian, and mixed systems alike, it
has been thought equitable to allow recovery for wasted pre-contractual
expenditure in *some* circumstances, though there is quite a divergence in
specifying which circumstances and in the level of recovery, some systems
having even proven willing to allow incomplete contracts to be perfected
rather than simply compensating a party for wasted expenditure.

Where liability for pre-contractual losses is seen as arising voluntarily, the notion that the party incurring the liability has promised (perhaps impliedly) to compensate the other has been thought amenable to
providing a conceptual explanation for its basis in some systems. On
the other hand, it can be argued that the requirement of a promise is
somewhat restrictive so far as pre-contractual expenditure is concerned,
given that expenditure is sometimes reasonably incurred without any
promise having been made by the other party. Promise certainly cannot explain the expansive recovery in German law under the doctrine of
culpa in contrahendo (where the stress is upon fault rather than promise).
A non-promissory basis for an obligation to compensate for wasted pre-
contractual expenditure might be argued to lie in a tortious duty not to
harm the other's interests, or in the fact that negotiating parties are in a
relationship which generates trust and good faith.

(a)   A Common law solution to the problem of pre-contractual expenditure: promissory and proprietary estoppel

One branch of the Common law capable of dealing with the problem of
wasted pre-contractual expenditure is the law of estoppel. There are various forms of estoppel recognised in the Common law world, all of them
being linked broadly by the idea that it is in some cases unconscionable
to allow a party to adopt a position which is at odds with a position previously adopted by it. Though the English courts have been strongly against
the view that a single doctrine of estoppel exists, of which the various
types are merely subsets, it has nonetheless been judicially remarked that
'it is unconscionability which provides the link between them'.[3]

Of the various forms of estoppel recognised by the Common law,
some arise at common law, and some in equity. Not all can be conceived
of in promissory terms. There is disagreement among the Common law

---

[3] In this respect there is, as will be seen in Ch. 7, a connection with the Scottish doctrine
of personal bar, in which the idea of unfairness is a constant linking the various forms of
personal bar.

jurisdictions as to whether various forms of estoppel can create rights or not, and whether or not they give rise to a cause of action or merely a defence. The summary which follows takes English law as the starting point, though differences of approach in other Common law jurisdictions will be noted at various points.

As to the types of estoppel recognised in common law and equity, at common law estoppel by representation provides a defence against a party seeking to deny a representation of fact which it has previously made.[4] Equity recognises promissory estoppel and proprietary estoppel, both varieties preventing a party which has made a promise from acting inconsistently with that prior promise; proprietary estoppel concerns promises made by an owner of land, promissory estoppel any other type of promise (including a promise made by a prospective purchaser of land). The two varieties of equitable estoppel, being promissory based, are clearly of the greatest relevance to a discussion on the idea of promise within contract law. Proprietary estoppel is discussed later in this chapter; it is promissory estoppel to which attention is first given.

The doctrine of promissory estoppel holds that if A has made a clear or unequivocal promise (or an assurance tantamount to a promise) to B which has affected B's position, and if it would be inequitable to allow A to go back on such promise, then A will be prevented from acting inconsistently with the promise.[5] This may mean either, as in US Common law, that B is given a direct right to enforce A's promise by raising a claim against A (thus, in effect, bypassing the requirement of consideration), or, as in England, that B is given a defence to any action by A to enforce a position contrary to A's promise (or sometimes that A is prevented from relying on a defence which might otherwise be available to it, if that would be contrary to A's promise).[6] In England, the courts have restricted the doctrine to cases where the promise relates to a right stemming from a pre-existing

---

[4] Peel, *Treitel on Contract*, paras. 3–090–091.

[5] The requirement of a promise – a statement of future undertaking – distinguishes promissory estoppel from estoppel by representation, which proceeds from a statement of existing fact. As such, promissory estoppel has more in common with common law forbearance than with estoppel by representation, given that both promissory estoppel and forbearance 'are concerned with the legal effects of promises rather than with proof of disputed facts' (Peel, *Treitel on Contract*, para. 3–091).

[6] In cases where the doctrine deprives the promisor of utilising a defence which might otherwise be available to it, promissory estoppel has a more active character (see Peel, *Treitel on Contract*, para. 3–089). However, the cause of action against the promisor must have arisen independently of the promise, because in English law promissory estoppel does not itself create any new cause of action (see *Combe* v. *Combe* [1951] 2 KB 215, 219).

legal relationship between the parties,[7] though that is not a requirement in all Common law jurisdictions (it is not so in the US, nor in Australia, where a belief that a legal relationship will exist in future may suffice).[8] In jurisdictions where the promise made need not relate to a pre-existing right between the parties, this evidently opens the way for promissory estoppel to play a role in relation to liability for pre-contractual expenditure: if A has incurred expenditure on the basis of a promise by B that a contract will be entered into between the parties, then such a promise can be used to trigger the doctrine of promissory estoppel (as will be seen in the discussion below of the *Hoffman* v. *Red Owl* case). On the other hand, if, as in English law, a pre-existing legal relationship must exist between the parties, promissory estoppel has no obvious scope of application to promises made during contractual negotiations.

The need for promissory estoppel to deal with cases of unenforceable unilateral promises and gratuitous contracts which, in other jurisdictions, would give rise to valid obligations, means that the doctrine must do a great deal more legal work than, say, the doctrine of personal bar in Scots law, where, given a much wider enforcement of promises, the focus of personal bar can be the prevention of unconscionable, inconsistent conduct without the need for the presence of a promise. If English law were to abolish the requirement of consideration, such a development in the law of estoppel would seem a likely possibility.[9]

(i)   Promissory estoppel: promissory or reliance-based principle?

Promissory estoppel has been argued by some to be a clear example of the reliance rather than the promissory principle at work in the law, in

---

[7] See Beale, *Chitty on Contracts*, para. 3–088; Peel, *Treitel on Contract*, paras. 3–079, 3–088.

[8] In *Waltons Stores (Interstate) Ltd* v. *Maher* (1988) 164 CLR 387, 428, Brennan J stated: 'to establish an equitable estoppel, it is necessary for a plaintiff to prove that (1) the plaintiff assumed that a particular legal relationship then existed between the plaintiff and the defendant *or expected that a particular legal relationship would exist between them* and, in the latter case, that the defendant would not be free to withdraw from the expected legal relationship; (2) the defendant has induced the plaintiff to adopt that assumption or expectation; (3) the plaintiff acts or abstains from acting in reliance on the assumption or expectation; (4) the defendant knew or intended him to do so; (5) the plaintiff's action or inaction will occasion detriment if the assumption or expectation is not fulfilled; and (6) the defendant has failed to act to avoid that detriment whether by fulfilling the assumption or expectation or otherwise' (italicised emphasis added). Brennan J does not use the word 'promissory' in this summary, and some have argued that Australian law is developing a more generalised doctrine of estoppel than exists under English law's compartmentalised approach.

[9] As arguably is already happening in Australia, a development discussed below at p. 188.

that it operates to protect the detrimental reliance of one in whose favour an undertaking is made.[10] However, given that, before application of the doctrine is triggered, a promise must be present, and one which (in English law at least) relates to a pre-existing right between the parties, it seems more plausible to say that it is actually about an attempt to solve a technical problem of promissory liability caused by the doctrine of consideration.[11] Such a promissory view of the doctrine is supported by an historical analysis of the development of the ideas of consideration and promissory estoppel.[12] As the nineteenth-century conception of consideration as a performance given under an exchange or bargain proved to be very restrictive, an impetus was created for developing the doctrine of promissory estoppel in order to mitigate perceived unjust results of the consideration rule. In England, Sir Frederick Pollock argued for an extension of the idea of a bargain to include a 'bargained for detriment'.[13] This suggestion was made in order to explain the enforcement of promises made in respect of marriage settlements, gratuitous loans and deposit. A related, but somewhat different, approach was taken with regard to the US Common law by Samuel Williston, who argued that marriage settlements were in fact enforced because of detrimental reliance, the promisee having changed his or her position in reliance on the promise by marrying.[14] Williston called the principle that he developed to explain this sort of liability 'promissory estoppel'.[15]

The promissory basis of promissory estoppel is evident in the judgment of Denning J (as he then was) in *Central London Property Trust Ltd* v. *High Trees*.[16] In fact, it can be argued that Denning J was attempting not just to establish the judgment on the basis of estoppel, but to develop a free-standing unilateral promissory form of liability. Denning J stated the basis for holding the landlord to his undertaking to accept a reduced rent not merely as the landlord being estopped from denying later contrary statements, but rather because

> a promise was made which was intended to create legal relations, and to the knowledge of the person making the promise, was going to be

---

[10] See Atiyah, *Promises, Morals and Law*, pp. 196–7.
[11] In *Waltons Stores (Interstate) Ltd* v. *Maher* (1988) 164 CLR 387, 402, Mason CJ and Wilson J noted in their joint judgment the tendency of promissory estoppel to 'occupy ground left vacant due to the constraints affecting consideration'.
[12] See Gordley, 'Enforcing Promises', pp. 562–6.
[13] Pollock, *Principles of Contract* (10th edn, 1936), p. 164.
[14] Evidently a fictional assumption in a great many cases, where the parties would have married even without the marriage settlement.
[15] Williston, *The Law of Contracts*, vol. 1, §§100, 139.   [16] [1947] 1 KB 130.

acted on by the person to whom it was made and which was in fact so
acted on.[17]

This comes quite close to an argument for outright unilateral promissory
liability, albeit with the caveat that it must be intended to produce reliance
and must in fact do so. There is no suggestion by Denning J that what is
created is merely a defence, but rather a full blown right which can be
enforced by the promisee under the conditions stipulated for its creation.
In fact, however, later more conservative interpretation of the *High Trees*
case saw it as embedding a defence of promissory estoppel in English law,
and not as creating positive promissory liability per se.

Nonetheless, despite the later restrictive interpretation of *High Trees*,
it has been remarked that other features of the current practice of the
English courts indicate the fundamentally promissory, rather than reliance, nature of promissory estoppel. Thus, it has been noted[18] that, as in
the US, English courts also seem to infer reliance, a practice which further suggests that the reliance aspect of the liability is being somewhat
downplayed. If promissory estoppel were genuinely a species of reliance-
based liability, one would expect an examination of whether such reliance
was actually present to be a crucial part of the court's analysis. The fact
that this does not occur tends to support the view that promissory estoppel is at heart an expression of the promissory principle. Furthermore,
true reliance-based liability would require some detriment to be caused to
the party acting in reliance, whereas the English cases demonstrate only
a need to prove that the party was affected by the promise, not that it has
suffered any loss.[19] Where promissory estoppel operates, it seems correct
to view it as promissory in nature.

Smith has characterised modern English law as being unclear as to
whether it is only promises which can found promissory estoppel or
whether representations indicating intention short of promise can also do
so too,[20] a lack of clarity, he argues, stemming from the fact that the language used by parties is often ambiguous. Thus, in *High Trees*, the landlord stated that he 'confirm[ed] … the ground rent should be reduced …
to £1,250 per annum', language which might prima facie be considered
either promissory or alternatively as merely expressive of a future intention. Yet, while language may at first appear ambiguous, it surely ought
to be the case that, if an obligation is to be considered as having been
assumed voluntarily by a party rather than as being imposed tortiously,

---

[17] [1947] 1 KB 130, 134.   [18] Smith, *Contract Theory*, p. 237.
[19] Beale, *Chitty on Contracts*, para. 3–094.   [20] Smith, *Contract Theory*, p. 236.

such language should be clearly expressive of an intention to be bound to the obligation, and not simply indicate an intention to be bound at some point in the future,[21] no matter whether it is called a promise or something else. Denning J clearly took the view in *High Trees* that what the landlord had said had indicated promissory intent, so there was no question of finding voluntary liability merely as a result of a statement of future intention. It seems right in principle that liability in promissory estoppel ought only to arise in cases where there is present a clear intention to be bound to an undertaking, whatever the exact words used.[22] Of course, were promises lacking consideration able to be directly enforced in English law, then promissory estoppel might develop in ways not restrained by the need to demonstrate the presence of a promise, but such development remains, for the moment, a feature of Common law jurisdictions other than that of England.

What then of the application of promissory estoppel to the field of failed pre-contractual negotiations and wasted expenditure associated with these?

(ii) Promissory estoppel and failed contractual negotiations

It is useful, in considering the potential relevance of promissory estoppel to the issue of wasted pre-contractual expenditure to have in mind a concrete example. One such is the famous US case *Hoffman v. Red Owl Stores*.[23] Hoffman had received various assurances from Red Owl that the latter would grant him a franchise in the Red Owl grocery store brand. On the faith of these assurances, Hoffman sold existing concerns he had, including a bakery. At one stage, an assurance from Red Owl was given that 'everything is ready to go. Get your money together and we are set'. This assurance turned out to be inaccurate, as a later telegram from Red Owl Head Office shown to Hoffman by the local Red Owl representative indicated: the telegram stipulated that only if Hoffman could find a further sum, in addition to that already required of him for promotional purposes, could the deal go through. Further conditions were added, and

---

[21] The view is taken in Beale, *Chitty on Contracts*, that either a promise, or an assurance or representation 'in the nature of a promise', must have been given (para. 3–089).

[22] If it is a question of whether an estoppel by representation of fact has been made, then of course representations other than of promissory intent may be relevant (see further Bower, *Estoppel by Representation*).

[23] *Hoffman v. Red Owl Stores, Inc.*, 26 Wis.2d 683, 133 N.W.2d 267 (1965). An interesting article, based partly upon interviews conducted with the plaintiff, is Whitford and Macaulay, 'Hoffman v. Red Owl Stores: The Rest of the Story'.

the negotiations collapsed. Hoffman sued Red Owl for his wasted expenditure, which amounted in total to around $20,000. The Wisconsin court found in favour of Hoffman on the basis of promissory estoppel, stating that Hoffman had reasonably and detrimentally relied on the promises made by Red Owl.

Fried argues that the decision was not actually about liability on a promise, because 'Red Owl was held liable not in order to force it to perform a promise, which it had never made, but rather to recompense Hoffman for losses he suffered'.[24] That seems however to miss an important point about promissory estoppel: while it is true that damages were not assessed in the performance measure, and nor was actual enforcement of any promise made, neither of these is necessary for the establishment of liability in promissory estoppel. That point aside, however, the correctness of the court's promissory estoppel analysis is evidently dependent upon there being some promise upon which to base liability for the subsequent losses of Hoffman: what then was the relevant promise (or promises) upon which Hoffman relied? The court stated that '[t]he record here discloses a number of promises and assurances given to Hoffman ... in behalf of Red Owl upon which plaintiffs relied and acted upon to their detriment. Foremost were the promises that for the sum of $18,000 Red Owl would establish Hoffman in a store'.[25] In so stating, the court emphasised that it was not the case that any promise would have to be so comprehensive as to meet the requirements of a contractual offer.[26]

Promissory estoppel, in the form applied in this case, is evidently capable of providing a basis for recovery of pre-contractual wasted expenditure in qualifying cases. Its qualifications are the need to identify (i) a promise made by the defendant, and (ii) losses flowing from reliance on this promise.[27] While most losses claimed by a negotiating party are likely to fulfil those criteria, if it transpires that the losses were incurred purely as a result of the decision of the party incurring them, without reference to anything said or done by the other party, they will be irrecoverable. That

---

[24] Fried, *Contract as Promise*, p. 24.
[25] 26 Wis.2d at 697, 133 N.W.2d at 274.   [26] 133 N.W. 2d at 275.
[27] Subsequent to the *Hoffman* decision, §90 of the Restatement (Second) Contracts was passed, the section stating: 'A promise which the promisor should reasonably expect to induce action or forbearance on the part of the promisee or a third person and which does induce such action or forbearance is binding if injustice can be avoided only by enforcement of the promise. The remedy granted for breach may be limited as justice requires.'

seems equitable, given that such losses are both risky as well as causally unrelated to anything the other party has done.

The *Red Owl* remedy has not been adopted in English law as a means of remedying wasted pre-contractual expenditure, given English insistence upon a prior legal relationship between the parties to which the promise must relate. However, in Australian Common law a radically developed version of promissory estoppel (argued by some to have transformed into a new, wider doctrine of 'equitable estoppel'[28]) has been held applicable in instances of failed contractual negotiations. In *Waltons Stores (Interstate) Ltd* v. *Maher*,[29] advanced negotiations for the lease of land were in place between the parties. The draft terms of the contract had been agreed, the prospective tenant's solicitors having assured the prospective landlord's solicitors that, if last minute amendments suggested by the landlord were not agreed to, then this would be intimated the following day. No such intimation was made, and the landlord's solicitors subsequently despatched a copy of the lease signed by its clients. Without any counter-signature by the tenant, the landlord (to the tenant's knowledge) began demolishing an existing building and the construction of a new one in order to comply with the terms of the envisaged lease. The tenant never signed the lease, and subsequently attempted to renege on the agreement. The High Court, however, held that a contract existed on the basis of promissory estoppel, noting that, given the unconscionability of withdrawing from the agreement, the tenant was 'estopped in all the circumstances from retreating from its implied promise to complete the agreement'.[30] The Court's discussion of the inequity of withdrawal, together with the focus on the implied assurance given by the tenant, bears close comparison not only with the *Red Owl* case, but also with the hallmarks of the Scottish approach to pre-contractual assurances discussed below, though with the difference that in the Australian decision the court treated the circumstances as being *as if a contract existed* between the parties,[31] damages being awarded for its breach, rather than mere recovery of wasted expenditure being awarded. The Australian approach takes promissory estoppel beyond its traditional role of providing a limited defence against conduct inconsistent with a prior promise and into the territory of enforcing informal promises in order to prevent inequity resulting from the non-enforcement of such promises. Such a radical approach is also

---

[28] Spence, *Protecting Reliance: The Emergent Doctrine of Equitable Estoppel.*
[29] (1988) 164 CLR 387. [30] Per Mason CJ and Wilson J, (1988) 164 CLR 387, 408.
[31] See judgment of Brennan J, para. 35: 'equity is to be satisfied by treating Waltons as though it had done what it induced Mr Maher to expect that it would do'.

visible in the view of the Australian courts concerning liability for breaking off contractual negotiations, discussed further below.

(iii)   Proprietary estoppel and failed contractual negotiations

English law has traditionally deemed that, if the right which the claimant
is seeking to establish relates to land, the relevant claim will lie in proprietary estoppel, not promissory estoppel, even though, in essence, the
foundation of the claim remains that the claimant was led by the defendant's promise to believe that a certain state of affairs existed, and, on the
faith of this, undertook expenditure which turned out to be wasted given
that no such state of affairs actually existed. The mere fact that the right
concerned is proprietary traditionally means that the claim is treated as a
separate type of estoppel, distinct from promissory estoppel, and with the
crucial difference that, in English law at least, it can operate as a cause of
action not just a defence.[32] It has thus traditionally proven useful in cases
where, for instance, B believes that it has acquired a proprietary right from
A but, because of some failure to comply with formalities, no valid right
has in fact been conferred upon B, circumstances which in some jurisdictions would give rise to a statutory remedial entitlement.[33] The traditional law in this area was thrown into doubt by the decision of the House
of Lords in *Yeoman's Row Management Ltd* v. *Cobbe*,[34] which seemed to
suggest that proprietary estoppel was a mere sub-species of promissory
estoppel.[35] However, subsequently, in *Thorner* v. *Major*,[36] the traditional
position was reaffirmed that proprietary estoppel is not simply a sub-
type of promissory estoppel, and that each form of estoppel has distinct
requirements. English law thus continues to take a different approach to
that of some other parts of the Common law world, where there has been a
growing tendency to view promissory and proprietary estoppel as simply
two varieties of equitable estoppel.[37] For the moment, where a proprietary
estoppel claim is available in English law, it presents the benefit in relation
to a claim for wasted pre-contractual expenditure that the claimant has a
cause of action rather than merely a defence.

---

[32] In Australia and the United States both proprietary *and* promissory estoppel can give
rise to rights, not simply a defence, so that the need to distinguish the two doctrines has
been rendered largely obsolete.

[33] As they do in Scotland, for instance, by means of what is referred to as a statutory form of
personal bar: see the Requirements of Writing (Scotland) Act 1995, s. 1(3), (4).

[34] [2008] UKHL 55.   [35] See judgment of Lord Scott at para. 14.

[36] [2009] UKHL 18.

[37] See Spence, *Protecting Reliance: The Emergent Doctrine of Equitable Estoppel.*

(iv)   Conclusion on estoppel and pre-contractual expenditure

It is clear that either promissory or proprietary estoppel is theoretically capable of dealing with certain claims relating to wasted pre-contractual expenditure. In fact, in a successful claim of proprietary estoppel, it is not simply that wasted expenditure is recovered, but rather that the right in land is itself upheld (in *Thorner*, the claimant was awarded the property itself, not simply wasted expenditure he had undertaken in the belief he was owner). That provides protection not merely of the restoration but the performance interest. By contrast, the utility of promissory estoppel varies jurisdictionally so far as wasted pre-contractual expenditure is concerned: in English law, it is unavailable, given the need for a pre-existing legal relationship and the further restriction that promissory estoppel claims are a defence rather than a foundation of rights; in US law, promissory estoppel may found a claim for wasted pre-contractual expenditure, as the *Red Owl* case shows; in Australia, promissory estoppel may not only found a claim but may be used to enforce an exchange of promises which lack only the legally required form.

Promissory estoppel is clearly one way to remedy the problem of informally made promises. It is only a partial solution, however, and the underlying question remains as to why only promises which are marked by reciprocal consideration or which give rise to reliance should be considered worthy of enforcement. Or to put it another way, if proper respect is given to personal autonomy and freedom of the will, why ought not all promises, if seriously uttered, be enforced according to their terms? One might also question whether, despite the views of their Lordships in *Thorner*, there is any overriding need to continue to insist that promissory and proprietary estoppel remain independent doctrines, given the similar functions they play in English law in preventing unconscionable denial of a prior promise by the promisor. If enforcement of both unilateral and gratuitous promises were permitted in English law, then estoppel would have to do a lot less work and would no longer have to be tied to the idea of promise. Indeed, in Australia, the traditional promissory nature of promissory and proprietary estoppel is arguably changing in just such a way,[38] through development into a doctrine characterised less by promise and more by the prevention of inconsistent conduct causing loss to another. Such a development would give it a very similar characteristic to that of personal bar in Scots law.

---

[38] See Robertson, 'Estoppels and Right-Creating Events'.

(b)   A civilian solution to wasted pre-contractual expenditure: culpa in
contrahendo *and bad faith termination of contractual negotiations*

The German doctrine of *culpa in contrahendo* ('fault in contracting') has
been described as arising as follows:

> Once parties enter into negotiations for a contract ... a relationship of
> trust and confidence comes into existence irrespective of whether they
> succeed or fail. Thus, protection is afforded against blameworthy con-
> duct which prevents the consummation of a contract. A party is liable
> for negligently creating the expectation that a contract would be forth-
> coming although he knows or should know that the expectation cannot
> be realized. Furthermore, the parties are bound to take such precaution-
> ary measures as are necessary for the protection of each other's person or
> property.[39]

Described in this way, the possible boundaries of liability in *culpa in contrahendo* are quite wide, and might certainly encompass any bad faith
termination of intended contractual relations. Taken at its widest, the
doctrine would have the potential to destroy the freedom *not* to contract
and might put parties off negotiating contracts in the first place without
having formed a preliminary contract determining how the negotiating
process for the substantive contract was to be conducted. The doctrine
has been criticised for ignoring the reality that negotiating parties look to
their own interests; expecting them to protect the other party's position
has been said to be unrealistic.

Culpa in contrahendo was proposed by the German jurist Rudolf von
Jhering, who saw it as based upon the trust which exists between negotiating parties.[40] While the doctrine was originally accepted into German
law in uncodified form, it was incorporated into the BGB as a general
form of liability in the most recent revision of the Code.[41] Even before
this general incorporation there were, however, what could be classified
as specific, narrower instances of *culpa in contrahendo*, for instance §119
on contracts avoided for mistake, which provides that a party avoiding a
contract must pay damages to the other party for losses which that other
party suffers 'as a result of relying on the validity of the declaration [of
intent of the other party]'.

The now general provision on *culpa in contrahendo* (§311(2)) states that
an obligation under §241(2) – that is, an obligation obliging 'each party to

---

[39]   Kessler and Fine, 'Culpa in Contrahendo', p. 404.
[40]   Von Jhering, 'Culpa in Contrahendo', pp. 1–112.   [41]   See §311(2) BGB.

take account of the rights, legal interests and other interests of the other party' – comes into existence by:

(1) the commencement of contract negotiations,
(2) the initiation of a contract where one party, with regard to a potential contractual relationship, gives the other party the possibility of affecting his rights, legal interests and other interests, or entrusts these to him, or
(3) similar business contacts.

This codification has been described as 'utterly vague' and liable to perpetuate differing academic views on the nature of *culpa in contrahendo*.[42] Such differing views are quite substantial, not least in respect of the underlying nature of liability which is created by the doctrine. While there is general agreement that the new provision in the BGB is *not* promissory-based liability, but rather a continuation of the trust-based liability of the former uncodified law, there is no agreement on whether liability in *culpa in contrahendo* is best seen as lying in contract, in tort, or somewhere between those two obligations.[43]

A substantial part of the difficulty in deciding where taxonomically to place *culpa in contrahendo* stems from the quite varied circumstances which can trigger the doctrine, as well as from the nature and extent of recovery available. As to the different factual circumstances triggering liability, these include:

(1) claims for harm caused in circumstances which are almost delictual, but where there is a contractual background: these cases are typically of harm for personal injury caused to A while contemplating contracting with B. Examples include the famous cases of a linoleum roll falling on to a potential customer,[44] and the child of a shopper slipping on a vegetable leaf;[45]
(2) claims by A for his being worse off as a result of not entering a contract with B;

---

[42] Markesinis *et al.*, *The German Law of Contract*, p. 93.
[43] See Zimmermann, *Law of Obligations*, p. 245, who states that *culpa in contrahendo* 'falls squarely into the grey area between the law of contract and the law of delict … there is much to be said for the proposition that it does not fit neatly into either of these, but rather forms an integral part of a third "track" of liability'. For citation in German of the different literature expounding the various views, see Schlechtriem, *Schuldrecht*, p. 13; for a discussion in English of the issues, see Dietrich, 'Classifying Precontractual Liability', pp. 174f.
[44] RGZ 78, 239.   [45] BGHZ 66, 51.

(3) claims by A for his being worse off as a result of B's inducing him to contract with C;

(4) claims by A for having entered a contract with B on unfavourable terms; and

(5) claims under §311(3), that is claims against agents or those acting like agents in facilitating the conclusion of a contract.

In all these types of claim, damages are available, though usually only if the harm caused was the result of the fault of the breaching party.[46] There are, however, some instances of strict liability for *culpa in contrahendo*, for instance in the case mentioned earlier of damages under §122 for contracts avoided for mistake. Damages essentially protect the restoration interest, though in some types of case the award can approach compensation in the performance measure,[47] adding further confusion to the proper classification of the doctrine.

What will be noticed from the different types of factual circumstance listed above capable of giving rise to claims of *culpa in contrahendo* is that types (1), (3) and (4) would usually be settled in tort by most systems, sometimes through claims of misrepresentation (the German solution thus closing a gap in the codal provisions on error, discussed later). Type (1) is problematic for German tort law because of the terms of §831 which allow a vendor to evade liability if he showed care in employing and supervising the employee (in other words, which limit what would be called vicarious liability for employee's torts in some systems). Styling this *culpa in contrahendo*, and giving it a pre-contractual nature, means that the §278 contractual liability for employees can be used. Types (3) and (4) have been developed to deal largely with cases of negligent misrepresentation causing pure economic loss, as German tort law does not allow recovery in such cases.

Type (2) cases raise the most interesting issues for the idea of promise, or rather the freedom *not* to promise. It is this type which the *Red Owl* facts fall into. Considering possible liability in this type of case prompts one to ask whether negotiating parties owe each other any duties on account of negotiations breaking down. In German law, the answer is yes (as will be seen more fully in a discussion of such duties later in this chapter), the principle of trust and good faith giving rise to such duties, and the breach of good faith creating liability in *culpa in contrahendo*. German case law

---

[46] See §280(1) BGB.   [47] See, for instance, BGH NJW 1965, 812.

has demonstrated that in such type (2) cases four requirements must be met before liability can be established:

(a) A and B entered into negotiations for the conclusion of a contract;
(b) A had a legitimate expectation that a contract would be concluded with B;
(c) in reliance on this legitimate expectation, A incurred expenses or otherwise suffered loss which stems from the failure to conclude the contract; and
(d) B broke off the contract negotiations without good cause.

Thus, for instance, negotiations conducted by a party in bad faith, with no intention of contracting with the other party, would fall squarely within this category. Liability would also arise where, for instance, the vendor of a house, having arranged a visit to the property with a prospective purchaser, omitted to inform the prospective purchaser that the house has been sold, thus causing the prospective purchaser wasted travelling expenses.[48]

Many legal systems might well find liability in the terms defined by German law in type (2) cases controversial. Consider the criteria which must be met: these include that A has a 'legitimate expectation' that a contract will be concluded, and that B must break off negotiations 'without good cause' (*ohne triftigen Grund*). As to the first, it seems odd, in a system which says that once an offer is made it cannot usually be withdrawn, to consider that it is ever legitimate to expect that a contract will be concluded if an offer has *not* yet been forthcoming (if it has, that will provide the basis of liability in any event). As to the second, it seems problematic attempting to assess objectively what may or may not be a good cause for breaking off negotiations. Clear bad faith may be easy to identify (the fraudulently conducted negotiations, for instance), but what of less clear-cut cases? This surely is asking courts to dabble in business decisions and assumes that the motivating factors of commerce are susceptible to scrutiny by reference to judicial norms. Such a process must be fraught with difficulty and liable to claims of judicial interference in non-judicial matters. Ultimately, the underlying legitimate concern about liability in this type (2) case is that it seems to infringe the freedom of parties not to contract. While under *culpa in contrahendo* there would most certainly have been liability on the *Red Owl* facts, there would also be so in many

---

[48] This example is cited by Kessler and Fine, 'Culpa in Contrahendo', p. 405.

other cases which, under the Common law or in mixed legal systems, would not give rise to liability.

Some of the other types of case where recovery is allowed seem, however, less controversial to non-German eyes: for instance, leading another to think that contract formalities need not be complied with may well create liability in other systems under estoppel or personal bar; contracts which are void or *contra bonos mores* also seem less controversial cases in terms of some sort of accounting between the parties, assuming that a blameworthy party can be identified.[49] But that leaves the challenging cases, especially cases where liability is established for losses caused in reliance on a contract being formed, but where the contractual negotiations have been broken off by a party in some way deemed culpable.

Lest it be thought that German law is unique in creating liability in this type (2) case, when there is simply a bad faith, unilateral breaking off of contractual negotiations, mention could be made of other civilian systems, but also of some jurisdictions within the Common law world, to indicate that this is not so. Dutch jurisprudence, for instance, distinguishes three stages in the contract negotiation process: at stage one, the stage of preliminary enquiry, both parties are entirely free to break off negotiations; at stage two, during substantive negotiation, a party may still break off negotiations, but will have to pay the other's expenses if it does so; at stage three, as negotiations draw to a close, if one party has been reasonably led to believe that a contract will be concluded between the parties, the parties will no longer be free to break off negotiations and, if this occurs, either damages will be due in the performance measure or the party in default may even be ordered to continue with negotiations.[50] Liability under Dutch law in these later stages of negotiation has been based upon the good faith relationship said to exist between the parties.[51] The Dutch approach clearly poses a much greater threat to freedom not to contract, given the possibility of compelling parties to continue negotiation (something which must surely be impractical if trust has broken down between the parties).

Yet it is not just civilian systems which are pushing the boundaries of pre-contractual liability beyond what arguably is equitable. In

---

[49] See Markesinis *et al.*, *German Law of Contract*, p. 100.
[50] See the *Plas/Valburg* case, HR 18 June 1982, NJ 1983, 723; though, taking the more restrictive view that a breach in negotiations may sometimes be justified even at a late stage, see HR 14 June 1996, NJ 1997, 481.
[51] HR 16 June 1995, NJ 1995, 705.

Australia, the decision of the New South Wales Court of Appeal in
Sabemo v. *North Sydney Municipal Council*[52] also gives grounds for concern, a concern voiced in the English courts in the *Regalian Properties*
case.[53] In *Sabemo*, the plaintiff company had tendered to undertake
work on land owned by the defendant. The contract negotiations were
prolonged, lasting some three years, but the defendant eventually
decided to abandon the development and broke off negotiations with
the plaintiff. The plaintiff had spent large sums of money during the
negotiation process, which it now claimed from the defendant. In his
judgment, Sheppard J held that the plaintiff was entitled to recover, on
the basis of the principle that

> where two parties proceed upon the joint assumption that a contract will
> be entered into between them, and one does work beneficial for the project, and thus in the interests of the two parties, which work he would not
> be expected, in other circumstances, to do gratuitously, he will be entitled
> to compensation or restitution, if the other party unilaterally decides to
> abandon the project, not for any reason associated with bona fide disagreement concerning the terms of the contract to be entered into, but for
> reasons which, however valid, pertain only to his own position and do not
> relate at all to that other party.[54]

Such liability cannot reasonably be characterised as voluntary in basis,
given that Sheppard J talked of 'imposing' it for the imputed fault of the
defendants, an imposition which he was willing to make 'irrespective of
the common intention of the parties'.[55] Though not strictly classed as tortious, it certainly has an air of tortious liability about it. It also has much
in common with the good faith approach of civilian systems. This is especially evident from the fact that Sheppard J went as far as to comment
that, while the defendant might have had 'good reasons' for dropping the
proposal, these were irrelevant because 'they had nothing to do with the
plaintiff', which had 'in good faith ... worked assiduously' towards the
conclusion of a contractual relationship.[56]

The principle enunciated in *Sabemo* is startling. It would seem to suggest that, for instance, if during protracted contract negotiations, one of
the party's financial circumstances alter so that the intended contract

---

[52] [1977] 2 NSWLR 880.
[53] See comments of Rattee J in *Regalian Properties plc* v. *London Docklands Development Corporation* [1995] 1 All ER 1005, 1024.
[54] [1977] 2 NSWLR 880, at 902–3.
[55] *Ibid.*, at 900.   [56] *Ibid.*

is no longer financially feasible for it, it is precluded from withdrawing (such a reason being valid but only pertaining to it) without compensating the other for any losses it may have suffered. Many will feel that this is far too great an interference with freedom of contract, though whatever view is taken, this development of the Common law of Australia in *Sabemo* has remarkable parallels with the *culpa in contrahendo* liability of German law.

As a final remark, it is interesting to note that the Louisiana courts have flirted with the idea of establishing liability based upon the idea of *culpa in contrahendo*. The Louisiana Supreme Court did so in *Coleman* v. *Bossier City*,[57] in which, due to certain contracts being held invalid on account of a failure to comply with state statutes (a potential invalidity of which the Court felt the defendants ought to have known), developers of property were left substantially impoverished. Because the defendant municipality had benefited from the developer's loss, a claim in unjustified enrichment was thought able to furnish a remedy for the plaintiff. This meant that the majority of the Court felt that 'we need not now decide whether recovery may be allowable under the doctrine of *culpa in contrahendo*'.[58] This statement offers a tantalising glimpse of what might have been the first example of *culpa in contrahendo* liability in Louisiana, but the possibility of such development has not been taken up by the courts, and the subsequent enactment[59] of a codal provision that amounts to promissory estoppel may perhaps be perceived as having removed any pressing need to revisit the idea of *culpa in contrahendo*. Were the possibility of so developing the law to be reconsidered at some point, then there are Louisiana cases other than *Coleman* which might be looked to for assistance. The early twentieth-century case of *Kaplan* v. *Whitworth*[60] could, for instance, provide a basis for developing *culpa in contrahendo*. In the opinion of the court in that case, though an agreement between the parties did not amount to a valid contract of sale, the litigation was remitted for further procedure on the question of whether the plaintiff's losses incurred in reliance on the belief, fostered by the defendant, that the land would be sold could be proved. If the plaintiff could so prove, said the court, '[t]hese actual losses, we think, he may be entitled to recover'.[61] The affinity of the facts of the case with the doctrine of *culpa in contrahendo* are evident.

---

[57] 305 So 2d 444 (La 1974).   [58] Per Tate J, for the majority, at 447.
[59] CC Art. 1967.   [60] 40 So 723 (La 1905).   [61] Per Monroe J at 725.

(c)   A mixed legal system solution to wasted pre-contractual expenditure: liability from an implied assurance that a valid contract exists

A mixed legal system solution to the problem of wasted pre-contractual expenditure has been fashioned around the core idea that liability should arise when an implied but false assurance has been given by one negotiating party to the other that a contract exists, such assurance leading to detrimental reliance on the part of the other party. Where this occurs, then, under Scots law, recovery will exceptionally be allowed for the wasted pre-contractual expenditure incurred in reliance on the assurance.

This remedial entitlement was developed in a line of cases beginning with *Walker* v. *Milne*.[62] Its restricted availability was explained in *Dawson International plc* v. *Coats Paton plc*,[63] when Lord Cullen identified the three requirements for a claim by A as being that: (1) B has given an implied assurance to A that a valid contract has been entered into by the parties; (2) this assurance is false, no valid contract in fact existing between them; and (3) A has incurred expenditure in reliance on the assurance given by B. In a subsequent action it was further judicially remarked that, because the remedy is equitable in nature, in order to claim, A must have no other remedy available to it for recovery of its wasted expenditure.[64] These requirements evidently restrict the utility of the remedy quite extensively. In particular, given that there must have been at least an implied assurance that a contract *already* exists, it will be obvious that a mere promise that the other party intends to contract is insufficient, as is a mere breaking off of negotiations without any promise or assurance of any kind having been given. Though the remedy has been argued to be based on good faith, if that is so it is a narrower expression of that idea than in *culpa in contrahendo*.

The remedy was pled recently in a Scottish version of the *Red Owl* facts in the case of *Khaliq* v. *Londis (Holdings) Ltd*.[65] As in *Red Owl*, the facts also concerned a shopkeeper who was keen to expand his business interests by joining a franchise. Like Mr Hoffman, Mr Khaliq's negotiations, and his substantial expenditure in preparation for joining the franchise, also proved fruitless. On the facts of the case, the Inner House of the Court of Session took the view that Mr Khaliq did not meet the requirements for a claim under the *Walker* v. *Milne* type of liability. In the

---

[62] (1823) 2 S 379.   [63] 1988 SLT 854.
[64] *Bank of Scotland* v. *3i plc* 1990 SC 215.   [65] [2010] CSIH 13.

principal judgment of the court, Lord Osborne classified the expenditure undertaken by Mr Khaliq as not made in reliance on any duty which he believed he was under in terms of a supposed contract between the parties, but rather as spent simply on the recommendation of the defender's representative.[66] This statement is somewhat controversial, as it suggests that, to trigger the equitable remedy established by *Walker* v. *Milne*, the expenditure must have been undertaken in the belief that it was made in fulfilment of such a contractual duty, yet prior to *Khaliq* none of the cases relating to this type of recovery have imposed such a requirement. All that hitherto has been insisted upon by the courts is that the wasted pre-contractual expenditure must have been undertaken in reliance on the existence of a contract, or, to put it another way, that the belief of the pursuer in the existence of the contract was the cause-in-fact of the expenditure. Lord Osborne's amended requirement goes further than those prior authorities.

A further troubling aspect of the *Khaliq* decision are judicial remarks made by two of the judges which cast doubt on the very continued availability of the remedy for wasted pre-contractual expenditure. Both Lord Osborne and Lord Marnoch doubted whether, given various changes in the law, there remained any need for the availability of the equitable remedy for wasted pre-contractual expenditure.[67] Yet the changes referred to would not have assisted Mr Khaliq, none of them being suitable to provide him with a remedy on the facts of his case. Mr Khaliq's claim boiled down to the fact that various implied assurances made by Londis had led him reasonably to believe that the parties were in a contractual relationship, a belief which was erroneous. Only Londis could have appraised him of the correct position, but it did not do so until after he had undertaken substantial expenditure on the basis of the false belief which they had created in his mind. Such circumstances have traditionally constituted grounds for equitable recovery, and it would be regrettable if the established remedy permitting such were now to be deemed to have been superseded. Fortunately, the judges in *Khaliq* did not go so far as to declare the remedy

---

[66] Lord Osborne also added that Mr Khaliq, having had two neighbouring shops he owned refitted as part of the works he carried out, was continuing to derive a benefit from the refitting of one of those shops, from which he continued to trade, and that therefore it would be inequitable to allow recovery of the refurbishment costs of that shop (amounting to some £25,000 of the total expenditure).

[67] See Lord Osborne's judgment at para. 26, and Lord Marnoch's judgment at para. 37. The legal developments referred to by the court are the passage of s. 1 of the Civil Evidence (Scotland) Act 1988, ss. 1 and 2 of the Requirements of Writing (Scotland) Act 1995, and changes in the law relating to negligent misrepresentation.

superseded, and it is to be hoped that in a future case the courts will reaffirm its continued existence and desirability. To repeal the remedy would leave an equitable gap in the law and would deprive Scots law of a result achieved in both the Common law and German law.

Admittedly, some (though not all) of the Scottish cases which might previously have been solved using the *Walker* v. *Milne* common law action for wasted pre-contractual expenditure could now more advantageously be solved by the application of the statutory form of personal bar found in the Requirements of Writing (Scotland) Act 1995 to which Lord Osborne referred in *Khaliq*. This form of personal bar allows, inter alia, a party which has detrimentally relied upon a contract relating to a real right in land to prevent the other party to the contract from denying its validity on account of a want of proper form so long as that other party knew of and acquiesced in the reliance of the first party.[68] What this means is that in cases where it is only a want of proper form which hinders the contract formation, a party may now seek to enforce the contract concerned, thereby protecting its performance interest, rather than simply falling back on the recovery of wasted expenditure undertaken in the belief that the contract existed. Though the point has not been specifically addressed by the courts, it would seem to follow from judicial statements that the equitable, common law remedy is an exceptional one, available only where the pursuer has no other avenue of legal redress – that a potential pursuer is now required to enforce the contract through use of the statutory personal bar, rather than claim its wasted expenses, in cases where the statutory remedy is available. In other words, in cases where the problem is a want of proper form, statutory personal bar now appears to have replaced the recovery of wasted pre-contractual expenditure.

---

[68] Section 1(3), (4). Interestingly, the provision says only that the party seeking to enforce the contract must have 'acted or refrained from acting in reliance on the contract'. It does not say that such reliance must have been reasonable. There is, thus, no definitive position adopted by the statute in relation to the question of whether the particular claimant ought to have known that contracts relating to land but not in the written proper form are invalid, and ought therefore to be precluded from triggering personal bar on the premise that its reliance was unreasonable. By way of contrast, in *Yeoman's Row* v. *Cobbe* [2008] UKHL 55, Lord Scott made a point of noting in his speech (at para. 27) that it 'would be an unusually unsophisticated negotiator who was not well aware that oral agreements relating to such an acquisition are by statute unenforceable and that no express reservation to make them so is needed. [The claimant] was an experienced property developer ...', such a consideration seeming to add weight to Lord Scott's decision not to permit reliance by the claimant on the doctrine of proprietary estoppel.

The Scottish approach has not been followed in other mixed legal systems. As discussed in Chapter 2, Louisiana already has a form of promissory estoppel[69] inspired by the US Common law, which may explain the lack of any evident perception that recovery in this area requires to be expanded. Promissory estoppel was not received into South Africa, which recognises only estoppel by representation. In both of these jurisdictions it has been argued by some that there was (or is) no need for a doctrine of promissory estoppel,[70] but this rather overlooks the point that no express acceptance of a promissory undertaking is required before promissory estoppel can apply, whereas such an acceptance (whether by word or conduct) would be required before a gratuitous contract might be concluded in either jurisdiction. On the circumstances prevailing in *Red Owl*, it seems unlikely that there would have been any liability in South African law for Hoffman's wasted expenditure, whereas such liability would have arisen under Article 1967 of the Louisiana Code.

As for *express* but false assurances that a contract exists, the obvious answer is that such can be treated as an actionable misrepresentation in delict/tort. That solution is available in the Common law as well as in the mixed legal systems too. Such a claim evidently presupposes that the defendant has expressly held out to the claimant, either by words or conduct, that a contract exists between them, that such a statement is false, and that the defendant reasonably relied upon it to his loss. Such prerequisites will not be met in every case.[71] Indeed, it does not seem clear from the reported facts of *Red Owl* that any of the representations made to Hoffman were false when made, albeit that Red Owl kept changing their requirements as time went on. If the case is simply one of a defendant who repeatedly changes its mind, then the facts will not give rise to any actionable misrepresentation.

---

[69] See CC Art. 1967. It has been argued that the application of this provision to solve facts such as those in *Red Owl* would be unnecessary, given that Louisiana law does not require consideration to enforce a promise and thus, it is said, does not need a doctrine of promissory estoppel: see Gordley, 'Louisiana and the Common Law: *Le jour de gloire, est-il passé?*'. For a discussion of promissory estoppel as an alleged cause of action in Louisiana and comparative law, see Larroumet, 'Detrimental Reliance and Promissory Estoppel'.

[70] See for Louisiana, Gordley, 'Louisiana and the Civil Law: *Le jour de gloire, est-il passé?*', 205; for South Africa, see Sonnekus, *The Law of Estoppel in South Africa*, p. 94.

[71] Though there may be the possibility in some cases of alleging other types of misrepresentation during the negotiating process: thus, in *Walford* v. *Miles* [1992] 2 AC 128, the one successful portion of the plaintiffs' case was a misrepresentation claim (amounting to £700 for wasted expenditure) based upon the false statement of the defendants that they were not negotiating with a third party.

(d) Other solutions to the problem of pre-contractual liability

The Draft Common Frame of Reference (DCFR) provision on liability for wasted pre-contractual expenditure draws on the good faith element evident in a number of the solutions discussed above, and of those solutions is closest in nature to the German approach.[72] While parties are in general free to negotiate and not liable for failure to reach agreement,[73] the negotiating process gives rise to a duty to negotiate in accordance with good faith and fair dealing, and not to break off negotiations contrary to such good faith and fair dealing.[74] A specific example of conduct in breach of the duty is stated in the Article to be entering into or continuing negotiations with no real intention of reaching an agreement.[75] Breach of the duty imposed by the Article results in liability for any resultant losses.[76] The enunciation of such a duty in a model Code such as the DCFR avoids the need to classify the duty imposed as promissory, contractual, or tortious in nature – it merely arises as a result of the relevant provision – though the stated measure of losses recoverable ('any loss caused') certainly appears wide enough to encompass both what could be styled as 'performance measure' losses (lost profit, for instance) as well as the 'restoration measure' losses typically argued to be constituted by wasted pre-contractual expenditure.[77] The DCFR approach does, however, raise questions about the uncertainty surrounding the question when a party may walk away from negotiations, an uncertainty inherent in any duty defined in good faith terms. These questions are discussed more fully in the discussion in Chapter 6 on good faith in relation to performance (as well as, to some extent, in the following section on duties of disclosure).

A further possible solution, conceivably maintainable in any jurisdiction, would be to argue for the existence of a preliminary contract

---

[72] The Italian Civil Code also contains a specific duty to negotiate a contract in good faith: Codice civile Art. 1337.

[73] DCFR Art. II.-3.301(1).

[74] DCFR Art. II.-3:301(2). The Article states that this duty cannot be excluded or limited by contract (or, one assumes, a unilateral promise made by one party to the other that it shall not enforce the duty).

[75] Art. II.-3:301(4).   [76] Art. II.-3:301(3).

[77] The official commentary to the Article states that recovery encompasses expenses incurred, work done, loss on transactions made in reliance of the expected contract, and 'in some cases loss of opportunities', though 'the aggrieved party cannot claim to be put in to the position in which that party would have been if the contract had been duly concluded' (see para. H of the Official Commentary to Art. II.-3:301). Why such an exclusion applies given the breadth of the wording of the Article is not explained.

governing the question of liability for negotiating costs. In the *Red Owl* case, for instance, might such a contract have been argued to have existed based upon the communications issued by Red Owl? Such an argument would have been unlikely to have been successful, given that the assurances issued by Red Owl made no mention of responsibility for any preliminary expenditure. On the other hand, there is no reason why negotiating parties might not theoretically enter into such a preliminary agreement. Indeed, the Common law and mixed legal system use of the device of an implied contract, under which a *quantum meruit* must be paid, is capable of utilisation in cases where work has been done, but no clear express contractual intent may be gleaned from the parties' dealing.[78]

A final possible approach would simply be to argue that, in a case like *Red Owl*, there ought *not* to be any liability, given the absence of any explicit assumption of responsibility by Red Owl for any of Hoffman's expenditure. Mr Hoffman should, it might be argued, have been more cautious before embarking on extensive expenditure with no certainty of any contract at the end of it. This approach of denying voluntarily based precontractual liability is largely the approach of English law. Promissory estoppel has a much narrower application in England than in the US, English law insisting that its use must relate to some pre-existing right of the claimant and, moreover, that it may only act as a defence but not a cause of action. No pre-existing right was present on the facts of *Red Owl*, nor was Mr Hoffman seeking simply to raise a defence to a claim by Red Owl. English law would therefore have been unlikely to grant Mr Hoffman the recovery he sought.

Such a view on the likely English approach is consistent with the decision in *Regalian Properties plc* v. *London Docklands Development Corporation*,[79] where the court took the view that, unless some benefit is conferred by one negotiating party on the other which is capable of founding a claim in restitution, expenditure undertaken by the first party merely in prospect of a contractual relationship is irrecoverable in English law. It is a view which is also consistent with the English law position that there will in general be no common law duty imposed on contracting parties to negotiate a contract in good faith, or to use 'best endeavours' or

---

[78] For a summary of the approach of the English courts, see the judgment of Christopher Clarke J (at para. 171) in *MSM Consulting Ltd* v. *United Republic of Tanzania* [2009] EWHC 121 (QB), (2009) 123 Con LR 154. For Scotland, see *Pillans & Wilson* v. *Castlecary Fireclay Co Ltd* 1931 SLT 532.

[79] [1995] 1 WLR 212, [1995] 1 All ER 1005 (Ch).

'reasonable endeavours/diligence' to reach agreement,[80] and that parties are therefore generally free to walk away from contract negotiations without incurring any liability to each other for so doing. That position was strongly asserted by the House of Lords in *Walford* v. *Miles*,[81] though an express duty to negotiate a specific contractual matter may be enforceable in English law if the matter to be negotiated is capable of precise and objective determination,[82] a view which is supported by the fact that express duties to use best efforts or endeavours to reach an agreement have been enforced in the English courts.[83] That has also been the recently expressed view of the Scottish courts, which have upheld undertakings to use reasonable endeavours to reach contractual agreement so long as objective criteria exist against which to measure the reasonableness of the parties' endeavours.[84] What the remedy ought to be for breach of such an obligation is, however, a trickier matter.[85]

(e) Conclusion on pre-contractual liability

It will be apparent, having regard to the comparative excursus undertaken above, that there remains a high degree of jurisdictional divergence

---

[80] *Scandinavian Trading Tanker Co. AB* v. *Flota Petrolera Ecuatoriana* ('*The Scaptrade*') [1981] 2 Lloyd's Rep 425, 432; *Star Steamship Society* v. *Beogradska Plovidba* ('*The Junior K*') [1988] 2 Lloyd's Rep 583; *Antclizo Shipping Corp.* v. *Food Corp. of India No. 2* ('*The Antclizo*') [1992] 1 Lloyd's Rep 558.

[81] [1992] 2 AC 128, HL. It is a view shared by other Common law jurisdictions: see, for instance, *Coal Cliff Collieries Pty Ltd* v. *Sijehama Pty Ltd* (1991) 24 NSWLR 1.

[82] See *Petromec Inc* v. *Petroleo Brasileiro SA Petrobas* [2005] EWCA Civ 891, [2006] 1 Lloyd's Rep 121. In Australia, such an undertaking may also be valid, assuming it is precise enough: see the judgment of Kirby P in *Coal Cliff Collieries Pty Ltd* v. *Sijehama Pty Ltd* (1991) 24 NSWLR 1; likewise, in Scotland, *McCall's Entertainments (Ayr) Ltd* v. *South Ayrshire Council (No. 1)* 1998 SLT 1403.

[83] *Re Anglo-Russian Merchant Traders Ltd* [1917] 2 KB 679; *Coloniale Import-Export* v. *Loumidis Sons* [1978] 2 Lloyd's Rep 560. See also the Australian case of *Hospital Products Ltd* v. *United States Surgical Corp* (1984) 156 CLR 41.

[84] *R & D Construction Group Ltd* v. *Hallam Land Management Ltd* [2009] CSOH 128, where a duty on a party to 'use reasonable endeavours' to agree a price for the sale of land was deemed an enforceable obligation; cf. *Scottish Coal Co Ltd* v. *Danish Forestry Co Ltd* [2009] CSOH 171, where an obligation to conclude a ranking agreement between the seller of a coal mine and the purchaser's bank, analysed by the court as an agreement to agree, was held *not* enforceable because of the absence of any objective criterion to judge the reasonableness of the endeavours of the parties to agree (see the judgment of Lord Glennie at para. 66).

[85] Specific enforcement of the obligation may well be impractical, which leaves damages. Presumably damages will require to be measured either on a loss of a chance basis, or by reference to wasted expenditure.

in the field of pre-contractual liability. At one extreme, English law shows a preference for the bright line approach of denying liability for wasted expenditure in cases of failed contracts, promissory and proprietary estoppel being capable of dealing with only a very limited number of cases. US Common law has shown more enthusiasm for recovery, by developing the remedy of promissory estoppel to allow claims in cases where some promise that a contract will be forthcoming have been made. Despite such remedy being argued by some to be reliance-based in nature, it is more plausible to see the concept of promise as the basis of liability, albeit that the recovery is in the restoration measure.[86] Scots law reaches a somewhat similar result, by providing an equitable remedy for recovery of wasted pre-contractual expenditure, but this may only be claimed in the rather restrictive case where there has been an implied but false assurance by the other party that a contract has been concluded between them. It might be going too far to characterise such a remedy as promise-based, though it would not be improper to suggest that it is a form of voluntary liability, given the requirement of assurances made by the defender. Some have alternatively argued that the nature of the Scottish remedy lies in good faith, a view which, if correct, would draw comparisons with the more extensive German good faith based remedy of *culpa in contrahendo* and with similar good faith based solutions in other civilian systems.

Harmonisation of the law in this field is likely to be somewhat problematic, given the differing jurisdictional conceptions of where risk and, with it, loss should properly fall during the negotiation of a contract. The solution suggested in the DCFR would be far from uncontroversial.

2. Pre-contractual duties of disclosure

The discussion in the immediately preceding section on pre-contractual liability has touched on the question of one specific type of pre-contractual duty, that of a duty not to break off contractual negotiations (and the resulting duty to pay the cost of wasted expenditure if one does), or, to put it another way, a duty to continue negotiating in good faith. In addition to such a duty there may be other duties alleged to exist at the pre-contractual

---

[86] It is a fallacy to assume that promissory based liability can only ever give recovery in the performance measure; on the contrary, while the performance measure is the primary interest protected by voluntary obligations, the restoration and restitutionary measures are exceptionally protected in appropriate cases. See further Hogg, *Obligations*, paras. 1.35–9.

stage. One such further possible, though controversial, duty is the duty to disclose such information to the other party concerning the contract, or the contractual negotiations, as that other party might reasonably wish to enable it properly to conduct negotiations. A duty of this type, if it exists, is less likely to be justified in terms of the idea of a promise, though it is not impossible to argue that there is an implied promise that full and appropriate disclosure will have been made by negotiating parties to each other. Such an argument does rely, however, on an evident fiction, and it is more common to find a duty of disclosure justified on the basis of the alleged good faith relationship of the parties at the negotiation stage.

But when, if at all, should such duties exist? The controversy generated by that question is not new. Cicero posed as a dilemma the question of whether a corn merchant should attempt to get the highest price he could from a starving population, or whether he was bound to disclose that further cargoes of corn were about to arrive and in so doing imperil the value of his own cargo.[87] Any duty to provide information to another negotiating party arguably interferes with the first party's right to seek the most advantageous bargain it can, is inconsistent with the Common law's 'arms' length' view of negotiation, may well presuppose an unrealistic level of altruism, and may be difficult to delimit in practice. Consider, for instance, an example mentioned by Fried:[88] an oil company, having done geological investigation of a locality, spots a potentially valuable area of land which it wants to explore for mining rights. It buys the land, through an agent, for little cost from a farmer, and makes a huge profit when a good source of oil is discovered on the land. Fried suggests that our sympathies may lie with the farmer, but he also rightly notes that in such a case the oil company will have spent money on its geological investigations and is taking a risk in buying the land. Why should it be forced to disclose its identity and motives to the farmer who may then decide not to sell, or only to do so for a vastly higher sum, thereby allowing him to gain from another's work in identifying the potential of the land? Fried's concerns with imposing a duty of disclosure in such a case seem reasonable. After

---

[87] Cicero, *De officiis* III.12. Cicero's view was that concealment was not the conduct of an open, frank, honest and good man (III.13). A not dissimilar real world example is found in the US case *Laidlaw* v. *Organ* 15 US 178 (1817), concerning a tobacco merchant who had early news of the signature of a peace treaty, an event which was likely to lead to a rise in tobacco prices. He immediately ordered 50 tons of tobacco, and thus profited from the ensuing sharp rise in price. The Supreme Court, in contrast to the Ciceronian displeasure at such behaviour, held that the merchant's purchase of the tobacco was a valid contract.

[88] Fried, *Contract as Promise*, p. 79.

all, had the farmer wished to, he could have carried out his own investigations to see whether his land might more profitably be put to other use, yet he did not. Why should he be able to subvert the results of that choice not to act, and instead free ride off the ingenuity and work of the oil company? The Common law view is that he should not. The oil company has simply made a good bargain, using its superior knowledge of the facts.

A different perspective is taken in civilian systems. German law, for instance, will on occasion impose duties to disclose information during the negotiation of a contract (*Ausklärungspflichten*). The German courts have justified the imposition of such a duty on the basis of the good faith relationship of negotiating parties. Such a duty of disclosure can be seen as an aspect of the more general duty of one party to protect the other party's interests (*Schutzpflicht*). This protective duty was codified in §241(2) BGB in the following terms:

> An obligation may also, depending on its contents, oblige each party to take account of the rights, legal interests and other interests of the other party.

Even respected German jurists recognise the danger posed by the breadth of this provision: as Markesinis has commented, 'it cannot be doubted that it creates insecurity in the law'.[89] Examples of specific manifestations of the duty to take account of the other party's interests have, on the facts of the case, been found by German courts to include a duty to assist the other party with performance,[90] a duty to assist the other party in advancing some claim external to the contract,[91] and, most pertinently for the present discussion, a duty to provide the other party with documentation.[92]

In respect of the duty to provide the other party with certain information or documentation, this can arise where specific information has been the subject of questions from the other party,[93] and, more controversially, where the information is of evident and overwhelming importance to the other party[94] or is required because of a relationship of trust, even if it has not been requested. Such a relationship of trust may arise between family members, or between professional and client, but has even been said to

---

[89] Markesinis *et al.*, *German Law of Contract*, p. 128.
[90] RGZ 101, 47.   [91] RGZ 108, 1, 7.
[92] BGH NJW 1992, 1965; BGH NJW 1973, 1793.   [93] BGHZ 74, 383, 392.
[94] In particular, 'information must be given about those circumstances which could frustrate the purpose of the contract, and which therefore are of substantial importance for the other party' (comment of the BGH in BGH NJW-RR 1996, 429, at para. II-2).

arise between commercial parties simply on account of a long-standing relationship.[95] Thus, in contracts of sale, a seller is not permitted to withhold information about serious defects in the goods sold,[96] and may even have to declare a likelihood that such defects may arise in the future in respect of the goods in question.[97] Some of these types of case would be dealt with in the Common law and mixed systems as cases of misrepresentation, or breach of a professional duty of care, others as breaches of statutory duty (for instance, under the Sale of Goods Act 1979). But some instances of the duty would not exist at all, as good faith would not be utilised to impose duties to inform merely because information was of great importance to the other party, the position being adopted that, if the information were indeed so important, the other party ought to have asked for it.

The German law's requirement that a negotiating party be required to provide information of crucial importance to the other party has been described as, at one and the same time, 'paternalistic' and 'utterly vague'.[98] Moreover, if one considers a typical case in which the rule was applied it will be seen that its application can be said to represent, in many cases, the encouragement of fecklessness in business. The case in question (a judgment of the BGH) concerned the sale of a business.[99] The buyer, having paid some of the purchase price, refused to pay the remainder on the basis that it had been deceived by the seller in that the seller had not disclosed that the business had suffered a 40 per cent drop in business in the preceding six months. This was held by the Bundesgerichtshof to be information of such importance to the buyer that it ought to have been disclosed. Yet, surely, if this sort of information is so crucial to the decision to buy a business, it will be one of the crucial pieces of information that the buyer ought actively to request and to obtain from the seller before buying the business. A buyer's failure to do so represents an astounding lack of business sense. Why should such a careless attitude to business be protected by a good faith duty of disclosure imposed on the seller? While consumers may need protecting from the consequences of their failure to request information, it is hard to see why the same policy should extend to businesses. It has been suggested by one German author that the preferable

---

[95] In BGH LM §123 BGB Nr. 52 such a relationship of trust between business parties was held to exist by the BGH because 'the parties had been in intensive long-standing business relationships, and besides this in relationships of personal friendliness' in which they pursued business opportunities 'in the common interest' (para. 3 of the judgment).

[96] BGH NJW 1990, 975.   [97] BGH NJW 1993, 1323.

[98] Markesinis et al., German Law of Contract, p. 309.   [99] BGH NJW-RR 1996, 429.

approach should be for a court to consider how difficult it would be for the party to obtain the information for itself:[100] easily obtained information should not give a party a right to enforce a good faith duty to provide it with such. Such a criterion, had it been applied in the case above, would surely have resulted in no good faith duty to provide the information in question being imposed by the law, given that the information might easily have been obtained by the buyer through a request for a comprehensive set of accounts.

To a Common or mixed system lawyer the German approach appears not only to encourage feckless commercial practices, but also to strike at the fundamental right to act self-interestedly when entering in to contracts. Such self-interest, limited by certain clearly defined tortious acts, is arguably the principal means by which mercantile society has flourished. How can one pursue one's own interests in a contract, if one has to look after the other party's? Is a contracting party to be his brother's keeper?[101] In the Common law, as well indeed as in mixed legal systems, such concerns have meant that only exceptionally is there held to be imposed a duty of disclosure at the pre-contractual stage, such a duty exceptionally arising in contracts *uberrimae fidei* (of the utmost good faith), such as insurance contracts, in fiduciary relationships, and where such disclosure is necessary in order to correct a misleading impression that would otherwise be given or to correct previously issued information which is now misleading or incorrect. The general position, however, in both the Common law and mixed systems is that there are no other pre-contractual duties of disclosure.

Even in the case of contracts *uberrimei fidei*, regard must be had to the specific nature of the information which it is alleged ought to have

---

[100] Lorenz, *Der Schutz vor dem unerwünschten Vertrag*, p. 421. An alternative suggestion has been made that it is information which is material to the other party which should be the subject of the duty of disclosure, except that an exception should be made for information which is 'productive' (in the sense of conducive to a better use of labour and capital) and was costly to obtain: see Kötz, 'Precontractual Duties of Disclosure'. It is not entirely clear from Kotz's argument, however, whether 'productivity' relates to resources in society at large, or whether the withholder of information is entitled to look primarily to the productive use of his own resources, in which case conceivably most information might be withheld. While Kötz says that a party is entitled to make use of knowledge of the likely rise or fall in demand for a product, later on the same page (p. 16) he suggests that this does not apply to information obtained 'very shortly before it becomes public'. This suggests a dividing line which would be very hard to apply in practice, and lead to uncertainty.

[101] Gen. 4:9: 'And the Lord said to Cain: Where is thy brother Abel? And he answered: I know not: am I my brother's keeper?'

been disclosed to see whether it is relevant to the losses claimed. That is clear from the decision of the House of Lords in *Banque Financière de la Cité SA v. Skandia (UK) Insurance Co Ltd*.[102] The plaintiffs were a syndicate of banks which had advanced loan monies to companies owned or controlled by a businessman. In security for the loans, insurance policies issued by the defendant were offered, the banks being named as co-insureds in order to protect their interests in the loans. The insurance policies were arranged by the banks through an insurance agent which it employed, who deceived the banks as to the extent of cover in place. The defendant was aware of the deception, but did not warn the plaintiffs of the true position. In reliance on the misstated position, the banks issued loan funds to the companies. When the companies defaulted in payment, the plaintiffs suffered losses, which they subsequently claimed from the defendants. As the facts related to a contract *uberrimae fidei*, one might have expected that the defendant would have been held to be under a duty to disclose the fraud of the agent of which it knew. However, the House of Lords held that, because the fraud of the agent was not information which would have enabled the insurance company to repudiate the policies, it did not fall within its duty of disclosure, even if it might otherwise have been relevant to the bank's commercial interest in the contemplated loans. As Lord Templeman put it:

> No authority was cited for the proposition that a negotiating party owes a duty to disclose to the opposite party information that the agent of the opposite party had committed a breach of the duty he owed to his principal … a duty to disclose sounding in damages for breach would give rise to great difficulties. The information may be unreliable or doubtful or inconclusive. Disclosure may expose the informer to criticism or litigation.

The rationale offered for holding no such duty exists may look unconvincing to a civilian lawyer armed with the knowledge that, in his own system, information of the type raised in this case would be likely to be considered just the sort of information which would be considered to affect legally relevant interests of the other party. The rationale is, however, entirely consistent with the cautious attitude of the Common law to imposing duties of disclosure on contracting parties beyond that for which there is clearly established precedent. In this area too, there is a clear gulf between the attitude of English law and civilian systems.

---

[102] [1991] 2 AC 249.

The DCFR recognises the differing approaches in national legal systems, commenting in its Principles that any model law 'may need to go beyond the general contract law of some Member States and impose positive duties to give information to the uninformed party'.[103] This suggestion is reflected in Chapter 3 of Book II, which imposes certain duties of disclosure on business parties in relation to intended contracts with consumers.[104] The drafters have, however, shied away from imposing such duties between parties of presumed equal bargaining strength and knowledge, so that business-to-business and entirely private contracts do not fall within the ambit of the provisions. Given differing national practice, extending duties of disclosure to such cases may well have appeared too radical. In relation purely to insurance contracts, the Principles of European Insurance Contract Law (PEICL) suggest a number of specific duties to warn on the part of the insurer, as well as a duty of disclosure on the prospective insured.[105]

3.   Offer and acceptance

(a)   Offer and acceptance as conditional promise

Given the definition of promise proposed in Chapter 1, both an offer (including a counter-offer) and an acceptance could be characterised as conditional promises, in that each can be described as a promise of performance made on the condition of, or given in exchange for, a pledge of counter-performance by the other party.[106] The type of condition involved relates not simply to performance by the other party, but also to the obligatory effect of the undertaking. In other words, the condition is suspensive of the obligation, because no obligation is intended unless and until a counter-pledge of performance (the other party's promise) is forthcoming.

Of course, in the classic case of an exchange of offer made by A and an acceptance of that offer by B, acceptance will normally follow on chronologically after the offer, so that the sequence of events might be described as follows:

---

[103] DCFR, Princ. 8.
[104] DCFR, Arts. II.-3:101–9. More specific provisions relating to pre-contractual duties to warn are found at Arts. IV.C.-2:102 (service contracts) and IV.C-6:102 (design contracts).
[105] PEICL, Arts. 2.101 (insured's duty of disclosure), 2.202–3 (insurance company's duties to warn).
[106] Or, in the case of the offer of a gratuitous contract, as a promise given on the condition of an acceptance by the other party.

Stage 1: A's offer, issued first, is classifiable as a promise, the obligatory nature of which is conditional upon a valid acceptance, also a promise, being given by B in return.

Stage 2: The offer is followed by the issuing of B's acceptance. But need this be seen as a *conditional* promise? Given that A's counter-pledge of performance, contained in A's offer, has already been received by B, any condition on B's part that A make such a pledge of performance seems redundant. B's acceptance could thus be seen as an unconditional promise, immediately binding on him. On the other hand, as it may be rather arbitrary who issues the offer first and who subsequently the acceptance, it may be simpler to maintain the view that both parties make conditional promises, and to say that each undertaking is given in exchange for, and thus on the condition of, the other's undertaking.[107]

Not all contracts though are formed by a process of an offer followed by an acceptance. Can the conditional promise characterisation be maintained in respect of other types of formation scenario? What, for instance, of a case where each contracting party signs a contractual document previously prepared by a third party? In such a case it seems no less plausible to describe each party as having made a conditional promise to the other. Indeed, it seems easier to do so in the absence of separate documents of offer and acceptance which follow chronologically on each other.

It is not difficult to see why, in a late scholastic intellectual climate where promise was still the dominant analysis of voluntary undertakings, and where an acceptance was widely seen as essential to a binding promise, the two-stage approach to the undertaking of a voluntary duty was thought amenable to describing not only the formation of promises but subsequently the negotiation process leading to a contract. An enforceable promise and a contract could both be described as accepted promises, the only difference being that a contract usually imposed duties on the promisee as well (duties specified in the offer's promise as conditions for the promise). One must add the caveat 'usually', because if there is no requirement of mutual consideration, then evidently it is possible to have a gratuitous contract.

---

[107] Fried maintains the view that each party makes a conditional promise, though his explanation gets overly complicated when he asserts that B's acceptance, as a conditional promise, must itself be accepted, something which he explains automatically and implicitly occurs when it is communicated to A, as A has bound himself to accept it when he issued the offer: see Fried, *Contract as Promise*, p. 48.

(b)   The traditional offer and acceptance model
as a unilateral dictation of terms

The traditional conception of contract formation described in the previous section, which sees offer and acceptance as conditional promises, and
in terms of which an offeror proposes all the contract terms and the offeree
simply agrees to or rejects them, is a very unilateral model of contract formation in that it puts the power to dictate the content of the obligation
proposed in the hands of one party. To be sure, negotiation can come in,
but, every time a counter-offer is made, the circumstances are treated as if
a new promise of performance has been offered by the party making the
proposed changes to the terms. An offeree must agree absolutely to the
undertaking proposed by the offeror, or else there is no contract. There is
no room for any active alteration to the proposal, or the offeree is treated
as having rejected the offeror's promised performance and is rather said
to be making a new offer himself.

The traditional model described above is quite different to the DCFR
(and PECL) conception, where core terms can be distilled from negotiations and others omitted. Thus, in the DCFR, the traditional approach to
formation of contract – that any alterations to an offer by the offeree kill off
the offer – is modified, so that it is only a response which 'states or implies
additional or different terms which materially alter the terms of the offer'[108]
which amounts to a rejection of the original offer and hence constitutes a
new offer. Where alterations or additions are not material, they become
part of the contract unless the offer limited acceptance strictly to its terms,
the additions or alterations are objected to by the offeror without undue
delay, or the offeree itself seeks assent from the offeror to the additions
or alterations.[109] A not dissimilar approach is proposed in the DCFR for
standard form negotiations, though here the change from the traditional
model is even more radical, a contract being formed from the terms in the
conflicting terms which are 'common in substance'.[110] These model provisions are almost identical to those previously proposed in the PECL.[111]

---

[108] DCFR Art. II.-4:208(1).   [109] DCFR Art. II.-4:208(2), (3).
[110] The 'common in substance' test seems fraught with difficulty, given its vague formulation. There is no attempt in the provisions of the DCFR to explain the notion of 'substance', though the official commentary to the Article states that the idea 'conveys that it
is identity in result not in formulation that counts'. That clarification dodges the question
of how one resolves disputes about what result was intended, and indeed the official commentary observes that 'what is "common in substance" will not always be easy to decide'.
[111] PECL Arts. 2:208 and 2:209.

This new approach to contract formation is a much more genuinely consensual one. It will strike many as radical, perhaps too radical, because we remain largely wedded to contract formation thinking which derives from the older promissory paradigm described earlier, a paradigm which sees offeror and counter-offeror as making a promise to contract on certain terms, the promissory undertaking being given on the condition that it is the exact terms offered, and only those, to which the promisor will be bound. Only if the new view displaces the older approach will the contract formation process have moved from a conception which, despite the oft repeated emphasis on agreement and consensus, continues to rest upon the promissory idea, to something more genuinely cooperative and mutual.

(c) Distinguishing offer from conditional promise

The fact that, as discussed in the previous section, a contractual offer can be characterised in promissory terms is not without attendant difficulties. These are particularly evident in cases where conceivably something might either be an enforceable unilateral promise or else an offer, and a determination is required as to which analysis must be adopted. This problem is most acute in a system like Scots law where unilateral promise is recognised as a separate form of valid obligation, though, as in most systems some instances of unilateral promise are exceptionally enforced, it is not a uniquely Scottish problem.[112] Wherever the possibility of seeing something either as a unilateral promise or as an offer exists, how can one tell whether a particular statement is intended as an immediately binding unilateral promise (albeit a conditional one), an offer requiring an acceptance before any obligation is constituted, or perhaps even a statement which is intended as neither of those things?

Consider, for instance, the following case. An insurance company, whose client has allegedly injured a third party, writes formally to the third party saying: 'We accept that our client is liable for the damages you have suffered. We will pay damages, to be assessed when we receive details of your injuries.' Is this an offer to pay damages, a unilateral promise to do so, or simply a non-contractual and non-promissory admission of liability?[113]

---

[112] It will be recalled from Ch. 3 that Pufendorf discussed the question in his *De iure naturae et gentium*: see p. 134.

[113] The example is based on the facts of the Scottish case *Van Klaveren* v. *Servisair UK Ltd* [2009] CSIH 37. In that case, the court held that the statement was a mere extra-judicial

What factors should determine the nature of such a statement?[114] Does one look at the ordinary meaning of the words used, the objective impression conveyed to a third party observer, or the subjective effect produced by such words in the mind of the hearer? If there is a presumption against unilateral promise, then cases of ambiguity might be resolved in favour of an offer analysis (assuming that the statement is capable of constituting an offer), but whether something is an ambiguous case presupposes that the rules for interpreting the statement in question provide no clear answer, and this itself suggests that there are clear rules in force. That may not, in a particular legal system, be so. Apart from judicial statements that it is the intention of the party which is crucial in determining whether an offer or a promise is intended[115] (hardly especially helpful, given that it will usually be precisely such intention which is doubtful), it seems sensible to suggest that the context of the statement will be important (a mercantile context for the statement making it more likely that an offer rather than a promise was intended), as well as whether the condition attached will bring any direct benefit to the maker of the statement (if it does, this again suggests that an offer is more likely to have been intended).[116]

Clearly in most systems, where a promise cannot give rise to a binding obligation without any acceptance being given to the promise, the need to distinguish a promise from an offer is much less pressing. If no unaccepted promise is binding, then a promise can only ever be an offer and one must look to see if the offer has been clearly and unequivocally accepted. Where exceptions to such an approach arise, then they will apply only to clearly delineated types of statement, such as the offer of reward (where an acceptance is usually presumed from conduct).

---

admission of liability, not productive of any civil obligation, and so could be withdrawn prior to commencement of legal proceedings before the courts.

[114] A rule, for instance, that a unilateral undertaking must be in a particular form (in deed form, for instance), does not necessarily determine the outcome: the lack of the correct form may preclude the statement from being a binding unilateral promise, but it does not then follow that the statement was meant as an offer, capable of acceptance.

[115] See, for instance, *Morton's Tr* v. *Aged Christian Friend Society of Scotland* (1899) 2 F 82, per Lord Kinnear at 85.

[116] In *Smith* v. *Oliver* 1911 SC 103, (1910) 2 SLT 304, in relation to the question of whether the statement of a woman pledging money to a church on condition of certain works being undertaken in accordance with her wishes was a promise or an offer, Lord Dunedin said 'so far as mutual contract is concerned, the lady was getting no benefit except in the sense in which anybody may be said to get something when anything is done in which he is interested' (1911 SC at 111). The court, influenced by this idea that the woman had not acted with any reciprocal benefit being given to her in mind, favoured a promissory rather than a contractual analysis of the statement.

(d)   Problem cases for a promissory analysis of offer and acceptance

Given what has been said above about the traditional characterisation of offer and acceptance as conditional promise, a further question may be posed: does such characterisation ever seem not to work?

One problematic case appears to be that where a contract is onerous (that is, imposes duties on both parties) but not mutual (because none of A's obligations are the reciprocal or counterpart of any of B's obligations). In such a case might it be said that neither A nor B has *conditionally* promised to perform its obligations? Both have made promises, but each promise seems to be unconditional, so that neither offer nor acceptance can be characterised as being made conditionally on counter-performance by the other party. While that is true, it can at least be said that each party is only offering to do what it has pledged to on the condition that the other undertake a separate, stipulated promise, albeit not one which is conceived of as mutual in nature. Given this, a conditional promissory analysis is still valid in respect of onerous but non-mutual contracts.

Another apparently problematic scenario is the example of the contract where formation and performance occur simultaneously (what might be called 'simultaneous transactions'). These types of contract were mentioned briefly in Chapter 1 as potentially posing a problem for a promissory analysis of contract.[117] Take, for instance, a sale of goods contract, where a customer selects goods for purchase in a store, presents them for payment at the till, such payment being immediately accepted by the seller. In such a case, the duties of each party (payment and delivery of the goods) appear to be performed simultaneously with the acts constituting the offer and acceptance of the contract. Given this, it seems, on the face of it, not to make sense to talk of the contracting parties having promised to do anything here, a promise being a pledge of *future* rather than immediate performance. Does this mean that the promissory analysis of contract breaks down in such a case? One answer is to accept this argument as valid, but to continue to maintain a general promissory analysis of contract by removing the class of transactions where formation and performance occur simultaneously from the category of contracts. This is the approach taken by Smith.[118] This, it is suggested, however, too readily concedes the point and, moreover, fails to accord with the attitude of the law, which continues to treat such transactions as contracts. The point is too readily conceded for two reasons. Firstly, in the example

[117]   See Ch.1, at p. 23.   [118]   Smith, *Contract Theory*, pp. 62–3.

given, the promise of the buyer to pay and performance will not necessarily be simultaneous. The buyer who presents goods for payment at a till is at that instant making a promise to pay for them. The cashier accepts the buyer's offer by taking the goods from the customer and ringing them up, thereby making a reciprocal promise to deliver the goods to the buyer. At that point, the contract is concluded. Only then does the buyer fulfil its promise by paying for the goods, handing over cash or offering another method of payment, and only then does the seller fulfil its promise of delivery, when the cashier hands the goods back to the customer. So, even in cases of apparent simultaneous formation and performance, on closer examination there may well be promises to perform which predate actual performance, even if only by a few seconds. Secondly, even if payment is in fact contemporaneous with the buyer's offer (because, for instance, the buyer hands over both the goods and a cash payment together), though it seems to be redundant to adopt a promissory analysis in such a case, no great conceptual harm is done by accepting that performance may occur contemporaneously with the promise to perform. Such transactions are no doubt anomalous, but their status as an anomaly need not be seen as undermining a general theory which continues to provide a satisfactory explanation for the field of obligations overall. Lastly, even in cases where performance occurs simultaneously with formation, there may be duties other than the primary duty of performance which are incurred under the contract. Thus, if it transpires that payment has not properly been made (for instance, because forged currency has been given, or a cheque tendered in payment does not clear) or that the goods delivered are defective, duties to correct the defective performance may be enforced, and such duties can be referred to as express or implied promises incumbent upon the parties and enforceable at a later point in time (when the defective performance is discovered). This last point is a somewhat weaker one, however, because it may be more realistic (as suggested later in this chapter) to see implied terms as stemming from legal rules and not any imagined promises of the parties.

If none of these arguments concerning simultaneous transactions are accepted, then the conclusion must be either that such transactions are not contracts (an undesirable one, it is suggested, given the universal view that such transactions *are* contracts), or that promising is not the only way of contracting. The latter view might, for instance, lead to the conclusion that both promising and also other conduct demonstrating an intention to be bound to an obligation are equally valid methods of forming valid contracts. Such a view would not represent, as some might claim, a fundamental attack on the idea of promise as a normative act, but merely a shift in focus from the idea of promise to that of behaviour demonstrative of obligatory intent, of which promise would be one (and perhaps the clearest) example.

(e)   Conceiving of offers as binding

In the Common law and mixed legal systems, the default status of an offer is that it does not give rise to any binding obligations, and may be withdrawn at any time before acceptance.[119] It may be possible to make the offer binding, but this is an exceptional position. By contrast, in German law, once an offer has been issued it is binding in the sense that it cannot be withdrawn, unless the power to do so has been reserved by the offeror, during the period of time for which the offeror might expect to receive a reply in ordinary circumstances.[120] Why is it that offers are seen as binding in Germany? Like so many other of the BGB provisions giving a legal effect to unilateral acts, this provision owes its origins to the position favoured by Franz von Kübel, editor of the draft contract provisions of the original text of the BGB. Von Kübel headed his submission to the first drafting Commission of the BGB on the topic of contractual offers with the words 'The unilateral promise as grounding the obligation to keep one's word (contractual offer)',[121] thereby making his views

---

[119] Though the law of the mixed legal system of Quebec is not a subject of study of this work, it is interesting that the Quebec Civil Code adopts a somewhat different default position in relation to offers than that taken in the mixed legal systems studied in this work. Article 1396 of the Code provides that '[a]n offer to contract made to a determinate person constitutes a promise to enter into the proposed contract from the moment that the offeree clearly indicates to the offeror that he intends to consider the offer and reply to it within a reasonable time or within the time stated therein'. Quebec law thus conceives of the following stages in the contract formation process: (1) the offer is issued (it may still be revoked at this stage); (2) the offeree indicates he is considering the offer – the offer is now a 'promise' to contract (and thus cannot be withdrawn), this 'promise' amounting to an option to contract (the 'option' label is in fact used later in Article 1396 to describe the nature of the offeree's right); (3) the promise to contract is accepted, this creating a contract.

[120] §§145–7 BGB. In the case of an offer made to a party who is present at the time the offer is made, it must be accepted immediately or it falls (§147(1)); where a time limit for acceptance is specified, that limit applies (§148).The Swiss Code of Obligations applies similar rules (see Arts. 3–5), as does Austrian Law (see §862 AGBG).

[121] My translation of von Kübel's German text, which read: 'Das einseitige Versprechen als Grund der Verpflichtung zum Worthalten (Vertragsantrag)' (von Kübel, in Schubert, *Die Vorlagen der Redaktoren*, pp. 1145 f). To somewhat similar effect is the following view of the Belgian Cour de Cassation: 'The binding character of an offer … is founded upon

on the desired nature and effect of an offer quite clear. This automatically binding effect may at first seem strange to non-civilian lawyers, as it is a position not maintained even in Scots Law, with its obligation of unilateral promise. In Scotland (as is discussed more fully later) an offeror must expressly promise to keep an offer open for a specified time before it can be held to be irrevocable, demonstrating the Scots law view that a simple offer of itself discloses no intention of the offeror unilaterally to be bound, not even to his keeping the offer on the table for acceptance. The DCFR position is somewhat similar to the Scottish approach.[122] The German position does not, of course, bind the offeror to the terms of a contract – for that, an acceptance is required – it only binds him to keeping the offer on the table for the other party to accept or not as it sees fit. The offeror is held to have committed himself unconditionally to the negotiations, though not the contract proposed (the condition for that commitment being the acceptance of the offeree). As such, any unilateral binding effect can be described as procedural rather than substantive.

As to a related matter, a waiver of the need for an acceptance, it should be appreciated that the fact that a legal system may hold an offeror to be entitled to waive the need for communication of an acceptance[123] does not turn the offer into a sort of quasi-unilateral promise, binding on the offeror without acceptance. That is so because waiver of an acceptance does not negate the need for acceptance, merely the need for it to be communicated. Were it otherwise, an offeror could, by waiving the need for communication of the acceptance, bind an unwilling offeree to the contract. Waiver of acceptance most commonly occurs in cases of parties involved in an ongoing, prolonged relationship. Thus, the window cleaner, who contracts on a repeated basis to clean a householder's windows once a week while he is at work, will be taken to have waived the need for an acceptance to be communicated to his standing offer to clean the windows every week. In such a case, the householder's acceptance, though not communicated after the initial occasion of cleaning, will be deemed to be manifested on each subsequent occasion by his conduct in tacitly allowing the cleaner access to the property to carry out the work. Proof that an intention to accept has been manifested in some way, though not communicated, may be disputed in some cases. Moreover, the further

---

an undertaking resulting from the unilateral will of the person making the offer' (9 May 1980, Pas. 1980 I 1127), though the word promise is not used in the court's reasoning.

[122] DCFR Art. 4:202 (discussed below, at p. 227).

[123] As is the case in, for instance, England, Scotland and Germany.

rule that silence does not constitute an acceptance, is also likely to lead to disputes about whether in particular cases the conduct of a party has or has not amounted to acceptance by conduct of an offer which waived the need for acceptance to be communicated.

4. Enforcement of auction/tender conditions

A common problem in many jurisdictions is how to hold a party to a statement in which is set out conditions concerning how bids in an auction for the sale of property or tenders for the award of a contract will be dealt with. The problem that usually arises is a claim by an unsuccessful bidder/tenderer that its offer was improperly excluded from the process or that its offer ought to have been accepted rather than that of another party. The prima facie problem that such claims face is that, because the claimant has not been successful in its offer it has no contract and therefore no contractual means to complain about the alleged improper behaviour of the defendant. In stating this problem, it is important to note that the party inviting the bids or tenders is not usually itself seen as having made an offer; rather, it has invited the bidders to make offers from which it will choose one to accept.

A simple way to solve this problem would be to analyse the conditions stipulated by the party inviting the offers, and which are to govern the bidding process, as unilateral promises on its part. Such conditions, if promises, might for instance bind the promisor to consider all bids submitted by a certain date (or not to consider any bids submitted after that date), or not to collude with a specific bidder against the other bidders, or not to communicate with bidders after the closing date except in certain ways. Such conditions might go even further and bind the party inviting bids to sell to the highest bidder (in an auction), or to award the contract to the tenderer submitting the lowest price for the desired work. The attraction of a unilateral promise analysis is that such promises would be seen as independent from the anticipated contract to be concluded with the successful bidder, thus enabling any bidder to complain of a breach of the conditions even if it was not successful in its bid.

Of course, unilateral promises have an established place in only one of the systems under consideration, that being Scotland, though their place in the DCFR would also make a promissory analysis possible. In the other systems, if a solution is to be found to the perceived problem, then it must be by virtue of some other analytical route. In English law, two solutions have been adopted. One has been adopted in auctions where bidders have been assured that the highest bid would be accepted. In such a case, the English courts have said that the party inviting bids has made an offer (and not just an invitation to treat), the offer being to sell to the highest bidder. Such an offer is only capable of being accepted by the highest bidder, and, in making a bid, that bidder therefore accepts the offer and concludes the contract of sale. Such was the decision in *Harvela Investments Ltd* v. *Royal Trust of Canada Ltd*,[124] in which the highest bidder, whose claim was improperly rejected by the seller, was held entitled by the House of Lords to the shares which were the subject of the auction. The analysis of the House of Lords was that the offer to sell to the highest bidder was a 'unilateral contract', binding on the party selling the shares immediately the invitation to submit bids was issued. This unilateral contract was transformed into a bilateral or synallagmatic contract when the successful bid was received. This concept of a unilateral contract is clearly an exceptional one, and indeed one which strikes at the very heart of the Common law's understanding that a contract (other than one by deed) is a bargain requiring mutual consideration to be valid. A unilateral contract which comes into existence the instant an invitation is issued to bidders is hardly characterised by mutual consideration (the price to be offered by the highest bidder for the shares being most naturally seen as consideration for the shares themselves, and not for the promise to sell to the highest bidder). The approach of the House of Lords must therefore be seen as stretching the rules almost to breaking point, albeit that it represents an imaginative response to the absence of an obligation of unilateral promise in English law.

A second Common law solution has been adopted in cases where the party inviting bids has not bound itself to sell to the highest or any other particular bidder, but has broken a condition relating to the submission and handling of the bids. In one such reported case, *Blackpool Aero Club* v. *Blackpool & Fylde District Council*,[125] rather than hold the invitation to tender to be an offer (as in *Harvela*), the court held it to be an invitation to treat. However, it added that the conditions of tender contained in the invitation to treat themselves constituted the offer of a subsidiary or secondary contract to govern the tendering process. Each tenderer who submitted a bid therefore not only submitted a bid or offer for the contract, but through tendering was also accepting the offer of the subsidiary contract to govern the tendering process. This meant that the plaintiff, who had had his tender improperly excluded from the tendering process due

---

[124] [1986] AC 207.   [125] [1990] 3 All ER 25.

to an erroneous belief on the defendant's part that it had been submitted late, was held entitled *as a matter of contract* (that is, under the subsidiary contract) to complain about the breach of the defendant's statement that it would not consider late bids (interpreted further to mean that it *would* consider timely bids). The final settlement of the claim is not reported, but it would not have been so easy for a court to determine as in the earlier *Harvela* case. As the defendant had not undertaken to award the contract to a specific party, the plaintiff was not arguing that it ought to have been awarded the contract; rather it was seeking damages for the lost opportunity of being awarded the contract, even though the quantum of that claim was somewhat difficult to compute. This case demonstrates a further imaginative use of contract law to solve a problem that seems more naturally classifiable as one of breach of a unilateral promise by the defendant.[126]

The Canadian Supreme Court in *R v. Ron Engineering*[127] considered matters from the perspective of the other party, when it bound a tenderer to a tender condition not to withdraw the tender before a specified date. As with the English courts, this solution was achieved by reference to the idea of a preliminary, subsidiary, or unilateral contract, governing the tendering process. *Ron Engineering* was just the beginning of the development of Canadian law in this field, as in subsequent decisions it has been held that the preliminary contract can contain reciprocal obligations, either expressly or impliedly,[128] and that such obligations include an implied obligation on the party inviting tenders to treat all tenderers fairly and equally.[129] This implied obligation has been characterised as embodying a requirement of good faith.[130] It has been held, for instance, that accepting a bid by a party ineligible to bid under the conditions laid down for the bidding process is in breach of this implied good faith obligation.[131] In the same judgment it was also held that a clause purporting to exclude

---

[126] The case concerned facts that occurred prior to the UK implementation of the EU rules dealing with tendering for public works contracts. Those rules would now govern the circumstances of the *Blackpool* case. However, were a similar dispute to arise again between private parties, it would require to be solved using the *Blackpool* logic.

[127] *R v. Ron Engineering & Construction (Eastern) Ltd* [1981] SCR 111.

[128] *Martel Building Ltd v. Canada* [2000] 2 SCR 860, at para. 83.

[129] *Ibid.*, para. 88.

[130] *Tarmac Canada Inc. v. Hamilton-Wentworth (Regional Municipality)* 1999 Carswell Ont 2761. There are many recent examples, see for instance *Force Construction Ltd v. Nova Scotia (Attorney General)* [2008] NSJ No. 490.

[131] *Tercon Contractors Ltd v. British Columbia (Ministry of Transportation & Highways)* 2010 SCC 4.

liability to bidders for losses which might arise from participation in the bidding process did not exclude a claim by an unsuccessful bidder, for the somewhat controversial causal reason that the appellant's losses arose not from participation in the bidding process but rather from the respondent's dealings with the ineligible bidder.[132]

Some Canadian developments have, however, surely gone too far in imposing allegedly fair outcomes. It has, for instance, been decided by the Ontario Court of Appeal that even if a party inviting tenders has expressly stated that it does *not* bind itself to accept the lowest tender, the courts may ignore such a statement and imply a term that the lowest tender *will* be accepted, if such an implication can be said to be necessary to ensure fairness in the tendering process. Such an approach is tantamount to rewriting a contract for the parties, and shows no regard for the promises made by them or the contract they intended.[133]

The German courts have also to some extent considered tendering problems. In a case concerning the auction of a car on a third party website, the seller refused to sell the car to the highest bidder, even though under the terms of the auction he had stated that he would do so.[134] The Bundesgerichtshof (BGH) considered whether a contract of sale had been concluded by the parties. Unlike the court below, the BGH was not prepared definitively to state that the seller had made an offer, and the buyer an acceptance.[135] Nonetheless, applying the German rule that a contractual obligation requires the declaration of will of two parties, it held that each party had issued such a declaration, although expressing the view that in the case of the seller his declaration might in fact have been a (legally permissible) prior acceptance of whichever bid made was the highest. The BGH decisively rejected the view that the seller's statements on the website amounted only to a non-binding invitation to treat: on the contrary, the information he had had to submit to the website in order to advertise the sale of his car was a precise and unequivocal commitment

---

[132] The Supreme Court's judgment was a 5–4 majority.
[133] See *Chinook Aggregates Ltd* v. *Abbotsford* (1989) 35 CLR 241 (Ontario Court of Appeal). In that case, despite the party inviting tenders stating clearly that 'the lowest or any tender will not necessarily be accepted', the Appeal Court implied a term that the lowest qualifying bid would be accepted. It did so in order, it said, to negate the effect of an undisclosed, and thus unfair, policy of the party inviting tenders that local contractors bids would be favoured if they were within 10% of the lowest bid.
[134] NJW 2002, 363.
[135] However, in a similar case from 2005, the BGH expressed the view that it was the seller who had made the offer, and the buyer the acceptance when it submitted the highest bid: BGH JZ 2005, 464; NJW 2005, 53.

to enter into a sale with the highest bidder. The result reached here by the German court is comparable to that reached in the English *Harvela* case, albeit that the German court expressed some doubt as to which party had made the offer and which the acceptance. That point did not require a specific ruling, given that the concepts of offer and acceptance are merely two manifestations of the more fundamental idea of a *Willenserklärung* (declaration of will).

More problematic for German law would be how to deal with a *Blackpool* type scenario, that is a case where the party making the complaint cannot convince a court that the breach of the condition complained of has deprived it of a contract which it ought to be awarded. If the condition is only, as in *Blackpool*, to consider a timely bid, but not to award the contract to any specific bidder, and consideration of such a timely bid has not occurred, does that failure constitute the breach of any contractual or other right possessed by the disgruntled bidder? One solution in German law would be to argue that, when parties submit bids on the basis of stated conditions, subsidiary contracts are being entered into between each bidder and the party inviting the bids, so that any bidder who suffers as a result of a breach of any of the conditions would be entitled to seek damages for its loss under the subsidiary contract. Alternatively, but less elegantly, the contractual bidding process might be described as a prize competition, and thus governed by §661 BGB, on the basis that each bidder could be said to be competing for the prize of being awarded the contract. On that basis, §661(2) would seem to oblige consideration of an 'entry submitted within the period of time' specified, failure to do so being a breach of this obligation. This second solution would, however, be to apply a section of the Code to circumstances which stretch the idea of a 'prize competition' somewhat beyond the usual understanding of that term.[136] Of the two suggestions, the better seems to be the concept of the subsidiary contract, the same approach used by the English court in the *Blackpool* case.

5. The firm or irrevocable offer

(a) Characterising the firm offer

A firm or irrevocable offer is one which the offeror has bound himself to keep open for a specified period of time. It is conceivable that, if such

[136] Though the §661 route is the natural solution for breach of conditions laid down in genuine prize competitions, such as the architectural prize competition which was at issue in BGH NJW 1983, 442.

undertaking is recognised as binding by a legal system, the binding effect could be conceived of as promissory in nature (though, as will be seen, that is not necessarily the view adopted by national legal systems). After all, it is the offeror alone who comes under any duty (not to revoke the offer during the stated time), the offeree remaining free to accept or reject the offer as he sees fit, circumstances which have a unilateral promissory aspect to them.

There is a variety of differing treatments of firm offers among legal systems. Some conceive of all offers, by default, as firm. It was discussed earlier how this is the position of German law.[137] The justification for the default position given by the framers of the BGB at the end of the nineteenth-century was that, if offers were not deemed irrevocable, commerce would become more difficult and the economy contract.[138] This seems fanciful in retrospect, given the thriving economy of a late nineteenth-century England in which binding offers were almost unknown. Whether the rationale is convincing or not, the default German position places a higher promissory value on the proposal of an offeror. Such a party is held at least to have promised to keep the offer open for acceptance for a certain time, even if he has not absolutely promised to perform the contract but merely conditionally promised to do so if an acceptance is forthcoming. Though the relevant provision of the BGB (§145) does not expressly use the language of promise in describing the default binding effect of an offer, a promissory interpretation of the nature of a binding offer is supported by the background to the adoption of §145.[139]

At the other end of the scale in terms of the default position regarding binding offers is the Common law approach, which refuses to give effect to a party's clearly expressed wish to bind itself to keep an offer open unless some consideration is provided for such an undertaking.[140] The offeror in Common law is thus able, in most cases, to revoke his offer freely, and will not even need to do that if there has been a fundamental change in circumstances since the offer was made: such a change is held to annul the offer without the offeror even having to withdraw it.[141] The harshness of

---

[137] See above at p. 217.

[138] 'Motive', pp. 165–6 (in Mugdan, *Die gesammten Materialien*).

[139] See above at p. 217.

[140] *Dickinson v. Dodds* [1876] 2 Ch D 463. The Law Revision Committee's Sixth Interim Report (1937, Cmnd 5449) recommended (see para. 38) that firm offers made without mutual consideration should be enforceable, but this recommendation was not acted upon.

[141] *Nielsen v. Dysart Timbers Ltd* [2009] NZSC 43.

the English unwillingness to hold offers irrevocable is somewhat softened by the rule that a revocation of an offer is not effective until communicated to the offeree.[142] An offeree thus knows that until he receives definite notice of withdrawal he is free to accept the offer, albeit not to rely upon it in other ways.

The Common law has developed in the US, under the doctrine of promissory estoppel, to allow a binding offer to have effect so long as the offeree has placed some reliance on it. Where that is so, the offeror is deemed to have made a subsidiary promise not to revoke the offer of the bilateral contract. Even this improved Common law position is far from ideal though, requiring as it does some proof by an offeree of reliance, a requirement which seems both unnecessary and likely to be difficult to prove in some cases. Moreover, the promissory estoppel approach founds only a right to damages for wasted expenditure if the offer is revoked, but does not render the offer irrevocable as such.[143] Though the damages route has been argued to be the likely course of action even in German law,[144] it is surely preferable to give the offeree the right to hold the offeror to his offer if the offeree so wishes, even if the offeree may not choose to exercise that right in cases where trust between the parties has broken down. The promissory estoppel solution has often been applied in the US to cases where main contractors have relied on offers by subcontractors to do work for a certain price. The main contractor, pricing its own work in accordance with the subcontractor's bid, is entitled to rely on that bid, and can sue the subcontractor in damages if the bid is withdrawn and the main contractor is obliged to hire someone else at greater cost.[145]

---

[142] For application of the English rule, see *Byrne & Co.* v. *Leon van Tienhoven* (1880) 5 CPD 344. A similar rule was established in Scots law in *Thomson* v. *James* (1855) 18 D 1. The DCFR is somewhat vague on the time when the revocation of an offer takes effect: Art. II.-4:203 states that an offer may be revoked if the revocation reaches the offeree before acceptance is despatched, but this does not tell us whether, in such a case, the revocation takes effect when it was posted or when it arrives, though presumably the latter was the intention of the drafters.

[143] The damages route was considered by the drafters of the BGB, but rejected as being not in the interests of commerce, given that it is more cumbersome and less certain than making the offer irrevocable: see 'Motive', pp. 165–6 (in Mugdan, *Die gesammten Materialien*).

[144] Markesinis *et al.*, *German Law of Contract*, pp. 66–7.

[145] See *Drennan* v. *Star Paving Co.* 51 Cal 2d 409, 333 P 2d 757 (Cal. 1958). Under §87(2) of the Restatement (Second) of Contracts, these circumstances would now be treated as giving rise to an option contract, so that recourse to promissory estoppel would no longer be necessary. The Uniform Commercial Code contains a provision (§2–205) making firm offers by merchants to buy or sell goods enforceable for the stated period of time (not exceeding three months).

Lying between the German and English positions, Scots law takes the view that, while offers by default are revocable at will, an offeror may bind himself to keep an offer open for a specific period of time. Such an undertaking is seen as a unilateral promise separate from, but attached to, the offer itself.[146] No consideration is required for the giving of such an undertaking. The offeree, as the recipient of such a promise by the offeror to keep the offer open, can enforce this promise by accepting the offer within the time limit, any attempted withdrawal of the offer being ineffective. Scots law thus gives effect to the intention of an offeror to bind himself unilaterally, doing so not by changing the default nature of the offer from a mere proposal of terms to something itself binding, but by attaching to the offer an additional obligation constituted by way of unilateral promise. This has the desired effect of making the offer binding, though those from outside the Scottish legal system might find the analysis of a separate promise to keep the offer open a somewhat convoluted approach.

Like Scotland, the mixed legal system of Louisiana also gives effect to a binding offer,[147] but it does so simply by virtue of a provision of the Civil Code stating that an 'offer that specifies a period of time for acceptance is irrevocable during that time'.[148] Like the provision from the BGB on the binding effect of offers, this provision gives no clue as to how the irrevocable effect of an offer is to be characterised, but, given the absence from Louisiana law of a category of unilateral promise, it is hard to see how a promissory analysis of this provision might be argued for. The general view is that the provision is also not to be seen as giving rise to an option.[149] Given the codal status of the provision, there may perhaps be no need to enquire further as to the nature of the binding effect of irrevocable offers.

In some systems, however, the firm offer is indeed treated as a type of option. South Africa is one example of a jurisdiction which has adopted the option analysis, an option in South African law being a type of contract.[150] Given this settled view that an offer can only be made firm by embodying it in an option contract subsidiary to the intended main

---

[146] *Littlejohn* v. *Hadwen* (1882) 20 SLR 5; *Paterson* v. *Highland Railway Co.* 1927 SC (HL) 32, 38, per Lord Dunedin.

[147] For a comparative analysis of the Louisiana rules on offer and acceptance, see Litvinoff, 'Offer and Acceptance in Louisiana Law'.

[148] CC Art. 1928.   [149] See Litvinoff, and Scalise, *Law of Obligations*, pp. 64–5.

[150] See *Anglo Carpets (Pty) Ltd.* v. *Snyman* 1978 (3) SA 582 (T); *Kotze* v. *Newmont SA Ltd* 1977 (3) SA 368 (NC); *Oos-Vrystaat Kaap Bedryf Bpk.* v. *Van Aswegen* 2005 (4) SA 417.

contract, the decision in the South African Labour appeal court case *University of the North* v. *Franks*[151] that a unilateral undertaking not to revoke an offer might 'in its context contain a waiver of the normal requirement of acceptance by the offeree'[152] must be considered suspect. This suggestion that a firm offer might be undertaken unilaterally is contradicted by other decisions supporting the view that a unilateral statement that an offer is irrevocable or held open for a certain time is of no effect.[153] While some have tried to argue the contrary view in favour of unilaterally binding firm offers,[154] this position is unsupported by the cases. Others have tried to argue for a watered-down version of the necessary acceptance of an option contract,[155] but again this is not convincing.[156] A final suggestion has been that a unilateral declaration that an offer will be kept open for a certain time might give rise to expectations on the part of the offeree, the doctrine of estoppel allowing the offeree to argue that the offeror cannot withdraw during that period of time.[157]

The DCFR makes provision both for revocable and irrevocable offers.[158] The default position is that an offer is revocable until the point the offeree despatches the acceptance.[159] However, an offer may be stated to be irrevocable or open for acceptance for a fixed time, in which case the offer is irrevocable.[160] Mirroring somewhat the US position, an offer is also irrevocable if 'it was reasonable for the offeree to rely on the offer as being irrevocable and the offeree has acted in reliance on the offer'.[161] Unlike the US Common law approach however, this rule does not simply give rise to a right to damages if it is broken, but ensures that the offeror will be bound to the offer by virtue of the offeree's entitlement to accept it should he wish. However, in stating none of this is the term promise or unilateral promise used. So, as with the German law on offers, these provisions of the DCFR are not expressly promissory in nature, though they achieve a unilateral binding effect. This is consistent with the DCFR's conception that there are unilateral undertakings other than unilateral promises.[162]

---

[151] [2002] 8 BLLR 701 (LAC).   [152] *Ibid.*, paras. 47–8.
[153] *Garnier & Co.* v. *Wright* 20 SC 421.
[154] See R. H. Christie, *The Law of Contract in South Africa*, pp. 52–3.
[155] See Zeffertt, 'Some Thoughts on Options'; Kritzinger, 'The Irrevocable Offer'.
[156] See Hogg and Lubbe, 'Formation of Contract', p. 55.
[157] Christie, *The Law of Contract in South Africa*, p. 53.
[158] Art. II.-4:202.   [159] Art. II.-4:202(1).   [160] Art. II.-4:202(3)(a),(b).
[161] Art. II.-4:202(3)(c).   [162] Art. II.-1:101 and 1:103(2).

(b) Promises of reward

One type of offer which in some systems is conceived of as irrevocable is an offer of reward for the performance of some act. A contractual analysis is maintained by most legal systems of this fact situation, even though (unless the reward is offered to a specific party) the promisee is unlikely to accept the offer before performing the task which is the condition for claiming the reward. Alternatively, a promise of reward can be viewed in unilateral promissory terms, an analysis for which there is authority in Germany as well as Scotland.

In the Common law, promises of reward (whether issued to one party or to persons generally) are considered 'unilateral contracts', binding on the part of the offeror alone. The party to whom the offer of reward is made (or any member of the public generally, in the case of public offers) has the option of performing the conduct stipulated in the offer of reward, and, if he does, he then becomes entitled to claim the reward. The offeror is prevented from withdrawing the offer once the offeree has begun to perform the stipulated conduct.[163] Because of the contractual analysis adopted by the Common law, this means that (unlike in German and Scots law) someone who performs the conduct in ignorance of the reward cannot subsequently claim the reward.[164] The adoption of an offer analysis also means that, as is generally the case under English law, the offer can be revoked at any time until it is accepted by the offeree. This creates potential problems for English law: what is the position where an offeror, seeing a member of the public walking towards his house with the offeror's lost dog, shouts out of the window 'I revoke my offer of reward' (a problem avoided in the DCFR by the provision that revocation of an offer made to the public must occur in the same way in which the offer was made[165])? The answer which has been suggested is that the offeree who begins to perform the conduct stipulated has validly accepted the offer,[166] though in Australia

---

[163] *Daulia Ltd* v. *Four Millbank Nominees Ltd* [1978] Ch 213. For an Australian example, see *Veivers* v. *Cordingley* [1989] 2 Qd R 278; an attempt to withdraw the offer of reward in a case where performance has begun will render the offeror liable to pay the reward in full: *Abbot* v. *Lance* (1860) Legge 1283 (NSWSC).

[164] There is no English case clearly setting out this view, though it would seem to follow from the general principles applicable to acceptances. For an Australian case adopting this view, see *R* v. *Clarke* (1927) 40 CLR 227; to similar effect, see the South African case of *Bloom* v. *American Swiss Watch Co.* (1915) AD 100.

[165] DCFR Art. II.-4:202(2).

[166] No decision of the courts definitively sets out this view, though the comments of Denning LJ in *Errington* v. *Errington* [1952] 1 KB 290 (CA), 295, support it. For

the Full Federal Court has opined that it may not always be unjust for an offeror to revoke an offer once the offeree has begun performance.[167] The dilemma would be avoided by adoption of a binding unilateral promissory analysis.

In German law, a promise of reward to a specific party is likely to be governed by whichever of the BGB provisions on service contracts,[168] work contracts,[169] or contracts to transact business,[170] is applicable given the nature of the contract entered into by the parties.[171] For a public offer of reward (*Auslobung*), special provision is made in §657 BGB, which states:

> *Binding promise*:
>
> Anyone offering by means of public announcement a reward for undertaking an act, including without limitation for producing an outcome, is obliged to pay the reward to the person who has undertaken the act, even if that person did not act with a view to the promise of a reward.

Unlike the default rule for offers in general in German law (that the offer may not be revoked, unless it is specifically stated to be revocable), §658 states the opposite: the promise of reward may be revoked until the act is undertaken, unless it is stated to be irrevocable. That the *Auslobung* is seen as a type of unilateral promise, and not an offer which may simply be accepted by conduct, is further confirmed by the fact that it does not matter if the promisee knew of the existence of the reward when he carried out the conduct which is the subject of the reward.[172] This puts German law on the same footing as Scots Law, in terms of which it is possible to view a promise of reward as a unilateral promise and therefore one which binds without any mental appreciation of, or acceptance by, the promisee. The contrast with the Common law position discussed earlier will be obvious.

In Scots law a promise of reward, whether made to the public or a specific person, can be characterised as an example of a unilateral promise. If such a promissory character is intended by the party issuing the reward, then, like any other example of a unilateral promise in Scotland, once issued the promise of reward cannot be revoked (unless power to do so has been retained), so that the difficulties of a promisor who subsequently

---

a discussion of the issues, see Peel, *Treitel on Contract*, pp. 41–3, and Furmston and Tolhurst, *Contract Formation*, paras. 3.79–99.

[167] *Mobil Oil Australia Ltd* v. *Lyndel Nominees Pty Ltd* (1998) 153 ALR 198.

[168] §§611–30.   [169] §§631–51.   [170] §675.

[171] See Gordley, *The Enforceability of Promises in European Contract Law*, pp. 308–9.

[172] §657.

tries to avoid paying a reward by revoking it are avoided. On the other hand, one practical problem with a promissory approach to cases of reward is that, unless the reward is offered in the course of business, it has to be in subscribed written form in order to be validly constituted.[173] That would be unusual for an offer of reward, many of which appear simply on photocopied notices of reward, or as advertisements in newspapers or in shop windows. This problem can be avoided if recourse is had to the English offer analysis, and in fact, under English influence, some Scottish courts have taken just such a view, describing offers of reward made to the public as contractual offers capable of acceptance by conduct.[174]

Again under the influence of the Common law, in South Africa the offer of reward is regarded as an offer capable of acceptance by performance of the act prescribed as the condition for the reward, a view set out in *Dietrichsen* v. *Dietrichsen*[175] and affirmed in *Bloom* v. *The American Swiss Watch Company*.[176] In Louisiana, the relevant codal provision on offers of reward made to the public describes them as offers, but provides that they are binding on the offeror.[177] The nature of this exceptional binding effect of an offer of reward is not explained, being simply provided for in the Code. It comes close to a unilateral promise, however, in that it is further provided that the offer is binding 'even if the one who performs the requested act does not know of the offer', which is not a commonly adopted position in relation to offers of reward conceived of in offer (rather than promissory) terms. The result is that, in form, Louisiana appears to adopt an offer analysis in respect of cases of reward but, in effect, treats them like unilateral promises. The result is a practical, though hardly elegant, one.

6. Options

There is no single way to define the concept of an 'option'. To make the term meaningful, however, it must be taken to signify more than just the right of someone who holds a revocable offer to accept it, otherwise option would mean no more than offer and *vice versa*. One could say that a firm or irrevocable offer is an option:[178] on that view then, for instance,

---

[173] See the Requirements of Writing (Scotland) Act 1995, s 1(2)(a)(ii).
[174] *Hunter* v. *General Accident Corp.* 1909 SC 344, affd 1909 SC (HL) 30; *Hunter* v. *Hunter* (1904) 7 F 136.
[175] 1911 TPD 486.   [176] 1915 AD 100.   [177] CC Art. 1944.
[178] As the Dutch Civil Code (BW) does: 'A stipulation whereby one party binds himself to enter into a certain contract with another party at the latter's option is deemed to be an

in German law all offers would be, by default, 'options', because they give the offeree a right to accept the offer enforceable against the offeror if the offeror tries to revoke the offer. In fact, however, German law does not call such an irrevocable offer an option, reserving the description of offers for options contracts. Similarly, Louisiana distinguishes firm options and options, there being separate codal provisions for the two.[179]

For present comparative purposes, an inclusive definition of an option will be taken, that being as follows:

> a right granted by A under either under a firm offer, or a contract, or a unilateral promise (but not merely one which is the subject of a revocable offer), giving to B a discretionary right either to compel A to enter into a further contract with B or else to confer some other benefit upon B.

An option might then theoretically be either bilateral (because it was a contractual option, binding both parties to the agreement) or unilateral (binding only the party granting it). Consider the following example:

> A grants an option to B, for no consideration, permitting B to purchase some land in A's ownership, such option to be exercised within one year. When B exercises the option nine months later, A reneges on the option.

How should the undertaking of A under such an option be characterised: is it a unilateral promise, a contractual undertaking, or something else? No assistance can be derived from the DCFR, which contains no provision dealing specifically with the nature of options.

German law recognises the validity of an option contract (*Optionsvertrag*), this being a contract in terms of which one party is given the right to require the other party to enter into a further contract with him, though no specific provision is made for such a contract in the BGB. Though the contract therefore creates circumstances which may be gratuitous (conferring rights only on one party), the option may only be obtained by the usual contractual method and not through any unilateral juridical act. If the option concerns the sale of land, it would have to comply with the provisions of §311b on land contracts and would thus require notarial authentication.

In English law, the principal hurdle to the creation of options is, as in the case of a firm offer, the requirement that a valid option have some

---

irrevocable offer' (BW, Art 6:219(3)). See also the Restatement (Second) Contracts, §25, which provides: 'An option contract is a promise which meets the requirements for the formation of a contract and limits the promisor's power to revoke an offer.'

179 The German and Louisiana positions are discussed further below, at pp. 231, 233.

reciprocal consideration for its grant. Given, however, the willingness of the courts to find ever more imaginary instances of consideration, a potential purchaser of land under an option might, for instance, very well be seen as having provided consideration for the option by instructing a survey to assess the suitability of the land for an intended purpose. In the absence of some type of consideration, however, no matter how strained or convoluted it may be, a genuinely *gratis* option would clearly be invalid. Where options are validly created in English law, they are conceived of as a species of so-called 'unilateral contract', since they create binding duties on only one party. As unilateral contracts they are said to transform into bilateral or synallagmatic contracts once the option is exercised.[180] So English law, in trying to describe an essentially unilateral and gratuitous obligation, has to give it the clothing of contract in order for it to be accommodated within the Common law obligational model.

What of the mixed legal systems? In Scots law, the nature of an option can be that of a firm offer (which, as noted above, is an offer with a promise attached to it to keep the offer open) requiring acceptance,[181] or simply a promise, plain and simple, not requiring any acceptance (though still evidently requiring to be exercised by some sort of notification on the promisee's part). Scots law thus has no difficulty with saying that an option can be constituted by a unilateral promise; indeed the reported cases seem to indicate a preference for such a promissory view. If the option relates to a real right in land, it has to be in subscribed writing,[182] but where the option is in promissory rather than contractual form, only the promise itself has to be in such a form, the exercise of the option need not be.[183]

In both South African and Louisiana law, an option must be embodied in contractual form in order to be valid. A problem for South African law, as it is in many other systems, is whether the option is sufficiently precise in its terms to be enforceable: an option contract may be invalid for lack of certainty, for instance if it does not specify aspects of the substantive contract to be entered into by the parties with sufficient precision.[184] It has though been suggested that an option which does not specify a time limit on its exercise is not void for uncertainty, but is rather to be taken as of unlimited duration, though it may expire after a

---

[180] See Lord Diplock in *Sudbrook Trading Estate Ltd* v. *Eggleton* [1983] 1 AC 444, 477A–B.
[181] For a case of an option conceived of as a firm offer see *Hamilton* v. *Lochrane* (1899) 1 F 478.
[182] Requirements of Writing Act (Scotland) 1995, s. 1(2)(a)(i).
[183] *Stone* v. *Macdonald* 1979 SC 363 (CSOH).
[184] See *Letaba Sawmills (Edms) Bpk.* v. *Majovi (Edms) Bpk.* 1993 (1) SA 768 (A).

reasonable time.[185] If the grantor of an option contract tries to revoke it, the option holder is entitled to enforce the option against the grantor by means of an interdict. Alternatively, the option holder may claim damages in an amount designed to put him in to the position he would have been in had the option been exercised, so long as he can demonstrate, on the balance of probabilities, that he would have exercised the option.[186] An additional complexity of South African law is that it appears that the South African courts make a distinction between options contracts and so-called 'preference contracts', the latter relating to rights of pre-emption, because, according to the courts, an option contract is a contract to keep an offer open but in the case of a right of pre-emption no offer exists at the time of the grant, and the grantor is not obliged to make any offer unless and until he decides to sell the property. This means that while the acceptance of the offer covered by the option contract is sufficient for the exercise of the option, the exercising of a right of pre-emption requires bilateral action, that is the making of an offer and acceptance.

In Louisiana law, an option is a 'contract whereby the parties agree that the offeror is bound by his offer for a specified period of time and that the offeree may accept within that time'.[187] As with all contracts in Louisiana, no consideration is required for an option contract; however, as with other contracts, 'cause' is required.[188] The Louisiana codal provision looks, somewhat confusingly, like the description given earlier to a firm offer, but the difference is that a firm offer is not a contractual right, there being no contract until such a firm offer is accepted, whereas an option contract is a concluded contract, in which one party is given the option, exercisable for a specified period of time, of entering into a further contract. What this means, in the opinion of Litvinoff and Scalise, is that a 'closer scrutiny reveals that an option is a contract that actually contains a promise to make another contract later.' They add that, as the promise 'binds only the grantor – since the grantee remains free to accept or reject – an option is or consists of a unilateral promise to contract.'[189] This is somewhat hard to reconcile with the traditional Louisiana jurisprudential view that unilateral promises have no legal effect, although,

---

[185] See Van der Merwe *et al.*, *Contract*, p. 83. In *Hanekom* v. *Mouton* 1959 (3) SA 35, Watermeyer J indicated that authority exists that a *pactum de contrahendo* may endure indefinitely.

[186] *Sommer* v. *Wilding* 1984 (3) SA 647 (A).   [187] CC Art. 1933.

[188] Art. 1966 states that '[a]n obligation cannot exist without a lawful cause'.

[189] Litvinoff and Scalise, *Law of Obligations*, p. 64.

if an accurate description, it would seem to suggest that there is at least one valid manifestation of such a promise in Louisiana law. A less radical view might be to characterise an option contract in Louisiana law as a contract which contains an irrevocable offer by A in favour of B, B having, for a stated period of time, the right to accept the offer and thereby require A to enter into a further contract with him. Putting it that way would give effect to Article 1933 of the Code on options contracts, without having to utilise the idea of a unilateral promise. However, that Litvinoff and Scalise felt compelled to use the description of a 'unilateral promise' to describe an option contract is perhaps not so surprising: as the above general discussion of options has shown, they are indeed, in essence, unilateral promises. The unequivocal recognition of this in Louisiana might constitute a first step towards a more general recognition of the utility of such an obligational form.

Whatever the classification of options adopted by specific jurisdictions, every system conceivably faces the problem of whether the option creates a right specific enough to be enforced. Whether that is so will depend on the nature of the right conferred upon the option holder. If the obligation is simply, for instance, that A will transfer to B the ownership of certain goods for a fixed price, that is likely to be a specific enough obligation to be enforceable under an option. Land contracts, on the other hand, may create more problems, if the option gives the holder the right to purchase the land under a contract of sale to be agreed between the parties, for what if the parties cannot agree? The grantor of the option may argue that, in good faith, he tried to negotiate a contract, but failed to reach agreement, so that he has exhausted his promissory undertaking. A way to avoid such an alleged failure to agree and consequent failure of the option would be to ensure that, when the option is granted, a draft of the future contract envisaged between the parties is attached to the option, thereby reducing to a minimum the number of terms of the further contract which require to be settled between the parties.

Although the model of contract does not pose any insuperable problems for classifying options, especially in systems where there is no requirement of mutual consideration, the option is nonetheless a prime candidate for analysis in a unilateral promissory way. The granting of an option occurs in circumstances where, typically, the grantor of the option intends unilaterally and immediately to bind himself, and may conceivably wish to do so for no consideration. A unilateral promissory analysis avoids arguments about when options in offer form expire, whether they have been accepted, and whether a specific form is required for the acceptance. Options certainly represent one type of transaction to which the DCFR's general recognition of unilateral binding undertakings can easily be put to good use.

7. Letters of intent and preliminary contracts

In most jurisdictions, an indication of a future intention to contract which falls short of a clear offer to contract at the present time will not give rise to any legal effect, and will not be capable of being accepted in order to conclude a contract. This follows logically from the requirement that a party must demonstrate a willingness to be bound at law, either unconditionally (in the case of a unilateral promise) or conditionally upon the other party's reciprocal willingness (in the case of an offer), before a legal obligation can arise. Consequently, what is commonly referred to as a 'letter of intent',[190] if it is objectively a mere indication of future intention to contract rather than a promise or an offer (which it might be, despite being referred to by the issuing party as a letter of intent), will have no effect in law, whatever psychological comfort it may provide to the recipient. This position has been affirmed in, amongst other jurisdictions, Germany,[191] England,[192] and Scotland;[193] by contrast, the DCFR does not specifically address the phenomenon. The inclusion of a statement that the contents of such a letter of intent are 'subject to contract' will usually assist in a finding against contractual liability resulting from the letter, the same holding true if the statement is to the effect that the parties have reached an agreement 'in principle'.[194]

---

[190] Letters of intent are sometimes referred to as 'comfort letters', though there is also a tradition of restricting the latter term to cases where the intent expressed relates to the provision of a security or other financial undertakings. On this more restricted type of comfort letter, see Furmston and Tolhurst, *Contract Formation,* paras. 10.58–68. For a comparative discussion of letters of intent, see Moss, 'The Functions of Letters of Intent'.

[191] See the standard German work by Lutter, *Der Letter of Intent*.

[192] *British Steel Corporation* v. *Cleveland Bridge and Engineering Co. Ltd* [1984] 1 All ER 504.

[193] *Uniroyal Ltd* v. *Miller & Co. Ltd* 1985 SLT 101.

[194] This position has been affirmed by the South African courts: see *Titaco Projects (Pty) Ltd* v. *AA Alloy Foundry (Pty) Ltd* 1996 (3) SA 320 (W), at 331. In *Kenilworth Palace Investments (Pty) Ltd* v. *Ingala* 1984 (2) SA 1 (C) parties who were acting under a bona fide but mistaken belief that they had reached an agreement were held not to be in a contractual relationship. Their position was not assisted by the inclusion in the defective agreement of terms that the parties 'accept that it may be necessary to alter the structure upon which [the purported agreement] is based' and for the purported agreement 'to be converted into a full and comprehensive agreement'.

Whether a party intends to issue a genuine letter of intent, expressing merely its non-binding intention to contract in the future, or has gone further than this, will depend upon the proper interpretation of its words and conduct in the circumstances of the case. That interpretative process may disclose a different intention, including the following:

(a)   An intent to contract

Sometimes, despite the use of the language of a letter of intent by one or both parties, the parties are held to have demonstrated sufficient contractual intent to have concluded the contract which they were negotiating.[195] This demonstrates that courts are looking not simply at the language used, but at the whole circumstances of the negotiations to determine the objectively manifested intentions of the parties.

(b)   A preliminary contract, envisaging a further contract

Though the language of a letter of intent may have been used, the party issuing it may be held to have issued a valid contractual offer, so long as what is contained in the communication demonstrates enough by way of minimum contractual content and a clear intention to be bound to constitute such an offer. That may be the case even if the intention is to enter in to a further, more detailed contractual relationship, to supersede the first, once the terms of this further contract have been negotiated and settled by the parties. In other words, the parties may have envisaged entering a holding or preliminary contract to govern their relationship *pro tem*, even if the language of a letter of intent was used.[196] One qualification to this is that, if what is envisaged at the preliminary stage is the granting

---

[195] *Uniroyal Ltd* v. *Miller & Co. Ltd* 1985 SLT 101; *Damon Cia SA* v. *Hapag-Lloyd International SA ('The Blackenstein')* [1985] 1 All ER 475; *Canada Square Corp. Ltd* v. *Versa Food Services Ltd* (1981) 130 DLR (2d) 205, 34 OR (2d) 250.

[196] See, for instance, the UK Supreme Court case *RTS Flexible Systems Ltd* v. *Molkerei Alois Müller GmbH & Co. KG (UK Production)* [2010] UKSC 14, in which the letter of intent was held to form the basis of a 'letter of intent contract'. For Scotland, see *Robertson Group (Construction) Ltd* v. *Amey-Miller (Edinburgh) Joint Venture* [2005] CSIH 89, where even though a letter from the defender contained the wording 'while it is our intention to enter into a contract with you', the letter was nonetheless held to be an offer of a preliminary contract capable of acceptance by the conduct of the pursuer in commencing work on site. See also *Newport Limited* v. *Sears, Roebuck & Co.*, 6 F. 3d 1058 (5th Cir. 1993), in which the Fifth Circuit of the US Court of Appeals, applying Louisiana law, held a letter of intent the basis of a valid contract.

of a discretionary right to another party, such a circumstance is usually classed as the grant of an option (or option contract), a subject discussed in the previous section.

Can any preliminary contract contain, or indeed be constituted solely by, an obligation to negotiate a further contractual relationship of indeterminate content at some point in the future? The traditional answer of the Common law to that question has been in the negative: a duty to negotiate a future contract of indeterminate content cannot be made binding in law, whatever its moral status may be, even if such duty is stated in good faith terms. Such an obligation, it is said, would be too uncertain to be enforceable at law, a position enunciated by the House of Lords in a decision discussed earlier in relation to the question of duties arising during the contract negotiation stage, *Walford* v. *Miles*.[197] A similar position is adopted in Scotland[198] and South Africa.[199] Matters may be otherwise if parties provide in a preliminary agreement for the negotiation of a contract, failing consensus on which terms are to be settled through some mechanism such as the decision of a third party arbiter. Given the provision of a mechanism for determination of outstanding matters, such a contract would not be void for uncertainty.

While the negative attitude towards a duty of good faith demonstrated in *Walford* v. *Miles* is in stark contrast to the principle of good faith embodied in §157 BGB, the position of German law in relation to contracts to negotiate is otherwise quite similar to that of English law. In Germany, parties may enter a 'pre-contract' (*Vorvertrag*) in which they undertake to enter into a further contract, but only so long as the terms of the further contract are determined or determinable under the pre-contract; if they are not, the alleged pre-contract is void.[200]

(c)   An expectation of a formal contract

A further alternative interpretation of what has been intended by parties is that, while one party intended to make an offer, expecting an acceptance to be forthcoming in turn, this may have been on the understanding

---

[197] [1992] 2 AC 128.

[198] *R & D Construction Group Ltd* v. *Hallam Land Management Ltd* [2009] CSOH 128.

[199] See *Shell SA (Pty) Ltd* v. *Corbitt* 1986 (4) SA 523 (C). For recent approval of this view, see *Shoprite Checkers (Pty) Ltd* v. *Everfresh Market Virginia (Pty) Ltd t/a Wild Break 166 (Pty) Ltd* [2010] ZAKZPHC 34.

[200] See the decision in RGZ 124, 81, for an example of a contract held to be void for just such a reason.

that no binding contract would arise until the agreement was embodied in formal documentation. That may have been the intention whether or not the law requires a contract of the type in question to comply with such formalities. In such a case, though we are not dealing with a classic letter of intent, a contract will nonetheless not arise until compliance with the relevant formalities is achieved.

(d) An expression of intention to do something other than contract

Yet a further possibility is that a communication may express the intention of a party to do something without that something necessarily being to enter into contract with the recipient of the communication. For instance, at the request of B, A may express to C its intention to pay C a sum of money. Unless the circumstances disclose that C has an enforceable third party right under a contract between A and B, could the mere communication of A to C found any claim by C to payment? In jurisdictions with a requirement of mutual consideration, this seems very unlikely. But even in those without such a requirement, it may be hard to view A's statement as in any sense binding. While it might, for instance under Scots law, amount to a unilateral promise, again it would be a question of interpreting the precise language used by A to ascertain whether A ought to be held objectively to have intended to bind himself through the words used. In one Scottish case,[201] a letter sent by A to C stated:

> We confirm receipt of a letter ... from [B] a copy of which is attached, requesting us to amend remittance instructions [i.e. by paying C rather than B]. We undertake that we shall comply with [B's] irrevocable instructions therein.

A subsequently failed to pay C as it had 'undertaken' it would. The court held that A's undertaking should not be interpreted as a promise, because it was unlikely that A would have intended to grant such a promissory right to C, a party with whom it had had no prior dealings. A's letter was rather a non-binding confirmation of its intention to act, and gave rise to no legal duties. The English courts have taken a similar attitude to a comfort letter issued to a party with whom the issuer has had no prior relationship.[202] In a subsequent Scottish case, an undertaking by a board of trustees expressing its intention to transfer funds to a party was again held non-promissory in nature.[203]

---

[201] *Krupp Uhde GmbH* v. *Weir Westgarth Ltd* 31 May 2002 (unreported).
[202] *Kleinwort Benson Ltd* v. *Malaysia Mining Corp. Bhd.* [1989] 1 All ER 785.
[203] *Cawdor* v. *Cawdor* [2007] CSIH 3, 2007 SLT 152.

Contrary to the results reached in such cases, Atiyah has argued that when institutions, corporate bodies and the like announce their decisions 'the line between a mere statement of intent and a promise becomes somewhat blurred. A public announcement in the form "The Committee [Board, Government, etc.] has decided ..." is much closer to being a promise than a comparable statement by a private individual.'[204] Atiyah's explanation for the view that statements by such bodies as to their decisions are more likely to be promises is that 'decisions of this character are usually more trustworthy than declarations of intent by a single individual',[205] but that seems an entirely impressionistic assertion which finds little, if any, support from the case law.

(e) A genuine unilateral promissory intention

It is rarely suggested that a letter of intent may be a simple, unilateral promise. However, if, as some courts have suggested, what may be called a letter of intent is capable of being a contractual offer, then in theory there would be nothing to prevent a letter of intent being, in the alternative, a promise, if that were the objectively determinable intention of the party issuing the letter. However, as most letters of intent are issued in a commercial context in which the issuer of the letter expects to receive something in return, it is unlikely that, if any binding obligation was intended at all, a unilateral promise will have been intended. In Scotland, with a separate obligation of unilateral promise, what case law there has been on the matter has not favoured a promissory analysis of letters of intent,[206] though of course everything turns on the intention of the specific party issuing the letter in any case.

8. Error in formation of contract

Error is commonly considered a difficult or troubling part of the law of contract.[207] The difficulty or trouble for legal systems lies in deciding first what types of error the consideration of justice mandates correcting, and second in developing a classification which accurately achieves the mandated outcome when applied to the facts of individual cases. Too often legal systems appear not to have reflected sufficiently on either the first

---

[204] Atiyah, *Promises, Morals and Law*, p. 152.   [205] *Ibid.*, p. 152.
[206] *Ritchie* v. *Cowan and Kinghorn* (1901) 3 F 1071.
[207] Pollock summed up the matter well: 'The whole topic is surrounded with a great deal of confusion in our books' (Pollock, *Principles of Contract*, p. 357).

or second of these matters. As to the first, unless one has decided when the requirements of justice mandate the correction of error, any classification will be hopelessly confused; as to the second, even if there is an underlying sense of what justice requires, the classification chosen, unless based on consistent criteria, may not properly reflect the policies said to be favoured by the system and will certainly be harder to apply in practice.

(a)   Choosing the policies which inform the rules on error

As to the first question, legal systems typically build corrective policies concerning error upon a preferred approach to a number of common issues. Foremost, there is the fundamental consideration of whether to give priority to the actual, subjective intentions of parties (the promises they in fact intended) or rather to the objectively manifested consent of the parties (the promises they appeared, to a reasonable person in the other party's shoes, to have made). A preference for the former over the latter will tend to allow a much wider field of relevant errors to be pled. The choice between subjectivity or objectivity is likely to be determined by the underlying contract theory favoured by a system, although what approach the chosen theory mandates is a moot question. Thus, while a strong preference for will (or promissory) theory has been said by some to favour a preference for subjectivity in the approach to error, other will theorists would argue that the will cannot be divorced from its external manifestation, so that a preference for objective declarations of the will should be favoured, with a consequently narrower field of relevant error. Reliance theorists will naturally have a preference for an objective approach, given that what matters is said to be the effect (the reliance) produced on one party by the manifested behaviour of the other. Apart from underlying contractual theory, other considerations can affect a preference for objectivity or subjectivity. Thus, a preference for commercial certainty and for not disturbing settled transactions will tend towards the choice of an objective approach. A preference for consumer protection may perhaps favour a variable approach, with a focus on subjective intention when it is the consumer's behaviour which is in question but objectively manifested intention when it is the commercial party's behaviour which is in issue.

Apart from the objective/subjective debate, another approach to constructing a legal system's policy on error is to focus on the culpability of the error. On this approach, a general preference is often made for treating induced errors rather than uninduced (or unilateral) errors as relevant.

Such an approach does of course raise the tricky question of discerning the cause of a contractual error, that is what precisely persuaded a party to contract. Because error describes a psychological state of a contracting party, the question of whether an inducement to contract was or was not operative comes down to an attempt to analyse the thought processes of that party: what made the party decide to contract? That is evidently a difficult question: not only is it hard to separate out different possible reasons why parties contract, but there is the question of whether or not one believes the reasons alleged for the decision to contract. Though this is a difficult question, systems with a developed doctrine of misrepresentation would likely argue that it is a not insurmountable one, and that such an approach reflects an intuitive sense that parties should accept the risk of their own mistaken assumptions but not assumptions based upon false information or impressions for which the other party was responsible.

A further policy question, though one which tends not to be given such prominence as the ones above, is the question of the extent to which contracts are viewed purely as private acts, or as having a public aspect to them. If the former view prevails, then it will seem more acceptable to allow parties who share an erroneous assumption (such as the meaning of a word) to adhere to that mistake, given the private nature of their contract, even if this flies in the face of the commonly understood meaning of a word; if the latter, then such parties may be governed by the objective meaning of their agreement, even if neither would wish such an interpretation to prevail. If third parties are affected by a contract, or if the contract is to be registered in a public register, then there is evidently stronger pressure upon a legal system to hold there to be (at least in some cases) a public, rather than a purely private, aspect to the parties' contract. A preference for a view that contracts have a public aspect also makes it easier for courts to justify application of external community norms such as fairness or good faith when analysing the process of formation or the contents of the contract.

If legal systems were to choose just one of the above policy considerations as the guiding principle for constructing classifications of error, a classification giving effect to such a policy would theoretically be relatively easy to construct, given the single division it would create between types of case. Thus, a simple preference for induced errors over unilateral errors could lead to a classification of error which held that where a contracting party had been affected to any extent by misleading information provided by the other this would result in the contract being challengeable, but not otherwise. However, legal systems usually wish to give some effect to more than one policy when constructing a taxonomy of error. Most systems use a combination of policies, which inevitably poses complications for classifying the types of case and may lead to tensions between the policies implemented. Thus, a system which wanted both to correct induced errors, but also to favour objectivity for reasons of commercial certainty, would be faced with a tension in the result to be reached in a case where a party appeared to consent to a contract, but later argued that it was misled by the other party; a tension would similarly exist if a system wanted to favour subjectivity, at the same time as protecting third parties. Such tensions are not always incapable of solution, as a decision can be taken that one policy trumps another where they conflict (for instance, by preferring the prevention of misrepresentation over the certainty of settled transactions, or vice versa), but self-evidently just solutions are sometimes more elusive given the complexity of the factual situations in which error is pled.

(b)   Constructing workable classifications which implement the policies chosen

Sometimes adopted classifications seem not to embody any clearly thought-out policies of the legal system in question, or occasionally, even if there appear to be clear policies, the classification chosen is not very adept at implementing those policies.

(i)   Roman Law

One searches in vain in classical Roman law for any clear policy on error. It did not occur to classical Roman jurists or courts to construct a single concept of error across contract law given that there was no law of contract as such but distinct actions. That law was concerned with the form of what was done: if the prescribed form had been complied with, there was an irrebuttable presumption that this represented the will of the parties. However, by the Justinianic period, a discernible doctrine of error had developed, this resting upon certain types of mistake which could be said to preclude consensus. Thus, in D. 18.1.9, we find it stated that, in contracts of sale, an error as to the substance of the subject being transacted precludes consent.[208] The natural place for the beginnings of a generalised

---

[208] 'It is obvious that agreement is of the essence in sale and purchase; the purchase is not valid if there be disagreement over the contract itself, the price, or any other element of the sale' (*In venditionibus et emptionibus consensum debere intercedere palam est: ceterum sive in ipsa emptione dissentient sive in pretio sive in quo alio, emptio imperfecta est*).

consensual law of error was in the treatment of consensual contracts like sale, given their foundation on the consent of the parties rather than mere compliance with a particular form.

The classification worked out for consensual contracts saw operative errors as falling in to one of a number of types:

(1) Errors as to the subject matter, as in the example narrated in D. 18.1.9 of an error relating to a plot of land to be sold. This category embodied the concern that what counts is the 'substance' or 'essence' of the thing in question (for instance, whether it is wine as compared to vinegar), with the view being taken that sales of things believed to be of one substance, but which were in fact of another, were invalid.[209] There has been some rather inconclusive debate over whether the authors of the Roman legal texts which make reference to the idea of the 'substance' of a thing may or may not have had in mind the Aristotelian conception of substance, though that is certainly how medieval scholars interpreted the Roman texts.[210]

(2) Errors as to the price.[211]

(3) Errors as to the nature of the transaction. The Digest uses the example of parties who are confused as to whether money has been handed over as a deposit or as a loan: given the irresolvable difference of their opinions on this point, there can be no contract in such a case.[212]

(4) Errors as to the identity of the other contracting party.[213]

In this Justinianic classification, it seems not to matter whether one party was mistaken, or both were,[214] or that one of the parties may have been at fault in arriving at, or in inducing, the error. The Justinianic scheme was to be heavily influential in forming the treatment of error in later civilian and mixed legal systems, right down to the twentieth century, in many systems the view being taken that any of the four types of error listed above constituted 'essential' error, in the sense of being relevant error. However, the Roman scheme has now largely lost its attraction. The reason for this is a simple one: a classification of error according to subject matter, price, nature of the transaction and identity of the parties, though focusing on matters which are doubtless important to the

---

Zimmermann speculates, *Law of Obligations*, pp. 588–9, that classical law would have been the same.

[209] D. 18.1.9.2. [210] Gordley, 'Mistake in Contract Formation'.
[211] As the text of D. 18.1.9 shows. [212] D. 12.1.18.1. [213] D. 19.1.9.pr.
[214] Some texts clearly indicate cases of a mistake shared by both parties, for instance D. 18.1.14 and D. 18.1.41.1.

parties, is a classification which does not explain why sometimes an error apparently falling into one these types is thought to be relevant, but sometimes not. For instance, in the modern law, the view is taken that a party who buys vinegar thinking it is wine will *not* always be able to avoid the contract. But to explain why this is so one needs to have regard to matters other than the subject matter of the contract, in particular *how* the party arrived at its erroneous view. The Roman classification is based entirely on a non-fault, subjective understanding approach to error, and as such does not embody all the policy considerations that the modern law would wish to implement in constructing its rules on error. Even in the Justinianic period, the limitations of the classification were already obvious, it not always being clear when, for instance, an object was of a particular 'substance' or not.[215]

<h4 style="text-align:center">(ii)   The Common law</h4>

The Common law, like Roman law, was originally a law built upon actions, again making it difficult for single, contract-wide policies on error to emerge, the division between law and equity also enabling some policies to flourish in equity but not in law. Indeed, it has been remarked by a number of observers that until the middle of the nineteenth century English courts provided almost no analysis of contract based upon the idea of consent or mistake,[216] a position which contrasts starkly with the civilian systems.

While one might draw within the ambit of mistake, widely defined, a large category of cases (including, for instance, promissory estoppel, which might be said to be based on the reliance placed on an erroneously created impression), for the moment it is useful to mention just the classic cases of remediable mistake in the Common law. The types of such mistake fall into narrowly drawn categories:

(1) *unilateral error*: unilateral error provides only very limited grounds for correction in English law. Where a mistake by one party, known about by the other, is taken advantage of by the other, then the contract may be avoided, but only where the mistake concerns a matter

---

[215] The Digest itself contains discussion of borderline cases. For instance, an object sold as gold but which is only gilded is nonetheless seen in D. 18.1.14 as a valid sale, but this view of Ulpian contradicts the opposite approach of Julian given in D. 18.1.41.1. This shows the limitations of the concept of the essence or substance of a thing.

[216] See Gordley, *Philosophical Origins*, p. 144; Ibbetson, *A Historical Introduction*, pp. 226–9. Ibbetson notes that the first writer to provide a mistake-based analysis was Macpherson in 1860, writing on Anglo-Indian contract law, followed by Leake in 1867.

which has been made a term of the contract.[217] This point was affirmed recently in *Statoil ASA* v. *Louis Dreyfus Energy Services LP*,[218] where the wrong date for an event was used by one party to calculate the contract price, a mistake known about by the other party, who simply chose to remain silent. The court found that the mistake in question, as to the date of the relevant event, was not itself a term of the contract, and therefore that it did not found a ground for avoiding the contract on the basis of unilateral error.[219] Of course, even if the matter has been made a term of the contract – price being a clear example – if the other party does not know that the wrong price was indicated (as will usually be the case with fixed price contracts), then it can hardly have taken advantage of the mistake, and the contract will stand.[220]

(2) *induced error*: where a misrepresentation has been made, the contract may be avoided. A misrepresentation is a misleading or untrue statement of fact made by one party to the other which has, to some extent, persuaded that other party to enter into the contract (in other words, there must be demonstrable reliance on the misrepresentation[221]). It is crucial to note, however, that the doctrine of misrepresentation is an aspect of tort law: the tortious act allows avoidance of the contract. The tortious nature of misrepresentation demonstrates the emphasis upon the wrongful aspect of the error rather than just the mere fact of the error, and demonstrates the operation of a strong policy concerning the allocation of blame and risk in the law of error.

(3) *common or shared error*: this is a mistake on a fundamental matter (interpreted narrowly) which is common to both parties' intentions, that is they share a subjective mistake about the objective nature of the contract or some matter pertaining to it.[222] Thus a sale of non-existent goods which the parties mistakenly believe exist is void, as this shared view does not reflect the reality of the circumstances.[223]

---

[217] There must be an error in transaction, rather than an error as to motive, to put it in Germanic terms.

[218] [2008] EHWC 2257 (Comm).

[219] Reference was made in the court's judgment to the Singaporean case *Chwee Kin Keong* v. *Digilandmall.com Pte Ltd* [2005] SGCA 2, in which a party taking advantage of a misquoted price it knew to be wrong was not allowed to hold the contract as concluded. That case was distinguished on the basis that the error related to a term of the contract, the price.

[220] *Centrovincial Estates plc* v. *Merchant Investors Assurance Co. Ltd* [1983] Com LR 158.

[221] *Pan Atlantic Insurance Co. Ltd* v. *Pine Top Insurance Co. Ltd* [1995] 1 AC 501.

[222] *Bell* v. *Lever Bros Ltd* [1932] AC 161 (HL); *Grains & Fourrages SA* v. *Huyton* [1997] 1 Lloyd's Rep 628; *Great Peace Shipping Ltd* v. *Tsavliris Salvage* [2003] QB 679 (CA).

[223] *Couturier* v. *Hastie* (1856) 5 HLC 673.

As in Roman law however, difficulties arise in determining when one is dealing with a mistake about a fundamental matter. There is, for instance, a difficulty of deciding when a thing is not the thing the parties thought it was, and when it is merely different in quality without that difference amounting to a difference in the type of thing (a matter which does not create a relevant mistake, though it may found remedies under relevant sales legislation, for instance[224]).

(4) *mutual error*: this concerns cases where parties are at cross purposes on some matter which they have made a term of the contract, and neither view can be said objectively to be the correct one. Because in a sense neither party is actually in error, each simply holding a perfectly reasonable though incompatible intention, these cases of alleged error are normally explained in doctrinal terms as a failure to reach consensus. Thus, if both parties stipulate for the purchase of goods aboard a named ship in a particular harbour, but there are two ships with such a name, each party reasonably meaning a different ship, there is no subjective or objective agreement and thus no contract.[225] Such cases are rare, as often one party's view of a matter is thought by courts to be objectively the reasonable one, and thus that view is preferred and the other party held to it.[226] Moreover, if the matter over which parties are at odds was not put forward as being part of the agreement, a disagreement on it will be irrelevant.

The overall character of the modern Common law of mistake shows a preference for enforcing objectively declared intentions, while allowing subjective intent (or sometimes, more strictly, presumed subjective intent)[227] to be pled in the face of an objective declaration of consent where

---

[224] Under the Sale of Goods Act 1979, s. 14.

[225] *Raffles* v. *Wichelhaus* (1864) 2 H&C 906, 159 ER 375.

[226] *Smith* v. *Hughes* (1871) LR 6 QB 597.

[227] What is meant is that, unless a party was acting unconsciously, it can always be said to have intended subjectively what it in fact did. So, to capture more accurately the nature of some relevant pleas of error, one requires to say that what the party is arguing is that, had it known the true position, it would subjectively have intended some other result (either no contract, or a different contract), and it is this alternative, counterfactual, and thus presumed subjective intent, which ought to prevail: for shorthand purposes, this can simply be referred to as its 'subjective intent'. The same distinction can be said to arise in cases of extortion: though one can argue that a party subject to extortion *did* subjectively intend to do what it did (by choosing to avoid the threats made against it), and indeed German law takes this view, what such party is arguing is that it would not subjectively have intended to do what it did in the absence of the extortion, and it is such alternate or presumed subjective intent which ought to prevail (see further the discussion of extortion below at pp. 257ff).

either (i) the party not in error was in some sense culpable as respects the other party's subjective error (either by inducing it, or taking advantage of it) or (ii) a shared subjective intention concerning a fundamental contractual matter is at odds with objective reality (as in the common error cases). Additionally, use is made of the idea of dissensus to deal with cases where the 'error' is no more than incompatible but equally justified beliefs about the proposed basis of the contract (as in cases of mutual error).

The approach to mistake in the Common law is sometimes argued to present a problem for will or promissory theories of contract, for two principal reasons. First, it is argued that, where objective intention is enforced in the face of genuine subjective error, this demonstrates that it is not the will which really grounds contract, but reliance. This argument was rejected in an earlier chapter, so no more need be said of it here save by way of reminder that the alternative view has been maintained that objective declarations of the will can normally be said to be the most reliable and genuine manifestations of such will. Second, it has been argued that because objective declarations of will are sometimes ignored in favour of subjective intentions, this shows an inconsistency in approach, and that either objective or subjective manifestations of the will should be enforced, but not one or the other on different occasions. To this objection, it may be answered that, exceptionally, there are valid considerations in some cases justifying the view that proven subjective intent (or presumed subjective intent) is a better indication of genuine intent than erroneously generated objective declarations. The overall approach may be said to demonstrate a preference for, but not a slavish adherence to, the enforcement of objectively manifested consent and an objective interpretation of contract terms.[228]

The Common law of error (and it has been the approach of Scots law too since the late nineteenth century) produces results which on the whole are perceived to be fair, but it must be said that the classification of errors does not commend itself as especially systematic or logical. Such classification mixes up issues of different natures, namely whether parties' views accord with an objectively correct view of matters external to their own subjective intentions (such as the erroneous view that the subject matter of the contract exists at the time of contracting), the process by which parties have reached an erroneous factual understanding (whether as a result of their own considerations or what the other party has said), and whether perfectly reasonable (and thus not really erroneous) views

---

[228] See further on this point Fried, *Contract as Promise*, Ch. 5.

fail to coalesce and thus prevent consensus being reached. These matters are of a quite different nature, and sit together very uneasily in a single taxonomy. What the Common law's classification does not do is to distinguish clearly issues of motivation from the substance of the contract, or to make it obvious why some types of relevant error have to relate to contract terms (unilateral and mutual error), others to fundamental matters (common error), and others yet simply to any matter which persuaded a party to contract (misrepresentation). The strong impression is conveyed of a law of contractual error which has been cobbled together from disparate considerations and cases, and added to over time in a not especially systematic way. That characterisation, if true, would suggest that rationalisation of the law of mistake would be desirable in the interests of legal science.

(iii)   The mixed legal systems

As mentioned above, Scots law has since the late nineteenth century followed a similar classification of errors as that utilised in English law, having grafted on to an earlier concept of 'substantial'[229] or 'essential'[230] error largely derived from Roman law, the Common law's stress on induced errors, as well as a stress on the commercial importance of upholding objectively manifested consent rather than the internal workings of the human mind. Recently, however, it has been suggested that the traditional scheme should be abandoned in favour of a taxonomy based upon the Germanic division between errors in motive and errors in transaction.[231] The basic justification for such a division is that motive is generally not relevant to assessing what someone has done in law (including what someone has promised), and it is precisely the matter of what someone has promised (or should be taken to have promised) which is argued to be the proper enquiry for the law. In that enquiry, the question of what constitutes the transaction takes on a primary importance.[232]

---

[229] Stair I.x.13.

[230] Erskine, *Institute*, III.i.16; Bell, *Principles*, s. 11 (Bell saw an error in the substantials as one relating to the subject of the contract, the parties, the price, the quality of the thing in question, or the nature of the contract. The similarities with the Louisiana law, discussed next in the main text, are notable).

[231] See Law Society of Scotland, *The Laws of Scotland*, vol. 15, para. 686; MacQueen and Thomson, *Contract Law in Scotland*, paras. 4.45–66; Cameron *et al.*, *The Law of Scotland*, paras. 6.21–34. The Germanic classification is discussed further below at pp. 251–4.

[232] The fullest explanation of what that means can be provided by considering the approach to error of German law, discussed below.

In Louisiana,[233] the Civil Code (whose provisions on error are, like much else, based on French law) provides that error 'vitiates consent only when it concerns a cause without which the obligation would not have been incurred and that cause was known or should have been known to the other party',[234] it being further provided that error concerns a cause when 'it bears on the nature of the contract, or the thing that is the contractual object or a substantial quality of that thing, or the person or the qualities of the other party, or the law, or any other circumstance that the parties regarded, or should in good faith have regarded, as a cause of the obligation'.[235] There are overtones in these provisions of Scot's law's 'essential error', both in its original form as relating to certain fundamental aspects of the contract (the *substantia*, a concern which perpetuates the earlier concern of the Roman law with the substance of the contract), as well as in the form as reinterpreted by the nineteenth-century courts to mean an error without which the contracting party would not have contracted. There are also some similarities to the approach of the DCFR (discussed below). The overall effect is that there is an attempt to meld both the idea of a list of essential qualities relating to contracts (the Justinianic Roman law approach) with the further idea that the error must have a causal effect upon the transaction. Operative error is clearly more than the merely private 'error in motive'[236] of German law discussed below, but must be an error which is either shared by both parties[237] or else an error of A known of (or which ought to have been known of) by B.[238] The Louisiana provisions pack a mixture of concerns into very terse provisions, and the effect is something of a muddle of different types of consideration. In addition, as in other systems, some cases of what can be styled error are treated as evidencing a lack of agreement and thus as disclosing no concluded contract between the parties.[239] The overall approach to error is broadly similar to that of Scots law.

---

[233] See Hoff, 'Error in the Formation of Contracts'. This article considers the provisions of the former Louisiana Code; the error provisions in the new Code are a much slimmed down version of the former, more complex, provisions.

[234] CC Art. 1949.   [235] CC Art .1950.

[236] Thus, in a contract for the purchase of a house, a private motive not disclosed by buyers to sellers was held irrelevant as a basis for challenging the contract: *Bordelon* v. *Kopicki* 524 So 2d 847 (La App 3 Cir 1988).

[237] Referred to in the Louisiana textbooks as 'mutual error', though it is what would be called 'common error' by the Common law. For an example, see *Calhoul* v. *Teal* 106 La 47, 30 So 288 (1901).

[238] *Deutschmann* v. *Standard Fur Co. Inc.* 331 So 2d 219 (La App 4 Cir 1976); *Marcello* v. *Bussiere* 284 So 2d 892 (La 1973); *Universal Iron Works Inc.* v. *Falgout Refrigeration Inc.* 419 So 2d 1272 (La App 1 Cir 1982).

[239] *LaBorde* v. *Aymond* 172 La 905, 135 So 913 (1931); *Paterson* v. *Koops* 10 Teiss 266 (La App Orl Cir 1913).

In South African law, there has been a traditional tendency in favour of focusing on the subjective meeting of the parties' minds in deciding whether a contract has been formed.[240] However, a doctrine of what is called *justus error* has been developed to inject an objective element in to the exercise, this doctrine allowing A to plead that it made a justifiable error in assuming that B appeared objectively to consent to the contract even though A later claims that it did not subjectively so assent. The effect of the doctrine is to protect A's reasonable reliance upon the objectively manifested consent of B.[241] The enquiry relevant to the doctrine of *justus error* has been stated as being whether

> the first party – the one who is trying to resile – [has] been to blame in the sense that by his conduct he has led the other party, as a reasonable man, to believe that he was binding himself.[242]

There is thus, in South African law, a role for objectivity in preventing a contracting party through its conduct from misleading its negotiating partner.[243] As in the other systems, there are also cases which are viewed as evincing dissensus and thus no concluded contract.[244]

All three mixed systems, though they adopt differing analyses and terminology in their attempts to separate relevant from irrelevant errors concerning the formation of contract, reach similar positions in practice: each holds that if parties are genuinely and reasonably in disagreement on essential aspects of the contract, then there will be a lack of consensus and no agreement; each holds that if A creates a reasonable impression in B's mind that consensus has been reached, A cannot seek to have the contract annulled; and each stresses that such impression in B's mind must be reasonable, disallowing B from taking advantage of a mistake by A if that error was known of by B. While the results may be similar, the analysis of each of the mixed systems has developed in a somewhat haphazard fashion. They would each benefit from a fresh look at the subject of error in order to adopt a more coherent taxonomy, perhaps along the lines of the Germanic analysis now to be considered.

---

[240] See Hogg and Lubbe, 'Formation of Contract', pp. 40–1.
[241] Such reliance must be reasonable. Taking advantage of a known error is unreasonable, and will not found the basis of a valid claim: see *Horty Investments (Pty) Ltd* v. *Interior Acoustics (Pty) Ltd* 1984 (3) SA 537 (W).
[242] *George* v. *Fairmead (Pty) Ltd* 1958 (2) SA 465 (A), 471.
[243] As occurred in *National & Overseas Distributors Corp. (Pty) Ltd* v. *Potato Board* 1958 (2) SA 473 (A).
[244] *Maritz* v. *Pratley* (1894) 11 SC 345.

(iv) German law

The provisions on error in the BGB, found at §§119–24, are relatively succinct, and set out simply and clearly. As in most systems, the rules adopted represent a compromise between subjectivity and objectivity, between a declaration of consent and actual consent.

The background to the form and content of the German rules is that they represent, by and large, the view of Savigny (and later Windscheid) that those errors which matter are errors which result in a party's will not being properly reflected in its declaration of intent: they are errors in the expression of the will. By contrast, Savigny saw errors of motive – the reasons why a party wants to enter into a contract – as largely irrelevant (except in cases of deception by the other contracting party).[245] These two categories of error indicate that it is the will, and the expression of that will, which is the crucial concept in the German law of error. The traditional Roman analysis of error into errors *in negotio, in persona*, and *in substantia*, thus finds only a very limited place in the BGB.[246]

Savigny's simple approach was adopted by the drafters of the BGB. In the adopted regime it is, note, irrelevant to whether or not a contract can be avoided for mistake that one party knew of another's mistake,[247] whether the mistake was a 'common' or shared one, or whether an error was self-induced (unilateral) or induced by another party (for instance, by a misrepresentation).

The primary BGB provision, §119(1), may be paraphrased as providing that a party who, when making a declaration of intent, was (i) mistaken about its contents, or (ii) had no intention whatsoever of making a declaration with the content in question, may avoid the declaration if it can be shown that he would not have made the declaration had he been properly appraised of the circumstances. The result of voidability, rather than voidness, supports the prima facie value of the promises as made by the parties, even if such promises are susceptible to avoidance at the instance of one of the parties if the terms of §119 are met. Where avoidance occurs, the parties must be restored to their original positions, and this is achieved, if compulsion is required, using an unjustified enrichment remedy (the *Leistungskondiktion*).

---

[245] As to cases of deception, see §123, discussed in the main text below.

[246] Errors of substance are mentioned in §119(2): see discussion in the main text, immediately following.

[247] Though it is not irrelevant, as will be seen, to the question of damages under §122.

The nod to errors *in substantia* comes in §119(2), where it is added that mistakes about those matters commonly regarded as essential characteristics of a person or thing are to be treated as declaration mistakes. What this seems to mean is that if a party makes a mistake about such an essential characteristic then, even if he does not declare it, the error can be pled. §119(2) thus appears to be an exception to the general rule that errors in motive are irrelevant. The provision is, for that reason, controversial, though the courts have restricted its application by holding that it does not extend to the price of an object, nor to cases where the claim in question is of a type covered by the regime of seller's liability for breach of contract, nor to the creditworthiness of the other party.[248]

Overall, where there is a discrepancy between objectively declared intent and actual subjective consent, §119 shows a preference for the latter, so long as the disparity between the two manifests itself in what a party declared (rather than in its motives). It thus becomes crucial to see what was stated by a party in its declaration of intent, what the party expressed itself as intending to do.

The concession to objectivism comes in §122, which provides that a party seeking to avoid its declaration of intent must pay damages to the other party (or, failing this, to a third party) for losses caused in reliance on the validity of the declaration. Such liability is avoided if the party suffering the losses knew, or ought to have known, about the factor justifying the avoidance. This provision might at first look odd to non-German lawyers – why should the party who has suffered the error be the one to pay damages? – but it must be remembered that it excludes such a duty to pay damages where the other party was at fault. So, it is only in cases where a party wants to avoid a contract with a party who was not in fault, that the disturbance of the settled transaction triggers the duty to pay damages.

An example often given in German law to exemplify the distinction between relevant and irrelevant errors is a mistake in the price offered for a contract. If, for instance, A intends to bid €500, but mistakenly says he is bidding €5,000, this is a mistaken declaration which can be avoided.[249] This is an example of a mistake as to content, the first of the two relevant types of error mentioned in §119(1). As seen earlier, this result would not prevail in the Common law, on the bare facts stated, given that such a

---

[248] See Markesinis *et al.*, *German Law of Contract*, pp. 297–301.
[249] An example of this sort of case is seen in the decision of the Landgericht Hanau, NJW 1979, 721.

mistake would not be evident to the other party. Another type of declaration error is the second type mentioned in §119(2), that is one where a party had no intention at all of making a declaration of consent in the form expressed by the declaration, for instance where a party signs a contract of guarantee but is ignorant as to the nature of what it entails because he cannot understand the language it is written in.[250] By contrast, if the mistake creeps in at the pre-offer preparation stage, during the offeror's calculations, and eventually results in an offer being made which the offeror would not have wanted to make, this is said to be an error in motive and irrelevant. While that result would also be reached in Scotland and England, the view has been expressed by some authors that such a difference in result is hard to reconcile with the terms of §119(2).[251]

So-called (in English law) common errors are not specifically addressed in the German provisions. What is the position then if both parties share an error which is not reflected in objective reality? Some common errors are dealt with by means of interpretation: a shared mistake as to the meaning of a term may result in the courts applying the mistaken meaning to the contract, rather than the objectively correct meaning.[252] If the shared mistake only affects motivation, however, (for instance, the mistaken belief that a certain transaction will exploit a perceived valuable need in the market), it will be irrelevant. Further cases may trigger application of the doctrine of the failure of the foundation of the transaction,[253] thus giving a right to adjustment of the contract or termination.

There are questions of how §119 fits with §118, the latter providing that a declaration of intent not seriously intended, and made in the expectation that its lack of serious intention will not be misunderstood, is void. The point is that on some facts it may be unclear whether someone intended no obligation at all (in which case it is a §118 case of the apparent declaration being void) or whether some obligation was intended, but simply not one of this nature (in which case it is a §119 case of a voidable contract). The same act, from the view of the other party, may have the appearance of either of these two situations. So, for instance, a party might issue a letter intending it to be merely informal and not binding. This course of action might conceivably fall under §118 or alternatively be considered as a case of a declaration of intent intended to have one effect but in fact giving the appearance of another (and thus falling under §119). The BGH

---

[250] An example is the decision in BGH NJW 1995, 190.
[251] See Markesinis *et al.*, *German Law of Contract*, p. 283.   [252] RGZ 99, 147.
[253] Markesinis *et al.*, *German Law of Contract*, pp. 346ff.

struggled with this issue in a case concerning a letter from a bank, not intended by it to have any binding effect, but which gave the appearance of a guarantee.[254] The court decided to impute an intention to make a declaration of intent, albeit not one of the character which the objective terms it used conveyed (thus the matter was for determination under §119).

Though motive is generally irrelevant in the rules on error, it is relevant to cases of deceit (or unlawful duress) under §123: a person who has been induced to make a declaration of intent as a result of such deceit is given an absolute right to avoid the declaration, and there is no requirement that the party deceived be labouring under an error as to the contents of the declaration. Deceit means, however, wilful or intentional misrepresentation, and does not cover a careless or innocent misrepresentation. There is thus, from a Common law or mixed legal perspective, a gap in the provisions of the BGB. In practice, however, *culpa in contrahendo* (discussed earlier) is used to tackle some such cases, namely those where a party has negligently persuaded another to enter into a contract. That still leaves the innocent misrepresentation largely irremediable, however. Cases of extortion will be discussed in the next section.

Overall, the German approach, though not solving all difficulties in the field, by adopting a simple, single division in the category of relevant and irrelevant error, results in a taxonomy whose two categories are determined by criteria of the same type and one which is able to implement relatively easily the preferred policy of what may be called 'selective subjectivism', that being a preference for the subjective will over objective declaration so long as the disparity between the two is manifested in a matter which forms part of the declaration of the party in error. The German approach is not without its flaws, the inclusion of the substantial error provision of §119(2) commonly being thought of us such a flaw, but the analysis it provides is at least clearer than that offered under both the English and Scottish approaches.

(v)   An ideal approach to promissory error?

Is there an ideal approach to dealing with errors affecting promises? To pose such a question assumes that one knows what is meant by a promise and one might imagine that, a definition of promise having been adopted in Chapter 1 of this work, such an assumption would be justified. But what that definition necessarily obscures is the detail of the debates about what it means to have promised something which are the very essence of

---

[254] BGHZ 91, 324.

the doctrine of error. What therefore is required, before a legal system can construct a rational and desirable approach to dealing with error, is for it to adopt a general approach to determining what will be considered to have been constituted by a promise. This means considering whether what a party should be taken to have promised should be what it reasonably appears to have promised, what it subjectively thought it was promising, what it would subjectively have promised had it been appraised of the correct facts, some mixture of these approaches for different circumstances, or some entirely different approach altogether.

It is suggested that a sensible and principled approach might be as follows:

(1) that promises be judged objectively – this may be called the 'general approach to assessing the content of voluntary obligations' – but

(2) a deviation from this approach in favour of actual subjective intention should be permitted when such subjective intention does not align with the manifestation of that intention given in terms of the declaration of consent – this may be called the 'general policy concerning error'. Matters on which a party thus remains silent, or which were not expressed as part of what it was agreeing to, or which merely form the background reasons for it contracting (save in cases of induced error), will thus not properly be able to form the subject of a relevant plea of error.

Such an approach is essentially the Germanic approach to error, and it is one which is beginning to find favour in non-Germanic systems.[255] It is consistent with a high regard for the value of promises as acts of will, in so far as such acts of will are generally judged by the objective manifestation of such acts of will, but it reverts to underlying subjective expressions of will in order to deal with circumstances in which it is judged that it would be unjust to ignore a discrepancy between the objective appearance of consent and the underlying subjective will of parties. Approached in such a fashion, the field of error need not be viewed as exposing alleged weakness of a will approach to contractual liability; rather, the issues posed by error problems simply reflect a deeper and ever present tension in the law as to whether juristic consequences should follow from manifested behaviour or from underlying psychological consent (however that is judged). That difficult question is one which affects all theories of contract law, and not just will or promissory theories.

[255] It has, for instance, been proposed as a workable taxonomy in Scotland: see n. 231 above.

Is this suggested approach adopted by the DCFR? Not in these terms, though the same result is arrived at. The DCFR approach to error is based not simply upon the corrective rules of the section on mistake (II.-7.2), but also in the preventive policies embodied in the duties imposed on negotiating parties to provide certain information at the pre-contractual stage. The provision of such information ought, so the overall plan of the DCFR suggests, to prevent a great many errors from arising in the first place. As for the rules on error themselves, they do not mirror the Germanic taxonomy of errors in transaction and motive suggested above as an ideal approach. Adopting this approach may well have been perceived to represent too much of an imposition of one system's view in a field with very divergent national approaches. Instead, the DCFR provisions are a mixture of elements taken from a number of systems: there is, for instance, a distinction drawn between mistake in general[256] and those mistakes which are the result of reliance placed upon inaccurate information (essentially misrepresentation), the latter giving a right to damages,[257] a distinction redolent of the Common law; there is also a component of the general DCFR provision on mistake which renders mistake relevant only if, but for the mistake, the contract would not have been concluded, or would only have been so on fundamentally different terms, a requirement which is redolent of the concern of Louisiana law that the mistake be causally operative on the behaviour of the innocent party.[258] This requirement of a causally operative mistake takes the place of any requirement that the error relate to the 'substance' of the contract, a concept which (sensibly it is suggested) appears not to have found favour with the drafters of the DCFR. Private errors in motive are irrelevant, because it is only errors of which the other party knew, or could reasonably be expected to have known, that count.[259] Such errors, known of and taken advantage of by the other party who remains silent, are described in the provisions as being 'contrary to good faith and fair dealing', a characterisation which echoes the view of the Scottish courts about such errors.[260] What might be characterised as 'substantial error' is not wholly irrelevant, however, as while the error rules provide for avoidance of contracts affected by error, it is clear from the earlier provisions on formation of contract (which require 'a sufficient agreement')[261] that, in an appropriate case, a divergence of understanding by the parties on a fundamental aspect of

---

[256] Art. II.-7:201.   [257] Art. II.-7:204.
[258] CC Art. 1949, discussed above at p. 249.   [259] Art. II.-7:201(1).
[260] See cases cited in MacQueen and Thomson, *Contract Law in Scotland*, para 4.55.
[261] Art. II.-4:101(b).

the proposed contract sufficient to indicate a failure to agree could be pled in order to argue that no contract existed to begin with.

The DCFR provisions represent a reasonable attempt to reach a pan-European consensus on the subject of the proper analysis of error. However, as a compromise which culls elements from a number of traditions, the principled approach to error suggested above does not clearly shine through the DCFR provisions.

9. Extortion in the formation of contract

If contract is a voluntary exercise of the parties' free will and consent, then it would seem to follow that a contract which has been extorted[262] or coerced by B from A as a result of improper pressure applied by B (or under 'duress', as Common lawyers would say) is not a valid contract because it is not the result of an exercise of A's free will. That, however, would be to simplify the question of extortion in a way which ignores some difficult questions. Chief among those questions which are of relevance to the idea of promise and contract is the question of whether, where extortion is present, there is deemed to be an exercise of the victim's will or not. A party who chooses to give in to extortion rather than to resist the pressure exerted on him to contract, might be said to have exercised his will to contract. On such a view, he has consented to the contract, albeit that his consent might be said to be distorted, because he has exercised his will in a way which he perceives will avoid the undesirable consequences threatened. He has, to put it colloquially, chosen the lesser of two evils. Such a view was adopted by some members of the natural law school, including Molina,[263] Lessius[264] and Grotius,[265] though they recognised that the prima facie valid contracts formed as a result of extortion were able to be avoided on account of the coercion used to achieve them.[266] This

---

[262] The term extortion is susceptible to a number of meanings, but in a broad sense it signifies the obtaining of something from another by improper means in such a way that sufficient fear is created in the victim to persuade him to acquiesce in the demand made of him.

[263] Molina, *De iustitia et iure*, disp. 352.   [264] Lessius, *De iustitia et iure*, 2.17.6.

[265] Grotius, *De jure belli ac pacis*, II.xi.7. Pufendorf took the slightly different line that, though coerced consent was still given voluntarily, it did not give rise to any obligation: *De jure naturae et gentium*, III.vii.10–14.

[266] Though whether such a contract ought to be avoided is another matter: Adam Smith took the view that, even if a promise had been coerced from someone by a highwayman, breach of such a promise would involve some ignominy, as such a breach would be 'at least a departure from the highest and noblest maxims of magnanimity and honour. A brave man ought to die, rather than make a promise which he can neither keep without folly, nor violate without ignominy' (Smith, *Theory of Moral Sentiments*, vii.4).

view is also largely that of modern legal systems, as will be seen below. An alternative view is that to call extorted consent valid consent distorts the idea of free will: consent made under improper pressure should be seen as *not* freely given, and thus as no consent at all.[267] As will be seen, whether the will is seen as overborne or merely as tainted as a result of extortion, the continuing relevance of a will-based analysis of the victim's position is becoming somewhat eclipsed by the rise of solutions focusing on the objectively objectionable conduct of the extorting party regardless of the effect it has on the vicim's promissory intent.

It is important to appreciate that, where there is no improper pressure exerted upon a party to contract, then the question of extortion does not arise. In opposition to this understanding, Fried has suggested that cases where, in emergency circumstances, people have to contract at high prices should also be seen as instances of duress.[268] Yet this suggestion surely distorts the idea of duress, given that no pressure is involved in such cases, merely a failure on the part of the exploiting party to behave in a just fashion. If therefore such cases are objectionable, they should not be seen as such for reasons of duress but for some other reason. Indeed, as discussed below, the rise of doctrines such as undue influence have located the objectionable element in many transactions not in the effect upon the will of the weaker party, but in the undesirable nature of the conduct of the other party.

An appreciation of the position adopted by modern legal systems in relation to extortion requires an understanding of the historical development of the law. In this regard, one must look to Roman law, to the natural law idea of the just exchange, and to the subsequent eclipse of earlier attitudes through the rise of the idea of the will. In early Roman law, there was little one could do to attack transactions allegedly affected by compulsion.[269] In the classical period, however, the law developed through a *formula Octaviana* in the prateorian edict aimed at recovery of what had been given under force and/or fear (*per vim et/aut metum*),[270] and through the praetorian *edictum perpetuum* of Hadrian that the praetor would not

---

[267] Other theoretical questions have to be addressed, including what amounts to 'improper' or 'unlawful' pressure, and whether there should be a presumption that such pressure has been operative in cases where it is present, but, as these questions are of less relevance to the present discussion, they are not considered in any detail in the main text.

[268] Fried, *Contract as Promise*, p. 110.

[269] Du Plessis, *Compulsion and Restitution*, pp. 5–6.

[270] It is unclear whether *vis et metus* or *vis aut metus* was the prevailing doctrine: there are references in Ciceronian texts to each expression (*Verrine Orations II* 3.65.152 and *Ad Quint. fratr.* 1.1.7.21).

uphold what was done in consequence of fear (*quod metus causa gestum erit*).[271] Since Roman times there has been scholarly disagreement as to whether the idea of *vis et metus* indicated a single doctrine describing the act of the active party and the related effect upon the passive party, or whether it denotes two separate triggers for the doctrine (force *or* fear), a debate which is unlikely to be resolved given the lack of textual corroboration for one view over the other. In the medieval period, the debate was conducted by reference to terminology developed to differentiate the degree of *vis* (force) which might be operative, whether *vis absoluta* (that is, bodily force which completely negated the will) or the lesser *vis compulsiva* (lesser force which merely bent the will of the victim, but did not overcome it, a threat of force being an example of such).[272] The differing views reflected a division between whether extortion was seen as denoting an absence of the will (in which case there would be no contract) or merely a bending of the will (in which case there would be a voidable contract).

A related but distinct approach to the problem of oppressive conduct adopted by late Roman law is seen in a text from the Codex[273] which deals with a specific type of exploitation in the contract of sale, and permits an owner of land who had sold his land for less than half its true value to rescind the contract. Though the text is very specific, it clearly embodies a principle of exploitation, as well as an idea of a 'just price' (*iustum pretium*), which was capable of extension to other circumstances. Such an extension occurred in medieval jurisprudence, such that what developed came to be known as the doctrine of *laesio enormis*.[274] This medieval doctrine offered protection in cases of sale to buyers as well as sellers, and was extended to other types of contract, though it continued to be applied by reference to the somewhat arbitrary trigger of half the just price. The doctrine flourished because of the Aristotelian concept of commutative justice[275] and the Thomist stress on the idea of the just price.[276]

With the eclipse of natural law and the rise of the concept of the will, came a reticence on the part of the courts to enquire into the justice or

---

[271] See du Plessis, *Compulsion and Restitution*, pp. 6–13.

[272] On the distinction see Hartkamp, *Der Zwang in römischen Privatrecht*, pp. 3 ff. For the relevant medieval debate, see Azo, *Summa*, in C. 2,19 (20) *de his quae vi metusve causa gesta sunt*, § *in primis*, 38; *Glossa ordinaria, gl. vi atroci ad* D. 4.2.1, *gl. non videor* and *per vim ad* D. 4.2.9 pr.; Baldus, *Commentaria super Decretalibus, in c. quae causa, X, de his quae vi metusve causa fiunt*, n. 6–7, f.171rb.

[273] C. 4.44.2.   [274] See Watson, 'The Hidden Origins of Enorm Lesion'.

[275] *Nicomachean Ethics*, 1130 b ff.   [276] *Summa Theologica*, II-II, Q. 77, Art. 1.

otherwise of the contract price. This naturally led, in time, to the super-session of the doctrine of *laesio enormis*. It was not incorporated into the BGB and it was statutorily abolished in South Africa.[277] It did, however, persist in muted form in both French[278] and Scots law.[279] Instead, the law was left with a belief in the importance of a free exchange of consents and the related idea of extortion embodied in the concept of *vis et metus*: where such free consent was absent, as a result of extortion by another, the trans-action affected might be declared invalid (though whether void, as one might expect if there were no free consent, or voidable, is a matter of jurisdictional dispute).

(a)   English law

Early protection against duress in English law was piecemeal, and lay largely in Chancery's protection against imprisonment and threats of ser-ious physical injury as means of procuring a contract. Such behaviour was seen as undermining consent and overbearing the will.[280] Such an effect was not presumed from the mere force, however, but had, if challenged, to be demonstrated.[281]

However, it was not until the second half of the nineteenth century (around the time of the fusing of the legal and equitable jurisdictions) that cases of duress came to be treated consistently and conceptually as such. Published in 1867, Leake's *Elements of Contract Law* was the first English work to deal systematically with the subject, Leake describing the circumstances of duress as being 'where one of the parties to the agree-ment was induced to consent by fear and intimidation, imposed by the violence or threats of the other party'.[282] The presence of the elements of both *vis* and *metus* in this statement may be noted, though the Roman ter-minology is not used. The effect was that the innocent party might avoid the contract, the will not being conceived of as entirely absent, as in cases of mistake or insanity.

Though such cases of duress might be explained by reference to the will theory (the will being compromised by the threats), it has been observed that historically there was in fact a tendency to explain the reasons given for relief in terms of public policy (on the basis that a man should not be

---

[277] General Law Amendment Act 1952, s. 25.
[278] Where the doctrine is, as in Roman law, restricted to the case of a sale of land: see *Code civil* Arts. 1118, 1674 (the loss must be greater than 7/12ths of the value of the land).
[279] See discussion below, at p. 263.   [280] Ibbetson, *A Historical Introduction*, pp. 71–3.
[281] *Ibid.*, pp. 71–2.   [282] Leake, *Elements of Contract Law*, p. 205.

allowed to profit from his wrongs).[283] Still, it is not unheard of for modern courts to use the language of the will in relation to duress. Thus, for instance, Lord Simon of Glaisdale said of duress that it 'deflects without destroying, the will of one of the contracting parties',[284] thereby offering an explanation of why the effect is that of voidability rather than voidness. To similar effect, Lord Scarman stated that the 'classic case of duress is, however, not the lack of will to submit but the victim's intentional submission arising from the realisation that there is no practical choice open to him'.[285]

From the late 1970s, the English courts began to accept that duress might be constituted by more than false imprisonment or threats of physical violence, and developed a concept of economic duress. Such economic duress has, in the reported cases, often been constituted by the threat to terminate a contract unless the party making the threat receives greater remuneration for its pledged performance.[286] In one case, money was demanded by a union from an employer on behalf of employees, the threat being to blockade the employer's ship in port.[287] The question of when economic pressure may amount to duress raises even more starkly the conceptual difficulties lying at the heart of extortion, especially the question of whether certain conduct (such as a threatened breach of contract) will, by its very nature, amount to such illegitimate pressure so as to constitute extortion, or whether a specific effect upon the mind of the party threatened is still required (as seems to be the case).[288]

(b) The mixed legal systems

In Scotland, rules against extortion have a long pedigree. There is some debate about what properly falls within the category of extortion, however, and how the idea of extortion relates to the established doctrine of 'force and fear' (a doctrine which reflects the Roman law's *vis et metus*, discussed earlier). It can be argued that the category of extortion is a wide

---

[283] Ibbetson, *A Historical Introduction*, p. 235.
[284] Lord Simon in *Lynch* v. *DPP of Northern Ireland* [1975] AC 653, 695.
[285] Lord Scarman in *Universe Tankships of Monrovia* v. *ITWF* [1980] AC 614, 636.
[286] *North Ocean Shipping Co. Ltd* v. *Hyundai Construction Co. Ltd* [1979] QB 705; *Pao On* v. *Lau Yiu Long* [1980] AC 614.
[287] *Universe Tankships of Monrovia* v. *ITWF* [1980] AC 614, revd. [1983] AC 366.
[288] See Lord Scarman's discussion in *Pao On* [1980] AC 614, 635, of the question of the practicality of alternative courses of action that victims might choose to exercise. The practicality of alternative arrangements also features heavily in a recent judgment of the Privy Council, *Borelli and others* v. *Ting and others* [2010] UKPC 21.

one, covering not only 'force and fear' but also the doctrines of undue influence, enorm lesion, and facility and circumvention, some of which are discussed below. On the other hand, some commentators equate force and fear with extortion (often on the basis that where extortion occurs, the will is wholly overborne), seeing the other doctrines as examples of improperly obtained consent but not extortion properly so called.[289]

Whether the doctrine of force and fear is the only form of extortion properly so called, it seems clear that, in the modern law, the courts' principal concern in deciding whether a case of force and fear has been made out is whether the victim has acted out of fear; having determined that, the court will then consider whether some improper pressure (an illegal or unwarrantable threat) has been used to induce such fear in the victim, force or the threat of force being one (but not the only) such improper means. *Metus* is thus the primary concern, with *vis* being merely one improper way of inducing *metus*. There is a debate however as to whether or not, in a case of force and fear, the victim's will is properly seen as being absent, it having been wholly overpowered by the other party. McBryde takes the view that in a case of force and fear, consent is indeed absent: the 'essence of a case of extortion is that a deed was granted or a contract entered into without consent'.[290] While agreeing that there are indeed cases where the force is so great that the will is indeed absent, du Plessis has argued that these should not properly be called cases of force and fear because, where *vis absoluta* is present, it amounts to 'applying force in a way which excludes any decision of will of the victim', his fear thus being irrelevant.[291] Under this argument, it is only *vis compulsiva* which triggers the doctrine of force and fear, the result being an impaired exercise of the victim's will. While therefore there is agreement that there are cases where the will is indeed absent, there is disagreement as to whether these fall under the established doctrine of 'force and fear' or not. Whatever one calls cases where the will is considered to be absent, they appear to include circumstances such as those where someone's hand is seized and forced to sign a contract, where the victim is put into a hypnotic trance, or where there is an immediate threat of personal violence: in each such case, there is a complete lack of contractual will and thus no contract is seen as formed.[292] By contrast, where a lesser state of fear is produced, such as in cases where economic threats are issued, consent is usually seen

---

[289] See further McBryde, *The Law of Contract*, Ch. 17.
[290] *Ibid.*, para. 17–03.   [291] Du Plessis, *Compulsion and Restitution*, p. 124.
[292] Ibid., pp. 126–7, and sources cited there.

as being present, but it is voidable given the presence of the fear produced by the threat. Examples of the types of case which fall into each category seem, however, not to be wholly determinative of the analysis applied in the case, the courts being more concerned with the effect produced on the victim in question. The adoption of such an approach discloses a judicial interest in the subjective state of mind of an apparently contracting party which marks a divergence from the usual concern for the objective appearance of consent.

Apart from the doctrine of force and fear, the doctrine of *laesio enormis* persists (under the nomenclature of 'enorm lesion'), but only in relation to contracts entered into by minors.[293] Otherwise, courts have taken the view that, absent any extortion or undue influence, the price determined by parties under a contract should not be interfered with. As Lord Blackburn put it in one Scottish appeal to the House of Lords:

> If a man chooses to bargain that he will pay ten times the value of a thing I do not think you have, in the absence of undue influence, any right to cut down the price to the tenth part of what was agreed upon.[294]

As in England, a recognised exception to the unwillingness of the courts to interfere in unconscionable contracts is in relation to penalty clauses, where the justification has been given that such a clause puts the party subject to the stipulated penalty *in terrorem* of it and thus renders it contrary to public policy.[295] There has also been development, discussed later, of the doctrine of good faith. This doctrine, together with statutory regulation of unconscionable bargains,[296] is a solution to the problems of unfairness which is not founded upon the idea of lack of free will but rather upon the oppressive nature of the conduct of the other party. As in England, there has been a shift away from explaining problematic cases in terms of will and towards judicial and legislative paternalism, though this has occurred largely by grafting ideas of fairness onto the will model rather than by developing a new model of contract law.[297]

In South Africa, though the English term 'duress' is used, the law is largely based on Roman-Dutch foundations. *Vis absoluta* (where actual physical force is used to procure a contract) negates consent entirely; *vis*

---

[293] See McBryde, *Contract Law*, pp. 449–450.
[294] *Caledonian Railway Co. v. North British Railway Co.* (1881) 8 R (HL) 23, 31.
[295] See later discussion of penalty clauses in Ch. 6, at pp. 394ff.
[296] For instance, under the UK-wide Consumer Credit Act 1974.
[297] See, to the same effect in English legal development, Ibbetson, *A Historical Introduction*, p. 261.

compulsiva merely renders the contract voidable. In cases of *vis compulsiva*, it is clear that the will operates, though it is impaired. As De Villiers CJ put it,

> it cannot be said that there is a total absence of consent – but inasmuch as his consent is forced and not free, the payment is treated as involuntary, and therefore subject to restitution.[298]

The threats used to procure the contract must be unlawful or *contra bonos mores* (the equivalent of the illegal/unwarrantable criterion of Scots law), and the fear must be a reasonable and not an ungrounded one.[299] The use of terminology such as 'economic duress', suggestive of certain interests protected in the law of duress, has been criticised as likely to confuse, the established and more generalised terminology of unlawfulness/*contra bonos mores* being preferable.[300]

Laesio enormis has not survived in modern South African law, having been abolished by statute in 1952.[301] However, other statutory provisions have been implemented to deal with oppressive contracts, among them the Credit Agreements Act,[302] the Usury Act,[303] the Alienation of Land Act,[304] and section 3 of the Conventional Penalties Act.[305] Such provisions, as with similar statutory developments in the UK, focus on the undesirable conduct of the contracting party in question, rather than on the effect upon the will of the other party.

In Louisiana, Article 1478 of the Civil Code provides that a 'donation *inter vivos* or *mortis causa* shall be declared null upon proof that it is the product of fraud or duress'. More generally, Article 1948 (discussed earlier) provides triple protection against error, fraud and duress in relation to contracts. Each of these factors vitiates consent, rendering the contract voidable. Additionally, duress applied by a third party may vitiate consent.[306] It is hard conceptually to justify why an act of donation should be void on account of duress, but a contract merely voidable, especially when, in Louisiana, acts of donation are treated as bilateral, and thus in a similar way to contracts. One conceivable justification may be that acts of donation, being gratuitous, are considered deserving of a higher level of protection than contracts in general. Article 1948, in adopting the

---

[298] Per De Villiers CJ, in *White Bros.* v. *Treasurer-General* (1883) 2 SC 322, 351.
[299] See du Plessis, *Compulsion and Restitution*, pp. 101–2.
[300] Du Plessis and McBryde, 'Defects of Consent', pp. 127–8.
[301] Section 25 of the General Law Amendment Act No. 32 of 1952.
[302] Act 75 of 1980.   [303] Act 73 of 1968.   [304] Act 68 of 1981.
[305] Act 15 of 1962 (considered further in Ch. 6).   [306] CC Art. 1961.

language of vitiated consent, clearly locates the essential issue in the will of the party affected by the duress.

(c)   German law

It is noteworthy that, under §123 of the BGB, contracts subject to extortion are not seen as void, even in extreme cases, as they might be in some other systems in the event of threats of physical violence, but are in every case categorised as valid but avoidable. So, despite what may be extreme threats by another party, the consent to contract is still seen as having been validly given and a contract thus validly formed, the will having been operative, albeit coerced, and not absent.

The BGB provides that the coercion must have been 'unlawful', a requirement which has produced a substantial body of case law, including cases on economic coercion. The concept of unlawfulness has proved a flexible one in the hands of the courts, which, as in other jurisdictions, have to tread a fine line between the prevention of conduct which infringes societal norms and sharp, aggressive, yet lawful, business practices. As with the approach in other systems, German courts have held that coercion may exist if what is threatened is unlawful (for instance, physical violence) or if what the party making the threats seeks to gain is illegitimate or unwarrantable (for instance, the receipt of a benefit which would otherwise not accrue to it). There have also been trickier cases where neither of these criteria is met, for instance where A has threatened to report B to the police for commission of a crime if B does not do something for A which B might conceivably have done for A in any event. In some such cases coercion has been held to be present, but in others not.[307]

(d)   Conclusion on extortion

Legislative developments in English law and the mixed legal system since the 1970s have developed the law of extortion beyond a focus on the effect of certain illegitimate forms of pre-contractual behaviour on the will of the victim. The modern approach of the systems studied shows a mixed

---

[307] In BAG NJW 1999, 2059, a cashier had been defrauding her employer, and the employer insisted that she enter into a contract to repay the money or else the employer would go to the police. This was held not to amount to coercion. A similar threat would probably amount to coercion if the benefit the employer had requested had no connection with the employee's conduct.

pattern of continued judicial explanation of the established fact patterns in terms of vitiated consent or distorted will together with application of statutory regimes focusing on certain undesirable types of behaviour regardless of (or subordinate to) the actual effect of such behaviour. Earlier concerns about whether promises reflect the true will of the contracting parties now mix with legislative paternalism directed against bad faith and unconscionable conduct.

In the DCFR, the old tradition of seeing extortion as relating to the impaired will or consent of the party affected is continued. This comes out most clearly in one of the provisions relating to unjustified enrichment, which provides that 'coercion' and 'threats' directed against the disadvantaged party are two of the factors giving rise to a lack of free consent by that party.[308] No definition is, however, given of either factor, so that it is unclear from the text of the DCFR why the idea of coercion is not itself conceived of as wide enough to include threats within it, though the textual implication must be that it is possible to coerce without threatening.[309] The distinction between coercion and threats is maintained in the contractual provisions of the DCFR, where it is provided that the use of coercion or the threat of an imminent and serious harm which it is wrongful to inflict, or wrongful to use, renders a contract voidable.[310] There is no restriction of the harm threatened to cases of physical harm so that economic harm might equally be relevant. The threat is not relevant if the threatened party had a reasonable alternative.[311] The overall tenor of the DCFR approach is summed up in the Principles as being a mixture of concern for lack of true consent as well as the prevention of gains made through undesirable conduct.[312] That being so, it is clear that this particular model law shows the same mixed pattern of concerns as do the national systems studied.

10.　Implied terms

It is sometimes said that the implication by courts of terms into contracts, whether with or without legislative authority, represents a fundamental

---

[308]　DCFR Art. VII.-2:103.

[309]　Indeed, that this is the conception is made clear by the official Commentary to the DCFR, which states that '[n]ormally coercion will involve the use of threats, but this is not necessarily so' (DCFR, Full Edition, commentary, p. 500).

[310]　DCFR Art. II.-7:206(1).

[311]　DCFR Art II.-7:206(2). See the earlier remark on English judicial comments concerning this matter at n. 288.

[312]　DCFR Princ. 42.

problem for a promissory view of contractual obligations. The problem is said to be that, where such implication occurs, this demonstrates that not all of the parties' obligations are referable to the promises they have made. This in turn, it is said, must call into question whether it is correct to see *any* of the obligations of the parties as stemming from promises made by them, for, if obligations can be imposed on parties and yet be called contractual in nature, the essence of contractual duties must lie in something other than the promises of the parties.

This argument merits some consideration. As a preliminary remark, however, it is worth stating that the implication of terms was not always thought to be a problem for seeing contractual duties as stemming from the promises or the will of the parties. The late scholastics and natural lawyers did not see the will of the parties and 'natural terms' (as implied terms were often then referred to, on the understanding that they derived from the nature of the contract) in opposition; on the contrary, it was believed that to hold parties to such 'natural terms' was to effectuate their will.[313] Such a view was, of course, tied to the idea that the various types of contract had certain fundamental purposes, and that from their purposes flowed certain implicit duties which could be attributed to the supposed will of the parties given the specific ends of the type of contract concerned. Gordley has remarked that:

> This way of analysing the content of a contractual obligation has become strange to us. It has become strange because the Aristotelian metaphysics of essences on which it was based fell from favour at the very time the northern natural law school was disseminating the doctrines of the late scholastics.[314]

This is an accurate observation on the death of Aristotelian metaphysics, though this has not resulted in a complete collapse of the idea that certain types of implied term 'naturally' arise in certain types of contractual relationship. That idea persists both in codified systems, where different classes of contract (such as hire, partnership, sale and so forth) are commonly treated in separate parts of civil codes, each specifying certain obligations as implicit adjuncts of the type of contract in question, but also in uncodified systems, such as England and Scotland, where there is a tradition of distinguishing terms implied in law from terms implied in fact. The former type of term are said to arise in a specific class of contract, and will be implied in every instance of contract falling within the class,

---

[313] See Gordley, *Philosophical Origins*, p. 109. [314] *Ibid.*, p. 111.

unless excluded by the parties (if such exclusion is permitted at law). Thus, while Aristotelian teleology may have fallen out of legal discourse, the idea that there are types or class of contract under which certain obligations will, by default, apply between the parties, has survived the extinction of the Aristotelian worldview.

It has, however, become less common to attempt to connect every implication of a term – whether in a class of contract, or an individual contract – to the supposed or tacit will of the parties. It has become more common in some jurisdictions to assert that, at least where an implication is made in a class of contracts, such implication follows from a policy-based rule, regardless (or even in spite of) the will of the parties. Thus, for instance, the implication of a particular standard of quality of goods in contracts for the sale or hire of goods is often made in the face of a desire by the seller or hirer *not* to guarantee any particular quality. Nonetheless, the policy underlying the implication (usually now an implication stemming from legislation) is said to justify the relevant implication, without the need to refer to the will or the promises of the parties.

Such a situation need not, however, create problems for a promissory view of contractual obligations. As explained earlier in this work, while the origins of contract are quite properly located in the freely exchanged promises of the parties, there is no necessity to see the entire content of the contract as based on specific promises of the parties. Some promises may be invalid or unenforceable because they contravene rules of law, and so will be struck out; other undertakings may be added in, because a targeted legal policy dictates that they are held to be implicit in the class of contract,[315] or because, with the policy interest of encouraging and supporting commerce in mind, it is thought necessary for a court to imply the term into a specific contract in order to address a matter to which the parties did not turn their minds.

It is not realistic to see all such contractual omissions and additions as somehow based on the will of the parties: arguments to that effect, whether medieval, nineteenth-century, or contemporary, are unconvincing. It must simply be accepted that the whole content of a contract is not, in every case, referable to the objectively ascertained will of the parties, a reality recognised in the provisions of the DCFR.[316] This admission need

---

[315] Or as virtue theorists might argue, because implication of a term into a class of contracts gives effect to Aristotelian virtues, such as justice or good faith: see Gordley, *Foundations of Private Law*, pp. 376–9.

[316] See DCFR Art. II.-9:101(1), which provides that the terms of a contract may be derived from the express or tacit agreement of the parties, rules of law, practices established between the parties, or usages.

not, however, be seen as abandoning the idea that the very existence of the contract, as well as any term which does result from express agreement of the parties, derives from a promissory undertaking. It merely recognises that the ability to promise, and thereby to assume contractual obligations, is a power which operates within bounds determined by the legal system. Voluntary contractual capacity is a derivative, not an absolute, power: the individual contracting party is free to bind himself only to the extent permitted by the law. Contract is, and remains, promissory in nature, but what can or cannot be promised is subject to limitations imposed by the sovereign lawmaker. There is no need to concede, as some promissory theorists have done, that certain types of implication of terms cannot be made to fit with a promissory theory of contract.[317] While it is true that a duty which is implied cannot in every case be referred to the promise, express or implicit, of the party upon whom it is imposed, promissory theory need not attempt to argue that every contract term must be so referable: when the proper source of promissory capacity is recognised as a derivative power granted to parties, one which it is legitimate to constrain in certain ways, then it is rightly recognised that only the existence of the contract at all, and such duties as are legitimately assumed by the parties, needs to be referable to the promises of the parties. Some duties which take effect contractually arise by virtue of imposition, and not agreement.

Before, however, dismissing the idea that any implied terms can be referred to the will of the parties, it may be sensible to take account of the variety of reasons for, and circumstances in which, terms are implied into contracts. When considering the whole field of implied terms, it may be possible to argue that at least *some* implied terms can be referred to the unexpressed will of the parties. Indeed, it is typical of many legal systems to attempt to describe at least terms implied into specific contracts, rather than a class of contracts, as referable to the unexpressed will of the parties. Thus, a South African court could describe a term implied into an individual contract as

> an unexpressed provision of the contract which derives from the common intention of the parties, as inferred by the Court from the express terms of the contract and the surrounding circumstances. In supplying such an implied term the Court, in truth, declares the whole contract entered into by the parties.[318]

[317] A concession made by Smith (see *Contract Theory*, p. 68).
[318] *Alfred McAlpine & Son (Pty) Ltd* v. *Transvaal Provincial Administration* 1974 (3) SA 506 (A), per Corbett AJA at 531–2.

Indeed, so strong are these sentiments in South African law, that terms implied into specific contracts are usually referred to as 'tacit terms' rather than implied terms. The attraction of such an attitude for courts is that it maintains the theory that judges are not making contracts for parties, but are merely drawing out what was implicit, but unexpressed, in the parties' express agreement.

The same theory has found a place in English law, and underlies both the 'business efficacy' and 'officious bystander' tests developed by the English courts. The former test, developed in *The Moorcock*,[319] and said to rest on 'what must obviously have been the intention of the parties', justifies the implication of a term in a contract in order to give 'the transaction such efficacy as both parties must have intended that at all events it should have', but which it lacks without the argued for implication.[320] It is thus said to be a test of necessity, in the sense that the implication is necessary to support the admitted intention of the parties to enter into a contract. Taking a slightly different approach to drawing out the presumed intention of the parties, the 'officious bystander' test, developed in those terms in *Shirlaw* v. *Southern Foundries (1926) Ltd*, states the approach to be taken as follows:

> *Prima facie* that which in any contract is left to be implied and need not be expressed is something so obvious that it goes without saying; so that, if while the parties were making their bargain, an officious bystander were to suggest some express provision for it in the agreement, they would suppress him with a common, 'oh, of course.'[321]

Both formulations of when a term should be implied into a specific contract evidently rest upon a judicial supposition and presumption as to what the parties' intentions were. Yet might it not equally, and perhaps more realistically, be suggested that in such instances the parties simply had *no* intention concerning the specific matter in question, having forgotten to consider it or having deliberately decided not to agree on it out of a realisation that agreement would be unlikely and in the hope that the matter would not fall into dispute? If that is, in some cases, a more realistic assessment of the facts, then judicial assumptions as to tacit intentions of the parties will be no more than fictions, designed to achieve a commercially sensible end but one which in reality is not referable to either

---

[319] (1889) 14 PD 64.
[320] See the judgment of Bowen LJ, at 68. See also the judgment of Scrutton LJ in *Reigate* v. *Union Manufacturing Co. (Ramsbottom)* [1918] 1 KB 592, 605.
[321] [1939] 2 KB 206, 207, per Mackinnon LJ.

the objective or subjective intention of the parties. The judicial practice of not implying terms unless they are reasonable and equitable[322] would seems to reinforce this conclusion: if the real intentions of the parties were at issue, then on occasion it might well be that an inequitable term would have to be included, given that many parties do not always act in good faith.

While some cases of implication may reasonably be said, on the facts, to be referable to an unexpressed intention of the parties (perhaps because circumstantial evidence would, if it were admissible, confirm that the parties had assumed, but simply omitted to express, a matter), it does seem that to conceive of *all* implications in fact as referable to the unexpressed but nonetheless present intention of the parties is a fiction, adopted to suit the ends of justice and commerce. Equally unconvincing is the recent radical reformulation of the judicial task when implying terms suggested by Lord Hoffmann in the Privy Council Appeal *Attorney General of Belize* v. *Belize Telecom Ltd*.[323] In essence, Lord Hoffmann suggested that the implication of terms into a written contract is essentially a process of interpreting the contract as a reasonable person would. Reviewing the existing tests of implication of terms in fact, Lord Hoffmann characterised these not as a series of independent tests but 'a collection of different ways in which judges have tried to express the central idea that the proposed implied term must spell out what the contract actually means'.[324] This seems, with respect to his Lordship, to miss the point that very often the express terms before a court will quite simply not give any clues to whether or not a suggested implication should be made. If the parties have simply forgotten to address a matter, then the express terms may be resolutely silent on the question of what the contract 'means' in relation to the omitted matter. In such cases, to suggest that an interpretative approach will solve the matter of whether or not a specific implication should be made seems overly optimistic. True, drawing out the assumed intention of the parties through interpreting the express terms may well work in some cases,[325] but not all. The suggested approach of Lord Hoffmann does not seem to offer a comprehensive solution to the problem of implication.

---

[322] As Lord Simon said in *BP Refinery (Westernport) Pty Ltd* v. *Shire of Hastings* (1977) 180 CLR 266, 283, 1978 ALJR 20, 26, 'for a term to be implied … it must be reasonable and equitable'.

[323] [2009] UKPC 10. [324] See judgment of Lord Hoffmann, para. 27.

[325] As, for instance, it did in the recent decision of the Court of Appeal in *Mediterranean Salvage & Towage Ltd* v. *Seamar Trading & Commerce Inc.* [2009] EWCA Civ 531, [2010] 1 All ER (Comm) 1.

It seems realistic to accept that one cannot explain all terms implied into individual contracts as resting either upon the tacit, unexpressed intentions of the parties or on a reasonable interpretation of the express terms of the contract. Some instances of implication seem to constitute judicially crafted reasonable solutions designed to uphold the intention of the parties to enter into a contractual relationship. When one moves into the field of terms implied into classes of contract, then it seems reasonably clear that such implications are made for policy reasons, for instance to create an equitable balance of duties between landlord and tenant under a lease,[326] rather than because the implication gives expression to the parties' presumed intentions. This is most evidently the case where the implication is required to be made as a result of legislative provision, but even judicial implications of terms into classes of contract at common law can only with great artificiality be explained as deriving from the parties' will. Even to call such terms (as some jurisdictions do) 'natural terms', deriving from the type of contract concerned and thus its presumed purpose, does not greatly assist in the argument that it is the will of the parties which gives rise to the natural implication, unless one argues that to will the specific end of the type of contract in question (for instance, hire) is by implication to will the natural terms which are said to apply to such a type of contract. But that rather overemphasises the idea of the human will, when what is crucial in the idea of 'natural terms' is the purpose and nature of the contract, and thus what pertains to that nature.

When one arrives at terms which the courts have suggested ought to be implied into *every* contract, then one is arguably dealing with a default rule of contract law, rather than an implied term, though both conceptions seem maintainable depending upon the jurisdiction in question. Thus, while a mutual duty upon contracting parties to cooperate to ensure that the contract's ends are achieved can be expressed as a term to be implied into all contracts,[327] such a duty of mutual cooperation might alternatively be described as a default rule of contract law, perhaps one inspired by the fundamental principle of good faith.[328] The same debate might be had in relation, for instance, to a duty to exercise discretionary

---

[326] *Liverpool City Council* v. *Irwin* [1977] AC 239.

[327] As it was, for instance, by the House of Lords in the Scottish appeal *McKay* v. *Dick and Stevenson* (1881) 8 R (HL) 37, 40, per Lord Blackburn.

[328] The DCFR specifies in contracts for services various 'rules' concerning cooperation between the parties: see Art. IV. C.- 2:103. The stipulation of these obligations as 'rules' seems to underline their fundamental nature to the contractual relationship, and suggest that their importance goes beyond the presumed will of the parties.

contractual powers (such as that to terminate for breach) in a reasonable and non-oppressive manner.[329]

Exact comparison between the English and mixed legal systems approach to the implication of terms and that of the German courts is not possible, as the categories of implication in fact and in law have no precise equivalents. However, German courts will have regard to the tacit intention of parties in considering whether a specific contract ought to be taken to include a non-express term, an exercise which can be said to be functionally equivalent to implication in fact. This Germanic approach is referred to as completive contract interpretation (*ergänzende Vertragsauslegung*),[330] justified by reference to §157 BGB. Such an approach is based upon the idea that there is a gap which requires to be filled in order to fulfil the purposes of the contract;[331] the similarity with the business efficacy test of the Common law is notable. The reasonableness of the term is not thought to be sufficient to justify implication, as it is not in the British jurisprudence.[332] No implication based upon a tacit intention can contradict an express term.[333]

As for the German equivalent of so-called terms implied in law, it is much clearer that these stem from underlying policy considerations, rather than imagined promises of the parties, because they are seen as default rules of the law rather than implied terms. This is a much more realistic approach, and one which, it was suggested above, would make for a more honest explanation of implications of terms in classes of contract in the UK. Thus, while contractual duties of care on parties are usually treated as implied terms at law in the UK, they derive from provisions of the BGB in German law.[334] The good faith principle embodied in §242 can justify further implications, though it has been remarked that in a codified system such as Germany, 'such judicial activism is bound to be seen as (more) suspicious and in need of justification'.[335] On the other hand, even in Germany the courts have on occasion sought to conceal essentially policy driven developments by disguising such developments as terms implied in fact rather than as default rules. A clear example is the

---

[329] See the later discussion, in Ch. 6, pp. 403ff, of whether the right to terminate must be preceded by the granting of a second chance to the defaulting party.

[330] See, for examples, RGZ 117, 176, 180; RGZ 131, 274; RGZ 161, 330.

[331] Markesinis *et al.*, *German Law of Contract*, p. 141.

[332] Ulmer, 'Teilunwirksamkeit von teilweise unangemessenen AGB-Klauseln?'; *Münchener Kommentar* – Mayer-Maly and Busche, §157 Rn 38.

[333] BGHZ 9, 273; BGH NJW 1984, 1177.   [334] For instance, §618 BGB.

[335] Markesinis *et al.*, *German Law of Contract*, p. 142.

development of the doctrine of contracts with protective effect towards third parties (*Verträge mit Schutzwirkung für Dritten*), which was developed by reference to §157 and completive interpretation, even though it is a clear example of a policy driven default rule rather than the tacit intention of the contracting parties.

In all of the systems studied, there is to a varying degree evidence of judicial willingness to disguise policy driven rules as deriving from the presumed or tacit intentions of the parties. This is more evident in Britain, where there remain judicial expressions of the idea that *all* implications, whether at fact or in law, are referable to party intentions. This is mere judicial fiction, designed to justify lawmaking by the courts, albeit out of a laudable desire to arrive at equitable results. It would be more honest, even in a jurisdiction like Germany where many default policy rules of contract law are codified, to accept that there may arise occasions when courts will wish to reflect the changing mores and nature of relationships by developing contract law in ways which cannot reasonably be tied to the unexpressed wishes of the parties. Such occasions require an honest expression of the policy factors which justify the legal development, something which is made more difficult if the language of implied terms is maintained.

11.   Consideration

(a)   *The Common law*[336]

Much of the difficulty with giving effect to promises in their own right stems from the doctrine of consideration (or, more accurately, of 'mutual consideration'). The fundamental objection to the doctrine of consideration is that, though it persists in some jurisdictions as part of the historical development of contract law, there seems no good theoretical reason why, in order to demonstrate a serious intention to enter a binding contractual obligation, consideration should be required to have been received for the commitment intended, or why, if it is present, intention is often presumed without further investigation.[337] Many legal systems

---

[336] See further Eisenberg, 'The Principles of Consideration'.

[337] The presence of consideration has been said necessarily to prove an intention to contract: *Williston on Contracts* (Rochester, NY: 4th edn, vol. 1, 1990), §3.5. To similar effect, as earlier editions of Anson's *Principles of Contract* used to state, 'Consideration ... is the only test of the intention of the promisor to bind himself by contract' (see 16th edn, p. 130). The present edition (28th) less restrictively states

manage perfectly well (indeed, better) without the doctrine of mutual consideration, and have other ways of testing seriousness of contractual intent. Indeed, the leading proponent of the doctrine, English law (and through it, other Commonwealth jurisdictions), has itself developed a separate rule that parties must demonstrate an intention to enter into legal relations.[338] Once such a separate rule was developed, any reason for continuing to insist upon mutual consideration was obviated. Intention forms a principal plank of English law's recent legislation on third party rights, the lack of consideration given by the third party having been ignored in the statutory conferral of rights on such third parties.[339] The logical conclusion is that the doctrine of mutual consideration, in terms of which a reciprocal performance is required for a valid contract, should go,[340] as Lord Wright convincingly argued as far back as 1936.[341] In continuing to insist on consideration, the Common law persists in getting matters back to front: it insists upon mutual consideration, while ignoring a genuine enquiry into the serious intention to be bound, when it should be insisting precisely on such serious intention, while dropping a separate requirement of consideration.

How is seriousness of intent to contract demonstrated in systems which lack a doctrine of consideration?

(p. 88) that 'consideration reflects a variety of policies', though one such policy identified remains seriousness of intent.

[338] See, for instance, *Rose & Frank Co.* v. *J. R. Compton & Bros. Ltd* [1923] 2 KB 261. Assessing such intention is an objective exercise: see Blanchard J in *Fletcher Challenge Energy Ltd* v. *Electricity Corporation of New Zealand Ltd* [2002] 2 NZLR 433, para. 54: 'Whether the parties intended to enter into a contract and whether they have succeeded in doing so are questions to be determined objectively.' Intention to contract is often (but not always) presumed to be absent in certain types of agreement, for instance domestic arrangements between spouses, or social arrangements between friends: see, for instance, *Balfour* v. *Balfour* [1919] 2 KB 571 (husband and wife); *Jones* v. *Padavatton* [1969] 1 WLR 328 (mother and daughter); cf. *Raffaele* v. *Raffaele* [1962] WAR 29 (where a contract was held to have been intended between a son and his parents). For further authority, see Furmston and Tolhurst, *Contract Formation*, paras. 10.19–32.

[339] See the Contracts (Rights of Third Parties) Act 1999.

[340] That is not necessarily to conclude that contract law no longer needs need a doctrine of *causa* (the issue is discussed elsewhere in this text).

[341] Wright, 'Ought the Doctrine of Consideration to be Abolished from the Common Law?'. Abolition was also recommended in The Law Revision Committee's Sixth Interim Report (1937), and by Chloros, 'The Doctrine of Consideration and Reform of the Law of Contract'. Cf., however, Gold, 'Consideration and the Morality of Promising', who argues that abolition would have undesirable consequences for a moral understanding of promising.

(b)   The mixed legal systems

None of the three mixed legal systems studied has a requirement of mutual consideration; instead, all require that parties to a contract (or to a unilateral promise, where this is permitted) must demonstrate an intention to be bound to the obligation. In none of the systems does the lack of a doctrine of consideration cause any problems. Indeed, in South African law the requirement of consideration was consciously jettisoned from the law in order to improve it.[342] Scots law both lacks a doctrine of mutual consideration for contracts, and also enforces unilateral promises, emphasising in both the need to determine whether there has been expressed an intention by a party to bind itself to an obligation. The courts have continuously emphasised the importance of determining what objectively was intended by the party in question:[343] did it intend unilaterally and immediately to bind itself, or did it intend to make an offer to the other party? This simple focus on objective intention, however, glosses over potential problems, especially where the distinction between conditional unilateral promises and offers are concerned. Because either might take the form 'I promise to do x if ...', the difficulties in distinguishing the two on the facts of a case will be evident. It was suggested earlier that the context of a party's statement ought to be important (for instance, a commercial content will naturally give rise to the assumption that an offer rather than a promise was the likely intention), as well as whether the condition attached to the promise will bring any direct benefit to the maker of the statement (if it does, this again suggests that an offer is more likely to have been intended). It is, however, difficult to find any extensive judicial treatment of these theoretical problems.

In practice, when in Scotland difficulties in determining whether contractual intention was present or not have arisen, it is striking that it is often in cases where there is no question of the intended consideration being uncertain. A number of reported cases relate to facts where a clear price *had* been agreed between the parties, but the facts were held to demonstrate that no intention to be bound contractually had yet been

---

[342] The rejection of the doctrine of consideration in South African law was finally confirmed in *Conradie* v. *Rossouw* 1919 AD 279.

[343] See, for instance, Lord Hodge in *Baillie Estates Ltd.* v. *Du Pont (UK) Ltd* [2009] CSOH 95, at para. 25: 'the court has to address not only whether the parties have agreed all of the legally essential elements of a bargain, or the means of achieving that agreement, in their negotiations but also whether they have manifested an intention to be immediately bound.'

demonstrated by one or both of them. In one such case, this was because the parties' prior dealings indicated that a subscribed written agreement had been intended, such an agreement being absent.[344] In another, it was alleged that discussions between negotiating parties at a meeting constituted an oral contract between the parties. However, the behaviour of the party so alleging, in continuing to engage in protracted negotiations and insisting on a written contract being concluded between the parties, objectively suggested to the court that that party did not consider a contract to have been concluded by virtue of the discussions at the meeting.[345]

South African law similarly requires parties to a contract to demonstrate an intention to be bound, a requirement which (as in German law) is not conceived of as the equivalent to the *causa* of the contract.[346] As Mason J stated in *Rood* v. *Wallach*, the essential elements of a contract are:

> the promise to do or forbear some act made by one and accepted by the other party and the intention that the legal relations of the parties shall be governed by the promise in matters to which it relates, or, as it is sometimes put, there must be consent and an intention to create legal relations.[347]

Such an intention to contract (*animus contrahendi*) is judged objectively, as Innes J explained in *Pieters & Co.* v. *Salomon*: 'When a man makes an offer in plain and unambiguous language, which is understood in the ordinary sense by the person to whom it is addressed, and accepted by him bona fide in that sense, then there is a concluded contract.'[348] Undertakings made in jest or anger do not demonstrate such an intent,[349] nor are family or social arrangements likely to. Statements which appear to narrate no more than facts (such as 'All goods supplied are manufactured according to the company's standard manufacturing procedures and techniques')[350] may nonetheless disclose the requisite *animus contrahendi*, given the context of the statement.

---

[344] *Karoulias* v. *The Drambuie Liqueur Co. Ltd* [2005] CSOH 112, 2005 SLT 813.

[345] *Aisling Developments Ltd* v. *Persimmon Homes Ltd* [2008] CSOH 140.

[346] See Jansen JA in *Saambou-Nasionale Bouvereniging* v. *Fridman* 1979 (3) SA 978, 991G; also Van Winsen J in *Hottentots Holland Motors (Pty) Ltd* v. *R* 1956 (1) PH K22.

[347] 1904 TS 187, 219. Mason J is clearly using the idea of a 'promise to do or forbear' as a synonym for an offer.

[348] 1911 AD 121, 137.   [349] See Christie, *Law of Contract in South Africa*, p. 30.

[350] The quoted statement was held to disclose an intention to be bound to an obligation in *Consol Ltd* v. *Twee Jongen Gezellen (Pty) Ltd* 2005 (6) SA 1 (SCA).

In Louisiana, a contract requires the consent of the parties.[351] Such consent must not only demonstrate agreement to the terms of the contract, but must also demonstrate a consent, or intention, to be bound to the obligation.[352] The parties' intentions are judged objectively, as a number of provisions in the Civil Code demonstrate.[353] In addition to contract formation, the process of interpreting a contract is explicitly stated in the Code to be 'the determination of the common intent of the parties'.[354] As in the other mixed systems, the context in which words are used is crucial, so that, for instance, words used in jest will not be held to demonstrate the necessary intention to be bound.[355]

Where the mixed legal systems sometimes struggle to deal with certain types of intention (as, for instance, South Africa does with options), this is not because of the lack of a doctrine of consideration, but rather because of the lack of a general means of enforcing seriously intended unilateral promises (those lacking an acceptance). The mixed systems all demonstrate that contract law functions quite happily without a requirement of mutual consideration.

(c)   German law

In modern German law, seriousness of intent is not judged by a doctrine of consideration, for there is none, nor by reference to the idea of *causa*.[356] Instead, there is in the BGB the negative statement that a 'declaration of intent not seriously intended which is made in the expectation that its lack of serious intention will not be misunderstood is void',[357] so that, for instance, what was plainly intended as a joke could not be an offer. The other side of the coin is that the provision suggests that a serious intention to contract is a requirement for a valid offer, though the BGB tells us nothing of how such seriousness of intent is to be judged. Some practical considerations can assist in so judging. For instance, agreements may require a certain form (a matter discussed below). Furthermore, agreements supported by mutual consideration are seldom questioned by the courts as to

---

[351] CC Art. 1927.

[352] Thus, if an offer is to be irrevocable for a period of time, intention that this be so must be demonstrated by the offeror: CC Art. 1928.

[353] For instance, under Art. 1942, silence may (exceptionally) constitute a valid acceptance of an offer, if the offeror is led 'reasonably to believe that a contract has been formed'. Such emphasis on the reasonable appearance given to the offeror demonstrates a concern for objectivity.

[354] CC Art. 2045.   [355] Litvinoff and Scalise, *Law of Obligations*, p. 28.

[356] See further Markesinis *et al.*, *German Law of Contract*, p. 87.   [357] §118 BGB.

lack of serious intent. Ultimately, a German court looks at the transaction in question and seeks objectively to judge what intention is disclosed by the behaviour of the parties, an approach shared with the mixed systems.

Occasionally in German law, perceived structural problems with the law distort findings of intention to contract. Thus, in order to avoid §823(1) of the BGB (the provision excluding liability for pure economic loss in tort), courts have sometimes contrived to discover contractual intention when a service is provided, even where it seems reasonably clear that no such intention was present. In one decision of the BGH, company A, which had allowed company B the free use of a chauffeur driven car, was held to have intended to contract with B, and, in so doing, was held to have assumed legal responsibility (*Rechtsbindungswille*) towards B, thereby rendering it liable in damages for its failure to provide a competent driver for the car.[358] This decision draws strong similarities with the artificial 'assumption of responsibility' approach adopted in English tort law, which is criticised elsewhere in this work as distorting the nature of tortious liability.[359] It is suggested that, as German courts appear eager to avoid the rule against recovery in pure economic loss by finding fictitious intent to contract, it might be better to adopt the more honest approach of amending the provisions of §823(1) to allow wider recovery of pure economic loss in tort rather than perpetuating artificial findings of contractual intent.

The same artificial approach has been used in relation to §675(2) of the BGB, which excludes liability for the financial consequences of giving advice to another unless a contract, tort, or statutory provision founds such liability. Given the tortious exclusion of liability for pure economic loss just discussed, German courts have in some cases found a party giving advice to have been in a contractual relationship with the recipient of the advice in order to trigger the application of §675(2).[360] Criticism of the artificial nature of such imputed contractual intent may again be made.

(d) Model law

All of the national systems studied emphasise the intention of the parties to be bound to an obligation as essential to enforcing promises (whether of the unilateral or contractual variety). Though the Common law also

---

[358] BGHZ 21, 102. The decision was followed in later cases.
[359] See discussion of *White* v. *Jones* [1995] 2 AC 207 in Ch. 5, p. 300.
[360] See discussion in Markesinis *et al.*, *German Law of Contract*, p. 91.

insists upon a requirement of mutual consideration as a further means of demonstrating seriousness of intent, this seems to add nothing to the law, and in fact hampers the adoption of obvious promissory solutions to some problems, problems which must instead seek other, less suitable, means of resolution.

The provisions of the DCFR sensibly do not require mutual consideration for a valid contract, stipulating instead two required elements: (i) an intention to enter into a binding legal relationship or to bring about some other legal effect, and (ii) a sufficient agreement.[361] The intentional element in this provision reinforces the terms of the earlier Article II.-1:101(1), which provides that a 'contract is an agreement which is intended to give rise to a binding legal relationship or to have some other legal effect'.[362] The emphasis in these provisions upon intention as the unique constitutive mode of contracting underpins the adherence of the DCFR to a will-based approach to contract law: contracts are not constituted merely by any effect they might produce, such as the conferral of a benefit or the creation of detrimental reliance, or simply through consensus on proposed terms. Similarly, Article II-1:103 locates the force of a unilateral promise in the intention of the promisor to be legally bound.

The position proposed by the DCFR, insisting upon an intention to be bound rather than any requirement of mutual consideration as the determinant of seriousness of intent, is both desirable and practicable. As to its practicability, as the editors of the DCFR commented generally of European legal systems, those systems which do enforce unilateral promissory undertakings 'do not in general encounter problems.'[363]

12.   Requirements of form: unwarranted restrictions on promising?

As a leading European legal academic has remarked, the modern trend is to informality, as least so far as the core areas of private law are concerned.[364]

---

[361]   DCFR Art II.-4:101.

[362]   It is noteworthy that the wording of this Article in the interim edition of the text conceived of as intention as merely one of the ways to create a contract: 'A contract is an agreement which gives rise to, or is intended to give rise to, a binding legal relationship or which has, or is intended to have, some other legal effect.' The revised wording confers upon the intention of the parties a unique constitutive role.

[363]   DCFR, Full Edition, Comments to Art. II-I:103 (p. 133).

[364]   Zimmermann, *Law of Obligations*, p. 86. Zimmermann's view of a preference for formlessness that 'its general intellectual background is one of superabundance and profusion of material, spinelessness and mental exhaustion' is somewhat hard to grasp.

Even when specific form is required for the constitution of an obligation, 'a tendency is often observable in the practice of the courts to water down such rules'.[365] Examples of such watering down may be found in a number of systems.[366]

As a general statement, it is suggested that the fewer formalities stand in the way of the enforcement of seriously intended and clearly expressed promises, the more a system can be said to value promises and to treat them seriously. The contrary argument, that rules on formality are there to protect people against unforeseen consequences, and thus ensure that frivolous undertakings are not treated as serious promises, represents one form of legal paternalism. The field of formalities is thus a classic battle-ground between the positions of legal libertarianism and paternalism. It has, for instance, been said of German law that:

> on the whole, in German law the rules about formality are meant to pro-tect the parties by ensuring that they enter legal transactions only after serious consideration of the consequences of their acts.[367]

This view encapsulates a systemic belief that sometimes parties require to be protected from themselves, because promising can be a risky thing if done hurriedly or without proper contemplation of the consequences. This is a not uncommon view, and therefore unsurprisingly a number of transactions which are promissory in nature are deemed to require some formalities in German law (as well as other systems). Thus, the promise of a gift requires notarial recording,[368] the guarantee of a surety requires writing,[369] and a will made by a testator himself, rather than by declar-ation to a notary, requires to be in his handwriting and signed by him.[370] Given the variety of different transactions which require adherence to some formality, it is evident that it is not just promises which are con-ceived of as giving rise to the risk of impetuous undertakings, though such danger is conceived of largely as affecting transactions which are

One could, by way of rejoinder, argue that a preference for giving force to all promises, regardless of form, rather reflects a profound respect for the moral force and worth of promises, such as is visible in the canon law's attitude.

[365] *Ibid.*, p. 86.

[366] For instance, in French law, the notarial requirement of Art. 1341 of the *Code civil* has been watered down by the doctrine of 'commencement de preuve par écrit', by which the testimony of witnesses to an obligation is admitted, so long as there is a foundation of a written document; in Germany, the BGH has shown itself willing to enforce con-tracts for the sale of land which lack the form required by §311b BGB, if good faith so requires.

[367] Markesinis, *German Law of Contract*, p. 81.   [368] §518(1).

[369] §766.   [370] §2247(1).

either unilateral in nature or which relate to a subject matter deemed of fundamental significance (such as land transfers).

Oddly enough, however, (at least from the perspective of a non-German lawyer), not all acts of a unilaterally binding nature enforced under the BGB require compliance with a formality: the issuing of public offers of reward do not, nor indeed, in general, do offers, even though the default rule is that offers are binding unless the power to revoke them is reserved. So a party making an offer without properly considering its position takes the risk of being unable to withdraw from the offer if it subsequently considers it to have been made foolishly. To a non-German lawyer, it is puzzling that some such instances of unilateral acts capable of binding a party do *not* require any particular formality, while others do. The answer doubtless lies in the view that, even though offers are binding, because they require some reciprocal act by the promisee to complete them, the consequences of foolish behaviour on the part of the offeror are not so grave as in those cases where the BGB prescribes formalities. German law is, moreover, not alone in stipulating different requirements for similar types of act: in Scotland, for instance, private unilateral promises must be in writing, but those given in a business context need not be.[371] Again, a paternalistic concern for the private party envisaged as being perhaps unadvised provides the reason for the different treatment, though one might question whether business parties and private individuals are really in that different a position so far as the contemplation of their intended undertakings are concerned.

Failure to fulfil some of the formalities stipulated by legal systems can be cured by subsequent conduct. Thus, in German law, failure to comply with the formalities for the making of a gift will not invalidate the gift if the donor's performance subsequently occurs.[372] The same is true of an informally constituted obligation of surety: discharge of the surety's duty cures the defect.[373] The prolonged labours of a party on land the owner-ship of which it was promised has been held to cure the absence of a nota-rised contract of sale.[374] These examples are doubtless best characterised in general as protecting the reasonable reliance of the promisee, rather than as bolstering promissory liability per se, given that they refer to cir-cumstances where the conduct concerned follows on from the promise.[375]

---

[371] Requirements of Writing (Scotland) Act 1995, s. 1.
[372] §518(2).   [373] §766 (sentence 3).   [374] BGHZ 12, 286.
[375] However, at least in respect of cases pled under §311b(1), requiring notarial recording of contracts for the transfer of land, the German courts have even shown themselves will-ing to enforce performance in defective contracts which have remained at the executory

Comparisons may be drawn with the Common law of proprietary estoppel, or the Scottish provisions on statutory personal bar applicable to land transactions, in that each allows defective land contracts to be enforced in circumstances where reliance has been placed upon the validity of an informally constituted transaction. The DCFR does not go so far as to allow the cure of informalities by subsequent conduct: instead, it goes for the less far-reaching solution of allowing a party which has reasonably relied on the validity of the contract to claim its reliance losses from the other party, if the other party knew of such reliance and allowed it to continue.[376]

The willingness of legal systems to consider subsequent conduct of parties, as well as the judicial watering down of some rules, doubtless mitigates against perceived overly paternalistic effects of formalism. Nonetheless, the continued existence of formal requirements must necessarily amount, to some extent, to a subversion of party autonomy. Such formalistic paternalism is, of course, part of a wider culture of increasing control of private contractual arrangements. Such control is likely only to increase, as successive national and EU legislative acts concerning consumer contracts impose new duties upon businesses to ensure that many transactions are committed to a certain form. The general approach of the DCFR – that its requirements can be excluded or derogated from – does not apply in the case of 'applicable mandatory rules',[377] requirements of form almost invariably falling under that heading (formal requirements for acts of donation being a prime example).[378]

Whether formal controls on promises are warranted, as the heading to this section of text asked, will inevitably depend upon one's own position in relation to the debate concerning legal libertarianism versus paternalism. In an age where personal responsibility is being blunted by the overarching protection of the state, it is suggested that the preference should be for party autonomy, though such a suggestion will not find universal acquiescence. Wherever the balance is to lie, it was suggested in Chapter 3 that a revitalised will theory of contract can happily coexist with such formal requirements as may be considered necessary to prevent ill-considered liberality.

---

stage, by compelling sellers who have assured buyers that the formality requirements have been complied with, when they have not, to transfer the land to the buyer: see for instance: BGHZ 48, 396; BGH NJW 1972, 1189.

[376] Art II.-1:106(2).   [377] Art II.-1:106(1).   [378] Art IV.H.-2:101.

5

Third party rights

1. The challenge to third party rights in contract

Any legal system which takes promises seriously would be expected to allow such promises to be enforced even if made by a contracting party to a non-contracting party, so long as the promise was seriously intended to confer enforceable rights upon that third party. After all, if a promise can be enforced outside the context of a contract (as happens when a unilateral promise is enforced), why should it not be possible for A to contract with B and, within the context of that contract, also make a promise to C. This, however, is to presuppose that the right of a third party to enforce a right given to it under a contract (a *stipulatio alteri* or *jus quaesitum tertio* as it is sometimes called) should be cast in promissory terms. As will be seen below, however, other characterisations of a directly enforceable third party right are conceivable.

Opposition to direct claims to enforce contractual rights (or to obtain contractual benefits)[1] by third parties has typically rested upon one or more of the following objections: (i) the rule of privity of contract; (ii) the lack of consideration offered by the third party; and (iii) the absence of any pecuniary interest on the part of the stipulator (the party requesting the creation of the third party's right) in the third party's entitlement, a concern of Roman law origins. These objections are discussed, and dismissed, below. Where prohibition of the direct enforcement by third parties of rights conceived in their favour is maintained by a legal system, it is invariably the case that methods for avoiding the prohibition are developed (as the Roman and English experiences narrated below

---

[1] The claim to enforce a right or to obtain a benefit are two different possible conceptions of a third party's entitlement. Some legal systems appear to treat the two as synonymous, on the unspoken understanding that what a third party will be seeking, in enforcing a right given to it, is a benefit in its favour. Conceivably, however, there might be cases where the right given to a third party is not beneficial in nature for it, so that a sufficiently widely drawn conception of third party rights would require to encompass such a right (as is the case in both England and Scotland, for instance).

will demonstrate). Such avoidance measures are a natural development of the desire of stipulators to achieve their wish that another be entitled to enforce a right in its favour. Where a consistent expression of the will manifests itself in a society, human ingenuity usually manages to find a way around juristic apathy or opposition.

To argue, as will be argued here, that the right of a third party under a contract to enforce a benefit in its favour is promissory in nature might mean one of two things. It might mean that such a benefit 'derives from' a promise. That is true in the sense that any right of a third party under a contract can only arise because the contracting parties themselves have undertaken promises to each other, one of which is the source of the third party's entitlement. It might, however, additionally mean something more, which is where the controversy over the nature of third party rights arises. It might mean that the third party is itself a promisee, having been promised by one (or perhaps both) of the contracting parties that it will receive the stated benefit. In this second sense, the third party's right would not simply arise out of promise (the contractual promise) but would itself have the nature of a promise. Such a promise might either be enforceable directly by the third party even though it was not made directly to it, or else it might be seen as the assignee of the contracting party to whom the promise was made, two conceptually distinct analyses.

The possible characterisation of a third party right as not simply arising out of promise but as itself being promissory in nature is controversial. Some would dispute that third parties are in reality the recipients of any promise, and so dismiss the promissory characterisation of third party rights.[2] Others would argue that, while it might be possible to adopt such a promissory characterisation, other characterisations of third party rights are preferable. The arguments for the different positions are considered below.

The possible characterisation of a third party's right as promissory was introduced in Chapter 1,[3] where it was noted that two distinct situations might arise: (i) a case where A promises to B that he will confer some performance upon C, and (ii) a case where A states in front of B (without appearing to promise B anything) that he is promising to confer some performance upon C. It was argued in Chapter 1 that the second case is one

---

[2] Thus, in his article 'Contracts for the Benefit of Third Parties', Smith specifically rejects the idea that a third party can be conceived of as having been the recipient of a promise in its favour and thus, unsurprisingly, defends the traditional pre-1999 English law position that a third party has no right to make any claim under the contract.

[3] See pp. 23–5.

of a valid promise to C (but not B), C simply being absent at the time the promise is made. That, however, is not really a case of a third party right as commonly conceived, for the simple reason that C, though absent, is the promisee, and not a third party, B simply being in effect a witness to the promise (B may, for instance, be a notary). It is the former case which raises the possible promissory characterisation of a third party right, but the question to be answered is: has A in fact, in his promise to B, also undertaken a promise to C? Only if he has, can it be said that the right of the third party is promissory in nature; if not, then any enforceable right which the third party has must have some other character. The argument that A has made a promise to C may be put in one of a number of ways, depending on the facts of the case:

(1) The promise of A to B that he will perform in C's favour might make it plain that he is also concurrently making a promise to C. Thus, A may state to B 'I promise to you [or I agree with you] that I undertake to pay C £100'. That sort of statement can be said to amount to a promise to, or contractual agreement with, B which also contains a promise to C. This sort of wording may be unusual, but it is not inconceivable. On such a view, the promise to C would be constituted at the time that the promise is uttered to B, even if C were absent. The result is that A has made two promises, one to B and one to C. If A's statement to B is contained within a contract, then evidently the promise to B is contractual in nature; on the other hand, if the intention of A is that he will immediately be bound to C, his promise to C is in the nature of a unilateral promise.

(2) The promise of A to B that he will perform in C's favour may not be express but may rather be implied from A's words of commitment to B or even from the whole context of the agreement between A and B (so that it may reasonably be concluded that A intended the commitment in C's favour). Thus, a statement of A to B that 'I promise to pay C £100' may be interpreted as manifesting an intention on A's part not only to commit himself to B but also to commit himself to performance in favour of C, even though the promissory language used is only, on the face of it, directed at B. Again, under this argument, it can be maintained that the promise to C comes into existence at the time A utters the relevant commitment to B. Some may baulk at interpreting A's promise to B as also incorporating a promise to C, and take the view that this is not a reasonable interpretation of such language: why should a promise to B, which simply happens to

mention C, be treated also as a promise to C? But once the theoretical objection to the idea that a promise can be made to an absent party is overcome,[4] then the possibility arises of circumstances where A may wish to express a binding commitment in favour of C to another party (in the case of third party rights in contract, to a contracting party). There is no reason relating to the nature of a promise why A's contract with B should not be allowed to contain a promise to C. Naturally, everything must depend upon a construction of the intention of the parties concerned as disclosed in the language used by them, and it is not argued that every statement in which A undertakes to B that something will be done for C should be interpreted as a promise to C,[5] but even non-promissory conceptions of third party rights are based on the belief that A can in an agreement with B effect a binding commitment to C: if non-promissory conceptions of third party rights are capable of bearing such an obligatory intention on A's part, why not promissory ones?

(3) Some may still object that, in either of the above scenarios, the promise in favour of an absent C remains, at the time it is uttered, an essentially private arrangement between A and B (unless B is a public official such as, as suggested above, a notary), and that such a private arrangement should not be capable of giving rise to rights in another's favour. If that private characteristic of the behaviour of A and B were thought to be true, a promissory view might still be taken of C's right by insisting in both circumstances (1) and (2) that a promise in favour of C would not come into existence until the right conceived in C's favour was intimated to it. Jurisdictions with a promissory view of third party rights differ on whether such a requirement is insisted upon: Scots law, for instance, insists upon intimation to the third party before the promise in its favour is held to have been constituted; by contrast, French law holds that the third party's right exists immediately the promise is made to the stipulator.

Whether the commitment to C is stated in terms which narrate an express promise to C as promisee, or whether such a promise to C can be inferred from A's promise to B to benefit C, such a commitment seems

---

[4] A promise in favour of an absent party was, at an early stage, not seen as problematic in Scotland. See Stair, I.x.5: 'So a promise, though gratuitous, made in favour of a third party, that party, albeit not present, nor accepting, was found to have right thereby' (Stair cites, in support, *Achinmoutie* v. *Hay*, Mor. 12126).

[5] And indeed, perhaps in the majority of cases this will *not* be the intention of A.

classifiable as a promise, bearing in mind the definition of a promise adopted in Chapter 1 as a 'statement by which one person commits to some future beneficial performance, or the beneficial withholding of a performance, in favour of another person'. Given this definition of promise, it is quite possible to see A's commitment to benefit C in promissory terms, with all the consequences that such a promissory analysis entails.

A third party conception of C's status characterises C as standing apart from both of the contracting parties, that is to say, as having no contractual relationship with either. Certainly the third party cannot be a party to the contract between A and B without the circumstances simply being that of a multi-party contract.[6] It is conceivable, however, that a third party might be in a different contractual relationship with one of the parties: thus, two contracts, A–B and B–C, might exist, C being a third party so far as the contract A–B is concerned. The contracts A–B and B–C might be connected, as part of a so-called 'contract chain', or they might not. As later discussion will demonstrate, arguments of third party rights in such dual contract scenarios have tended to arise in the context of claims that C is the beneficiary of a right conferred by contract A–B of a negative nature, for instance an indemnity against legal action. As a promise can be of a negative kind, a promise *not* to do something, there would seem to be no objection in principle (if a promissory view of third party rights is taken) to a third party being the beneficiary of such a negative promise. Such scenarios can raise complex issues, which are discussed further below.

The utility of the promissory conception over other conceptions of third party rights may be seen when considering a paradigm case of third party rights, that of the beneficiary under a policy of life insurance. In such a paradigm case, A (the stipulator) wishes to take out an insurance policy on his life with insurance company B (the debtor). In the policy, he stipulates that the benefits accruing under the policy are to be paid over to his spouse (the third party) upon his death. The insurance company contacts the spouse to inform her of the benefit in her favour, and to indicate the circumstances in which it will be made over to her. The spouse takes note of the arrangement, but does not communicate with the insurance company in relation to it. Upon the death of the stipulator, the spouse claims the benefit in her favour and the insurance company is obligated to pay the sums to her. A traditional promissory analysis of this situation holds that, by virtue of the contract of insurance, the insurance company

---

[6] This is the approach taken by modern Dutch law: see further below, p. 290.

has agreed with the insured party that it will confer the benefit upon the spouse after the insured's death. Either at that moment, or, depending on the view taken, in communicating with the spouse in the terms in which it has, it has made a promise to pay the spouse. If the promise in favour of the third party is seen as arising at the very moment that the contract between A and B is made, then either the view can be taken that the third party is being permitted to enforce a promise made to the stipulator *qua* promisee, or, given that promises can be made to absent parties, that the third party is enforcing a promise made to her *qua* promisee (a promise contained within the promise made to the stipulator). If the view is taken that the promise arises when the third party is informed of the right in her favour, then it seems more certain that the third party is herself the promisee, a promise having been communicated to her which is additional to any promise given to the stipulator. In addition (and one of the systems under examination holds as much), it might be said that the stipulator has also made certain promises to the third party, at least an implied promise to assist the third party in any way necessary to enable her to advance her claim.

A unilateral promissory analysis of the third party's rights under an insurance policy seems apposite because it can be said that the insurance company has voluntarily undertaken a commitment to the spouse to pay her the proceeds of the insurance policy in due course. Such a commitment expresses a willingness to be subject to the duty to pay in accordance with the terms agreed with the stipulator. By contrast, such a promise imposes no duties on the third party.[7] Only a mutual promise by the spouse to undertake duties could do so. No such mutual promise has been forthcoming, and none seems necessary to enable the stipulator's intentions to be fulfilled. The spouse can of course reject the benefit in her favour if she wishes, and if she does so the right is considered to be annulled. A valid promise having been constituted, it cannot unilaterally be revoked by the debtor (the insurance company) or by the stipulator, or by the contracting parties together, unless a power to do so has been retained within the contract to permit this. All of this flows from promissory principles, although specific legal systems may amend the position in certain ways. The promissory conception has the merit of capturing the unilateral and gratuitous

---

[7] Some jurisdictions have taken the view that a third party *can* come under certain duties. The French courts, for instance, have decided that, after confirmation of the right in favour of the third party, the third party can come under certain obligations: see Cass civ 1st, 8 December 1987, Bull civ I, no. 343, at 246.

nature of the benefit conferred upon the third party and the means by which such conferral is achieved. It emphasises that the right comes into existence as a result of the will of the parties, and not merely by virtue of any reliance created or benefit conferred. It also enables undertakings to be made in favour of third parties who are not yet in existence, whether natural or juristic persons, as such parties need not accept the promise for it to become binding. Thus, to continue the insurance policy example, the stipulator might validly stipulate for the proceeds to go to his as yet unborn child. Similarly, in South African law, the *stipulatio alteri* is often used as a vehicle for making pre-incorporation undertakings in favour of companies which have not yet been set up. Non-promissory analyses of third party rights do not capture the essence of the nature of the third party right, are deficient in certain regards (as the description of alternative conceptions following will indicate), and lack the flexibility and utility of the promissory analysis.[8]

The promissory conception of third party rights has been adopted by some jurisdictions. However, the promissory route is not the only conceivable analysis of an enforceable third party right, and other conceptions have been advanced for the third party's right:

(1) *The full contracting party analysis*: it is possible, especially if an acceptance by the third party is insisted upon, to conceive of the third party as itself becoming a party to the contract between A and B, or to a new contract with the debtor (B), though an insistence upon the presence of such an acceptance does not necessarily entail that C has the status of a contracting party. Such a contractual solution does not strictly create a third party right, however, but confers upon the third party the status of a full contracting party. This contractual conception is unusual in modern legal systems, though it is the position of Dutch law.[9] Clearly, it is an analysis which cannot describe third party rights in those systems in which no acceptance is required by the third party.

(2) *The assignment view*: the third party can be conceived as an assignee/cedent, to whom is assigned a benefit originally promised to the

---

[8] Proponents of a sui generis view of third party rights would argue that that conception also possesses the benefits which a promissory conception has. However, if that is so, it is only achieved through the creation of an entirely separate, compartmentalised category for third party rights, something which unnecessarily complicates the taxonomy of obligations law.

[9] BW Art. 6:254(1). The result is a tripartite contract, governed by the Code's rules on multiparty contracts, in particular Art. 6:279.

assignor. This evidently provides a solution to the third party rights question in circumstances where a classic *stipulatio alteri* is not permitted, though it is a quite different conception of the parties' relationships, and presupposes an intention of a party to contract for its own benefit initially, and only a subsequent intention to transfer the benefit to a third party. The institution of assignment is treated separately at the end of this chapter.

(3) *The agency view*: the third party can be seen as a principal, for whom the stipulator has been acting as agent. This analysis does not seem, however, to describe very well the intentions of most stipulators, who would not see themselves as acting as an agent in the conduct of another's affairs.

(4) *The* negotiorum gestio *view*: the relationship can be seen as one where the stipulator has been managing the affairs of the third party without authorisation, the acceptance by the third party of the benefit in its favour being conceived of as ratification of such unauthorised management. This analysis does not seem apt to describe many third party rights, however, given that, until the contracting parties agree, the third party has no right, and thus no affairs which can be considered as being 'managed'.

(5) *The sui generis view*: the status and the nature of the rights of the third party may be seen as sui generis. While such a view is perfectly possible, it is not preferable to categorise rights within the field of obligations law as sui generis unless none of the existing characterisations is apt to describe such rights. Thus, if a promissory analysis of third party rights is possible, it is preferable to adopt such an analysis.

As a supplement to the above possible conceptions, the idea that a third party right may also be donative in substance has been recognised in a number of legal systems. If, for instance, a stipulator wishes a right conferred upon a third party purely as a gift to the third party, such a conferral can be described as donative in nature; on the other hand, the stipulator may wish the right conferred upon the third party in order to settle some debt of the stipulator's, such circumstances clearly being indicative of the conferral of a third party right upon a party who stands in the position of a creditor in relation to the stipulator. While a donative characterisation of some third party rights is thus possible, few systems appear to have insisted that in such cases of donation the requirements applicable to donations should prevail where differing from those generally governing third party rights.[10] To do so would be to make the regime for the creation of third party rights unnecessarily restrictive, given the requirements of form or notarisation often applied by national legal systems to donations.

Conceptions of tripartite relationships such as agency or trust, while involving third parties, are distinct legal relationships, and are thus not the focus of the following discussion. The existence of such other tripartite relationships has inevitably impacted upon the theory and practice of third party rights in contract, though it is not possible in the present discussion to explore this complex issue.

Whichever conception of third party rights is chosen has, in the past, been in part to do with finding a way of getting around the traditional antagonism of Roman law, discussed in the following section, towards conferring enforceable rights upon third parties. As that antagonism faded, to be replaced by a desire to make parties adhere to their word, promise became the favoured means to permit the upholding of someone's word, given to a non-contracting party, that he would confer a benefit upon that party.

2.   The historical legal background

In Chapter 3 it was seen how the *stipulatio*, a formal promise, was one of the major components of Roman contract law. Classical Roman law prohibited any stipulation in favour of a third party, whether the stipulator had an interest in the performance or not. This rule was embodied in the maxim *alteri stipulari dari nemo potest* (no one may stipulate that something be given to a third party).[11] In later Roman law, the position was amended to allow for a valid stipulation in favour of a third party so long as the stipulator had an interest in the performance of the promise. The maxim had by then come to be expressed somewhat differently as *alteri stipulari nemo potest* (no one may stipulate on behalf of another),[12] though this amended wording does not convey the change in view. An interest of the stipulator in performance meant circumstances where such performance would have a direct pecuniary effect upon the stipulator's position. The position of the later Roman law regarding the *stipulatio* is explained in the Digest as being that 'obligations of this kind were devised in order

---

[10] Louisiana is one system where donative rules are held to apply to donations of third party rights.

[11] See Hallebeek and Dondorp, *Contracts for a Third Party Beneficiary*, p. 10.

[12] D. 45.1.38.17.

that each man should acquire for himself what is of benefit to him'.[13] Such a benefit could be provided through stipulating that non-performance would result in a penalty being incurred by the promisor, the penalty to be paid to the stipulator.[14] The absence of any conception that an 'interest' in another's performance might extend beyond material interests to, for instance, an affective interest (such as a friendly concern for another) proved to be a continuing stumbling block against third party rights even in the post-Roman period.

The Digest provides examples in the later law of instances where an interest of the stipulator in a third party performance might arise. For instance, the example is given of a tutor stipulating with a replacement for the benefit of the pupil.[15] Here there was a valid stipulation: because the old tutor would be liable if the pupil's affairs were not properly administered, the old tutor had an interest in the stipulation. Further examples given are of a slave stipulating for his master, or a son for his father.[16] The Institutes mention a debtor stipulating for his creditor.[17] Even where a valid interest arose, so that stipulation might require performance to be made to a third party, it was the stipulator alone who could complain about defective or non-performance, not the third party.

In post-classical Roman law, certain exceptional cases were admitted where a third party might have a direct action to enforce a right in its favour. One such case was that of the *donatio sub modo*: a direct action was permitted by a third party donee to whom a donation was meant to have been transferred after a certain time.[18]

Under influence of the canonists, a movement began in favour of allowing a more generalised enforcement by third parties of benefits in their favour. The discussion in Chapter 2 has already disclosed the canonical stress upon the importance of a party keeping its word, and that there be no falsity in parties' words. Such emphases proved crucial in developing a more favourable view of commitments made in favour of third parties. The canonist de Butrio argued that a promise made by A to B to perform in favour of C, an absent third party, could be enforced by C against the promisor by means of the canonical *denunciatio evangelica*,[19] a view with which later canonists concurred. Though the third party had no legal

---

[13] *Ibid.*

[14] This use of *stipulationes poenae*, to provide tangential enforcement of third party rights, is explained in the latter part of D. 45.1.38.17.

[15] D. 45.1.38.20.   [16] D. 45.1.38.17.

[17] Inst. 3.19.20.   [18] C. 8.54.3 (see also C 3.42.8).

[19] De Butrio, *Ad proemium* no. 69 (*Super librum I–V decretalium commentaria*).

right, not being the promisee, he had a natural right to hold the promisor to his word, and this natural right might be enforced in the ecclesiastical courts.[20]

Matters moved beyond natural obligations in the Kingdom of Castile, where a law of 1348, the ley 'Paresciendo' of the Ordenamiendo de Alcalá, provided that a party intending to bind himself to another through a promise, contract, or by some other means, was obliged to perform what he had promised. The legal duty created by this provision was enforceable by the beneficiary, regardless of whether the obligation was entered into with another party. The law further provided that it was no defence that the formalities of the law, including those for a stipulation, had not been made. Under this Castilian law, a stipulator no longer required an interest in the performance in favour of the third party. The phraseology of the law was sufficiently wide to encompass both contracts concluded by an agent in favour of a principal as well as genuine third party rights (that is, contracts between A and B as principals, with a provision in favour of third party C).

In the seventeenth century, natural law arguments were brought to bear in favour of the stipulatio alteri by Hugo Grotius. In his De jure belli as pacis, Grotius argued that stipulations in favour of third parties were agreeable to the natural law, remarking that

> by the Law of Nature I acquire a Right of accepting, that thereby the Right of demanding the Performance of the Promise may pass to another, if he also will accept of it.[21]

The requirement that the third party accept before the obligation is constituted in his favour is consistent with Grotius's general view of the need for an acceptance before a promise binds. This passage does not go so far as to suggest that the third party is conceived of as being the recipient of a direct promise in his favour; on the contrary, the language used, of the right to demand the performance 'passing' to another, suggests that, while the third party acquires a right to demand performance, this occurs through some sort of transfer from stipulator to third party. That conceptualisation differs from what appears to be Grotius's analysis in his Inleidinge, in which he states that, out of a concern for equity, 'a third party may accept a promise, and thereby acquire a right, unless the promisor has revoked his promise before the third party has accepted it.'[22] Grotius's support for direct enforcement by third parties of rights in

---

[20] See further Hallebeek and Dondorp, Contracts for a Third Party Beneficiary, pp. 22–9.
[21] II.xi.18.   [22] Inleidinge, III.iii.38.

their favour came to be applied by the Dutch courts.[23] A similar approach was adopted by Scots law, without the need for an acceptance by the third party, a development discussed below.

The historical antipathy to direct claims by third parties in English law is well known.[24] There were a number of reasons for this. One that must not be ignored is the Common law institution of the trust, which itself provides a vehicle for the conferral on a right upon a third party, the beneficiary under the trust. Another is the institution of agency, whereby B may conclude a contract with C on behalf of A. It is not proposed to discuss these institutions in any detail here, but merely to note that their existence explains in part the absence from English law of the *jus quaesitum tertio*. These two institutions apart, the English law approach to contracts was that only parties to, or beneficiaries under, formal contracts could bring an action under them, and that only those who had given consideration for a right under an informal contract could raise an action. In exceptional cases, such as claims permitted by C, a creditor of B, to whom A had promised to pay C, a promissory analysis was at least maintained as the basis of the claim, even if the courts ignored the fact that consideration had not moved from C to A as it was meant to.[25] The creation in the nineteenth century of a general contractual architecture out of the medieval actions allowed the various old rules against third party claims to be systematised under a single concept of privity of contract: a person who was not a party to a contract could derive neither rights nor come under duties in respect of the contract. A third party, not being such a contracting party (the third party, after all, had issued no acceptance of any contractual offer) was thus excluded by the privity principle from deriving any enforceable rights under it. The privity rule was entrenched in the decision of the Queen's Bench in *Tweddle* v. *Atkinson*,[26] which held that a promise by a man to pay money to the son of another was not directly enforceable by the son.

The entrenchment of the privity rule in English law created an incentive for avoidance techniques and exceptions. Some exceptions were provided for statutorily;[27] some were developed by the courts, such as in relation

---

[23] Hallebeek and Dondorp, *Contracts for a Third Party Beneficiary*, p. 63.

[24] *Ibid.*, Ch. 5; also Palmer, *The Paths to Privity*.

[25] Hallebeek and Dondorp, *Contracts for a Third Party Beneficiary*, p. 106.

[26] (1861) 1 B & S 393, 30 LJQB 265, 4 LT 468, 9 WR 781.

[27] For instance, under the Third Parties (Rights Against Insurers) Act 1930 and the Restrictive Trade Practices Act 1956.

to the 'negative' rights contained within exclusion clauses,[28] though an early willingness to protect third parties in this area was later subject to restriction, which itself produced a change in contract drafting procedure to create third parties as principals acting through the medium of an agent.[29] Sometimes the courts were willing to hold that someone who appeared to be a third party was in fact in a direct contractual relationship with a promisor;[30] sometimes liability in tort furnished a remedy for defective performance to a third party, if not non-performance.[31] These various ways proved, however, of limited assistance in filling the gap left by a genuine third party right in contract. The problem was not eventually remedied until the Contracts (Rights of Third Parties) Act 1999, which provided for the direct enforcement by a third party of a right conceived in its favour. This development is discussed further below.

More might be said of the historical development of third party rights, and indeed something more is said below in relation to nineteenth- and twentieth-century development, but it will already be appreciated from the history narrated above that there has been a long-standing antipathy in many legal systems to granting a non-contracting party title to sue under a contract in respect of a right which one of the contracting parties has stipulated for the other to confer upon the third party. In some instances, this was because of a view that a promisee did not have any recognised interest in the stipulated performance in favour of the third party. If that were so, however, why would such a performance have been requested in the first place? The traditional arguments failed to give sufficient value to the simple desire of the stipulator for the requested performance and to the objectively manifested commitment of the promisor to undertake the promised act. In some instances, the objection was on the grounds that any promise was made to the stipulator, and not to the third party. This objection presupposes that the third party has had no promise communicated to it, but if such communication has been undertaken, then this argument clearly has no force; naturally, if the third party has not been the recipient of any such promise made to it, then the argument is a good one. Sometimes the objection was that the third party had given nothing for the right in its favour. That, however, was an argument which was subject to all the criticisms of the doctrine of consideration

---

[28] *Elder Dempster & Co.* v. *Paterson Zochonis & Co. Ltd* [1924] AC 522.
[29] The clause so drafted was referred to as a 'Himalaya clause', after the name of the ship involved in important litigation on this issue (see *Adler* v. *Dickson* [1955] 1 QB 158).
[30] *Shanklin Pier* v. *Detel Products Ltd* [1951] 2 KB 854.
[31] See for instance *Hedley Byrne & Co.* v. *Heller & Partners Ltd* [1964] AC 465.

that have already been narrated at various points in this work. Finally, the objection has sometimes been that only parties to a contract ought to be affected, whether positively or negatively, by the contractual relationship. The rationale of the 'privity' of contractual relationships has an obvious merit to it where it protects non-contracting parties from having unwanted duties thrust upon them. As regards benefits conceived in their favour, however, it serves no obvious useful function, so long as a separate rule is recognised that no one can have a benefit thrust upon him against his will. Such a rule is operative in some systems in respect of unwanted donations, and it would equally serve to protect third parties under contract without the need for a more restrictive rule against enforceable third party benefits.

3.   Third party rights in modern contract law

(a)   The Common law[32]

Within the Common law world, England lagged behind many of its sister jurisdictions in granting general recognition to directly enforceable third party rights in contract.[33] Starting in 1969, various parts of Australia passed legislation to recognise the *stipulatio alteri*,[34] New Zealand following suit in 1982.[35] Most of such Commonwealth legislation is drafted

---

[32] A useful history of the Common law tradition in relation to third party beneficiaries in contract is found in Palmer, *The Paths to Privity*.

[33] Canada alone (saving of course Quebec) among the major Common law jurisdictions continues to deny third party beneficiary claims in contract, despite arguments for reform (see for instance the report in favour of reform submitted by M. Lavelle, 'Privity of Contract and Third Party Beneficiaries', to the Uniform Law Conference of Canada (www.ulcc.ca) in September 2007).

[34] See the Western Australian Property Law Act 1969, s.11(2) ('where a contract expressly in its terms purports to confer a benefit directly on a person who is not named as a party to the contract, the contract is ... enforceable by that person in his own name'), the Queensland Property Law Act 1974, s. 55 ('A promisor who, for a valuable consideration moving from the promisee, promises to do or to refrain from doing an act or acts for the benefit of a beneficiary shall, upon acceptance by the beneficiary, be subject to a duty enforceable by the beneficiary to perform that promise'), and the Northern Territory Law of Property Act 2000, s. 56(1) ('A promisor who, for valuable consideration moving from the promisee, promises to do or to refrain from doing an act or acts for the benefit of a beneficiary is, on acceptance by the beneficiary, subject to a duty enforceable by the beneficiary to perform that promise'). In addition, the Australian Commonwealth Insurance Contracts Act 1984 allows third party beneficiaries to enforce contracts of insurance.

[35] See the Contracts (Privity Act) 1982, s.4, which states: 'Where a promise contained in a deed or contract confers, or purports to confer, a benefit on a person, designated by name, description or reference to a class, who is not a party to the deed or contract ... the

in promissory terms. In the United States the recognition of third party rights came even earlier, and was achieved by the courts without the need for legislation. The first decision in which such rights were clearly enforced was the New York Court of Appeals decision in *Lawrence* v. *Fox* in 1859.[36] Some US states subsequently chose to entrench third party rights in legislation, as did the Restatement (Second) of Contracts.[37] One such legislative enactment is section 1559 of the California Civil Code, which provides that a contract 'made expressly for the benefit of a third person, may be enforced by him at any time before the parties thereto rescind it'. US Common law jurisprudence, like that of other jurisdictions, has recognised that a third party may be the recipient of, and may enforce, a negative right in its favour.[38]

English law finally broke decisively with the rigidity of the doctrine of privity, favouring instead the intention of the parties, when it passed the the Contract (Rights of Third Parties) Act 1999. The Act calls the traditional stipulator the promisee, and the party by whom the benefit is to be conferred on the third party the promisor. This identifies the promise to benefit the third party as made to the other contracting party, but says nothing about whether additionally any promise is made to the third party or whether the third party is simply seen as exceptionally being granted the right to enforce a promise made to another. In fact, the Act does not specify the nature of the third party's right other than to say that the third party is permitted 'in his own right [to] enforce a term of the contract'.[39] The lack of any language characterising the third party's right as a promise is not necessarily conclusive of the third party's right *not* being promissory in nature, and indeed it seems that in general the third party is conceived of as enforcing a promissory right,[40] though without any clarification as to whether the promise is considered as made to it also or just to the promisee. It is consistent with this promissory view that the Act is considered to permit promises to be made in favour of unborn

---

promisor shall be under an obligation, enforceable at the suit of that person, to perform that promise.'

[36] 20 NY 268 (1859).   [37] Restatement (Second) of Contracts, §302.

[38] Thus, for instance, it is possible for a third party to take the benefit of an exclusion clause: see *Carle & Montanari Inc.* v. *American Export Isbrandtsen Lines Inc.* 275 F Supp 76 (1967). On negative benefits, see the Restatement (Second) of Contracts, §306.

[39] S. 1(1).

[40] Peel, *Treitel on Contract*, para. 14–095, describes the contracting party which is obliged to the third party as 'the person who makes the promise which the third party is claiming to enforce (the promisor)', a description which certainly seems to conceive of the third party as enforcing a promissory right.

parties, and as yet unincorporated corporate bodies.[41] There is nothing in the Act itself to suggest that, as is possible under Scots law, a third party right might not be intended to arise between indirectly related parties in a contract chain, though some have suggested that such chains are incompatible with an intention by contracting parties to confer such rights upon more distant parties in such a chain.[42] However, an early decision under the Act suggested that the mere fact that another remedy might be open to a third party did not mean that the contracting parties cannot have intended to confer a right under the Act.[43]

The third party is certainly not a full contracting party, though for remedial purposes is treated as if it were: section 1(5) says that there is available to the third party 'any remedy that would have been available to him in an action for breach of contract *if he had been a party to the contract*' (emphasis added). The Act takes a dualist approach to the creation of the third party's right to enforce a term of the contract. It can arise either because the contract expressly states that the third party has such a right of enforcement, or because a term of the contract purports to confer a benefit upon him.[44] There is thus an emphasis both upon the express intention of the parties as well as upon a beneficial result for the third party. This latter route needs no express intention of the contracting parties to be present; rather, it in effect presumes that an intention to confer the benefit was the tacit intention of the contracting parties. The assumption of such a tacit intention can be overcome, as one would expect, by contra-indications in the contract.[45] Though it might be argued that the non-intention based nature of this route for the creation of a third party right indicates that the third party's right is not promissory in nature, it ought to be recalled that jurisdictions taking a promissory view of the nature of the right, such as that in Scotland, also maintain that the intention to confer a benefit on the third party may arise tacitly.

No acceptance of the right is required to be given by the third party in order for the right to exist in its favour, again supporting the view that the third party is not the recipient of a contractual offer. However,

---

[41] *Ibid.*, para. 14–100.   [42] See, for instance, McKendrick, *Contract Law*, p. 118.

[43] *Nisshin Shipping Co. Ltd* v. *Cleaves & Co. Ltd* [2003] EWHC 2602 (the alternative possible remedy for the third party in that case being as beneficiary under the trust of a promise).

[44] s. 1(1).

[45] s. 1(2). It seems that, despite this subsection, contracting parties subject to English law are concerned at the possibility of third party rights being held to exist where none were intended, the regular practice being to exclude the application of the Act, the parties preferring in many cases to rely upon the use of contractual warranties as the means of conferring rights upon third parties.

a 'communication of assent' by the third party to the term in its favour
is one of the means by which the right may be made irrevocable (mere
intimation of the term, or delivery of the contract, is not enough, in contrast with the position in Scotland), the other two methods of irrevocability relating to the reliance of the third party.[46]

While it might be supposed that the absence from English law of a
generalised third party rights doctrine prior to 1999 was the spur to
development of the law of tort in certain ways to protect third parties, it
should not be forgotten that those developments in the field of tort were
in part the result of the decision in the Scottish appeal *Junior Books Ltd* v.
Veitchi Co. Ltd.[47] As Scots law had a third party rights rule at the time of
that decision, it cannot be said that all of the tortious developments were
solutions to a perceived failure of contract law to provide equitable solutions to perceived problems of unfairness. The absence of any attempt
to argue a contractual solution (whether liability across the contract
chain or a third party right) in *Junior Books* is puzzling. The decision
is perhaps best explicable as part of an expansionist attitude at the time
to tort liability, an expansion that was later reined back in *Murphy* v.
Brentwood District Council.[48] However, despite this later reining back
of tort liability, and the subsequent introduction of third party rights
to English law, some subsequent developments in tort law are cause for
concern that tort might once again be trying to stray into the rightful sphere of contract in relation to third parties. In this respect, the
House of Lords' decision in *White* v. *Jones*[49] marked a worrying development. It is obvious that, had the defendant in *White v Jones* been asked
whether he was 'assuming a responsibility' to the third party plaintiffs,
he would have replied in the negative. It is also clear that, had he wished
to make the plaintiffs any promises concerning his contract with their
father, he might have chosen to do so; he did not. For the House of Lords
to ignore this and create liability in tort based upon a wholly fictional
'assumption of responsibility' was tantamount to implying promises
on the part of the defendant to third parties to the contract with his
client. In effect, the plaintiffs were treated as having a third party right,
even though it was recognised by Lord Goff that 'the ordinary law could
not provide a simple answer to the problems which arise in the present
case, which appears at first sight to require the imposition of something

---

[46] s. 2(1).   [47] 1982 SC (HL) 244, [1983] 1 AC 520.
[48] [1991] 1 AC 398, [1990] 2 All ER 908 (HL).
[49] [1995] 2 AC 207, [1995] 1 All ER 691 (HL).

like a contractual liability which is beyond the scope of the ordinary *jus quaesitum tertio*.'[50]

If it is indeed correct that a *stipulatio alteri* would not arise on *White* v. *Jones* facts, then it seems highly dubious to allow tort to circumvent this failure. However, now that English law does indeed give general recognition to third party rights, a proper judicial analysis of whether such rights would be appropriate to the situation of the disappointed beneficiary under a will would be welcome. There are, of course, some evident objections to such beneficiaries being considered third parties in contract, such as that the testator appears to be both promisor and promisee in relation to the third party's expected benefit, that the alleged right of the beneficiary is only a *spes successionis*, and that the solicitor only intends to benefit his client, not a third party. These objections are sufficiently weighty to suggest that the better view may simply be that the plaintiffs in *White* v. *Jones* ought not to have recovered at all. As Lord Mustill said of possible recovery by the plaintiffs in his dissenting speech, this is 'undoubtedly a possible result, but I would wish to counsel against assuming too readily that it so reflects the moral imperatives of the situation that the law of delict should be strained to bring it about'.[51] Interestingly, if *White* v. *Jones* does indeed represent an incursion by tort into the proper sphere of contract in order to remedy perceived gaps in contract law protection, this would represent a mirror image of aspects of German law, where, as discussed below, the doctrine of the contract with protective effect for third parties has been used to supplement the protection offered by German tort law.

(b) The mixed legal systems

South African law recognises what is called a contract in favour of a third party, and has done since the mid-nineteenth century. Following the position of Roman-Dutch law (narrated above), the acceptance of the right by the third party is seen as essential to the creation of the right.

The nineteenth- and early twentieth-century cases on the subject developed the view of the third party as the recipient of a promise made in its favour. In the first of these cases, *Louisa and Protector of Slaves* v. *Van den Berg*,[52] De Villiers CJ analysed the circumstances of a *stipulatio alteri* as giving rise to a promise accepted by both stipulator and third party. A

---

[50] [1995] 2 AC 207, 263A.   [51] [1995] 2 AC at 278H–279A.
[52] (1830) 1 Menz 471.

number of subsequent cases adopted the same analysis, the position being confirmed in *McCullough* v. *Fernwood Estate Ltd.*[53] Reference was made in these decisions to Roman-Dutch sources on promise, especially to Grotius and his treatment of promise and its required acceptance.[54] This requirement for an acceptance was disputed by the prominent contract scholar J. C. de Wet,[55] but this opposition to the established judicial view did not find favour with the courts. Despite this early foundation of the third party's right in promise, it has been observed that later authorities have used a plethora of terminology to describe the third party's right, not all of it suggestive of a promise.[56] The need for an acceptance appears to have favoured a contractual rather than a promissory approach in later cases.

As in Scots law, the intention of the contracting parties to confer the right on the third party was recognised as being required to create the third party's right; the mere incidental accrual of a benefit by a third party is not enough to create such right. This position emphasises that the doctrine of third party rights in South African law is clearly will-based and not benefit-based.

More recently, the traditional promissory analysis has been criticised by Sutherland and Johnston, who have argued that the

> terminology that South African courts use is imprecise and confusing. The cases variously state that the third party must accept a stipulation, promise, contract, benefit, the benefits of the contract, or an offer of a benefit. The only sense that can be made of all these expressions is that the third party accepts an offer. The courts approach then fits perfectly with orthodox principles of contractual liability.[57]

Such an offer, argue the authors, gives the third party an option to enter into a contract with the party offering to confer the right on the third party.[58] The result is two contracts: one between A and B, in which B has promised to confer the right upon C, and one between A and C, formed by the making of an offer by A to C (giving rise to an option) which C must accept to complete the envisaged relationship. This is a bold reinterpretation of the existing South African jurisprudence, though, as the authors recognise, it does not provide the legal system with the mechanism which is suggested by the terminology of a *stipulatio alteri*.[59] Having

---

[53] 1920 AD 204.   [54] Grotius, *De Jure Belli ac Pacis*, II.xi.18.
[55] De Wet, 'Die ontwikkeling van die ooreenkoms ten behoewe van 'n derde'.
[56] Sutherland and Johnston, 'Contracts for the Benefit of Third Parties', p. 214.
[57] *Ibid.*, p. 214.   [58] *Ibid.*, p. 215.   [59] *Ibid.*, p. 215.

characterised the *stipulatio alteri* as an option, it is somewhat unclear why the authors later choose to describe the true third party contract as 'sui generis', as an option does not merit such a description.[60]

The analysis of Sutherland and Johnston was offered as a way of making sense of a confusing array of judicial analyses by the South African courts of the nature of the *stipulatio alteri*. In offering their new analysis, however, they might be said too readily to dismiss the inherited Roman-Dutch analysis of the third party as the recipient of a promise, albeit one that has to be accepted before it takes effect. One can appreciate why such a promissory view may be unattractive in the present age: modern South African law does not generally recognise the promise as a distinct and binding obligation. It thinks in terms of contracts, and so any continued description of enforceable rights as promissory in nature, rather than contractual, would be to perpetuate an anomalous hangover from an age when the *ius commune* was still familiar with the idea of the promise. Yet, if South African law were to restore promise to a central position in its law of obligations, as it has been suggested at various points in this work that all the legal systems studied ought to, there would be no need to dismiss a promissory view of the *stipulatio alteri*. Far from being an anomaly, it would be one example of a number of circumstances which might usefully be analysed in promissory terms. That usefulness, in the field of third party rights, lies not least in the ability to characterise the third party as the recipient of rights only, without the need to conceive of its coming under any duties (though of course if it is desired to burden a third party with duties, then there is nothing to prevent that third party being created as a full contracting party by the normal route).

In Louisiana, following the lead of the somewhat limited provision in the French Civil Code concerning the *stipulation pour autrui*,[61] the Louisiana Civil Code provides that a 'contracting party may stipulate a benefit for a third person called a third party beneficiary'.[62] The Code does

---

[60] *Ibid.*, p. 217.
[61] *Code civil* Art. 1121 (the terms of which were taken, almost verbatim, from Pothier). Following the lead of Roman law, French law at the time of the drafting of the Code was essentially against the idea of a *stipulatio alteri*. The terms of Art. 1121 were therefore drafted in a very restricted way, permitting a *stipulation pour autrui* only where 'it is the condition of a stipulation which one makes for oneself or of a gift which one makes to another'. Modern French law has been developed by the courts to allow a wide enforcement of third party rights.
[62] CC Art. 1978.

not require the acceptance of the third party as a constitutive element,[63] nor does it insist (as Roman law did) that the stipulator have any interest in the performance to the third party. The Louisiana jurisprudence has located the essentials of the *stipulation pour autrui* as being a clear intention to benefit the third party, the specification of a clear benefit to be conferred, and a benefit which is not merely an incidental one.[64] The codal provision also provides that a manifestation of intention by the third party to avail itself of the benefit prevents the contracting parties from dissolving the contract without the third party's agreement.[65] Such manifestation of consent has the additional effect that the stipulation in favour of the third party cannot be revoked; before this point, the stipulator is able to revoke the stipulation.[66] The provisions do not permit any duties to be imposed upon a third party, though in a separate provision (again following the lead of the French Code)[67] the Code provides that, if a contracting party promises third party performance and this does not occur, the contracting party is itself liable for such performance.[68]

The Louisiana Code describes the nature of the right given to the third party as that of demanding performance from the promisor. Beyond that, it does not describe how this right is conferred; specifically, it does not say whether it is conferred by means of a promise. However, given that the provisions in the Louisiana Code derive from those of the French Code, it is generally recognised in Louisiana that, like the French Code, Louisiana's *stipulation pour autrui* can be analysed in promissory terms. The promise is conceived of as having been made to the stipulator however, not to the third party beneficiary, that third party being allowed to enforce the promise conceived of in its favour though made to the stipulator.[69] It is recognised that the stipulation of a third party right may

---

[63] Again, this position mirrors that of French law. The French courts had settled in 1888 that the third party's right comes in to existence at the moment that the promisor has made the promise to the third party: see judgments of February and March 1888, DP 88.1.193.

[64] See *Joseph* v. *Hospital District No. 2*, 939 So 2d 1206 (La 2006). The third of these requirements seems superfluous, given the first requirement of a clear intention to confer the benefit: if a benefit is intentionally conferred, it surely cannot be merely incidental.

[65] CC Art. 1978.

[66] CC Art. 1979. If the promisor has an interest in performing, the stipulation cannot be revoked without his consent.

[67] *Code civil* Art. 1120.   [68] CC Art. 1977.

[69] *Ibid*. In *Joseph* v. *Hospital Service District No. 2*, 939 So 2d 1206 (La 2006), Weimer J commented that '[a] true third party beneficiary is never a party to the contract in question; he is never a promisee.' This comment of course equates promisee with contracting party, and (consistently with Louisiana law) does not recognise that there may be unilateral promisees.

amount to a donation, with the result that the donative provisions of the
Code concerning revocation, reduction, and so forth, apply to such a
stipulation.[70]

In Scots law, the right of a third party to enforce a benefit conceived
of by contracting parties was recognised at an early stage in legal
development.[71] In the seminal legal analysis of Scots law, that of Stair,
the *stipulatio alteri* is conceived of as a species of unilateral promise,
Stair discussing the *jus quaesitum tertio* as part of his treatment of such
promises. Stair refers to the opinion of the Spanish scholastic Molina in
support of the *stipulatio alteri*, and states that

> It is likewise the opinion of Molina and it quadrates with our customs
> that when parties contract, if there be any article in favour of a third
> party,[72] at any time, *est jus quaesitum tertio*, which cannot be recalled
> by either or both of the contractors, but he may compel either of them
> to exhibit the contract, and thereupon the obliged may be compelled to
> perform.[73]

The break with Roman law, and the alignment with the natural law tradition of the late scholastics, is significant. Stair's remarks have not been
without subsequent interpretative disputes, however. Specifically, the
words 'which cannot be recalled' have given rise to a debate as to whether
'irrevocability' is a prerequisite in Scots law for the constitution of a *jus
quaesitum tertio*. That was said to be the case by the House of Lords in
Carmichael v. *Carmichael's Executrix*,[74] a decision thought by many to
be based upon a mis-reading of Stair.[75] The matter is complicated by confusion about whether the idea of irrevocability relates to the nature of
the right conferred, or to the act by which the right is constituted. With
that distinction in mind, it seems to be the case that (i) the nature of the
right conferred will usually be irrevocable (that is, it is a right which, once

---

[70] See Litvinoff and Scalise, *Law of Obligations*, p. 326.
[71] Morison's Dictionary, an early repository of case reports, contains case reports under the
heading of *jus quaesitum tertio* from 1591 onwards.
[72] The idea of a contract term being 'in favour of a third party' seems wide enough to
encompass both terms conferring a tangible benefit upon a third party, as well as terms
conferring a right upon a third party which does not necessarily confer any tangible
benefit upon it (for instance, a right to make a determination about the performance of
the contract or the obligations of the contracting parties).
[73] I.x.5.   [74] 1920 SC (HL) 195.
[75] For various views on this matter, see Cameron, 'Jus Quaesitum Tertio; The True Meaning
of Stair I.x.5'; Rodger, 'Molina, Stair and the Jus Quaesitum Tertio'; MacCormack, 'A
Note on Stair's Use of the Term *Pollicitatio*'.

given, cannot be taken back) *unless* the power of revocation is reserved when the right is first conferred,[76] and (ii) as to the act by which the right is conferred, some irrevocable act must occur before the right comes into existence: in an oral contract, such an act is constituted by the third party being informed of the right; in a written contract, either the party must be given a copy of the contract or else some act equivalent to delivery must occur.

The requirement of informing the third party, or of delivering the contract to him, is an additional requirement to those applying in the ordinary law of promises. Given this relatively modern requirement of delivery or an equivalent, it seems that in Scots law the third party can today be seen as being the recipient of a promise made directly to it at the time of such delivery or an equivalent. Before this requirement was added to the law, one might have treated the third party in the same way as any other absent promisee, that is as gaining its promissory right at the very moment that the promisor indicated his intention to be bound (the same moment that the contract between stipulator and debtor is concluded).

As in other systems, the genesis of the third party's right is said to lie in the intention of the parties to confer the right upon it, a mere incidental benefit being insufficient. It has been said that this intention of the parties may be expressly stated in the contract, or may be implied from it.[77] Merely mentioning the third party's name, as a party affected by the contract, will not be enough of itself to demonstrate such an intention. Arguments about whether such an intention is present is evidently a factual investigation, based upon the specific contract before the court. In Scots law, such arguments have not infrequently arisen in cases involving contract chains, where the argument is advanced that C, a party to contract B–C, was also intended as a third party under contract A–B, often as a means of allowing it to sue for defective performance by A,[78] as well as cases involving negative benefits, where C is claiming the benefit of an alleged indemnity from liability.[79] Such arguments have usually failed, the courts being unpersuaded that any intention to create C as a third

---

[76] As to such as revocable right, see *Love v. Amalgamated Society of Lithographic Printers* 1912 2 SLT 50 (IH).

[77] McBryde, *Contract*, para. 10–12.

[78] *Scott Lithgow Ltd v. GEC Electrical Projects Ltd* 1989 SC 412, 1992 SLT 244 (CSOH); *Strathford East Kilbride Ltd v. HLM Design Ltd* 1997 SCLR 877 (CSOH).

[79] *Aberdeen Harbour Board v. Heating Enterprises Aberdeen Ltd* 1990 SLT 416, 1989 SCLR 716 (CSIH).

party existed in the circumstances of the case,[80] though the courts have not approved of suggestions that in contract chain cases the very existence of the chain must indicate that parties only intend to confer rights upon those next to them in the chain and not on third parties further up or down the chain.[81] Moreover, there is no reason to suppose that the mere possibility of an assignation must be taken to indicate that no third party right could have been intended.

Stair's conception of the third party's right as a species of promise has been supported by commentators[82] and by the courts. In the leading encyclopaedia of the law, *The Laws of Scotland*, it has been suggested that not only is the party obliged to perform (the debtor) in favour of the third party (the tertius) held to make a promise to the tertius, but that the party requesting performance (the stipulator) may also be considered to have, at least impliedly, made a promise, not of performance but of an accessory nature.[83] This goes further in a promissory analysis than any other jurisdiction appears to.

Despite the traditional conception of a *stipulatio alteri* in Scots law in promissory terms, it has been questioned by some whether this description is entirely apt. The author of the leading scholarly contract monograph, McBryde, has opined of the right of a third party that its nature is 'uncertain', and has suggested that it 'may be better to treat jus quaesitum tertio as an independent right, which shares some of the characteristics of other contractual rights but also has special features'.[84] Assessing the promissory view of the *stipulatio alteri*, McBryde believes that it is no longer necessary to rely on this view any more than it is necessary to see a contract as an exchange of promises.[85] This rather presupposes that there is something undesirable or unhelpful in viewing either the *stipulatio alteri* or the contract in promissory terms which, it will be evident from this work, it is suggested there is not.

---

[80] There have been some successes however: see *Melrose* v. *Davidson & Robertson* 1993 SC 288, 1993 SLT 611 (CSIH), where the defenders won on the *jus quaesitum tertio* point, but lost the action on other grounds.

[81] As is demonstrated by the willingness of the court to consider a possible *jus quaesitum tertio* in the contract chain case *Scott Lithgow Ltd* v. *GEC Electrical Projects Ltd* 1989 SC 412, 1992 SLT 224 (CSOH).

[82] Smith, *Studies Critical and Comparative*, pp. 172, 177, 184, 185, 196, 197; Scottish Law Commission, Memorandum No. 38, pp. 12–15; MacQueen, 'Jus Quaesitum Tertio', para. 827.

[83] MacQueen, *ibid.*, para. 827. Stair had remarked that either of the contracting parties could be compelled upon by the third party to exhibit the contract (I.x.5).

[84] McBryde, *Contract*, para. 10–07.   [85] *Ibid.*

(c)   German law

The BGB contains a cluster of provisions[86] entitled 'the promise of performance to a third party' (*Versprechen der Leistung an einen Dritten*). This title would seem to suggest that the nature of the relationship with the third party is that someone (one or both of the contracting parties) promises a performance to him, given that it speaks of a promise of performance 'to a third party' (*an einen Dritten*). But is this description justified by the substance of the articles which appear in the title or by the jurisprudence relating to the articles?

The words promise, promisor (*der Versprechender*), or promisee (*der Versprechensempfänger*), appear in various sections under this title of the BGB, but in §331, for instance, the reference to promising is clearly conceived of as being a promise made by one of the contracting parties to the other:

> §331(1): If the performance for the third party is to occur after the death of the person to whom it is promised, the third party acquires the right to the performance, in case of doubt, upon the death of the promisee.

Promisor and promisee here signify the principal contracting parties, and not the third party. So, under this section, a contracting party is taken to make a promise to the other (which is just as the English legislation describes the situation). But this tells us nothing of the nature of the right in favour of the third party. In fact, the other articles use promissory language in precisely the same way, that is to say they never do so in relation to the third party.

The provisions allow for termination or alteration of the third party's right. §328(2) states that, in the absence of a provision governing the matter, it is a matter of inference from the circumstances, in particular the purpose of the contract, 'whether the power is to be reserved for the parties to the contract to terminate or alter the right of the third party without his approval'. Does this suggest that the third party's right cannot be promissory in nature? Not necessarily. As discussed above, a *stipulatio alteri* can be made revocable in Scotland, where the third party's right has nonetheless traditionally been understood in promissory terms.

In fact, as a whole, the text of the relevant sections of the BGB do not shed any light on what the relationship is between the principal contracting

---

[86]   Book 2, Division 3, Title 3, comprising §§328–35.

parties and the third party, whether it is to be understood as contractual, promissory, or as having some other nature.

The views of academics are also inconclusive as to the understanding of the nature of the third party's right. Markesinis has remarked that in German law 'it is generally agreed (but not expressly stated) that the acquisition of a right by the third party depends upon the intention of *the promisor* and *the promisee*'.[87] But this still does not tell us what the nature of the third party's right to performance is. A view has been advanced that the relationship between promisor and third party is 'quasi-contractual' (*vertragsähnlich*),[88] by which it seems is meant a right akin to a contractual one (rather than one arising under unjustified enrichment).

The uncertain position which prevails today need not have been the case. The codal provision concerning the rights of third parties was originally suggested to be an example of a unilateral promise in favour of the third party, but this approach did not win out. This approach had been promoted by von Kübel, the editor of the contract portions of the draft of the BGB. Von Kübel saw the third party's right as arising without any involvement on the part of the third party, by virtue of a unilateral promise in its favour. He rejected the view that the third party should be seen as being the recipient of an offer, one which it would be required to accept before liability on the promisor's part could arise. Von Kübel's promissory approach was however not maintained as the drafting process continued. This resulted in the promissory link between promises of reward (which did make it into the BGB as rare examples of an enforceable unilateral promise) and the right of a third party under a contract being lost.[89] Nor, however, was the final position that an acceptance by the third party was required: no such acceptance is needed, though the third party is entitled to reject the benefit.[90]

The loss of von Kübel's position, which would clearly have defined the nature of the third party's right in German law, means that the most that it seems possible to say about the right of a third party under a contract in German law is that it is a right which, though not that of a contracting party, arises under contract.

As to the uses to which German law puts third party rights in contract, Markesinis has identified eleven fact situations which have commonly

---

[87] Markesinis *et al.*, *German Law of Contract*, p. 197 (the authors' italics).
[88] See Hallebeeek and Dondorp, *Contracts for a Third Party Beneficiary*, p. 156.
[89] For a summary of the relevant history, see Zimmermann, 'Vertrag und Versprechen', pp. 473–4.
[90] BGB §333.

been held to fall under the regime of contracts in favour of third parties.[91] Some of these would also clearly be treated as enforceable third party right scenarios in Britain. Thus, widows' insurance schemes and workers' retirement schemes, insurance contracts stipulating for performance to a third party, and travel contracts where family members are to benefit as well as the contracting party, would be so categorised, under a mixture of common law (in Scotland) and statute (in Scotland and England).[92] Others, however, would be less likely to fall within a third party rights regime: most cases concerning medical treatment are regarded as tortious/delictual, as they concern treatment by agents of the National Health Service with whom no contract will normally arise, though private medical contracts for the treatment of a third party might conceivably give rise to an enforceable third party contractual right; consignees of goods which are damaged in transit also fall within the German regime, whereas in the UK, while such parties might recover their losses indirectly at common law under the principle of 'transferred loss' discussed below,[93] that is not an independent third party claim as such.[94]

Whatever the nature of the right in favour of the third party in German law, it seems clear that another institution often discussed alongside it, that of the contract with protective effect for third parties (*Vertrag mit Schutzwirkung für Dritte*, or 'VSD' for short), cannot be characterised as arising out of promise, except if one were to say that contractual promises are being extended for policy reasons to offer protection for third parties.[95] But essentially this aspect of German law uses contract to perform what would be dealt with tortiously/delictually (with one notable exception, discussed below) in other legal systems. So, a major tranche of the cases under the VSD doctrine relate to personal injury or physical damage caused by a contracting party to third parties or their property. The VSD operates here to supplement a very narrow provision of the BGB relating

---

[91] Markesinis *et al.*, *German Law of Contract*, p. 187.

[92] Many cases are now dealt in England under the Contracts (Rights of Third Parties) Act 1999. However, more specific statutes govern certain factual cases, including the Married Women's Property Act 1882, s. 1(1) of the Marine Insurance Act 1906, the Third Parties (Rights Against Insurers) Act 1930, s. 47 of the Law of Property Act 1925, and s. 148(7) of the Road Traffic Act 1988.

[93] See further below at pp. 320ff.

[94] In German law, the relevant law is found in Book 4, Part 4 (§§407–75h) of the Commercial Code (HGB), the contract of carriage being seen as a contract for the benefit of a third party.

[95] For a summary of the relevant law, see Markesinis *et al.*, *German Law of Contract*, pp. 204–14.

to vicarious liability for the torts of employees.[96] The other major tranche of cases dealt with under the VSD relates to pure economic loss, and was developed from the 1960s onwards, beginning with a famous case imposing liability on a notary towards disappointed beneficiaries of a testator (and thus similar to *White* v. *Jones*) referred to as the *Testamentfall* case.[97] These cases were developed to overcome the exclusion of liability for negligently inflicted pure economic loss under §823(1) BGB. The notable exception to the fact that the VSD covers cases that would normally be classified tortiously elsewhere is the exclusion clause conceived in favour of a third party. This is treated in German Law as a type of contract with protective effect for third parties,[98] mirroring the contractual (and not tortious) treatment meted out to such clauses in England (under the 1999 Act) and Scotland (at common law).

(d)   Model law

Principle 4 to the DCFR explains that the DCFR takes what Common lawyers would style contractual privity for granted: it is said to be 'self-evident that parties can contract only for themselves, unless otherwise provided, and that contracts, as a rule, regulate only the rights and obligations between the parties who conclude them'. The DCFR spells out exceptions to this position, one of these exceptions being the *stipulatio alteri*. Article II.-9:301(1) provides that the

> parties to a contract may, by the contract, confer a right or other benefit on a third party. The third party need not be in existence or identified at the time the contract is concluded.[99]

This article does not spell out positively the nature of the third party's entitlement (as promissory, sui generis, or whatever). In fact, Art II.-9:301(2) adds that the 'nature and content of the third party's right or benefit are determined by the contract'. This would suggest that parties may, if they want, confer a right which is in the nature of a unilateral promise on a third party. That possibility seems to be confirmed by Article II.-9:302, which provides for the default position, applicable in cases where one of the contracting parties is required to render a performance to the third party, that (in the absence of anything to the contrary in the contract)

[96] §831.   [97] BGH NJW 1965, 1955.
[98] See Markesinis and Unberath, *German Law of Torts*, p. 540.
[99] The provisions notably include both right and benefit conceptions of a third party's right: see earlier discussion at n. 1 to this ch.

the third party has the same rights to performance and remedies for non-performance as if the contracting party was bound to render the performance under a binding unilateral undertaking in favour of the third party.

The taxonomic approach of this default provision is noteworthy: in effect, it treats a third party who is the intended recipient of a performance as a promisee under a unilateral promise. The default nature of the right given to other third parties (those who are not to receive a performance from one of the parties) is not clarified, however, so that, for instance, a third party upon whom an indemnity was conferred would not automatically be characterised as a promisee under a unilateral promise, though (given the permissive terms of Article II.-9:302) there would seem to be nothing preventing the parties from providing positively that such an indemnity is in the nature of a unilateral promise by one of the parties not to hold the third party liable.

Whatever else the contracting parties may provide, it appears that it would be inconsistent with the terms of the DCFR's articles on third party rights to conceive of the third party as accepting a contractual offer in its favour. Such an inconsistency would seem to arise from the fact that (i) third party rights may be conferred upon parties who are not yet even in existence – that could only be so if no acceptance were required to constitute the third party's entitlement; and (ii) the third party is entitled to reject the right or benefit,[100] suggesting that such right or benefit does not arise as a result of the agreement of the third party (were that so, such an entitlement would be unnecessary, as the third party could simply fail to accept the intended entitlement if it did not wish it).

The DCFR framework for third party rights leaves the nature of the third party's rights to be determined by the contracting parties, conceivably in a promissory way. This is consistent with the broad approach of other parts of the DCFR in seeking to permit as many possible characterisations of circumstances as is consistent with the coherence of the law of obligations as a whole.

(e)   Conclusion on third party rights under contract

A simple conclusion on the above comparative analysis of third party rights under contract is that, while all the systems studied now recognise (in contrast with the Roman law and Common law prior to 1999) a

---

[100]   Provided for in Art. II.-9:303(1).

generalised right of third parties to a contract to enforce in their own name a right conceived under the contract in their favour, there is no agreement on the exact nature of such a right. In some systems, there is at least a majority (if not universal) view that the nature of the third party's right is promissory. Such an analysis is founded on the *ius commune* promissory tradition. Of the mixed systems, Scots law is clearly in this camp, Louisiana is arguably so, but South Africa, while once taking a clearly promissory view, now arguably adopts a contractual option approach. In German law the promissory view was almost adopted when the BGB was enacted, but it lost out to a non-specific characterisation of the third party's right. Under English law, though the 1999 Act at no point states expressly that the third party is enforcing a promise conceived in its favour, the import of the Act would appear to be to that effect. Only in Scots law has the tradition clearly been that the third party is a direct recipient of a promise made to it, one arising upon delivery of the contract or when an equivalent to delivery occurs; in the other systems adopting a promissory view, it is arguable that the third party is, exceptionally, being given a right to enforce a promise made to the other contracting party, rather than to enforce a promise made directly to it, though this point seems not to have been explored sufficiently to draw any firm conclusions on the matter.

In each of the systems studied, it is clear that the impetus for the recognition of third party rights was in large part a concern that those who undertake to confer a benefit on a third party should be held to their word, with a secondary concern being to protect the third party's reliance placed upon the promise in its favour. The development of third party rights thus represents an equitable development of the law beyond the confines of the default rule that only parties to a contract derive rights under it. Such a development is laudable as upholding the intention of the promisor; less so are developments in some systems which have led to a protection of the performance interest of third parties through extensions to the law of tort. Such developments run the risk of blurring the boundaries between contract and tort, especially where quasi-promissory language such as 'assumption of responsibility' is used to describe non-voluntary tortious duties. The DCFR's approach marks a commendable way forward in this field of contract law.

4. Assignment

The relationship between third party rights narrowly so called (the subject of the discussion thus far) and assignment is a complex one. There is an evident similarity between the two institutions, in that both allow a third party to enforce rights under a contract. The distinction is that, with third party rights narrowly so called, the contracting parties intend to confer upon a non-contracting third party distinct rights of its own; in the case of assignment, one of the contracting parties forms an intention to transfer its own pre-existing rights to a third party, who takes the place of the transferor as holder of the rights in question. The distinction rests upon the intention of the parties, thus locating the essence of both doctrines in the will of the contracting parties. The answer to an enquiry as to which status was intended for a third party, that of assignee or tertius, ought therefore to depend upon a factual enquiry as to such intention.

An assignment (or assignation, cession, or transfer of rights, depending upon jurisdictional terminology), like donation, is a transfer of something (in the case of assignment, personal rights) to another party. Where it is duties rather than rights which are transferred, the terms 'delegation' or 'substitution of debtor' may be used, though one also encounters the term assignment being applied to transfers of debts.[101] Though any personal rights might be the subject of an assignment, in what follows the discussion will be restricted to contractual rights.

Considering the matter purely as one of principle, the question may be put whether a high regard for a strict enforcement of promises according to their terms ought to lead to a prohibition on assignment save by express agreement of the original contracting parties. On one view, it ought not. This view posits that a contractual right promised to a party forms part of that party's assets, and that one should be able to dispose freely of one's assets as one wishes, unless there are sound policy reasons for preventing such a free disposal. A claim which one has to a contractual performance ought therefore, on this view, to be as readily disposable as any other part of one's assets. This argument is persuasive to an extent, though it ignores the fact that the peculiar feature of a promise as an asset is that a promise is an undertaking of A's to perform in favour of B and (unless otherwise stipulated) B alone: it is not an undertaking of A to perform in favour of C or anyone else, and it seems irrelevant to A that B might wish C to receive the benefit of the pledged performance. Recognition of this special feature of promises as assets might be argued to mitigate against any free right to assign the benefits of a contractual performance to another

---

[101] The substitution of one debtor for another can alternatively be achieved by novation, though in that case the original debt is seen as being extinguished and replaced by a new debt.

person. In practice, however, many jurisdictions do permit transfers of rights by B in C's favour even without the consent of A, as will be seen from the discussion below. As for the delegation of duties, a duty is clearly not part of one's assets. In the case of delegation therefore, the case in principle for a general prohibition seems even stronger: if B promises A a performance, then it is B that is bound by that promise and B cannot expect to be released from such a promise simply by agreeing with C that C will perform the promise rather than B. Legal systems follow principle here, and are generally unwilling to allow substitutions of debtors without the consent of the creditor.

Classical Roman law did not permit assignment. Instead, two alternative routes were used to achieve an effect similar to assignment.[102] First, novation might be used: a creditor might authorise a debtor to undertake a fresh obligation to a third party, such obligation replacing the original duty. Second, a creditor could authorise someone to sue in his own name and to keep the proceeds of such legal claim, such a person being styled a *procurator in rem suam*. Neither method was ideal, though it preserved the integrity of the contracting parties' rights from interference by third parties. By the Justinianic period, assignees were given a right to sue on their own behalf by virtue of an *actio utilis*, though the apparent incompatibility of this form with the *procurator in rem suam* led some later civilian jurists to doubt whether the *actio utilis* genuinely permitted an assignee to claim in his own right.

In theory, one might view an assignment of rights simply as a unilateral act of transfer, protection against unwanted assignment being achieved by giving the assignee a right to reject the right assigned; on the other hand, assignment might be conceived of as a bilateral juridical act, requiring a declaration of the will of both parties to effect the transfer. Quite apart from the act of transfer itself, there might also be a prior promise or contract to assign contractual rights, that being an optional, prior juridical act separate from the juridical act of transfer itself.

As for transfers of duties in the modern law, given that the transferee is, through the act of transfer, having duties imposed upon him, there is great pressure, even in those systems which permit unilateral assignments of rights, for tolerating such a transfer of duties only by way of a consensual arrangement between transferor and transferee, as well as by requiring the consent of the creditor before the transfer of duties takes effect.

[102] See Zimmermann, *Law of Obligations*, pp. 60–2.

(a)   English law[103]

In modern English law, assignments are governed by section 136 of the Law of Property Act 1925, which stipulates that they must be constituted 'by writing under the hand of the assignor', though a failure to comply with this requirement (or the further requirement of written notification of the assignment by the assignor or assignee to the debtor) may nonetheless create an equitable assignment for which nothing more is required than an act which demonstrates the clear intention of the assignor to assign the rights in question.[104] An equitable assignment, which may be in any form, is undertaken either by intimation of the assignment by assignor to assignee, or by assignor requesting the debtor to perform in favour of the assignee.[105]

The nature of both assignments complying with the Law of Property Act as well as equitable assignments is therefore that of a unilateral judicial act undertaken by the assignor. While, in addition, intimation to the debtor is desirable for equitable assignments and required for statutory ones, the consent of either debtor or assignee is not (unless the contract or statute so specifies) required as a constitutive part of the assignment.

An assignment might, of course, be required by virtue of an obligation in a preceding contract between A and C requiring A to effect the assignation in C's favour, though if the circumstances permitting such an assignment in C's favour are the subject of control in A's contract with B, compliance with such controls will be necessary if the assignment is to be valid.[106]

(b)   The mixed legal systems

In Scotland, an assignation is a bilateral juridical act (though not a contract) requiring both an intentional conveyance of a claim by the cedent and acceptance of the assignation by the assignee.[107] In addition,

---

[103] See, on English law, Smith, *Law of Assignment*; Tolhurst, *The Assignment of Contractual Rights*.

[104] However, if the assignment is an equitable one, the debtor continues to receive a valid discharge of his debt through payment to the assignor rather than the assignee until notification of the assignment is made to him.

[105] See Beale, *Chitty on Contracts*, para. 19–021.

[106] *St Martin's Property Corporation Ltd* v. *Sir Robert McAlpine & Sons Ltd* [1994] 1 AC 85, [1993] 3 WLR 408, [1993] 3 All ER 417.

[107] Anderson, *Assignation*, para. 1–02.

intimation of the assignation to the debtor must be made by either assignor or assignee before the act of transfer is effected. The general rule is that (subject to any restrictions or prohibition in the contract) assignation is permitted, and that both the assignation and the intimation of it to the debtor may be constituted in any form. Thus an assignation might be made orally by the assignor (a simple statement such as 'I hereby assign all my rights under this contract to you' would suffice), or constituted in a handwritten or typed document, whether signed by the assignor or not. Formalities apply in the case of the assignation of certain types of right, principally real rights relating to land.[108] While the transfer of the rights may be preceded by a contract or unilateral promise by which the assignor undertakes to effect the assignation, that is not a requirement of a valid assignation. The act of transfer which constitutes the assignation of rights in Scots law is thus not itself promissory in nature, though it may be preceded by a promise to assign.

In South Africa, there is, as in Scotland and England, a general presumption in favour of cession (as South African law calls assignment) without the need for the debtor's consent, again subject to any agreed or statutory restrictions. The act of cession itself (often referred to as the *pactum cessionis*) is, as in Scotland, a type of bilateral juridical act, dependent therefore upon the declarations of will of both cedent (assignor) and cessionary (assignee). It is not, however, a contract, though it is characterised by both the intention of the cedent to effect the transfer and the concurrence in, or acceptance of, such act by the cessionary, and hence can be described as characterised by 'agreement' in a broad sense.[109] The principal difference from the Scottish approach is that notice to the debtor is not a requirement of the cessionary act, but merely something which acts as a precaution designed to prevent the debtor's performance to the wrong party. Cession may be preceded by, or occur simultaneously with, a contract of cession by which the cedent undertakes to effect the transfer, but this is not a necessary requirement. As in Scotland, therefore, the act of cession in South African law is not itself promissory in nature, even though it may be preceded by a contractual promise to effect the cession.

---

[108] Requirements of Writing (Scotland) Act 1995, s. 1(2)(a)(i), (b).

[109] See Scott, *Cession*, p. 7: 'As cession is an act of transfer, it is incorrect to refer to cession as a contract.' She notes (p. 8), however, that the act of cession is often embodied in the same document as the contract in terms of which the cedent undertakes to effect the transfer.

In Louisiana, the Civil Code provides[110] that all rights may be assigned save those 'pertaining to obligations which are purely personal', that is to say obligations which are intended to be enforceable only by a specific party or against a specific party,[111] though the right to assign a right may be excluded in the contract.[112] The codal provision further provides that the assignee 'is subrogated to the rights of the assignor against the debtor',[113] subrogation being defined[114] as 'the substitution of one person to the rights of another' either conventionally or legally. This, however, leaves unsettled the question of whether an assignment is seen as a bilateral (and possibly contractual) or unilateral juridical act. The answer appears to be that Louisiana law conceives of assignment as a contract, though such a conclusion requires to be pieced together from a number of observations: (i) the provisions on assignment are located within the title on sale, suggesting that assignment is conceived of as a kind of sale, sale being of course one specific type of contract; (ii) the current provisions on assignment derive from the provisions of the French Code on assignment[115] and, while those provisions are themselves unclear on the contractual nature of assignment, the secondary commentary to them makes the contractual analysis clear; (iii) Article 2649 of the Louisiana Code makes a tangential reference to the nature of assignment as a contract when it provides that when 'the assignor of a right did not warrant the solvency of the debtor but knew of his insolvency, the assignee without such knowledge may obtain rescission of the contract'; and (iv) there are several cases which similarly tangentially refer to assignment as a contract.[116] Taken together, these observations lead reasonably to the view that assignment in Louisiana is a contract, thus requiring the consent of both parties before it takes effect.

(c)   German law

German law requires that an assignment of rights (as well as a delegation of duties) be achieved via contract. §398 BGB provides that a 'claim may

---

[110] CC Art. 2642.
[111] 'Strictly personal obligations' are defined in CC Art. 1766. As an example of an obligation which is strictly personal on the part of the obligee, Art. 1766 mentions one where 'the performance is intended for the benefit of the obligee exclusively'.
[112] CC Art. 2653.   [113] CC Art. 2642.
[114] CC Art. 1825.   [115] Code civil Arts. 1689–1701.
[116] See, for instance, Succession of Delassize, 8 Rob. 259 (La 1844), in which, discussing proof of assignment, it was held that no writing was required since '[a]ll contracts which are not expressly required to be reduced to writing, can, we apprehend, be made verbally'.

be transferred by the obligee to another person by contract with that person', adding that the transfer takes effect at the point at which the contract of assignment is entered into. Such a contract of transfer is separate to any preceding contract for the assignment which may precede the latter contract of transfer. The contract of transfer however merely affects the position of the assignor and assignee inter se: until the debtor receives notification of the assignment, he remains free to tender performance to the assignor.[117] In other words, intimation of the assignment to the debtor is required to bring the assignee and debtor in to a formal relationship. Assignment may be prohibited by the parties in their contract.[118]

There is separate provision in the BGB for the transfer of duties, which again requires to be achieved under a contract,[119] as well as a further provision stipulating that any such transfer requires the ratification of the party to whom the debt is due before the transfer becomes effective.[120]

(d)   Model law

In the DCFR, the general rule is that all rights to performance are assignable unless otherwise provided by law.[121] Substitution of debtors is treated separately.[122] The general rule on assignment is worked out in a quite radical way through the further provision that a contractual prohibition or restriction on assignment does not prevent such assignment.[123] This puts the DCFR position at odds with the position in a number of national systems that the parties are free to prohibit assignment if they so stipulate in their contract and that such a prohibition is effective to prevent an assignment. The DCFR position may be argued to undermine the right of a promisor to determine the nature of the promise undertaken by it, in that it restricts the promisor's right to determine to whom the promise is to be performed. A sop to the freedom of the promisor to determine the nature of the right promised is offered by way of the fact that 'personal rights' may not be assigned unless with the permission of the creditor,

---

[117] §407(1) BGB.   [118] §399 BGB.   [119] §414 BGB.   [120] §415 BGB.

[121] Art. III.-5:105(1). The applicability of the regime on assignment only to rights of performance is somewhat limiting. For instance, in a case where A lets property to B, and B then sublets the property to C, a right in the lease between A and B entitling B to trigger arbitration in relation to a matter (such as whether the property is in need of repair by A) by an agreed arbiter would appear not to be able to be assigned to C, even if it might be C who has a direct interest in such an arbitration, because such a right is not to a 'right to performance' by A.

[122] See Arts. III.-5:201 to III.-5:209.   [123] Art. III.-5:108(1).

such personal rights being those 'to a performance which the debtor, by reason of the nature of the relationship between the debtor and creditor, could not reasonably be required to render to anyone except that creditor', but such a concession is not great and prevails in many jurisdictions anyway (it mirrors the rule of *delectus personae* in Scots law, and that affecting so-called 'personal contracts' in the Common law and Louisiana).

The DCFR requires that the assignee be entitled to the transfer by virtue of a contract or other juridical act,[124] and that the transfer occurs by means of a 'valid act of assignment'.[125] The act of assignment is in the form of a contract or another juridical act, and may be the same contract or act from which the assignee's entitlement to the transfer arose.[126] These rules on the act of assignment seem therefore to indicate the need either for a bilateral contractual form for the act of transfer, or conceivably a unilateral act of transfer (given the stipulation that the act may be by way of a juridical act other than a contract). This view that a unilateral act of assignment may be possible is bolstered by the fact that Article III.-5:110 states that the rules of Book II on the formation and validity of contracts and other juridical acts apply to acts of assignment. Those Book II rules encompass not just contract but also the provision generally giving legal effect to unilateral undertakings binding without acceptance. It would seem to follow from all of this then that in the DCFR regime an act of assignment could, if that were the intention of the transferor, be classed as a unilateral act of transfer not requiring the acceptance of the assignee. Such a unilateral juridical act would not, however, be a unilateral promise, as the transferor under such an act is undertaking a present transfer of rights rather than making a promise of a future transfer.

5.   The problem of transferred loss

(a)   English law

The *stipulatio alteri* is a promise obtained for another's benefit, a distinctive feature of such a promise being that it is the third party for whom the benefit of the promise was conceived upon whom title to sue is conferred. This title extends both to enforcing performance of the promise as well as to recovering damages in respect of any defective performance rendered.

---

[124] Art. III.-5:104(1)(d).   [125] Art. III.-5:104(1)(e).   [126] Art. III.-5:104(3).

In English law another type of promise benefitting a third party has exceptionally been recognised by the courts, though with such promises the third party is neither given a right to sue nor is it enforcement of the promise which is sought but rather damages suffered by the third party as a result of breach of the promise. This type of exceptional recovery has been referred to as 'transferred loss' recovery.[127]

Any recovery for a third party's losses in contract must be exceptional for the fundamental reason that the default rule for assessing the quantum of recoverable contractual damages by A under its contract with B is that only such losses of A as are reasonably foreseeable to B may be recovered by it. Both unforeseeable losses of A, as well as losses of any party other than A, fall outside this rule. The reason for the losses of other parties being excluded stems from the privity or 'parties only' rule of contract law. If only A gets rights under its contracts with B, to allow A to claim for another's losses would be to subvert that rule by potentially allowing C to claim through A and thus to derive, albeit tangentially, rights from a contract to which it is not a party.[128] Transferred loss claims clearly amount to a subversion of the rule and ought therefore to be permitted only for an overriding policy reason determined by the courts or implemented in relevant legislation. Such a policy reason has been held to be constituted by an equitable concern that contract breakers should not be permitted to escape liability for damage purely on account of a post-contractual division between two parties of title to sue and incidence of loss.

The circumstances in which a transferred loss claim has been thought permissible by the English courts may be stated as follows. Where A and B contract, and B's breach of contract causes loss to C (a third party who has no right under the contract to sue for those losses) but not to B (the party who has a right to sue under the contract but has suffered no loss), then A

---

[127] In English law, the term 'transferred loss' was first used by Robert Goff LJ (later Lord Goff of Chieveley) in *The Aliakmon* [1985] QB 350. See generally on this type of claim, Unberath, *Transferred Loss*.

[128] In *The Albazero* [1977] AC 774, Lord Diplock remarked (at 841) that the 'general rule' against recovering third party losses was not, in English law, one of great antiquity. His Lordship illustrated this remark by commenting that, until the early nineteenth century, a plaintiff in an action of assumpsit relating to non-delivery of goods was entitled to recover for the full value of the goods or the full amount of the damage, notwithstanding the fact that the goods were not his own and that he had sustained no loss himself as a result of the defendant's breach of contract. However, this remark on the alleged recent origins of the general rule fails properly to distinguish the history of actions of debt or *indebitatus assumpsit* (where loss to the plaintiff was indeed irrelevant) from actions of special assumpsit (where demonstration of loss by the plaintiff was required): see on the relevant history, Ibbetson, *A Historical Introduction*, pp. 148–51, 243–4.

and B may be taken to have entered into the contract on the basis that A
will be able to sue for C's losses on C's behalf. Two types of fact situation
have given rise to most transferred loss claims: (i) cases where goods are
committed to transit by an original owner of them (A), the goods being
damaged or destroyed in transit in breach of contract by the carrier (B) to
the loss of the new owner (C), and (ii) cases where a building is constructed
by a builder (B) for a customer (A), the building being sold as construction is ongoing to a third party buyer (C), who suffers loss when the building is subsequently discovered to be defective. In both such cases, A will
have received full value for the goods or building at the time of sale (no
damage or defect having yet arisen at that point), thus suffering no loss;
C, on the other hand, suffers the economic loss of getting damaged goods
or a defective building, but appears to have no claim against the carrier/
contractor as it is not in a contractual relationship with such party. The
concern of the courts in both such cases is that, if some route to recovery
by C is not found, losses which can be said to have 'transferred' from A
to C will fall into a so-called legal 'black hole', and the party which has
breached its contract will be allowed to escape the consequence of having
done so. Such a result is considered to be inequitable, and thus as meriting
a remedy. This equitable concern is similar to that which mandates recovery of third party losses in cases of bailment and of beneficiaries under
the trust over a promise, and which is operative in subrogation claims
by insurers, a similarity which it has been argued by Unberath indicates
that transferred loss cases in English law should not be seen as the unique
example of recovery for third party losses as some have suggested.[129]

A seemingly obvious way to achieve recovery in the problematic circumstances outlined in the previous paragraph would be for A to assign
its claim against B to C, thus ensuring that C has not only suffered a loss
but also possesses title to sue. However, before transferred loss recovery is
permitted such an assignment must be impossible, either because assignment is not permitted under the contract or because, though permitted,
B's consent is required for such an assignment and it is being lawfully
withheld (in such a case, any purported assignment by A will be invalid).
If assignment is not possible, then a further conceivable avenue could be
for C to argue that it is the third party beneficiary under a *stipulatio alteri*.
However, a problem with that potential route is that, in many cases, at

---

[129] See Unberath, *Transferred Loss*, pp. 143–63. Recovery for third party losses by a bailor is
one of the recognised cases of recovery in German law justified by reference to the principle of transferred loss: see later discussion in the main text at p. 331.

the time the contract was made no identifiable third party was intended
by both A and B as the recipient of an enforceable benefit under the contract. This is certainly so in typical cases of the consignation of goods,
or the construction of a building, subsequently sold to a third party. In
most jurisdictions, delict or tort is not likely to provide a solution either,
as the losses suffered by an owner of defective goods or a defective building will be treated as pure economic loss and thus likely to be irrecoverable. A more radical solution in contract, by which more than nominal
losses would be held to have been suffered by a claimant not by virtue of
any pecuniary effect upon that claimant but simply by virtue of the fact
that the claimant did not receive the bargained for performance, has not
found favour with the courts.[130] Given the difficulty of utilising any of
these different avenues of claim, the English courts developed transferred
loss claims as an equitable and exceptional type of claim which would
allow A to sue for C's losses.

Initially such an exceptional claim was permitted only in cases of
contracts for the carriage of goods sold by the owner while in transit but
subsequently damaged or lost by the carrier. The right of the former owner
to sue the carrier in such circumstances for the losses of the new owner[131]
was established in *The Albazero*.[132] The principle justifying recovery in
that case was described by Lord Diplock as being that

> in a commercial contract concerning goods where it is in the contem-
> plation of the parties that the proprietary interests in the goods may be
> transferred from one owner to another after the contract has been entered
> into and before the breach which causes loss or damage to the goods, an
> original party, if such be the intention of them both, is to be treated in law

---

[130] Such a radical reformation of the principle of the assessment of damages (subsequently
dubbed the 'broad approach') was suggested by Lord Griffiths in *St Martin's Property
Corporation Ltd* v. *Sir Alfred McAlpine & Sons Ltd* [1994] 1 AC 85, 96–97, and reiter-
ated by Lord Goff in *Alfred McApline Construction Ltd* v. *Panatown Ltd* [2001] 1 AC
518, 546–7. These two attempts to promote the broad approach have however not found
favour with the wider bench.

[131] Any direct claim which the new owner in *The Albazero* might have had under the bill
of lading had prescribed (after one year) in accordance with the relevant prescriptive
period specified under the Hague Rules of 1924 on the carriage of goods by sea.

[132] [1977] AC 774, [1976] 3 All ER 129. In the earlier nineteenth-century Scottish case,
Dunlop v. *Lambert* (1839) 6 Cl & F 600, (1839) Macl & R 663, which was highly influential in the minds of their Lordships in *The Albazero*, it had been suggested by Lord
Chancellor Cottenham that circumstances might arise where a consignor of goods was
permitted to sue in respect of loss of or damage to them without the need to demonstrate
ownership of the goods (and therefore, by implication, without the need to show any
losses which it had suffered).

as having entered into the contract for the benefit of all persons who have
or may acquire an interest in the goods before they are lost or damaged,
and is entitled to recover by way of damages for breach of contract the
actual losses sustained by those for whose benefit the contract is entered
into.[133]

It will be remarked from this description that a blend of elements from
both the *stipulatio alteri* (note the emphasis upon the parties' contemplation of a third party and of their intentions) and agency (note that the
non-breaching contracting party is said to have entered into a contract
for the benefit of others) is used in order to create an equitable solution
which amounts to neither a *stipulatio alteri* nor agency but rather to a new
solution for the specific third party problem raised by the facts.

Lord Diplock's summary of *The Albazero* principle suggests the following required elements to a claim:

(1) there must be a 'commercial contract' between A and B concern-
     ing goods (in fact, the strict ratio of the case does not extend beyond
     commercial contracts for the carriage of goods at sea);
(2) both parties must 'contemplate' the possible sale of the goods by A to
     C at a point after formation of the A–B contract but before breach by
     B. Note therefore that, unlike a *stipulatio alteri*, no definite intention
     that there be a third party who will have rights is necessary, merely a
     contemplation that there *might* be such a third party; and
(3) both parties must 'intend' that, where such a sale takes place, A will
     be treated as having entered into the contract with B 'for the benefit
     of' *all* persons (not just C, but conceivably further buyers D, E, etc.)
     who may acquire an interest in the goods before they are damaged or
     lost.

If (1) – (3) apply, then A is entitled (though note, is not forced)[134] to recover
C's (or D's etc.) contractual losses on its behalf. The elements to the claim
are quite narrow. There is, for instance, no question of the principle being
applicable to the recovery of damage arising out of a tort committed by B
which happens to harm C, or for a breach of contract by B which causes A
loss but, also, in addition, further loss to B.

---

[133] Lord Diplock, [1977] AC at 847.
[134] This marks a distinction with German law, to be discussed below, where the courts have
said that C may compel A to transfer its claim to C, thereby ensuring that its interests
are protected. The reliance, in English law, of C upon A's willingness to raise the claim is
clearly a weak link in the protection afforded to C.

No mention is made in Lord Diplock's remarks of how C will recover these losses from A, but later decisions have held that A holds any recovered damages in trust for C.[135] It is obvious, however, that a crucial element to the claim described by Lord Diplock is A's and B's joint intention to allow A to claim on behalf of C. But how is such an intention to be judged? Is one to have regard to the express contract terms and thus attempt to judge the actual intention of the parties? Or does the mere possibility of an onward sale by A to C justify an inference that A and B must have intended to give A the right to sue for C's losses unless there is some contra-indication against such an inference? When *The Albazero* was decided there was no possibility in English law of C being the beneficiary under a *stipulatio alteri*, but now that such a status is possible for C it will, in the absence of any express statement in the contract, be a difficult task for a court to decide whether A and B intended C to be a tertius (and thus gain a direct right to sue for any losses) or whether they intended only that A might sue on behalf of C.

The problem raised in *The Albazero* of loss caused during shipment to a new owner of goods having no contractual title to sue for the loss was subsequently addressed in the Carriage of Goods by Sea Act 1992, which provided a statutory footing for a claim by the contracting party on the new owner's behalf.[136] However, the common law principle developed in *The Albazero* did not disappear with the passage of the Act.[137] In fact, the principle was later extended beyond cases concerning goods damaged in transit to cases of a defective building erected under a contract between A and B, ownership of which building is transferred by A to C together with a purported but invalid assignment by A of its rights under the contract with B. This extension of the transferred loss exception was effected in *St Martin's Property Corporation Ltd v. Sir Robert McAlpine & Sons Ltd.*[138] In that case, a building was sold by A to C for full value, so that A suffered no loss when the building was discovered to be defective. However, the

---

[135] This was the view taken by the Court of Appeal in *Darlington Borough Council* v. *Wiltshier Northern Ltd* [1995] 1 WLR 68. An alternative would be to see a claim as lying in unjustified enrichment.

[136] The Carriage of Goods by Sea Act 1992, s. 2(4).

[137] The statutory remedy under the 1992 Act is, for instance, inapplicable to cases in which there is no bill of lading relating to the goods. Moreover, *The Albazero* common law remedy remains of continued potential use in cases of carriage of goods by land which result in transferred loss.

[138] [1994] 1 AC 85, [1993] 3 WLR 408, [1993] 3 All ER 417 (HL). Similarities may be drawn between such circumstances and the German cases of indirect representation discussed in the main text below at p. 331.

purported but invalid assignment[139] of A's contractual rights potentially opened A up to liability in damages for breach of contract with C: why was this potentially substantial loss on A's part not claimable by A as actual losses of its own against B? The House of Lords took the view that this was because such losses would be unforeseeable so far as B was concerned, and therefore irrecoverable (B could not be expected to have foreseen that A would fail to seek its permission for the assignment, as the contract required). As on these facts, C's losses potentially fell into the same sort of black hole as in the cases of the consignment of goods, their Lordships decided to extend *The Albazero* exception to the facts of the case before them.

The principle so extended to the *St Martin's* facts was, however, analysed differently in two respects (quite apart from the extension of the principle beyond the field of carriage of goods by sea) to the analysis adopted in *The Albazero*:

(1) The rationale for the claim was said in *St Martin's* to rest upon the 'presumed intention' of A and B that A would be treated as having a right to sue on C's behalf, rather than on an actual intention that that be so, as Lord Diplock had required in *The Albazero*. This might at first glance be thought to be an improvement on the earlier formulation, as discovering actual intention in such cases is likely to be a difficult, if not fruitless exercise. However, even the reference to a presumed intention faces two objections. First, in *St Martin's* Lord Browne-Wilkinson comes close to suggesting that such an intention could be presumed from the fact that the project was a 'large development of property which ... was going to be occupied, and possibly purchased, by third parties and [A]'.[140] This suggests that a small development might not have benefited from the presumption. It also suggests that the mere possibility of a sale to some third party founds the intention, but such a possibility must surely exist in almost all developments with the result that the requisite intention will be nearly universally assumed. Such a position suggests that presumed intention is being used as a mask for an underlying but unexpressed judicial policy. Second, in *St Martin's* the parties had *expressly* intended a means by which a party in C's shoes might acquire rights, namely the assignment provided for (but not effectively undertaken) in the contract.

---

[139] The assignment was invalid because B's consent to it had not been obtained, as the contract between A and B required. This rendered the assignment invalid.

[140] [1994] 1 AC at 114.

Given such an express intention to permit assignment as a means of conferring rights upon C, C's acquiral of rights via the route of a claim by A on C's behalf was arguably contrary to this express intention regarding third party rights. If the parties had wanted A to be allowed to sue on behalf of C, why include an assignment clause in the contract? This argument shows up the weakness in basing transferred loss analysis on the will and intention of the parties. A better solution would be to recognise that entitlement to a transferred loss claim rests upon legal policy. This was indeed recognised by Lord Clyde in the subsequent transferred loss case of *Alfred McAlpine Construction Ltd v. Panatown Ltd*,[141] who said of the *Albazero* principle that 'it is preferable to regard it as a solution imposed by the law and not as arising from the supposed intention of the parties, who may in reality not have applied their minds to the point.'[142]

(2) The second difference from *The Albazero* was the focus on the question of the invalid assignment. In Lord Diplock's judgment in *The Albazero*, there is no mention of the subject of a possible assignment of the charterer's claim under the charterparty, and no consideration of whether, on the facts, that party might have assigned its right under the contract of charterparty to the new owner of the goods as an alternative to claiming damages on the new owner's behalf.[143] Assignment was at issue in *St Martin's*, however, and such an assignment was attempted unsuccessfully. This makes a remark by one of the judges in *St Martin's*, Lord Browne-Wilkinson, somewhat puzzling: his Lordship stated that it was proper to permit a transferred loss remedy because C was a party 'who, under the terms of the contract, could not acquire any right to hold [B] liable for breach'.[144] Such a statement is factually incorrect: C could certainly have acquired a right of its own to sue for its losses had the procedure for effecting a valid assignment been followed by A. In arguing for the equities of fashioning the remedy which their Lordships did, the plaintiff's disability appears to have been exaggerated by Lord Browne-Wilkinson.

---

[141] [2001] 1 AC 518 (HL).

[142] [2001] 1 AC 518, at 530. The same legal policy analysis was adopted in a Scottish transferred loss case: see the judgment of Lord Drummond Young in *McLaren Murdoch & Hamilton Ltd* v. *The Abercromby Motor Group Ltd* (2003) SCLR 323 (CSOH) at para. 42.

[143] The judgments in the case at the lower levels do however narrate that any direct claim by the new owner of the cargo under the bill of lading had prescribed (though no such claim had in any event been raised).

[144] [1994] 1 AC at 114.

Assignment was certainly, in theory, an alternative, though one which A had failed properly to utilise.

The possibility of an assignment in the latter case somewhat throws doubt on whether there was any absolute need to apply the *Albazero* principle to the *St Martin's* facts; the better result may have been simply to refuse the claim, on the basis that A had had a way of benefiting C (through assignment) which it simply failed properly to exercise. Subsequently, in *Panatown* the House of Lords held that there was no sufficient reason to extend the *Albazero* principle to a case where the third party had an alternative means of suing under a collateral warranty in its favour relating to defects in a building. On the other hand, in *Darlington Borough Council* v. *Wiltshier Northern Ltd*[145] a transferred loss claim by a financial intermediary which had never been the owner of the defective building was permitted, thus arguably extending the field of application of the principle in construction cases to any circumstances where A is indirectly representing C.[146] With such an extension of the principle, it is the idea of transferred loss alone which seems capable of explaining the variety of cases said to be explicable by reference to the *Albazero* principle.

A transferred loss claim was not permitted in *Panatown* because such a claim was held to be the exception, not available where another avenue of recovery existed (even if that other avenue was potentially less remunerative to the third party). It is clear from the cases that if, on the facts of a case, an assignment, a third party right claim in contract, a tort claim,[147] or a claim under a collateral warranty is available,[148] the courts will insist that such an alternative avenue is utilised. This seems a reasonable conclusion given that transferred loss is seen as an equitable gap-filler (closing a deemed legal loophole or black hole), whereas directly enforceable third party rights, while also an exception to the privity or parties only rule, are not conceived of in such an exceptional manner, but as deriving from the intention of the parties.

It has been argued in the foregoing discussion that the preferable characterisation for a transferred loss claim is not as one which stems from

---

[145] [1995] 1 WLR 68. Similarities may be drawn between such a case and the German cases of indirect representation discussed in the main text below at p. 331.

[146] If the representation were direct, then the circumstances would be those of agency.

[147] In *Riyad Bank* v. *Ahli United Bank (UK) plc* [2006] EWCA Civ 780, [2006] 2 Lloyd's Rep 292, the Court of Appeal held it unnecessary to consider a transferred loss claim against the defendants as they were in any event found liable in tort.

[148] As was the case in *Alfred McAlpine* v. *Panatown*.

the express or presumed intention of the parties, but rather as a policy-based exceptional deviation from the ordinary compensatory principle of the assessment of damages. The exception is based upon a judicial policy of preventing loss caused by a breaching party from being unclaimable merely on account of the division of the elements of loss and title to sue between two parties, the loss being borne by a party other than that which would have borne it before such division. Transferred loss is not thus promissory based: the third party is *not* the recipient of any promise, nor is the contracting party enforcing a promise made in favour of such third party. Rather, the third party is simply the beneficiary of a very limited policy exception to the default rule that a party may only claim for its own losses in contract. Though the promissory idea is a useful one in relation to *stipulationes alteri*, it cannot explain every aspect of contractual claims to benefit third parties.

(b)   The mixed legal systems

Little needs to be said on Scots law and transferred loss, as it is a subject which has hardly been litigated upon. Despite a relative dearth of authority, the Scottish courts have nonetheless recognised and awarded damages based upon transferred loss reasoning,[149] and in so doing have expressly followed the English authorities discussed above (as well as referring to the nineteenth-century Scottish case of *Dunlop* v. *Lambert*[150]). It should perhaps be added that there are some cases where conceivably, given the priority given to performance over damage in Scotland, an order of specific implement might be sought by A against B in preference to a damages claim, thereby obviating the need for reliance upon the transferred loss principle. Such an alternative would not, of course, be possible in the case of the complete loss of goods in transit, though it might be more feasible in some cases of defective buildings.

South Africa does not recognise transferred loss claims at common law, and insists that, under its contract with B, A is permitted only to sue in respect of its own losses. However, as with the similar statutory development in the UK, relatively recent legislation has addressed the specific problem raised on the facts of *The Albazero*. Section 4 of The Sea Transport Documents Act[151] provides that the holder of a sea transport

---

[149] *McLaren Murdoch & Hamilton Ltd* v. *The Abercromby Motor Group Ltd* 2003 SCLR 323 (CSOH).
[150] (1839) 6 Cl & F 600, (1839) Macl & R 663.   [151] No. 65 of 2000.

document such as a bill of lading is entitled to the same rights against the party issuing the document (usually the owner of the ship, or its agent) as if it were a party to a contract with that person on the terms of the document, and is furthermore to be regarded as a cessionary (that is, assignee) of all rights of action for loss of or damage to the goods referred to in such a document, whether arising from the contract of carriage, ownership of the goods, or otherwise. This provision would have allowed the new owner of the goods in *The Albazero* to have had a direct claim against the shipowner, thus obviating the need for the exceptional transferred loss claim permitted by the House of Lords. This statutory provision is limited to the field of carriage of goods by sea, however, and would thus evidently fail to protect a third party to a construction contract (such as the new owner of the building in *St Martin's*).

In Louisiana, the Civil Code enshrines the principle that damages in contract are to compensate both the creditor's actual losses (*damnum emergens*) as well as his loss of expected profit (*lucrum cessans*).[152] The provision makes no reference to a right, even exceptionally, to claim in respect of the losses of any other party. Moreover, in the particular case of carriage of goods at sea, the US Carriage of Goods by Sea Act[153] (applicable in all the states of the US) contains no provision equivalent to that in the UK's Carriage of Goods by Sea Act specifying for third party damage claims in respect of goods, though it does contain a permissive provision entitling carrier and shipper to agree 'any terms as to the responsibility and liability of the carrier for such goods', such terms conceivably encompassing one allowing the shipper to claim in respect of third party losses.

(c)   German law

In German law, there is no provision in the BGB for transferred loss (or *Drittschadensliquidation* as it is called), but a body of case law has grown up recognising the doctrine as an exception to the ordinary rule that a creditor may sue to protect its own interest alone.[154] The claim has been described as being available where 'all the damage due to the harmful conduct of the obligor is suffered by a third party rather than by the person with title to sue', and only so in such cases where there is one injury, suffered by the third party, which would have been suffered by the promisee but which has shifted to the third party as a result of the contractual

---

[152] CC Art. 1995.   [153] 28 USC §1306 concerns agreements as to particular goods.
[154] See Unberath, *Transferred Loss*, pp. 85–91.

interest vesting in that third party.[155] The similarities with the English legal idea of transferred loss is notable. As in English law, it is A who sues for damages on behalf of C, A being required to account to C for the damages recovered. The German courts have also said, however, that an alternative conception is to regard C as being entitled to require A to assign its right to sue for damages to C, something which comes close to a subrogation of A's claim. If this were seen as a general entitlement, it would be hard to reconcile with a more limited right of assignment which might exist under a contract, such as the limited right which existed in the *St Martin's* case. However, the courts have not settled on a single description of transferred loss claims to the exclusion of all others.

As in England, development of third party claims has tended to cluster around certain fact situations. Three principal groups of case have emerged, those being: (1) claims in relation to the transportation of goods, decided cases in this class having typically related to claims by cargo owners in cases of carriage of goods by land for the benefit of a third party,[156] claims by the forwarder of goods against the carrier in respect of losses suffered by the consignor or consignee,[157] and claims against carriers of goods by sea in respect of losses suffered by third parties having an interest in the goods (such as a new owner of the goods);[158] (2) claims in respect of damage to goods which are the subject of a contract of bailment;[159] and (3) claims arising out of so-called 'indirect representation' (*mittelbare Stellvertretung*), such as claims by an agent under a contract of commission for losses suffered by his principal[160] and claims in some construction scenarios,[161] sufficiently akin to the English construction cases discussed earlier to suggest that, in similar circumstances to those English cases, the German courts would also apply transferred loss analysis.[162] Recovery in circumstances other than these three types of case is controversial, the courts being cautious about adding to the exceptions.[163]

Unlike in English law, transferred loss claims in German law are not seen as a last recourse, available only where no other claim is possible. In

---

[155] See for these statements of the nature of the claim, BGHZ 40, 91.

[156] In this type of case, *Drittschadensliquidation* has been entrenched in a provision of the HGB (§421).

[157] For instance, RGZ 75, 169; 115, 419; BGH NJW 1989, 3099.

[158] For instance, BGHZ 25, 250.   [159] BGH NJW 1985, 2411.

[160] The principal has a right to have the agent's claim assigned to him: §384(2) HGB.

[161] BGH NJW 1972, 288; BGH VersR 1972, 274.

[162] So argues Unberath, *Transferred Loss*, p. 222.   [163] BGHZ 133, 36.

many of the factual circumstances which might justify a transferred loss claim, an alternative claim in tort might be available to the third party for its loss.[164] A further contrast with English law might be said to lie in the preference given by German law, as with Scots law, to performance remedies. This has the effect that there are circumstances where the question of damages simply does not arise, the party in default being required to remedy its breach (or opting so to remedy, as it may sometimes do under German law[165]). This may be one reason why a case like *St Martin's* has not, as yet, arisen in German law.

Sensibly, it is suggested, German law has moved away from an earlier analysis of transferred loss claims as resting upon the supposed intention of the parties, said to give rise to an implied term that third party losses would be recoverable,[166] in favour of the view that objective policy requirements mandate transferred loss claims.[167] It was argued earlier that English law would do well to entrench an emerging similar view.

6.   Conclusion on third parties

As the discussion in this chapter has shown, there is quite a diverse treatment in the jurisdictions studied in the treatment of third parties to a contract. A universal phenomenon, however, even in systems like Roman law with a clear antipathy if not objection to the rights of third parties, is the invention by contracting parties of ways to avoid legal restrictions on conferring rights on third parties. The reason for such party-led developments is clear: contracting parties wish to be able to benefit third parties and will take whatever steps they can, using any available institutions and rules, to see that their will is given effect to. Even in those systems where third parties have historically been viewed with suspicion, the law has been forced to respond to the evident desire to benefit such third parties by (sometimes grudgingly) developing the law: so, for instance, because the right of legal representation in Roman law through appointment of a *procurator in rem suam* could not meet the needs of commerce, the concepts of agency and cession were developed. Development of a right given to an extra-contractual third party to enforce in its own name a benefit conceived in its favour required a longer period of gestation, but the

---

[164]   BGH NJW 1985, 2411.   [165]   See for instance, §635 BGB.

[166]   See for examples of the subjective, intention view of transferred loss liability, RGZ 170, 246 and BGHZ 15, 224.

[167]   BGHZ 40, 91.

importance attached by the canon law to the keeping of one's word, and thus to enforcement of promises made even in favour of third parties, justified the eventual development of the *stipulatio alteri*, albeit very belatedly in the Common law. As has been discussed, it is possible – though not the reality in every system – to view such a directly enforceable third party right in promissory terms. The same, however, cannot be said of assignment or transferred loss claims, their having the alternative classifications noted above.

That not every case where a third party derives a benefit from a contracting party should be seen in promissory terms is unsurprising. The very fact that a third party is *not* a party to the contractual relationship from which an alleged right derives should already suffice to indicate that any right which it might derive from the relationship might take one of a number of forms, perhaps promissory, but equally perhaps tortious, restitutionary, or sui generis in nature, depending upon the precise circumstances of the connection. In the same way, the variety of types of third party rights have no invariable connection with the idea of detrimental reliance or the conferment of a benefit. *Some* such rights, such as certain tort claims, depend upon a demonstration of reliance by a third party, but not all do; the same may be said of the receipt of a benefit, for whilst it has some relevance to the establishment of certain third party rights, that is not invariably so. The idea of a third party right, in the widest sense of that term, is simply too extensive to attract a single obligational classification. That does not mean, however, that promise cannot provide a useful and appropriate characterisation of certain types of third party right. In the case of the *stipulatio alteri*, it has been suggested that it can.

6

Contractual remedies

The field of remedies provides fertile ground for analysing whether legal systems have a high regard for the promises made by parties to a contract, or indeed the promises made by a unilateral promisor (the same remedies generally being available for such promises), or whether instead what is sought is the achievement of goals other than promissory ones.

One would expect a high regard for promise in any legal system to be reflected both in a ready availability of remedies designed to secure actual enforcement of what has been promised (whether the performance promised was an act or forbearance from an act) as well as in substitutionary remedies which reflect, so far as is possible in substitutionary form, the so-called 'performance interest' of the parties (as defined below). If, however, enforcement of performance is an exceptional remedy, or if substitutionary remedies do not achieve the equivalent of enforcement but protect instead some other interest of the promisee, doubts must be raised as to whether a high regard for the value of promise is a hallmark of the system in question.

The issue of what requires to occur before remedies may be claimed for breach of promise also deserves attention. In Common law and mixed legal systems, it is generally the case that any failure to comply strictly with the terms of a promise will trigger the availability of the remedy of damages, but termination is confined to cases where deviation from the promise has been substantial. By contrast, in German law, for instance, fault requires to be present before damages are available, yet the right to terminate is not tied to the severity of breach. Systems can appear to give out mixed messages regarding the value accorded to promises, something which is discussed further below in relation to specific remedies.

1. The 'interests' protected by remedies

There are a number of so-called 'interests' protected in the law of obligations, and these interests may conceivably be protected through various judicial remedies, notably specific performance, damages and restitution following termination. Though it is possible to frame definitions of such interests purely in relation to breach of contract (as, for instance, Fuller and Perdue did in their seminal article[1] on contractual damages), it is suggested that it makes more sense to attempt to define the relevant interests in a way which allows them to be used across the field of obligations. That being the case, the following three interests are suggested as the fundamental interests of parties protected in the law of obligations:[2]

(1) *performance interest*: the interest B has in having its position improved through an expected performance to be rendered by A. Such an expected performance might be due either under a contract or a unilateral promise, but should not be applicable in the case of a tort/delict. The performance interest is the primary interest protected by contract, though the other two interests defined below are protected in many systems in some contractual circumstances. The term performance interest is preferable to 'expectation interest', as expectation is a term which can conceivably be used to describe any of the various interests protected in the law, because, for instance, a party may 'expect' to receive the gains made by another through an unjustified enrichment (the restitutionary interest), or may 'expect' to be restored to the position it was in before harm was culpably done to it (the restoration interest). Given then that the term 'expectation' may cause confusion, 'performance interest' is suggested as the preferable term. It is the performance interest which most clearly embodies the values and goals of promising, given that a promise is an obligation which embodies a duty of performance in favour of another. The extent to which any legal system's rules concerning remedies are therefore geared, as far as possible, towards support of the performance interest will justify a description of it as pro-promissory or not, as the case may be.

(2) *restoration (or status quo ante) interest*: the interest B has in being restored to the position it was in prior to loss caused by the conduct of A. This is the primary interest protected by tort/delict and *negotiorum gestio*, as well as being a secondary interest protected in some cases of breach of contract.[3] Note that the interest so defined is wider than the

---

[1] Fuller and Perdue, 'The Reliance Interest in Contract Damages'.
[2] The scheme suggested here is one which I previously set out in *Obligations*, paras. 1.34–9.
[3] This interest is of particular relevance to the discussion in this chapter of damages claims for wasted contractual expenditure.

so-called 'reliance interest' coined by Fuller and Perdue, which they defined as being concerned only with losses suffered through change of position in reliance on a promise.[4] The terms 'reliance interest' and 'reliance damages', quite therefore apart from describing a narrower field than that encompassed by the concept of 'restoration interest' suggested here, are also apt to confuse: given that we can be said to be entitled to 'rely' on performance occurring under a contract, the idea of reliance could therefore be argued to encompass the protection of an expected performance, but that would lead to confusion with the performance interest. The term 'reliance interest' is thus best avoided.

(3) *restitutionary (or disgorgement) interest*: the interest B has in gains made by A. This is the interest usually protected by unjustified enrichment, either through restitution of property in the hands of B to A or in a monetary award reflecting gains made by A at B's expense. The interest may also, very exceptionally, be protected under contract, though not every system permits gains made by A to be claimed following termination or other failure of contract.

The above suggested names and definitions of the relevant interests protected by the law of obligations differ from those suggested previously by others. Fuller and Perdue, as noted earlier, suggested their own scheme with the US Common law in mind, but did so solely for the purposes of analysing contract damages. In German law, it is common to distinguish the 'negative' (or 'reliance') interest (often conceived along the lines of Fuller and Perdue's concept) from the 'positive' (or 'expectation') interest, the restitutionary interest (not protected in German contract law), and also an 'interest in the integrity of one's rights' (*Integritätsinteresse*), violation of which entitles the aggrieved party to be 'put into a position in which he would now have been had the violation of the interest not occurred'.[5] This interest appears very similar to the restoration interest as defined here, as it seeks to put a party into the position it would have been in had violation of its interest(s) not occurred. Indeed, examples sometimes given of types of loss it might protect against – for instance, personal injury caused by defective goods, or losses caused by poor performance of services to other property owned by the party suffering the breach[6] – are things that would naturally seem to fall under the restoration interest. Only if the 'reliance interest' is defined as purely concerning damages suffered in reliance on

[4] See Fuller and Perdue, 'The Reliance Interest in Contract Damages', p. 53.
[5] Markesinis *et al.*, *German Law of Contract*, p. 469.   [6] *Ibid.*, p. 471.

the contract is there a need to have a further 'integrity interest' to deal with such cases.

There is, however, no one objectively correct set of terms or definitions for the interests protected by the law. Different schemes might equally be capable of explaining the results produced by the courts. It does seem, however, that a scheme like Fuller and Perdue's, conceived only with damages for breach of contract in mind, is too narrow, given that there are types of contractual remedy other than damages, and that there is an increasing tendency in all jurisdictions to consider the field of obligations in the round. It would be preferable to suggest a scheme which can be used across the field of obligations. That being so, the scheme suggested here may commend itself. Whatever scheme is used, however, the important thing for present purposes is to be able to identify whether the remedial regime in different jurisdictions is supportive of the value of promises. To explore whether that is so, the classification suggested above will be adopted, though competing classifications would be likely to produce the same conclusions.

2. Mutuality of promises and withholding of performance

Is A entitled to withhold performance under its promise because B has not performed a promise made by it in favour of A?[7] Such an entitlement (sometimes referred to under Roman law's *exceptio non adimpleti contractus*) will usually be held to exist if performance of A's duty is conditional or contingent on performance of B's ('I promise to do *x* if you do *y*'), if that is, to put it another way, the relevant promises of the parties are mutual, synallagmatic, or reciprocal (the terms may be used interchangeably). If such mutuality characterises an undertaking, then it is perfectly consistent with respect for the nature of the promise in question to allow the promisor *not* to perform if the condition of counter-performance has not been met, given that all such a course of action does is to construe the promise strictly according to its conditional nature. On the other hand, if mutuality is not a characteristic of the undertaking, then respect for the nature of the promise suggests that the promisor should be compelled to perform absolutely, this again doing no more than holding the promisor to the promise according to its unconditional nature. As will be seen

---

[7] Evidently this issue does not arise in the case of gratuitous contracts (in those jurisdictions where such contracts are permitted), as in such contracts the promisor is not entitled to any counter-performance.

below, however, in German law at least, a promisor may even be entitled to avoid performance of an unconditional promise simply because an independent promise made by the promisee arising out of the same legal relationship has not been performed.

A condition or contingency might be made explicit (as where an express promise exists to the effect that 'I promise to do x on condition that you do y') or it might be held to be implicit from the relationship of the parties, as for instance it often is with regard to the primary duties in contracts of sale.

Some legal systems consider cases where there is held to be a mutuality of parties' promises under a contract as demonstrating the existence of a 'principle' of mutuality of contract. However, in systems where such a legal principle exists, strictly speaking it is a principle of the mutuality of *obligation* rather than of the mutuality of the contract in general, because the reciprocity relates to specific obligations (in the sense of pairings of duties) under the contract rather than to all of the obligations. It has quite rightly been judicially remarked that there is

> a danger of focusing on the expression 'mutuality of contract' rather than on 'mutuality of obligation' ... Within a single contract, there may be obligations which are mutually dependent upon each other and can truly be described as reciprocal. There may also be within that single contract an obligation, or obligations, in respect of which there is no direct recip-rocal counterpart.[8]

This comment is a useful reminder that not every duty on one side of a contract may have a counterpart on the other side of the relationship.

The idea of mutuality of obligation does not itself tell us, however, whether there are or ought to be any presumptions entertained by a legal system as to whether, and if so which, duties on one side will be held to be the counterpart of duties on the other. A legal system might conceivably adopt one of a number of positions in relation to the question of how the principle of obligational mutuality will operate in relation to individual contracts:

(1) there may be no presumption in law as to the mutuality or reci-procity of terms in specific contracts, it being entirely a matter for the parties to such a contract whether, and if so which, promises on the one side are the counterparts of promises on the other, and it

---

[8] Lord Clarke, in *Inveresk plc* v. *Tullis Russell Papermakers* [2009] CSIH 56.

being for the party bringing any claim to prove what the intention of the parties was;

(2) the independence of contract terms may be presumed, that is to say it may be presumed that no specific obligation on the one side is the counterpart of any specific obligation on the other, it being for the party bringing any claim to overturn such a presumption if it so wishes and is so able;

(3) 'general mutuality' may be presumed, which is to say that all the obligations on one side may be deemed to be the counterpart of all the obligations on the other side, such that failure to perform any obligation by A would give the right to B to withhold any or all of the obligations on its side; or

(4) 'targeted mutuality' may be presumed, which is to say that specific obligations on A's part may be deemed to be the counterpart of specific obligations on B's part, so that only breach of specifically countervailing obligations would give rise to a right to withhold performance. How presumed targeting would operate, that is to say, how precisely the presumed pairings of obligations would be determined, would usually be expected to depend on the type or class of contract in question (for instance, sale, employment, and so forth).

Conceivably a mixture of approach (3) and (4) may operate, by applying general mutuality except in the case of certain types of contract, where targeted mutuality could apply. For instance, if mutuality were to be presumed generally, it might thus apply in the case of a lump-sum contract, where a number of tasks were to be performed in exchange for a single sum of money, but targeted mutuality could be presumed in contracts for staged works, those being contracts where various tasks are each to be performed in stages in exchange for a specified portion of the overall price, in which case each portion would be presumed to be the counterpart only of the specific task for which it was to be tendered.

In applying the idea of mutuality of obligation, it is usually significant when performance falls due under a contract. If a promisor is required to perform its promise ahead of the other party's counter-performance, then such a promisor must perform first and can have no justifiable reason for withholding performance, unless it is by virtue of a jurisdictional rule that a reasonable apprehension that the other party is going to be unable to perform allows the withholding of performance.

The question of the position adopted by various jurisdictions is now considered.

(a)   The Common law

In English law, despite the existence of the requirement of consideration – a requirement about the need for *mutual* consideration – no independent doctrine of mutuality as such exists in the modern law. There does exist, however, a classification of contract terms into conditions precedent, concurrent conditions and independent promises, intended to deal with the question posed above of whether performance may ever justifiably be withheld by a promisor. This classification hinges on the proper interpretation of the intended nature of the promise in question. There is no general, default rule about the mutuality of terms, or the order of performance of terms, though certain presumptions have been developed through precedent and under legislation over time.

Under the English classification, a contract term is a 'condition precedent' if the duty it embodies must be fulfilled in order for a duty on the other side to become exigible. As explained above, such conditionality may be expressly stated ('I promise to do x if and only if you do y'), but it may also be inferred from the conduct and statements of the parties.[9] On the other hand, the promise of each party may fall due concurrently, so that neither A nor B need perform the relevant duty until the other performs as well, and neither may withhold performance on the basis that the other is supposed to perform first. Finally, a contractual promise on the one side will be independent of a promise on the other if the former promise may be enforced even though the latter has been breached. Which position is to prevail in respect of a particular contract term is a matter for the parties, though certain presumptions applicable to different types of contract exist, either as a result of judicial decision or statutory provision. Thus, in sales of goods contracts, delivery of the goods and payment of the price are concurrent conditions,[10] whereas in leases the duty of the tenant to pay the rent and the duty of the landlord to undertake repairs to the property are promises independent of the other.[11]

Because the third position, that of independent promises, creates a risk for a party that it may have to perform even if the other has breached (leaving it only with the route of raising a claim against the party in breach), English courts have been reticent to reach the conclusion that

---

[9] *Trans Trust SPRL* v. *Danubian Trading Co.* [1952] 2 QB 297.
[10] Sale of Goods Act 1979, s. 28.
[11] Beale, *Chitty on Contracts*, para. 21–038. However, in a case of a breach by a landlord of his duty to undertake repairs, the tenant may be entitled to an equitable set-off of the rent due.

such a position was intended by the parties,[12] preferring to hold, in cases of doubt, that, where simultaneous performance is possible, the parties must have intended concurrent performance (unless a promise is very minor, in which case it may be classified as an independent promise[13]). This preference, in cases of doubt, for favouring an interpretation of intended simultaneous performance is also the position adopted in §234(1) of the US Restatement (Second) of Contract.

(b) Mixed legal systems

The mixed legal systems, drawing upon their civilian heritage, operate local forms of the *exceptio non adimpleti contractus*. Its use is subject to control, either by reference to the severity of the breach of the party in default or by reference to an equitable control which is not unlike the restraints on withholding of performance which applies in civilian countries as a result of the doctrine of good faith.

In Scotland it is is generally asserted that onerous contracts are governed by the principle of mutuality, but the issue of whether a specific obligation of a contract is the counterpart of a specific obligation on the other side is a question of the intention of the parties. There has been some debate over the past fifteen years or so as to whether or not a presumption of general mutuality of terms exists in respect of all onerous contracts. In a decision of the House of Lords in 1998, *Bank of East Asia Ltd* v. *Scottish Enterprise*,[14] no such presumption was held to exist. However, more recently, following a number of judgments in favour of such a presumption[15] and another against,[16] the Supreme Court reassessed the earlier view of the House of Lords and held in its decision in *Inveresk plc* v. *Tullis Russell Papermakers Ltd*[17] that in every case 'the analysis should start from the position that all the obligations that [a contract] embraces are to be regarded as counterparts of each other unless there is a clear indication to the contrary'.[18] The judges however reasserted that there may be contracts, such as that which arose in the *Bank of East Asia* case,

---

[12] See Peel, *Treitel on Contract*, para. 17–020.
[13] *Huntoon Co.* v. *Kolynos (Inc.)* [1930] 1 Ch 528.   [14] 1997 SLT 1213 (HL).
[15] See the judgments of Lord Drummond Young in: *A* v. *B* 2003 SLT 242, 249; *Hoult* v. *Turpie* 2004 SLT 308, 312–316; *Purac Ltd* v. *Byzak Ltd* 2005 SLT 37, 40. See also the judgment of Lord Marnoch in *Macari* v. *Celtic Football & Athletic Co. Ltd* 1999 SC 628, 655.
[16] *Robertson Construction Central Ltd* v. *Glasgow Metro LLP* [2009] CSOH 71, per Lord Hodge at para. 30.
[17] [2010] UKSC 19, 2010 SCLR 396, [2010] All ER (D) 18.
[18] *Ibid.*, per Lord Hope at para. 42.

where the presumption will not apply, but a more specific pairing of duties on each side will operate given the staged nature of performance by each party.[19] The right to withhold performance for a breach of this mutuality principle, that is for defective or non-performance on the other side, may be exercised (it seems) for any failure of the reciprocal performance which is more than trivial.[20]

Withholding of performance by A of a duty due by it in favour of B under one contract may be exercised in respect of a failure by B of its duty due to A under another contract if the two contracts are so closely related that they form part of one overall transaction.[21] A similar result may be reached by different means in English law, where a cross-claim may give rise to an equitable set-off if it flows out of and is inseparably connected with the dealings and transactions which give rise to the claim: there can be a sufficiently close connection even though the claim and cross-claim arise out of two different contracts.[22]

An apparent limitation on the right to withhold performance in Scotland is that there is no authority for its use otherwise than where the whole of the obligation due is to be retained: in other words, there is no authority for a combination (at common law) of part-withholding and part-performance of an obligation due under a contract. By contrast, the DCFR specifically permits such part-withholding.[23]

The Scottish approach is somewhat similar to that taken in South Africa. Mutuality is presumed in bilateral contracts, such as sale, exchange, letting and hire.[24] This presumption – that, in bilateral contracts, the obligations will be reciprocal – is, however, only a presumption, and the determining factor is, as Cloete JA noted in *Man Truck & Bus* v. *Dorbyl*,[25] the intention of the parties:

---

[19] *Ibid.*, per Lord Hope at para. 43.

[20] Judgment of Lord Hope, *ibid.*, para. 43; McBryde, *Contract*, paras. 20–47, 20–60.

[21] *Inveresk plc* v. *Tullis Russell Papermakers Ltd* [2010] UKSC 19, 2010 SCLR 396, [2010] All ER (D) 18.

[22] Per Lord Collins in *Inveresk plc* v. *Tullis Russell* [2010] UKSC 19, citing *Bank of Boston Connecticut* v. *European Grain & Shipping Co.* [1989] AC 1056, 1102, and *BIM Kemi AB* v. *Blackburn Chemicals Ltd (No. 1)* [2001] 2 Lloyd's Rep 93 (CA).

[23] DCFR Art. III.-3:401(4).

[24] 'Where a contract is bilateral the obligations on the two sides are *prima facie* reciprocal, unless the contrary intention clearly appears from a consideration of the terms of the contract' (per Cloete JA, in *Man Truck & Bus (SA)(Pty) Ltd* v. *Dorbyl Ltd t/a Dorbyl Transport Products & Busaf* 2004 (5) SA 226, 233 (SCA)).

[25] *Man Truck & Bus (SA)(Pty) Ltd* v. *Dorbyl Ltd t/a Dorbyl Transport Products & Busaf* 2004 (5) SA 226 (SCA).

The overriding consideration is the intention of the parties; and the question whether the performance of respective obligations was reciprocal, depends upon the intention of the parties as evident from the terms of their agreement seen in conjunction with the relevant background circumstances.[26]

The *Man Truck* case concerned facts where the appellant and defendant had entered into a risk-sharing agreement. Under this agreement, the appellant had undertaken to maintain a number of buses (which it had leased to a third party), while the defendant had agreed, if the third party defaulted on the lease agreement, to make certain guaranteed payments to the appellant. The third party defaulted under the lease, and the appellant sued the defendant for the guaranteed payments it claimed were therefore due. One of the questions for the court was whether the defendant's duty to make the payments was the reciprocal counterpart of the duty to maintain the buses, the court holding that it was.

As in Scotland, the right of a contracting party under South African law to withhold its performance for the non-performance of the other party's mutual undertaking is designed to act as a spur to the other party to perform, without providing any guarantee of the remedying of that non-performance. It thus acts as a 'self-help' means to protect the performance interest,[27] but other solutions will evidently require to be called in to play if the defaulting party does not cure its default. The right to withhold counter-performance is in principle not tied to any requirement as to the degree of non-performance on the other party's part, so the withholding of performance can in theory occur even for minor defects in the other party's performance.[28] In order to prevent abuse of the right, however, an equitable control of the right may be exercised by the courts in cases where B has utilised A's defective performance to its advantage.[29] Where the discretion is exercised, and the right of B to withhold performance denied, there are thus two conceivable outcomes for B: (i) if A's performance can be rectified, the contract price less the cost of remedying the defect will be awarded to A; or (ii) if defective performance cannot be rectified, then, rather than a claim for a reduced contract price being awarded to A, an equitable award will be made to give A a fair recovery

---

[26] *Ibid.*, 233.

[27] 'A general opinion is that [the right to withhold counter-performance] is an instrument for enforcing specific performance' (Van der Merwe *et al.*, *Contract*, p. 390).

[28] *BK Tooling (Edms) Bpk.* v. *Scope Precision Engineering (Edms) Bpk.* 1979 (1) SA 391 (A).

[29] *Ibid.*

for the performance rendered.[30] While it might be argued that, by conceivably forcing B to perform even where it has not received the precise mutual performance for which it bargained, this equitable control fails fully to respect the promissory undertakings of the parties, it is surely hard to refer the circumstances arising in such cases to any promises actually made by the parties: as they evidently did not consider possible non-conforming outcomes (or else they would have provided for them in the contract), the court simply has to fashion a solution to the problem. The South African approach has at least the merit that it does not purport to operate by way of the artificial device of presumed promises.

As for Louisiana, the Civil Code provides for a category of 'commutative' contracts, these being contracts in which 'the performance of the obligation of each party is correlative to the performance of the other'.[31] Is a contract presumed to be commutative when there are obligations to be performed on each side? Though the Code does not make this clear, the courts have had occasion to express an opinion of the matter. In *Stockstill* v. *Byrd*, it was said that

> The courts at the present day incline strongly against the construction of promises as independent; and, in the absence of clear language to the contrary, promises which form the consideration for each other will be held to be concurrent or dependent, and not independent, so that a failure of one party to perform will discharge the other, [and] so that one cannot maintain an action against the other without showing the performance or tender of performance on his part.[32]

This view has been approved of in subsequent cases, including by the US Court of Appeals,[33] which, applying this approach to litigation before them, concluded that it meant that the plaintiffs' and defendant's several undertakings 'would therefore be considered as dependent and part of the whole agreement absent language indicating the contrary'.[34] The logical result of a contract's being commutative is spelt out in a codal expression of the right to withhold performance: 'Either party to a commutative contract may refuse to perform his obligation if the other has failed

---

[30] See Van der Merwe *et al.*, *Contract*, p. 396. There is a similarity here with the Scottish approach to awarding price less cost of cure in cases of non-material defects, but utilising an unjustified enrichment award in cases of material defects: see Hogg, *Obligations*, paras. 4.175–82.

[31] CC Art. 1911.   [32] 132 La. 404, 407, 61 So. 446, 447 (1913).

[33] *Gregory* v. *Popeyes Famous Fried Chicken and Biscuits Inc.* 857 F 2d 1474 (1988).

[34] *Ibid.*, para. 14 of the Court's judgment.

to perform or does not offer to perform his own at the same time, if the performances are due simultaneously.'[35]

As will be appreciated from the above, the law in the three mixed systems on this topic is broadly similar.

(c)   German law

The German law of justified withholding of performance is split between two central provisions of the BGB, §§320 and 273. The first of these creates a right similar to the right to withhold performance which operates in other jurisdictions; the latter goes further than such a comparative right, as it provides for a right to withhold performance even in respect of non-synallagmatic or non-mutual obligations.

§320(1) BGB provides that a party to a reciprocal (or 'mutual' or 'synallagmatic') contract may refuse to perform his part until the other party tenders performance, unless advance performance has been stipulated. What the provision is thus essentially dealing with is reciprocal obligations, rather than reciprocal contracts, as the focus is on specific pairings of obligations rather than the nature of the contract as a whole. Though the provision provides for what is called a right of retention in some other jurisdictions (Scotland being one), in German law the term 'right of retention' is usually reserved for the more general right of retention provided for under §273(1) applicable not just in cases of synallagmatic obligations.[36] §273 provides that, if a debtor (A) has a claim against a creditor (B) arising out of the same legal relationship as that on which A's debt is based, then A may refuse to perform the duty until the performance due to him by B is tendered. This provision, it will be noted, stipulates no requirement that the two duties be synallagmatic, so that performance of an independent obligation of A can be withheld because of the non-performance by B of its independent obligation under the same relationship. This section is thus noteworthy in providing for a much wider right of justified non-performance than exists in most jurisdictions.

How do §§320 and 273 interact? §273 can conceivably operate in respect of any contract, as a contract with no reciprocal obligations would still be subject to §273. However, if a contract has both reciprocal and non-reciprocal obligations, the former obligations are governed by the regime of §320, the latter by that of §273. This means that, in contracts with at least some reciprocal obligations, it is necessary to determine which obligations

---

[35] CC Art. 2022.   [36] §273 also provides for a right of lien: see §273(2).

on the one side are the synallagma, or counterpart obligations, of which obligations on the other side, and which obligations (if any) on either side are free-standing, independent obligations. There is thus, in contracts with reciprocal obligations, no assumption of 'general mutuality' (as it was termed earlier), the question on which reciprocal pairings exist being a matter of fact to be determined in the circumstances of the case and by reference to the intentions of the parties. For those obligations which are deemed synallagmatic, the §320 regime is triggered, this providing for somewhat different conditions under which the right to withhold performance may be exercised than does the more general right granted by §273. For instance, whereas under §273 the right of retention may be excluded by a debtor through the provision of security, this does not apply to the synallagmatic duties which are the subject of §320.[37] Some types of contract are not considered to give rise to synallagmatic obligations at all (unless exceptionally provided for), an example being the contract of mandate, where the mandatory's duty to act on behalf of the mandant in relation to the specified matter is not reciprocal to the mandant's duty to reimburse expenses incurred by the mandatory.

The effect of §320 is to provide for a default rule requiring contemporaneous performance of synallagmatic obligations, though the default position can be varied by a requirement in the contract that one of the parties perform first. The BGB also contains a number of exceptions to the default rule. Some of these are in precisely the areas where non-codified systems have generated case law on the question of whether retention is justified. So, for instance, in building contracts under which the work is to be performed in stages, the remuneration due for each stage of the works falls due at the time the work is 'accepted'.[38] This will be deemed to be the point when the customer physically receives the work with the express or tacit declaration that it constitutes performance,[39] unless the contract stipulates some other point. Standard form building contracts usually regulate the matter more precisely, and make it clear which part of the overall remuneration is applicable to the various stages of the work. In such a case, performance of a specific stage of the work is seen as the mutual counterpart of the duty to pay the relevant specific portion of the price. One protection for a party obliged to perform first is that, if, after the contract is entered into, it becomes apparent that his entitlement to consideration is jeopardised by the inability to perform of the other party, performance by the party obliged to perform first may be refused.[40]

---

[37] §320(1).   [38] §641(1).   [39] RGZ 110, 404, 406–7.   [40] §321(1).

Under §320(2), if withholding performance would be in bad faith, this is not permitted. When bad faith might preclude the right to withhold being exercised is not specified, save that such bad faith is specified as particularly including the case where a defaulting party is in default in only a 'relatively trivial' way. That would seem to result in an identical practice to that operating in the mixed legal systems, where trivial defective performance will also prevent the exercise of the right to terminate.

Considered overall, the German rules in §§320 and 273 provide for one of the most pro-creditor regimes in respect of withholding of performance. Not only may performance of a promise be withheld if the reciprocal promise for which it was given is not performed, but, under the general provision of §273, performance of an independent obligation may be withheld if any non-reciprocal duty of the other party is unfulfilled. This latter entitlement causes problems from a theoretical promissory point of view: if a promise is made unconditionally, one would expect it to be enforceable regardless of whether the promisee fails to fulfil an independent promise of its own. One way to attempt to justify §273 would be to see it as a kind of set-off, though this is not an entirely convincing explanation given that the operation of set-off in the Common law requires the relative value of each performance to be weighed, whereas the German rule would allow A to withhold performance even where its duty was of a far lesser value than B's duty.

(d)   Model law

The article of the DCFR specifically dealing with withholding of performance of a reciprocal obligation must be read in conjunction with earlier provisions on the concept of reciprocity and the time for performance of obligations. Article III.-1:102 defines an obligation as reciprocal if (i) performance of the one obligation is due in exchange for performance of the other obligation, (ii) it is an obligation to facilitate or accept performance of the other obligation, or (iii) it is so clearly connected to the other obligation or its subject matter that the performances can be regarded as interdependent.[41] There is nothing in this definition to prevent an obligation from one contract being the reciprocal of an obligation in another contract. The DCFR also provides that, unless there is a stipulation to the contrary, parties are bound to perform reciprocal obligations simultaneously.[42] Taken together these provisions mean that there is no

---

[41] DCFR Art. III.-1:102(4).   [42] DCFR Art. III.-2:104.

automatic presumption of reciprocity (or mutuality), as in some of the national systems mentioned above (though there are three widely defined circumstances in which obligations will be taken to be mutual), and that where obligations are reciprocal the default position is that they must be performed simultaneously. Failure by A to effect a performance which requires to occur either simultaneously or before B's performance triggers an entitlement on B's part to withhold performance until the reciprocal performance due by A has occurred.[43] Part of, as well as the whole of, a performance may be withheld if that is reasonable in the circumstances.[44]

The DCFR regime is consistent with the basic idea of the conditionality of a promise, that a promise may be made only on condition that the promisee also does something. It follows from that idea that if the promisee does not meet the condition, the promisor should not require to do what it has promised. The absence of any more extensive right to withhold performance (as in the BGB) is consistent with the idea that an unconditional promise must be performed regardless of any failings of the promisee.

3.   Specific performance

Any system claiming to place a high value on promises would, one would expect, ensure that there was a robust legal remedy available to compel performance by the promisor if such compulsion became necessary. Such a remedy – specific performance – one would expect to be available as of right, and not merely at the discretion of the courts, and would expect to be a primary and not simply a secondary entitlement of the promisee's. One would also expect that the circumstances where judicially ordered performance was *not* granted would be limited to those cases where to order it would be impractical or impossible, such a practicability limitation not undermining the theory underpinning the remedy. All of such expectations flow from an understanding of the nature of promise as a commitment to performance, so that any system claiming to respect the nature of promise would thus be expected to ensure that, despite a breach of the duty to perform, promisors would still be expected to honour their obligations and be compelled to perform, where possible. Such compulsion is consistent with the promisor giving its pledged performance legal and not simply moral normative form.

---

[43] DCFR Art. III.-3:401(1).   [44] DCFR Art. III.-3:401(3).

As the following discussion shows, the totality of these expectations is not met in all jurisdictions: typically, in both civilian and mixed legal systems there is a primary entitlement to performance under a contract,[45] whereas in the Common law the primary right is to damages, with specific performance only a secondary entitlement.[46] However, in all legal families it is at least largely the case that the practicability test is used to determine when specific performance will not be granted.

(a) English law

In English Law, the order of specific performance is discretionary in nature, and equitable in origin (perhaps originally a borrowing from canon law[47]). Whilst the discretionary nature of the remedy is a feature which is shared with some of the other systems studied (so that all such systems can be said to be marginalising the performance interest of the promisee to some extent),[48] those systems have not, as English law has, historically treated specific performance as an extraordinary or supplementary entitlement of a claimant, and thus as one in relation to which the judicial discretion to grant the remedy should be used sparingly. Though in practice many (but not all) pleas for specific performance receive the same treatment in England as they would in other systems, the extraordinary nature of the remedy has created a perception that the right to performance is undervalued in the Common law. Some legal theorists have even argued that the extraordinary nature of the entitlement means that the alleged duty in the Common law to adhere to contractual duties is no more than an undertaking to pay damages if one does not so adhere.[49] While such a view of duties of performance as essentially discretionary in nature is an absurdly distorted one, it reflects a legal climate where damages have historically been of much greater significance and where, as a result, courts have been ambivalent towards the idea that a recalcitrant promisor should, where possible, be required to perform.

---

[45] This being the case in Quebec (Civil Code Art. 1590), the Netherlands (BW, Art. 3:296), Italy (*Codice civile*, Art. 1453), Germany (BGB §241), and France (*Code civil*, Art. 1184; see also Law No. 91–650 of 9 July 1991 on civil procedure for execution of judgments).

[46] Uniform Commercial Code §2–716; Restatement (Second) Contracts, §§357, 359.

[47] See the view of Martinez-Torron, noted earlier in Ch. 2, at p. 82, n. 77.

[48] The point being that it would, alternatively, be quite possible to state that specific performance is a legal entitlement, save in a specified class of cases. Such a conception of the remedy as a legal rather than a discretionary entitlement would place a higher value on promise as a pledge of performance.

[49] To this effect, see Holmes, 'The Path of the Law', p. 462.

The nature of specific performance as a discretionary remedy puts the spotlight firmly upon the courts: the way in which their discretion is exercised has the ability to champion promissory liability (if the remedy, when requested, is granted widely) or to marginalise it (if the remedy, when requested, is granted only sparingly). In this respect, one must take note of the established English judicial view that the remedy ought not to be granted whenever damages would be an adequate remedy. This has given rise, for instance, to a practice of granting the remedy in cases where delivery of unique goods (or land) is required, but of only awarding damages in the case of duplicate goods easily obtainable on the market. Such a distinction raises some rather under-explored assumptions about the idea of the 'adequacy' of a remedy. On one view, damages could be said always to be an inadequate, second-best, remedy, as self-evidently they merely substitute for the actual performance desired by the promisee, though such an attitude is clearly not shared by the courts.

Even where it is clear that, according to traditional ideas of adequacy, damages would *not* be adequate, sometimes courts have nonetheless refused the request for specific performance on the grounds that the order would have to be constantly supervised by the courts.[50] This point was raised in the important case of *Co-operative Insurance Society* v. *Argyll Stores (Holding) Ltd*,[51] where the order was refused. Though the case concerned the specific question of the enforcement of a so-called 'keep-open' provision in a lease, it is symbolic of the generally reserved attitude of English law to specific performance. The contrast between the decision and that in the similar fact Scots case *Retail Parks Investments Ltd* v. *Royal Bank of Scotland plc (No. 2)*,[52] discussed below, is marked.

In the *Co-operative* case, Lord Hoffmann explained the judicial concern about possible constant supervision as relating to the possibility that courts may have to give an indefinite series of rulings concerning compliance with a specific performance order. Such a possibility derives, in a case of a keep-open clause, from the fact that keeping a business open is an ongoing, rather than a one-off, matter. Yet the courts already require to ensure ongoing compliance with other orders, such as maintenance or child support orders, and perform this task without apparently insuperable difficulty. Lord Hoffmann also worried about difficulties relating to the precision required for drafting the order. Yet surely the real problem

---

[50] See for an older case stating this *Powell Duffryn Steam Coal Co.* v. *Taff Vale Railway* (1874) LR 9 Ch 331.
[51] [1998] AC 1.   [52] 1996 SC 227, 1996 SLT 669.

is in testing whether there has been a breach of the order, not in drafting it. The wording of the order simply requires to mirror the term in the contract. If that term is itself somewhat vague, then naturally there may be difficulty in assessing whether there has been a breach of the order, but the correct response to a vaguely or widely drafted clause is, arguably, to allow the party bound by it a degree of discretion in its implementation. Consider the clause in the *Co-operative* case, which obliged the tenant to

> keep the demised premises open for retail trade during the usual hours of business in the locality and the display windows properly dressed in a suitable manner in keeping with a good class parade of shops.

Lord Hoffmann worried that this clause said nothing about the level of trade, the kind of trade, and so forth. But this surely means no more than that the clause gives the tenant a wide discretion as to how to act, so that, so long as it stays within that wide discretion, it will not have breached the order. True, the clause does not say what 'usual hours of business' means, but again surely that gives the tenant a reasonable discretion on that matter. The tenant might decide to stay open from 7 a.m. to 8 p.m. six days a week, or only 9 a.m. to 5 p.m. five days a week, but so long as the hours chosen are similar to the hours of opening of other shops in the locality (especially the other units in the shopping centre) it surely ought to be the case that the order should not be seen as having been broken.

Lord Hoffmann also worried about yoking parties together who were now in a grudging contractual relationship, and one which might be causing loss to one of them through its continuation.[53] But, as to the loss point, is this not a risk that all contracting parties take when then they contract? To release a party from such consequences is to excuse a party from the negative consequences of that risk, and to readjust the balance of risk in the relationship. If a party who has agreed to sell something at a price which turns out, by the date of performance, to be much lower than the market rate is held to that contract, why not also the tenant who has over-estimated his ability to trade profitably?

Overall, Lord Hoffmann's judgment fails to appreciate the inadequacy of the remedy of damages in the case, given the impossibility of calculating accurately the losses which might reasonably be contemplated by the parties as likely to flow from the throwing up of the lease by an anchor tenant, and thus the crucial importance to the landlord of that tenant remaining.

---

[53] [1998] AC 1, see Lord Hoffmann, at paras. 15–16.

A fundamental criticism of the English approach to specific perform-ance is that it can be said to convey the impression that breach of con-tract prima facie destroys the right to performance, and the impression that, only if a party convinces a court to restore the right, can such per-formance be compelled. This not only communicates a low regard for the normative value of promises (and bolsters the views of reliance theorists), but can be said not to take sufficiently seriously the unlawful behaviour which is breach of contract. The toleration of a position which begins from allowing parties in breach to kill off the right to performance is tan-tamount to penalising the innocent party and to preferring the behaviour of the breaching party. The justification advanced recently by Smith for the Common law's reluctance to award specific performance – that such orders are 'prima facie intrusive of personal liberty',[54] in that they often compel people to render services that they no longer wish to provide, and thus are akin to servitude – is unconvincing. Contracting parties, in the very act of contracting, have already restricted their personal liberty by each binding themselves voluntarily to do something for the other, so the enforcement by courts of duties of performance does no more than affirm the parties' own targeted restrictions of their personal freedom. The logical conclusion of Smith's objection would be that all contracts, or at least those pledging personal services, are a kind of servitude, an argu-ment which is unlikely to convince anyone except perhaps the diehard anarchist.

(b) Mixed legal systems

In the mixed legal systems, a higher theoretical value is placed upon the promises undertaken by contracting parties. This is reflected in, amongst other things, a doctrinal predisposition towards granting remedies designed to enforce performance, foremost among them the remedy of specific performance (or specific implement, as it is referred to in Scotland). In Scotland, South Africa and Louisiana, specific performance/implement is often said to be a 'primary' or 'default' remedy, that is to say there is a prima facie entitlement to seek the remedy without demonstrat-ing (as in English law) why damages would not be an adequate remedy.[55]

---

[54] Smith, *Contract Theory*, p. 402.
[55] *PIK Facilities Ltd* v. *Shell UK Ltd* 2005 SCLR 958; *Benson* v. *SA Mutual Life Assurance Society* 1986 (1) SA 776 (A); *Concise Oil & Gas Partnership* v. *Louisiana Intrastate Gas Corp.* 986 F 2d 1463 (1993).

There are differences in emphasis between the jurisdictions, however. In Louisiana, the remedy has been described as a 'substantive right' and as 'the preferred remedy for breach of contract'.[56] On the other hand, in Scotland a more Common law approach is noticeable in judicial remarks that 'it must always be in the discretion of the Court to say whether the remedy of specific implement or one of damages is the proper and suitable remedy in the circumstances',[57] and there is a tradition of refusing to grant the remedy if to do so would be inequitable.[58] In South Africa, though the right to specific performance has been judicially described as a cornerstone of the law, in the same judgment it was noted that (as in Scotland) there is a discretion on the part of the court in whether or not to grant the remedy.[59] In practice, in the mixed jurisdictions there are a number of similar recognised circumstances in which the remedy will *not* be granted,[60] such that differences in emphasis in the general descriptions of the entitlement to the remedy ought not to be over-emphasised. Even though there may be a theoretical 'preference' for the remedy, a creditor is not compelled to seek performance, and may utilise other remedies, such as damages, should it so wish.

In Scotland, because ultimately a party refusing to comply with an order of specific implement may be imprisoned, the order is unavailable in respect of breach of monetary debts, imprisonment for civil debt having been abolished.[61] Instead, in the case of monetary debts, the relevant action for enforcement is an action for payment. This contrasts with South Africa, where both monetary as well as non-monetary obligations are classified as falling within specific performance, though again imprisonment for failure to satisfy an order to pay a monetary debt has been abolished.[62] The non-availability of specific implement in Scotland

---

[56] *J. Weingarten, Inc. v. Northgate Mall, Inc.* 404 So 2d 896, 897, 899 (La 1981).

[57] *Moore v Paterson* (1881) 9 R 337, 351, per Lord Shand.

[58] See McBryde, *Contract*, paras. 23–15, 23–22, and authorities cited there.

[59] *Benson* v. *SA Mutual Life Assurance Society* 1986 (1) SA 776 (A).

[60] For instance, if performance is impossible, would be impractical, would cause undue hardship to the debtor, or where the inconvenience to the debtor outweighs the advantage to the creditor: see, for instance, *Austin's of Monroe, Inc.* v. *Brown* 474 So 2d 1383 (La App 2nd Cir 1985); *Stewart* v. *Kennedy* (1890) 17 R (HL) 1; *Amend* v. *McCabe* 649 So 2d 1059 (La App 3rd Cir 1995). In certain classes of contract involving a close personal relationship (such as employment contracts) courts may refuse enforcement if the relationship has broken down: *McArthur* v. *Lawson* (1877) 4 R 1134; *Nationwide Airlines (Pty) Ltd* v. *Roediger & Anor* 2008 (1) SA 293 (W).

[61] Debtors (Scotland) Act 1880, s. 4.

[62] The Abolition of Civil Imprisonment Act 2 of 1977 (see also the earlier Civil Imprisonment Restriction Act 21 of 1942).

for monetary debts should not be seen as undermining a high regard for the performance interest of the creditor, given that various forms of judicial enforcement (collectively called 'diligence') are still available for breach of a court order to pay, but should rather be viewed as an appreciation of the futility of imprisonment as a means of debt collection in many cases.

The reticence of English law noted earlier to enforce tenants' duties to trade from premises by means of specific performance on the alleged ground of the non-specificity and uncertainty of the duty involved is absent from the Scottish approach. Just such a keep-open and trade provision in a commercial lease was enforced in *Retail Parks Investment Ltd* v. *Royal Bank of Scotland plc (No. 2)*.[63] In his judgment, Lord McCluskey made the important comment in relation to orders of specific implement that

> An order of the court may in effect specify the end to be achieved but leave open the precise means whereby the defender is to achieve the specified end; to that extent, at least, the order may contain a degree of flexibility.[64]

Such judicial flexibility is of crucial assistance to a promisee, the promise in favour of whom lacks detail as to the method of performance (for instance, how precisely a tenant must trade) but specifies a clear objective (trading in general terms). Such promisees will be entitled to enforce the promise in question, and will not be required to make do with the remedy of damages, a remedy which is often inadequate in cases of non-occupation of premises by keystone tenants.

The decision of the Inner House in *Retail Parks* marked a movement away from prior Scottish decisions in which the courts had been unwilling to enforce similar duties on the alleged ground of their vagueness and imprecision.[65] The new approach reinforces the high value accorded to the promised performance of a positive obligation. The resulting contrast with the English decisions in leasehold cases is such that the more friendly environment for promisees under Scots law would perhaps make it desirable for English landlords to consider whether they might wish to make Scots law the *lex contractus* if not the *lex fori* for their leases.

---

[63] 1996 SC 227, 1996 SLT 669.   [64] 1996 SC 227, 241.

[65] For instance, *Grosvenor Developments (Scotland) plc* v. *Argyll Stores Ltd* 1987 SLT 738.

(c)   German law[66]

The German law on contractual remedies was reformed by amendments to the BGB in force as of 1 January 2002. The overall effect of the reforms has been to make it much easier to describe general principles and rules concerning the remedy of damages, the enforcement of performance (specific performance) and termination. Prior to the reform, such description was much harder, as available remedies and the conditions affecting their availability were largely tied to the individual parts of the BGB dealing with specific types of contract rather than set out in the general part.[67]

§241(1) BGB states that by 'virtue of an obligation an obligee is entitled to claim performance from the obligor. The performance may also consist in forbearance'. This provision means that the creditor has a primary right to performance in German law, which, of course, is consistent with the deep roots of the *pacta sunt servanda* principle in civil law systems. It may be noted that before the secondary right of damages is permitted under §281, a reasonable period of grace (*Nachfrist*) must be offered to the debtor to allow him to attempt to correct his imperfect performance: so the defaulting party has to get (in most cases) a second bite at the performance cherry before damages may be claimed.[68] The requirement of a *Nachfrist* is not imposed in cases where performance would be impossible,[69] and in some other cases.[70] The right to claim performance ends only when and if a damages claim is raised.[71]

German law distinguishes between orders to pay money (this includes, however, both a sum due as a debt but also sums claimed as damages) and orders to do something other than pay a sum of money. Obligations to hand over specific things are dealt with in the Code of Civil Procedure (the 'ZPO'). If the obligation is to perform an act, and this can be performed by some other party, an order will allow the creditor to have the act done by someone else, at the debtor's expense,[72] which thus effectively

---

[66] For a comparison of the treatment of the primary remedial right in German Law, English Law and the DCFR, see Weller, 'Die Struktur des Erfüllungsanspruchs'. That article distills ideas expounded in greater length in the author's monograph *Die Vertragstreue*.

[67] There are also further rules concerning performance in the German Code of Civil Procedure (ZPO), §§ 883–90. On the remedial reforms in German law, see Zimmermann, *New German Law of Obligations*, as well as Markesinis *et al.*, *German Law of Contract*, Chs. 8–10.

[68] The similarity with the controversial Scottish case of *Lindley Catering* v. *Hibernian F.C.* 1975 SLT (Notes) 56 is noticeable, though the status of that judgment is uncertain: see discussion at p. 408.

[69] §275 BGB.   [70] §281(2) BGB.   [71] §281(4) BGB.   [72] §887(1) ZPO.

turns the duty to perform into a compensatory claim: this contrasts with the Common law, where the ability of some other party to perform an act would make it much less likely that an order of specific performance would be granted and, if it were granted, it would only be enforceable against the party who had contracted to perform the act. If the order to perform the act can only be performed by the debtor, then failure to do so will result in fines or possible imprisonment.[73] Any fines go to the State, not the promisor, however, so this cannot be said directly to protect the promisor's interests. There are a number of cases where execution in this manner will not be granted, including promises made in marriage, and (significantly) the duties of an employee under a contract of service.

A claim for performance is excluded where it is impossible for the obligor or any other person to perform.[74] Importantly, however, such circumstances do not exclude a claim for damages, because §275(4) provides that in such an event the rights of the obligee are governed by other sections of the Code.[75] This seems somewhat odd to a non-German lawyer: why should a duty which it is impossible to perform give rise to a duty to compensate for such non-performance? The logic of so providing has been explained[76] as being that what impossibility really entails in German law is only the prevention of a claim for non-performance, but not the negation of the duty to perform itself; thus, because that duty still exists, other claims may lie for the failure to perform, such as damages. While this does have a certain logic to it, it still looks odd to hold a party liable in damages if it is impossible for it to perform its contractual duties.[77] Impossibility can mean impossibility either before or after the contract is concluded,[78] and can include something for which the debtor was responsible, or not. Objective impossibility (where no one could perform the contract) and subjective impossibility (where it is just the party concerned who cannot perform, for instance because it does not in fact own the item it contracted to sell and the current owner is refusing to sell the item to it) are both included. However, if the debtor can overcome a subjective problem, for instance by buying the goods, even if at

---

[73] §888(1) ZPO.   [74] §275(1) BGB.

[75] Including §280 BGB, on damages for breach.

[76] Markesinis *et al.*, *German Law of Contract*, p. 407.

[77] In Common law and mixed legal systems, post-formation impossibility of performance would frustrate the future performance of the contract, a result which would not give rise to a right to damages.

[78] By comparison, in English and Scots law pre-contractual impossibility would prevent the contract coming into being, which was the same position taken by the pre-reform German law.

a high price, it is expected to do so and this does not constitute subject-ive impossibility.[79] However, this is subject to the further rule of §275(2), that where the cost of performance becomes 'grossly disproportionate' in comparison to the interest of the creditor in receiving performance, this allows the debtor to refuse to perform (and thus creates a sort of deemed impossibility of performance, or what was before the reforms referred to as 'economic impossibility'). Evidently, the line between efforts which are grossly disproportionate (and which therefore justify non-performance) and those which are not will be hard to determine and predict.[80] The Common law also faces the issue of determining when cases of alleged economic impossibility sufficient to trigger the doctrine of frustration exist, but those cases do not involve an uncertain sliding scale of eco-nomic hardship but rather a determination of whether the very under-lying purpose of the contract no longer exists.

Because, if the conditions are met, §275(1) effectively releases the party affected from the duty to perform, §326(1) provides that in such a case the party released from the duty to perform does not have the right to claim the price. This general rule of the release of both parties in case of impos-sibility is subject to some exceptions.[81]

As the particular case of keep-open provisions in leases has been men-tioned in relation to other jurisdictions, it may be noted that, as might be expected given the narrative of the general approach of German law above, German courts have compelled tenants to keep open and run busi-nesses in accordance with lease terms obliging them to do so,[82] though the specific circumstances of some cases have been held to mitigate against such enforcement.[83]

It will be appreciated that German law generally places a high regard upon the performance interest of the promisee, and stresses that the promisor is expected to do what it has promised. There are though quirks, from an outside perspective, of German law which have been noted: the second chance to be offered to cure non-conforming performance; the promisee's right to have an act performed by another party (where pos-sible) with the cost charged to the promisor; and impossibility precluding claims for performance, but not for damages.

---

[79] Markesinis et al., German Law of Contract, p. 409.
[80] See further Zimmermann, New German Law of Obligations, pp. 47–8.
[81] Discussed by Markesinis et al., German Law of Contract, pp. 409–11.
[82] See OLG Celle NJW-RR 1996, 585.
[83] See OLG Naumburg NJW-RR 1998, 873.

(d)   Model law

One would expect any model system claiming to place a high value upon promises to designate specific performance as a primary legal entitlement. Both PECL Article 9:102(2) and DCFR Articles III.-3:101 and 3:302 do so, the right to enforce performance being not a secondary but a primary legal entitlement in both model codes.

Of the two model codes, the DCFR takes perhaps the strongest pro-performance stance, as, unlike PECL, it does not exclude the remedy of specific performance just because the aggrieved party might reasonably obtain performance from another source.[84] The other cases where specific performance is excluded in the DCFR broadly reflect exclusions already operative in the national systems examined.[85] The DCFR's statement that the creditor 'is entitled' to enforce specific performance of an obligation puts the matter as one of legal right and not discretion, and, in so doing, reflects a conception of the fundamental nature of promise as a pledge of performance and not merely as a pledge to pay damages if performance of an expected outcome is not achieved.

4.   Perfect or substantial performance of contractual promises

Ought a trivial defect in performance to preclude a party from claiming the price due under the contract for such performance? In jurisdictions with a so-called doctrine of 'substantial performance', so long as substantial, though not perfect, performance occurs, the price may still be claimed, but is subject to a deduction (either for the losses caused to the other party or for the difference in value between what was contracted for and actual performance). Whether such a doctrine of substantial performance is consistent with a high regard for promises is debatable. On the one hand, it has traditionally been said that promises ought to be enforced strictly, and that any rule which permits deviation by the promisor from the terms of the promise while preserving a right to claim for the value of what has been rendered undermines the sanctity of the promise and is tantamount to rewriting it. On the other hand, an alternative view is that to deny a promisor a claim for the value of what he has performed where

---

[84] Contrast PECL Art. 9:102(2) with DCFR Art. III.-3:302(3).
[85] DCFR Art. III.-3:302(3) excludes specific performance where it would be unlawful or impossible, unreasonably burdensome or expensive, or would be of such a personal character as to make it unreasonable to enforce it.

only trivial defects exist in relation to such performance allows promisees to 'free ride' off the back of substantial performance and may discourage promising in the first place. The concern embodied in this alternative point of view could be somewhat met by allowing defective performance to give rise not to a claim in contract but in unjustified enrichment, thus preserving the sanctity of promise while allowing for an equitable solution to the free-riding problem. At least two of the jurisdictions considered below choose to employ unjustified enrichment to solve some of the problems created by defective performance.

The approach taken by particular legal systems to the issue of perfect or substantial performance often depends on whether or not the contract in question is one for the provision of goods or services: typically perfect performance tends to be required in sale of goods contracts, whereas substantial performance may be sufficient in contracts for services.[86] Even where perfect performance is required, if the promisee elects to keep the benefit of substantial performance, then he usually has to pay something for the performance that has been tendered.

(a)   Contracts for services

Consider this troubling factual example, based upon the facts of a reported case:

> A builder undertakes building work under a lump sum contract[87] which is entirely in conformity with the agreed contract, except that he uses a different type of mortar for the work than that agreed in the contract. The finished work therefore, though it is of a high quality and value, is nonetheless not in conformity with the terms of the contract. The customer refuses to pay anything for the work done.[88]

In Scotland, there is no doctrine of substantial performance such as prevails in English law. The approach taken by the courts has been to hold that material defects in performance deprive the contractor from suing for the price in contract: instead a claim may be made in unjustified enrichment

---

[86] For an analysis of the different approaches in sales of good contracts and services contracts, largely from a US perspective, see Rakoff, 'The Implied Terms of Contracts', pp. 203 ff.

[87] That is, one where the contract is for payment of a single sum in respect of all the work to be undertaken. If the contract provides for payment in stages for various portions of the work, then payment will be due for all stages of the work completed properly, even if work done under one or more of the other stages is defective.

[88] The facts are from the Scottish case *Steel* v. *Young* 1907 SC 360.

for the value of the work conferred,[89] a somewhat controversial approach which some might argue undermines the sanctity of the contract.[90] On the other hand, if the defect in performance is classified as immaterial, then an action for the price may be maintained, subject to a deduction (though how such deduction is to be calculated, has not been definitely settled[91]), which is in effect a substantial performance position though not referred to in Scots law as such. The decision of the Scottish court on the facts of the example above was that the deviation was material because it could only be remedied by demolishing the works and starting again, and the builder's claim in contract for the price was therefore rejected. That seems a not entirely satisfactory way of assessing material deviation, as it does not compare disparity between the work done and the work contracted for (as one might expect) but rather the ease of correction of the defect. But many defects may be hard to cure even if different in only trivial respects from the contract specification: does that mean they must be material defects?

In German law, work is free of material defects if it is of the agreed quality.[92] If the quality has not been agreed, then work is not materially defective so long as it is suitable for the use envisaged in the contract, or else it is suitable for the customary use to which such work is put and is of a quality that is customary in works of the same type,[93] it being further stated in the BGB that it is 'equivalent to a material defect if the contractor produces a work that is different from the work ordered or too small an amount of the work'.[94] So, on the basis either of the BGB's requirement that work done be of the 'agreed quality', or else that it not be 'different from the work ordered', the example given above would also likely result in the same determination as that made by the Scottish court, that being that the work done was materially defective, albeit for a different reason.

---

[89] *Ramsay v. Brand* (1898) 25 R 1212, (1898) 35 SLR 927. It was also said in the case that the customer may instead reject the substantially defective work done and ask the builder to remove it, though such an entitlement may be subject to equitable control by the courts (if, for instance, costs of removal would be inordinate). One must also consider the possible role of an architect in all of this: if an architect employed by the customer has approved work done as it is completed, this might very well negate any right of the customer to reject work later found to be defective.

[90] Evidently, such a claim in unjustified enrichment cannot be maintained if the party to whom performance is to be rendered is seeking to enforce perfect performance through an order of specific implement. If such an order were granted, the obligation to tender full payment of the price would have to be met by the customer.

[91] A debate exists as to whether the deduction should represent the difference in value of the work done from that contracted for, or the cost of cure of the defect.

[92] §633(2) BGB.   [93] *Ibid.*   [94] *Ibid.*

Various rights are given by German law to the customer in such a case of materially defective performance: it may demand cure; it may remedy the defect itself and demand reimbursement for the work done; it may withdraw from the contract or reduce the payment due; or it may demand damages.[95] Note that it is not permitted simply to refuse to pay, leaving the contractor to seek some remedy in unjustified enrichment. The German approach to the case of the materially defective performance of a builder thus preserves a contractual solution to the problem: if the client wishes to keep the benefit of the defective work it must pay a reduced price for it, such reduction being computed on a difference in value basis.[96]

In English law, there is a reasonably established line of authority for the existence of a doctrine of substantial completion,[97] but this has been criticised in leading commentaries on the law as unnecessary, given the existence of the concept of 'entire' obligations.[98] Under English law, an obligation in a contract may be intended to be entire, that is, perfect performance of the obligation may be stipulated as a pre-requisite for payment being due in respect of it; on the other hand, if the obligation is not intended to be entire, then a claim may be allowed in respect of it even if it has not been performed exactly according to its terms. In other words, so the criticism goes, the proper way to approach such matters ought to be by way of judicial interpretation as to whether or not an obligation is entire, rather than by recognising a generally applicable doctrine of substantial performance. Despite this criticism, there is authority for the view that, while the builder who abandons a lump sum contract gets nothing,[99] the builder who substantially performs (this being a matter of fact) is entitled to recover the price subject to a deduction for the cost of cure.[100] This is a similar position to the Scottish one, save that in Scotland even the builder whose work is materially defective still gets something under unjustified enrichment, whereas the English builder does not. The English position on this latter point is more in keeping with the sanctity of the contractual promises undertaken by the parties, acts as a spur to proper performance

---

[95] §634 BGB.   [96] §638(2) BGB.

[97] *Dakin* v. *Oxley* (1864) 15 CB (NS) 646, 664–5; *Dakin* v. *Lee* [1916] 1 KB 566; *Bolton* v. *Mahadeva* [1972] 1 WLR 1009; *Sim* v. *Rotherham MBC* [1987] Ch 216, 253; *Wiluszynski* v. *Tower Hamlets LBC* [1989] ICR 493, 499; *Williams* v. *Roffey* [1991] 1 QB 1, 8–10, 17.

[98] See criticism in Peel, *Treitel on Contract*, para. 17–039; Beale, *Chitty on Contracts*, paras. 21–032–21–033.

[99] *Sumpter* v. *Hedges* [1898] 1 QB 673.

[100] *Dakin* v. *Lee* [1916] 1 KB 566; *Hoenig* v. *Isaacs* [1952] 2 All ER 176; *Kiely & Sons* v. *Medcraft* (1965) 109 SJ 829; *Bolton* v. *Mahadeva* [1972] 1 WLR 1009.

by the builder, and discourages builders from simply throwing up contracts if they perceive that more profitable work can be undertaken elsewhere. But, in defence of the Scots position, it might be said to possess the merit of providing an equitable solution in cases where correcting defective performance might be prohibitively expensive, and ensures that a customer does not take the benefit of work conferred for nothing. An ideal solution might perhaps be the middle ground of providing a more limited right to unjustified enrichment, available only in some cases (for instance, where cost of cure would be prohibitive but where work undertaken by a builder acting in good faith has conferred more than trivial value on the customer).

The Louisiana Civil Code provides that contracts may be dissolved for non-performance,[101] but adds a substantial performance caveat which stipulates that the right to dissolution does not apply where the debtor has rendered a substantial part of the performance and the part not rendered does not substantially impair the interest of the creditor.[102] If, therefore, a performance had been substantially performed, the party tendering such performance would still be entitled to claim the price, although a counterclaim for damages would be maintainable by the other party in respect of the losses caused by the defective performance.

The South African courts have adopted a similar view to the Scottish courts: in *BK Tooling (Edms) Bpk.* v. *Scope Precision Engineering (Edms) Bpk.*[103] the Appellate Division held that, where a contract cannot be cancelled on account of breach (because the breach does not go 'to the root of the contract'),[104] a contractual action for a reduced price lies; on the other hand, if the contract is terminated for breach, an action lies in unjustified enrichment for the value of any performance which cannot be restored to the innocent party.

The DCFR provides a simple and unitary solution to the problem of the value due for non-conforming performance in contracts in its general part. In Article III.-3:601, it is provided that a 'creditor who accepts a performance not conforming to the terms regulating the obligation may reduce the price', the reduction reflecting, as in German law, the difference of value between what was contracted for and what was received. There is a further provision, in the section on construction contracts, requiring

---

[101] CC Art. 2013.   [102] CC Art. 2014.   [103] 1979 (1) SA 391 (A).

[104] As to breaches going 'to the root of the contract', see *Oatarian Properties (Pty) Ltd* v. *Maroun* 1973 (3) SA 779 (A), and *Elgin Brown & Hamer (Pty) Ltd* v. *Industrial Machinery Suppliers (Pty) Ltd* 1993 (3) SA 424 (A).

a constructor to ensure that the structure is of the quality and description required by the contract, is fit for a particular purpose expressly or impliedly made known to the contractor, and fit for purposes of which a structure of the same description would ordinarily be used.[105] Again, there is a marked similarity to the approach in the BGB. To apply these provisions to the example given earlier, assuming that the type of mortar to be used had been specified in the contract, deviation from this description would mean the building was not in conformity with the contract. Thus, the particular articles on construction contracts would affirm the result reached under the general DCFR rule, and entitle the customer to a reduction in price affecting the reduction in value (if any) of the building as constructed.

(b)   Sales of goods

The harsh decision of the US Supreme Court in the case of *Filley* v. *Pope*,[106] referred to approvingly in later Supreme Court decisions, might be thought to go against the substantial performance position. In that case, a contract was concluded for the sale of 500 tons of pig iron, at the price of $26 per ton, to be shipped from Glasgow to New Orleans as soon as possible. The seller had trouble finding a vessel to ship the iron, but eventually found one which was able to transport it from the port of Leith, near Edinburgh, rather than Glasgow. The iron was shipped from Leith to New Orleans, but the seller refused to accept and pay for the iron as shipped from Leith. The Court held that the stipulated port of embarkation of the goods was a 'warranty' (or 'condition precedent') of the contract, failure to fulfil which entitled the buyer to 'repudiate' (in other words, terminate) the contract. Such a result of course leaves the seller, who has performed at some considerable cost to himself, with no way to claim the price from a buyer unwilling to accept the goods simply on account of a matter which has no bearing on the quality of the goods at all.

In English law (which has its own late nineteenth-century equivalent of the *Filley* decision),[107] as in US Common law, a distinction is made between those types of term which entitle a party to terminate a contract (called a 'condition'), and those which do not (called a 'warranty', despite equation

---

[105]   Art. IV.C.-3:104.   [106]   115 US 213.

[107]   *Bowes* v. *Shand* (1877) 2 App Cas 455, where the deviation from the contract terms was as to the date upon which goods were to be shipped. The House of Lords held the date of shipment to be an integral part of the description of the goods sold.

of the terms 'warranty' and 'condition' in *Filley*). A third category (an 'innominate term') may give a right to terminate, but only if the breach is deemed severe enough.[108] Determining which character a term will have is essentially a matter of interpreting what the parties intended (a point emphasised in the case of sale of goods contracts by section 11 of the Sale of Goods Act 1979, which states that such determination 'depends in each case on the construction of the contract').[109] Assuming that the same facts as arose in *Filley* were to obtain in an English case, the outcome would depend on whether the parties had intended the port of embarkation of the goods to be a condition of the contract, something which could not be assumed merely from the inclusion of the name of the port in the contract. The case for arguing that the inclusion of the port of embarkation of the goods was a condition would be sealed if it could be argued that it was part of the description of the goods, that is if the goods to be sold by the seller were not just '500 tons of pig iron' but '500 tons of pig iron to be shipped from Leith'. The significance of finding that the description of the goods to be sold included the phrase 'to be shipped from Glasgow' would be that, were the goods to be shipped from Leith instead, what would be delivered would not be the goods as described in the contract. This would mean that there would be a breach of section 13(1) of the Sale of Goods Act, the section which provides that where there is 'a contract for the sale of goods by description, there is an implied term that the goods will correspond with the description', breach of this section being deemed a condition of the contract.[110] The approach of the US Supreme Court in *Filley* was certainly to see the stipulation as to the port of embarkation as part of the description of the goods sold, a similar approach taken by the House of Lords in a case from 1877.[111] On the other hand, in the present era an English court might well be less likely to consider such a stipulation as part of the description of the goods.[112]

If goods shipped from the wrong port were nonetheless kept by the buyer, it would certainly have to pay for them. Moreover, it is extremely

---

[108] *Hong Kong Fir Shipping Co. Ltd* v. *Kawasaki Kisen Kaisha Ltd* [1962] 2 QB 26.

[109] SOGA, s. 11(3) (not applicable in Scotland).

[110] SOGA, s. 13(2). [111] *Bowes* v. *Shand* (1877) 2 App Cas 455.

[112] In *Harlingdon & Leinster Enterprises Ltd* v. *Christopher Hull Fine Art Ltd* [1991] 1 QB 564, the description a 'Gabriele Münter' applied to a painting was held not have been intended by the parties to be a term of the contract, so that the contract was not one of sale by description in terms of s. 13 of the Sale of Goods Act 1979. Such a view suggests that the specification of a port of loading for goods may be equally unlikely to be held a condition of a contract.

unlikely that such a breach of the contract terms could be argued to render the goods 'defective' in some way. They would not be defective in England (or Scotland) under section 14 of the Sale of Goods Act 1979, which concerns the quality of goods, and there would thus be no entitlement on the buyer's part to a reduction in price.[113] Nor would they be defective under German law. Under §433 of the BGB a seller is obliged, among other things, to procure the thing for the buyer free of material and legal defects, the concepts of material and legal defects being explained at §§434 and 435. As the goods shipped from the wrong port would still be suitable for the use intended under the contract, and for customary uses, they would not be materially defective under §434; and, as third parties could assert no rights over the goods, they would also be free of legal defect under §435. As the goods would not be defective, §441 on reduction of the price of the goods for defects would also be inapplicable, this provision allowing for a reduction in price in case of reduced value, the reduction to be 'in the proportion in which the value of the thing free of defects would, at the time when the contract was entered into, have had to the actual value'.[114]

In the DCFR, the *Filley* problem would again boil down to whether or not the port of embarkation were part of the description of the goods. Article IV.A.-2:301 provides that goods do not conform with the contract unless, inter alia, they are of the description required by the contract, and are packaged in the manner required by the contract. The Commentary to the DCFR gives no hint as to the likely application of the relevant rules to a case like *Filley*, but, as suggested earlier, a modern court is unlikely to adopt the narrow point of view that the port of embarkation was intended by the parties as part of the description of the goods. A finding that it was would arguably ratify bad faith on the buyer's part.

5.   Injunction (interdict)

Traditionally, the Common law and mixed systems have provided for separate remedies to enforce positive obligations (obligations to do something) and negative obligations (obligations not to do something). The former are enforced by specific performance (or specific implement as it is sometimes called), or, in the case of monetary sums, actions for an agreed

---

[113] So far as consumer contracts are concerned, SOGA, s. 48C stipulates simply that the price is to be reduced to an 'appropriate amount', without saying how the calculation of such an amount is to be undertaken.

[114] §441(3) BGB.

price, the latter by injunction (or interdict as it is sometimes called). Injunction/interdict is also the appropriate remedy to prevent any action (whether obligatory in nature or not) which would put a party in contravention of an obligation it owes.[115] A perfectly valid claim may be, and frequently has been, defeated by a litigant's choice of the wrong remedy. To avoid refusing claims for such a procedural nicety, there may be sense in the suggestion that all claims to enforce duties, whether of a positive or negative type, ought to be amalgamated in to a single remedy. German Law takes such an approach, providing for a single procedural remedy (the *Leistungsklage*) applicable in all cases in which a party is seeking enforcement of an express obligation of another to do or not to do something.[116] This approach is also adopted by the PECL [117] and the DCFR.[118]

The question of whether actions to amalgamate both positive and negative obligations into a single remedy is an interesting one, though not of primary relevance for the present examination of the value of promises. Of greater relevance is perhaps the more fundamental question of whether it ought to be possible, as it presently is, to prevent by injunction threatened acts by B in favour of C which are merely inconsistent with an express promise made by B in favour of A. That it should be possible might seem to be so obviously the case as not to merit consideration, but given the traditional approach of some legal systems to construing promises strictly in accordance with the reasonable objective impression conveyed only by the words used, it is surely at least questionable to hold that a party who has promised merely to do x should also be held tacitly to have promised not to do y, an act inconsistent with x. Although most legal systems *do* adopt such an attitude[119] through the grant of injunctions to prevent a threatened occurrence of y from taking place, it is perhaps somewhat inconsistent that, if the likelihood of y occurring is not discovered ahead

---

[115] For instance, in South African law, interdicts are available not only to ensure compliance with a negative contractual duty but also 'to restrain the debtor from doing something which may prevent him from complying with his duties' (Van der Merwe *et al.*, *Contract*, p. 387).

[116] Anticipated actions which would be inconsistent with the obligation in question may be prevented by use of an injunction (*Unterlassungsklage*).

[117] Specific performance is available to enforce obligations 'to do or not to do an act': see comment A to Art. 9:102 of PECL.

[118] The DCFR simply states that the creditor is entitled to enforce specific performance of 'an obligation', without specifying whether it is to do or not to do something.

[119] Indeed, in a slightly different context (one not involving a third party), the principle of preventing acts inconsistent with a prior promise is the whole basis of the law of promissory estoppel.

of time, but B simply goes ahead and does *y*, it does not necessarily follow that *y* is held to have no legal effect. Take, for instance, a case where B has a contract to sell his car to A. If A discovers that B, in contravention of his contractual duty to sell the car to A, is about to sell the car to C, A can prevent this act by means of an injunction. On the other hand, if A merely subsequently discovers that B has entered into such a contract with C, the contract between B and C is not deemed to be void, as one might expect; on the contrary, it is a valid contract, albeit one that will put B in the unenviable position of having to breach either his contract with A or C. This position often strikes law students as puzzling: why should B, who has already promised to sell to A, still be allowed validly to contract to sell to C also? The injustice of this being permitted seems even greater when it is explained that A can prevent ahead of time an inconsistent promise from being given effect to, but cannot prevent C from taking the benefit of such a promise if performance has already been effected in C's favour.[120] An explanation sometimes offered for this apparent discrepancy of approach is that this simply demonstrates that the law is compelled to take account of the reality of transactions which have already happened. That, however, seems less convincing an explanation when one considers that purported transfers of stolen goods are treated as wholly invalid regardless of the 'reality' of what has occurred.

What position then ought the law to adopt in relation to these issues? It certainly seems reasonable that a promise by B to A to do *x* should be taken to mean that B is also bound not to do *y*, an act inconsistent with *x*. One can explain this either by reference to an implicit or tacit further promise by B (along the lines of 'I promise to do *x*. I also promise not to do *y*') or by reference to an external limitation on B's promissory capacity, given the nature of B's first promise, imposed by the requirements of justice. Either seems feasible, though the latter explanation has the benefit of avoiding the use of a legal fiction. If such a restriction on B's promissory capacity seems reasonable, however, then it would also seem reasonable to deal with such a limitation consistently by holding that B can not only be injuncted from doing *y* but also that any attempt to do *y* should be treated as invalid so long as the prior promise to do *x* remains in force. Such a conclusion would not agree with the position adopted in many legal systems, however, where the contrary view is taken that, while B may be injuncted

---

[120] Except in limited cases: for instance, in terms of the UK Sale of Goods Act 1979, some (but not all) transfers of goods to third parties in contravention of A's rights can be prevented by A even after the purported transfer has occurred.

from doing *y*, a promise made by B to a third party to do *y* is not otherwise invalid (though it may be ineffectual in exceptional cases). The position adopted by such systems seems to be justified on the basis that, from C's point of view, if B does not appear to lack contractual capacity to do *y*, the promise to do *y* should be held valid even though inconsistent with the prior promise to do *x*. As remarked earlier, however, such a policy of third party protection does not apply in the case of transactions tainted by *vitium reale* (that is, theft), which suggests a degree of inconsistency.

6.   Damages

The law of damages is a vast subject about which whole treatises have been written. Fortunately, the majority of the issues contained in such works are not of present concern. The principal matter which the remedy of damages raises for the current discussion is whether the general policies concerning the law of contractual damages adopted by jurisdictions can be said to show a high regard for promises, including through adequate substitutionary redress in cases of breach of promise.

The concern in the present section of the text is with default damages, that is to say, with the damages that will be awarded by a court in an action for breach of contract in the absence of any express provision concerning the assessment of damages which the parties may have provided for in their contract (such express damages clauses are discussed separately below). In codified systems, it is (as one would expect) the Code which specifies how such damages are to be assessed; in uncodified systems, the courts have developed various rules to assist in the assessment process. As will be seen from the discussion below, in no system is the view taken in the modern law that such default damages rules rest upon a presumed or tacit promise by the defaulting party to pay damages according to a certain measure. Such reasoning, while it may have been adopted in the past,[121] now has an air of extreme artificiality about it, given that it is quite evident that, in those cases where no express damages clause was adopted by parties, parties simply failed to consider (or perhaps even chose to ignore) the question. The farthest that legal systems presently get towards having regard to the intention or will of the parties, when framing default rules as to damages, is in referring, as they often do, to what the parties

---

[121] See for instance the remark of Bovill CJ in *British Columbia etc. Sawmill Co. Ltd* v. *Nettleship* (1868) LR 3 CP 499, 505, that the defendant was liable for those damages 'to which he assented expressly or impliedly by entering the contract'.

might reasonably be supposed to have contemplated as the likely losses which would flow from an act of non-performance of the contract.[122] Because such foreseeable loss can, in appropriate cases,[123] be measured according to the cost of cure of imperfect performance, it is evident that legal systems consider it to be consistent with the nature of a promise that the promisee may seek performance by an alternative party or the costs of itself effecting a cure if the promisor defaults, even if strictly the promisor only promised its own performance rather than that of another party in cases of default.[124]

The origins of the tradition of tying default damages to foreseeable losses appears to lie in a discussion of an old Roman text on recoverable damage in Molinaeus's *Tractatus de eo quod interest*.[125] This discussion of foreseeability was generalised by Pothier, in his statement that 'the person who owes a performance is only liable for the damages that one could have foreseen at the time of the contract that the party owed a performance would suffer'.[126] Pothier's view was explicitly borrowed by the court in the seminal case of *Hadley* v. *Baxendale*,[127] which enshrined the foreseeability approach in English law. Though foreseeability was, in the formulation penned by Alderson B in *Hadley*, equated with the more causal notion of loss 'arising naturally, i.e. according to the usual course of things',[128] in the long run the accepted view has become that the formulation proposed two types of recoverable damage: (i) any damage reasonably contemplated as a matter of fact by both parties (this encompassing unusual types of damage), and (ii) any damage of a type ordinarily caused by the type of breach in question (and thus of a type foresight of which might reasonably be imputed to the parties). Reasonable foreseeability thus became the touchstone, though it would be assumed by courts in the case of ordinary types of loss.[129]

This common idea of 'foreseeability of loss' does not go so far as to posit that parties *intended* a specific quantum of damages to be recoverable,

---

[122] See Gordley, 'The Foreseeability Limitation on Liability in Contract Law'.

[123] In those cases where cure is practicable, and is intended by the promisee.

[124] An issue which arose in the English case *Ruxley Electronics* v. *Forsyth* [1996] AC 344, discussed below at p. 379.

[125] Molinaeus, *Tractatus de eo quod interest*, §60.

[126] Pothier, *Treatise on Obligations*, §160.

[127] (1854) 9 Exch 341.   [128] *Ibid.*, per Alderson B at 354.

[129] In *Victoria Laundry (Windsor) Ltd* v. *Newman Industries Ltd* (1949) 2 KB 528, Asquith J stated (at 539) that knowledge was either imputed or actual, the knowledge of the reasonable person being imputed to the contract breaker. Knowledge of special, unusual facts would require to be demonstrated as a matter of fact.

but, insofar as it posits that the parties might reasonably be supposed to have foreseen a certain quantum and type of loss as likely and did nothing to restrict or exclude the recoverability of such loss, it does at least attempt to provide a justification for awarding such foreseeable loss which has some connection with the minds (if not the actual intentions) of the parties. It is noteworthy that the *Hadley* v. *Baxendale* formulation requires likely losses to have been contemplated by *both* parties before they may be recoverable (albeit that such contemplation is assumed for losses of an ordinary type). There must thus be some sort of 'agreement', as least in that the parties' contemplations of likely loss must 'agree' in a loose sense, before the losses are recoverable: a unilateral conception by one party that it is likely to suffer a particular type of loss in the event of breach which is not shared by, or communicated to, the other party is not enough to make the loss foreseeable.[130] Nonetheless, there is evidently something of a leap to be made from conceiving of a loss as likely to imagining that this somehow demonstrates an intention of the defaulting party to pay for it. Realistically, any such conceptual leap is too great: foreseeability of loss as a basis for imposing liability for damages cannot sensibly be said to rest upon an intention or a promise by the defaulting party to pay for the loss it has caused. Rather, the use of foreseeability must be seen as functioning both as a judicial policy that a party *ought* to pay for some losses, as well as a recognition that there must be some sort of limitation placed upon the extent of the liability for such losses.

A foreseeability test as such a break on damages has of course the potential drawback that, if A and B foresee very onerous and, some might argue, disproportionate losses as arising in the event of breach of contract by A, simply by that act of foresight A will have incurred liability for such losses.[131] Such limitations on the usefulness of foreseeability to arrive at arguably 'fair' results have been judicially commented upon: as one English judge has recently remarked 'the concept of reasonable foreseeability is not a complete guide to the circumstances in which damages are recoverable as a matter of law'.[132] Such concerns have led to attempts

---

[130] *Ibid.* For a Scottish example of the application of the rule that both parties must contemplate the likely losses, see *Balfour Beatty Construction (Scotland) Ltd* v. *Scottish Power plc* 1994 SC (HL) 20.

[131] An oft-used example is the taxi driver who knows that delivering his client late to his destination may result in heavy business losses: see Peel, 'Remoteness Revisited', p. 10; Hoffmann, '*The Achilleas*: Custom and Practice or Foreseeability?', p. 59.

[132] Sir Anthony Evans in *Mulvenna* v. *Royal Bank of Scotland plc* [2003] EWCA Civ 1112, para. 33.

to marginalise foreseeability as the proper test for remoteness of damages in recent English cases,[133] without a clear alternative test yet emerging. Lord Hoffmann's attempt to postulate an alternative test of 'assumption of responsibility'[134] is unlikely to help, as such a test has the tendency to act as one of vague application and uncertain content under which to hide a general equitable allocation of risks.[135] It is, moreover, prima facie unsuited to the many problematic cases where it is unclear precisely whether or not a party's behaviour indicates its acceptance of bearing the consequences of a risk materialising.

The fact that the availability of default damages in breach of contract cases derives from legal rules and not from the promises (express or tacit) of the parties does not mean, however, that the remedy of damages has no relationship with the promisee's interest in performance. As a substitutionary remedy for a promised but unfulfilled performance, damages are intended to protect the interest that the innocent party has in that performance by putting it, as far as possible, in that position which can be equated in pecuniary terms with the position in which it would have been had performance occurred. To the extent then that damages reflect such performance interest, they are referable to the promise made by the other party to perform. Though it has become fashionable of late among so-called rights theorists to argue that contractual damages are *not* a substitutionary remedy to compensate a claimant for the loss resulting from non-conforming performance, but rather constitute compensation for infringement of, or loss of, a right to performance,[136] such an alternative view does not reflect decisions of the courts emphasising that it is not the value of the right lost but the pecuniary and non-pecuniary losses caused

---

[133] *Transfield Shipping Inc.* v. *Mercator Shipping Inc.* ('*The Achilleas*') [2009] 1 AC 61; *Supershield Ltd* v. *Siemens Building Technologies FE Ltd* [2010] EWCA Civ 7.

[134] See Lord Hoffmann's speech in *The Achilleas* [2009] 1 AC 61. Considerations of market expectations, such as those that operated in *The Achilleas*, may well however be a relevant factor in determining the proper result in some cases.

[135] See O'Sullivan, 'Damages for Lost Profits for Late Redelivery', p. 36. See also critical remarks in McGregor, *McGregor on Damages*, para. 6–171.

[136] The rights theorist Robert Stevens has argued that the standard award of damages in both tort and breach of contract is not compensatory, but rather provides a substitute for the infringement of the right in question. On this view, the value of the award is thus not measured according to the harm done to person, property, or other patrimony, but by relation to the value of the infringement of the right. This theory's fundamental problem is that it assumes that rights have an objective value capable of determination, whereas (as discussed in Ch. 2) the view of modern economics is that value is a subjective quality. For Stevens' views, see 'Damages and the Right to Performance: A Golden Victory or Not?'; also, generally, Stevens, *Torts and Rights*.

by breach which are important,[137] though it evidently represents what some commentators would wish the law to be.

If the challenge of rights theorists does not accord with the stated approach of the courts, what of the problem that courts do on occasion award damages that do not reflect the performance interest, but some other interest of the innocent party? Do such awards fundamentally undermine a 'substitution for performance' based view of contractual damages?

(a) Contractual damages and interests other than the performance interest

In most legal systems, the performance measure of damages for breach of contract is conceived of as encompassing both actual losses suffered by the innocent party as a result of the breach (what is sometimes called *damnum emergens*) as well as lost opportunities to profit by the expected performance (what is sometimes called *lucrum cessans*). As discussed further below, wasted expenditure in preparing for a contract (an aspect of the actual, rather than speculative, loss) is usually factored in as part of the net claim made by the claimant. Both *damnum emergens* and *lucrum cessans* are rightly seen as legitimate monetary compensation for the position which the innocent party *would* have been in had the contract been performed properly: the innocent party *would* have avoided the losses it has suffered, and *would* have made the profit it has been deprived of. As Lord Chancellor Haldane put it in *British Westinghouse Electric and Manufacturing Co. Ltd* v. *Underground Electric Railways Co. of London Ltd*,[138] 'as far as possible, he who has proved a breach of a bargain to supply what he contracted to get is to be placed, as far as money can do it, in as good a situation as if the contract had been performed. The fundamental basis is thus compensation for pecuniary loss naturally flowing from the breach.' Given the construction by courts of the hypothetical circumstances that would have prevailed upon proper performance, the idea of a 'performance measure' of damages (or the 'performance interest' of the claimant) makes sense, though it ought to be borne in mind that courts,

---

[137] As demonstrated recently, for instance, in *The Golden Victory* [2007] UKHL 12, where the House of Lords assessed damages in a breach of contract case at the time of the claim, thus including consequential losses after the date of breach, rather than at the time of breach. Had the latter approach been adopted, then the case for arguing that damages compensate for loss of the right to performance would have been strengthened.

[138] [1912] AC 673, 689.

when deciding the issue of damages, do not always, or even usually, talk in terms of performance 'measure' or 'interest' when making their awards, but simply rather 'what would have happened' had performance occurred, or (to put it in the negative) what the parties 'might reasonably have foreseen' as the outcome had proper performance *not* occurred. Evidently, counterfactual judicial conceptions of the outcome of the case had proper performance occurred mean that, where claimed, both *damnum emergens* and *lucrum cessans* must be proven to be connected causally with the defendant's breach of contract using the ordinary tests of causation.

As will be seen in the discussion below, however, sometimes contracting parties are exceptionally permitted to raise a claim which does not reflect protection of the performance interest. One of the arguments levelled against a promissory, will-based approach to contract theory is that because exceptionally there is recovery of damages in the restoration and restitutionary interests, rather than the performance interest, this shows that contractual liability is not based exclusively (or even at all) on the will of the parties, otherwise the performance measure of damages would be awarded in every case. What may be said in response to such a criticism?

First, it should be noted that damages is not in every jurisdiction the primary (or default) remedy – in most civilian and mixed systems, it is not substitutionary remedies but actual performance which is conceived of as the primary entitlement of an aggrieved party. Where that is so, the will is clearly given greater prominence, which helps to counter any suggestion that the availability of non-performance measures of damages in certain cases somehow indicates a jurisdictional lack of respect for the will of the parties. Second, it should not be forgotten that the performance measure is the primary measure of damages, even though (like other obligations) there may be another interest which is protected apart from the primary interest. Protection of another interest may be awarded in some cases because, for instance, no evident measure of performance can be determined, in which event the restoration interest often seems a reasonable fall back measure of recovery,[139] or because the performance measure would be inadequate because, for instance, breach has caused foreseeable harm to the other party in excess of the performance measure. Recourse to non-performance damages is, however, exceptional and only available to support specific, limited objectives which do not detract from a general emphasis upon performance.

---

[139] See, for instance, *McRae* v. *Commonwealth Disposals Commission* (1951) 84 CLR 377 and *Anglia Television Ltd* v. *Reed* [1972] 1 QB 60.

As to wasted contractual expenditure, such expenditure on the part of the party suffering a breach of contract will usually be absorbed into a claim for damages made by reference to the performance measure, because what will be claimed is the gross amount which that party expected to gain by the other's performance (the contract price, for instance, if a seller is the claimant). Alternatively, though the claim is seldom presented that way, net profits together with wasted expenditure may be claimed. However, gross profits *and* wasted expenditure cannot both be claimed, as such expenditure would have had to have been incurred in any event to make the gross profit. Thus, if A expected to make £5,000 gross profit on a contract (this being the contract price charged by A) and to incur £1,000 in costs related to the performance, if B breaks the contract then either the gross profit/contract price of £5,000 *or* the £4,000 net profit together with the £1,000 expenditure can be claimed by A, but not the £5,000 gross profit/contract price and the £1,000 costs. A difficulty arises in cases where, unluckily for A, following formation of the contract with B, A's costs rise to such an extent that they exceed the price agreed for A's services. What, thus, if by the eve of performance, A's costs have risen to £6,000, and B then breaches the contract: can A choose to claim these wasted costs rather than the contract price? If A is so permitted, then it will be able to avoid a bad bargain, and to recover costs which would have had to have been incurred as part of its contractual duties in any event had the contract not been breached by B. For that reason, such wasted costs ought not to be recoverable by A, and all A should get is the £5,000 price agreed for its performance. In other words, a proper respect for the contract, and for the allocation of risk between the contracting parties, should mean that there is no free choice between the performance measure and restoration measure where the latter would permit recovery in excess of the former.[140]

What of a choice between performance and restitutionary measures? The restitutionary interest is hardly ever protected in contractual damages, in any jurisdiction. Even the notable and exceptional recent protection of the restitutionary interest by English law in *Attorney-General* v. *Blake*[141] concerned not the remedy of damages but the remedy of an account of profits, a remedy the granting of which was said to be justified given the exceptional, quasi-fiduciary nature of the relationship

---

[140] This is, in any event, the approach of English law: *CCC Films (London) Ltd* v. *Impact Quadrant Films Ltd* [1985] QB 16.

[141] [2001] 1 AC 268, [2000] 4 All ER 385.

in question.[142] It is a fundamental principle of contractual damages that such damages should measure the actual losses suffered by the aggrieved party rather than any gain made by the party in breach.[143] Whilst there are some voices arguing that penal damages should be recoverable in some instances of breach of contract,[144] or that restitutionary damages should be available in cases of 'cynical' breach of contract, while the Common law (and mixed systems) maintain the view, discussed further below, that damages for breach of contract are not a fault based remedy, but a strict one, it seems equitable that loss rather than gain should remain the fundamental touchstone of the assessment exercise. In addition, it is noteworthy that, following a breach of contract, an innocent party is not usually permitted to seek financial recompense by abandoning a claim for damages in contract and instead raising a potentially more advantageous claim in unjustified enrichment.[145]

In English law, the principle that damages reflect actual loss has been exceptionally deviated from in cases involving a breach of a specific covenant, where, though a party undertook not to do something, it has done the very thing it covenanted not to, profiting thereby. In such cases, the courts have permitted recovery in damages in a fictional measure (without the need to demonstrate any loss), that measure being in an amount which the aggrieved party might reasonably be imagined to have charged for a relaxation or waiver of the covenant.[146] It must not be thought, however, that this exceptional recovery somehow represents compensation in the restitutionary measure: there is no question of any gains made by the contract breaker being used as the basis upon which recovery is

---

[142] The *Blake* approach was also adopted in *Esso Petroleum* v. *Niad* [2001] EWHC 6 (Ch), though given that this case did not involve any fiduciary or similar relationship between the parties, the decision is hard to square with an orthodox approach to damages. For a similar decision to *Blake* in US Common law, see *Snepp* v. *United States* 444 US 507 (1980).

[143] *Tito* v. *Waddell (No. 2)* [1977] Ch 106.

[144] In Canadian Common law, penal damages for breach, though rare, may be awarded: *Vorvis* v. *Insurance Corp. of British Columbia* [1989] 1 SCR 1085.

[145] In some systems this rule is enforced via a principle that unjustified enrichment remedies are 'subsidiary' to, or 'postponed' to, remedies under other branches of the law of obligations, so that where a remedy exists under another such branch, an enrichment remedy is precluded. Even if no such principle of subsidiarity is recognised, another rule or rules typically operates to exclude enrichment remedies if the remedy of damages for breach of contract is available.

[146] *Wrotham Park Estate Co. Ltd* v. *Parkside Homes Ltd* [1974] 1 WLR 798 (Ch); *Amec Development Ltd* v. *Jury's Hotel Management (UK) Ltd* [2001] 1 EGLR 81 (Ch); *Experience Hendrix LLC* v. *PPX Enterprises Inc.* [2003] EMLR 25 (CA). See also the Privy Council Appeal *Pell Frischman Engineering* v. *Bow Valley Iran* [2009] UKPC 45.

measured. On the contrary, damages are assessed according to a deemed performance interest loss by the claimant. This is an entirely fictional approach, as the claimant is not required to show that it would have agreed to the waiver if it had been sought (indeed, the recovery is available even if the evidence indicates that it would *not* have agreed to the waiver). Appreciating this, the exceptional approach adopted in breach of covenant cases should not be seen as a radical departure from the traditional assessment of damages.

(b) Damages for mere breach of contract, or for fault?

Making damages dependent upon the demonstration of fault in every case can be said to be at odds with the promissory principle: quite often a promisor does not promise to do something 'if he is able' or 'unless he is prevented', but simply to do it. Any failure is thus a breach of that promise, yet an invariable fault requirement for damages claims would exclude from compensation breaches of such simple and unconditional promises. One could argue that caveats such as 'if I am able' or 'unless I am prevented' should be read into promises, but such implications seem improper in the face of the practice of adding such caveats only where promisors wish that to be the case.

As seen below in the discussion of German law, automatic fault-based liability in damages has been argued to be an 'ethically superior' position by some, but such claims seem spurious. A more promising way of justifying a fault requirement in damages claims might be to argue as follows. When a promisor undertakes to do (or not do) something in a promise, that is a strict and unqualified undertaking. For that reason, the remedy of enforced performance does not require the fault of the promisor to be shown. However, promisors often say nothing about the circumstances in which they will or will not be willing to pay damages instead of performing, and one should not assume that the willingness to pay damages will also be a strict undertaking. Of course, if strict liability to pay damages is stated (in a so-called 'penalty' or 'liquidated damages' clause) then that position ought to prevail, given the principle of *pacta sunt servanda*. But, if no such choice is expressly made, it could place too heavy a burden on the promisor to impose strict liability to pay damages; on the contrary, and acting consistently with the approach in delict, the duty to pay should only be held to arise where fault on the promisor's part can be demonstrated.

A critical appraisal of this justification would seem to depend at least in part on how the default duty to pay damages is seen as arising: does it derive from an implied or tacit agreement of the parties, or is it a duty imposed by law (unless excluded by the parties)? If the duty arises by implied or tacit agreement of the parties, then it might seem somewhat harsh to impose a strict standard of liability on the promisor. In effect one would be saying that the promisor had promised as follows: 'I promise to do x [the express part of the promise]; in the event that I do not do x, for whatever reason, I promise to pay damages for not doing x [the implied promise]'.[147] It might be argued that if one is going to imply a promise on the promisor's part, such implication should be of no more onerous a duty than is necessary to provide reasonable protection of the promisee's interests. If correct, that would suggest the implication of a fault-based duty to pay damages would be sufficient protection. However, it is far from obvious that the duty to pay damages should be seen as arising from an implied promise to pay. Especially in systems where a civil code is the source of the duty to pay damages, but even in those where the duty to pay damages is imposed by courts as a result of the unwritten law, it seems equally if not more plausible to suggest that the nature of the duty to pay damages is that of a default legal rule, and one which ought therefore to be able to embody a policy of either strict or fault-based liability as the particular legal system sees fit. Whilst some of those who support promissory based liability might not approve of this view, given that it diminishes the extent of contractual duties conceived of as resting upon the promises of the parties rather than externally imposed legal policy, it avoids the fiction of implied promises, a fiction which too often brings promissory liability into disrepute.

If this view – that the duty to pay damages derives not from an implied promise, but by application of a default legal rule to pay – is correct, then there need be no concern about trying to tie either strict or fault-based liability to the supposed wishes of a promisor, nor is there any force in the idea that an absence of a harsher regime for deliberate breaches of contract undermines a promissory view of contract.[148] The

---

[147] Smith, *Contract Theory*, pp. 384–6, takes the view that, in the Common law, the duty to pay damages is a 'conjunctive obligation' (that is, a secondary obligation applicable in cases of default of performance) agreed to by the parties, thus rooting the duty to pay damages in implied promises of the parties.

[148] Even if the default obligation to pay damages were conceived of as resting upon an implied promise to pay damages, rather than a legal rule that they be paid, an absence of penal damages in a legal system would not undermine a promissory view of contract for

promisor is simply subject to a duty to pay imposed by the law, unless and to the extent that the promisor varies or excludes such a default duty.[149] That still leaves the question of *which* policy should be adopted by the default legal rule. This brings us back to the first point made in this discussion, namely that this ought to depend upon the nature of the promise made by the promisor. If, as often happens, a promisor has made an unqualified promise of performance to achieve a particular result, then the remedial position which most respects such a promise is a position which makes available contract remedies for any deviation from the promised performance. Thus, if A says to B 'I promise to deliver the goods to your depot by 9 a.m. on Monday morning', then, short of the operation of *force majeure*, any failure to meet that promise ought to trigger liability in damages (or the availability of other remedies). On the other hand, if A only promises to act with skill and care in achieving delivery of the goods – so that end result x is subject to a fault-based caveat – or if no specific end or result is specified as act x, but the promise made is simply one to act generally with skill and care in the interests of the promisee (for instance, 'I hereby undertake to perform with ordinary skill and care such legal services on your behalf as you may instruct me in relation to'), then it would be consistent with respect for the nature of that type of promise to permit a damages claim only where the promisor has demonstrated the necessary want of skill or care. What is suggested therefore is that it is the nature of the promise undertaken which should determine the type of liability, strict or fault-based, which triggers the remedy of damages. Such an approach, flexible according to the nature of the promise made, is that which would seem to be most respectful of the nature of promissory liability. Most legal systems appear to show some appreciation of the wisdom of such a view, but those which begin from a default position of fault-based damages run the greater risk of failing to show respect for the precise nature of the promises made, because they have the greatest difficulty in dealing with those promises which on their face promise strict achievement of a specific outcome.

the simple reason that a penal response to a breach of a promise is by no means a necessary or obvious response. On the contrary, it is just as consistent with a proper response to a breach of promise that some remedial or restorative remedy be imposed, rather than a penal one.

[149] Though such an ability to vary or exclude liability in damages is itself subject to external control in some cases, by virtue of statutory control of potentially unfair terms.

(c)   English law

Various aspects of English law (including the use of foreseeability as a break on recoverable damages) have already been discussed in the introductory remarks to this discussion of damages, and reference is therefore made to those earlier remarks, particularly those indicating that English law generally awards contract damages in the performance measure.[150] Two matters will be discussed further at this point, namely damages for loss of amenity, and the Common law's theoretical subjugation of specific performance to damages.

As to the first issue, the decision of the House of Lords in *Ruxley Electronics* v. *Forsyth*[151] awarding damages for 'loss of amenity' as a result of a breach of contract is sometimes said to demonstrate that contract is *not* about the performance of a promise, or, in default, the award of a substitutionary remedy to compensate for non-conforming performance, given that Mr Ruxley did not get such a substitutionary award for his loss. When Mr Ruxley was sued for payment under a contract for the construction of a swimming pool, he counterclaimed for damages for the loss he had suffered through the non-conforming performance of the builder (the pool was not of the contracted-for depth). While the Court of Appeal awarded Mr Ruxley the costs of rebuilding the pool to the correct depth, the House of Lords overturned this award, given that the evidence showed that Mr Ruxley had no intention of so rebuilding the pool; to award him damages for costs of rebuilding would thus have been to overcompensate him. The alternative common measure of damages in building cases, difference in value, was also rejected, on the basis that the value of the pool that had been constructed was no different to that which ought to have been built; to award him this measure would be to undercompensate him. Despite both these ordinary measures of damages being rejected, Mr Ruxley was held still to be entitled to damages for his 'loss of amenity', such reflecting the reduced pleasure he obtained from the pool as built compared to the pleasure he would have derived had the contract been performed properly.[152] It is suggested that the judgment does not undermine a performance-based view of contract in relation to compensation for skimped performance. Rather, it demonstrates that in some cases the English courts do not consider it reasonable to award damages

---

[150]   For a pro-performance view of remedies, including damages, in English law, see Webb, 'Justifying Damages'.
[151]   [1996] AC 344.   [152]   *Ibid.*, see speech of Lord Lloyd at 373–4.

by virtue of one of the measures ordinarily adopted to compensate for non-conforming performance in construction cases, but will instead, where the case concerns the construction of a 'pleasurable amenity', have regard to a third measure which can equally be said to be performance-based, given that performance was intended to provide the claimant with a certain measure of pleasure of which he has been deprived. Assessment of the quantum of such measure will inevitably be a somewhat uncertain exercise for the courts, but this does not detract from the point that it is the loss occasioned by the skimped performance of a pleasurable amenity which they are attempting to assess.

As to the second issue, it was suggested earlier that the English law approach that damages are the primary contractual remedy under-values the promises of performance made by contracting parties, and tacitly condones the behaviour of those who break their contractual promises. The place of damages as the primary remedy gives the impression that English law adopts the attitude that breach kills off the right to performance, and that damages are simply compensation for having lost that right to perform. Such an entrenched attitude created a legal environment in which the important (though dissenting) ideas of Lord Goff in *Alfred McAlpine Construction Ltd* v. *Panatown Ltd*[153] concerning the nature of damages might be advanced. In the context of a so-called 'transferred loss' claim,[154] his Lordship proposed a radical restatement of the purpose and assessment of contractual damages in general.[155] According to Lord Goff, the loss which a party suffers as a result of a breach of contract, and for which it ought to be compensated, lies in not having received the performance it bargained for. It does not matter, in Lord Goff's view, that, having not received the bargained-for perform-ance, a party is no worse off in the sense of suffering a pecuniary loss, because the real loss is the failure to receive the expected performance. That loss of a bargained-for performance might arise equally in cases where the performance is to be tendered to a third party, as much as where it is to be tendered to the party suffering the breach. Such a theory of the nature of the loss suffered in breach of contract cases was able to

---

[153] [2001] 1 AC 518; [2000] 4 All ER 97; [2000] 3 WLR 946.

[154] See discussion of this topic in the previous chapter, at pp. 320–32.

[155] Lord Goff's new approach was developed in part by reference to the broad approach to damages claims in respect of third party loss of Lord Griffiths in *St Martin's Property Corp. Ltd* v. *Sir Robert McAlpine & Sons Ltd* [1994] 1 AC 85. Lord Griffiths had remarked (at 97) of a hypothetical claim for such damages that the claim would arise because the party claiming 'did not receive the bargain for which he had contracted'.

explain, in Lord Goff's view, why recovery of damages was permissible in transferred loss cases.

Lord Goff attempted to find support for his radical redefinition of the nature of loss and the assessment of damages in breach of contract cases from contemporary academic re-emphasis on the protection of the performance interest.[156] But is his redefinition in fact consistent with a high regard for performance and the promises of the parties? Lord Goff's approach seems essentially to compensate a claimant for having lost the rights bargained for in the contract. But this ignores the fact that a party's contractual rights are *not* lost by the other party's breach; on the contrary, the innocent party can still insist upon performance, or, if it chooses, to seek a substitute for performance (monetary damages). True, this point is more easily made in civilian or mixed systems, with their emphasis upon performance remedies, but even in English law damages are properly viewed as substitutionary performance, not compensation for the loss of contractual rights. Lord Goff's theory concedes too much to the contract breaker, who does not have a unilateral power to extinguish the other party's contractual rights. As Lord Clyde correctly put it in *Panatown*, a 'failure in performance of a contractual obligation does not entail a loss of the bargained-for contractual rights'.[157]

Lord Goff's approach has not been followed in later judgments of the English courts. On the contrary, the line of transferred loss cases was described in a later decision of the Court of Appeal as demonstrating a concern that 'where a real loss has been caused by a real breach of contract, then there should if at all possible be a real remedy which directs recovery from the defendant towards the party which has suffered the loss'.[158] Such a characterisation, in emphasising the idea of a 'real loss', shows a preference for not conceiving of the mere failure to receive a promised performance as in itself a loss. While Lord Goff's approach purported to be based upon respect for the performance interest, in fact it could be said to undermine a genuine respect for performance given its approval of the idea that a defaulting party has in effect destroyed the other party's entitlement to performance. It is also hard to reconcile with the traditional stress in the assessment of damages on the position which the parties would have been in had the contract not been broken:[159] if damages are, in Lord Goff's view,

---

[156] See Lord Goff, [2001] 1 AC 518, 546C.   [157] See Lord Clyde, [2001] 1 AC 518, 534.

[158] *Offer-Hoar and others v. Larkstore Ltd and another* [2006] EWCA Civ 1079; [2006] 1 WLR 2926, per Mummery LJ at para. 85.

[159] *Golden Strait Corporation v. Nipon Yusen Kubishika Kaisha ('The Golden Victory')* [2007] UKHL 12; [2007] 2 AC 353; [2007] 3 All ER 1.

to represent the loss of contractual rights, then it is not obvious why the counterfactual situation which would have prevailed had there been no breach is relevant to an assessment of loss.

Lord Goff's approach would not be sanctioned by systems such as German law or Scots law,[160] neither of which would concede that a party in breach can unilaterally kill of the other party's right to performance; on the contrary, that right is properly seen as subsisting unless and until the innocent party relinquishes it. Both of those systems place a strong emphasis upon the performance interest of contracting parties, but they recognise that it is entirely consistent with that interest that, where its protection finds expression in the substitutionary remedy of damages, it is properly measured by reference to the actual loss occasioned to the innocent party and not by reference to some supposedly abstract value to be attached to a failure to receive the performance bargained for.

(d)   Mixed legal systems

As a general point, it may be noted that, as in English law, none of the mixed systems requires fault on the promisor's part to be shown before a claim for damages may be made.

In South African law, damages are usually measured according to the performance interest (or what is usually called in South Africa the 'positive interest') of the party suffering the breach.[161] Can, however, a party choose to claim damages reflecting a protection of the 'negative interest' (that is, the restoration or *status quo ante* interest) instead?[162] Although the Supreme Court has yet to rule definitively on this, there are judgments from a number of the divisions of the High Court supporting the view that the negative interest can be recovered,[163] though in the judgment

---

[160] The Goff approach was explicitly criticised in the Scottish case *McLaren Murdoch & Hamilton Ltd* v. *The Abercromby Motor Group Ltd* 2003 SCLR 323 (OH).

[161] *Thoroughbred Breeders' Association* v. *Price Waterhouse* 2001 (4) SA 551 (SCA).

[162] Appropriate terminology to cover the restitutionary interest appears, not yet, to have been developed in South African jurisprudence. This is doubtless because the South African courts have not thus far recognised any distinct protection for this interest in damages. Perhaps, to fit with the existing terms 'negative' and 'positive', 'restitutive' might be appropriate, unless the South African courts adopt supranational terminology, such as that advocated in this work.

[163] See judgments of the Witwatersrand division of the High Court in *Tweedie* v. *Park Travel Agency* 1998 (4) SA 802 (W) and the Cape Division in *Mainline Carriers (Pty) Ltd* v. *Jaad Investments CC* 1998 (2) SA 468 (C).

of the Cape Division it was held that the amount of the positive interest should act as a ceiling on a negative interest claim.

The alternative view has been advanced academically that it is fundamentally wrong for South African courts to allow computation of damages according to the negative or so-called reliance interest when breach of contract is the cause of action,[164] the argument being that doing so both compensates the plaintiff for having entered into the contract at all, as well as affords an avenue of escape from the consequences of a party's own bad bargaining. Instead, it is argued, so-called 'reliance losses' should be seen as an important component of positive damages; it is the unfounded belief that such losses are recoverable only as part of a party's negative interest which is responsible for the confusion in some of the South African cases. What is to be made of this argument? It is certainly true that it is possible to see many damages claims for protection of the performance interest as including an element of recovery of wasted expenditure, given that (as mentioned earlier) a claim for lost gross profits can alternatively be framed as one for lost net profits plus wasted preliminary expenditure.[165] On the other hand, it is only if claimants are always allowed to opt for protection of the restoration interest over the performance interest, in a way that might permit them to claim more via the former route, that there is a danger of bad bargains being freely avoidable. If, on the other hand, claiming the restoration interest is an exceptional route (as in England and Scotland), or, even if generally available, is capped by the amount of the performance interest (as suggested by the Cape High Court), this danger should not arise. Moreover, a prohibition of claims in any circumstances for the restoration interest would leave claimants in cases where it is impossible to calculate with any precision what performance interest protection is worth with no remedy, which seems inequitable.

In Scotland also, the performance measure is the primary measure of contractual damages, and the starting point for calculating an award of damages. As in other systems, the performance measure encompasses both *damnum emergens* and *lucrum cessans*.[166] The *Hadley* v. *Baxendale* rule is applied to limit recoverable damages. Damages based upon any profit made by a contract breaker are specifically irrecoverable (even if

---

[164] See Clive and Hutchison, 'Breach of Contract'.

[165] See earlier discussion of this point at p. 374.

[166] Though there is no established Scottish tradition of the usage of such terms by the courts in their decisions, it is clear from those decisions that both types of loss may be claimed for.

they are foreseeable),[167] and there are no punitive damages for breach of contract.[168] There is no definitive Scottish authority on whether a pursuer has a free choice between performance or restoration measure, a choice which might allow bad bargains of the type discussed above to be avoided. However, in *Daejan Developments* v. *Armia*,[169] the Scottish court followed a similar approach to that adopted in the Australian case of *McRae* v. *Commonwealth Disposals Commission*.[170] In *McRae*, expected profits in relation to the salvage of what transpired to be a non-existent vessel were deemed too speculative, the court instead awarding damages for wasted expenditure. In *Daejan*, the defenders were unable to transfer ownership of certain property to the pursuers due to a defect in title. The pursuers were permitted to claim wasted expenditure incurred in expectation of the purchase, and were not required to formulate a claim based upon what would have been speculative loss of profit. Though the decision sets down no clear rules as to when such an alternative claim for wasted expenditure may be made, it seems reasonable to assume that the Scottish approach supports recovery of the restoration measure only in exceptional cases. To allow a free choice in every case would be to open up the risk of allowing avoidance of bad bargains, and would permit recovery of sums that would not have been recouped had the contract been performed according to its terms.[171]

In Louisiana, damages are, as in the other systems studied, designed to compensate the innocent party for its losses: as Article 1995 of the Civil Code puts it, damages are 'measured by the loss sustained by the obligee and the profit of which he has been deprived', thus expressly permitting recovery for both *damnum emergens* and *lucrum cessans*. The liability to pay damages arises as a result of the debtor's 'failure to perform a conventional obligation', such failure encompassing non-performance, defective performance, as well as delayed performance.[172] The text of the current article is notably different from that of the 1870 Code, where liability was said to depend upon the 'default' of the obligor,[173] a condition

---

[167] *Teacher* v. *Calder* (1898) 25 R 661.

[168] The sole exception being a penal measure of damages for unauthorised continuation of possession of leasehold property beyond the expiry of the lease, such damages being referred to as 'violent profits' and typically being in the measure of twice the amount of rent under the lease.

[169] 1981 SC 48 (OH).   [170] (1951) 84 CLR 377; [1951] 25 ALJ 425.

[171] Abortive expenditure which would have been incurred even if the contract had been performed cannot therefore form the substance of a damages claim under the restoration measure: see *Dawson International plc* v. *Coats Paton plc (No. 2)* 1993 SLT 80.

[172] CC Art. 1994.   [173] CC of 1870, Art. 1930.

which was taken as providing for fault-based liability (as in French law), albeit that fault was usually presumed as a result of non-performance. No requirement of fault is stipulated in the present wording of the Code. As Article 1995 is tied to the loss of the plaintiff, there is no question of so-called 'restitutionary damages' (providing for disgorgement of any gain made by the defendant through non-performance) being awarded, as the famous decision of the Louisiana Supreme Court in *City of New Orleans* v. *Firemen's Charitable Association*[174] is said to show.

Given the wording of the right to damages under Article 1995, it is evident that damages are seen as protecting the innocent party's performance interest. So-called 'reliance damages' are the proper province of recovery under the promissory estoppel provision of Article 1967, though occasionally the term 'reliance damages' appears to have been used by the courts to refer to the *damnum emergens* element of a damages claim which has, overall, the characteristic of a protection of the performance interest.[175] As an example of the calculation of the performance interest, one may take the case of a defendant who refuses to accept and pay for goods it has ordered: the ordinary rule in such cases is that the quantum of damages to which the plaintiff is entitled is the difference between the contract price and the market price of the goods at the date of breach. Thus, in a case where a defendant refused to purchase scrap metal for an agreed price, the plaintiff's losses were calculated based on the drop of the market value in the metal between the contract date and the date of delivery.[176] In so awarding damages, the Court compensated the plaintiff for the likely loss of profit which it would now suffer on a resale (though this ordinary rule is not applied in all cases).[177] Because in this case the contract breaker was not in bad faith, the rule that recoverable damages were to be those 'foreseeable at the time the contract was made' was applied.[178] On the other hand, if the contract breaker is in bad faith (which might be so in the case of

---

[174] (1891) 9 So 486. The plaintiff was seeking repetition not damages, however.

[175] So, for instance, in *Southern Tire Services Inc.* v. *Virtual Point Development LLC* 798 So 2d 303 (La App 2001), the Fourth Circuit of the Court of Appeal upheld an arbitrator's award of damages amounting to $135,000 for 'estimated net lost sales and reliance damages'.

[176] *Friedman Iron & Supply Co.* v. *J.B. Beaird Co. Inc.* 63 So 2d 144 (1952).

[177] The rule is not applied if there is no ordinary market price of the goods; instead, full anticipated profits are awarded: see *Interstate Electric Co.* v *Frank Adam Electric Co.* 136 So 2d 283 (1931); *Security National Bank of Shreveport* v *Terrell* 482 So 2d 919 (La App 2 Cir 1986).

[178] This rule is found in CC Art. 1996.

a deliberate breach of contract), all losses that are a direct consequence of the failure to perform are recoverable, whether foreseeable or not (so-called consequential damages).[179] Drawing a distinction between foreseeable consequences and direct consequences based upon whether the defaulter was acting in good faith or bad faith is a unique approach in the systems studied in this work, a position deriving from French law.[180] It is evidently a rule which has no reference to what the party in default may be imagined to have promised or to have foreseen that he would pay, but rather reflects a legislative policy of penalising bad faith. The current Louisiana codal provisions on good faith/bad faith damages do not, however, explicitly state whether certain possible losses may be *presumed* to have been foreseen, or whether actual proof of foresight for even commonplace losses must be demonstrated by the plaintiff.[181] However, it is the established view of the courts that natural or ordinary damages are presumed to be foreseeable and thus to have been contemplated by the parties.

Though damages in Louisiana are geared towards the performance measure, one must not overlook a provision of the Code which states that, where damages are insusceptible of precise measurement, much discretion is to be left to the court for the reasonable assessment of these damages.[182] This discretionary power could conceivably allow a Louisiana court to fashion damages approximating to the restoration measure in a case where it felt such a measure to be an appropriate response to circumstances of imprecisely measurable loss, a case raising facts like those in *Anglia Television* v. *Reed*,[183] perhaps. Given, however, that damages are tied to the concept of loss, it would seem to follow that disgorgement of gains should never feature in an award made by a Louisiana court under this provision.

---

[179] CC Art. 1997. See *Womack v Sternberg* 172 So 2d 683 (1965). Apart from the more generous measure of damages against bad faith defaulters, Louisiana does not generally favour penal (or 'exemplary') damages; such are available only in those limited circumstances provided for by statute (see for instance La Rev Stat Ann §22:656, relating to failure by life insurance providers to pay policy proceeds to a beneficiary within a specified time).

[180] See *Code civil* Art. 1150.

[181] The relevant provision of the Code of 1870 relating to damages payable where bad faith was not present, stated that the debtor was liable for such damages 'as were contemplated, or may reasonably be supposed to have entered into the contemplation of the parties at the time of the contract', reflecting Pothier's formulation.

[182] CC Art. 1999.   [183] [1972] 1 QB 60, discussed below at p. 391.

(e)   German law

It is important first of all to note that in German law the basic principle is that there must be fault before a claim can be raised for damages (the so-called fault principle or *Verschuldensprinzip*). Fault means either intention or negligence.[184] This evidently marks an important difference in principle with the approach taken by the Common law and mixed systems, where any non-conforming performance gives rise to liability for damages, whether it was the breaching party's fault or not (with an exception applicable to cases of frustration). Justifications that have been offered for the German approach are that it is ethically superior[185] or fairer,[186] but such claims seem to be predicated on the supposition that a promisor only makes himself responsible for fault-based failures, which is highly questionable given the nature of some promises. The alleged superiority of the German view also seems to be based upon a supposition that the Common law of contract invariably imposes strict guarantees on promisors concerning their contractual performances, whereas the English courts have been quite careful to distinguish those contractual undertakings which amount to guarantees of a specific result from those which impose only fault-based liability,[187] the point being that, contrary to the German characterisation of the Common law, it does not hold all contractual duties to be of the former type.

There are, however, a number of ways in which the German apparent insistence on fault as a prerequisite for a damages claim is softened. For instance, contracting parties are held implicitly to have guaranteed that they have the skill necessary to perform the duties they have promised to fulfil, so that it is no defence to a claim for work improperly carried out that the promisor did 'his best' and was thus not at fault in lacking the necessary skill.[188] Furthermore, strict liability is recognised in relation to certain types of breach of duty, such as monetary debts and delivery of generic goods, and in general a plea will not be entertained that a debtor was financially unable to perform a duty.[189] Also, it ought not to be forgotten that §276(1) BGB allows parties to impose a regime of strict liability

---

[184]   §276(1) BGB.   [185]   Heldrich *et al., Festschrift für Claus-Wilhelm Canaris*, pp. 1, 22.

[186]   Huber, *Leistungsstörungen*, vol. 1, p. 31.

[187]   An example of a contract term imposing only fault-based liability would be one in a contract for professional services in terms of which the professional party undertakes to provide the services with due skill and care.

[188]   BGH NJW 2000, 2812.

[189]   See further Markesinis *et al., German Law of Contract*, pp. 448–9.

for breach if they so desire. The fault of a party engaged by a promisor to undertake a duty is imputed to the promisor.[190] While these exceptions go some way to dealing with cases where promisors appear to have accepted liability for the absolute achievement of certain outcomes, they are somewhat sporadic and do not achieve a proper differentiation between strict duties and fault-based duties.

The second thing to note about the German law is that, as in Scots law but not English law, there is a primary right to performance; damages is a secondary remedy. But German law goes even further. While in Scotland there is a primary entitlement to enforcement, the German regime may be called one of mandatory performance – a creditor is, following breach by the debtor, required to make at least one further attempt to keep the contract alive after breach, before resorting to damages.[191] Damages are also a subordinated remedy in a second way, namely that, according to §249(1) BGB, a person who is obliged to compensate for damage must effect a restoration to the position that would have existed if the circumstance obliging him to effect such compensation had not occurred. Effecting restoration in kind is thus a prior duty of the debtor (unless this is not possible, when damages are automatically available): §250 states that only if such restoration does not occur within a reasonable time does the party become liable for monetary compensation (*Schadensersatz in Geld*), that is, damages.

Damages are primarily compensatory,[192] so are to reflect the loss of the promisee. So, as in other systems, damages do not disgorge gains made by the other party, nor do they penalise the other party.[193] As §252 BGB makes clear, damages may include expected lost profits, either arising in the normal course of events or by virtue of special circumstances.[194] Damages may be claimed, as in other systems, alongside the right to terminate the contract.

There is no exact equivalent in German law of the Common law concept of foreseeability of loss as a brake on recoverable damages. Instead, limitation on recoverable damages is based upon the principle of causality.[195]

---

[190] §278 BGB.   [191] Markesinis *et al.*, *German Law of Contract*, p. 381.

[192] *Ibid.*, p. 443; Lange and Schiemann, *Schadenersatz*, p. 9.

[193] See, however, the discussion below at pp. 401f concerning the extent to which penalty clauses are permissible in German law.

[194] An interesting comparison may be drawn here with the English case of *Victoria Laundry (Windsor) Ltd* v. *Newman Industries Ltd* [1949] 2 KB 528, where ordinary lost profits of a business were claimable but not profits from unusually lucrative contracts, as these could not have been foreseen by the party in breach.

[195] Markesinis *et al.*, *German Law of Contract*, p. 473.

This requires, in addition to *sine qua non* causation, a demonstration that the defendant's breach of contract was an 'adequate cause' of the loss (the *Adäquanztheorie* of causation), though an alternative theory suggests that the extent of liability should depend upon the purpose of the rule imposing liability for breach (the purposive approach).[196] There is some disagreement about whether the purposive approach to loss can be compared to foreseeability, and indeed, if foreseeability is conceived of as meaning reasonably foreseeable as a possible or probable outcome,[197] then a plausible comparison with causation will be evident. The BGH has, however, stated that the theory of adequate causation is less a causal doctrine and more about determining the boundaries 'within which the originator of a condition can equitably be presumed liable for its consequences'.[198] Adequate causes, said the court, are those which increase the objective probability of an occurrence of the type which happened (the damage), such objective probability being determined by the observations of an imaginary 'optimal observer' at the time of the breach. Put this way, there do appear to be comparisons between the question of what the contracting parties might have foreseen about the outcome and the observations of an optimal observer about the probability of damage, though clearly the former formulation is a subjective one and the latter an objective one. As an objective exercise, the German approach to limiting damages demonstrates even less possibility of linkage with some presumed promise of the contract breaker than does the Common law approach.

The revised BGB damages provisions have made damages for non-performance of contractual duties easier to claim: no longer does the innocent party have to serve a warning notice requiring performance in every case, and no longer does the innocent party himself have to threaten not to perform after the expiry of the reasonable period set for performance.[199] The revised provisions, in making damages easier to claim, can therefore be said to have increased pressure on the debtor to perform his obligation, and are therefore more supportive of promissory liability.[200]

The BGB contains provisions regulating the claiming of damages in specific circumstances, including cases of: (a) 'simple damages' (or

---

[196] Rabel, *Recht des Warenkaufs*, pp. 495 f.
[197] See *Koufos* v. *C Czarnikow Ltd* ('*The Heron II*') [1969] 1 AC 350; [1967] 3 All ER 686.
[198] BGHZ 3, 261.   [199] As to which, see now §281(1) BGB.
[200] See further on the change in emphasis in the new damages provisions, Schulte-Nölke, 'Vertragsfreiheit und Informationszwang', pp. 72 f, and Schulte-Nölke and Schulze, 'Schuldrechtsreform und Gemeinschaftsrecht', pp. 3 f.

damages alongside performance);[201] (b) damages in lieu of performance;[202] (c) damages for delay;[203] (d) damages for wasted expenditure;[204] and (e) damages in case of mistake.[205] These separate provisions provide for results largely equivalent to those arrived at by courts in systems without the benefit of a code. Thus, types (a), (b), and (c), are generally conceived of as providing an entitlement to damages protecting the performance interest (*Erfüllungsinteresse*) and not the restoration interest (*Vertrauensschaden*).

Protection of the restoration interest is applicable only under type (d) claims, those for wasted expenditure. §284 BGB provides that 'in place of damages in lieu of performance, the creditor may demand reimbursement of the expenses which he has made and in all fairness was entitled to make in reliance on receiving performance, unless the purpose of the expenses would not have been achieved, even if the debtor had not breached his duty.' A comparison is often drawn between this type of recovery and so-called 'reliance damages' in the Common law. However, as has been remarked,[206] the wording of §284 – that the reliance be 'of receiving performance under the contract' – is narrower than the reliance normally required in the Common law, which is merely reliance generally on the contract (thus allowing a claim for all losses flowing from the breach).[207]

A further difference from Common law restoration damages is that §284 does not limit the right to claim damages to cases where it is impossible to calculate compensatory damages, or to cases where restoration damages are less than compensatory ones, limitations which apply to a claim for wasted contractual expenditure in English law. In German law, the creditor can choose the claim which is most advantageous to him.

---

[201] §280(1) BGB. This section also encompasses damages for *culpa in contrahendo*, though in such a case damages are not restricted to the performance interest.

[202] §§280(3), 281 BGB. Damages in lieu of performance may be claimed if the creditor has set a reasonable period for the debtor to perform, he has not done so, and the breach is material (§281(1)). As soon as damages are demanded in lieu of performance, the claim to actual performance is excluded (§281(4)), as one would expect.

[203] §§280(2), 286 BGB. As to such damages, Zumbansen has written that '[t]he creditor can claim compensation for all damages resulting from this delay, such as lost profits or substitution costs' (Zumbansen, 'The Law of Contracts', p. 193). This type of claim is designed to put the creditor in as good a position as if the debtor had performed correctly and fully (*ibid.*, p. 194).

[204] §284 BGB.   [205] §122 BGB.

[206] Markesinis *et al.*, *German Law of Contract*, pp. 461–2.

[207] As Lord Denning MR put it in *Anglia Television Ltd* v. *Reed* [1972] 1 QB 60, 64, the party suffering the breach may 'claim … the expenditure which has been thrown away, that is, wasted, by reason of the breach'.

As Zumbansen has commented, the creditor 'will calculate whether the damages for faulty performance or non-performance exceed her incurred costs and will choose her remedy accordingly'.[208]

Despite these differences, comparisons can be be drawn between §284 and some claims of damages for wasted expenditure which are permitted in the Common law: for instance, the wasted expenditure recovered in *Anglia Television Ltd v Reed*,[209] expenditure which had been incurred by a television company in preparing to perform its contractual duties with an actor, would similarly be recoverable under §284. Although a similar result would be reached in Germany on such facts, this type of recovery was (prior to the reform of remedies under the BGB) rationalised by German courts as a kind of performance interest damages, the wasted expenses being fictionally presumed to be amounts that would have been recovered as profits had the contract been performed.[210] This conceptualisation reflected a fundamental antagonism in German law to permitting the 'reliance damages' awarded by the Common law; indeed the recommendation of the Commission looking at the reform of remedies in the BGB that a general 'reliance' damages provision be introduced was rejected.[211] However, given that §284 now expressly covers wasted expenditure, as well as the fact that it covers cases where any contractual profit may be very speculative (circumstances like the *Anglia Television* case) and cases where the contract was not even entered into with any intention of making a profit, the former rationalisation now looks very strained. The most accurate description of §284 liability would perhaps be that it provides for limited (or targeted) protection of the restoration interest. The narrow focus of §284 is a reflection of the German preference for performance, something which restricts the extent to which the BGB is willing to permit recovery for wasted expenditure.

As to the last specific type of damages mentioned above, type (e) – damages for mistake – these are designed to compensate for losses suffered as a result of the reliance of the other party on the validity of the declaration of the avoiding party.[212] The overall effect of this provision

[208] Zumbansen, 'The Law of Contracts', p. 194.
[209] [1972] 1 QB 60.   [210] BGH NJW 2000, 2342.
[211] German Federal Ministry of Justice, *Final Report of the Commission to Revise the Law of Obligations* (1992), p. 173; rejected, *Bundestags-Drucksache* 14/6040, 144.
[212] §122(1). Such damages for reliance are not permitted to exceed the interest which the non-rescinding party has in the validity of the declaration, i.e. they cannot give him more than he would have got had the contract been performed according to its objective meaning.

would seem to be to allow a wide discretion to a court in assessing a damages claim in cases of error: it might conceivably be a claim for expenditure wasted in preparing to perform (classic restoration interest damages) or it might be a claim for lost expected profit (classic performance interest damages), given that both such types of loss could be said to flow from reliance on the validity of the declaration of the other party.

Though the foregoing gives only a flavour of the complex subject of the German law of damages, when taken with the stress in German law placed upon performance, the law can be said to be generally supportive of the performance measure (even if the duty to pay default damages cannot be said to rest upon the promises of the parties). Even where a claim under §282 for wasted expenditure is permitted, it is limited to expenditure in reliance on the expected performance. The high regard for the performance pledged by a promisor is clear. On the other hand, the theoretical barrier of demonstrating fault before damages can be claimed is a deviation from the high respect given to promises, as it fails to differentiate between strict promises to achieve a result and fault-based promissory duties.

(f)   Model law

Under the DCFR, the right to damages is available for 'loss caused by non-performance of an obligation'.[213] The stipulation of loss as the basis of damages clearly excludes gain-based damages being claimed under this provision.

There is no hint in the DCFR provisions on damages of Lord Goff's radical view that loss in breach of contract cases means loss of the right to performance. Instead, without the idea of loss being exhaustively defined, it is clear from the statements in Article III.-3:701(3) that loss for non-performance of an obligation includes economic and non-economic loss, and that economic loss includes loss of income or profit, burdens incurred, and a reduction in the value of property. The traditional view is taken that it is a demonstrable and measurable effect upon the patrimony of the claimant by which the value of economic loss is to be judged. As to the measure of damages, Article III.-3:702 grounds this firmly in the performance measure by stating that the 'general measure' of damages is 'such sum as will put the creditor as nearly as possible into the position

---

[213]   Art. III.-3:701(1).

in which the creditor would have been if the obligation had been duly performed'.[214] This commendably clear statement is evidently highly supportive of contractual parties' promises. The choice of the phrase 'general measure' is, however, suggestive of the fact that another measure may in exceptional circumstances be appropriate, though what such alternative measure might be is not specified.[215] It seems reasonable to suggest that such measure might, in an appropriate case, be the restoration (or *status quo ante*) measure, in terms of which recovery of wasted expenditure undertaken in preparation for performance might be sought. It would, however, have been useful to have seen an explicit statement in the text of the DCFR that such an exceptional claim is permissible.

Damages are available for all failures to perform an obligation unless 'the non-performance is excused'.[216] Does this impose a fault-based requirement upon damages claims? To answer that question, regard must be had to Article III.-3.104 which concerns excuses for non-performance due to impediments. The Article provides that 'impediments beyond the debtor's control' which the debtor 'could not reasonably be expected to have avoided or overcome' [217] excuse the debtor from performance. An impediment so described is evidently one in relation to which the debtor cannot be at fault, as one cannot be responsible (and thus at fault) for events beyond one's control. So, the DCFR damages provision, taken together with the provision on impediments, means that non-performance due to matters beyond a party's control excuses the duty to pay damages. That does not mean, however, that the general regime of damages under the DCFR is in consequence fault-based, as there are many circumstances

---

[214] By focusing on the creditor's position, and taking into account the way in which loss is measured, this statement of the general measure of damages would seem to exclude transferred loss claims. Special provision is made for cases where, following termination for non-performance, the creditor undertakes a replacement transaction to cover for such non-performance: the measure of damages is the difference between the two contract prices (Art. III.-3:706).

[215] The Official Commentary to the DCFR notes that certain provisions on damages resulting from circumstances other than non-performance give rise to a right to reliance-based damages designed to restore the party prejudiced to the position it was previously in (the *status quo ante* position), Art. II.-7:204 being an example of such a provision. The Commentary does not, however, give any further information as to when such damages might apply under Art. III.-3:702, save to note somewhat cryptically that the Article leaves open the possibility that 'a rule relating to a particular kind of obligation could provide for a special measure of damages' (Comment E to Art. III.-3:702).

[216] Art. III.-3:701(1).

[217] Though where the impediment is permanent, the obligations is extinguished: Art. III.-3:104(4). This describes what in Common law terms would be called frustration.

within the control of the debtor the occurrence of which might nonetheless occur without any fault on the debtor's part. The occurrence of such circumstances, if they constitute non-performance of a duty, will trigger a right to damages on the creditor's part, an entitlement explained more fully in the official commentary to Article III.-3:701. The DCFR damages is, in consequence, not fault-based.[218]

7.   Liquidated damages: penalty clauses

Arguably, any legal system which considers itself as according a high level of respect for seriously intended contractual promises would enforce a so-called 'penalty clause' (*stipulatio poenae*), being a clause for the payment or forfeiture of a sum of money in the event of a breach of contract, regardless of any possible harsh effect which such a clause might have, so long as the clause could be said to represent the freely given consent of the contracting parties. If parties wish to provide for clauses which have an effect which others might deem harsh, this need not necessarily be any concern of the courts. Indeed, such clauses can be argued to be useful, in that they both serve as a spur to performance as well as to pre-empt unnecessary judicial investigation into the assessment of damages which may be due in the event of a breach of contract.

In practice, however, many jurisdictions will not enforce such penalty clauses in every case, for instance in cases where the penalty promised does not reflect the loss which the promisee is likely to suffer or does suffer at the time the application of the clause is triggered. Such interference in penalty clauses might conceivably be justified on a number of grounds, such as the underlying purpose of contract law (to facilitate advantageous arrangements rather than to inflict punishment), the protection of weak parties, the prevention of unconscionable conduct (or the promotion of virtuous conduct), or the requirement of good faith, among others.

In Roman law, a *stipulatio poenae* was enforceable. Such a clause might be of two types: the first was very much like the modern penalty clause, namely an accessory obligation that became due in the event of non-performance of a primary obligation; the second was a peculiar usage of Roman law, and provided for penalties as a means of achieving tangentially that which could not lawfully be done directly.[219] With the first type

---

[218] DCFR, Official Commentary to Art. III.-3:701, Comment C.

[219] For instance, while a *jus quaesitum tertio* was not directly enforceable by a third party, the promisee could stipulate for a penalty if performance was not rendered to the third

(accessory penalty stipulations), it seems that, in the Roman law, once the penalty became enforceable, the prior obligation to which it was related could no longer be sued upon: that, in any event, is the import of a text of Paul at D. 44.7.44.6. Some modern systems, such as Swiss and German law take a different approach, in that they provide that a party can still use its primary action of damages if the penalty turns out to be inadequate. The German provision is discussed further below.

(a)   English law

As mentioned in Chapter 3, conditional bonds were popular in medieval English law as a way of ensuring fulfilment of an obligation, the courts simply awarding the amount of the bond without question. The effect of such judicial enforcement was often a penal one so far as debtors were concerned. Eventually equity provided relief in such cases, which led first to the decline of the conditional bond and in time to the rejection by English law of penalties payable upon breach of contract which were *in terrorem* of the other contracting party.[220] These developments led English law to adopt a comparable approach to that of civilian systems, with the principal difference being that, while in the civil law an agreed penalty may be modified, in English law a stipulated damages clause is either enforced or struck down entirely. The idea of altering the agreement of the parties to reflect a more equitable position is anathema to a Common law view preference for clearly stated and limited public policy oversight of contracts rather than an open-ended, good faith based judicial discretion.

Many of the principles regularly applied by the English courts in relation to penalty clauses were first suggested in *Dunlop Pneumatic Tyre Co. Ltd* v. *New Garage and Motor Co Ltd*.[221] The decision of the House of Lords solidified in English law a distinction between a genuine liquidated damages clause (one that pre-estimates the parties' losses) and a penalty clause (one that is not such a genuine pre-estimate). This distinction is not made in civilian legal systems, which generally choose to class all designated damages clauses together, while allowing some judicial discretion to refuse to enforce certain such clauses. A somewhat problematic aspect to the *Dunlop* decision, however, was that Lord Dunedin contrasted non-opposites when describing the essence of penalties and liquidated

---

party, thus providing for an indirect means of securing the benefit in favour of the third party: see Zimmermann, *Law of Obligations*, p. 97.

[220]   *Ibid.*, p. 97, n. 10.   [221]   [1915] AC 79.

damage clauses. First, he stated that a penalty clause is identifiable by the fact that it is a sum 'stipulated as *in terrorem* of the offending party', and thus suggested that the essence of such a clause lies in the oppressive and frightening effect which it has upon the mind of that party. One may assume, though his Lordship did not say as much, that such a terrorising effect stems from the fact that the clause specifies an inordinately high sum to be paid in the event of breach (an excessively small sum would hardly terrorise the other party). Indeed, such an assumption is borne out by some of the examples that Lord Dunedin gives of such clauses. Such a clause *in terrorem* of the other party might conceivably be seen as one to which, because of its oppressive nature, no genuine consent was given, though Lord Dunedin does not analyse matters in that way: the preference in the judgments of Lord Dunedin and his colleagues is for an analysis in terms of 'unconscionability', which stresses the equitable, public policy nature of the approach, rather than a promissory, will-based analysis. The opposite to a penalty clause, the enforceable liquidated damages clause, was not, however, defined by Lord Dunedin simply as a clause which is *not* stipulated *in terrorem* of the other party; rather it was described as one which 'is a genuine pre-estimate of damage'. This definition says nothing of the subjective effect upon the mind of the offending party, but rather looks at the objectively ascertainable question of whether there was any attempt by the parties to consider the likely outcome of possible breaches of contract. Conceivably, under this approach, a patent *under*-assessment of damages might qualify as a penalty clause (even if such an under-assessment would not naturally fit with the idea of penalising someone), given that it would, as much as an over-assessment, constitute a failure to assess likely loss in the event of breach.

Lord Dunedin's differing definitions of the distinction between a penalty and a genuine liquidated damages clause have the potential to cause confusion, unless either the two elements identified by Lord Dunedin (failure to pre-estimate loss, and a terrorising effect) are combined to produce a dual requirement for a penalty clause, or one element is preferred as the test and the other discarded. In fact, in subsequent cases the courts have located the essence of the distinction between enforceable and unenforceable clauses in the element of the pre-estimation of loss, rather than in any terrorising effect. In *Bridge* v. *Campbell Discount Co. Ltd*,[222] Lord Radcliffe criticised the notion of a clause being *in terrorem* of another party, saying that the phrase 'obscures the fact penalties may

[222] [1962] AC 600.

quite readily be undertaken by parties who are not in the least terrorised by the prospect of having to pay them and yet are ... entitled to claim the protection of the court when they are called on to make good their promise'.[223] The essence therefore of identifying a penalty lies in assessing whether a true pre-estimate of damages took place or not, a clause not reflecting such a true pre-estimate being just such an unenforceable penalty; where such an unenforceable penalty is identified, the party seeking recovery for any loss must instead rely upon common law damages.[224]

The Common law rule against penalty clauses is clearly an infringement of the sanctity of promise, but it is one which is judicially justified as necessary in order to prevent oppressive and unconscionable conduct. As was said in the Canadian Supreme Court,

> the power to strike down a penalty clause is a blatant interference with freedom of contract and is designed for the sole purpose of providing relief against oppression.[225]

Evidently the power to strike down is a discretionary one, and requires the courts to judge sensibly whether a reasonable attempt was made to assess likely losses. To that end, the adoption of guiding principles such as those in *Dunlop*, and the principle that, if a genuine assessment is difficult given the uncertainty of the likely loss, a court should be slow to intervene,[226] represent a wise attempt to bring some objective standards into what would otherwise run the risk of being a highly subjective, *ad hominem* judicial exercise.

(b) Mixed legal systems

In Roman-Dutch law, under the influence of the canon law, a penalty was only enforceable if it was reasonable in relation to the resulting damage. Subsequently, in South African law the courts introduced the Common

---

[223] [1962] AC 600, 622.

[224] *Scandinavian Trading Tanker Co., AB* v. *Flota Petrolera Ecuatoriana ('The Scaptrade')* [1983] 2 AC 694, 702; cf. however, the alternative view that what occurs is enforcement of the penalty clause, but only up to the amount of the actual loss suffered: *Jobson* v. *Johnson* [1989] 1 WLR 1026, 1040. This latter view would cause difficulties in application if the penalty were a patent under-valuation, however, as the actual loss suffered would exceed the penalty.

[225] *Elsey* v. *J. G. Collins Insurance Agencies Ltd* (1978) 83 DLR 1, 15; [1978] 2 SCR 916, 937 (opinion of the Court, delivered by Dickson J).

[226] *Clydebank Engineering and Shipbuilding Co. Ltd* v. *Castaneda* (1904) 7 F (HL) 77; [1905] AC 6 (a Scottish authority, applied in England also).

law position, but, when this development was strongly criticised by the Appellate Division,[227] the Conventional Penalties Act was passed.[228] The Act provides that a penalty clause is enforceable,[229] but that if the penalty is out of proportion[230] to the prejudice suffered by the innocent party, a court may reduce the penalty to a level which is equitable in the circumstances.[231] The Act restored the culture of the old Roman-Dutch law, which had been founded upon Voet's view that excessive penalties might be moderated by replacing them with a provision which was *ad bonum et aequum*.[232] It is noteworthy that the Act talks about 'reducing' the amount of a penalty. This means that a party who claims that a penalty clause is out of proportion to the prejudice suffered because it is *too low* in comparison with the actual loss suffered cannot argue that the amount payable under the penalty clause should be increased (a result which can theoretically happen in Scotland, where, if a penalty clause is found not to be a genuine pre-estimate, it can be struck down and a *higher* sum of damages claimed at common law).

In Louisiana, §2117 of the Civil Code formerly dealt with what were referred to as 'penal clauses', but are now, under the replacement §2005, styled stipulated damages, though nothing of substance turns on the change of terminology. §2005 states that parties

> may stipulate the damages to be recovered in case of nonperformance, defective performance, or delay in performance of an obligation.

In adding that such a stipulation 'gives rise to a secondary obligation for the purpose of enforcing the principal one', the provision makes clear the accessory characterisation of such clauses.

A court may only interfere in such a stipulated damages clause if the damages specified are 'so manifestly unreasonable as to be contrary to public policy'.[233] Where this test is met, the clause may be amended by the

---

[227] See *Baines Motors* v. *Piek* 1955 (1) SA 534 (A).   [228] Act 15 of 1962.

[229] s. 1. A penalty is defined so as to include any agreed sum (or the delivery or performance of anything) due upon breach as liquidated damages or as a penalty.

[230] The onus is on the debtor under the penalty clause to demonstrate that it is out of proportion. In *Western Credit Bank Ltd* v. *Kajee* 1967 (4) SA 386 (N) the phrase 'out of proportion' was interpreted by the court to mean 'markedly, not infinitesimally' out of proportion.

[231] s. 3.   [232] See Zimmermann, *Law of Obligations*, p. 109.

[233] CC Art. 2012. Because the unreasonableness must be 'manifest', stipulated damages may exceed, to some degree found reasonable by the court, the actual damages, without breaching public policy (*Mobley* v. *Mobley* 852 So 2d 1136 (La App 2nd Cir 2003).

court by a downward adjustment of the damages payable.[234] The courts have had occasion to consider when a stipulated damages clause might be contrary to public policy, and have formulated the position that, in assessing public policy, it is proper to consider both (i) the amount of actual loss when compared with the stipulated damages, and (ii) whether the damages stipulated were a reasonable assessment of the likely losses. In *Carney* v. *Coles*,[235] for instance, Sexton J emphasised the first of these two considerations, noting that when 'stipulated damages in a contract do not bear any reasonable relation to the actual damages suffered, courts have reduced the amount of damages recoverable'.[236] On the other hand, in *American Leasing Company of Monroe Inc.* v. *Lannon E. Miller & Son*, Marvin J emphasised the second, stating that the task of the court was to 'determine the reasonableness of the amount of stipulated damages by inquiring whether the parties attempted to approximate actual damages in confecting the stipulated damages provision of the agreement'.[237] This consideration is further emphasised in official comment (c) to Article 2005, which states that a 'stipulated damages clause is given effect if the court deems it to be a true approximation of actual damages'. The Louisiana approach is thus wider than that taken by the British courts, where judicial regard is had only to the second consideration (the reasonableness of the estimation of likely losses at the time the contract was made) and not to whether there is any discrepancy between stipulated damages and actual loss suffered. The making of a claim for stipulated damages precludes a claim for performance, unless the stipulated damages are due only for delay.[238]

In addition to the above accessory function of stipulated damages clauses, the Louisiana Civil Code also provides for what are styled 'penal clauses in submission'.[239] These are penalties which parties may provide for in the event of a failure to adhere to an arbitration award, such penalties being designed to encourage adherence to the award rather than the making of a further appeal (such an appeal triggering payment of the penalty by the appellant).[240] This function of penalty clauses was known in Roman law.

---

[234] The wording of the codal provision would also seem theoretically to permit an upward revision of a damages clause, assuming an argument could be made out that public policy required such an uplift.

[235] 643 So 2d 339 (La App 2nd Cir 1994).   [236] 643 So 2d 339, 343.

[237] *American Leasing Company of Monroe, Inc.* v. *Lannon E. Miller & Son, General Contracting, Inc.* 469 So. 2d 325 (La App 2nd Cir 1985).

[238] CC Art. 2007.   [239] CC Art. 3106.

[240] CC Art. 3130. The Roman usage of penalties in such circumstances was discussed above in the main text, at p. 394.

The Scottish position on stipulated damages, deriving from *Dunlop Pneumatic Tyre Co.* v. *New Garage and Motor Co.*,[241] remains, for the moment,[242] identical to that of the English law discussed earlier, namely that a stipulated damages clause will be enforced by a court if, and only if, it represented at the time the contract was formed a reasonable estimation of the losses likely to be suffered by the party entitled to claim under the clause. If it is struck down, it is styled a 'penalty clause', regardless of whether it was stated in the contract to be a liquidated damages clause and not a penalty. The reasonableness of the clause is judged at the time the contract is made. This judicial power to review damages clauses is in two senses narrower than that given to courts in Louisiana and South Africa. It is narrower, firstly, in that it is no part of the judicial consideration of the clause whether the actual loss suffered by the relevant party deviates from the stipulated amount; all that matters is whether the assessment of *likely* losses was carried out in a reasonable fashion. It is narrower, secondly, in that a Scottish court cannot amend a stipulated damages clause: either the clause is enforced or it is struck down entirely, the innocent party then being forced to rely on a common law damages claim. Occasionally, it may benefit the innocent party to have the clause struck down, this being so where the actual losses suffered turn out to be much greater than those predicted at the time the clause was agreed. Courts are not unaware of cynical attempts by innocent parties to have agreed damages clauses struck down simply in order to be able to claim more than was agreed, and maintain a strict assessment of the reasonableness of the clause at the time the contract was concluded.

Because only clauses which provide for payment or another performance (including forfeiture of a sum already paid) in the event of a breach of contract fall within the penalty clause rule it is possible to provide for disguised penalties, that is clauses which have a penal effect but are not tied to breach. Hence, rather than penalise a contractor for late completion of a construction project, an employer might instead specify that a

---

[241] [1915] AC 79 (HL).

[242] In 2010, the Scottish Government conducted a consultation exercise on whether to change the law. It proposed a new regime whereby enforceable liquidated damages clauses would no longer have to be a genuine pre-estimate of likely loss, but clauses would be unenforceable if 'manifestly excessive' (though in such a case, a court would be entitled to alter the terms of the clause so as to make it enforceable): see the the proposed Penalty Clauses (Scotland) Bill, included in the Scottish Government Consultation on Penalty Clauses (July 2010). These proposals are somewhat similar to the provisions of the DCFR noted in the main text below, at p. 403.

charge for occupying the premises must be paid by the contractor for any period of time beyond the intended completion date. Such a clause, operating in effect as a penalty, could not be struck down as a penalty clause as it does not provide for any payment dependent upon breach. Likewise, a sum of money due upon the insolvency of a contracting party would not be caught under the existing penalty clause regime.[243] The forfeiture of a deposit might conceivably amount to a penalty, but not if its purpose was an earnest and guarantee of payment.[244]

Of the varying positions adopted by the three mixed systems, the one which arguably accords most with a respect for the parties' promises is the Scottish position. That is so because it is only in Scotland, when assessing whether a damages clause should be upheld, that regard is had to the circumstances prevailing at the time of contract formation alone. In the other two systems, a divergence between the actual losses suffered and the agreed damages payable may be taken into account in deciding whether or not to uphold the clause. This extra consideration, in providing a wider basis upon which to attack stipulated damages clauses, clearly has a greater potential to undermine the agreement of the parties.

(c) German law

German law, like other systems, ties the concept of a penalty clause to a sum of money payable in the event of non-conforming performance of any kind (that is, in Common law terms, breach). Under §339 BGB, the general rule is that such penalty clauses are enforceable, though, as with the provisions in the BGB concerning damages in general, such penalties may only be claimed if the debtor was at fault in not fulfilling the relevant obligation.[245] As is the position in the Common law, if a damages clause stipulates for payment of a sum in the event of non-performance, should the creditor choose to claim such sum he is then barred from suing for performance.[246] That position has an evident logic to it: it would

---

[243] The Scottish Law Commission suggested extending the law to cover penalties occurring on occasions other than breach of contract: see Scottish Law Commission, *Report on Penalty Clauses*. This proposed change has been included in the Bill proposed by the Scottish Government (see n. 242).

[244] *Zemhunt (Holdings) Ltd* v. *Control Securities plc* 1992 SLT 151.

[245] This follows from the reference to the debtor being 'in default' in §339: default entails fault because §286(4) states that the debtor is 'not in default for as long as performance is not made as the result of a circumstance for which he is not responsible'.

[246] §340(1).

be nonsensical to allow a party to claim a sum stipulated as payable for non-performance, if that party were able at the same time to force performance of the primary duty. The claim for other penalty sums, for instance for late or defective performance, does not of course prohibit a concurrent claim for performance.

As in the Common law, penalty clauses are subject to scrutiny by the courts, though the criterion for, and method of, such scrutiny is different. The BGB provides that, if application is made to the court before the penalty is paid, a penalty which is 'disproportionately high' can be reduced to a 'reasonable amount'. Such a trigger for scrutiny is somewhat different to that under the Common law, where the court's jurisdiction to consider agreed damages clauses is founded upon the question of whether the clause represents a genuine pre-estimate of loss at the time the contract was made: if it is, then even if at the time of the breach the damages payable may be 'disproportionately high' in relation to actual loss suffered, the clause will stand; on the other hand, if the clause was not a genuine pre-estimate of likely losses, it will be struck out of the contract (not amended), the party suffering the breach having instead to fall back upon a common law damages claim. However, the outcome of the Common law approach may not be so different to the German approach: a disproportionately high German penalty clause can be altered to provide 'reasonable' recovery (reasonableness, naturally suggesting some reference to the loss actually suffered), and an English common law damages award is based upon assessment of damages at the time of the trial by reference to the actual loss suffered by the party. The English approach is to look at the good faith nature of the term as agreed by the parties, the German approach to consider the practical effect of the clause at the time a complaint is raised. To that extent, the English approach may be said to pay more regard to the nature of the promise as made.

Unlike the position in the Common law and mixed legal systems, a stipulated penalty may not in German law be the full extent of what may be claimed by the creditor: the creditor is entitled to claim the penalty as the 'minimum amount' of damages, but is permitted to claim further damages if his loss exceeds the amount of the penalty.[247] This is at odds with the Common law approach, where, if parties commit their agreement as to exigible damages to a valid liquidated damages clause, the amount stipulated is that which is required to be paid by the party in breach, regardless of whether the actual amount of damages suffered

[247] §340(2).

is greater or less than the sum fixed in the clause. Again, the Common law approach may be said to pay more regard to the express terms of the promise as made by the promisor, the German approach to the fairness of the outcome at the time of the breach.

(d) Model law

Under the DCFR, liquidated damages clauses are to be given effect to, the creditor being entitled to the sum stipulated in the clause regardless of the actual loss suffered.[248] However, as in many of the national systems discussed above, such clauses are subject to moderation in order to prevent the use of excessive penalties. If the amount stipulated is grossly excessive in relation to the loss suffered, then the amount recoverable may be reduced to a reasonable amount.[249] This solution is symbolic of the DCFR's general attitude towards the autonomy of parties: respect tempered by moderation to curb perceived abuse.

The DCFR approach of judicial moderation, rather than (as in the Common law) the blunt instrument of striking down clauses, represents what appears to be an emerging preference of legal systems (it may, for instance become the Scottish approach in the near future).[250] It is, however, an approach which raises one serious objection, that being as to why judicial moderation requires to operate in commercial contracts. The case for protecting consumers against oppressive business practices may be reasonably well established, but that for interfering in the decision of commercial parties to include excessively penal clauses is far less robust. Arguably, it proposes an approach which goes too far in subjecting the promises of parties to the standards of commutative justice.

8.   Termination of contract for non-performance

As a prologue to this topic, it should be noted that there is a confusing array of terminology that is employed in the English language to describe the act of justified *ex nunc* (that is, prospective) termination of a contractual relationship. Such terms include cancellation, abrogation, annulment, rescission, repudiation, avoidance, withdrawal and resilement. Some of these can have specific meanings in individual legal systems, so their use to describe a general right to terminate future contractual relations

---

[248] Art. III.-3.712(1).   [249] Art. III.-3:712(2).   [250] See discussion above at n. 242.

is avoided in the following discussion, the largely jurisdiction-neutral term 'termination' being preferred. Even use of that term, without further clarification, runs the risk of conveying the idea that an act of termination by a party entirely annuls all rights and duties under the contract from the moment of termination onwards. That, as will be seen below, is not usually the case. Accrued but unfulfilled rights normally continue in force even after termination, and termination may not bring to an end all future rights. Thus, the right to seek damages for past faulty performance will survive termination. That is consistent with one of the purposes of termination, which is to protect the position of the party exercising the right to terminate. It is clearly not inconsistent with that protective purpose to allow accrued rights to continue to be enforced, especially as it may be that the right to terminate is being exercised precisely because such accrued rights have not been properly fulfilled by the other party. Given all this, the concept of termination must be understood strictly to mean termination of future performance.

Under a strict theory of the sanctity of promise, it might be argued that a party to a contract ought not to be given a default right to avoid performance of its promise even if the other party fails to perform its duties, such a right properly arising only if expressly stipulated by the promisor at the time of the making of the promise. However, the appreciation that contractual promises are usually conditional, the condition being the proper performance by the other party of its duties, can be argued to justify a default right of termination by the innocent party. The concept of mutuality is thus useful in accommodating a right to terminate within a structure which remains respectful of the high value to be accorded to promises.[251]

There are a number of potentially difficult issues relating to termination. Terminological ambiguity has the potential to pose substantive difficulties. Thus, for instance, where the right to terminate is tied to the idea of 'material' or 'fundamental' breach, as it is in some systems, there is the potential for confusion as to whether it is only the gravity of the breach of contract which is important, whether it is the importance of the clause which has been breached, or whether a combination of the two. Does a minor breach of an important term trigger the right to terminate? What of an important breach of a minor term? Naturally this problem can be

---

[251] Though there remains the theoretical problem of how to justify a default entitlement to terminate in non-mutual contracts, but such a right may simply have to be accepted as an anomaly in a system designed with mutual contracts primarily in mind.

avoided if the contract clearly stipulates which breaches will give rise to the right to terminate, and which not, but contracts do not always do so, and where they do not there ought to be a clear default rule. Most systems have serendipitously resolved the matter by holding that a material breach must go 'to the root of the contract', suggesting that it is the overall effect upon the parties' relationship which counts (so that an important breach of a minor term would *not* amount to material breach of the contract). A further potentially difficult issue is whether, in cases of remediable breach of contract, good faith requires that the party in breach should be given an opportunity to attempt to remedy the breach before the other party terminates the contract, a matter discussed further below.

(a) Historical origins of the right to terminate

Even in classical Roman law, there was an acceptance that not every pledged contractual performance had to be rendered: for instance, a tenant could terminate a lease if the landlord did not comply with his duties, and a landlord could terminate if the tenant did not pay his rent;[252] a purchaser under a contract of sale could terminate the purchase in the event of a defect which triggered the *actio redhibitoria*; and, in later Imperial law, the rule of *laesio enormis* allowed sales of land for less than half their real worth to be cancelled by the seller.[253]

Later, the canon law rule of *frangenti fidem fides non est servanda* ('to him who breaches fidelity, fidelity is no longer owed') was extended into the general law to provide a principle of wide application allowing termination for breach. This tradition of a wide termination right has been continued into a number of, though not all, modern legal systems.

(b) English law

As noted earlier in the discussion on perfect or substantial performance, in English law the right to terminate a contract for breach of contract depends upon whether the term breached is classified as a condition or a warranty: breach of the former class of term (along with *some* breaches of so-called 'innominate terms') gives a right to terminate, breach of the latter type does not.[254] As in other systems, termination for breach has an

---

[252] Zimmermann, *Law of Obligations*, p. 356.   [253] C. 4.44.2.
[254] See earlier discussion at p. 363.

ex nunc (prospective) but not *ex tunc* (retrospective) effect.[255] Damages for loss caused by breach may be claimed whether or not the contract is terminated.

The innocent party faced with breach of a condition may elect to terminate or not, as it sees fit, and once the decision is made the alternative course of action cannot be resurrected.[256] If an election is made to terminate, the decision to terminate must be communicated in some unequivocal way (which may be by means of conduct) to the party in breach.[257] Unlike in German law and Louisiana law, there is no requirement at Common law that the party in breach be given a second chance to remedy a breach which is remediable. However, in cases of consumer sales, the buyer now has the right to require that the seller repair (if possible) or replace the goods, so in this class of case a second attempt at proper performance can be compelled by the innocent party, though not required by the party in breach.[258]

(c)   Mixed legal systems

As in many systems, in South Africa termination for breach (or rescission, as it is known) has a prospective, not retrospective, effect. Accrued but unfulfilled rights are not terminated by the rescission, and a claim may still be maintained in respect of them.[259] The right to terminate is available in respect of those breaches of contract which are sufficiently material, and which are thus said to 'go to the root of the contract'.[260]

In South African law, the courts have had occasion to reject the convoluted and artificial view that the power of termination of a contract for breach arises by virtue of an offer from the breaching party to end the contract.[261] Such a theory was rejected by Jansen JA in *Stewart Wrightson*

---

[255] *Photo Production Ltd* v. *Securicor Transport Ltd* [1980] AC 827.
[256] *Johnson* v. *Agnew* [1980] AC 367. The language of 'waiver' is sometimes employed to describe the fact that the alternative course of action cannot be resurrected once the election has been made (a usage also encountered in South African law).
[257] *Vitol SA* v. *Norelf Ltd* [1996] AC 800.
[258] Sale of Goods Act 1979, s. 48A (this section applies in Scotland also).
[259] *Thomas Construction (Pty) Ltd (in liquidation)* v. *Grafton Furniture Manufacturers (Pty) Ltd* 1986 (4) SA 510 (N), at 511 per Nienaber J.
[260] See authorities cited earlier in this chapter under heading 4, at p. 362.
[261] The theory that election to terminate is an acceptance of an offer to terminate from the breaching party finds its support from US Law, where it was the view of Williston, *Williston on Contracts*, §683.

(Pty) Ltd v. *Thorpe.*[262] Jansen JA, reviewing the Roman-Dutch law on the matter, said:

> In those instances where our old authorities did recognize the possibility of terminating a bilateral contract for a breach by the other party, it seems clear that this was considered to flow from the breach as of right, and not as a result of any application of a theory of offer and acceptance. In fact, it would be highly artificial to consider a breach as an offer to terminate, as in most instances termination is the very last result that the party in breach desires or intends ... The cases dealing with the giving of notice of an election also do not appear to support such a theory.[263]

While rejecting an offer and acceptance view of election to terminate, Jansen JA did not offer any definite view on the actual basis of the right. He did, however, confirm the need for such an election to be be made manifest to the other party, though again stressing that this requirement does not rest upon any need for *consensus* but 'must flow from other considerations, whatever they may be'.[264] The election to terminate may be manifested by a verbal communication, or by way of conduct.

Despite this fairly clear judicial view that the right to rescind for breach does not have to be explained as deriving from an offer to terminate from the breaching party, a variation on this idea is still maintained by some modern commentators. For instance, it has been argued that the right to elect to terminate 'is inferred from a contractual term, which comes into operation upon breach of contract. The relevant term will usually be an *ex lege* term.'[265] This seems a highly fictionalised and laboured approach, and a better alternative is suggested by the same authors as being that 'cancellation is a power (capacity or competence) that is simply bestowed by law on the victim of breach of contract'.[266] This alternative view is indeed preferable and, if correct, would align South African law with the view

---

[262] 1977 (2) SA 943 (A). See also *Datacolor International (Pty) Ltd* v. *Intamarket (Pty) Ltd* [2001] 1 All SA 581 (A), in which Nienaber JA was equally dismissive of the offer and acceptance analysis of the election to terminate.

[263] 1977 (2) SA 943, 953. Jansen JA refers to an earlier judicial comment in *Moyce* v. *Estate Taylor* 1948 (3) S.A. 822, 829 (AD) that 'election seems ... to stand on exactly the same footing as waiver: it is indeed a form of waiver', but says that this does not support an agreement theory of election to terminate.

[264] At 954, per Jansen JA. He adds that '[c]onceivably, questions of estoppel and *quasi* estoppel are relevant'.

[265] Van der Merwe *et al., Contract*, p. 399.

[266] *Ibid.*, p. 399, n. 115. In support of this alternative view, there is citation of O'Brien, 'Restitutio in integrum', pp. 285 f, and O'Brien and Reinecke, 'Restitusie na terugtrede weens kontrakbreuk', p. 563.

adopted in other systems. Whatever its nature, in South African law (as in Scots law) the right to terminate for breach of contract is a remedy which does not require the intervention of the courts (even if it is sanctioned by law, in a general sense).

In Scots law, it was traditionally said that a material breach of contract gave an absolute right to terminate. Thus, in *Municipal Council of Johannesburg* v. *D. Stewart & Co.*,[267] Lord Dunedin said:

> If the stipulation which is broken goes to the root and essence of the contract, the other party is entitled to say – now you have so broken the contract that I am entitled to say that it is at an end through your fault. I shall not perform any more of my stipulations because you have precluded me …[268]

Expressing the innocent party's entitlement in such a fashion leaves it somewhat unclear as to whether there is a need to offer the party in breach a second chance to adhere to its obligations. The inclusion of the idea that B's material breach may 'preclude' A from performing its reciprocal undertakings might, however, be said to justify a distinction between those material breaches which are irremediable, and so by their nature prevent the parties from continuing the contractual relationship, and those which, though material, might be remedied and thus permit the relationship to continue in being. Just such a distinction was said to exist in *Lindley Catering Investments Ltd* v. *Hibernian Football Club Ltd*,[269] a case in which the defender purported to terminate the contract between the parties on account of various alleged defects in the catering facilities offered by the pursuer at the defender's football ground. It was decided that there had been no material breach of the pursuer's duties, but the judge, Lord Thomson, gave his *obiter* view that, if a breach of contract

> is such by degree or circumstances that it can be remedied so that the contract as a whole can thereafter be implemented the innocent party is not entitled to treat the contract as rescinded without giving to the other party an opportunity to remedy the breach.

Though these remarks were merely *obiter*, the position suggested by Lord Thomson is similar to that of German law's *Nachfrist*, or 'second chance', discussed below. His specification of the 'degree or circumstances' that can warrant a second chance seems to have been intended to serve as a reminder that it is both material breaches short of a

---

[267] 1909 SC 860.   [268] 1909 SC at 877.   [269] 1975 SLT (Notes) 56.

repudiation ('degree') as well as the type of conduct constituting the breach ('circumstances') which are relevant in assessing whether the breach is remediable or not.

It is unfortunate that the view expressed in *Lindley* has not been authoritatively settled by the Appeal Court, but has merely been the subject of comment in later first instance judgments. In one such later judgment, *Charisma Properties* v. *Grayling (1994) Ltd*,[270] Lord Sutherland remarked that as a 'general rule, if there is a material breach of contract, the innocent party is entitled to rescind the contract forthwith'; on the other hand, in *Strathclyde Regional Council* v. *Border Engineering Contractors Ltd*,[271] Lady Cosgrove expressed a more favourable view of Lord Thomson's approach, commenting that 'it is a basic principle of the law of contract that if one party is in breach, the innocent party is not entitled to treat the contract as rescinded without giving the other party an opportunity to remedy the breach.' The issue, which represents one of the many unsettled contractual issues typical in a small uncodified jurisdiction like Scotland, requires to be settled definitively. Until such time, it seems wise for parties to continue to specify contractually when a breach will or will not be material, either by listing certain breaches as such or by providing for a notification procedure by which any breach by B may be the subject of a notice by A requiring B to remedy the breach within a specified time, failure so to remedy triggering an entitlement on A's part to rescind the contract forthwith. Such a notice procedure has the merits both of clarifying when the right to terminate arises as well as embodying the good faith which is inherent in a second chance process.

Finally, in Louisiana the right to terminate for breach (or to 'dissolution of the contract' for failure to perform, as the Code calls it) is the subject of the whole of chapter 9 of the Code. As partly discussed earlier in relation to substantial performance, if the debtor fails to perform, Article 2013 gives the creditor 'a right to judicial dissolution of the contract or, according to the circumstances, to regard the contract as dissolved'. The remedy thus has both a judicial and a self-help form. The right to damages is, in either case, reserved. Rather than stipulate that the right to terminate is dependent upon the seriousness of the breach, the Code looks at things the other way round, from the level of performance tendered: dissolution is not available where the debtor has rendered substantial performance.[272] As in the other mixed systems, the right to be remunerated for a partial

---

[270] 1996 SC 556.   [271] 1998 SLT 175.
[272] CC Art. 2014: see earlier discussion at p. 362.

performance already tendered, short of substantial performance, survives dissolution of the contract.[273]

In judicial proceedings, the defaulting party may be allowed a second chance to perform, because 'according to the circumstances' the court may grant it an additional time to perform. Evidently, such an additional time would not be granted where, for instance, the defective performance could not be remedied. In addition, where dissolution is sought as a self-help remedy, without recourse to the courts, a notice is to be issued by the innocent party to the defaulting party upon the latter's non-performance requiring performance within a specified reasonable time, and warning that if such performance is not forthcoming the contract shall be deemed to be dissolved.[274] The issuing of this notice is a necessary step if dissolution by the party, rather than the court, is sought, though an exception is made where delayed performance would no longer be of value to the innocent party or when it is evident that the party in default will not perform.[275] Though the requirement for a compliance notice evidently acts as a break on what is otherwise a clearly party-centred, will-based remedy, such a requirement is not unusual in a comparative context: the provisions of the Louisiana Code bear strong comparisons with German law's *Nachfrist*, discussed in the following section.

(d)   German law

The relevant portion of the BGB for present purposes concerns the right of termination for non-performance in §§323–6.[276] The principal section on termination, §323, is, it should be noted, only applicable to mutual or reciprocal contracts: it has no application to gratuitous contracts, which has a certain logic to it given that in such gratuitous contracts the promisee has no duties the breach of which might mandate conferral of the right to terminate on the promisor.[277] Unlike the right to claim damages or to enforce penalty clauses, there is no requirement that the right to

---

[273] CC Art. 2018: 'If partial performance has been rendered and that performance is of value to the party seeking to dissolve the contract, the dissolution does not preclude recovery for that performance.'

[274] CC Art. 2015.   [275] CC Art. 2016.

[276] Rescission for mistake has been dealt with earlier in Ch. 4, under the section on error.

[277] On the other hand, why should not, in theory, the promisee under a gratuitous contract have the right to terminate the contract for breach? Admittedly, it might seem that such a promisee does not need the protection of the right to terminate, given such a promisee has no duties which it might be compelled to undertake, but might there not be other valid reasons why such a promisee might wish to terminate the contract?

terminate may only be exercised in the event of the other party's fault, a discrepancy which further serves to question the need for the fault principle in damages claims. Termination and damages may be sought concurrently. In fact, as will be noticed, the regimes for termination and damages in lieu of performance are (the fault issue aside) similar in many respects.

As with the right to seek performance, the right to terminate for non-performance or non-conforming performance arising under §323 may only be exercised if an additional period of time has been specified for performance or cure and this has not occurred (the so-called *Nachfrist*, or 'second chance'). There are three exceptions specified from the requirement to give the breaching party a second chance: (i) the occurrence of what would be called repudiation in English or Scots law, that is where the debtor seriously and definitively refuses performance; (ii) where the creditor made it clear in the contract that performance by a specified time was essential, and this has not occurred – what would be termed in the Common law, making time 'of the essence'; and (iii) where there are 'special circumstances' which, on balance, justify immediate termination.[278]

Termination brings with it, under §346, the mutual duty to restore received performances to the other party (with certain exceptions). This is clearly seen as a contractual effect of termination, and is not a form of unjustified enrichment. The duty to restore is not applicable in cases of 'continuing contracts' (such as lease) where numerous acts of performance on each side may already have occurred, restoration in such cases being impracticable.[279]

One difference between German law and many other systems is that the §323(1) right to terminate is not dependent upon the seriousness of the breach by the other party: in theory any type of breach, whether major or minor, justifies the right to terminate, though evidently a minor breach is more likely to be remedied during the period of *Nachfrist* which must usually be given to the defaulting party. In other systems, typically only important or material breaches give a right to termination. In one respect, however, German law makes a concession to its 'any breach' position: §323(5) adds that in cases of non-conforming performance (but not of total failure to perform), the right to terminate does not apply if 'the breach of duty is trivial'. Trivial breaches would similarly not give rise to a default right to terminate in other systems, though such a right could in those systems (as it could in Germany) be reserved by the parties

---

[278] §323(2) BGB.   [279] Continuing contracts are regulated by §314 BGB.

through defining any breach of contract as serious and thus as triggering a right to terminate.[280] By comparison then, the default rule in Germany is that all breaches other than trivial ones give a right to terminate, while in England only material breaches give such a right. The difference thus lies in the treatment of the middle ground, that being the treatment of non-material but more than trivial breaches.[281]

As in the Common law and mixed systems, termination is available for anticipatory breach: a creditor may terminate the contract before performance becomes due if it is obvious that the requirements for termination will be met.[282] An obvious case would be a statement of the debtor ahead of the due date for performance that it will not perform when such performance falls due, but other objective indications of unwillingness or inability to perform would also trigger the right to terminate ahead of time. In the German law however, unlike the English law, any claim for damages following anticipatory termination must await the due date for performance.

Termination has only an *ex nunc* effect, so any performances due which have already been rendered are unaffected by termination and are not subject to the restitutionary regime considered in the next principal section of this chapter.

(e)   Model law

In the introduction to the DCFR, the opportunity is taken to affirm the important point made earlier in this chapter that, where breach of contract gives rise to a right to terminate, it is not the contract as a whole which is terminated but only specific rights and obligations arising under it.[283] This statement is a crucial reminder that termination for breach does not affect accrued rights, but has only an *ex nunc* or prospective effect.[284] The DCFR approach in relation to the right to

---

[280] So, for instance, though late performance of a duty to pay may not usually amount to a material breach of contract, the parties may agree that 'time is of the essence', meaning that exact conformity with the timetable must occur, and may provide that any failure in this respect will confer a right to terminate: see, for instance, *Union Eagle* v. *Golden Achievement* [1997] AC 514.

[281] This is on the assumption that such a thing as non-material but non-trivial breaches exist, which it is argued they do.

[282] §323(4) BGB.   [283] DCFR, *Introduction*, para. 51.

[284] The same position prevails in relation to termination by agreement: see Art. III.-1: 108(2)(a).

terminate is, rather than to talk loosely of 'material breach' or 'fundamental breach' as some systems do, to specify four different grounds justifying termination:

(1) fundamental non-performance;[285]
(2) non-fundamental delay in performance, following expiry of a period of notice requiring performance;[286]
(3) anticipated fundamental non-performance;[287] and
(4) inadequate assurance of due performance, following expiry of a period of notice requiring such assurance.[288]

What these grounds mean is fleshed out in the relevant article governing each ground. Importantly, 'fundamental non-performance' is not defined in terms which limit it to a culpable non-performance; rather, non-performance is fundamental if it 'deprives the creditor of what the creditor was entitled to expect under the contract', unless such a result was unforeseeable to the debtor at the time of contracting. This strict liability basis of the right to terminate is consistent with a law of contract which permits parties (if they wish) to promise that a specific end will be achieved, and not simply that best efforts will be employed in an attempt to achieve that end. A failure of a promise to achieve a specific end ought properly to give rise to a right to terminate for any failure to so achieve, and the DCFR provisions reflect this by giving a wide general right to terminate for non-performance. Consistent with the position in national systems relating to termination by the innocent party (rather than by a court), a notice of termination must be issued to the debtor.[289]

Not every circumstance where termination is permitted requires the party in default to be given a second chance to perform: of the four grounds of termination listed above, only termination under grounds (2) and (4) involve the innocent party first giving the party in default a period of time to remedy the problem. The DCFR has thus chosen to limit the 'second chance' approach (or *Nachfrist* in German terms) to a limited category of case.[290]

---

[285] Art. III.-3:502.   [286] Art. III.-3:503.   [287] Art. III.-3:504.
[288] Art. III.-3:505.   [289] Art. III.-3.507(1).
[290] Though in fact, in relation to ground (4), it is not so much that the debtor has breached the contract and is being asked to correct this, it is rather that a debtor who has shown signs of being unlikely to perform when the due time falls has been unable to give an adequate assurance of performance.

9.   Restitution following termination for non-performance

Following the termination of a contract for non-performance, A may wish, as an alternative (or perhaps in addition) to raising a claim for damages for any losses it has suffered, to seek the restitution of any performance it has tendered to B under the contract.[291] Though such a claim, if it is allowed, evidently protects the restitution interest of the party concerned, rather than the performance interest, to the extent that such right to restitution is held to be a species of contractual claim (rather than a type of unjustified enrichment) it can at least be said to be promissory in nature, given that its justification (from A's point of view) lies in the fact that, because B did not do what it promised to do, A ought to be able to get back what it gave to to B. Such a contractual restitutionary claim can be seen (as with the right to terminate itself) as a further remedial manifestation of the principle of mutuality of contract. As will be seen, however, in some jurisdictions the right to such restitution following breach of contract may be controversial or very restricted, or may be classifiable not as contractual in nature but as a type of enrichment claim.[292] Such an enrichment classification fails to recognise the promissory nature of the circumstances out of which the restitutionary remedy arises. Termination, after all, has only *ex nunc* effect; it is not, as with void contracts, as if the contract never existed at all.

(a)   English law

English law stands apart from civilian and most mixed systems in not generally allowing some form of restitution following termination for breach. In the Common law, restitution is available to a party which has given consideration under a contract only in cases of total failure of consideration, those being where the party has received no part of the reciprocal performance identified in the contract. This entitlement was established in *Fibrosa* v. *Fairbairn*,[293] and has been applied in a line of cases following it. The reason why failure of consideration must be total is that such consideration is conceived of as having been pledged as an indivisible whole for the other party's reciprocal consideration (unless

---

[291] See Fried, *Contract as Promise*, Ch. 8.

[292] Fried argues that the right to the return of what has been paid should be seen as non-contractual restitution: *ibid.*, pp. 117–18.

[293] *Fibrosa Spolka Akcynjna* v. *Fairbairn Lawson Combe Barbour Ltd* [1943] AC 32.

the parties stipulate otherwise), so that the receipt of any portion of the consideration precludes the restitution of what was given for it. The remedy, where claimable, is not seen as contractual in nature, but as an equitable measure to prevent the recipient's unjustified enrichment. The result is that the party who is the victim of the breach has the choice of using whichever of restitution or damages is more favourable in the circumstances, and therefore of potentially avoiding a bad bargain[294] (precisely the possibility denied to the pursuer in the Scottish case of *Connolly* v. *Simpson*, discussed below). As an equitable restitutionary remedy it is, of course, subject to the usual restitutionary defences, such as change of position, which would be inapplicable were the restoration seen as contractual in nature.

While partial failure of consideration can now also ground restitution by virtue of the provisions of the Law Reform (Frustrated Contracts) Act 1943, this only applies to frustrated contracts, not those terminated for breach, a distinction which can be productive of arguably unfair results. The hirer of a car destroyed in a storm one day into a fortnight's hire can seek restitution for partial failure of consideration, but the hirer whose vehicle irreparably breaks down after the same period of time because the vehicle has been inadequately maintained by the lessor cannot so recover and is restricted to a remedy in damages.[295] Such discrepancies of result are also obvious if one compares circumstances of breach with those where a contract is avoided for misrepresentation: although the facts of the case may be very similar, the treatment of those facts as giving rise to a case of misrepresentation will allow *restitutio in integrum* to be effected, even if consideration has only been reciprocated in part at the time the contract is avoided, but no restitution will be available if the facts are classified as breach of a contract term unless the failure of consideration has been total.

The extent of the availability of restitution for total failure of consideration is obviously very limited in practice, and such a limited remedy does not detract from the position of damages as the primary remedy for breach in the Common law. It is though a remedy which is at least undoubtedly available, unlike restitution following breach in Scots law.

---

[294] See further Peel, *Chitty on Contracts*, para. 29–059.

[295] The Law Commission however recommended keeping the rule as to total failure of consideration: see Law Commission Report, *Law of Contract: Pecuniary Restitution on Breach of Contract*.

(b) Mixed legal systems

In South African law, quite apart from any claim to damages which a plaintiff may have following termination for breach of contract, the plaintiff is also entitled to restitution of any sum or any thing transferred under the terminated contract.[296] This right to restitution following termination has traditionally been viewed as a contractual remedy, not one based in unjustified enrichment, though this view has been challenged by some commentators.[297] The challenge rests on the view that the effect produced by a remedy ought to be determinative of its classification, restitution therefore being argued to be an enrichment remedy. But this alternative view fails to take account of the fact that restitution is a remedy which is capable of operating in a number of spheres of law, including property law, where the vindicatory claim of an owner is an example of a restitutionary claim. It would seem odd to classify such a vindicatory claim stemming from ownership as concerning unjustified enrichment, but that is a conclusion whose adoption this alternative theory concerning restitution following breach would seem to compel. For that reason, it seems better to continue to classify remedies flowing from the enforcement of a valid contract, or one which, though valid, is terminated for breach, as contractual in nature, and reserve an enrichment classification only for cases where a contract is held never to have existed at all.

The operation of restitution following breach in South African law may be seen in the case of *Hall Thermotank Natal (Pty) Ltd* v. *Hardman*.[298] In that case, the plaintiff had supplied and fitted refrigeration facilities aboard a ship owned by the defendant. The defendant had made a part payment towards the total contract price before the ship sailed. Unfortunately, when an attempt was made to put the refrigeration facilities to use, they proved wholly defective. Before they could be repaired, the ship sank during a storm. When the plaintiff sued for the balance of the contract price, the defendant terminated the contract, claimed damages, and argued that it was entitled to set off the part payment it had made against any amount it might be found to owe the plaintiff. In the Supreme Court, it was held that: (i) the defendant was entitled to terminate the contract on account of the defect in the unit supplied, (ii) because

---

[296] Van der Merwe *et al.*, *Contract*, p. 422.
[297] Visser, 'Rethinking Unjustified Enrichment', pp. 225–9; Hutton, 'Remedies after Breach of Contract'.
[298] 1968 (4) SA 818 (D).

the defendant had received no benefit from what had been supplied, he was not obliged to compensate the plaintiff in money or kind for what had been lost in the storm, and (iii) given the valid termination of the contract, the defendant was entitled to restitution of the part payment he had made to the plaintiff. In this case, restitution only operated in one direction, though had the goods supplied not been lost in the storm, the defendant would have had to return them to the plaintiff following termination of the contract.

The question of restoration following termination for breach is one of the fields where Scots law manifests the weakness of being a non-codified system with a small body of case law. The law on this issue is muddled. Late nineteenth- and early twentieth-century academic views[299] and judgments[300] appeared to support the view that it was an established rule of Scots law that where an advance payment was made by one contracting party for a performance which was never received from the other, and the contract was then terminated for breach, the payment might be claimed back, albeit that the claim was seen as 'quasi-contractual' (or lying in unjustified enrichment, as we would now say) rather than contractual. Lord President Inglis famously characterised such a claim as a 'rule of the civil law, as adopted in all modern codes and systems', applying it in the case before him.[301]

Unfortunately, the general applicability of the rule in all cases of termination for breach was doubted in *Connelly* v. *Simpson*.[302] In *Connelly* the pursuer had paid £16,000 in advance for shares which were never transferred to him, initially because he asked for the transfer to be delayed and then latterly because the company was put into liquidation. At the time of liquidation, the shares were worth only £400. It seems that the pursuer attempted to rescind the contract for breach (though the judgments of the court are unclear whether this had occurred). It evidently made a great difference to the pursuer whether he was entitled to claim restoration to the pre-contractual position, when he would get his £16,000 back, or whether he had only a damages claim, in which case he would only get £400. The nineteenth-century authorities appeared to suggest that (assuming he had validly terminated the contract for breach) he was entitled to his money back. A majority of the appeal court held, however, that he was not, though their reasoning is somewhat confused. One judge

---

[299] Gloag, *Contract*, pp. 59–60.
[300] *Watson* v. *Shankland* (1871) 10 M 142; affirmed (1873) 11 M (HL) 51.
[301] See judgment of Lord President Inglis in *Watson* v. *Shankland* (1871) 10 M 142, 152.
[302] 1993 SC 391; 1994 SLT 1096.

argued that the pursuer got what he paid for: he paid for the right to have the shares transferred to him, he got such a right, and therefore he could not claim restitution on the ground that he paid in advance for what he did not get.[303] The other majority judge took the different view that 'in a breach of contract case, especially one where a long time has elapsed without performance ever having been demanded, [there is no room] for a remedy in the form of restitution of the price as such.'[304] The underlying concern of this judge appears to have been that, the pursuer having delayed for a long time to ask for the transfer to be effected, he had taken the risk of a decrease in the value of the shares. This view might suggest that, more generally, termination for breach ought not to give rise to a right to restitution of advance performance, but only to damages. If that is so, then it would put Scots law out of step with the other mixed systems and with civilian systems.

The law is in need of further clarification. It would be helpful for a clear judicial statement to be given to the effect that restitution following termination for breach is available in Scots law, such a remedy being seen (as in South African law) as contractual in nature. The denial of such a claim – if that is now the law following the unclear *Connelly* decision – puts the victim of a breach of contract in a disadvantageous position in relation to the contract breaker, which seems the reverse of the position suggested by the equities of the case. Moreover, the majority academic view is in favour of seeing the right to restitution in such a case as contractual, rather than enrichment, in nature.[305]

In Louisiana, the codal title on sale provides for a right on the buyer's part to restitution of the price if the contract is rescinded.[306] More generally, Article 2018 provides that: (a) where a contract is dissolved, the parties are to be be restored to the situation that existed before the contract was made; and (b) if such restoration in kind is impossible or impracticable, then a court is entitled to award damages.[307] This preference for restitution over damages is a feature shared with German law, as will be seen below. In cases where a partial performance has been rendered which is of

---

[303] See judgment of Lord Sutherland, 1993 SC at 414G–H; 1994 SLT at 1110G.
[304] Lord McCluskey 1993 SC at 407D–408A; 1994 SLT at 1106C–G.
[305] See Hogg, *Obligations*, paras. 4.164–9; R. Evans-Jones, *Unjustified Enrichment* (vol. 1), paras. 6.119–23.
[306] CC Art. 2497. See also Art. 2507 (restitution despite deterioration).
[307] An alternative approach would have been (as in German law) to have awarded the monetary equivalent of the thing which cannot be restored in kind, though in any event it might be argued that the loss to be compensated under a damages award includes the value of the non-returnable thing.

value to the party seeking to dissolve the contract, Article 2018 adds that dissolution of the contract does not preclude recovery for that performance 'whether in contract or quasi-contract'.

(c) German law

In German law, following termination of contract a so-called 'obligational restitutionary relationship' (*Rückgewährschuldverhältnis*) comes in to being. This regime is considered contractual in nature, and its operation precludes the use of unjustified enrichment remedies to adjust the parties' positions. The restitutionary regime applicable following termination is governed by §346 BGB. Restitution of any performance received is the first duty mandated by the provision,[308] though if that is not possible then monetary compensation is to be provided (this is not the same as damages for loss).[309] In addition to performance received, restitution must also be effected of 'emoluments' (or 'benefits') derived from such performance, such as use of an object. Restitution *in forma specifica* evidently cannot be effected in some cases, three being listed on §346(2) as being where: (i) the nature of the performance is incompatible with such restitution – usage of an object being just such a case, as evidently past usage of an object cannot be transferred; (ii) the object transferred has been consumed, disposed of, encumbered, processed, or redesigned; or (iii) the object transferred has deteriorated (ordinary wear and tear excepted) or been destroyed. Assessment of the appropriate monetary compensation uses the contract price (if one is specified) as the starting point, with appropriate modification (so, if a one-month hire of an object for €300 is terminated after only half a month, €150 would be an appropriate sum for the usage).[310] There is, furthermore, no duty to effect compensation in monetary terms as a substitute for restitution *in forma specifica* in three stated circumstances: (i) if the defect justifying termination only became apparent during processing or transformation of the object; (ii) if the party in breach was responsible for the deterioration or destruction, or the damage would have happened in any event if the object had stayed with that party; or (iii) in cases of a statutory right of termination (i.e. for breach of contract under §323), if the deterioration or destruction occurred in the terminating party's hands but that party showed the same care he customarily

---

[308] §346(1). [309] §346(2) BGB.
[310] See, for instance, BGH NJW 1991, 2484; BGH NJW-RR 1995, 364; BGH NJW 1996, 250.

took in relation to his own affairs. The only duty in such cases is to return any 'remaining enrichment'.

These provisions would make solution of circumstances such as those raised in the South African case *Hall Thermotank* v. *Hardman*,[311] discussed above, relatively straightforward under the German regime. Actual restitution of the refrigeration facilities would clearly be excluded by their destruction, making the defendant theoretically liable to compensate the plaintiff monetarily.[312] However, given that it appears that the defendant in *Hall* acted with customary care while the goods were in its possession (the loss of the refrigerator facilities and the ship being due to a storm), such a duty to make monetary compensation would be excluded. Furthermore, given complete loss of the ship and the refrigeration facilities, there would be no 'remaining enrichment' for the defendant to restore. On these facts then, the supplier would be entitled to nothing. From the customer's point of view however, the supplier would be required to return the advance payment to the customer.[313] German law would thus provide for the same solution as reached by the South African court, but the route to that conclusion in Germany would be much clearer than was the case in the South African decision, given the rules set out in §346 BGB.

An important exception to restitution following termination of contract in German law applies in the case of so-called 'continuing contracts' (*Dauerschuldverhältnis*), those being contracts where the parties are under a continuing, repeated obligation of performance. Examples of such contracts (regulated by §314 BGB) include lease, partnership and employment, though any contract which imposes continued performance will fall within the regime. Such contracts may be terminated without notice under §314(1) so long as a 'compelling reason' exists for their termination, the requirement of a compelling reason being explained as meaning circumstances where 'the terminating party, taking into account all the circumstances of the specific case and weighing the interests of both parties, cannot reasonably be expected to continue the contractual relationship until the agreed end or until the expiry of a notice period'. Damages are available following such termination, but not the restitutionary regime described above. So, past mutual performance under a continuing contract, for instance mutual performance in relation to rental periods now passed, would not be disturbed by means of restitution, but accrued and unfulfilled rights could still be claimed (for instance a claim for payment

---

[311] 1968 (4) SA 818 (D).   [312] §346(2)(3) BGB.   [313] §346(1) BGB.

might be made for unpaid rent).[314] That position equates to the approach taken in Common law and mixed systems.

(d) Model law

The DCFR follows the German approach in clearly permitting restitution following termination for breach, in classifying this as a contractual and not an enrichment remedy, and in providing for substitutionary methods of effecting such restitution if exact restitution in kind cannot be achieved.[315] A change of position defence, such as would be maintainable if the claim were in unjustified enrichment, is not permitted: where a benefit cannot be returned because, for instance, it has been consumed, payment for the value of the benefit must be made.[316] Restitution is not required in respect of a performance that has been met with a reciprocal conforming performance of the other party,[317] so that, for instance, payments under a staged contract for portions of work which have been properly performed would be irrecoverable. Adoption of the DCFR approach would be to the manifest benefit of both English and Scots law, in providing both clarity and equity to the law's treatment of restitution following termination for breach.

10. Good faith and contractual remedies

The doctrine of good faith is evidently not a remedy as such, but rather a principle informing contract law generally and the rights created under contracts more particularly. Given that good faith is a principle which has been used to regulate the exercise of contractual remedies, it is appropriate to conclude the discussion of contractual remedies with an examination of how such regulation has operated in the systems studied.

On one view, good faith is of the very essence of all promises, whether contractual or unilateral. On this view, the existence of promissory liability is founded upon a relationship of trust existing between the promisor and promisee, the promisee taking the promisor at his word and thus placing his faith upon the pledged performance. Whether it is necessary to describe all promises in this fashion is, however, doubtful.[318] If a promisor becomes bound in law to honour a promise simply by uttering the

---

[314] Markesinis *et al.*, *German Law of Contract*, p. 437.
[315] DCFR Art. III.-3:510.   [316] Arts. III.-3:510(4) and III.-3:512.
[317] Art. III.-3:511(1).   [318] See Kimel, *From Promise to Contract*, pp.14–20.

promissory words with the intention that the undertaking becomes bind-ing on him, then it would seem to be irrelevant whether or not the prom-isee trusts the promisor to honour that undertaking: whether or not such trust exists as a matter of fact, the promisor is still required to honour his promise. On this view, while trust and faith may as a matter of fact flow from many promissory undertakings, they are not essential to the valid constitution of a promise. Given the definition of a promise sug-gested in Chapter 1, this seems the better view. Unless the need for trust and good faith are written into the very definition of a promise – so that a promise is defined as 'a statement by which one person, *in furtherance of a relationship of trust and good faith with another,* commits to some future beneficial performance, or the beneficial withholding of a performance, in favour of that other person' – then it does not seem correct to state that a promise requires the presence of trust and good faith before it can come into being. Indeed, in reality, many promisees may well be beneficiaries of promises from people in whom they have little if any faith or trust, yet the law considers them beneficiaries under valid promises nonetheless.

Even if good faith (and trust) are not necessary components of the very idea of a promise, however, promissory liability has nonetheless proven to be a fertile field in which good faith has put down roots. Particularly in civilian jurisprudence, the doctrine of good faith has been used to regulate the contract negotiation and formation process, to interpret the rights expressly undertaken by parties, to impose additional duties upon parties and, of most relevance for present purposes, to regulate the exercise of remedies in the event of breach. Such uses of the doctrine of good faith have caused concern among some promise theorists, espe-cially in the Common law. A high regard for the value of the express promises undertaken by promisors would seem to allow little, if any, room for external interference with such promises, including remedies for breach thereof: the more the obligations established by promises are regulated or varied by external normative concepts such as good faith, the less regard will be shown by a legal system for the autonomous will of the promisor. The struggle between the poles of party autonomy on the one hand and extra-promissory normative control on the other is part of a wider and more fundamental philosophical and political battle between legal libertarianism and paternalism which rages well beyond the field of contract law, but adjudicating that debate is beyond the scope of the current work.

It is important to remember, of course, that good faith is capable of manifesting itself in at least two different ways, one subjective and the other objective.[319] Those who have concerns at the threat good faith poses to the inviolability of promises usually object most strongly to the objective manifestation of good faith. In its subjective sense, good faith means the actual honesty and fair dealing of the party in question (whether the promisor or promisee): did that party know, for instance, about a mistake made by the other and take advantage of it? If so, that constitutes a subjective absence of good faith (or perhaps even the positive presence of bad faith) which would merit the application of corrective measures in most systems. In its subjective sense, good faith has an established and largely uncontroversial role in Common law, mixed and civilian legal systems. In its objective sense, good faith concerns not the actual behaviour or knowledge of the contracting parties, but rather external community norms concerning appropriate behaviour, such as preventing the exercise of contractual remedies in a manner considered oppressive, or the imposition of a duty upon contracting parties to provide each other with certain information, or the implied duty on parties to cooperate to ensure that the goals of the contract are achieved. It is the interference constituted by the external imposition of such controls that lead to accusations that promises are being increasingly undermined in some legal systems.

It is possible to accommodate the requirements of subjective good faith within a regime which shows a high degree of respect for the actual promises made by the parties and which insists upon a strict enforcement of those promises. As subjective good faith has as its core the notion that a party ought to behave honestly and truthfully towards the other party, it is not difficult to argue that such a duty will accord in every case with the actual promises made by parties: after all, there is an ancient tradition of equating promising with truth-telling, as narrated in the earlier chapters of this book. Fried, for instance, has argued that the classic definition of good faith is honesty in fact,[320] and that such honesty is the hallmark of the principle of contractual autonomy.[321] On the other hand, it is harder to attempt to accommodate objective good faith, of the type which imposes normative controls on the exercise of remedies, in a way which is consistent with respect for the promises made by the parties. If, for instance, parties specify that termination for breach is to be available automatically in certain circumstances, why, if one of those circumstances arises, should the party in breach be required to be given a second chance to perform (as

[319] See Hesselink, 'The Concept of Good Faith', 471.
[320] See the Uniform Commercial Code, §1–201(b)(20).
[321] Fried, *Contract as Promise*, p. 77. Fried argues that to this idea of honesty must be added the idea of loyalty.

German law so requires)? This, it might be said, undermines the stipulated requirement of performance, and provides for a right to cure imperfect performance which the parties might have chosen for themselves but did not.

The potential for objective good faith to regulate, or one might say interfere with, the operation of contractual remedies is seen most clearly in civilian systems. German law provides, in §242 BGB, that a debtor has a duty to perform according to the requirements of good faith, taking customary practice into consideration. Though this provision is *ex facie* limited to performance of the debtor's duty, the German courts have been active in using the provision to create a wide ranging duty of good faith capable of creating pre-contractual duties, imposing further duties on the parties, and restricting the creditor's exercise of its rights, among other functions. As regards moderating the exercise of contractual rights and remedies, some decisions exist to the effect that, in extreme cases, a party may not be entitled to enforce a right if such exercise does not reflect a 'proper protection' of its interest, for instance because, though a breach existed originally, it was subsequently cured by the time of purported termination for breach.[322] In another case restricting an apparent unfettered right to terminate, it was held that if the exercise of the right occurs in circumstances where it breaches a constitutional right given to a party under the Basic Law (*Grundgesetz*), the exercise of the right can be said to breach the requirement of good faith imposed by §242.[323]

Such results are not unique to civilian systems, but may be seen in mixed legal systems also, especially in Louisiana with its code based upon the French Civil Code. Article 1759 of the Louisiana Civil Code provides that good faith is to 'govern the conduct of the obligor and the obligee in whatever pertains to the obligation'.[324] This provision has been used, inter alia, to restrict remedial entitlement. Thus, the Louisiana Appeal Court held in one case that a trial court had not erred in finding that A had

---

[322] BGHZ 90, 198.
[323] See BAG NZA 1994, 1080, where an unfettered right to terminate the contract was held to have been exercised against the requirement of good faith because it was motivated by reason of a dislike for the terminated party's sexual orientation (whose expression found constitutional protection as an aspect of his right of personality).
[324] Levasseur argues that this provision provides a 'general principle' which pervades the entire law of the Civil Code, and has an 'underlying presence' (*Louisiana Law of Obligations*, para. 1.4.2), adding that the Code contains more specific manifestations of good faith, which demonstrate two of its aspects, namely the duty of loyalty and the duty of cooperation. See generally on good faith in a Louisiana and comparative context, Litvinoff, 'Good Faith'.

breached a contract with B, in contravention of Article 1759, because A had terminated the at-will contract with B in order to award the contract to C.[325] Such a result seems consistent with the approach of the German courts, which have similarly looked at the motivation for the exercise of remedies.

In South Africa, good faith is said to be an expression of constitutional values, but the precise way in which it operates has been somewhat controversial. Good faith was specifically mentioned in the concurring minority judgment of Olivier JA in *First National Bank* v. *Saayman* as a justification for setting aside a suretyship agreement (the majority took a different approach, saying that the agreement was void for lack of capacity). Olivier JA said: 'I am convinced that the principles of good faith, founded in public policy, still play, and must continue to play, a significant role in our law of contract.'[326] Applying those principles to the case before him, Olivier JA thought the bank ought to have ensured that the grantor of the surety had a sufficient understanding of the nature of what she was undertaking. It has been questioned whether such an approach means that good faith should be seen as providing a separate, independent ground for setting aside contracts, or not.[327] Subsequently, in *Brisley* v. *Drotsky*[328] the Supreme Court of Appeal warned that Olivier JA's judgment should be approached with caution. The majority expressed their agreement with the view of Dale Hutchison that while good faith has a creative, controlling and legitimating or explanatory function, it is not the only principle underlying contract law, nor perhaps even the most important one.[329] The majority held that another such value is *pacta sunt servanda*, a value which is often in competition with good faith. When the values conflict, the court must perform a balancing act. So, if a particular rule or principle is regarded as unfair, it can be amended, but such amendment can only operate within the bounds of *stare decisis*, and where it does occur must happen incrementally and with caution. Individual judges are not authorised to refuse to give effect to contracts merely because they find them unfair.

English law has been even more reticent than South African law to give good faith any general, explicit role in constraining the exercise of

---

[325] *N-Y Assocs* v. *Board of Commissioners* 926 So. 2d 20 (La App 4 Cir 2006), writ denied 930 So. 2d 231 (La 2006).

[326] 1997 (4) SA 302 (A), 326G.

[327] See Brand and Brodie, 'Good Faith in Contract Law'.

[328] 2002 (4) SA 1 (SCA).

[329] See Hutchison, 'Good Faith in the South African Law of Contract'.

contractual remedies. What limited explicit role the concept performs derives largely from the implementation of the European Directive on unfair terms in consumer contracts, transposed into national law in the Unfair Terms in Consumer Contracts Regulations 1999.[330] Good faith also operates explicitly within the restricted context of insurance contracts (contracts *uberrimae fidei*, or the 'utmost good faith'), though in this context it founds, rather than restricts, the remedial entitlement to terminate such contracts for non-disclosure of any matter affecting the insured risk (such non-disclosure being deemed a breach of the requirement of the utmost good faith). Beyond this, however, good faith has little explicit role in the field of remedial enforcement, though it has been argued that many aspects of the English law of remedies reflect, under different guises, concerns which in other systems would be described as good faith in nature.[331] Similar arguments have been made about Scots law, where again any role for good faith in the field of remedies is at best a latent rather than a patent one,[332] despite a reference in the House of Lords in a Scottish appeal to 'the broad principle in the field of contract law of fair dealing in good faith'.[333] Such attempts to recast established rules and constraints in good faith terms are controversial, and any radical development in English or Scots law towards a more explicit good faith position is unlikely to precede a European harmonisation of contract law.

The recent proposals for harmonised contract law have all enshrined good faith within them, as references to a number of good faith provisions of the DCFR at various points in this work indicate.[334] Typically, as in the case of the DCFR, this is by way of a general good faith provision,[335] as well as by way of more specific manifestations of the good faith principle in relation to specific contract rules.[336] The general provision in the DCFR (Article III.-1:103) makes clear the application of good faith to the control of remedies, by stating that the duty to act in good faith extends

---

[330] See Reg. 5(1), which states that a 'contractual term which has not been individually negotiated shall be regarded as unfair if, contrary to the requirement of good faith, it causes a significant imbalance in the parties' rights and obligations arising under the contract, to the detriment of the consumer'.

[331] See Friedmann, 'Good Faith and Remedies for Breach of Contract'.

[332] See MacQueen, 'Good Faith in the Scots Law of Contract'.

[333] Per Lord Clyde in *Smith* v. *Bank of Scotland* 1997 SC (HL) 111, 121.

[334] See, for instance the discussion on the duty to negotiate in good faith in Ch. 4, at p. 201.

[335] DCFR Art. III.-1:103.

[336] Such as the duty to negotiate in good faith: Art. II.-3:301(2). This approach of a general, but also more specific, enunciation of good faith duties is not without its difficulties: see Beale, 'General Clauses and Specific Rules in the Principles of European Contract Law'.

to 'exercising a right to performance, in pursuing or defending a remedy for non-performance, or in exercising a right to terminate an obligation or contractual relationship'. Such a statement, while clearly very much in the tradition of civilian systems, goes well beyond what English law or the mixed systems (with the exception of Louisiana) would consider an appropriate restraint on party autonomy. It is reflective of a view of contract law which sees party autonomy, and thus the rights promised by parties to each other, as requiring to be regulated in the interests of justice and fairness. This view is likely to gain ground as a result of the increased impact of EU law into national contract law as well as the increasing influence of the model codes. Whatever the merits or otherwise of such a development, it must be admitted that it represents a major challenge to the earlier paradigm of contract law as being mostly about what contracting parties have promised each other, though, as suggested at the end of Chapter 3, a reinvigorated will theory of contract law is able to accommodate such external control of party autonomy if that is considered desirable.

7

The renunciation of contractual rights

If a party undertakes to renounce its contractual rights, or at least creates in the other party's mind the reasonable impression that it is doing so, can such a course of action be characterised as a promise? Alternatively, if liability arises in such a situation, does it derive from the reliance placed upon the impression conveyed to the other party? The proper characterisation of the renunciation of contractual rights is considered in this chapter.

1. Terminology

It is important, before attempting to answer these questions, to note that different English language terms are used to describe an undertaking (express or implied) by one party not to enforce its contractual rights against the other. These terms have often been used inconsistently and interchangeably, making analysis of this area of law very difficult. There are some general patterns of usage of terminology which can be discerned, though if European private law is at some stage to be harmonised this is one area where uniformity of terminology would be of great benefit.

Where the undertaking occurs by means of a valid contract, contractual variation, or unilateral act, it is common for one of the following terms to be used to describe the undertaking: renunciation, release, discharge, remission, acceptilation,[1] *pactum de non petendo*,[2] or the more generic 'alteration of contract' (a term which is evidently capable of describing more than just alterations which have the effect of releasing a contracting party from a duty). Where the undertaking arises not by virtue of a valid contract or unilateral undertaking, but nonetheless by virtue of conduct

---

[1] The term deriving from Roman law's *acceptilatio*, an oral form of the dissolution of an obligation.

[2] A term used to describe agreements not to enforce rights temporarily, rather than cases of the absolute discharge of the debtor.

of the party deemed to have given the impression that it was renouncing its rights, the circumstances are more often referred to as personal bar, promissory estoppel, waiver, or acquiescence.

Some of the terms encountered (such as renunciation and waiver) are more suggestive of a unilateral act by the party renouncing its rights, whereas other terms (such as release and discharge) are more suggestive of a consensual arrangement as the basis of the renunciation, but one should not assume that the use of a particular term necessarily imports what it might appear to suggest, as the terminology used is not always consistent with the nature of the underlying act. Sometimes a term (for instance, renunciation, release and discharge) may be more suggestive of an undertaking that is intended wholly to extinguish the creditor's rights, whereas others (such as personal bar, waiver and estoppel) of a mere undertaking not to enforce rights *pro tem*. Whether a bilateral or unilateral arrangement is meant, and whether it is to be permanent or merely temporary, is ultimately a question of interpreting what was intended by the parties, though this can be a tricky matter. Does, for instance, a landlord who gives a struggling commercial tenant a rent rebate for six months intend to renounce entirely the claim for the unpaid rent, or merely to postpone collection of it until a later date? Clearly, examination of the words used, as well as all the surrounding circumstances of the case (where this is permitted), will be crucial in answering such a question.

Sometimes the party in whose favour a renunciation operates will not be given any right to raise a claim against the renouncing party, but only a defence which it can raise if enforcement of the rights is sought. This effect often, depending on the jurisdiction in question, follows from the characterisation of the renunciation as arising from the conduct of the relevant party (as is the case with 'personal bar' or 'estoppel', discussed below).

In theory any type of contractual right might be renounced by the creditor, whether it be to payment, to enforce some other performance, to damages for late, defective, or non performance, to terminate for breach, to refer a matter to arbitration, or as to some other matter. There may, however, be statutory restrictions on the right to waive in specific circumstances, for instance restrictions designed to protect a consumer from waiving his rights.

2.   Bilateral or unilateral renunciations

In Roman law, the release of a contractual debtor was a bilateral act, achieved (apart from by performance) either under a *pactum de non petendo* (which operated not to extinguish the rights in question, but merely as an undertaking by the creditor not to enforce them) or by means of an *acceptilatio* (an oral question and answer, much like the *stipulatio*, which extinguished the debt).[3]

In modern legal systems which recognise unilateral promises whether generally or exceptionally, it may be possible to see an express renunciation of rights in either a promissory or a contractual way. But even in systems where a unilateral promise is not conceived of as a species of obligation, the concept of a unilateral juridical act may be utilised to explain a renunciation of rights which takes effect unilaterally, without the cooperation of the debtor. Those systems which permit a unilateral release by a creditor of a debtor's obligation include Scotland, Spain, Italy and the Nordic countries, a position also adopted in the PECL and the DCFR.[4] By contrast, France,[5] Germany,[6] the Netherlands[7] and Switzerland,[8] among others, permit release of a debtor only by agreement of the parties, this also being the position adopted in the UNIDROIT Principles of International Commercial Contracts (the PICC).[9] Whilst growing toleration of a unilateral approach has been observed,[10] this trend seems to amount to no more than the practice of presuming an acceptance to an offer of release rather than as a strictly genuine unilateral form of release.

Those jurisdictions which require the agreement of creditor and debtor, and thus reject a unilateral characterisation of release, often cite the concern that a benefit should not be thrust on an unwilling beneficiary, though a right of rejection of an unwanted benefit is as amenable to avoiding such an outcome as is a requirement of acceptance of a renunciation.[11] However, because, in the case of gratuitous releases, many jurisdictions deem an acceptance to have been given where an offer of release is not

---

[3] Zimmermann, *Law of Obligations*, pp. 754–8.
[4] For Scotland, see discussion below at p. 434; for Italy, *Codice civile* Art. 1236; PECL Art. 2:107; DCFR Art. II.-1:103(2).
[5] For the French position, see Terré *et al.*, *Droit civil*, no. 1459.   [6] §397 BGB.
[7] BW Art. 6:160(1).   [8] Code of Obligations Art. 115.   [9] Art. 5.1.9.
[10] See Kleinschmidt, 'Erlass einer Forderung'.
[11] Such a right of rejection exists in Scotland and Italy (for Italy, see *Codice civile* Art. 1236). There may be rare cases where release of a debtor from an obligation may make the debtor worse off overall, so that he will wish to refuse the 'benefit' of such a release, though it is hard to imagine what the facts of such cases might be. More conceivably, a debtor may have a moral reason for not wishing to be released from his debts, namely that he considers it consistent with honesty and good faith that he discharge in full duties he has undertaken.

rejected, the strictly bilateral model tends to be unilateral in its practical application.[12]

3.   Characterising undertakings not to enforce contractual rights

Given the possibility of both unilateral and bilateral characterisations of renunciations of rights, this means that, in cases where there is an express undertaking not to enforce contractual rights, there are a number of distinct possible ways of analysing what is happening:[13]

(1) *the contractual conception*: the contracting parties may be seen as having, by means of a contractual amendment or a further contract, altered the original contract to provide for a renunciation of a right, such a course of action requiring the distinct assent of both parties. Where the party in whose favour the renunciation is conceived agrees immediately, then a contractual variation clearly occurs at once; on the other hand, if the acceptance of this party is not immediately forthcoming, or is not (if permitted) presumed, the question arises of whether some sort of option (to accept the waiver) exists, or whether the offer to renounce may be revoked at the whim of the offeror;

(2) *the unilateral promissory conception*: the party renouncing its rights may have made a unilateral promise not to enforce those rights in the future;

(3) *the unilateral juridical act conception*: the party renouncing its rights may be seen as having undertaken, if not any obligation in the form of a unilateral contract or promise, a unilateral juridical act which has the effect of terminating the right in its favour;

(4) *the personal bar/estoppel conception*: even if none of the first three characterisations can be maintained, the party giving the undertaking may be 'personally barred' or 'estopped' from raising any future claim (or have 'acquiesced' in the other party's failure of duty), meaning that it is precluded from adopting a course of action which would contradict the impression it gave that it would not enforce the rights in question. This usually has the effect that the other party is entitled

---

[12] The position of a presumed acceptance prevails statutorily in the Netherlands and Switzerland, and by virtue of decision of the courts in Austria, France, and Germany.

[13] In fact, there is a further analytical possibility to those listed here, that being that a renunciation of rights can be conceived of as forming part of such a substantial revision of the contract that such revision is considered to be a novation, but this possibility is not considered further in the main text.

to raise a defence against any such claim, though not itself to raise an action founded on the estopped rights. Such an analysis may be compelled in relation to express undertakings if, as in the Common law jurisdictions, there is a requirement of mutual consideration before an enforceable contract of waiver can exist and such consideration is lacking; in jurisdictions allowing gratuitous contracts or unilateral promises, however, it is largely superfluous to use this analysis to deal with express undertakings to waive contractual rights; or

(5) *the donation conception*: one might conceivably characterise a renunciation of contractual rights as a species of donation, on the basis that what the renouncing party is doing is gifting to the other a release from the latter's contractual duties. In Roman law, a renunciation of rights was conceived of as a kind of donation, a tradition carried over into some modern legal systems. Under such an approach, the rules on the form of a donation are determinative of the required form for a renunciation.

In cases where there is no express undertaking not to enforce contractual rights, but merely words or conduct which create a reasonable impression in the other party's mind that the rights will not be enforced, which impression is relied upon to that other party's detriment, then while an express contractual or unilateral promissory explanation is not amenable to describing what has happened, the analysis of personal bar or estoppel can still be used to explain the defence given to the second party.

4.   Express contractual or promissory renunciation of rights

(a)   The Common law

From the sixteenth century onwards, the view was taken by the English courts that a mere agreement to vary a contract was not enforceable, including a variation by which a creditor undertook to renounce some or all of its rights.[14] This view was a simple conclusion from the application

---

[14] For instance, Comyns, *Digest of the Laws of England*, cites (p. 127) the case of *Lynn* v. *Bruce* 2 H. Bl. 317 (1794), in which a declaration had been made by A that he had, at B's request, agreed to accept from B a composition of so much in the pound upon a certain sum of money owing by B in full satisfaction and discharge of B's debt. It was held that B's promise to pay this composition was not a good consideration to support an assumpsit against B, 'a mere accord not being a ground of action'.

of the rule requiring mutual consideration.[15] It means that, for instance, a bare promise made by a creditor to accept part payment in full settlement of a debt is not contractually enforceable, and the creditor is able to go back on such a promise, it being no argument that he may have received the 'practical benefit' of securing some payment rather than none from a financially distressed debtor.[16] However, even a change in time or place of performance can constitute valid consideration,[17] and, as eighteenth- and nineteenth-century courts were increasingly willing to hold, even a slight benefit in the creditor's favour can count as valid consideration. More recently, it has been held that a variation which may benefit or prejudice either party is enforceable,[18] though arguments about whether factually this may or may not be so create undesirable uncertainty about the enforcement of a variation. The decision in *Williams* v. *Roffey Bros.*[19] that a promise to pay *more* for services already due is an enforceable variation makes continued insistence on the non-binding nature of a promise to pay a reduced sum in settlement of a debt seem inconsistent. In either case a seriously intended renegotiation of an existing duty is at stake, and the alleged valid consideration in *Williams* v. *Roffey* of the acquiral by the promisor of the benefit of the completion of work by a promisee who may have been unable to complete the works without the extra payment[20] represents such a fictional manifestation of consideration as seriously to call in to doubt the continued insistence for such consideration when contractual duties are renegotiated.[21] As Ibbetson has remarked of the basis of liability in the case, the 'real test of liability was that provided by the Will Theory: so long as the parties had freely agreed, without duress, that the higher sum would be paid, the court would hold them to their agreement.'[22] A lot has changed in the thirty years since Fried argued that consideration was still a dominant doctrine within contract law. The decision in *Williams* v. *Roffey* surely suggests that it would not be too great a leap for the English courts to continue that development by recognising

---

[15] On the historical background, see Ibbetson, *A Historical Introduction*, p. 240, and cases there cited.

[16] *Foakes* v. *Beer* (1884) 9 App Cas 605 (HL); *Selectmove, Re* [1995] 1 WLR 474.

[17] *Pinnel's Case* (1602) 5 Co Rep 117a.

[18] *Alan & Co. Ltd* v. *El Nasr Export & Import Co.* [1972] 2 QB 189.

[19] [1991] 1 QB 1.   [20] *Ibid.*, judgment of Glidewell LJ at 15–16.

[21] Waddams has remarked of the present, post-*Roffey* position, that it is now 'very difficult to state what principles govern modification of contracts' (Waddams, 'Principle in Contract Law', p. 61). Such uncertainty would seem to be an inevitable effect of the chipping away at the doctrine of consideration without taking the bold step of abolishing it.

[22] Ibbetson, *A Historical Introduction*, p. 240.

that all promises seriously intended should, as a matter of principle, be enforceable at law, and to carve out any exceptions from that principle which were thought desirable.

In the absence of any mutual consideration, a valid renunciation could previously be made under seal, or now, since the abolition of the requirement of the seal, in a deed. If, however, neither consideration nor deed routes are available, recourse will have to be had, if available on the facts, to common law forbearance or one of the various forms of estoppel (discussed below), which is the closest English law comes in practice to enforcing, albeit tangentially, a unilateral promise to renounce contractual rights.

(b)   Mixed legal systems

In Scotland, with its separate obligations of contract and promise, both a contractual and promissory analysis of renunciation of rights is possible, and the renunciation may be either an undertaking not to enforce the right in question *pro tem* or an outright termination of the right. Thus, parties may either agree by contractual variation or by a new contract to vary previously constituted rights,[23] or one party may unilaterally promise for the future not to enforce its rights against another (either for a specified period of time or for the entire remaining period of the contract). Alternatively, a contract may contain a clause entitling a party to waive one of the contractual rights in its favour, such a right, though being constituted by contractual agreement, effectively allowing a unilateral renunciation to occur.[24]

In addition, it is conceivable that, without either party entering into a contract or making a promise, one party may simply, by a unilateral

---

[23] Such renunciations have a long pedigree. For instance, some late medieval examples of renunciations of rights are narrated in the Protocol Book of Sir Alexander Gaw, including the following: 'Memorandum narrating that Robert Scot acknowledged that he had granted his permission to Egidia Lesslie and Stephen Arnot, her son, to labour and till two parts of Estir Pitgrugny, and denied that he had given to them right and title of his possession within the bounds of the lands, but promised that he would not cite or pursue them for the permitted labouring of the lands before any judges, because the lands were in dispute between him and a certain Peter Balvard (1st January 1550)'.

[24] A conceptually tricky case is the right of waiver of a suspensive condition in a contract. If such a right is given to both parties, case law indicates that a unilateral renunciation of the right by either may only be made if the right is designed purely for that party's benefit and is severable from the rest of the contract: see *Manheath Ltd* v. *Banks & Co. Ltd* 1996 SC 42.

declaratory act, immediately renounce its rights in favour of another, such declaration sometimes being referred to as a type of 'express waiver'.[25] Such unilateral acts of renunciation are not just possible in respect of contractual rights, but in relation to other rights too.[26]

As Scots law lacks a doctrine of mutual consideration, there was no need for Scotland to develop a doctrine of promissory estoppel to deal with cases of gratuitous renunciation of rights: such cases can be dealt with either as gratuitous contracts of renunciation, gratuitous promises to renounce, or simple unilateral declarations of renunciation, depending on the precise circumstances. There is also, however, a doctrine of personal bar which operates in Scots law, not just in contract but in other fields of law too (for instance, property law), and it is applicable to some of the circumstances that would fall under promissory estoppel or waiver in English law (a fact discussed further below).

Turning to Louisiana law, one encounters no general definition of a renunciation (or 'remission' as it is often styled) of contractual rights.[27] The Civil Code seems to assume an understanding of the concept when it provides in Article 1888 that a 'remission of debt by an obligee extinguishes the obligation', adding that the remission 'may be express or tacit'. Such a remission is most likely to be given gratuitously, though conceivably some consideration may have been provided by the debtor.[28] The terms of Article 1888 tell us nothing of whether the remission is conceived of as a unilateral or bilateral act, or whether it is to be viewed as a contract, a unilateral promise, or in some other way. Article 1890 however tells us that the remission of debt is effective 'when the obligor receives the communication from the obligee'. This not only makes it clear that communication of the remission is essential, but it might be thought to suggest,

---

[25] Where the waiver is not expressly made, but is arguably to be implied from conduct, then the circumstances are properly described as implied waiver, a species of personal bar discussed later: see further discussion in main text, below at p. 447.

[26] For instance, the right of ownership in property law may be unilaterally renounced, the effect being that the property concerned is held to be abandoned and ownership passes to the Crown; the benefited proprietor under a real burden may unilaterally renounce it; succession rights may unilaterally be renounced.

[27] 'The Louisiana Civil Code, which regulates nominate contracts and juridical acts in detail, does not provide definition or regulation for a contract or act of waiver' (the view of the US Court of Appeals, Fifth Circuit, in its judgment in *Shaw Constructors* v. *ICF Kaiser Engineers* 395 F 3d 533).

[28] A gratuitous release does not, however, constitute a valid contract of compromise in Louisiana law and therefore cannot be founded upon to bar litigation between the parties: *Bielkiewicz* v. *Rudisill* 201 So 2d 136 (La 1967).

given that the remission is said to take effect as soon as such communication is effected, that remission is by its nature a unilateral act (though not a unilateral promise).

Such a unilateral conception of remission would be flawed, however. Article 1890 states that '[a]cceptance of a remission is always presumed unless the obligor rejects the remission within a reasonable time'. This reference to 'acceptance' is indicative of a contractual conception of remission, albeit with the acceptance being presumed. Though this contractual basis of remission is less clearly spelt out than it was in an earlier legislative form of the provision on remission (which distinguished 'conventional' and 'tacit' remissions, rather than the present distinction between 'express' and 'tacit' remissions),[29] the accepted view remains that remission is 'not a unilateral act' but rather 'requires the concurrence of the wills of creditor and debtor'.[30]

For the sake of completeness, it should be noted that in the Louisiana Code there is provision for a so-called 'contract of giving in payment' (also known as a 'dation'), such a contract being one under which a debtor gives a thing to his creditor in fulfilment of a debt due by the debtor. The effect of such a contract is to remit wholly the debtor's debt (unless the parties agree that only a partial remission is to be given).[31]

Lastly, there is the South African position. In South Africa, a renunciation of contractual rights (or 'waiver' as it is often called) must itself be undertaken contractually. Hence an offer to renounce rights must be accepted by the party in whose favour the offer is conceived, such acceptance constituting a contractual agreement. The justification for this view has been located in a conception of a renunciation of rights as a type of donation, donation requiring acceptance before it can be effective. This position was adopted by Munnik AJ in *Union Free State Mining and Finance Corporation Ltd* v. *Union Free State Gold and Diamond Corporation Ltd:*[32]

> I do not think that a creditor can by the mere exercise of his will terminate the obligation without the concurrence of the debtor because, as both Wessels and Pothier point out, a release, waiver or abandonment is tantamount to making a donation to the debtor of the obligation from which he is to be released and until that donation has been accepted it has not been perfected.

---

[29] See the now repealed Art. 2199 of the Civil Code.
[30] Litvinoff and Scalise, *Law of Obligations*, p. 205.
[31] *Dunaway* v. *Spain* 493 So 2d 577 (La 1986).   [32] 1960 (4) SA 547, 549 (W).

Munnik AJ added the practical point that 'for a variety of reasons it may not suit him [the debtor] to be released'. Given the conception of renunciation as the making of a new contract, Munnik AJ felt himself justified in concluding that to allow a unilateral renunciation would be 'tantamount to creating a contract at the will of one party which is a foreign concept to our jurisprudence'. At first glance, there is quite a startling contrast between this South African view and the Scots law view that conferring a benefit unilaterally on another by means of a promise is perfectly permissible. However, given that South African jurisprudence, like that of Louisiana, accepts that an offer to waive contractual rights may be tacitly accepted, the position of the two systems on this point may in practice not be as different as the theory suggests.

There must be a clear intention to renounce the rights in question. This may be evinced from express words to that effect, or may be implied from a conduct demonstrating such an intent. Thus, a landlord who accepts payment of rent from a tenant who has committed a breach of lease that would entitle the landlord to terminate the lease, may be held to have waived the right to terminate,[33] though the facts of the case are crucial (for instance, acceptance of rent after a clear indication of an intention to terminate will negate any implication of the waiver of the right to terminate).[34] In Scots law, such cases of implied waiver by landlords are not seen as tacit contractual undertakings, but operate as a type of personal bar, and in English law such facts might give rise to an equitable estoppel, as discussed further below.

(c)   German law[35]

While it seems that practice in eighteenth-century Germany was to regard a unilateral release from contractual duties as perfectly valid,[36] the common view is that this was not the approach taken by the framers of the BGB. There are a number of provisions in the BGB relating to the renunciation (*Verzicht*) of rights, though some are not of direct relevance to the present work (for instance, waiver of inheritance rights). One example

---

[33]   *Watts* v. *Goodman* 1929 WLD 199, 212–4; *Penny's Properties Ltd* v. *SA Cabinet Works Ltd* 1947 (2) SA 302 (C); *Ralph* v. *Hayes* 1948 (1) SA 46 (N); *Soffiantini* v. *Berman* 1958 (30 SA 426 (E).

[34]   *Franks* v. *Thelma Court Flats (Pty) Ltd* 1943 CPD 530; *Central Investment Co. (Pty) Ltd* v. *Shaikjee* 1945 TPD 428.

[35]   See further on the German Law, Kleinschmidt, 'Erlass', and 'Erlass einer Forderung'.

[36]   See Kleinschmidt, 'Verzicht'.

of renunciation is found in a provision in the title on donation[37] which stipulates that the right to revoke a donation on account of the ingratitude of the donee can only be waived once the party entitled so to revoke becomes aware of the donee's ingratitude. The provision does not, however, tells us what the nature of such waiver is. Again, the provision on the revocation of public offers of reward[38] states that the right of the offeror to revoke the offer until performance occurs may be waived, without stating the nature of such a waiver. In this case, however, given that an offer of reward is conceived of as one of the few examples in the BGB of a genuine unilateral promise, it would seem to follow that the waiver of the right to revoke should also be conceived of as a type of unilateral juridical act, or legal transaction (*Rechtsgeschäft*) as the BGB puts it.

The most important provision on renunciation of rights in the BGB is however §397, the heading to which is somewhat obliquely translated in the official Federal Ministry of Justice English version of the BGB as 'Forgiveness', by which is meant the release of contractual debts. The provision provides that an obligation is terminated if, by contractual agreement of the parties, the creditor either releases the debtor or acknowledges that the debt does not exist. The two methods specified thus cover both the express release of a debtor and the release which is to be implied from the creditor's statement that he no longer considers the debtor to be under the obligation. Both methods have the effect of terminating the obligation in question, not simply of suspending the duty of performance temporarily, though there is no reason why contracting parties might not alternatively provide for such a temporary suspension by contactual agreement.

The wording of §397 appears, on the face of it, to be quite unequivocal as to the need for a contractual agreement, unlike the exceptional unilateral method permitted in the case of the waiver of the right to revoke an offer of reward. As a contract is prescribed, then the ordinary rules on contractual formation will apply, including the default rule of the irrevocable offer,[39] something which provides the debtor with some opportunity to consider the renunciation offered before deciding whether or not to accept it.

It has, however, recently been argued by Kleinschmidt that the apparent wording of the provision may not be as prescriptive as first appears to be the case, and that in practice the courts assume acceptance or simply

---

[37] §533 BGB.   [38] §658 BGB.   [39] Discussed in Ch. 4, p. 217.

overlook consideration of the matter.[40] Kleinschmidt argues that §397 is permissive rather than prescriptive: it allows for contractual renunciation, but does not forbid a unilateral renunciation. He further argues that, though §311(1) seems as a general principle to require a contractual route for the creation and variation of obligations, if the purpose of that provision is considered (it being designed to encapsulate freedom of contract), then it is consistent with that purpose to recognise unilateral renunciations, if that is the form which the renouncing party wishes to give the renunciation. In support of this argument, Kleinschmidt points out that under §423, an agreement between a creditor and one of a number of joint debtors can have the effect of extinguishing the whole debt, the renunciation of the debt taking effect against the other debtors unilaterally, even without their consent. If then renunciation of contractual debts can effectively occur unilaterally so far as co-debtors are concerned, it cannot be the case that there is any theoretical objection to such renunciations in favour of a sole debtor.

Though Kleinschmidt's position that unilateral renunciations are presently permissible under the existing provisions of the BGB has not persuaded all commentators,[41] most have recognised that the case he has put for recognising such renunciations is a convincing one. If German courts are in effect permitting such unilateral renunciations, it would surely be more honest for the legal system to recognise them for what they are and to cease to force essentially unilateral acts into a bilateral contractual model.

5. Forbearance, promissory estoppel and personal bar

Having considered renunciations of rights which are recognised as valid contractual or promissory alterations, it is necessary also to say something about those renunciations which are given effect as a result of a party's behaviour preventing it from acting at odds with consent which it is deemed to have given to an undertaking. The idea of using promise to explain this result has been influential in a number of legal systems, but it has not been the only explanation for the basis of liability. Alternatively, it can be argued either that it is the principle of good faith

---

[40] See Kleinschmidt, *Der Verzicht im Schuldrecht*. Kleinschmidt's argument has generated support from the following (among others): Zimmermann, 'Europa und das römische Recht', 243, 270; Schulze, in *Anwaltkommentar zum BGB*, §§145–147, n. 15; Stoll, 'Review of *Der Verzicht im Schuldrecht*'; Kramer, *Münchener Kommentar*, 'Einleitung' n. 55.

[41] Some feel that his argument stretches the plain meaning of the text of the BGB.

which requires parties not to act in a way which is at odds with their prior behaviour, or that this is mandated by the reliance placed upon such behaviour by others.

(a)   The Common law

The position of the Common law with respect to non-agreement based renunciations (including variations) of rights is complicated by the availability of different claims in common law and equity each of which have the character of a promise.

(i)   Forbearance at common law

At common law, the doctrine of forbearance can operate to prevent a party enforcing its rights (either absolutely or *pro tem*) in respect of performance due under the contract.[42] A forbearance denotes an indication of willingness on the part of a party not to enforce its rights strictly in terms of the contract, but, in response to some request that it do so, to accept some altered performance (for instance, late delivery of goods or payment of a lesser sum due under the contract) or indeed no performance. The act of forbearance must be unequivocal, and must be acted upon by the party in whose favour it is conceived.[43] If such an indication of willingness is unsupported by consideration, though it cannot constitute a contractual variation, it will operate at common law to prevent a claim by the party which has indicated a willingness to forbear for damages for non-conforming performance, and to preclude that party from refusing such altered performance (if any) in accordance with the terms of its promised forbearance.[44]

Where the forbearing party has made some express declaration of its willingness, such declaration can be conceived of as a promise, though it may not strictly be couched in promissory terms. Thus, to state 'I am willing to accept delivery one week late' can be read as meaning 'I promise

---

[42] See further Peel, *Treitel on Contract*, paras. 3–069–075; Beale, *Chitty on Contracts*, paras. 3–057–060, 22–040–047. The prevention may operate *pro tem* if, for instance, a specified period of acceptable late performance has been specified. A creditor may withdraw a temporary forbearance by the giving of reasonable notice to the debtor: *Banning* v. *Wright* [1972] 1 WLR 972, 981; *Ficom SA* v. *Sociedad Cadex Ltda* [1980] 2 Lloyd's Rep 118, 131; *Bremer Handelsgesellschaft mbH* v. *Raiffeisen Hauptgenossenschaft EG* [1982] 1 Lloyds Rep 599. Alternatively, forbearance may operate absolutely if, for instance, goods of a different standard have been accepted by the buyer as conforming goods.

[43] See Beale, *Chitty on Contracts*, para. 22–044, and numerous cases cited there.

[44] See Beale, *Chitty on Contracts*, 22–042; Peel, *Treitel on Contract*, 3–072.

that I shall not exercise any remedies for late delivery for a period of a week.' The same is equally true of conduct indicating forbearance: if such conduct is made in response to a request to forbear, then there is no theoretical difficulty in seeing the conduct as indicative of a promise to forbear if it is unequivocally referable to such an intention.[45]

The benefit from a creditor's view of pleading forbearance is that consideration does not need to have been given for the forbearance, unlike the case of a full contractual renunciation.[46] Whether a statement is intended to operate as a contractual renunciation (and thus to require consideration to be valid) or as forbearance is said to depend on the party's intentions,[47] though sometimes courts have, *ex post facto*, interpreted statements not supported by consideration as forbearance in order to give them some limited effect.[48]

Given the promissory nature which may be accorded to acts of forbearance, they are comparable to equitable estoppel, which is also a promissory based doctrine. Indeed, there seems to be little to distinguish common law forbearance from equitable estoppel: while it is a requirement of equitable estoppel (but not forbearance) that it be inequitable for the promisor to go back on its promise, given that this requirement of equitable estoppel is deemed to be satisfied if the promisee has relied on the promise, and that it is also a requirement of forbearance that the party granted the forbearance must have relied or at least acted on it, the two requirements seem essentially to state the same thing. That being so, all that would seem to distinguish forbearance from equitable estoppel is that the *intention* of the party forbearing is crucial to the former, whereas it is the *conduct* of the promisor which is essential to the latter. This distinction, between intent (assessed objectively) and conduct (also assessed objectively) seems a slender basis upon which to set up two distinct doctrines. This may be one example of where the common law/equity division has created an unnecessary duplication of solutions.

(ii) Forbearance in equity: promissory estoppel in English law

As discussed in Chapter 4 in relation to contract formation, in addition to common law rules, equity also developed remedies to prevent a party

[45] *Bremer Handelssgesellchaft mbH* v. *Vanden Avenne-Izegem PVBA* [1978] 2 Lloyd's Rep 109.
[46] See Beale, *Chitty on Contracts*, para. 3–084.
[47] *Stead* v. *Dawber* (1839) 10 A & E 57, 64.
[48] Beale, *Chitty on Contracts*, para. 3–084.

reneging on a prior position adopted by it, such equitable remedies taking the form of various types of equitable estoppel. It is the particular form of promissory estoppel which is of prime interest for present purposes. As noted in the earlier discussion, promissory estoppel is often utilised to deal with cases where, were it not for the absence of mutual consideration, there would otherwise be a valid contract. Promissory estoppel is thus evidently able to prevent a party which has stated that it will vary a contract in a particular way from acting in a way contrary to such a promise, as the following discussion will demonstrate.

It was in respect of a claim to prevent enforcement of informally waived contractual rights that the doctrine of promissory estoppel was first developed in English law. In *Hughes* v. *Metropolitan Railway Co.*,[49] a landlord had required its tenant to complete certain repairs to the leased property within six months. However, negotiations had thereafter commenced for the possible reversion of the tenant's interest to the landlord, though these had eventually broken down. At the conclusion of the six-month period, the landlord sought repossession of the property on the basis that the repairs had not been effected. The House of Lords held that the landlord was precluded from counting the period during which the negotiations had taken place from the six-month notice period, it having in effect (though not expressly) promised to the tenant to suspend the operation of the repairing notice in order to enter upon negotiations for the reversion of the lease. The subsequent claim of the landlord to enforce its rights strictly in accordance with the terms of the lease was precluded on the basis that to go against its promise would be inequitable.[50]

Subsequently, in *Central London Property Trust Ltd* v. *High Trees House*,[51] the doctrine was applied in a case of contractual renegotiation. A landlord had assured his tenant that, for the future, he would seek only a reduced amount of rent. No consideration was given for such statement of variation of the rent. In due course, a receiver acting for the landlord sought to claim the full rent as well as back payments for the shortfall since the agreement of the reduction. Denning J held that, given recent developments in the law, the time had come to assert that a promise of the type made by the landlord ought to be enforceable. Whilst he sought to argue that such enforcement was not simply a form of estoppel, later judicial interpretation of the decision has been to the effect that it amounts to

[49] (1877) 2 App Cas 439.　　[50] See comments of Lord Cairns at 448.
[51] [1947] 1 KB 130.

promissory estoppel and is not strictly a direct and full enforcement of the promise in the same way that a valid contractual promise would be.

In order for promised variations of contract such as those in *Hughes* and *High Trees* to operate as instances of promissory estoppel, English law has determined that certain requirements must be met: (i) the parties must be in a pre-existing legal relationship; (ii) a promise, or an equivalent assurance, must have been made by A; (iii) the promise must be clear and unequivocal, though it need not be express (as it was not in *Hughes* v. *Metropolitan Railway*). Acceptance by A of B's defective performance will not constitute such an unequivocal, deemed promise by A to treat such performance as fulfilling B's contractual duty so long as A reserves its strict contractual rights;[52] and (iv) B must have relied on the promise to some extent, so that it would be inequitable to allow A to go back on its promise.

(iii)   Promissory estoppel in American Common law

The development of promissory estoppel in modern American contract law has been no less dramatic than in English law. As noted in Chapter 4, the American courts proved themselves willing to assume reliance or overlook the need for it, effectively moving the law towards a position where promises which might be assumed to give rise to reliance were enforced. This development suggests the true nature of liability under promissory estoppel to be promise and not reliance. American courts have, for instance, either ignored or assumed the reliance requirement in cases of marriage settlements (where there has been no enquiry whether the promisee only married in reliance on the promise) and in the enforcement of promises to charitable organisations (where again there has been no enquiry of whether the charity relied on the promise). In fact, in these two specific areas, the Restatement (Second) of Contracts has legislated to the effect that the promise will be binding without proof of reliance (whether by action or forbearance).[53] From an outside perspective, it seems somewhat curious to select these two quite unrelated types of promise as alone being worthy of this presumption: why should other promisees not be equally worthy of the benefit of the provision?

---

[52] Failure to do so may constitute such deemed unequivocal promise to accept defective performance: see, for instance, *Bremer Handelsgesellchaft mbH* v. *Vanden Avenne-Izegem PVBA* [1978] 2 Lloyd's Rep 109.

[53] Restatement (Second) of Contracts, §90(2).

Promissory estoppel has also been held to apply in American jurisdictions to cases where a promise has been made to do some service gratuitously for the promisee, some cases involving promises made to the other contracting party after the contract was formed (and hence amounting to variations of existing duties), others promises to a third party.[54] As in English law, some commentators have argued that such cases demonstrate that promissory estoppel is in fact a species of reliance-based liability. However, it is striking that the promisee is often not required to show, or even allege in some cases, any detrimental reliance on the promise. It seems therefore more satisfactory to see them as indicative of a desire of American Common law to move towards a wider recognition of promissory liability in general, even in the absence of mutual consideration.[55]

It is significant that the provision in the Restatement (Second) of Contracts on 'Promises reasonably inducing action or forbearance' (§90) does not see promissory estoppel as a mere defence to a claim (as in English law) but rather provides that where a promise which the promisor should reasonably expect to induce action or forbearance on the part of the promisee or a third party, has just such an effect, it is binding if injustice can be avoided only by enforcement of the promise. Such a promise is thus fully binding on the promisor and gives the promisee title to sue as well as all the usual contractual remedies. This is clearly an even larger inroad to the rule of consideration than is the case with promissory estoppel in English law.

---

[54] Cases where promissory estoppel has been applied have included the following facts: a seller of property agreed to file papers to insure it (*Dalrymple* v. *Ed Shults Chevrolet, Inc.* 380 N.Y.S.2d 189, 190 (App Div 1976)); a railway company promised to help a customer by filing papers with the Government (*Carr* v. *Maine Central R.R. Co.* 102 A. 532 (N.H. 1917)); the holder of a security over property promised to insure it at the promisee's expense (*East Providence Credit Union* v. *Geremia* 239 A.2d 725 (R.I. 1968)); the senior creditor in a financing arrangement offered to give notice of default to the junior creditor (*Miles Homes Div. of Insilco Corp.* v. *First State Bank* 782 W.W.2d 798 (Mo. Ct. App. 1990)); a main contractor agreed to write cheques payable to the subcontractor's supplier, rather than to the supplier itself (*United Electric Corp.* v. *All Serv. Elec., Inc.* 256 N.W.2d 92, 95–96 (Min. 1977)). Further cases are mentioned by Gordley, 'Louisiana and the Common Law'.

[55] Gordley has argued of such cases that the 'doctrine of promissory estoppel does not explain these cases. The best explanation is that when the promisor enters into the sort of transaction which is known to civil law as mandate, his promise is enforceable without regard either to consideration or reliance' (Gordley, *ibid.*, p. 203).

(iv) Conclusion on promissory estoppel in the Common law

The existence of an equitable doctrine of promissory estoppel, though helpful in providing a way of enforcing renunciations of contractual rights, also causes problems of seemingly inconsistent results in law. If one compares the results in two cases mentioned earlier, *Foakes* v. *Beer* and *Central London Property Trust* v. *High Trees House*, it is very hard to see why opposite outcomes should have been reached merely because one claim was at law and one in equity. In *Foakes*, the common law position was applied that a creditor is not bound by a bare promise to accept less than the full debt owed by the debtor. This meant that Mrs Beer, who had assured her debtor that she would consider the debt satisfied if the principal amount was paid off over time in instalments, was not precluded from subsequently claiming interest in addition to this sum. By contrast, in *High Trees*, the landlord who had assured his tenant that the ground rent would be varied below that stated in the contract of lease, was precluded from going against this promise on account of the equitable defence pled by the debtor. Common law and equity seem to pull in different directions, in a way which is hard to justify. A better result would surely be reached if it were accepted that promises either to renounce or forego rights ought generally to be enforceable at law, however the claim is framed, and whether or not consideration has been given for the promise.

(b) Mixed legal systems

(i) South Africa

Because South Africa does not recognise a doctrine of promissory estoppel, clearly such a doctrine cannot support an argument that rights have been renounced as a result of the behaviour of a party incompatible with such rights. South African law, like English law, does, however, have a doctrine of estoppel by misrepresentation, though such a doctrine is evidently of limited use in explaining circumstances which could be characterised as a renunciation of rights by conduct, given that estoppel by misrepresentation relates to statements of present fact rather than of future conduct.

Renunciations of rights in South Africa are thus accommodated with ease only within an express, contractual setting (no consideration being required for the renunciation), though it should be noted that such contractual waiver (discussed earlier) may be undertaken impliedly, so long as there is clear evidence for such implied waiver.[56] There is thus some scope for accommodating conduct-based renunciations of rights in South African law, albeit that the conduct must indicate contractual intent.

(ii)   Louisiana

There ought to be, and indeed there is, much less need for a doctrine of promissory estoppel in Louisiana than in US Common law jurisdictions.[57] Louisiana, like the other mixed systems studied, has no mutual consideration doctrine, and it recognises the validity of irrevocable offers,[58] both of which solve some problems which promissory estoppel deals with in Common law systems. In the 1950s the Louisiana Supreme Court denied that there was any such doctrine as promissory estoppel in Louisiana law.[59] However, in the 1984 Codal revision a provision on detrimental reliance on a promise (in effect, promissory estoppel) was introduced. Article 1967 of the Civil Code provides that a party 'may be obligated by a promise when he knew or should have known that the promise would induce the other party to rely on it to his detriment and the other party was reasonable in so relying', though adding that reliance on a gratuitous promise lacking required formalities is not reasonable.[60]

While the need for a general doctrine of promissory estoppel in Louisiana law is questionable,[61] Article 1967 is clearly capable of explaining liability in circumstances in which no valid contractual renunciation has occurred but rights have been waived by one contracting party and such waiver has been relied upon by the other party.

---

[56] 'It is repeatedly emphasised by our courts that evidence of an alleged waiver of rights is required, particularly where an implied waiver has been made. It should be clear that the person acted with due notice of his rights and that his actions are inconsistent with the continued existence of such rights or with intent to enforce them' (per Corbett AJA, in *Borstlap* v. *Spangenberg* 1974 (3) SA 695, 704 (A), my translation from the Afrikaans).

[57] See further Snyder, 'Hunting Promissory Estoppel'.

[58] CC Art. 1928.   [59] *Ducote* v. *Oden* 59 So 2d 130, 132 (La 1952).

[60] Which contrasts with the statutory provisions on personal bar in Scots Law, which specifically permit reliance on a gratuitous promise lacking the proper formalities to found a claim of personal bar: see Requirements of Writing (Scotland) Act 1995, s. 1(3), (4).

[61] Though the provision has been used to explain, inter alia, certain commercial transactions, such as the so-called 'estoppel letters' which are used to elicit promises from businesses that they do not object to a planned merger: see Snyder, 'Hunting Promissory Estoppel', p. 310, who suggests that the Scottish unilateral promissory approach would be a preferable analysis of such transactions.

(iii)   Scotland

Scots law does not have a doctrine of promissory estoppel, the need for such being largely obviated by the lack of a doctrine of mutual consideration and the recognition of unilateral promises, but it does possess a doctrine of personal bar.[62] Personal bar is a doctrine of general legal application, applicable where A claims to have a right the exercise of which B claims is barred because, to B's knowledge, A behaved in a way which was inconsistent with the exercise of the right, A knew it had the right when it so behaved, and permitting the exercise of the right by A would both affect and be unfair to B.[63]

Personal bar operates in respect of many cases which in English law would fall under the heading of forbearance or implied waiver (that is waiver constituted not by an express statement but by conduct inconsistent with the right claimed). Thus, personal bar may be a relevant plea in cases where a creditor has on prior occasions accepted late payment of periodic sums due by a debtor, leading the debtor to believe that prompt payment will not be required on future occasions but where no contractual variation exists stating as such. A similar case is that of the landlord who fails timeously to activate a review of rent, in consequence barring itself from triggering the review when it realises its failure. In one such case, reference was made by the court to the English case law on waiver,[64] though as the authors of the leading work on personal bar have noted, while 'Scots and English law share the term and concept, certain important differences in the law of waiver should not be overlooked'.[65] One clear similarity is, however, that the doctrine of personal bar requires at least an underlying obligation upon which the claim can be based, and so is not applicable to complete an agreement where consensus is lacking. A further similarity is that personal bar is largely defensive, and cannot be used to create rights.[66]

---

[62] See further, on the complexities of the field as a whole, Reid and Blackie, *Personal Bar*. See also, for a comparison of Scots and Louisiana law, Snyder, 'Hunting Promissory Estoppel'.

[63] See Reid and Blackie, *Personal Bar*, para. 2–03, and Ch. 2 generally. Reid and Blackie list (at para. 2–03) a number of different ways in which unfairness may be demonstrated. A statutory form of personal bar applies to permit enforcement of informally constituted agreements relating to rights in land: see Requirements of Writing (Scotland) Act 1995, s. 1(3), (4).

[64] See *Banks* v. *Mecca Bookmakers (Scotland) Ltd* 1982 SC 7, 1982 SLT 150, where reference was made to *Banning* v. *Wright* (cited at n. 42 above).

[65] Reid and Blackie, *Personal Bar*, para. 3–40.   [66] *Ibid.*, paras. 5–21–25.

By way of contrast, however, given that the core of personal bar in Scots law lies in the idea of inconsistent conduct and unfairness, the idea of promise seems largely, perhaps wholly, irrelevant to the doctrine. Because of the comparative ease with which contractual promises and unilateral promises can be expressly enforced in Scotland, the field lying beyond these enforceable obligations within which personal bar operates does not, for the most part, include cases which have a promissory aspect but which simply fail to meet the requirements for a contract, as is the case with promissory estoppel in the Common law.

Liability in Scots law (based on the *Walker* v. *Milne* line of cases) for pre-contractual statements which give the impression that a contract has been concluded, when it has not, was discussed in Chapter 3.[67] Such liability is best not seen as a form of personal bar as such, given that what is claimed is wasted expenditure from failure to constitute a valid obligation rather than prevention of conduct inconsistent with a validly established obligation.

(c) German law

German law does not require mutual consideration for a contract to be binding. It also treats offers as binding unless they are stated to be otherwise. These features of contract law mean that many of the cases which in the Common law require the application of promissory estoppel, including variations to contracts, can be solved in an ordinary contractual manner in German law, as discussed earlier in this chapter.

In addition, German law also recognises that a party should not be entitled to go against its own prior conduct, a German manifestation of the Roman *venire contra factum proprium* doctrine known as *Verwirkung* or, in English, 'forfeiture', based upon the idea of good faith.[68] Some of the German cases of *Verwirkung* can be compared to promissory estoppel in the Common law, as in some the previous conduct was a promise made to another (as for instance in the case of a lawyer who was held not entitled to charge more than the amount he had suggested on a prior occasion[69]), but others have more of the

---

[67] See discussion in Ch. 4, pp. 197ff.
[68] For a full treatment, see Singer, *Das Verbot widersprüchlichen Verhaltens*; for a comparative analysis, see Vaquer, 'Verwirkung versus Laches'.
[69] BGHZ 34, 355.

appearance of Common law forbearance.[70] The same approach is taken in Austrian law.[71]

Lapse of time may lead to loss of a right even before the relevant period of prescription has expired, based upon *Verwirkung*.[72] This is controversial, as it seems to undermine the clear policy of the rules on prescription.

6. Model Law and renunciations of rights

The PECL do not specifically deal with renunciations of contractual rights, so there is no reason why such a release should not be seen as either contractual or promissory in nature, depending on the circumstances. The DCFR also does not specifically regulate renunciations, though Article III.-1:108 provides permissively that the variation or termination of a right, obligation or contract can occur 'by agreement' at any time. That statement need not be seen as prohibiting unilateral renunciations, however, and the general legal recognition in the DCFR of unilateral undertakings[73] seems quite capable of applying to a unilateral renunciation of contractual rights, either in the form of a unilateral promise to release or simply an immediate unilateral release.

Article 5.1.9(1) of the UNIDROIT Principles of International Commercial Contracts provides a contractual model for release by the creditor of its right against the debtor (such release requiring to be 'by agreement'). This naturally presupposes the usual methods for conclusion of such a contract, typically offer and acceptance. However, if the offer of release is a gratuitous one, then acceptance of it is deemed to have been made unless the obligor rejects the offer without delay once becoming aware of it.[74] No clear justification is available for the fictional consent approach of this provision, but it has been observed that a convincing rationale may be that, because a gratuitous release confers only benefits upon the creditor but no duties, there is no reason not to imply consent

---

[70] See further Markesinis *et al.*, *German Law of Contract*, p. 123.
[71] In Austria, the Court of the Federal Chamber of Commerce and Industry has allowed the defence of *Verwirkung*, based on the gap-filling principle of good faith, to assist a buyer who did not (as required under the contract) give timely notice of defects, because the seller at first did not insist upon such timely notice and had begun to renegotiate the contract (see Schlechtriem, 'Good Faith in German Law and in International Uniform Laws'). This approach, note, is based on good faith rather than promise.
[72] See discussion of the subject in Vaquer, 'Verwirkung versus Laches'.
[73] See Art. II.-1:103(2).   [74] Art. 5.1.9(2).

to such a beneficial arrangement.[75] It has been further remarked that the reasons for the UNIDROIT drafting committee's rejection of the possibility of unilateral release are 'not entirely clear',[76] especially in the light of such a unilateral route in some jurisdictions.

[75] Vorgenauer and Kleinheisterkamp, *Commentary on the UNIDROIT Principles*, p. 575.
[76] *Ibid.*, p. 573.

PART 3

The future

8

The future of promise in contract law

1. The restricted role of promise in the modern law

In Part 1 of this book, a study was made of the nature of promise and of the uses to which it has historically been put by Western moral and legal systems. It was explained how promise originally had a central normative role in the law, deriving partly from a stress upon the virtuous practice of keeping promises inherited from Greek thought, partly from promissory form and language inherited from Roman law, and partly from later canonical (and biblical) stress upon the duty of faithfulness to one's word. This latter canonical stress upon promise keeping was extended from the realm of the simple promise to that of contract law. Embodied in the maxim *pacta sunt servanda*, it resulted in generalised contractual enforcement rather than the particular enforcement of the old Roman *numerus clausus* of contracts. Promissory ideas thus breathed new life into contract, allowing it to replace the promise as the paradigm voluntary obligational undertaking. Promissory language was largely relegated to the role of explaining the nature of contract as an exchange of promises, though the bare or simple promise remained as an exceptionally recognised undertaking in most systems, and in one system (Scotland) as a discrete, generally enforceable undertaking (subject to requirements of proof and subsequently form).

In Part 2, selected aspects of the modern law of contract were examined in a number of Common law, civilian, and mixed legal systems from a promissory perspective. In the case of some such aspects, it was suggested that promise provided the most useful or most appropriate analysis of the nature of the circumstances studied; in others, it was suggested that promise could not provide the best explanation of why the law was structured the way it was, and that some other rationale explained the feature or rule of contract studied. The suggested appropriateness or usefulness of promise as an explanation of certain features of contract law was intended to signify either that the nature of the rule or transaction in question seemed intrinsically to depend upon the law's view that it was the will of the parties, as demonstrated in their exchanged contractual promises, which was determinative of the content of the rule or the structure of the transaction in question, or that, because the interaction of the parties in the circumstances revealed a unilaterally obligatory undertaking by one towards the other, promise (in the more restricted sense of a unilateral promise rather than an exchange of promises) was best able to characterise the nature of the obligation intended. As an example of the first type of obvious fitness of promise for explaining the law's approach, it was suggested that the preference given in some systems to performance remedies, and the generally adopted protection of the performance measure in relation to the remedy of damages, are explicable by reference to the high regard placed by the law upon the performance promised by the parties. As examples of the second type of obvious fitness of promise to explain the law, it was suggested that enforcement of duties undertaken at the contractual bargaining stage concerning how offers and tenders will be treated, options to contract, so-called 'firm' or 'irrevocable' offers, and offers of reward, each embody unilateral undertakings which are most appropriately and accurately analysed as unilateral promises. Where such undertakings are forced by legal systems into contractual form in order to be enforceable (if indeed they are enforceable at all), the resultant contractual form has a tendency to distort the nature of the transaction (often, for instance, requiring the use of the presumption of a fictional acceptance), can lead to a confused view of the relationship between the parties and in general does not assist a coherent taxonomy of the law or transparency within the legal system.[1] A more honest approach would be to recognise that such transactions are best analysed in unilateral promissory terms and for legal systems to accommodate such an analysis. Such accommodation might either be (as it is in Scots law) by way of the recognition of an obligation of promise separate from that of contract, able to be used generally in the law wherever that is so desired by promisors, or (if that is thought too radical an approach) at least by a willingness to recognise

---

[1] Any reverse tendency to distort genuinely bilateral arrangements by forcing them into unilateral form ought, of course, also to be resisted. In this respect one might note the dogged determination of English law to treat the standard contract of estate agency as a unilateral contract, imposing a duty upon the principal but none upon the agent (see Lord Russell of Killowen in *Luxor (Eastbourne) Ltd* v. *Cooper* [1941] AC 108, 124), when the natural analysis of the arrangement is surely that the estate agent should be seen as coming under a duty at least to use its best endeavours to market and sell the property. Watts and Reynold, *Bowstead and Reynolds on Agency* (para. 7–035), opine that this natural view would, on account of the *Luxor* decision, be 'difficult to establish'. Such a perverse position evidently requires to be revisited.

a greater number of exceptional circumstances where such unilateral promises will be enforceable.

In the final part of this book, some suggestions will be offered as to how the idea of promise might serve the future development of the law, partly from the internal perspective of individual legal systems, but also with harmonised legal development (particularly within the European context) in mind.

2. Future possible development of the law

If, as suggested above, it would be to the benefit of the law to recover the earlier significance accorded to promise, what would be necessary for this to happen? That question can be posed inter-jurisdictionally by reference to certain general considerations, but also in relation to the specific legal systems studied in this work.

(a) General remarks

There are a number of matters listed below which affect the general prospect of promise being accorded a greater role in contract law in all of the jurisdictions studied. However, a fundamental question is whether legal development is managed one jurisdiction at a time, or whether supranational, harmonised development becomes the preferred route. While factors such as globalisation, cost reduction, the ease of doing business, and the committal of many transactions to electronic form favour harmonisation, on the other hand legal nationalism, systemic differences between Common law and civilian systems, and lack of political will for harmonisation, all seem to pull in favour of single jurisdictional legal development. Which will win in the long term is uncertain, though a more prominent role for promise in contract law is most likely to be derived from supranational development and harmonisation, given the recognition accorded to promise in already published model law.

Whether in relation to national or supranational legal development, there are a number of obstacles to promise regaining the ground it once lost in legal thought and practice. Among such obstacles are the following:

(1) Any greater role for promise would first require an agreed understanding of basic obligational concepts essential to describing promises and other obligations. These concepts were considered in Chapter 1, and include qualities such as unilaterality and bilaterality, gratuitousness

and onerousness, and conditionality. Typically, codified systems already have a clear understanding and definition of such basic concepts, as Germany and Louisiana demonstrate. On the other hand, uncodified systems tend to lack such an agreed understanding and definitions: England and Scotland are both beset with this problem (consider the divergent views on what 'unilateral contract' means),[2] as is South Africa to a lesser though still not insignificant degree. There is a clear divergence in juridical and academic use of these fundamental terms in uncodified systems, a phenomenon which is naturally productive of confusion. Without clarification of such confusion and the adoption of uniform definitions of basic obligational ideas, the development of a greater role for promise will be hampered, as the analysis of fact situations and the characterisation of possible solutions to such situations will inevitably remain muddled.

(2) Even if terminology is agreed, there would remain a large antagonism in certain quarters to allowing promise a greater normative and explanatory role in the law. The relentless attacks of utilitarians since Bentham onwards have created a fundamental mistrust in the minds of many thinkers as to the value of promise, certainly in a normative but even in a descriptive role. Despite the appearance in recent years of different varieties of neo-promissory analysis (such as that of Fried and Smith) as well as of neo-virtue ethics, there remain many adherents of reliance theories and of other non-promissory theories of contract law. Critics of promise are bolstered in their views by modernist and post-modernist attacks on the idea of the importance of the human will. The resultant confusion means that some have despaired of adducing in the present age any coherent theory of contract law. Any attempt entirely to vanquish promissory sceptics in the academic field may well be fruitless, though an attempt was made in Part 1 of this work to enunciate a revived will theory capable of meeting many of the criticisms of anti-will theorists. It was also suggested how promise need not claim all of the ground which promissory theorists once attempted to, but rather how it can quite happily function as a description of the means by which human beings are permitted by the legislative sovereign to

---

[2] A 'unilateral' contract strictly refers in English law only to a contract in deed form, yet the courts have utilised the term in other conflicting senses, as earlier discussion in Chapter 4 indicated; in Scotland, there is no such thing as a unilateral contract (save as a misnomer for a gratuitous contract), though one encounters academic and judicial use of the term.

assume voluntary obligations, even if it does not explain the whole content of such obligations.

(3) Even if antagonism to promissory ideas in any form can be overcome, there would remain a deeply ingrained preference in many systems for the accepted promise, and a consequent rejection of the unaccepted promise as a basis for anything other than very exceptional types of liability. Overcoming such a general rejection of the unilateral promise would, again, not be easy. Antagonism to unilateral promises has a long tradition. Yet, the history of the law of the *ius commune* prior to around 1700, a law which *did* give to promise a primary role, is surely not itself an insignificant tradition: what would require to happen is not so much a complete abandonment of tradition, but the rediscovery and redevelopment of an older tradition. That older tradition of enforcing unilateral promises served many useful purposes, and might (as suggested at various points in this work) do so again. The more recent tradition would be hard, but not impossible, to change.

(4) Were a greater role to be given to promise by particular national legal systems or in a supranational code, a decision would require to be taken as to whether this should be by way of the development of a separate obligation of promise (as in Scots law), by way of treating the unilateral promise as generally enforceable without conceiving of it as a new nominate obligation, or by way of continuing to deny general recognition to such promises while increasing the exceptional cases in which they were enforceable. Though the first option is entirely possible, it would have the appearance of a radical alteration of the law and thus be unlikely to command widespread support. The second option has already found favour with the drafters of PECL, in which a unilateral promise is treated as a sort of unaccepted contract, and thus subject to the rules on contract with 'appropriate modifications' (whatever they may be).[3] The framers of the DCFR chose to follow a somewhat different approach. As their project had a wider canvas than merely contract, they were not obliged to try and squeeze promise in to provisions drafted with contract almost entirely in mind. They were instead able to give promise a place in the Book on 'Contracts and other juridical acts', the point being that the DCFR treats promise

---

[3] PECL Art. 1:107 states that the Principles 'apply with appropriate modifications to agreements to modify or end a contract, to unilateral promises and other statements and conduct indicating intention.' Art. II.-1:103(2) of the DCFR states that 'A valid unilateral undertaking is binding on the person giving it if it is intended to be legally binding without acceptance.'

not as a modified sort of contract but as one of the 'other juridical acts' (a unilateral juridical act). The approach of the DCFR, though it does not go so far as to recognise promise as a separate class of obligation, nonetheless gives it an independent life of its own by treating it as a generally enforceable type of undertaking. This seems a preferable approach to that taken in PECL, as many rules of contract law stated in contract codes such as PECL are redundant in the case of unilateral promise (the rules on offer and acceptance being an obvious example), but it is not always clear which apply to promises and which do not.[4] The last option, increasing the exceptional cases where unilateral promises are recognised (in some cases by applying promissory analysis to facts currently treated as contractual), is clearly practicable but has the disadvantage of requiring identification of specific transactions which the law is to consider sufficiently important to merit legal recognition rather than the much simpler process of allowing parties themselves to determine what is important to them. The result of applying an exceptional recognition approach is likely to be both piecemeal and to appear overly paternalistic.

(5) Assuming that some sort of change were desirable (under one of the models discussed in the preceding paragraph), the question of how to achieve it arises. Evidently in codified systems an alteration to the existing Code would be required. If general recognition of unilateral promises were to be allowed, a broad enabling provision could be inserted into the Code in question, and other more specific, exceptional provisions could be removed as being in consequence obsolete. In codified systems, preference already tends to be given to performance remedies (and thus to the protection of the promissory interest in a wider sense, not just in the narrower sense of unilateral promise), so that only minor codal changes might be needed to enhance the role of promise in that regard. In non-codified systems, the way forward for promise would be harder to plot. Short of wholesale change of private law to put it on a codified basis, development would have either to be led by the courts or through statutory change (a 'Contract Act', for instance, might, in modernising other aspects of contract law, give legal effect to unilateral promises). Any possible

---

[4] Take the rules on rescission for breach of contract, for instance: while a material or serious breach of contract will justify termination of a contract and restitution of a performance tendered, it is not evident that the detail of this principle applies *mutatis mutandis* to a case of a breach of a condition attaching to a unilateral promise such as might justify a unilateral promisor seeking restitution of his performance.

judicial development would encounter the large theoretical obstacle of the abolition of a mutual consideration requirement (where it exists in a specific system) and the rule that only mutual promises are enforced (a component of the privity rule), matters considered further below in relation to Common law development. Such a step might be perceived by many as too radical for the judicial branch of government to undertake. If that were so, then legislative development would be required to address the question, as, for instance the Contract (Rights of Third Parties) Act 1999 did for England and Wales in a restricted way by allowing enforcement of promises for the benefit of third parties.

(6) Assuming that promise were to be given a greater role in the law, care would have to be taken not to neuter the potential of gratuitous promise by subjecting it automatically to the legal regime applicable to donations. Were that to happen, then if the particular national regime for donations required compliance with strict formal or notarial rules, gratuitous promise would be prevented from fulfilling much of the potential which it has been suggested in this work it might have. However, the risk of that happening is not great, as many gratuitous promises do not relate to the transfer of ownership of a thing, and it is only such transfers which could be conceived of as donations. Gratuitous promise has a large field within which to operate which is not donative in nature.

(7) If supranational harmonisation of contract law or wider civil law is thought desirable, promissory reform might naturally find a place in any such harmonisation, as the examples of the PECL and DCFR indicate. Achieving such harmonisation would itself be problematic, however. There are not insignificant political and juristic objections to harmonisation, though evaluation of the scope and force of these lies outside this work. Nonetheless, assuming such hurdles can be overcome, the very existence of the PECL and DCFR texts shows that harmonisation is feasible, albeit that it would mean a significant degree of change to the laws and legal culture of some jurisdictions (particularly Common law ones). Outside Europe, the harmonisation of the laws of South Africa and Louisiana with other systems raises considerations different to those applicable within the European context. Though organisations such as the Pan African Lawyers' Union and the African Union actively promote legal harmonisation across the African Continent as a goal, such an enterprise is at the present time little more than an aspiration, and there is no African equivalent

of the PECL or DCFR to which South African law might contribute. In Louisiana, there is pressure from some quarters for the legal system to become more Common law in nature, but this has not thus far been reflected in changes to the legal system.[5]

(8) Lastly, mention must be made of the doctrine of good faith. The growth of good faith jurisprudence in recent years has been something of a mixed blessing for promise. On the one hand, some might argue that good faith mandates adherence to one's word and thus to promises seriously made, whether bilateral or unilateral, gratuitous or onerous. On this view, as Aristotelian virtues and the canon law supported the keeping of promises in earlier times, good faith can be argued to be a modern equivalent of such older structural underpinnings of the duty to keep promises. On such a view, the rise of good faith jurisprudence is an opportunity for promise, rather than a threat. This view can, however, be said too readily to equate promising with trustworthiness. It was suggested in Chapter 6 that trust, while it may accompany the making of many promises, is not a necessary component of a promise. As such, the operation of objective good faith, as applied by the courts, in order to moderate the promises strictly made by parties and to impose community values of justice and fairness represents a challenge to the possible re-establishment of promise as a central idea in the law. The challenge for a future law where both promise and good faith are required to coexist ought not to be underestimated.

(b)   The Common law

The granting of a more prominent role to promise in the Common law of obligations, and more particularly in contract law, faces the theoretical problems of the related doctrines of consideration and privity. The obstacle these doctrines present has been the subject of discussion earlier in this work: to recap, gratuitous contracts, promises made in favour of non-contracting parties, and unaccepted but seriously made promises (unilateral promises), are all theoretically denied enforcement in the Common law, unless some exceptional means can be found to enforce certain instances of them.

---

[5] For instance, Louisiana continues to refuse to implement section 2 of the Uniform Commercial Code (the section relating to sales of goods).

Both doctrines have been subject to much discussion by academics and judges, and there are various theories of the roles which consideration and privity are said to play in the law.[6] At various times, it has been suggested that English law should abandon the requirement of mutual consideration for a valid contract.[7] One critic suggested that such a move should form part of 'legislation ... to validate all contracts where there is genuine agreement and also to provide for various types of essentially unilateral promises such as gifts, promises relating to the performance of services and offers inviting the performance of certain acts'.[8] Such arguments have, in English law at least, not been acted upon. Whilst calls for the complete abandonment of the doctrine of privity have not been made, and are not likely to be for the very good reason that privity performs the useful function of preventing the imposition of duties upon third parties, the sensible abandonment of the rule against the conferral of enforceable third party benefits under contract has now been effected in most of the major Common law jurisdictions.[9] A further logical step, given this existing reform, would be to recognise that unaccepted but seriously made unilateral promises should also be accorded validity. Any perceived risks inherent in enforcing such unilateral promises are no greater than those inherent in allowing third party beneficiaries to enforce benefits conceived in their favour.

Although the general recognition of third party rights would at one time have been unthinkable in the Common law, the radical reform which achieved recognition of such rights surely suggests that reform of the doctrine of consideration might now also be within contemplation. The results of abolition of the doctrine would include, inter alia, both recognition of the validity of gratuitous contracts[10] as well as the placing of greater stress upon the already existing contractual requirement of an intention to undertake legally binding obligations. Both of these features are visible in civilian and mixed legal systems, and create no practical difficulties for distinguishing seriously intended obligations from extra-legal arrangements. The opening up of the doctrine of privity by recognising not just third party rights but also unilateral promises would bring

---

[6] For the various policies said to underlie the doctrine of consideration, see, for instance, Eisenberg, 'The Principles of Consideration'; in respect of the policies and functions of privity, see Palmer, *The Paths to Privity*, Ch. 2.

[7] See, for citation of advocates of this approach, Ch. 4, n. 341, of this work.

[8] Chloros, 'The Doctrine of Consideration', 165.

[9] See earlier discussion at p. 297.

[10] See Anson, *Principles of the Law of Contract* (28th edn), p. 125.

the benefits discussed in earlier chapters of this work, and need not entail any conceptual or practical difficulties. Such a development would greatly reduce, if not remove, the need for a doctrine of promissory estoppel, an equitable stop-gap which has been required to address the problems created by legal refusal to recognise the validity of unilateral promises. The recognition of the legal and not merely equitable status of such promises seems a natural step to take: if a promise is worthy of enforcement, why not recognise that at the level of a legal rule rather than at that of an equitable remedial entitlement?

The Common law has a great history of adaptability. This is seen in many ways, such as in the forging of the very field of contract law out of the diverse medieval actions, in the fusion of legal and equitable jurisdictions, in varied developments of the requirement of consideration, and in the development of doctrines such as equitable estoppel to remedy perceived flaws in the pre-existing hard edges of contract law. It would be regrettable if the great adaptability of the Common law were to have been lost in the present age, and for lawyers to feel that, if continued adherence to certain doctrines deprived the law of adaptability, this situation could not be amended merely because such doctrines were perceived to have a long tradition. Statutory reform has already given third parties a long overdue entitlement at law; if such reform is also needed in relation to consideration, then it should be undertaken. The problems caused by the requirement of consideration and the refusal to recognise unaccepted promises may have given rise to practical avoidance techniques, but a coherent legal system deserves more than such makeshifts.

(c)   The mixed legal systems

It will be evident from all that has been said in earlier chapters of this work that, though the mixed systems share a similar Roman-Common law heritage, how that heritage has translated into specific contractual rules, and especially the treatment of promises, differs. Scots law most explicitly values the unilateral promise, in giving it separate taxonomic status in the class of obligations; South Africa and Louisiana do not go so far, but do recognise the validity of gratuitous contracts. Even Scotland, however, restricts enforcement of unilateral promises by imposing a requirement of form[11] for the validity of non-business promises (itself a less serious

---

[11] Before statutory reform of the law in 1995, the requirement of form was instead an evidentiary requirement of proof, all seriously intended unilateral promises being valid but requiring proof by the writ (subscribed written document) or the oath of the promisor.

hurdle than the previous rule requiring proof by writ or oath). The rationale for this restriction is questionable, though there is no evident desire for its amendment at the present time. In South Africa and Louisiana, though the recognition of gratuitous contracts allows such contracts to be the vehicle for certain transactions (such as promises of reward, and gratuitous options to contract) which are only with greater conceptual difficulty accommodated in the Common law, the absence of a general recognition of the unilateral promise is still felt to some extent. This has been the subject of academic comment from a South African perspective in relation to firm offers.[12] Louisiana has avoided that particular problem by virtue of a codal provision enforcing firm offers,[13] though there is no explanation in the Code of the basis of this provision, with the result that it has an awkwardness in terms of its obligatory classification. It has already also been noted how Louisiana's provision on public offers, though framed in offer terms, is in effect unilaterally promissory in nature. It will come as no surprise, given the general thrust of this work, that it is suggested that such provisions would be better recognised and styled as unilateral promises, such a development allowing a clearer appreciation of why the relevant party is considered bound at law. Any such development would, of course, require either codal or other legislative reform or, in South Africa, adventurous judicial development of the law.

(d)   German law

German law does not know a doctrine of consideration, recognising in consequence gratuitous contracts; it places great stress upon performance remedies; and it has a developed and clear obligational terminology, allowing a logical classification of obligations and a precise analysis of their nature. Features such as these allow German law to give greater prominence to the idea of promise (widely defined). Earlier discussion in this work has, however, indicated how the early prospect of a relatively general recognition of unilateral promises in the BGB was thwarted before publication of the final text of the Code in 1900. The result was a relegation of the unilateral promise to a few recognised exceptional instances,[14] and the impermissibility of allowing it to be applied to new circumstances for which it might otherwise have been the ideal legal characterisation. Whilst the German courts have on occasions developed

---

[12]   See Hogg and Lubbe, 'Formation of Contract', p. 64.
[13]   CC Art. 1928. See earlier discussion of this issue in Ch. 4, p. 226.
[14]   See the discussion of such exceptional circumstances at p. 152.

new legal doctrines to address perceived problems not addressed in the Code,[15] it hardly seems likely that they will adopt such a course in respect of unilateral promise given that its general recognition was considered but explicitly rejected by the drafters of the Code. Any step to give unilateral promises wider and more general recognition in German law is thus likely to come about only by virtue of amendment to the text of the BGB. No widespread desire to effect such amendment in respect of promise seems discernible at the present time. While this doubtless reflects the fact that lack of a general recognition of unilateral promises seems not to cause any major problems in German law,[16] it can nonetheless be argued that a general promissory provision in the BGB would create greater consistency. This would be so because the current approach singles out some instances of seriously intended unilateral promises as worthy of protection, yet denying all other instances such protection, while demonstrating no evident reason for this casuistic approach. The only apparent defence of the present position is that the instances of unilateral promise which have been given protection in the BGB are those which most commonly arise. Yet why should frequency of occurrence of a particular type of promise determine its legal effectiveness? Are not less frequently occurring but seriously intended instances of unilateral promise equally worthy of being given effect to in law? The great unanswered question for German law is why, having accepted the principle of *pacta sunt servanda*, it does not apply the same logic to unilateral promises, but rather implements a principle that only some of these promises are enforced.

(e)   *The development of supranational model law*

The likelihood of any of the national systems studied unilaterally developing their law in a way which would give a more explicit and a greater role to promise is not great. That assessment is made on the basis that there does not appear to be any groundswell of opinion in any of the jurisdictions studied pressing for such development, albeit that in some jurisdictions promissory scholarship is attracting more attention in recent years than it has for some time. Realistically, it is to supranational model codes, and the possibility of the eventual adoption of such codes into law, that one must look to advance the cause of promise.

---

[15]   The judicial development of the doctrine of transferred loss (*Drittenschadensliquidation*), discussed at p. 330, being one such example.

[16]   As the discussion in (primarily) Ch. 4 has indicated.

The references in this work to, primarily, the provisions of the DCFR (as well as of the PECL) have indicated several things about the likely role of promise in a possible harmonised law of obligations in Europe:

(1) Promise, as a type of unilateral juristic undertaking, will be recognised in any future harmonised legal order. A general enabling provision of the type in the DCFR (Article II.-1:103(2)) would potentially allow promise a role in many of the specific topics considered in the earlier chapters of this work, a development which would have the potential to benefit both legal theory and practice.

(2) Promise is capable of offering a suitable explanation of unilateral undertakings to effect a donation.[17] The act of transfer effecting a donation, however, while a unilateral juristic act, is not itself promissory. This point emphasises the importance of appreciating the distinction between unilateral obligatory acts and unilateral acts of another nature, a point which finds a clearer expression in the DCFR and in some legal systems than it does in other national systems.

(3) It is conceivable that some sorts of undertaking may not be subject to specific regulation, an example being the option. This leaves a promissory conception as one (though not the only) possible analysis of the nature of the undertaking. Such possible freedom of analysis is welcome, as it allows national systems a degree of flexibility.

(4) Model law is unlikely to tackle the detail of any formal requirements which may be thought necessary in instances of promise. While this omission is unsurprising given the variety of formal requirements applied in different systems, it would be regrettable if national systems continued to limit the flexible uses to which promise can be put by unduly restrictive requirements of form. Such restrictions tend merely to foster attempts at avoidance through disguising essentially promissory relationships in some other form.

(5) Importantly, there are limitations to the utility of promise. In a future harmonised contract law, promise is, for instance, unlikely to continue to stamp upon offers their traditional character of unilaterally determined undertakings to contract upon certain terms: the DCFR approach of conceiving of offer and counter-offer as proposals from which a core agreement can be distilled presents the possibility of a quite different view of the negotiation process. Promise is also unlikely to provide a suitable explanation for the challenging field of

---

[17] See Hogg, 'Promise and Donation in Louisiana and Comparative Law'.

pre-contractual liability for wasted expenditure, where a sui generis solution, deriving its moral and legal force from the idea of good faith, is (as the PECL and DCFR approaches indicate) likely to be adopted, albeit that the idea of good faith will require very close monitoring if the solution it offers is to have the clarity and certainty needed to meet the demands of contracting parties.

3. Conclusion on the future of promise

The Introductory Principles to the DCFR include a principle entitled 'Minimal substantive restrictions'[18] defined as follows:

> The absence of any need for consideration or *causa* for the conclusion of an effective contract, the recognition that there can be binding unilateral undertakings and the recognition that contracts can confer rights on third parties all promote efficiency (and freedom!) by making it easier for parties to achieve the legal results they want in the way they want without the need to resort to legal devices or distortions.

This principle, it is suggested, correctly identifies personal autonomy and efficiency as two strong reasons for recognising both unilateral undertakings and third party rights (other manifestations of promise might similarly be justified), and the avoidance of distortion of the law as a strong reason for not forcing transactions to adopt inappropriate legal forms in an attempt to avoid structural barriers to validity. It is encouraging to see the drafters of the DCFR adopt this view, as it aligns with what has been argued throughout this work.

Promise seems, at the present time, to have relatively bright prospects in a future contract law. The attacks against it which were prevalent in the 1970s and 1980s have proved fleeting and ineffectual, as they were always likely to be, given the fundamental nature of promising to the operation of human societies. It is simply the case that, like other perennial features of human interaction, the pledging of a future performance in favour of another is something which people are likely to continue to wish to do in a legally effective manner. Legal systems which put the fewest barriers in the way of the legal recognition of promises will be those which most accurately and honestly reflect the societies which they govern.

None of this is to say that promise needs to be recognised as the whole of the law of contract, as once might have been argued. Promises, as

---

[18] DCFR, Principle 56.

manifestations of the human will, have a place within the law of voluntarily assumed obligations, but promise is not the source of all such obligations; other normative and descriptive concepts have their proper place too. Even where promise is properly recognised as the most appropriate form for an obligation, or where the performance interest equating to promise is protected in some remedial way in contract law, the law may quite properly constrain the private promises of parties or the performance interest by reference to other considerations, among them equity and good faith, albeit that the balancing act between personal autonomy and community interests is necessarily a difficult one to get right.

The Draft Common Frame of Reference, by recognising the importance of promise within the wider law of obligations, has provided encouragement to national systems to take up the promissory challenge and to recognise more fully the potential of the idea of promise for developing the law in a way which promotes personal autonomy, overcomes outmoded restrictions and rules, and provides a good match between the underlying nature of transactions and their legal classification.

BIBLIOGRAPHY

Addison, C. G., *Treatise on the Law of Contracts and Liabilities Ex Contractu* (London: 1847)

Aelian, *Historical Miscellany* (Harvard University Press, 1997)

Aeschines, *Speeches* (Cambridge, Mass.: Loeb, 1989)

Albright, W. F., *From Stone Age to Christianity* (New York: Doubleday, 1957)

Anderson, A., *Assignation* (Edinburgh: Edinburgh Legal Education Trust, 2008)

Anson, W. R., *Principles of the English Law of Contract* (Oxford: Clarendon Press, 1879); 28th edn, by Beatson, J. (Oxford University Press, 2002)

Aquinas, St. T., *Summa Theologica*, 22 vols., 2nd rev. edn (London: Burns Oates & Washbourne, 1920)

Árdal, P., 'And That's a Promise' (1968) **18** *The Philosophical Quarterly* 225–37

Aristotle, *Nicomachean Ethics*, being vol. 19 of *Aristotle in Twenty Three Volumes* (Harvard University Press, 1934)

Ashton Cross, D. I. C., 'Bare Promise in Scots Law' (1957) *Juridical Review* 138–50

Atiyah, P. S., *Essays on Contract* (Oxford University Press, 1986)
  Promises, Morals and Law (Oxford University Press, 1981)

Aubry, C. and Rau, C., *Cours de droit civil français* (Paris: 1869–1871)

Augustine of Hippo, St, *Enarrationes in Psalmos 101–150* (Vienna: Verlag der Österreichischen Akademie der Wissenschaften, 2001)

Austin, J. L., *How to Do Things with Words: The William James Lectures delivered at Harvard University in 1955* (Oxford University Press, 1962)

Azo di Bologna, P., *Summa super Codicem* (Pavia: 1506; Turin: Augustae Taurinorum, 1966)

Baldus de Ubaldis, *Commentaria super Codice* (Venice: 1577)
  Commentarius super Decretalibus (Lyon: 1551)

Baker, J. H., 'Origins of the 'Doctrine' of Consideration, 1535–1585', in M. S. Arnold *et al.* (eds.), *On the Laws and Customs of England* (University of North Carolina Press, 1981), pp. 336–58
  The Oxford History of the Laws of England, Vol. VI (Oxford University Press, 2003)

Ballow, H., *Treatise on Equity* (London: 1737)

Bankton, Lord (A. McDouall), *Institute of the Laws of Scotland*, 3 vols. (Edinburgh: 1751–3)

Bartolus de Saxoferrato, *Commentaria* (Venice: Baptista de Tortis, 1526; repr. Rome: Istituto giuridico Bartolo da Sassoferrato, 1996)

Beale, H., 'General Clauses and Specific Rules in the Principles of European Contract Law: The "Good Faith" Clause', in S. Grundmann and D. Mazeaud (eds.), *General Clauses and Standards in European Contract Law* (The Hague: Kluwer Law International, 2006), pp. 205–18

Beale, H. G., *Chitty on Contracts*, 2 vols. (London: Sweet & Maxwell, 2008)

Bechmann, A., *Der Kauf nach gemeinem Recht* (Erlangen: Andreas Deichert, 1884)

Bell, G., *Principles of the Law of Scotland*, 4th edn (Edinburgh: T. Clark, 1839)
  Commentaries on the Law of Scotland, 7th edn (Edinburgh: T. & T. Clark, 1870)

Bishop, J., *Believing by Faith: An Essay in the Epistemology and Ethics of Religious Belief* (Oxford University Press, 2007)

Blackstone, W., *Commentaries on the Laws of England*, 4 vols. (Oxford: Clarendon Press, 1765–9)

Bower, S., *The Law relating to Estoppel by Representation*, 4th edn (London: LexisNexis, 2004)

Brand, F. and Brodie, D., 'Good Faith in Contract Law', in R. Zimmermann, K. Reid and D. Visser (eds.), *Mixed Legal Systems in Comparative Perspective: Property and Obligations in Scotland and South Africa* (Oxford University Press, 2004), pp. 94–116

Carter, W. R., 'On Promising the Unwanted' (1973) **33** *Analysis* 88–92

Cairns, J. and du Plessis, P., *The Creation of the Ius Commune* (Edinburgh University Press, 2010)

Cairns, J., 'Ius Civile in Scotland, ca. 1600' (2004) **2** *Roman Legal Tradition* 136–70

Cajetan, T., *Commentaria* (Padua, 1698)

Campbell, A., 'Iran and Deception Modalities: The Reach of taqiyya, kitman, khod'eh and taarof' (2006) *National Observer* 25–48

Cameron, J. T., 'Jus Quaesitum Tertio; The True Meaning of Stair I. x. 5' (1961) *Juridical Review* 103–18

Cameron, J. T. (Lord Coulsfield), MacQueen, H. L. and Carey Miller, D. L., *The Law of Scotland by W. M. Gloag and R. Candlish Henderson*, 12th edn (Edinburgh: W. Green, 2007)

Chitty, J., *A Practical Treatise on the Law of Contracts* (London: S. Sweet, 1826)

Chloros, A. G., 'The Doctrine of Consideration and Reform of the Law of Contract' (1968) **17** *International and Comparative Law Quarterly* 137–66

Christie, R. H., *The Law of Contract in South Africa*, 5th edn (Cape Town: Butterworths, 2007)

Cicero, M. T., *De Officiis* (Harvard University Press, 1961)
  Epistulae ad Quintum Fratrem (Cambridge University Press, 2004)
  The Verrine Orations, 2 vols. (Harvard University Press, 1928–35)

Cimino, C., 'Virtue and Contract Law' (2010) *Oregon Law Review* 704–43

Clive, E. and Hutchison, D., 'Breach of Contract', in R. Zimmermann, K. Reid and D. Visser (eds.), *Mixed Legal Systems in Comparative Perspective* (OUP, 2005), pp. 176–207

Cohen, M. R., 'The Basis of Contract' (1933) **46** *Harvard Law Review* 553–92; reprinted in M. R. Cohen, *Law and Social Order: Essays in Legal Philosophy* (New Jersey: Transaction Publishers, 1982)

Colebrooke, H., *Treatise on Obligations and Contracts* (London: 1818)

Comyn, S., *The Law of Contracts and Promises* (London: 1807)

Comyns, Sir J., *A Digest of the Laws of England*, 4th edn (London: 1800)

Connanus, F., *Commentariorum juris civilis libri X* (Naples: 1724)

Coote, B., *Contract as Assumption* (Oxford: Hart Publishing, 2010)

Craswell, R., 'Contract Law, Default Rules and the Philosophy of Promising' (1989) *Michigan Law Review* 489–529

Darwall, S., (ed.), *Contractarianism/Contractualism* (Oxford: Blackwell, 2003)

De Butrio, A., *Super librum I–V decretalium commentaria* (Venice: 1578; repr. Turin: 1967)

De Wet, J. C., 'Die ontwikkeling van die ooreenkoms ten behoewe van 'n derde', unpublished PhD thesis, Leiden University, 1940

Demante, A., and Colmet de Santerre, E., *Cours analytique de Code Civil* (Paris: 1883)

Demolombe, J. C., *Cours de Code Napoléon* (Paris: 1854–82)

Dietrich, 'Classifying Precontractual Liability: A Comparative Analysis' (2001) **21** *Legal Studies* 153–91

Donaldson, G., 'The Church Courts', in G. C. H. Paton (ed.), *Introduction to Scottish Legal History* (Edinburgh: Stair Society, 1958)

Del Mar, M. and Bankowski, Z., *Law as Institutional Normative Order* (Farnham: Ashgate, 2009)

Downie, R. S., 'Three Accounts of Promising' (1985) **35** *Philosophical Quarterly* 259–71

Du Plessis, J., *Compulsion and Restitution* ((Edinburgh: The Stair Society, 2004)

Du Plessis, J. and McBryde, W. W., 'Defects of Consent', in R. Zimmermann, D. Visser and K. Reid, *Mixed Legal Systems in Comparative Perspective* (Oxford University Press, 2004), pp. 117–42

Duranton, M., *Cours de droit français* (Paris: 1834–7)

Eisenberg, M. A., 'The Principles of Consideration' (1982) **67** *Cornell Law Review* 640–65

Erskine, J., *An Institute of the Law of Scotland*, 2 vols., 5th edn (Edinburgh: Bell & Bradfute, 1812)

Evans-Jones, R., *Unjustified Enrichment*, vol. 1 (Edinburgh: W. Green, 2003)

Farnsworth, E.A., 'The Past of Promise: An Historical Introduction to Contract' (1969) **69** *Columbia Law Review* 576–607

Farrelly, C. and Solum, L., (eds.), *Virtue Jurisprudence* (Basingstoke: Palgrave Macmillan, 2008)

Fox, R. and Demarco, J., 'The Immorality of Promising' (1993) *Journal of Value Enquiry* 81–4

The Immorality of Promising (New York: Humanity Books, 2001)

Fried, C., *Contract as Promise* (Cambridge, Mass.: Harvard University Press, 1981)

Friedmann, D., 'Good Faith and Remedies for Breach of Contract', in J. Beatson and D. Friedmann (eds.), *Good Faith and Fault in Contract Law* (Oxford University Press, 1995), pp. 399–426

Fuller, L. L. and Perdue, W. R., 'The Reliance Interest in Contract Damages' (1936) **46** *Yale Law Journal* 52–96 (Pt.1), 373–420 (Pt. 2)

Furmston, M., *Cheshire, Fifoot and Furmston's Law of Contract*, 15th edn (Oxford University Press, 2006)

Furmston, M. and Tolhurst, G., *Contract Formation: Law and Practice* (Oxford University Press, 2010)

Gauthier, D., *Morals by Agreement* (Oxford University Press, 1986)

German Federal Ministry of Justice, *Final Report of the Commission to Revise the Law of Obligations* (*Abschlußbericht der Kommission zur Überarbeitung des Schuldrechts*) (1992)

Gilbert, J., *Treatise on Contract* (c.1720) BL MS Harg 265

Gilbert, M., 'Scanlon on Promissory Obligation: The Problem of Promisees' Rights' (2004) **101** *Journal of Philosophy* 83–109

Gilmore, G., *The Death of Contract* (Columbus, Ohio: Ohio State University Press, 1974)

Glanvill, R., *Treatise on the Laws and Customs of England*, new transl. into English by G. D. G. Hall (Oxford University Press, 1965, repr. 1993)

Gloag, W., *The Law of Contract*, 2nd edn (Edinburgh: W. Green, 1929)

Gold, A. S., 'Consideration and the Morality of Promising', in S. Neyers *et al.*, *Exploring Contract Law* (Oxford: Hart Publishing, 2009), pp. 115–37

Gordley, J., *The Philosophical Origins of Modern Contract Doctrine* (Oxford University Press, 1991)

'Enforcing Promises' (1995) **83** *California Law Review* 547–614

(ed.), *The Enforceability of Promises in European Contract Law* (Cambridge University Press, 2001)

'The Foreseeability Limitation on Liability in Contract Law', in A. Hartkamp *et al.* (eds.), *Towards a European Civil Code* (Nijmegen: Ars Aequi Libri/ Kluwer Law, 2004), Ch. 12

'Mistake in Contract Formation' (2004) **52** *American Journal of Comparative Law* 433–68

Foundations of Private Law (Oxford University Press, 2007)

'Louisiana and the Common Law: Le Jour de Gloire, Est-Il Passé?' (2009) **24** *Tulane European and Civil Law Forum* 191–206

Greaves, R. L., *Society and Religion in Elizabethan England* (University of Minnesota Press, 1981)

Grotius (de Groot, H.), *De iure belli ac pacis*, translation of the 1646 edition by F. W. Kelsey (Oxford University Press, 1925; reprinted by Hein & Co, New York, 1995)

   Inleidinge tot de Hollandsche Rechts-Geleerdheid, trans. R. W. Lee (Oxford University Press, 1926)

Hacker-Wright, J., 'Virtue Ethics without Right Action: Anscombe, Foot and Contemporary Virtue Ethics' (2010) **44** *Journal of Value Enquiry* 209–24

Hallebeek, J. and Dondorp, H., *Contracts for a Third Party Beneficiary: A Historical and Comparative Account* (Leiden: Martinus Nijhoff, 2008)

Hart, H. L. A., 'Are There Any Natural Rights?' (1955) **64** *Philosophical Review* 175–91

   The Concept of Law, 2nd edn (Oxford University Press, 1994)

Hartkamp, A., *Der Zwang im römischen Privatrecht* (Amsterdam: Hakkert, 1971)

Heldrich, A., Prölss, J. and Koller, I., *Festschrift für Claus-Wilhelm Canaris*, 2 vols. (Munich: C. H. Beck, 2007)

Helmholz, R. H., 'Assumpsit and Fidei Laesio' (1975) **91** *Law Quarterly Review* 406–32

   'Contracts and the Canon Law: Possible Points of Contact between England and the Continent', in J. Barton (ed.), *Towards a General Law of Contract*, (Berlin: Duncker and Humblot, 1990), pp 49–65

Herodotus, *Histories*, 4 vols., rev. edn (Cambridge, Mass.: Loeb, 1989)

Hesselink, M., 'The Concept of Good Faith', in A. Hartkamp *et al.*, *Towards a European Civil Code*, 3rd edn (Nijmegen: Kluwer Law International/Ars Aequi Libri, 2004), pp. 471–98

Hickey, R., 'A Promise is a Promise: On Speech Acts of Commitment in English' (1986) **28** *Studia Anglica Posnaniensia* 69–80

Hobbes, T., *Leviathan*, ed. R. Tuck (Cambridge University Press, 1996)

Hoff, T., 'Error in the Formation of Contracts in Louisiana: A Comparative Analysis' (1979) **53** *Tulane Law Review* 329–79

Hoffmann, Lord (L.), 'The Achilleas: Custom and Practice or Foreseeability? (2010) **14** *Edinburgh Law Review* 47–61

Hogg, M., 'Leases: Four Historical Portraits', in K. Reid and R. Zimmermann (eds.), *A History of Private Law in Scotland* (Oxford University Press, 2000), vol. 1, pp. 363–98

   Obligations, 2nd edn (Edinburgh: Avizandum, 2006)

   'Perspectives on Contract Theory from a Mixed Legal System' (2009) **29** *Oxford Journal of Legal Studies* 643–73

'Promise: The Neglected Obligation in European Contract Law' (2010) **59** *International and Comparative Law Quarterly* 461–79

'Promise and Donation in Louisiana and Comparative Law' (2011) *Tulane European & Civil Law Forum* (forthcoming)

Hogg, M. and Lubbe, G., 'Formation of Contract', in R. Zimmermann, D. Visser and K. Reid (eds.), *Mixed Legal Systems in Comparative Perspective* (Oxford University Press, 2004), pp. 34–65

Holmes, O. W., 'The Path of the Law' (1897) **10** *Harvard Law Review* 457–78

Homer, *The Iliad*, 2 vols., 2nd rev. edn (Cambridge, Mass.: Loeb, 1999)

Hostiensis (H. de Segusio), *Lectura* (Paris: printed by J. Schott and G. Übelin, 1512)

Summa aurea (Venice: printed by Gracioso Perchacino, 1605)

Howarth, W., 'The Meaning of Objectivity in Contract' (1984) **100** *Law Quarterly Review* 265–81

Huber, U., *Leistungsstörungen*, 2 vols. (Tübingen: Mohr Siebeck, 1999)

Hume, D., *A Treatise of Human Nature*, ed. by D. F. Norton and M. J. Norton (Oxford University Press, 2000)

'Of the Original Contract', repr. in E. Barker (ed.), *Social Contract* (Oxford University Press, 1960), pp. 145–66

Hutchison, D., 'Contract Formation', in R. Zimmermann and D. Visser (eds.), *Southern Cross: Civil and Common Law in South Africa* (Oxford University Press, 1996), pp. 165–94

'Good Faith in the South African Law of Contract', in R. Brownsword *et al.* (eds.), *Good Faith in Contract: Concept and Context* (Aldershot: Dartmouth Publishing, 1999), pp. 213–42

Hutton, S., 'Remedies after Breach of Contract: Rethinking the Conventional Jurisprudence' (1997) *Acta Juridica* 201–24

Hyland, R., 'Pacta Sunt Servanda: A Meditation' (1994) **34** *Virginia Journal of International Law* 405–33

Ibbetson, D., 'Consideration and the Theory of Contract in Sixteenth Century Common Law', in J. Barton (ed.), *Towards a General Law of Contract* (Berlin: Duncker and Humblot, 1990), pp. 67–124.

An Historical Introduction to the Law of Obligations (Oxford University Press, 1999)

Johnston, D., *Roman Law in Context* (Cambridge University Press, 1999)

Jones, W. R., 'The Two Laws in England: The Later Middle Ages' (1969) **11** *Journal of Church and State* 111–31

Kaiser, W., 'The Old Promise and the New Covenant: Jeremiah 31:31-34' (1972) **15**(1) *Journal of the Evangelical Theological Society* 12–23

Kames, Lord (H. Home), *Essays on the Principles of Morality and Natural Religion* (Edinburgh: Kincaid and Donaldson, 1751)

Principles of Equity, 2nd edn (Edinburgh: Kincaid and Bell, 1767)

Katz, A., 'The Strategic Structure of Offer and Acceptance: Game Theory and the Law of Contract Formation' (1990) **89** *Michigan Law Review* 215–95

Kessler, F. and Fine, E., 'Culpa in Contrahendo, Bargaining in Good Faith and Freedom of Contract: A Comparative Study' (1964) **77** *Harvard Law Review* 401–49

Kimel, D., *From Promise to Contract: Towards a Liberal Theory of Contract* (Oxford: Hart Publishing, 2003)

Kleinschmidt, J., 'Erlass', in R. Zimmermann (ed.), *Historisch-kritischer Kommentar zum BGB Band II: Schuldrecht. Allgemeiner Teil*, vol. 2 (Tübingen: Mohr Siebeck, 2003), pp. 2250–80

  Der Verzicht im Schuldrecht (Tübingen: Mohr Siebeck, 2004)

  'Erlass einer Forderung', in J. Basedow, K. Hopt and R. Zimmermann (eds.), *Handwörterbuch des Europäischen Privatrechts* (2009), Ch. 3 (English language edition forthcoming, 2011)

  'Verzicht', in J. Basedow, K. Hopt and R. Zimmermann (eds.), *Handwörterbuch des Europäischen Privatrechts* (2009) (English language edition forthcoming, 2011)

Koller, I., 'Wertpapierrecht', in Bundesminister der Justiz (ed.), *Gutachten und Vorschläge zur Überarbeitung des Schuldsrechts*, vol. 2 (1981)

Korn, J. and Korn, S., 'Where People Don't Promise'(1983) **93** *Ethics* 445–50

Kötz, H., 'Precontractual Duties of Disclosure: A Comparative and Economic Perspective' (2000) **9** *European Journal of Law and Economics* 5–19

Kramer, A. E., in *Münchener Kommentar zum Bürgerlichen Gesetzbuch*, vol. 2, 5th edn (Munich: Beck Juristischer Verlag, 2006)

Kritzinger, K. M., 'The Irrevocable Offer' (1983) **100** *South African Law Journal* 441–53

Kronman, A. T., 'Contract Law and Distributive Justice' (1980) **89** *Yale Law Journal* 472–511

Lange, H. and Schiemann, G., *Schadenersatz* (Tübingen: Mohr Siebeck, 2003)

Larenz, K., *Lehrbuch des Schuldrechts*, 14th edn (Munich: C. H. Beck, 1987)

Larombière, M. L., *Theorie et pratique des obligations* (Paris: 1857)

Larroumet, C., 'Detrimental Reliance and Promissory Estoppel as the Cause of Contracts in Louisiana and Comparative Law' (1986) **60** *Tulane Law Review* 1209–30

Laurent, F., *Principes de droit civil français* (Paris: 1869–78)

Lavelle, M., 'Privity of Contract and Third Party Beneficiaries', report submitted to Uniform Law Conference of Canada, Sept. 2007 (published online at www.ulcc.ca)

Law Commission of England and Wales, *Law of Contract: Pecuniary Restitution on Breach of Contract* (Law Com. No. 121, 1983)

Law Revision Committee, *Sixth Interim Report* (1937, Cmnd 5449)

Law Society of Scotland, *The Laws of Scotland: Stair Memorial Encyclopaedia*, 25 vols. and reissue vols. (Edinburgh: Butterworths, 1987–)

Leake, S. M., *The Elements of the Law of Contracts* (London: Stevens, 1867)

Lessius, L., *De iustitia et iure* (Paris: 1628)

Levasseur, A., *Louisiana Law of Obligations in General: A Précis,* 2nd edn (2008)

Litvinoff, S., 'Offer and Acceptance in Louisiana Law: A Comparative Analysis' (1967) **28** *Louisiana Law Review* 1–81 (pt. 1), 153–210 (pt. 2)

'Good Faith' (1997) **71** *Tulane Law Review* 1645–74

Litvinoff, S. and Scalise, R., *The Law of Obligations in the Louisiana Jurisprudence* (New Orleans: LSU Law Center, 2008)

Lorenz, S., *Der Schutz vor dem unerwünschten Vertrag* (Munich: C. H. Beck, 1997)

Lucy, W. N. R., 'Contract as a Mechanism of Distributive Justice' (1989) **9** *Oxford Journal of Legal Studies* 132–47

Lutter, M., *Der Letter of Intent,* 3rd edn (Cologne: Heymanns, 1998)

Lyons, D., *Forms and Limits of Utilitarianism* (Oxford University Press, 1965)

Macaulay, S., 'Relational Contracts Floating on a Sea of Custom? Thoughts about the Ideas of Ian Macneil and Lisa Bernstein' (2000) **94** *Northwestern University Law Review* 775–804

MacCormack, G., 'A Note on Stair's Use of the Term Pollicitatio' (1976) *Juridical Review* 121–6

'The Oral and Written Stipulation in the Institutes', in P. G. Stein (ed.), *Studies in Justinian's Institutes in memory of J. A. C. Thomas* (London: Sweet & Maxwell, 1983), pp. 96–108

MacCormick, D. N., 'Voluntary Obligations and Normative Powers I' (1972) **46** (Supp. vol.) *Proceedings of the Aristotelian Society* 59–78

Legal Right and Social Democracy (Oxford University Press, 1982)

Institutions of Law (Oxford University Press, 2007)

MacIntyre, A., *After Virtue,* 3rd edn (University of Notre Dame Press, 2007)

Macleod, J., 'Before Bell: The Roots of Error in the Scots Law of Contract' (2010) *Edinburgh Law Review* 385–417

Macpherson, W., *Outlines of the Law of Contracts as Administered in the Courts of British India* (London: 1860)

MacQueen, H. L., 'Jus Quaesitum Tertio', in The Law Society of Scotland, *The Laws of Scotland*, vol. 15 (Edinburgh: Butterworths, 1996)

'Good Faith in the Scots Law of Contract: An Undisclosed Principle?', in A. Forte (ed.), *Good Faith in Contract and Property* (Oxford: Hart Publishing, 1999), pp. 5–38

MacQueen, H. L. and Thomson, J., *Contract Law in Scotland,* 2nd edn (Edinburgh: Tottel, 2007)

Markesinis, B., and Unberath, H., *The German Law of Torts: A Comparative Treatise* (Oxford: Hart Publishing, 2002)

Markesinis, B., Unberath, H. and Johnston A., *The German Law of Contract* (Oxford: Hart Publishing, 2006)

Martínez-Torrón, J., *Anglo-American Law and Canon Law: Canonical Roots of the Common Law Tradition* (Berlin: Duncker & Humblot, 1998)

McBryde, W. W., *The Law of Contract in Scotland*, 3rd edn (Edinburgh: W. Green, 2007)

McCoubrey, H., *The Development of Naturalist Legal Theory* (Croom Helm: London, 1987)

McGregor, H., *McGregor on Damages*, 18th edn (London: Sweet & Maxwell, 2009)

McKendrick, E., *Contract Law*, 8th edn (Basingstoke: Palgrave Macmillan, 2009)

McNeilly, F. S., 'Promises De-Moralized' (1972) **81** *The Philosophical Review* 63–81

Meek, R. L., *Studies in the Labour Theory of Value* (London: Lawrence and Wishart, 1956)

Melden, A. I., 'On Promising' (1956) **65** *Mind* 49

Mersinis, T., 'Stair, Institutions, 1.10.5: A Linguistic Note' (1996) **1** *Edinburgh Law Review* 368–70

Meyer, E. A., *Legitimacy and Law in the Roman World: Tabulae in Roman Belief and Practice* (Cambridge University Press, 2004)

Mills, J. K., 'The Morality of Promising Made in Good Faith' (1995) *Journal of Value Enquiry* 573–4

Molina, L. de, *De iustitia et iure tractatus* (Venice: 1614)

Molinaeus, C. (du Moulin, C.), *Tractatus de eo quod interest* (Venice: 1574)

Moss, G. C., 'The Functions of Letters of Intent and Their Recognition in Modern Legal Systems', in R. Schulze, *New Features in Contract Law* (Munich: Sellier, 2007)

Mugdan, B., *Die gesammten Materialien zum Bürgerlichen Gesetzbuch* (1899) (repr. by Keip Verlag, 2005)

Münchener Kommentar zum BGB, 11 vols. (Munich: C. H. Beck, 2006–)

Nagel, T., *Equality and Partiality* (Oxford University Press, 1991)

Narveson, J., 'Promising, Expecting, and Utility' (1971) **1** *Canadian Journal of Philosophy* 207–33

The Libertarian Idea (Philadelphia: Temple University Press, 1988).

Nifong, W., 'Promises Past: Marcus Atilius Regulus and the Dialogue of Natural Law' **49** *Duke Law Journal* 1077–126.

Oakley, J., 'Varieties of Virtue Ethics' (1996) **9(2)** *Ratio* 128–152

O'Brien, P. H., 'Restitutio in integrum in die Suid-Afrikaanse reg', unpublished LLD thesis, Rand Afrikaans University, 1996

O'Brien, P. H. and Reinecke, M. F. B., 'Restitusie na terugtrede weens kontrakbreuk' (1998) **3** *Tydskrif vir die Suid-Afrikaanse reg* 561–9

O'Sullivan, J., 'Damages for Lost Profits for Late Redelivery: How Remote is Too Remote?' (2009) **68** *Cambridge Law Journal* 34–7

Paley, W., *Principles of Moral and Political Philosophy* (London: 1785)

Palmer, V., *The Paths to Privity: A History of Third Party Beneficiary Contracts at English Law* (San Francisco: Austin and Winfield, 1992)

Peel, E., *Treitel on the Law of Contract*, 12th edn (London: Sweet & Maxwell, 2007)

'Remoteness Revisited' (2009) *Law Quarterly Review* 6–12

Plato, *Laws*, 2 vols. (Cambridge, Mass.: Loeb, 1989)

Republic, being vols. 5 and 6 of *Plato in Twelve Volumes* (Harvard University Press, 1969)

Pollock, F., *Principles of Contract at Law and in Equity* (London: Stevens and Sons, 1876)

Pothier, R., *A Treatise on the Law of Obligations, or Contracts*, trans. by W. Evans, 2 vols. (London: J. Butterworth, 1806)

Pound, R., 'The Role of the Will in Law' (1954) **68** *Harvard Law Review* 1–19

Pratt, M., 'Promises, Contracts and Voluntary Obligations' (2007) *Law and Philosophy* 531–74

'Contract: Not Promise' (2008) **35** *Florida State University Law Review* 801–16

Puchta, G. F., *Pandekten* (Leipzig: 1844)

Pufendorf, S. von, *De Iure Naturae et Gentium*, 1688 edn, trans. by C. H. and W. A. Oldfather (Oxford University Press, 1934; reprinted by Hein & Co., 1995)

Elementorum Jurisprudentiae Universalis, 1672 edn, transl. by W. A. Oldfather (Oxford University Press, 1931; reprinted by Hein & Co., 1995)

Rabel, E. *Das Recht des Warenkaufs*, vol. 1 (Berlin: de Gruyter, 1936; repr. 1957)

Rakoff, T. D., 'The Implied Terms of Contracts: Of "Default Rules" and "Situation-Sense"', in J. Beatson and D. Friedmann (eds.), *Good Faith and Fault in Contract Law* (Oxford University Press, 1997), pp. 191–230

Rawls, J. A., *Theory of Justice*, rev. edn (Harvard University Press, 1999)

Raz, J., 'Promises and Obligations', in P. Hacker and J. Raz (eds.), *Law, Morality and Society* (Oxford University Press, 1977), pp. 210–28

Regelsberger, F., *Die Vorverhandlungen* (Weimar: 1868)

Reid, D., 'Thomas Aquinas and Viscount Stair: The Influence of Scholastic Moral Theology on Stair's Account of Restitution and Recompense' (2008) **29** *Journal of Legal History* 189–214

Reid, E. C. and Blackie, J. W. G., *Personal Bar* (Edinburgh: W. Green, 2006)

Reinach, A., 'Die apriorischen Grundlagen des bürgerlichen Rechts', *Jahrbuch für Philosophie und phänomenologische Forschung*, I/2, 685–847; also published as Separatum, (1913) and (1922); repr. in Reinach, A., *Gesammelte Schriften* (Halle: Max Niemeyer, 1921), pp. 166–350, English trans. as 'The Apriori Foundations of the Civil Law', by J. F. Crosby, in (1983) **3** *Aletheia* 1–142

Richter, A. and Friedberg, E. (eds.), *Corpus Iuris Canonici*, 2 vols., repr. (New Jersey: The Lawbook Exchange, 2000)

Richter, T., 'Did Stair know Pufendorf?' (2003) **7** *Edinburgh Law Review* 367–78

Robbins, M. H., *Promising, Intending and Moral Authority* (Cambridge University Press, 1984)

Robertson, A., 'Estoppels and Right-Creating Events: Beyond Wrongs and Promises', in J. Neyers *et al.* (eds.), *Exploring Contract Law* (Oxford: Hart Publishing, 2009), pp. 199–224

Rodger, A., 'Molina, Stair and the Ius Quaesitum Tertio' (1969) *Juridical Review* 34–44 and 128–51

Ruiter, D., 'A Basic Classification of Legal Institutions' (2001) **10** *Ratio Juris* 357–71

'Structuring Legal Institutions' (1998) **17** *Law and Philosophy* 215–32

Savigny, F. C. von, *System des heutigen Römischen Rechts* (Berlin: Veit & Co., 1840–8)

Scanlon, T. M., *What We Owe to Each Other* (Cambridge, Mass.: Harvard University Press, 1998)

Schermaier, M., *Materia: Beiträge zur Frage der Naturphilosophie im klassischen römischen Recht* (Vienna: Böhlau Verlag, 1992)

Schlechtriem, P., 'Good Faith in German law and in International Uniform Laws' (Address to Centro di Studi e Richerche di Diritto Comparato e Straniero, delivered February 1997)

Schuldrecht, Allgemeines Teil (Tübingen: Mohr, 1997)

Schlesinger, H. J., *Promises, Oaths and Vows: On the Psychology of Promising* (London: The Analytic Press, 2008)

Schmidt-Kessel, M. (ed.), *Principles of European Law: Donation* (Oxford: Oxford University Press, 2011)

Schulte-Nölke, H., 'Vertragsfreiheit und Informationszwang nach der Schuld-rechtsreform' (2002) *Zeitschrift für das gesamte Schuldrecht* 72–8

Schulte-Nölke, H. and Schulze, R., 'Schuldrechtsreform und Gemeinschaftsrecht', in R. Schulze and H. Schulte-Nölke (eds.) *Die Schuldrechtsreform vor dem Hintergrund des Gemeinschaftsrechts* (Tübingen: Mohr Siebeck, 2001)

Schulze, G., in *Anwaltkommentar zum BGB*, vol. 1 (Bonn: Deutscher Anwaltverlag, 2005)

Scott, S., *Cession* (Cape Town: Juta, 1991)

Scottish Law Commission, *Memorandum on Constitution and Proof of Voluntary Obligations – Stipulations in Favour of Third Parties* (Scot Law. Comm. No. 38, 1977)

Report on Penalty Clauses (Scot. Law Comm. No. 171, 1999)

Scottish Record Society, *Protocol Book of Sir Alexander Gaw* (Edinburgh: 1910)

Scrutton, T. E., *The Influence of the Roman Law on the law of England* (Cambridge University Press, 1885)

Searle, J. R., *Speech Acts: An Essay in the Philosophy of Language* (Cambridge University Press, 1970)

'A Taxonomy of Illocutionary Acts', in K. Günderson (ed.), *Language, Mind, and Knowledge* (University of Minnesota Press, 1975), vol. VII

Sellar, W. D. H., 'Promise', in K. Reid and R. Zimmermann (eds.), *A History of Private Law in Scotland*, 2 vols. (Oxford University Press, 2000), vol. 2, pp. 252–82

Sheng, C. L., 'On the Nature of Moral Principles' (1994) **28** *Journal of Value Enquiry* 503–18

Seneca, *De Beneficiis* (Cambridge, Mass.: Loeb, 1935)

Shiffrin, S., 'The Divergence of Contract and Promise' (2006) *Harvard Law Review* 708–53

Simpson, A. W. B., *A History of the Common Law of Contract* (Oxford University Press, 1975)

Singer, R., 'Das Verbot widersprüchlichen Verhaltens', unpublished Jur. Diss. (Munich:1992).

Skene, J., *Regiam Majestatem*, repr. (Edinburgh: Stair Society, 1947)

Slackman, M., 'The Fine Art of Hiding What You Mean To Say', *New York Times*, 6 August 2006 (Week In Review, p. 5)

Smith, A., *Lectures on Jurisprudence*, repr. (Oxford University Press, 1978)
  The Theory of Moral Sentiments (London: Printed for Millar, and Kincaid & Bell, 1759)

Smith, B., *John Searle* (Cambridge University Press, 2003)

Smith, H. M., 'A Paradox of Promising' (1997) **106** *The Philosophical Review* 153–96

Smith, M., *Law of Assignment: The Creation and Transfer of Choses in Action* (Oxford University Press, 2007)

Smith, S., 'Contracts for the Benefit of Third Parties: In Defence of the Third-Party Rule' (1997) *Oxford Journal of Legal Studies* 643–64
  Contract Theory (Oxford University Press, 2004)
  'The Limits of Contract', in J. Neyers *et al.* (eds.), *Exploring Contract Law* (Oxford: Hart Publishing, 2009)

Smith, T. B., 'Jus Quaesitum Tertio: Remedies of the "Tertius" in Scottish Law' (1956) *Juridical Review* 3–21
  Studies Critical and Comparative (Edinburgh: W. Green, 1962)

Snyder, D., 'Hunting Promissory Estoppel', in E. Reid and V. Palmer (eds.), *Mixed Jurisdictions Compared: Private Law in Louisiana and Scotland* (Edinburgh University Press, 2009), pp. 281–321

Sommerstein, A. H. and Fletcher, J., (eds.), *The Oath in Greek Society* (Exeter: Bristol Phoenix Press, 2007)

Sommerstein, A. H. *et al.*, *The Oath in Archaic and Classical Greece* (Berlin: De Gruyter, forthcoming, 2012)

Sonnekus, J. C., *The Law of Estoppel in South Africa* (Durban: Butterworths, 2000)

Sophocles, *Electra*, trans. A. Carson (Oxford University Press, 2001)
  Oedipus Tyrannus, trans. I. McAuslan and J. Affleck (Cambridge University Press, 2003)

Spence, M., *Protecting Reliance: The Emergent Doctrine of Equitable Estoppel* (Oxford: Hart Publishing, 1999)

Stair, Viscount (Dalrymple, J.), *Institutions of the Laws of Scotland*, 2nd edn of 1693 (repr. University Presses of Edinburgh and Glasgow, 1981)

Stevens, R., 'Damages and the Right to Performance: A Golden Victory or Not?', in J. Meyers (ed.), *Exploring Contract Law* (Oxford: Hart Publishing, 2009) *Torts and Rights* (Oxford University Press, 2007)

Stoll, H., 'Review of *Der Verzicht im Schuldrecht*' (2007) *Zeitschrift für Europäische Privatrecht* 396–8

Sutherland, P. and Johnston, D., 'Contracts for the Benefit of Third Parties', in R. Zimmermann, D. Visser and K. Reid (eds.), *Mixed Legal Systems in Comparative Perspective* (Oxford University Press, 2004), pp. 208–39

Swain, W., 'The Changing Nature of the Doctrine of Consideration 1750–1850' (2005) **26** *Journal of Legal History* 55–72.

Swain, W., 'The Classical Model of Contract: The Product of a Revolution in Legal Thought?' (2010) **30** *Legal Studies* 513–32

Terré, F., Lequette, Y. and Simler, P., *Droit civil: les obligations*, 9th edn (Dalloz, 2005)

Tolhurst, G., *The Assignment of Contractual Rights* (Oxford: Hart Publishing, 2006)

Ulmer, P., 'Teilunwirksamkeit von teilweise unangemessenen AGB-Klauseln?' (1981) *Neue Juristische Wochenschrift* 2025

Unberath, H., *Transferred Loss* (Oxford: Hart Publishing, 2003)

Van der Merwe, S. *et al.*, *Contract: General Principles*, 3rd edn (Lansdowne, South Africa: Juta, 2007)

Vaquer, A., 'Verwirkung versus Laches' (2006) **21** *Tulane European & Civil Law Forum* 53–72

Vinogradoff, P., 'Reason and Conscience in Sixteenth-Century Jurisprudence', in his *Collected Papers*, vol. 2 (Oxford University Press, 1928), pp. 190–204

Visser, D., 'Rethinking Unjustified Enrichment: A Perspective of the Competition between Contract and Enrichment Remedies' (1992) *Acta Juridica* 203–36

Von Bar, C. and Clive, E. (eds.), *Principles, Definitions, and Model Rules of European Private Law: Draft Common Frame of Reference*, 6 vols. (Munich: Sellier, 2009)

Von Jhering, R., 'Culpa in contrahendo oder Schadensersatz bei nichtigen oder nicht zur Perfektion gelangten Verträgen' (1861) 4 *Jheringsche Jahrbücher Zweck im Recht*, 3rd edn (Leipzig: Breitkopf & Härtel, 1898)

Von Kübel, F., 'Das einseitige Versprechen als Grund der Verpflichtung zur Erfüllung', in W. Schubert (ed.), *Die Vorlagen der Redaktoren für die Erste Kommission zur Ausarbeitung des Entwurfs eines Bürgerlichen Gesetzbuches, Recht der Schuldverhältnisse*, vol. 3 (Berlin: 1980)

Vorgenauer, S. and Kleinheisterkamp, J., (eds.), *Commentary on the Unidroit Principles of International Commercial Contracts (PICC)* (Oxford University Press, 2009)

Vorster, J., 'A Comment on the Meaning of Objectivity in Contract' (1987) **103** *Law Quarterly Review* 274–87

Waddams, S., 'Principle in Contract Law: The Doctrine of Consideration', in J. Neyers *et al.*, *Exploring Contract Law* (Oxford: Hart Publishing, 2009), pp. 51–75

Watson, A., *The Law of the Ancient Romans* (Southern Methodist University Press, 1970)

'The Hidden Origins of Enorm Lesion' (1981) **2** *Journal of Legal History* 186–93

Watts, P. and Reynolds, F. M. B., *Bowstead and Reynolds on Agency*, 19th edn (London: Sweet and Maxwell, 2010)

Webb, C., 'Justifying Damages', in J. Neyers *et al.*, *Exploring Contract Law* (Oxford: Hart Publishing, 2009), pp. 139–70

Weller, M.-P., 'Die Struktur des Erfüllungsangspruchs im BGB, common law und DCFR – ein kritischer Vergleich' (2008) *JuristenZeitung*, 764

Die Vertragstreue: Vertragsbindung – Naturalerfüllungsgrundsatz – Leistungstreue (Tübingen: Mohr Siebeck, 2009)

Whitford, W. and Macaulay, S., 'Hoffman v. Red Owl Stores: The Rest of the Story' (2010) **61** *Hastings Law Journal* 801–58

Williston, S., *The Law of Contracts*, 4 vols. (New York: Baker, Voorhis & Co., 1920)

Windscheid, B., *Lehrbuch des Pandektenrechts* (Frankfurt-am-Main: 1891)

Wright, Lord, 'Ought the Doctrine of Consideration to be Abolished from the Common Law?' (1936) **49** *Harvard Law Review* 1225–53

Zeffertt, D., 'Some Thoughts on Options' (1972) **89** *South African Law Journal* 152–8

Zimmermann, R., *The Law of Obligations: Roman Foundations of the Civilian Tradition* (Oxford University Press, 1996)

'Europa und das Römische Recht' (2002) **202** *Archiv für die Civilistische Praxis*

The New German Law of Obligations: Historical and Comparative Perspectives (Oxford University Press, 2005)

'Vertrag und Versprechen: Deutches Recht und Principles of European Contract Law in Vergleich', in *Festschrift für Andreas Heldrich* (Munich: C. H. Beck, 2005), pp. 467–86

Zumbansen, P., 'The Law of Contracts', in M. Reimann and J. Zekoll (eds.), *Introduction to German Law* (The Hague: Kluwer Law International, 2005)

INDEX